W9-CLF-195

Research in Psychology

**EIGHTH
EDITION**

METHODS AND DESIGN

Kerri A. Goodwin
Towson University

C. James Goodwin
Western Carolina University

WILEY

EXECUTIVE EDITOR	Veronica Visentin
PROJECT MANAGER	Gladys Soto
PROJECT SPECIALIST	Nichole Urban
CONTENT MANAGEMENT DIRECTOR	Lisa Wojcik
SENIOR CONTENT SPECIALIST	Nicole Repasky
PRODUCTION EDITOR	Arun Surendar
PHOTO RESEARCHER	Billy Ray
COVER PHOTO CREDIT	© Bruce Rolff/Shutterstock

This book was set in 10/12 Avenir LT Std by SPi Global and printed and bound by Quad/Graphics.

Founded in 1807, John Wiley & Sons, Inc. has been a valued source of knowledge and understanding for more than 200 years, helping people around the world meet their needs and fulfill their aspirations. Our company is built on a foundation of principles that include responsibility to the communities we serve and where we live and work. In 2008, we launched a Corporate Citizenship Initiative, a global effort to address the environmental, social, economic, and ethical challenges we face in our business. Among the issues we are addressing are carbon impact, paper specifications and procurement, ethical conduct within our business and among our vendors, and community and charitable support. For more information, please visit our website: www.wiley.com/go/citizenship.

Copyright © 2017, 2013, 2010, 2007, 2004 John Wiley & Sons, Inc. All rights reserved. No part of this publication may be reproduced, stored in a retrieval system, or transmitted in any form or by any means, electronic, mechanical, photocopying, recording, scanning or otherwise, except as permitted under Sections 107 or 108 of the 1976 United States Copyright Act, without either the prior written permission of the Publisher, or authorization through payment of the appropriate per-copy fee to the Copyright Clearance Center, Inc., 222 Rosewood Drive, Danvers, MA 01923 (Web site: www.copyright.com). Requests to the Publisher for permission should be addressed to the Permissions Department, John Wiley & Sons, Inc., 111 River Street, Hoboken, NJ 07030-5774, (201) 748-6011, fax (201) 748-6008, or online at: www.wiley.com/go/permissions.

Evaluation copies are provided to qualified academics and professionals for review purposes only, for use in their courses during the next academic year. These copies are licensed and may not be sold or transferred to a third party. Upon completion of the review period, please return the evaluation copy to Wiley. Return instructions and a free of charge return shipping label are available at: www.wiley.com/go/returnlabel. If you have chosen to adopt this textbook for use in your course, please accept this book as your complimentary desk copy. Outside of the United States, please contact your local sales representative.

ISBN: 978-1-119-33044-8 (PBK)
ISBN: 978-1-119-25730-1 (EVALC)

Library of Congress Cataloging in Publication Data:

LCCN: 2016036350

The inside back cover will contain printing identification and country of origin if omitted from this page. In addition, if the ISBN on the back cover differs from the ISBN on this page, the one on the back cover is correct.

SKY10033902_032322

KAG: To Dave, Jack, and Jimmy

CJG: To Susan

CONTENTS

10 NON-EXPERIMENTAL DESIGN II: OBSERVATIONAL AND ARCHIVAL METHODS   291

11 QUASI-EXPERIMENTAL DESIGNS AND APPLIED RESEARCH   313

Summary of Research Examples

PREFACE

THE PHILOSOPHY OF THE TEXT

Several strong beliefs have guided the writing of this book over its eight editions. First, it is important for students to develop a clear understanding of how psychologists think and how they do their work. Thus, students using this book will encounter thorough discussions of the nature of psychological science and how it differs from pseudoscience, the logic of scientific thinking, and the manner in which psychological scientists (a) develop ideas and shape hypotheses for research, (b) design their studies, (c) carry them out, (d) analyze them, and (e) draw proper conclusions from them. Second, students should understand that psychologists use a variety of methods in their attempts to understand psychological phenomena. Although the book's main focus is on the experimental method, it thoroughly discusses numerous other research designs as well. Third, because researchers must always be aware of the ethical dimensions of their research, students must also have a thorough understanding of research ethics. Thus, an ethics chapter appears early in the book (Chapter 2) and additional discussions of ethics (Ethics Boxes) appear in *every* subsequent chapter. Fourth, because nobody can understand psychology's present without knowing something of its past, we have incorporated certain aspects of the history of experimental psychology into the text. Recognizing that the text is for a methods course and not for a history course, however, we have included only historical information that illuminates important methodological concepts. Fifth, and perhaps most important, although we both believe that doing psychological science is a joyful activity, it has been our experience that some students enter the course with a sense of dread. They believe it will be boring, difficult, and not especially relevant for them. To counter this, we have taken pains to write a student-friendly book that is appealing (lots of interesting descriptions of real research), understandable (clear writing in an interactive, conversational style), and valuable (sharpening important critical thinking skills).

THE ORGANIZATION OF THE TEXT

The book includes 12 chapters, a brief epilogue, and 2 appendices. By thoroughly explaining the scientific way of thinking and contrasting it with nonscientific and pseudoscientific thinking, the opening chapter lays the groundwork for all that follows. Chapter 2 is devoted to research ethics and concerns how the American Psychological Association's most recent code of ethics applies to research with both human participants and animal subjects. The problem of scientific fraud is also discussed. Chapter 3 examines how ideas for research originate and explains the continually evolving relationship between theory and research. It also helps students learn to use psychology's most important electronic database (PsycINFO) and provides tips for reading empirical journal articles. Issues related to sampling, the measurement of psychological phenomena, and the statistical analysis of data are the focus of Chapter 4. The next four chapters deal primarily with the experimental method, psychology's most important method because of the kind of conclusion (causal) that can be drawn from it. There is a basic introduction to the experimental method (Chapter 5), a discussion of control problems in experimental research (Chapter 6), and two chapters devoted to experimental design (Chapter 7 on single-factor designs and Chapter 8 on factorial designs).

While much of the content and general organizational structure of the textbook remains the same as in past editions, we have altered the organization of the final four chapters of the text. Because we devoted two chapters to specific experimental methods (Chapters 7 and 8), we created two comparable non-experimental methods chapters focused on survey methods, correlation, and regression (Chapter 9) and observational and archival methods (Chapter 10). Chapter 11 is devoted to applied research, including program evaluation, and Chapter 12 describes small N designs, including the case study method and applied behavior analysis. In the current edition, both experimental and non-experimental chapters include descriptions of data analysis for specific experimental and nonexperimental designs. For example, in Chapter 8 we describe analysis of variance as a statistical tool for evaluating data from factorial designs, and in Chapter 10 we describe meta-analysis as an example of an archival research tool.

The two appendices describe how to prepare the (in)famous APA-style research report and provide feedback for some of the end-of-chapter applications exercises. Note the word *some*. So that you as instructors can use some of these materials for homework assignments, we have given students feedback on about half of the exercises in Appendix B. Answers to the remaining exercises can be found in the electronic Instructor's Resources.

At various points in the text are boxed sections of three general types. *Origins* boxes supply interesting information about the historical roots of psychological research and show how research concepts and methods (e.g., the Hawthorne effect) were created and have evolved over the years. *Classic Studies* boxes describe famous experiments (e.g., Bandura's Bobo doll studies) that illustrate particular research designs and/or methodological issues. Finally, the previously mentioned *Ethics* boxes reflect our belief that a consideration of research ethics should occur in more than just a single chapter. The ethics boxes address such topics as informed consent, the operation of subject pools, and the proper use of surveys.

It is not uncommon for methods texts to begin with simple descriptive methods (observation, survey, etc.), move through non-experimental methods, and eventually reach the experimental method. There is certainly some logic to this organizational structure, but it is not the structure we have chosen. Rather, when teaching the course, we have been disturbed by how late in the semester students were encountering such things as factorial designs—who wants to be figuring out interactions while digesting the Thanksgiving turkey? Such complex topics seem rushed within the course of a semester, so for us, it seemed better to teach about experimental designs earlier in the semester in order to spend sufficient time on them if students run into trouble. Also, because many of the course's lab activities used experimental designs, it seemed important for students to have some understanding of the studies they run during the semester. So the chapter organization reflects the way we teach the course—getting to experiments as soon as possible. Reviewers of the text have been divided on the issue, with most liking the current organization, but some preferring to start with non-experimental methods. It has been good to learn, however, that a number of reviewer/colleagues who like to begin the course with non-experimental methods have been using this text anyway, and simply changing the chapter sequence to suit themselves. Thus, it is worth noting that the text is to some degree modular and can be taught using several arrangements of chapters.

PEDAGOGICAL FEATURES OF THE TEXT

For the student, this text has several features designed to facilitate learning. These include:

- At the start of each chapter, a brief **Preview** of what is to be found in the chapter and a set of specific **Learning Objectives** for the chapter.

- Throughout each chapter, periodic **Self Tests**, set off in small boxes, enabling the student to test comprehension for a portion of a chapter just completed.

- At the end of each chapter, a comprehensive **Summary** of important points, a set of **Review Questions**, a set of **Applications Exercises**, and answers to the Self Tests. The review questions are short essay questions for discussion and reflection. These review questions are not just definitional; they ask students to apply concepts learned in the chapter and to think critically about them. The applications exercises include thought questions and problems to solve that require using the concepts learned in the chapter. Appendix B contains feedback on about half of these exercises. The online Instructor's Manual includes feedback for the remaining exercises, which enables instructors to assign some of the end-of-chapter exercises as graded homework.

- Key terms and concepts appear in **boldface** print throughout the textbook and they are collected in a Glossary which is found at the end of the book. To make it easier to find where the descriptions of the Glossary terms appear in the text, we have structured the Index so the text page where a glossary term is first defined is boldfaced.

- Throughout the text, numerous concrete examples of real research are used to illustrate methodological points and to enhance critical thinking. These include 41 detailed descriptions (Research Examples) and dozens of briefer descriptions. Of the Research Examples, 11 are new to this edition.

ELECTRONIC RESOURCES

Several electronic resources are available for students and instructors; these can be found here: www.wiley.com/college/goodwin

Simply go to the site, find the textbook and click on Student or Instructor Companion Sites. Students can get to the materials directly; instructors must register with Wiley because some of the materials are password-protected. Here's what can be found.

For the Instructor:

- An Instructor's Manual, organized by chapter, which provides numerous ideas for in-class exercises, lecture elaborations, homework, and so on (many taken from psychology's best journal for teachers, *Teaching of Psychology*). It also includes the answers for those end-of-chapter Applications Exercises students won't find in Appendix B.

- A Test Bank for each chapter that includes both objective (multiple choice, fill-in-the-blank) items and written questions (short essays and comprehensive, integrative essays).

- A set of PowerPoint slides to accompany the chapters.

- A Laboratory Manual—a set of materials and instructions that will enable you to collect data for 20 research projects.

For the Student:

- An electronic Study Guide that includes concept questions for students to answer as they work their way through chapters, sample objective test items (fill-ins, matching, and multiple choice) with detailed feedback, and applications exercises similar to the ones found at the ends of chapters in the main text.

- The Student Statistics Guide includes important aids for statistical analysis:

  - Detailed descriptions for calculating various statistical analyses by hand (e.g., t tests, ANOVA).
  - Step-by-step SPSS instructions because many departments rely on SPSS for statistical analysis.

ACKNOWLEDGMENTS

KAG: When I was a little girl, I used to love it when my dad would bring me to his office and I could play in the "playroom" with interesting toys and, sometimes, another child. Little did I know that my leisurely play was being observed by students in a classroom on the other side of a two-way mirror in a developmental psychology laboratory. I did not know then I would parallel my father's journey into teaching and research, and I am indebted to him and to my mom for instilling in me a sense of curiosity from an early age. As I grew older and more curious, I found myself majoring in psychology where I discovered a love for perception and cognition. I want to thank Dr. Janet Larson for giving me an initial road map into the world of experimental psychology. Even further down the road, I found I liked to share ideas of research with others and with students in particular. My graduate mentors, Dr. Mike Toglia and Dr. Colleen Kelley, remind me of the importance of life-long learning via teaching and research and the nobility in sharing ideas with others. Finally, I am most grateful to my husband, Dave. He has taken me on an off-shore journey of sorts, and I am forever indebted to his unique perspectives and loving support. Since our first date almost 20 years ago when we capsized a small sailboat, he has been the wind behind my sails and my anchor when at port.

CJG: This project would not have been started, much less completed and evolved into an eighth edition, without the encouragement and support of many people, most notably my dear wife of almost 50 years (Susan, retired now, but a former corporate internal auditor good at keeping me on task, yet willing to let me sneak out for an occasional round of mountain golf) and my children (Kerri, a university professor, cognitive psychologist, assistant department chair, mother of two, all-around wonder woman, and now the lead author of this text), and Charles (a geologist working as project manager for an environmental consulting firm). The hundreds of students who passed through my research methods course were my principal source of inspiration in starting the first edition of this book back in the 1990s. During those early years, many of them told me to stop complaining about the textbook being used at the time and write my own.

To Darryl Bruce, my dissertation director, I owe a great debt. He first showed me how exciting research in psychology could be during my grad school days in Tallahassee. And he taught me how to write. I still have the first draft of my master's thesis – his edits (accompanied by occasional exclamation points) decorated virtually every page. Up until just a few years ago, I would still send him drafts of my writing and he would reliably red pencil the daylights out of them. When Darryl died a few years ago, I lost a mentor and a close friend.

Finally, the editors, production team, and marketing staff at Wiley have very supportive. We are especially grateful for the support of Victoria Visentin, Gladys Soto, and Chris Johnson and for the skillful production work of Amy Jolin and Arun Surendar.

Scientific Thinking in Psychology

1

PREVIEW & CHAPTER OBJECTIVES

Welcome to what might be the most important course you will take as a psychology student. This opening chapter begins by trying to convince you that a research methods course is essential to your education, whether or not you have a future as a research psychologist. The chapter then proceeds with an introduction to the ways in which we come to know things in our world. Some of what we know comes from our reliance on authority figures, other knowledge results from our ability to reason, and we have often heard that experience is the best teacher. All these avenues to knowledge have merit, but each is flawed. Research psychologists rely on scientific thinking as a way to discover truth, and this opening chapter carefully examines the general nature of science, describes the scientific way of thinking, and contrasts it with pseudoscientific thinking. Distinguishing science from pseudoscience is especially important for psychology, because some things that are promoted as "psychological truth" (e.g., the ability to assess personality by examining someone's handwriting) are actually examples of pseudoscience rather than true science. The chapter closes by discussing the goals for a scientific psychology, and brief introductions to the work of two of experimental psychology's legendary stars, Eleanor Gibson and B. F. Skinner. They both showed the passion and commitment that psychological scientists have for their work. When you finish this chapter, you should be able to:

- Defend the need for a research methods course for psychology students.

- Explain how the overall purpose of a methods course differs from other psychology courses.

- Identify and evaluate nonscientific ways of knowing about things in the world—authority, reasoning, and experience.

- Describe the attributes of science as a way of knowing, which assumes determinism and discoverability; makes systematic observations; produces public, data-driven, but tentative knowledge; asks answerable questions; and develops theories that attempt to explain psychological phenomena.

- Distinguish science from pseudoscience and recognize the attributes of pseudoscientific thinking.

- Describe the main goals of research in psychology and relate them to various research strategies to be encountered later in the book.

In the preface to his weighty two-volume *Principles of Physiological Psychology*, published in 1874, the German physiologist Wilhelm Wundt boldly and unambiguously declared that his text represented "an attempt to mark out a new-domain of *science*" (Wundt, 1874/1904; italics added). Shortly after publishing the book, Wundt established his now famous psychology laboratory at Leipzig, Germany, attracting students from all over Europe as well as from the United States. American universities soon established their own laboratories, about 20 of them by 1892 (Sokal, 1992). In that same year the American Psychological Association (APA) was founded, and before long it ratified a constitution identifying its purpose as "the advancement of Psychology as a *science*. Those who are eligible for membership are engaged in this work" (Cattell, 1895, p. 150; italics added). Thus, for psychology's pioneers, both in Germany and in the United States, the "new psychology" was to be identified with laboratory science. It gradually forged an identity separate from the disciplines of physiology and philosophy to become the independent discipline it is today.

For early psychologists, the new psychology was to be a science of mental life, the goal being to understand exactly how human consciousness was structured and/or how it enabled people to adapt to their environments. In order to study the mind scientifically, however, generally agreed-upon methods had to be developed and taught. Hence, students of the new psychology found themselves in laboratories learning the basic procedures for studying mental processes. Indeed, one of psychology's most famous early texts was a highly detailed laboratory manual published right after the turn of the 20th century by Cornell's eminent experimental psychologist, E. B. Titchener, a student of Wundt's. The manuals were in use in lab courses well into the 1930s and they were instrumental in training a generation of research psychologists (Tweney, 1987).

Although the particular research methods have changed considerably over the years, today's psychology departments continue this long tradition of teaching the tools of the trade to psychology students. From the very beginning of psychology's history, teaching research methodology has been the heart and soul of the psychology curriculum. Of course, students understandably tend to be suspicious of the argument that they are required to take a research methods course because "we've always done it that way." There should be other reasons to justify taking the course. There are.

Why Take This Course?

The most obvious reason for taking a course in research methods is to begin the process of learning how to do research in psychology. Our ideal scenario would be for you to become fascinated by research while you are taking this course, decide that you would like to do some, get your feet wet as an undergraduate (e.g., collaborate with a professor and perhaps present your research at a research conference), go to graduate school and complete a doctorate in psychology, begin a career as a productive researcher, get lots of publications and win lots of grants, achieve tenure, and eventually be named recipient of the APA's annual award for "Distinguished Scientific Contributions"! Of course, we are also realists and know that most psychology majors have interests other than doing research, most do not go on to earn doctoral degrees, most who earn doctorates do not become productive researchers, and very few productive scholars win prestigious grants or awards. If you won't be a famous research psychologist someday, are there still reasons to take this course? Certainly!

For one thing, a course in research methods (accompanied by a statistics course) provides a solid foundation for understanding the information you will encounter in other psychology courses in more specific topic areas (social, cognitive, developmental, etc.). Research has shown that students who do well in statistics and methods courses go on to have higher GPAs in their other psychology courses than students doing poorly, and that methodology course grades in particular are good predictors of the overall knowledge about psychology gained by students during their careers as psychology majors (Freng, Webber, Blatter, Wing, & Scott, 2011). Thus, it is no surprise that your psychology department requires you to take statistics and methodology courses, and usually wants you to take them early in your career as a psychology major. The difference between the methods course and other courses in the psychology curriculum is essentially the difference between *process* and *content*. The methods course teaches a *process* of acquiring knowledge about psychological phenomena that is then applied to all the specific *content* areas represented by other courses in the psychology curriculum. A social psychology experiment in conformity might be worlds apart in subject matter from a cognitive psychology study on eyewitness memory, but their common thread is research methodology—the manner in which researchers gain their knowledge about these phenomena. Fully understanding textbook descriptions of research in psychology is much easier if you know something about the methods used to arrive at the conclusions.

To illustrate, take a minute and look at one of your other psychology textbooks. Chances are that virtually every paragraph makes some assertion about behavior that either includes a specific description of a research study or at least makes reference to one. For example, Myers's (1980) social psychology text includes the following description of a study about the effects of violent pornography on male aggression (Donnerstein, 1980). Myers wrote that the experimenter "showed 120 . . . men either a neutral, an erotic, or an aggressive-erotic (rape) film. Then the men, supposedly as part of another experiment, 'taught' a male or female confederate some nonsense syllables by choosing how much shock to administer for incorrect answers. The men who had watched the rape film administered markedly stronger shocks – but only toward female victims" (Myers, 1990, p. 393). While reading this description, someone unfamiliar with experimental design might get the general idea, but someone familiar with methodology would also be registering that the study was at the very least a 2 (sex of the confederate) x 3 (film condition) between-subjects factorial design resulting in a type of interaction effect that takes precedence over any main effects; that the two independent variables (film type, victim gender) were both manipulated variables, thereby strengthening the causal interpretation of the results; and that the "victims" were not really shocked but were clued in to the purposes of the study (i.e., they were confederates). Also, the thoughts "I wonder what would happen if there was more of a delay between viewing the film and the learning part of the study?" or "I wonder how female participants would react in a replication of the study?" might also float through the mind of someone in tune with the kind of "what do we do for the next experiment?" thinking that accompanies knowledge of research methodology. By the end of this course, you will be familiar with all the language found in the aggression study we just described and you will also be asking those "next step" kinds of questions that researchers ask.

A second reason for taking experimental psychology is that even if you never collect a single piece of data after completing this course, knowledge of research methods will make you a more informed and critical thinker. Any good course in psychology will improve your critical thinking skills, but a methodology course will be especially effective at enhancing your skills in evaluating research and claims about psychology that appear to be based on research. Bensley (2008) defines critical thinking in psychology as a form of precise thinking "in which a person reasons about relevant evidence to draw a sound or good conclusion" (p. 128). This requires being able to judge the quality of the evidence used to support a claim, being fair and unbiased when examining conflicting claims, and drawing reasonable conclusions based on the evidence at hand. A research methods course will help you do all of these things better.

The need for critical thinking about psychology is clear. We are continually exposed to claims about behavior from sources ranging from the people around us who are amateur psychologists to media accounts ranging from the sublime (an account in a reputable magazine about research on the relationship between video-game playing and aggressiveness) to the ridiculous (the tabloid headlines you read while waiting in line to pay for groceries). While the latter can be dismissed without much difficulty (for most people), a professional writer unaware of the important distinction between experimental and correlational research might have penned the video game study. Consequently, the article might describe a correlational study hinting at cause and effect more than is justified, a mistake you'll have no difficulty recognizing once you have finished Chapter 9. Another example might be a claim that while under hypnosis, people can be transported back to the moment of their birth, thereby gaining insight into the origins of their problems. When you learn about "parsimonious" explanations in Chapter 3, you will be highly suspicious about such a claim and able to think of several alternative explanations for the reports given by patients about their alleged birth experiences. Similarly, you will learn to become skeptical about the claims made by those who believe the "subliminal" messages in the recordings they just downloaded are the cause of the weight they just lost, or by those who believe that their child's IQ can be raised by listening to classical music (the so-called "Mozart effect").

Third, there is a very practical reason for taking a research methods course. Even if you have no desire to become a research psychologist, you might like to be a psychology practitioner someday. Like researchers, practitioners must earn an advanced degree, either a master's degree or a doctorate. Even for future clinical psychologists, counselors, and school psychologists, graduate school almost certainly means doing some research, so a course in methodology is an obvious first step to learning the necessary skills. Furthermore, your chances of getting into *any* type of graduate program in the first place are improved significantly if you (a) earned good grades in undergraduate research methods and statistics courses and (b) were involved in doing some research as an undergraduate. As Kuther (2006) put it in *The Psychology Major's Handbook*, graduate admissions committees "want applicants who are interested in the program, have research experience, and have a background in statistics, methodology, and science" (p. 206). Furthermore, Norcross, Hanych, and Terranova (1996) examined the undergraduate courses most likely to be required for admission to graduate school, and found that the methods course was ranked second, just behind statistics, while specific content courses (e.g., developmental and abnormal psychology) lagged far behind and were not even required by many programs.[1]

Should you become a professional psychologist, your research skills will be essential. Even if you don't become an active researcher, you will need to keep up with the latest research in your area of expertise and to be able to read and critically assess research. Furthermore, good clinical work involves essentially the same kind of thinking that characterizes the laboratory scientist—hypotheses about a client's problems are created and tested by trying out various treatments, and the outcomes are systematically evaluated. Also, if you work for a social service agency, you may find yourself dealing with accreditation boards or funding sources and they will want to know if your psychological services are effective. As you will discover in Chapter 11, research evaluating program effectiveness touches the lives of many professional psychologists.

Only a minority of psychology majors become professional psychologists with advanced degrees, yet a research methods course can help develop the kinds of skills that employers look for in bachelor's level job applicants. By the time you have completed this course, for example, you should be better at critical and analytical thinking, precise writing, and logical argument. In addition, you will know how to analyze, summarize, and interpret empirical data, search for information in libraries and electronic databases (e.g., PsycINFO), and present the results of your research in a clear and organized fashion. Your computer skills will also improve—you will either learn or increase your existing skill with some statistical software package (e.g., SPSS) and you

---

[1] In an analysis of 1554 graduate programs, it was found that 85.2% "required" or "preferred" statistics. The percentages were 66.0% for the research methods course, 35.9% for "childhood/developmental," and 32.5% for "abnormal/psychopathology."

might also become more familiar with presentation software (e.g., PowerPoint). To learn more about the kinds of skills you will begin to develop in the methods course, you might take a peek ahead to the Epilogue and the section called "what I learned in my research methods course."

Finally, a course in research methods introduces you to a particular type of thinking. As mentioned above, other psychology courses deal with specific content areas and concentrate on what is known about topic X. The methods course, however, focuses more on the process by which knowledge of X is acquired. That process is centered on scientific thinking, and it is deeply ingrained in all research psychologists. Before detailing the features of the scientific way of thinking, however, let us first describe some of the other ways in which we arrive at our knowledge of the world.

Ways of Knowing

Take a moment and reflect on something that you believe to be true. The belief could be something as simple as the conviction that lobster should be eaten only in Maine, or it could be something as profound as the belief in a personal God. How do we arrive at such beliefs? Have we learned it from others we view as experts, or did we use logical reasoning, or did we base our knowledge of our beliefs on our own experiences? These three alternatives represent three ways of knowing described below: authority, reason, and empiricism. And none are without their flaws.

Authority

Whenever we accept the validity of information from a source that we judge to be an expert, then we are relying on **authority** as a source of our knowledge. As children we are influenced by and believe what our parents tell us (at least for a while), as students we generally accept the authority of textbooks and professors, as patients we take the pills prescribed for us by doctors and believe they will have beneficial effects, and so on. Of course, relying on the authority of others to establish our beliefs overlooks the fact that authorities can be wrong. Some parents pass along harmful prejudices to their children, textbooks and professors are sometimes wrong or their knowledge may be incomplete or biased, and doctors can miss a diagnosis or prescribe the wrong medicine. An important aspect of the attitude of a critical thinker is the willingness to question authority.

On the other hand, we do learn important things from authority figures, especially those who are recognized as experts in particular fields. Thus, we read *Consumer Reports*, we watch the Weather Channel, and we (sometimes) pay attention when the medical community cautions us about our chronic lack of exercise and poor eating habits. Also, it doesn't stretch the concept of authority to consider the giants in the arts and literature as authority figures who can teach us much about ourselves and others. Who can read Shakespeare or Dickens or Austen without gaining valuable insights about human nature?

Use of Reason

We sometimes arrive at conclusions by using logic and reason. For example, given the statements (sometimes called premises):

Primates are capable of using language.

Bozo the chimp is a primate.

It is logical for us to conclude that Bozo the chimp has the ability to use language. Can you see the problem here? The logic is flawless, but the conclusion depends on the truth of the first two statements. The second one might be OK and easy to verify, but the first one could be subject to considerable debate, depending, among other things, on how language is defined. Psycholinguists have been arguing about the issue for years. The key point is that the value of a logically drawn conclusion depends on the truth of the premises, and it takes more than logic to determine whether the premises have merit.

The American pragmatist philosopher Charles Peirce pointed out another difficulty with the use of reason and logic—it can be used to reach opposing conclusions. Peirce labeled the use of reason, and a developing consensus among those debating the merits of one belief over another, the **a priori method** for acquiring knowledge. Beliefs are deduced from statements about what is thought to be true according to the rules of logic. That is, a belief develops as the result of logical argument, *before* a person has direct experience with the phenomenon at hand (*a priori* translates from the Latin as "from what comes before"). Peirce pointed out that the *a priori* method was favored by metaphysical philosophers, who could reason eloquently to reach some truth, only to be contradicted by other philosophers who reasoned just as eloquently to the opposite truth. On the question of whether the mind and the body are one or two different essences, for instance, a "dualist" philosopher might develop a sophisticated argument for the existence of two fundamentally different essences, the physical and the mental, while a "monist" might develop an equally compelling argument that mental phenomena can be reduced to physical phenomena (e.g., the mind *is* the brain). The outcome of the *a priori* approach, Peirce argued, is that philosophical beliefs go in and out of fashion, with no real "progress" toward truth.

Empiricism

Another important way of coming to know things is through our experiences in the world. This is **empiricism**—the process of learning things through direct observation or experience, and reflection on those experiences. You will see shortly that asking "empirical questions" is an important component of scientific thinking, and there is certainly some truth in the old saying that "experience is the best teacher." Yet it can be dangerous to rely uncritically and solely on one's experiences when trying to determine the truth of some matter. The difficulty is that our experiences are necessarily limited and our interpretations of our experiences can be influenced by a number of what social psychologists refer to as "social cognition biases." One of these biases is the **confirmation bias**: a tendency to seek and pay special attention to information that supports one's beliefs, while ignoring information that contradicts a belief (Wason & Johnson-Laird, 1972). For instance, persons believing in extrasensory perception (ESP) will keep close track of instances when they were "thinking about Mom, and then the phone rang and it was her!" Yet they ignore the far more numerous times when (a) they were thinking about Mom and she didn't call, and (b) they weren't thinking about Mom and she did call. They also fail to recognize that if they talk to Mom about every two weeks, their frequency of "thinking about Mom" will increase near the end of the two-week interval, thereby increasing the chances of Mom actually calling. Confirmation bias often combines with another preconception called **belief perseverance** (Lepper, Ross, & Lau, 1986). Motivated by a desire to be certain about one's knowledge, it is a tendency to hold on doggedly to a belief, even in the face of evidence that would convince most people that the belief is false. It is likely that these beliefs form when the individual hears some "truth" being continuously repeated, in the absence of contrary information. Thus, many college students in the 1960s strongly believed in the idea of a generation gap and accepted as gospel the saying "Don't trust anyone over the age of 30." (Of course, these same people are now pushing 70 and some of them are deeply suspicious of anyone younger than 30). Strongly held prejudices include both belief perseverance and confirmation bias. Those with racist attitudes, for example, refuse to consider evidence disconfirming the prejudice and seek out and pay attention to information consistent with the prejudicial belief. They will argue that experience is indeed the best teacher and that their experience has taught them about the superiority of their own group and the inferiority of members of another group.

Another social cognition bias is called the **availability heuristic**, and it occurs when we experience unusual or very memorable events and then overestimate how often such events typically occur (Tversky & Kahneman, 1973). Thus, people who watch a lot of crime shows on TV misjudge their chances of being crime victims, and because spectacular plane crashes are given more attention in the media than car accidents, some people cannot believe the fact that air travel is considerably safer than travel by automobile. An example of an availability heuristic of relevance to students is what happens when students change their answers on multiple-choice tests. Many students believe that the most frequent outcome of answer changing is that an initially correct answer will be changed to a wrong one. Students tend to hold that belief because when such an event does occur, it is painful and hence memorable (availability heuristic), perhaps making the difference between an A and a B on a test. Also, once the belief starts to develop, it is strengthened whenever the same kind of outcome does occur (confirmation bias), and it doesn't take too many instances before a strong belief about answer changing develops (belief perseverance begins). It is not uncommon to hear students tell others not to change answers but to "go with your initial gut feeling," a phenomenon that Kruger, Wirtz, and Miller (2005) call the "first instinct" fallacy. The problem is that students overlook cases when they change from one wrong multiple-choice alternate to another wrong one, or when they change from a wrong alternative to the correct one. It is only the memorable situation, changing from a right to a wrong answer that damages their score ("I had it right! And I changed it!").

When Kruger et al. (2005) asked students ($n = 1,561$) to estimate the percentages of the various outcomes of answer changing on a multiple-choice test, these were the results:

Changing from wrong to right   → 33%
Changing from right to wrong   → 42%
Changing from wrong to wrong   → 24%

But when Kruger and his colleagues calculated the actual percentages, measured by looking at erasures on multiple choice tests taken by the same students, these were the results:

Changing from wrong to right   → 51%
Changing from right to wrong   → 25%
Changing from wrong to wrong   → 23%

This of course is a huge difference—students were holding onto a strong belief ("Don't change answers—go with your first instinct!"), a belief they thought was based solidly on their direct experience, and yet the belief was completely false.[2] If you are saying to yourself there is no way this can be true, and I suspect you might indeed be saying that to yourself, then you have some idea of the strength of the combined forces of confirmation bias, belief perseverance, and the availability heuristic. Our experiences can be an indispensable and important guide to life's difficulties, but we also need to be aware of their limits. Social cognition biases such as the ones described here (not to mention several others—check out any social psychology textbook) can work together to distort the beliefs about and our interpretations of experiences in the world.

---

[2] People who should know better also fall prey to this first instinct fallacy. Kruger et al. (2005) opened their article by quoting from a well-known GRE test preparation guide (*Barron's*)—"Exercise great caution if you decide to change an answer. Experience indicates that many students who change answers change to the wrong answer" (p. 725). They also referred to an earlier study by Benjamin, Cavell, and Shallenberger (1984), which showed that the majority of *faculty* at Texas A&M University surveyed also endorsed the first instinct fallacy.

The Ways of Knowing and Science

The most reliable way to develop a belief, according to Charles Peirce, is through the method of **science**. Its procedures allow us to know "real things, whose characters are entirely independent of our opinions about them" (Tomas, 1957, p. 25). Thus, Peirce believed that the chief advantage of science is in its objectivity—for Peirce, to be objective meant to avoid completely any human bias or preconception. Modern philosophers of science recognize that, because scientists are just as human as everyone else, the ideal of a pure objectivity among scientists is impossible. To some degree, they rely on authority, they often logically argue with each other in an *a priori* fashion, and they are prone to social cognition biases in the process of learning from their experiences.

Concerning bias, scientists sometimes hold on to a pet theory or a favored methodology long after others have abandoned it, and they occasionally seem to be less than willing to entertain new ideas. Charles Darwin once wrote half seriously that it might be a good idea for scientists to die by age 60, because after that age, they "would be sure to oppose all new doctrines" (cited in Boorstin, 1985, p. 468). On the other hand, the historian of science Thomas Kuhn (1970) argued that refusing to give up on a theory, in the face of a few experiments questioning that theory's validity, can have the beneficial effect of ensuring that the theory receives a thorough evaluation. Thus, being a vigorous advocate for a theory can ensure that it will be pushed to its limits before being abandoned by the scientific community. The process by which theories are evaluated, evolve, and sometimes die will be elaborated in Chapter 3.

Research psychologists can also be influenced by authority. The "authorities" are usually other scientists, and experts are certainly more likely to be reliable sources than not. Nonetheless, researchers know better than to assume automatically that something is true simply because a reputable scientist said it was true. Rather, scientists are normally guided by the motto engraved on the entrance to the headquarters of the British Royal Society—"Nullius in Verba"—which encourages them to "take nobody's word for it; see for yourself" (cited in Boorstin, 1985, p. 394). Of course, "seeing for yourself" opens up the dangers of uncritically relying on experience, but scientists tend to be rather good at critical thinking.

Peirce's *a priori* method (the use of reason) is frequently found in science to the extent that scientists argue with each other, trying to reach a rational consensus on some issue, but often failing to do so (e.g., whether the computer provides a useful metaphor for memory). As you will see in Chapter 3, they also rely on the rules of logic and inductive/deductive reasoning to develop ideas for research and to evaluate research outcomes. Although scientific thinking includes elements of the nonscientific ways of knowing described thus far, it has a number of distinct attributes. It is to the nature of science that we now turn.

SELF TEST

1.1

1. Even if you never get involved in research after taking the research methods course, why is taking a research methods course valuable?
2. If you fail to question anything in this textbook, you will be relying too heavily on _____ as a way of knowing.
3. Some students think they should never change answers on multiple-choice tests. What does this have to do with the availability heuristic?

Science as a Way of Knowing

The way of knowing that constitutes science in general and psychological science in particular involves a number of interrelated assumptions and characteristics. First, researchers assume **determinism** and **discoverability**. Determinism simply means that events, including psychological ones, have causes, and discoverability means that by using agreed-upon scientific methods, these causes can be discovered with some degree of confidence. In psychology, we ultimately would like to know what causes behavior (determinism), and it is with the tools of science that we can discover those causes (discoverability). Even with the best of methods, research psychologists do not expect to predict psychological phenomena with 100% certainty, but they have faith that psychological phenomena occur with some regularity and that the regularities can be investigated successfully. Let us examine the determinism assumption in more detail. This will be followed by a discussion of the other attributes of science as a way of knowing.

Science Assumes Determinism

Students are often confused after reading that psychologists regard human behavior as "determined." They sometimes assume this means "predestined" or "predetermined," or that "determinism" is contrasted with "free will." These are not the definitions of determinism that scientists use. A believer in absolute predestination thinks that every event is determined ahead of time, perhaps by God, and develops a fatalistic conviction that one can do little but accept life as it presents itself. However, the traditional concept of determinism, as used in science, contends simply that all events have causes. Some philosophers have argued for a strict determinism, which holds that the causal structure of the universe enables the prediction of all events with 100% certainty, at least in principle. Most scientists, influenced by 20th-century developments in physics and the philosophy of science, take a more moderate view that could be called probabilistic or **statistical determinism**. This approach argues that events can be predicted, but only with a probability greater than chance. Research psychologists take this position and use this definition of determinism in their science.

The concept of determinism, even the "less than 100%" variety, is troubling because it seems to require that we abandon our belief in free will. If every event has a cause, so the argument goes, then how can one course of action be freely chosen over another? The psychologist would reply that if determinism is not true at least to some degree, then how can we ever know anything about behavior? Imagine for a moment what it would be like if human behavior was completely unpredictable. How could you decide whether to marry Ned or Ted? How could you decide whether or not to take a course from Professor Jones?

Of course, there are multiple factors influencing behavior, and it is difficult to know for sure what someone will do at any one moment. Nonetheless, behavior follows certain patterns and is clearly predictable. For example, because we know that children will often do things that work effectively for them, it is not hard to predict a tantrum in the toy department of a crowded store if that behavior has yielded toys for a child in the past. And because behavior learned in one setting tends to "generalize" to similar environments, it isn't hard to predict a tantrum in Wal-Mart for the child whose tantrums have worked effectively in Target.

Most research psychologists believe that the issue about the existence of free will cannot be settled one way or the other by science. Rather, whether the choices we make in life are freely made or not is a philosophical matter, and our personal belief about free will must be an individual decision, arrived at through the use of reason (perhaps supplemented with reflection on our experiences and/or the ideas of authority figures). The best that psychologists can do is to examine scientifically such topics as (a) the extent to which behavior is influenced by a strong belief in free will, (b) the degree to which some behaviors are more "free" than others (i.e., require more conscious decision making), and (c) what the limits might be on our "free choices" (Baumeister, 2008). As just one example of this line of research, Vohs and Schooler (2008) argued that a belief in free will has value, perhaps increasing the chances that people will behave ethically. In two studies, they found that encouraging a belief in determinism increased the tendency for subjects to cheat on academic-type tasks, whereas subjects believing in free will and reading statements promoting free will were less likely to cheat.

Science Makes Systematic Observations

A major attribute of science as a way of knowing is the manner in which science goes about the business of searching for regularities in nature. All of us do a lot of observing in our daily lives, and we draw conclusions about things based on those observations. But we also know, from the earlier discussion of empiricism as a way of knowing, that experience is susceptible to such biases as confirmation bias, belief perseverance, and the availability heuristic. Science also bases its findings on observations, but they are made much more systematically than our everyday observations. The scientist's systematic observations include using (a) precise definitions of the phenomena being measured, (b) reliable and valid measuring tools that yield useful and interpretable data, (c) generally accepted research methodologies, and (d) a system of logic for drawing conclusions and fitting those conclusions into general theories. The rest of this book is an elaboration of the sentence you just read.

Science Produces Public Knowledge

Another important characteristic of science as a way of knowing is that its procedures result in knowledge that can be publicly verified. This was the attribute that Peirce found most appealing about science—its **objectivity**. For Peirce, being objective meant eliminating such human factors as expectation and bias. The objective scientist was believed to be almost machine-like in the search for truth. Today, however, nobody believes that scientists can separate themselves from their already-existing attitudes, and to be objective does not mean to be devoid of such normal human characteristics. Rather, an objective observation, as the term is used in science, is simply one that can be verified by more than one observer. In science this usually takes the form of defining the terms and research procedures precisely enough so that any other person can repeat the study, presumably achieving the same observable outcome. That is, science produces knowledge that is public knowledge. This process of repeating a study to determine if its results occur reliably is called "replication" and you will learn more about it in Chapter 3. In general, as results are replicated, public confidence in the reality of some psychological phenomenon is increased. On the other hand, questions are raised when results cannot be replicated. As you will learn in the next chapter, a failure to replicate is also how scientific fraud is sometimes suspected and then uncovered.

Of course, in order to repeat a study, one must know precisely what was done in the original one. This is accomplished by means of a prescribed set of rules for describing research projects. These rules are presented in great detail in the *Publication Manual of the American Psychological Association* (American Psychological Association, 2010), a useful resource for anyone reporting research results or writing any other type of psychology paper. Appendix A, a guide to writing a research report in APA format, is based on the manual and provides a good introduction to writing the report.

Objectivity in psychological science has been a problem historically. When psychology first emerged as a new science, it defined itself as the "science of mental life" and one of its early methods was called **introspection**. This procedure varied considerably from one laboratory to another, but it was basically a form of precise self-report. Participants in an experiment would perform some task and then provide a detailed description of their conscious experience of the task. To give you some sense of what introspection was actually like, read Box 1.1 before going any further. It shows you an example of a verbatim introspective description in a 1913 experiment on attention, and it shows how the progress of science occurred when introspection was later abandoned for more objective measures of behavior.

BOX 1.1   ORIGINS—A Taste of Introspection

The following introspective account is from a 1913 study by Karl Dallenbach dealing with the phenomenon of attention. Introspectors were instructed to listen to two metronomes set at different speeds and to count the number of beats between coincident beats (i.e., both metronomes hitting at the same instant). While counting, they were also asked to perform some other task, such as continuously adding numbers out loud. Needless to say, these tasks severely tested the limits of attention. After finishing a session, one introspector reported:

> The sounds of the metronomes, as a series of discontinuous clicks, were clear in consciousness only four or five times during the experiment, and they were especially bothersome at first. They were accompanied by strain sensations and unpleasantness. The rest of the experiment my attention was on the adding, which was composed of auditory images of the numbers, visual images of the numbers, sometimes on a dark gray scale which was directly ahead and about three feet in front of me. . . . When these processes were clear in consciousness, the sounds of the metronomes were very vague or obscure. (Dallenbach, 1913, p. 467)

Notice that the introspector attempted to describe everything that happened in consciousness while performing the task, including sensory events ("strain"), emotion ("unpleasant"), and imagery, both auditory and visual. Also, the difficulty in keeping multiple tasks equally "clear in consciousness" led Dallenbach to conclude that attention

was severely limited, a finding later rediscovered by later research on "selective" attention (e.g., Broadbent, 1958).

The problem with introspection was that although introspectors underwent rigorous training that sought to eliminate bias in their self-observations, the method was fundamentally subjective—I cannot verify your introspections and you cannot verify mine. The problem was articulated nicely by John B. Watson, in a paper that came to be known as the "Behaviorist Manifesto" (Watson, 1913). As he put it:

> Take the case of sensation. A sensation is defined in terms of its attributes. One psychologist will state with readiness that the attributes of a visual sensation are *quality*, *extension*, *duration*, and *intensity*. Another will add *clearness*. Still another that of *order*. I doubt if any one psychologist can draw up a set of statements describing what he means by sensation which will be agreed to by three other psychologists of different training. (p. 164, emphasis in the original)

If psychology was to be truly "scientific," Watson argued, it needed to drop introspection and measure something that was directly observable and could therefore be verified objectively (i.e., by two or more observers). For Watson the answer was simple: just measure behavior. His argument that the basic data of psychology ought to be observable and measurable behavioral acts earned Watson the title of founder of behaviorism as a school of thought. Today, the term *behavior* is part of psychology's definition in every introductory psychology textbook.

With behavior as the data to be measured, the modern researcher investigating attention would not ask for detailed introspective accounts, as Dallenbach did in Box 1.1, but would design an experiment in which conclusions about attention could be drawn from some easily observed behavior in the Dallenbach task, such as the number of addition errors made while the participant was trying to keep track of the metronome activity. Presumably, two independent observers could agree on the number of errors that occurred in the task, making the experiment open to public verification.

Science Produces Data-Based Conclusions

Another attribute of science as a way of knowing is that researchers are **data driven**. That is, like the character in the middle at the bar in Figure 1.1, who is undoubtedly a scientist of some kind, research psychologists expect conclusions about behavior to be supported by evidence gathered through some systematic procedure. For instance, a claim made by a college admissions director that "this year's incoming class is better prepared than any in recent memory" (an annual claim at some schools) would compel the scientific thinker to respond, "Let's see the data for this year and the past few years," and "What do you mean by better prepared?" Furthermore, researchers try to judge whether the data given to support some claim are adequate for the claim to be made. Hence, if someone asserts that talking on a cell phone adversely affects driving, the scientist immediately begins to wonder about the type and amount of data collected, how the terms were defined in the study (e.g., driving performance), the exact procedures used to collect the data, the type of statistical analysis that was done, and so on.

This attitude about data can be detected easily in research psychologists. They even find themselves thinking about how data might bear on the problems they encounter in daily living. Even a neighbor's offhand observation about the tomato crop being better this year might generate in the researcher's mind a host of data-related questions to test the claim (How exactly did you count the tomatoes during the past 2 years? Did you measure the number picked per day or the number that ripened per day? How did you define "ripe"? What do you mean by "better"?). Of course, there are certain hazards resulting from this kind of thinking, including a tendency for the neighbor to begin avoiding you. Sometimes the "driven" (as in compelled) part of the term "data-driven" seems to be the operative term.

©The New Yorker Collection 1999 Edward Koren from cartoonbank.com. All Rights Reserved.

"Are you just pissing and moaning, or can you verify what you're saying with data?"

FIGURE 1.1
On the importance of data-based conclusions.

A personification of the data-driven attitude taken to extremes can be found in the life of Sir Francis Galton, a 19th-century British jack-of-all-sciences, whose interests ranged from geography to meteorology to psychology. His importance for correlational research will be examined in Chapter 9. Galton was obsessed with the idea of collecting data and making data-based conclusions. Thus, he once measured interest in various theater productions by counting the number of yawns that he could detect during performances; he studied association by counting the number of related ideas occurring to him on his morning walks; and he collected data on species differences and age-related hearing loss by inventing a device, called the "Galton whistle," that produced sounds of various pitches (Galton, 1883/1948).

Galton's (1872) most unusual attempt to draw a data-based conclusion was a controversial study on the "efficacy of prayer." Like his cousin, Charles Darwin, Galton was skeptical about religion and decided to test empirically the notion that prayers "worked." If prayers were effective, he reasoned, then sick people who pray for a return to health should recover sooner than those who do not. Similarly, people who do a lot of praying for a living (i.e., the clergy) or who are the object of a great deal of prayer (i.e., the king and queen of England) should live longer than the general population. None of these predictions were supported by the data, however. For instance, by digging through biographical dictionaries, Galton found that eminent members of the clergy lived for an average of 66.42 years and members of the royal family lasted 64.04 years; lawyers, on the other hand (presumably less likely to be the object of prayer), made it to a virtually identical average of 66.51 years (data from Forrest, 1974, p. 112). Galton was understandably criticized for his rather simplistic idea of the purpose of prayer, and his article on prayer was initially rejected (three times) as being "too terribly conclusive and offensive not to raise a hornet's nest" (cited in Forrest, 1974, p. 111), but the study certainly illustrates a conviction for drawing data-based conclusions.

Science Produces Tentative Conclusions

Related to the data-driven attitude that characterizes researchers is the recognition that conclusions drawn from data are always tentative, subject to revision based on future research. That is, science is a self-correcting enterprise and its conclusions are not absolute, yet there is confidence that research will eventually get one ever closer to the truth. The attitude was nicely described by Damasio (1994), in the context of research on the brain.

> I have a difficult time seeing scientific results, especially in neurobiology, as anything but provisional approximations, to be enjoyed for a while and discarded as soon as better accounts become available. But skepticism about the current reach of science, especially as it concerns the mind, does not imply diminished enthusiasm for the attempt to improve provisional explanations. (p. xviii)

The tentative nature of scientific research is a feature of scientific thinking that is often difficult for the general public to understand; people seem to believe that the outcome of well-executed scientific research will be authoritative and the final answer to some question. This belief is the basis for the frustration often felt when some new finding reported in the news seems to contradict what was reported just a few years before. You can probably think of many examples that have been in the news. For example, consider coffee and its main ingredient, caffeine, America's favorite drug. A Google search on the topic quickly yields newspaper headlines like the following: "Conflicting Views on Caffeine in Pregnancy" (*New York Times*, 17 July 2001); "Sorting out Coffee's Contradictions" (*New York Times*, 5 August 2008); and "Coffee: Good for Us? Or Bad for Us? Two New Studies Disagree" (*Los Angeles Times*, 19 August 2013). Reading these stories, one learns that coffee drinking by pregnant women might result in babies with low birth weight, but maybe it won't; that coffee can increase the risk for developing high blood pressure, but maybe it won't; or that coffee drinking can increase the chances of getting liver cancer, but maybe not. Coffee drinkers (i.e., most of us) reading these articles might be inclined to throw up their hands and say, "Why can't they (scientists) make up their minds?" The frustration is reasonable, but it is based on a fundamental misunderstanding of science. It is true that some findings have a greater degree of certainty than others, because they are based on a large body of evidence accumulated over a long period of time (e.g., the link between smoking and heart disease), but all findings are subject to rethinking, based on new research. Compared to most people, scientists have a relatively high tolerance for ambiguity and a willingness to be patient with the progress of science. In the long run, scientists have faith that the proficient use of science will lead to increasing confidence about the truth of some phenomenon.

The tentative nature of science contrasts sharply with the nonscientific thinking described in the previous section of this chapter. Beliefs not based in science tend to be resistant to change, because they bring social cognition biases into play. Beliefs rooted in scientific methodology, however, are always subject to change based on new data. Individual scientists might be reluctant to give up on their own data easily, but science as a whole proceeds because new information, if based on good science and replicated, eventually cannot be ignored. Finally, there is an important lesson here for everyday critical thinking—we should always be open to new data and new ideas, willing to change our minds in the face of good (i.e., scientifically sound) evidence.

Science Asks Answerable Questions

As mentioned earlier, *empiricism* is a term that refers to the process of learning things through direct observation or experience. **Empirical questions** are those that can be answered through the systematic observations and techniques that characterize scientific methodology. They are questions that are precise enough to allow specific predictions to be made. As you will learn in Chapter 3, asking questions is the first step of any research endeavor. How to develop a good empirical question and convert it into a testable hypothesis will be one theme of that chapter.

We can begin to get an idea about what constitutes empirical questions, however, by contrasting them with questions that cannot be answered empirically. For example, recall that Peirce used the mind-body question to illustrate the *a priori* method (use of reason). Philosophers argued both sides of the question for many years (they're still at it!), and Peirce wasn't optimistic about the issue ever being resolved. Whether the mind and the body are two separate essences or one is simply not an empirical question. However, a number of empirical questions *can* be asked that are related to the mind-body issue. For instance, it is possible to ask about the influence of mental activity (mind) on physical health (body) by asking the empirical question "What are the effects of psychological stress on the immune system?" Also, it is possible to investigate the body's influence on mental states by asking how physical fatigue affects performance on some task.

Science Develops Theories That Can Be Falsified

When designing research studies, an early step in the process is to reshape the empirical question into a *hypothesis*, which is a prediction about the study's outcome. That is, prior to having empirical data, the hypothesis is your best guess about the answer to your empirical question. For the two empirical questions just asked about the mind-body issue, for instance, we might develop these hypotheses:

- Because students experience high levels of stress during final exam week, they will be more likely to become ill if they are exposed to a virus than students not exposed to a virus.

- Students asked to exercise vigorously for an hour will perform more poorly on a test of creative problem solving than students not asked to exercise.

You will notice that empirical questions are just that, questions, whereas hypotheses are statements about what a scientists think may occur in a particular situation.

As you will learn in Chapter 3, hypotheses sometimes develop as logical deductions from a **theory**, which is a set of statements that summarize what is known about some phenomena and propose working explanations for those phenomena. A critically important attribute of a good theory is that it must be precise enough so that it can be refuted, at least in principle. This concept is often referred to as **falsification** (elaborated in Chapter 3—you could take a look ahead to Box 3.2 for a great historical example of falsification). That is, theories must generate hypotheses producing research results that could come out as the hypothesis predicts (i.e., support the hypothesis and increase confidence in the theory) or could come out differently (i.e., fail to support the hypothesis and raise questions about the theory). Research that consistently fails to support hypotheses derived from a theory eventually calls a theory into question and can lead to its modification or outright abandonment.

To sum up this section on science as a way of knowing, research psychologists can be described as "skeptical optimists." They are open to new ideas and optimistic about using scientific methods to test these ideas, but at the same time they are tough-minded—they won't accept claims without good evidence. Also, researchers are constantly thinking of ways to test ideas scientifically, they are confident that truth will emerge by asking and answering empirical questions, and they are willing (sometimes grudgingly) to alter their beliefs if the answers to their empirical questions are not what they expected.

One final point. Although we have been describing the attitudes and behaviors of psychological scientists, it is important to realize that virtually all of the points made in this section of the chapter are relevant to you as a developing critical thinker. To reiterate a point made earlier, it is not essential for you to become a researcher for the lessons of this book to have value for you. All of us could benefit from using the attributes of scientific thinking to be more critical and analytical about the information we are exposed to every day.

SELF TEST

1.2

1. Textbook definitions of psychology always include the term "behavior." What does this have to do with the concept of objectivity?
2. What is an empirical question? Give an example.
3. What is a hypothesis? Give an example.

Psychological Science and Pseudoscience

Because everyone is interested in human behavior, it is not surprising that many claims are made about its causes and inner workings. Many of those claims are based on legitimate scientific inquiry, of course, following the rules of the game that you will learn about in this text and carried out by the skeptical optimists we just described. That is, psychologists know a fair amount about behavior and mental life as a result of relying on the kinds of thinking and the specific methods that characterize legitimate science. However, many claims are made in the name of psychological science using methods and ways of thinking that are not truly scientific but merely pseudoscientific ("pseudo" is from the Greek word for "false"). In general, the term **pseudoscience** is applied to any field of inquiry that appears to use scientific methods and tries hard to give that impression, but is actually based on inadequate, unscientific methods and makes claims that are generally false or, at best, overly simplistic. The Sidney Harris cartoon in Figure 1.2 portrays an

FIGURE 1.2
The unfortunate popularity of pseudoscience.

unfortunate truth about pseudoscience—its popular appeal. What differentiates true science from pseudoscience is an important thing to know for a critical thinker in psychology.

Recognizing Pseudoscience

Those living in the late 19th-century could send away to the New York firm of Fowler and Wells for a "Symbolic Head and Phrenological Map" for 10 cents. For another $1.25, the head and map would be accompanied by a copy of *How to Read Character: A New Illustrated Handbook of Phrenology and Physiognomy* (Anonymous Advertisement, 1881). Thus equipped, people would then be in a position to measure character (theirs or that of others) "scientifically" through an analysis of skull shape.

Even today in the 21st century, we can visit any one of dozens of websites and learn about "graphology," the so-called science of analyzing personality by examining handwriting. At one site, for instance, for $29.95, you can buy a "Basic Steps to Graphoanalysis" kit, complete with workbook and DVD. Thus equipped, you would then be in a position to measure personality (yours or that of others) "scientifically" through an analysis of handwriting.

As these two examples suggest, people are willing to pay for self-knowledge, especially if the methods appear to be scientific and take little effort to implement and understand. Both 19th-century phrenology and 21st-century graphology are pseudoscientific, however, and both illustrate the main features of pseudoscience—they try hard to associate with true science, they rely primarily on anecdotal and testimonial evidence, they sidestep the all-important falsification criterion, and they take complex phenomena (e.g., character, personality) and try to convince you these phenomena can be understood by relying on simple-to-understand concepts (e.g., head shape, handwriting shape).

Associates with True Science

Proponents of pseudoscience do everything they can to give the appearance of being scientific. In some cases, the origins of a pseudoscience can be found in true science; in other instances, the pseudoscience confuses its concepts with genuine scientific ones. Phrenology illustrates the former, graphology the latter.

Phrenology originated in legitimate attempts to demonstrate that different parts of the brain had identifiably distinct functions, and it is considered one of the first systematic theories about the localization of brain function (Bakan, 1966). Phrenologists believed that (a) different personality and intellectual attributes ("faculties") were associated with different parts of the brain (see Figure 1.3), (b) particularly strong faculties resulted in larger brain areas, and (c) skull measurements yielded estimates of the relative strengths of faculties. By measuring skulls, therefore, one could measure the various faculties that made up one's personality.

Phrenology remained popular into the early years of the 20th-century, even though it had been discredited in a brilliant series of studies by the French physiologist Pierre Flourens by the mid-1800s (see Box 1.2). Yet in the second half of the 19th century, despite being abandoned by scientists, phrenology as a business enterprise flourished—phrenological societies were formed, popular journals were established, and phrenological analysis was used for everything from choosing a career to hiring an honest servant. Even if a theory is discredited within the scientific community, then, it can still find favor with the public. This creates special problems for psychology as a science, because it isn't difficult for virtually any type of theory about human behavior to have some popular appeal. The graphology business is a good recent example.

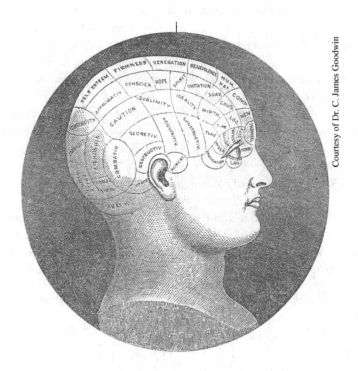

Courtesy of Dr. C. James Goodwin

FIGURE 1.3
A phrenological skull with faculties identified.

BOX 1.2   CLASSIC STUDIES—Falsifying Phrenology

In 1846, a brief volume (144 pages) with the title *Phrenology Examined* appeared. Its author was Pierre Flourens (1794–1867), a distinguished French physiologist and surgeon known for demonstrating the role of the ear's semicircular canals in balance, for locating the respiratory center in the medulla oblongata, and for discovering the anesthetic properties of chloroform (Kruta, 1972). He was also phrenology's worst enemy. He certainly did not mince words, declaring:

> The entire doctrine of [phrenology] is contained in two fundamental propositions, of which the first is, that understanding resides exclusively in the brain, and the second, that each particular faculty of the understanding is provided in the brain with an organ proper to itself.
>
> Now, of these two propositions, there is certainly nothing new in the first one, and perhaps nothing true in the second one. (Flourens, 1846/1978, p. 18)

To test the phrenologists' claims, Flourens took an experimental approach to the problem of localization, using the method of *ablation*. Rather than wait for natural experiments to occur in the form of accidental brain damage, Flourens removed specific sections of the brain and observed the effects. If the result of an ablation is an inability to see, then presumably the area of the removed portion has something to do with vision.

Flourens's attack on phrenology consisted of showing that specific areas of the brain that were alleged by phrenologists to serve one function in fact served another function, and that the cerebral cortex operated as an integrated whole rather than as a large collection of individual faculties located in specific places. One focus of his research was the cerebellum. To the phrenologists, this portion of the brain controlled sexual behavior and was the center of the faculty of "amativeness." In his celebrated *Outlines of Phrenology*, for instance, Johann G. Spurzheim (1832/1978) argued that sexuality "appears with the development of this part, and is in relation to its size" (p. 28). Apparently thinking of some anecdotal data, Spurzheim pointed out that sometimes the cerebellum "is of great magnitude in children, and then its special function, the propensity we treat of, appears in early life" (p. 28).

Flourens would have none of it. First, he ridiculed the circular logic of assigning "faculties" to a certain behavior and then explaining that same behavior by pointing to the faculties:

> [W]hat sort of philosophy is that, that thinks to explain a fact by a word? You observe . . . a penchant in an animal . . . a taste or talent in a man; *presto*, a particular faculty is produced for each one of the peculiarities, and you suppose the whole matter to be settled. You deceive yourself; your *faculty* is only a *word*,—it is the name of a fact,—and all the difficulty [of explanation] remains where it was before. (Flourens, 1846/1978, p. 39; italics in the original)

Flourens had little trouble ruling out (falsifying) the idea that the cerebellum had anything to do with sexual motivation. By carefully removing portions of the cerebellum, he showed that it was the center of motor coordination. Thus, pigeons deprived of the organ were unable to coordinate wing movements in order to fly, and dogs were unable to walk properly and were observed staggering, falling down, and bumping into objects they could normally avoid. Sexual motivation was unaffected. With other animals, Flourens removed varying amounts of the cerebral cortex and found a general relationship between the amount destroyed and the seriousness of the ensuing problem. He could find no indication of distinct functions ("faculties") residing in specific areas of the cortex.

Flourens effectively destroyed phrenology, but the issue of localization of function did not by any means disappear, and other physiologists soon demonstrated that the cortex had a greater degree of localization than Flourens was willing to grant. The French surgeon Paul Broca, for example, demonstrated that a relatively small area of the left frontal lobe of the cortex (later named for him), seemed to control the production of speech. For more on this issue of localization, take your department's courses in history and systems of psychology and/or biological psychology.

As for graphology, it has an even longer history than phrenology, dating at least as far back as the 17th century, when an Italian physician named Camillo Baldi wrote *Treatise on a Method to Recognize the Nature and Quality of a Writer from His Letters* (Nickell, 1922a). Various techniques for assessing handwriting developed over the years, and there are several modern versions, all having in common the belief that a close analysis of the components of handwriting will reveal stable personality traits. Graphology has an intuitive appeal, because handwriting styles do tend to be unique to the individual, so it is natural to assume that the style reflects something about the person—extroverts might write with larger letters than introverts, for instance. Graphologists have been employed in a number of settings, used by businesses for employee selection, for instance.

Advocates for graphology try to associate with true science in two different ways. First, there is a fairly high degree of complexity to the analysis itself, with measurements taken of such variables as slant, letter size, pen pressure, spacing between letters, etc. With actual physical measurements being made, one gets the impression of legitimacy. After all, science involves measuring things. Second, graphologists often confuse their pseudoscience with the legitimate science of document analysis, performed by professionals called "questioned document examiners" (Nickell, 1992b). This latter procedure is a respected branch of forensic science, involving the analysis of handwriting for identification purposes. That is, the document analyst tries to determine whether a particular person wrote or signed a specific document. This is accomplished by getting a handwriting sample from that person and seeing if it matches the document in question. The analyst is not the least bit interested in trying to assess personality from the handwriting. Yet graphologists sometimes point to the work of document examiners as a verification of the scientific status of their field.

Relies on Anecdotal Evidence

A second feature of pseudoscience, and one that helps explain its popularity, is the reliance on and uncritical acceptance of **anecdotal evidence**, specific instances that seem to provide evidence for some phenomenon. Thus, phrenology data consisted mostly of a catalog of examples: a thief with a large area of "acquisitiveness," a priest with an overdeveloped bump for "reverence," a prostitute with excessive "amativeness." Graphology advocates use the same approach. Their websites are filled with testimonials from people have had their handwriting analyzed and have been amazed at how accurate the graphologist's description of them appears to be. Anecdotal evidence in the form of testimonials has great appeal to the uncritical reader.

There is nothing wrong with accumulating evidence to support a theory; even anecdotal examples like the ones mentioned are not automatically disqualified. The problem occurs when one relies heavily on anecdotes or makes more of them than is warranted. The difficulty is that anecdotal evidence is selective; examples that don't fit are ignored (you might recognize this as another example of a confirmation bias). Hence, there may be some thieves with a particular skull shape, but in order to evaluate a specific relationship between skull configuration and thievery, one must know (a) how many people who are thieves do not have the configuration, and (b) how many people who have the configuration aren't thieves. Without having these two pieces of information, there is no way to determine if there is anything unusual about a particular thief or two with a particular skull shape. The identical problem occurs with graphology—the websites never report cases of people being given handwriting-based personality assessments that were wide of the mark.

One other reason to distrust a glowing testimonial is that it often results from a phenomenon familiar to social psychologists—**effort justification** (Aronson & Mills, 1959). Following from Leon Festinger's theory of cognitive dissonance (elaborated in the Chapter 3 discussion about theory), the idea is that after people expend significant effort, they feel compelled to convince themselves that the effort was worthwhile. After spending $30 on a handwriting analysis package, we don't like to think that we've thrown away hard-earned money and wasted valuable time.

To reduce the discomfort associated with the possibility that we've been had, we convince our-selves that the investment of time and money was a good one. That is, we justify the effort or cost we just expended by thinking it was worth it.

Sidesteps the Falsification Requirement

As you learned earlier in this chapter, one of the hallmarks of a good scientific theory is that it is stated precisely enough to be put to the stern test of falsification. In pseudoscience this does not occur, even though on the surface it would seem that both phrenology and graphology would be easy to falsify. Indeed, as far as the scientific community is concerned, falsification has occurred for both. As you know, Flourens effectively discredited phrenology (at least within the scientific community), and the same has occurred for graphology. Professional graphologists claim to have scientific support for their craft, but the studies are inevitably flawed. For example, they typically involve having subjects produce extensive handwriting samples, asking them to "write something about themselves." The content, of course, provides clues to the person. The graphologist might also interview the person before giving the final personality assessment. In addition, the so-called *Barnum effect* can operate. Numerous studies have shown that if subjects are given what they think is a valid personality test (but isn't) and are then given a personality description of themselves, filled with a mix of mostly positive traits, they will judge the analysis to be a good description of what they are like. This occurs even though *all* the subjects in a Barnum effect study get the exact same personality description, regardless of how they have filled out the phony personality test! So it is not difficult to imagine how a graphologist's analysis of a person might seem fairly accurate to that person. However, the proper study of graphology's validity requires (a) giving the grapholo-gist several writing samples about topics having nothing to do with the subjects participating in the study (e.g., asking subjects to copy the first three sentences of the Declaration of Independence), (b) assessing the subjects' personality with recognized tests of personality that have been shown to be reliable and valid (concepts you'll learn more about in Chapter 4), and then (c) determining whether the graphologist's personality descriptions match those from the real personality tests. Graphology always fails this kind of test (Karnes & Leonard, 1992).

Advocates of pseudosciences such as phrenology and graphology have had to face the skepti-cism of legitimate scientists. Not all thieves have bumps in just the right places and not everyone with tightly cramped handwriting is tight with their money. Apologists respond to these threats rather creatively. Instead of allowing an apparent contradiction to damage the theory, they side-step the problem by rearranging the theory a bit or by adding some elements to accommodate the anomaly. Consequently, the apparent falsification winds up being touted as further evidence in support of the theory! For example, if a known pacifist nonetheless had a large area of destruc-tiveness, a clever phrenologist would find even larger areas of cautiousness, benevolence, and reverence, and these would be said to offset or suppress the violent tendencies. Likewise, when responding to a case where a person was found to be a big spender, even with tightly cramped handwriting, the graphologist would look to some other aspects of the handwriting (remember, a wide range of factors are measured) to explain away the apparent anomaly ("yes, the handwriting is cramped, but the extreme slant and specific looping of the g's and p's offsets that cramping, and is indicative of a certain looseness with money"). Or the graphologist might say the big spender is unconsciously trying to disguise the tendency by writing in a way that is opposite to the trait.

Thus, for pseudoscience, any contradictory outcome can be explained or, more accurately, explained away. Yet a theory that explains all possible outcomes fails as a theory because it can never make specific predictions. If a pacifist can have either a large or a small area of destructive-ness, how can we use skull shape to predict whether someone will be a pacifist? If cramped writ-ing may or may not indicate stinginess, how can behavior be predicted from the writing? In general, if a theory is beyond the reach of the strong test of falsification, and is therefore incapa-ble of making predictions, it is of no value.

Another way that falsification is sidestepped by pseudoscience is that research reports in pseudoscientific areas are notoriously vague and they are never submitted to reputable journals with stringent peer review systems in place. As you recall, one of science's important features is that research produces public results, reported in books and journals that are available to anyone. More important, scientists describe their research with enough precision that others can replicate the experiment if they wish. This does not happen with pseudoscience, where the research reports are usually vague or incomplete and, as seen earlier, heavily dependent on anecdotal support.

Reduce Complex Phenomena to Overly Simplistic Concepts

A final characteristic of pseudoscience worth noting is that these doctrines take what is actually a very complicated phenomenon (the nature of human personality) and reduces it to overly simplistic concepts. This, of course, has great consumer appeal, especially in psychology. Trying to figure out and improve behavior is a universal human activity, and if the process can be simplified, either by measuring someone's head, interpreting someone's handwriting, or determining someone's astrological sign, then many people will be taken in by the apparent ease of the explanations. Please note that the actual simplicity of the explanatory concepts is often masked by an apparent complexity of the measuring devices used in many of the pseudosciences. Thus, the phrenologists went through an elaborate set of skull measurements to measure faculties and graphologists measure dozens of features of handwriting.

In sum, pseudoscience is characterized by (a) a false association with true science, (b) a misuse of the rules of evidence by relying excessively on anecdotal data, (c) a lack of specificity that avoids a true test of the theory, and (d) an oversimplification of complex processes. Perhaps because of our enormous interest in behavior, pseudoscientific approaches to psychology are not hard to find in any historical era, and many people seem to have difficulty seeing the inherent weaknesses in pseudoscientific doctrines. As you develop your skills as a critical thinker by taking this research methods course, however, you should be able to distinguish valid psychological science from that which merely pretends to be.

The Goals of Research in Psychology

Unlike pseudoscience, scientific research in psychology has four interrelated goals. Researchers hope to develop complete descriptions of behaviors, to be able to make predictions about future behavior, and to be able to provide reasonable explanations of behavior. Furthermore, they assume that the knowledge derived from their research will be applied so as to benefit people, either directly or eventually. Below we introduce you to each of these goals: description, prediction, explanation, and application. They will be discussed in more depth in later chapters of the book, and they form the structure of how we report our research to others (see Appendix A).

Describe

To provide a good **description** in psychology is to identify regularly occurring sequences of events, including both stimuli or environmental events and responses or behavioral events. For example, a description of aggressive behavior in some primate species might include a list of the situations in which fighting is most likely to occur (e.g., over food), the types of threat signals that might precede actual combat (e.g., baring teeth), and the form of the fight itself (e.g., attacks directed at non-vital areas like shoulders and haunches). Description also involves classification, as when someone attempts to classify various forms of aggressive behavior (e.g., fighting vs.

predation). Providing a clear, accurate description is an essential first step in any scientific endeavor; without it, predictions cannot be made and explanations are meaningless. Some research in psychology is primarily descriptive in nature. For example, most survey/questionnaire and observational research falls into this category. You will learn more about this research in Chapters 9 and 10.

Predict

To say that behavior follows **laws** is to say that regular and predictable relationships exist for psychological phenomena. The strength of these relationships allows **predictions** to be made with some degree of confidence. After describing numerous primate fights, for example, it might become clear that after two animals fight over food and one wins, the same two animals won't fight again. If they both spot a banana at the same time, the winner of the initial battle might display a threat gesture and the loser of that first fight will probably go away. If that series of events happened often enough, the researchers could make predictions about future encounters between these animals and, more generally, between animals who are winners and losers of fights. One of the primary strengths of research that uses correlation and regression, as you will learn in Chapter 9, is that it is useful for making predictions. A correlation between SAT scores and college GPA enables admissions departments at colleges to use SAT scores to predict success in college (up to a point).

Explain

The third goal of the experimenter is **explanation**. To explain some behavior is to know what caused it to happen. The concept of causality is immensely complex, and its nature has occupied philosophers for centuries. Psychological scientists recognize the tentative nature of explanations for behavior, but they are generally willing to conclude that X is causing Y to occur if they conduct an experiment in which they systematically vary X, control all other factors that could affect the results, and observe that Y occurs with some probability greater than chance and that variations of Y can be predicted from the variations in X. Furthermore, they will have confidence in the causal explanation to the extent that (a) the explanation makes sense with reference to some theory or some already existing sets of laws, and (b) other possible explanations for Y occurring in the presence of X can be ruled out. The process of theory building, and of how empirical research is derived from and affects the development of theory, will be elaborated in Chapter 3. For now, simply be aware that causality is a complicated process involving experimental control, a time sequence with cause preceding effect, a theoretical structure, and the ruling out of alternative explanations. As you will see, starting in Chapter 5, research psychologists believe that, within some limits, causal conclusions can be drawn from a type of research called experimental research.

Apply

This final goal of psychological science, **application,** refers simply to the various ways of applying those principles of behavior learned through research. Psychologists assume that because of the knowledge derived from the research they do, it is possible for people's lives to change for the better. Hence, research on the factors influencing depression enables therapists to help people diagnosed with depression, research on aggression can help parents raise their children more effectively, and so on. Pioneer cognitive psychologist George Miller (1969) concluded his presidential address to the APA stating

I can imagine nothing we could do that would be more relevant to human welfare, and nothing that could pose a greater challenge to the next generation of psychologists, than to discover how best to give psychology away. (p. 1074)

What Miller meant was that it is crucial for psychological scientists to share their work with the general public for the betterment of society. Researchers today in clinical psychology, for example, sometimes refer to their work as **translational research**, or research that is done for both better understanding of a particular phenomenon as well as for its application to promote physical and psychological well-being. Translational research will be elaborated in Chapter 11. In summary, it is certainly a goal for psychological scientists to follow Miller's lead to "[instill] our scientific results . . . in the public consciousness in a practical and useful form so that what we know can be applied by ordinary people" (p. 1068) or . . . "to give [psychology] away to the people who really need it—and that includes everyone" (p. 1071).

SELF TEST

1.3

1. How did pseudoscientific phrenologists get around the problem of falsification?
2. What is anecdotal evidence and what is the problem with using it as a way to support the truth of some claim?
3. In psychological science, what is a law, and with which goal is it associated?

A Passion for Research in Psychology

Near the end of his long and productive life, the renowned Russian physiologist Ivan Pavlov was asked to write a brief article for a student journal on what it takes to be a great scientist. Pavlov wrote that it took three things. The first was to be systematic in the search for knowledge and the second was to be modest and to always recognize one's basic ignorance. The third thing, he wrote, was "*passion*. Remember that science demands [your] whole life. And even if you could have two lives, they would not be sufficient. Science calls for tremendous effort and great passion. Be passionate in your work and in your search for truth" (quoted in Babkin, 1949, p. 110; italics added). A similar sentiment is evident in the words of cognitive psychologist Elizabeth Loftus. In graduate school, once she found a topic that excited her, the practical aspects of memory, Loftus

spent every free moment in [the] lab, setting up the experimental design, running subjects, tabulating the data, and analyzing the results. . . . I began to think of myself as a *research psychologist*. Oh, those were *lovely* words—I could design an experiment, set it up, and follow it through. I felt for the first time that I was a scientist, and I knew with ultimate clarity that it was exactly what I wanted to be doing with my life. (Loftus & Ketcham, 1991, p. 6; first italics in the original; second italics added)

Although your goal in life might not be to become a researcher, your education in psychological research and scientific thinking is invaluable, and it might very well give you some moments when you have some insight into the words of Pavlov and Loftus. It can be truly exciting to create a study to answer some question that interests you, and there is nothing like the great feeling of discovery that comes from the results of all your hard work. Perhaps the best reason for doing research in psychology is that it is can be enormously rewarding. Yes, it is challenging, frustrating at times, and there will be long hours in the lab, but few researchers would exchange their careers for another. What could be more satisfying than getting an idea about some aspect of human behavior, putting it to the test of a research study, and having the results come out just as you hoped?

Let us wrap up this opening chapter with brief examples of how two legendary experimental psychologists became devoted to their work and found great satisfaction in it.

Eleanor Gibson (1910–2002)

On June 23, 1992, Eleanor Gibson (Figure 1.4) was awarded the National Medal of Science by President George H. W. Bush. It is the highest honor a president can confer on a scientist. Gibson, then 82, was honored for a lifetime of research in developmental psychology, studying topics ranging from how we learn to read to how depth perception develops. She was perhaps best known to undergraduates for her "visual cliff" studies.

Gibson was the prototype of the devoted researcher who persevered even in the face of major obstacles. In her case the burden was sexism. This she discovered on arrival at Yale University in 1935, eager to work in the lab of Robert Yerkes, well known for his work in both comparative psychology and mental testing. She was astounded by her first interview with him. As she later recalled, "He stood up, walked to the door, held it open, and said, 'I have no women in my laboratory'" (Gibson, 1980, p. 246).

Undaunted, Gibson eventually convinced the great behaviorist Clark Hull she could be a scientist and finished her doctorate with him. Then in the late 1940s, she went to Cornell University with her husband, James Gibson (another famous name, this time in perception research). Eleanor labored there as an unpaid research associate for 16 years before being named professor.[3] It was

George Bush Presidential Library and Museum

FIGURE 1.4
Eleanor Gibson receiving the National Medal of Science by President George H. W. Bush in 1992.

---

[3] Cornell did not pay her a salary during this time, but she earned stipends via the many successful research grants that she wrote (e.g., from the Rockefeller Foundation, National Science Foundation, U.S. Office of Education).

during this period of uncertain status that she completed her work on perceptual development. Some sense of her excitement about this research is evident from her description of how the visual cliff experiments first came about.

The project evolved out of perceptual development research with rats that she was doing with a Cornell colleague, Richard Walk. They were both curious about depth perception. In the army, Walk had studied training programs for parachute jumpers, and at Cornell's "Behavior Farm," Gibson had observed newborn goats avoid falling from a raised platform. She also had a "long-standing aversion to cliffs, dating from a visit to the Grand Canyon" (Gibson, 1980, p. 258). With a lab assistant, Gibson

> hastily put together a contraption consisting of a sheet of glass held up by rods, with a piece of wallpaper under one side of it and nothing under the other side except the floor many feet below.
>
> A few rats left over from other experiments got the first try. . . . We put a board about three inches wide across the division between the surface with flooring and the unlined glass, and put the rats on the board. Would they descend randomly to either side?
>
> What ensued was better than we had dared expect. All the rats descended on the side with textured paper under the glass. We quickly inserted some paper under the other side and tried them again. This time they went either way. We built some proper apparatus after that, with carefully controlled lighting and so on. . . . *It worked beautifully*. (Gibson, 1980, p. 259; italics added)

Gibson and Walk (1960) went on to test numerous species, including, of course, humans. The visual cliff studies, showing the unwillingness of eight-month-olds to cross the "deep side," even with Mom on the other side, are now familiar to any student of introductory psychology.

B. F. Skinner (1904–1990)

If you ask students to name a famous psychologist other than Freud, many will say "B. F. Skinner" (Figure 1.5), psychology's most famous 20th-century scientist. His work on operant conditioning created an entire subculture within experimental psychology called the *experimental analysis of behavior*. Its philosophy and the methods associated with it will be explored in Chapter 12.

Skinner's autobiography (three-volumes—he wasn't shy) provides a marvelous view of his life and work, and the following quote illustrates his almost childlike fascination with making a new discovery. It is from a period when Skinner had just completed his doctorate at Harvard and was staying on there as a prestigious research fellow. In early 1932, he was studying a number of conditioning phenomena, including extinction. In his words:

> My first extinction curve showed up by accident. A rat was pressing the lever in an experiment on satiation when the pellet dispenser jammed. I was not there at the time, and when I returned *I found a beautiful curve*. The rat had gone on pressing although no pellets were received. . . .
>
> The change was more orderly than the extinction of a salivary reflex in Pavlov's setting, and *I was terribly excited*. It was a Friday afternoon and there was no one in the laboratory who I could tell. All that weekend I crossed streets with particular care and avoided all unnecessary risks to protect my discovery from loss through my accidental death. (Skinner, 1979, p. 95; italics added)

There is a thread that weaves together the work of Pavlov, Loftus, Gibson, and Skinner, and countless other researchers in psychology. Pavlov accurately identified this common feature when he exhorted students to be *passionate* about their work. You can detect this passion if you read

FIGURE 1.5
B. F. Skinner as an eager young graduate
student at Harvard, circa 1930.

carefully the quotes above. In both the Gibson and Skinner quotes, the concept of beauty appears. For Gibson, the first visual cliff experiments "worked *beautifully,*" and Skinner found "a *beautiful* curve." Similarly, when Loftus referred to her self-identity as a research psychologist as "*lovely* words" and knew she had found her life's work, that same intensity of feeling was being expressed.

Throughout the remainder of this book, you will be learning the tools of psychological science and will be reading about the research of other psychologists who are committed scientists in love with their work. Our greatest hope is that by the time you have completed this book and your methods course, you will be hooked on research and want to contribute to the growing collection of knowledge about what makes people behave the way they do.

CHAPTER SUMMARY

Why Take This Course?

The research methods course is at the core of the psychology curriculum. It should be taken by all psychology majors because it provides the foundation for doing research in psychology, serves as a basis for understanding other content courses in psychology, makes one a more critical thinker about research, is essential for admission to graduate studies, and teaches scientific thinking.

Ways of Knowing

Our knowledge of the world around us often derives from our experiences and how we interpret them, our reliance on the authority of others, and our use of reason. These sources of knowledge can be quite valuable, but they can also lead to error. Our experiences can be subject to social cognition biases (e.g., belief perseverance, availability heuristic, and confirmation bias), authorities can be wrong, and while reason and logic are essential for critical thinking, reasonable arguments in the absence of empirical evidence can be unproductive in the search for truth. Research psychologists rely heavily on scientific thinking as a way of knowing and understanding behavior.

Science as a Way of Knowing

Research psychologists assume that human behavior is lawful and predictable and that using scientific methods can lead to the discovery of regularities in behavior. Science relies on observations that are more systematic than those made in everyday life, and produces knowledge that is open to public verification (i.e., it is said to be objective—verifiable by more than a single observer); historically, the emphasis on objectivity led to a shift from using introspection as a method to using methods that measured specific behaviors.

UPI/Bettmann/©Corbis

Science also requires conclusions about the causes of behavior to be data-based, but scientists recognize that their data-based conclusions are tentative and could change, depending on the outcomes of future studies. The questions asked by scientific researchers are referred to as empirical questions—they are answerable through the use of recognized scientific methods. Scientists also develop theories that are precise enough to meet the test of falsification. Research psychologists are skeptical optimists—optimistic about discovering important things about behavior, but skeptical about claims made without solid empirical support.

Psychological Science and Pseudoscience

It is important to distinguish legitimate scientific inquiry from pseudoscience. The latter is characterized by a deliberate attempt to associate itself with true science, by relying on anecdotal evidence (e.g., glowing testimonials), by developing theories that are too vague to be adequately tested with scientific methods and fail the test of falsification, and by a tendency to explain complicated phenomena with overly simplistic concepts.

The Goals of Research in Psychology

Research in psychology aims to provide clear and detailed descriptions of behavioral phenomena, to develop laws that enable scientists to predict behavior with some probability greater than chance, and to provide adequate explanations of the causes of behavior. The results of psychological research can also be applied to change behavior directly.

A Passion for Research in Psychology

Psychological scientists tend to be intensely curious about behavior and passionate about their work. As a relatively young discipline, psychology has more questions than answers, so doing research in psychology can be enormously rewarding. The joy of doing research can be seen in the lives and work of famous psychologists such as Eleanor Gibson (the visual cliff studies) and B. F. Skinner (the discovery and promotion of operant conditioning).

CHAPTER REVIEW QUESTIONS

At the end of each chapter you will find a set of short essay questions for review. You should study the chapter thoroughly before attempting to answer them. You might consider working through them with a lab partner or with a study group. There are additional review questions, along with detailed feedback, at the online Study Guide on the Student Companion Site. The review material includes multiple choice, fill in the blanks, and matching items.

1. Explain why it would be a good idea to take a research methods course prior to taking courses in such areas as social, abnormal, developmental, and cognitive psychology.

2. As ways of knowing, what are the shortcomings of (a) authority and (b) what Peirce called the *a priori* method?

3. Explain how various social cognition biases should make us cautious about the old saying that "experience is the best teacher."

4. Using the historical example of introspection, explain how research psychologists use the term objectivity.

5. What is an empirical question? Give an example of an empirical question that would be of interest to someone studying the relationship between religion and health.

6. Distinguish between determinism and discoverability, as a research psychologist would use the terms.

7. Describe the essential attributes of science as a way of knowing.

8. Research psychologists are said to be "skeptical optimists." What does this mean?

9. Pseudosciences are criticized for relying on anecdotal evidence. What kind of evidence is this and why is it a problem?

10. Pseudosciences do what they can to appear scientific; use the graphology example to illustrate this point.

11. Research in psychology is said to have four related goals. Describe each.

12. In order for research psychologists to feel confident that they have found a "cause" for some phenomenon, what conditions have to be met?

APPLICATIONS EXERCISES

In addition to review questions, the end of each chapter will include "applications" exercises. These will be problems and questions that encourage you to think like a research psychologist and to apply what you have learned in a particular chapter. For each chapter, in order to give you some feedback, we will provide you with answers to some of the items (about half) in Appendix B. Your instructor will have a complete set of answers to all the exercises.

Exercise 1.1   Asking Empirical Questions

For each of the following non-empirical questions, think of an empirical question that would be related to the issue raised and lead to a potentially interesting scientific study.

1. Is God dead?

2. What is truth?

3. Are humans naturally good?

4. Are women morally superior to men?

5. What is beauty?

6. What is the meaning of life?

Exercise 1.2   Thinking Critically About an Old Saying

You have probably heard the old saying that "bad things come in threes." Use what you have learned about the various ways of knowing and about pseudoscientific thinking to explain how such a belief might be formed and why it is hard to convince a believer that there are problems with the saying. From what you have learned about scientific thinking, explain what needs to be made clearer in order to examine this "theory" more critically. That is, what needs to be precisely defined to determine if the saying is really true?

Exercise 1.3   Arriving at a Strong Belief

Consider people who have a strong belief in a personal God who, they believe, directs their daily lives. Using the various ways of knowing described in this chapter, explain how such a belief might form and be maintained.

Exercise 1.4   Subliminal Self-help

The basic idea behind the pseudoscientific subliminal self-help industry is that you can change some aspect of your behavior if you let your unconscious process motivational messages ("you can lose weight easily") that are sent to you "subliminally"—below the normal threshold for hearing. The process is said to be simple. You put on a CD that seems to have soothing music or gentle-waves-breaking-on-a-beach sounds and just relax. The subliminal messages will reach your unconscious and bring about some type of cognitive/attitudinal change that will lead directly to a change in behavior. The chief attraction is that you don't seem to have to do any work to lose weight, improve your memory, stop smoking, raise your self-esteem, etc.

Do a simple Google search for "subliminal self-help" or "subliminal CD." You will find dozens of sites. Examine two sites—one promoting subliminal techniques and one that provides a more skeptical analysis of them.

1. Consider each of the main aspects of pseudoscience described in the chapter. How does each apply in this case?

2. Even though we have not begun to discuss research design, you probably have some sense of what an experiment is like. Design a simple study that might be a good test of the claim that subliminal messages can change your life.

Exercise 1.5   Social Cognition and the Psychic Hotline

There are a surprising number of otherwise normal people who consult psychics for advice about how to live their lives. Explain how believing in someone who appears to have psychic ability might result from or be strengthened by:

1. belief perseverance

2. confirmation bias

3. the availability heuristic

ANSWERS TO SELF TESTS

✓ 1.1

1. Improves your ability to be a critical thinker when assessing claims made about human behavior and mental processes.
2. Authority.
3. When students change answers and happen to get the item wrong (statistically less likely than changing an answer and getting it right), the outcome sticks out in their memory because it is painful (loss of points).

✓ 1.2

1. Behaviors can be measured and agreement among observers can occur.
2. An empirical question is one that can be answered with data collected from a study using scientific procedures. An example: What percentage of students reading this book take the self-tests?
3. A hypothesis is a research prediction that can be deduced from a theory. An example: Students who have higher GPAs are more likely to take this textbook's self-tests than students who have lower GPAs.

✓ 1.3

1. Phrenologists sidestepped falsification by using combinations of faculties to explain the apparent anomaly.
2. Anecdotal evidence involves using specific examples to support a general claim (they are also known as testimonials); they are problematic because those using such evidence fail to report instances that do not support the claim.
3. A law is a regularly occurring relationship. It applies to the goal of prediction.

Ethics in Psychological Research

PREVIEW & CHAPTER OBJECTIVES

This second chapter will introduce you to the most recent version (2002) of the ethics code formulated by the American Psychological Association (APA). The code directs psychological scientists in the planning, execution, and reporting of their research, and it includes guidelines for psychological research that tests both human participants and animals.[1] Ethical issues are important to review early in this textbook because such issues must be addressed at all stages of the research process. When you finish this chapter, you should be able to:

- Describe the origins and evolution of the APA ethics code.

- Articulate the code's five general principles, especially as they apply to research in psychology.

- Describe the role of the Institutional Review Board (IRB) in the research process and what needs to be done by the researcher to achieve IRB approval of research.

- Explain when research proposals are exempt from IRB review, eligible for expedited review, or in need of a full formal review.

- Explain why the decision-making processes of IRBs have occasionally been controversial.

- Identify the essential features of a researcher's ethical responsibility when completing psychological research using adult human participants.

- Describe historical examples of research that raised serious ethical questions.

- Identify the ethical principles involved when completing research with children and those from special populations (e.g., prisoners and nursing home residents).

- Describe how the ethics code applies to research that involves using the Internet.

- Describe the arguments for and against the use of animals in psychological research.

- Identify the essential features of a researcher's ethical responsibility when completing psychological research using animal subjects.

- Identify the varieties of scientific dishonesty, how it can be detected, and understand some of the reasons why misconduct sometimes occurs in science.

---

[1] Humans are animals, too, of course. When we use the term *animal research*, we are referring to research with nonhuman animals.

A system of **ethics** is a set of "standards governing the conduct of a person or the members of a profession" (*American Heritage Dictionary*, 1992, p. 630). As members of the profession of psychology, researchers are obligated to follow the code of ethics established by the APA. When conducting research in psychology, our ethical obligations encompass several areas. Research psychologists must (a) treat human research participants with respect and in a way that maintains their rights and dignity, (b) care for the welfare of animals when they are the subjects of research, and (c) be scrupulously honest in the treatment of data. This chapter will examine each of these broad topics.

Before we describe the APA code of ethics, you should read Box 2.1, which describes one of psychology's best-known studies and two lesser-known experiments. The Little Albert experiment is often depicted as a pioneering investigation of how children develop fears, but it also serves well as a lesson in dubious ethical practice. Also, in the name of psychological science, other infants have been subjected to repeated pinpricks in a study on adaptation to pain and have spent up to 14 months in relative isolation.

BOX 2.1   CLASSIC STUDIES—Infants at Risk

In this chapter, you will learn about an ethics code that is elaborate and finely tuned. In fact, you might think the code is unnecessarily complex and the good judgment of psychological researchers would surely prevent research participants from coming to serious harm. After you read about the following three studies, which occurred before the code existed, it should be clear why one was needed.

One of psychology's most frequently cited studies (Watson & Rayner, 1920) has come to be known as the Little Albert study. The authors were the famous behaviorist John B. Watson and Rosalie Rayner, a graduate student who eventually became Watson's second wife. The study tested just one child, an 11-month-old boy referred to as Albert B. The purpose of the study was to see if Albert could be conditioned to be afraid. Despite serious methodological weaknesses and failed replication attempts (Harris, 1979), the study has become a "classic" in psychology, routinely appearing in general psychology textbooks in the chapter on conditioning.

In prior research, Watson had determined that most infants were naturally afraid of loud noises and loss of support (e.g., falling). Watson and Rayner (1920) decided to use loud noise, produced when Watson struck a steel bar with a hammer just behind the infant's head. To see if the fear could be attached to a neutral stimulus, a white rat, the conditioning procedure was to pair the loud noise with the rat. When Albert reached out to touch the rat, "the bar was

struck immediately behind his head" (p. 4). His response? "The infant jumped violently and fell forward, burying his face in the mattress" (p. 4). After several trials, the loud noise was no longer needed; Albert was now afraid of the rat. Because of generalization to similar stimuli, he was also fearful when shown a rabbit. Watson and Rayner made no attempt to remove the fear, although they made several suggestions for doing so.

It is difficult to hold Watson and Rayner responsible for ethical guidelines that were published several decades after they completed their study. Historical events must be evaluated in the context of their own times. They acknowledged, however, that "a certain responsibility attaches to such a procedure" (Watson & Rayner, 1920, p. 3). They decided to proceed because Albert seemed to be a strong, healthy child. Watson also justified the study by arguing that because Albert would learn such fears in real life *anyway*, he might as well learn them in a way that would advance behavioral science.

Watson and Rayner haven't been the only psychologists who used questionable judgment while studying infants. Two other examples are studies by Myrtle McGraw and by Wayne Dennis, both published in 1941. McGraw (1941) was interested in nervous system maturation, a legitimate topic of study. Her method was to apply repeated "pin pricks" to the cheeks, abdomens, arms, and legs of 75 children "at repeated intervals from birth to four years" (p. 31). The pin

(continued)

BOX 2.1   (CONTINUED)

pricks did not penetrate the skin, but they certainly caused distress, as is clear from McGraw's descriptions of the reactions to the stimulus. For example, she wrote that the "most characteristic response consists of diffuse bodily movements accompanied by crying, and possibly a local reflex withdrawal of the stimulated member" (p. 32). Eventually, just the mere sight of McGraw heading their way with a pin was enough to stress the children: "With advancing development, it will be observed that perception of the pin or of the approaching arm of the adult provokes fussing, crying, or withdrawal reactions on the part of this child" (p.33).

Dennis (1941) was interested in studying how early development would be affected by reducing environmental and social stimulation. From a local hospital, Dennis and his wife were able to "obtain" a pair of newborn female twins "because the mother was unable to provide for them" (p. 149). The Dennises offered the impoverished mother "temporary care of the twins in return for the privilege of studying them" (p. 149). The twins spent 14 months in the Dennis household, kept most of the time in a nursery room that afforded minimal views of the outside (sky and the top of a tree); the room contained little furniture and no toys. Dennis and his wife interacted with them only during feeding, bathing, and diaper changing, and "carefully refrained from rewarding or punishing the subjects for any action" (p. 150). Dennis reported delays in motor development for the girls but claimed no serious adverse effects resulted from the environmental deprivation. He concluded that during the first year, social interactions and environmental stimulation had minimal effect on children. He made little of the fact that the twins were slow in language development, an outcome that wouldn't surprise modern developmental psychologists. Today, research psychologists sometimes use animals in procedures that would not be considered appropriate for humans, and raising them briefly in isolation is an example. In 1941, however, Dennis had no misgivings about subjecting infants to an impoverished environment.

The Watson, McGraw, and Dennis studies were not completed by callous and unconcerned researchers but rather by people who believed they were advancing their science. But they were operating in the absence of a code of ethical conduct that might have given them pause. These studies make the need for an ethics code clear.

Developing a Code of Ethics for Psychological Science

After World War II, the United States and its allies conducted the Nuremberg trials to hold Nazi officers, doctors, and others associated with them accountable for various war atrocities. Included in those trials were the Doctors Trials which involved Nazi doctors' experimentation on human beings, including being injected with gasoline, deliberately infected with deadly diseases, and exposed to high levels of radiation for the purposes of sterilization and abortion. In addition, the implementation of the T-4 "Euthanasia" Program resulted in the systematic killing of individuals "unworthy of life" including children with physical or psychological disabilities between 1939 and 1945 (Weindling, 2004). One lasting legacy that emerged from these trials was the Nuremberg Code of ethics (1949), which emphasized the importance of voluntary consent from individuals involved in medical research. You can review the complete Nuremberg code online at the Student Companion Site or by doing a simple Google search.

Psychologists in the United States published their first formal code of ethics in 1953 (APA, 1953), and it was influenced by the Nuremberg code. The document was the outcome of about 15 years of discussion within the APA, which had created a temporary committee on scientific and professional ethics in the late 1930s. This soon became a standing committee to investigate complaints of unethical behavior (usually concerned with the professional practice of psychology) that occasionally were brought to its attention. In 1948, this group recommended the creation of a formal code of ethics. As a result, the APA formed a Committee on Ethical Standards for Psychologists, chaired by Edward Tolman (Hobbs, 1948).

In keeping with psychology's penchant for drawing data-based conclusions, the APA committee took an empirical approach when developing the code. Using a procedure called the

critical incidents technique, the committee surveyed the entire membership of the APA (about 7,500 members at the time), asking them to provide examples of "incidents" of unethical conduct they knew about firsthand and "to indicate what [they] perceived as being the ethical issue involved" (APA, 1953, p. 4). The request yielded over 1,000 replies. Although most concerned the practice of psychology (e.g., psychotherapy), some of the reported incidents involved the conduct of research (e.g., research participants not being treated well). A second committee, chaired by Nicholas Hobbs, then organized the replies into several drafts that were published in *American Psychologist*, APA's primary journal; readers were encouraged to comment on the drafts. The APA's council of directors accepted a final version of the code in 1952 and it was published the next year. Although it was concerned mainly with professional practice, one of its sections in this first ethics code was called "Ethical Standards in Research."

In the early 1960s, not long after APA created its first ethics code, a young, Yale psychologist named Stanley Milgram began a series of studies that became as well known for the questions they raised about research ethics as it did for their conclusions about human behavior. Milgram, who was Jewish, was motivated by questions about the Nazi Holocaust and deeply concerned about the problem of obedience to authority. (During the Nuremberg trials, a common defense used by Nazi war criminals was that they were just following orders.) Did the Holocaust reflect some basic flaw in the German psyche? Or is the tendency to obey authority found in all of us, produced when the circumstances are right? To answer his own questions, he developed his now famous research on obedience to authority. In the guise of a study on the effects of physical punishment on learning, Milgram induced volunteers to obey commands from an authority figure, the experimenter (who was actually a member of the research team and a high school biology teacher in real life). Playing the role of teachers, participants were told to deliver what they thought were high-voltage shocks (no shocks were actually given) to another apparent volunteer (also a member of the research team and a railroad payroll auditor in real life) who was trying, without much success, to accomplish a memory task (see Figure 2.1). A surprisingly high percentage of subjects complied with the "orders" from an experimenter to deliver shock and, in doing so, most subjects became quite distressed. In his original study, Milgram (1963) reported he had

Courtesy of Dr. C. James Goodwin

FIGURE 2.1
The shock apparatus used by Milgram in his obedience studies.

observed a mature and initially poised businessman enter the laboratory smiling and confident. Within 20 minutes he was reduced to a twitching, stuttering wreck, and was rapidly
approaching a point of nervous collapse. (p. 377)

As you might guess, Milgram's research has been controversial. He was sharply criticized for
exposing his volunteers to extreme levels of stress, for producing what could be long-term adverse
effects on their self-esteem and dignity, and, because of the degree of deception involved, for
destroying their trust in psychologists (Baumrind, 1964).

Milgram completed his obedience studies in the 1960s and early 1970s, which was a time in
the United States when significant societal changes were taking place. The Civil Rights Act
(1964) and the Voting Rights Act (1965) were passed by Congress and contributed to growing
movement toward civil rights for all Americans. In part, the civil rights movement in American
culture emphasized basic equality and dignity among individuals and created a heightened awareness of instances of inequality and mistreatment of vulnerable groups. One such group whose
plight had finally come to light in the 1970s included poor Black men from the area around
Tuskegee, Alabama, who were diagnosed with syphilis, but deliberately left untreated so that
researchers could study the development of the disease over time (see Box 2.2). The revelation of
the Tuskegee study in the early 1970s is one factor that led to the United States Congress to enact
the National Research Act in 1974, which created the National Commission for the Protection of
Human Subjects of Biomedical and Behavioral Research. In 1979, the commission published
what came to be called the Belmont Report, which includes three basic principles for research
with human subjects: Respect for persons, Beneficence, and Justice. You can review the entirety
of the Belmont Report online at the Student Companion Site or by doing a simple Google search.

Over the years, the APA ethics code has been revised several times, most recently in 2002. It
currently includes a set of 5 general principles and 89 standards, the latter clustered into the
10 general categories. The general principles are "aspirational" in their intent, designed to "guide
and inspire psychologists toward the very highest ideals of the profession" (APA, 2002, p. 1062),
while the standards establish specific rules of conduct and provide the basis for any charges of
unethical conduct.[2] The entire APA code can be found online at www.apa.org/ethics/code/.

The five general principles reflect the philosophical basis for the code as a whole. These principles apply broadly to the science and practice of psychology. As they apply to research, they
can be described as follows:

A. *Beneficence and Nonmaleficence* establishes the principle that psychologists must constantly weigh the benefits and the costs of the research they conduct and seek to achieve
   the greatest good in their research with little harm done to others.

B. *Fidelity and Responsibility* obligates researchers to be constantly aware of their responsibility to society and reminds them always to exemplify the highest standards of professional behavior in their role as researchers.

C. *Integrity* compels researchers to be scrupulously honest in all aspects of the research enterprise.

D. *Justice* obligates researchers to treat everyone involved in the research enterprise with fairness and to maintain a level of expertise that reduces the chances of their work showing
   any form of bias.

E. *Respect for People's Rights and Dignity* translates into a special need for research psychologists to be vigorous in their efforts to safeguard confidentiality and protect the rights
   of those volunteering as research participants.

---

[2] The APA has established procedures for evaluating claims of ethical misconduct and for punishing those found guilty of misconduct.
There is even a link allowing psychologists to report "critical incidents." For more information, visit http://www.apa.org/ethics/code/.

There are many similarities between the principles of the Belmont Report and those of the APA Code, including some very similar language. Now, we turn to how psychological scientists apply these ethical principles in their research.

SELF TEST

2.1

1. How was the critical incidents technique used when the first APA ethics code was being developed?
2. What was the ethical justification used by Watson and Rayner in the "Little Albert" study?
3. What are the three basic principles of the Belmont Report?
4. The first general principle of the APA ethics code is "beneficence and nonmaleficence." What does this mean for the researcher?

Ethical Guidelines for Research with Humans

In the 1960s, a portion of the original ethics code was elaborated into a separate code of ethics designed for research with human participants. Another APA committee, led by Stuart Cook, used the same critical incidents procedure and published an ethics code specifically for researchers in 1973 (APA, 1973); it was revised in 1982 (APA, 1982) and again as part of the general revisions of 1992 and 2002. The specific APA Standards regarding research are found in Category 8 of the code ("Research and Publications"); you can find the full text of Category 8 at the Student Companion Site. In general, the standards for research with human participants include making a judgment that the benefits of the research outweigh the costs, gaining the informed consent of those participating in the study, and treating the research volunteers well during the course of the study and after it has been completed.[3]

Weighing Benefits and Costs: The Role of the IRB

All research on human behavior imposes some burden on those participating in the study. At a minimum, people are asked to spend time in an experiment when they could be doing something else. At the other extreme, they are sometimes placed in potentially harmful situations. In the name of psychological science, human **research participants (or subjects[4])** have received electrical shocks, been told they failed some apparently easy test, and been embarrassed in any number of ways. That such experiences can be distressing is illustrated in Milgram's (1963, 1974) obedience studies described earlier.

---

[3] Another useful source of information about the ethical treatment of human research participants is the Office for Human Research Protections in the U. S. Department of Health and Human Services. Its website is www.hhs.gov/ohrp/.

[4] The question of what to call those who participate in psychological research has changed over the years. In the early 20th century, during the era of introspection (Chapter 1), participants were often called *observers* because their task was to observe what was going on in their minds during some task and then give an introspective report of it. As introspection went out of vogue, participants began to be called *subjects*. Starting with the fourth edition of its publication manual, in 1994, however, the APA mandated a change in this usage for articles published in APA journals. At least with regard to most humans (nonhuman animals and preverbal infants were still to be referred to as *subjects*), APA required writers to use *research participant* or *participant* instead of *subject*, apparently on the grounds that the latter term was somehow biased and dehumanizing. This change was widely criticized (e.g., Roediger, 2004) on the grounds that the term *subject* does not necessarily demean anyone, is more efficient linguistically (two as opposed to four syllables), and reflects historical continuity. In its most recent publication manual, APA (2010) has backed off and recognized the historical argument, noting that "for more than 100 years the term *subjects* has been used as a general starting point for describing a sample, and its use is appropriate (p. 73, italics in the original).

The basic dilemma faced by Milgram and every other researcher is to weigh the scientific value of the research being planned (a benefit) against the degree of intrusion on those contributing data to the study (a cost). On one hand, psychological scientists believe strongly in the need to conduct psychological research on a wide range of topics. Indeed, they believe that failing to investigate abdicates their responsibility as scientists. If the ultimate goal is to improve the human condition (the "Beneficence and Nonmaleficence" general principle), and if knowledge about behavior is essential for this to occur, then clearly it is essential to learn as much as possible. On the other hand, research can create discomfort for those participating in it, although few studies come anywhere near Milgram's experiments in terms of the level of stress experienced by subjects.

When planning a research study, the experimenter always faces the conflicting requirements of (a) producing meaningful research results that could ultimately increase our knowledge of behavior and add to the general good and (b) respecting the rights and welfare of the study's participants and causing them no harm. An integral part of the process of planning a study involves consulting with others. A good first step is to ask a researcher colleague whether your study has any ethical pitfalls. A formal process also exists, however, and it concerns a group called the **Institutional Review Board or IRB**. In a university or college setting, this group consists of at least five people, usually faculty members from several departments and including at least one member of the outside community and a minimum of one nonscientist (Department of Health and Human Services, 1983).[5] In 1974, as part of the National Research Act, the federal government mandated that IRBs be in place for any college or university receiving federal funds for research. Today, IRBs are found in virtually all colleges and universities, whether or not federal funding is involved. Because of the complexity of the regulations involving research with human subjects, IRB members often go through a training program—a number of web-based programs exist (e.g., the Collaborative Institutional Training Initiative or CITI, found at www. citiprogram.org/). One survey found, however, that only 22% of IRB members reported having a formal training program at their institution (Cook & Hoas, 2011).

Researchers seeking IRB approval typically submit a rationale for the study and a description of research procedures, a statement about potential risks to participants, how these risks will be alleviated and why they can be justified, a copy of the study's informed consent form, and copies of materials to be used in the experiment. IRBs distinguish between proposals that are *exempt* from full review, those eligible for *expedited review*, and those requiring a *full review*. For research in psychology, proposals that are exempt from full review include studies conducted in an educational setting for training purposes (e.g., asking students like you to test each other on reaction time in the lab as part of a course requirement), purely naturalistic observation studies of public behavior, survey research that does not assess sensitive topics, and archival research. Proposals receiving expedited review include many of the typical psychology laboratory experiments in basic processes such as memory, attention, or perception, in which participants will not experience uncomfortable levels of stress or have their behavior manipulated in any significant fashion. All other research usually requires a full review by the entire IRB committee.

As you might guess, there are gray areas concerning decisions about exempt, expedited, and full review. Hence, it is common practice for universities to ask that *all* research be given some degree of examination by the IRB. Sometimes, different members of an IRB are designated as "first step" decision makers; they identify those proposals that are exempt, grant approval (on behalf of the full board) for expedited proposals, and send on to the full board only those proposals in need of consideration by the entire group. At medium and large universities, where the number of proposals might overwhelm a single committee, departmental IRBs are sometimes created to handle the expedited reviews (Murphy, 1999).

---

[5] It is common practice for IRBs to include a research psychologist on the grounds that a substantial number of proposals come from psychology departments (Cook & Hoas, 2011).

An important component of an IRB's decision about a proposal involves determining the degree of **risk** to be encountered by participants. Sometimes, there is no risk at all, as when experimenters observe public behavior and do not intervene in any way. At other times, subjects in a study may be "at risk" or "at minimal risk." The distinction is not razor sharp but is based on the degree to which the people being studied find themselves in situations similar to "those ordinarily encountered in daily life or during the performance of routine physical or psychological examinations or tests" (Department of Health and Human Services, 1983, p. 297). Hence, subjects facing situations like those encountered in daily living that might involve some stress, but not a substantial amount, are considered to be "at minimal risk." If the risks, physical or mental, are greater than that, participants are said to be "at risk." For instance, people would be at minimal risk in a sports psychology study investigating whether training in visual imagery techniques leads to better athletic performance than the absence of such training. However, if that same study investigated whether the improvement due to training in imagery could be reduced by having participants ingest some drug, the degree of risk to participants would obviously be higher and require more careful scrutiny by an IRB.

When there is minimal or no risk, IRB approval is usually routinely granted through an expedited review, or the proposal will be judged exempt from review. However, when participants are "at risk," a full IRB review will occur and experimenters must convince the committee that (a) the value of the study outweighs the risk, (b) the study could not be completed in any other fashion, and (c) they will scrupulously follow the remaining ethical guidelines to ensure those contributing data are informed and well treated.

One final point about IRB approval is that when conducting research outside of the university environment, a researcher might have to satisfy more than a single review board. A health psychologist, for instance, might be using a local wellness center as a location for studying adherence to an exercise program. In addition to gaining university IRB approval, the researcher will usually need an OK from the center's research committee before proceeding with the study.

IRBs provide an effective safeguard for participants, researchers, and universities, but they are controversial for three reasons. One issue is the extent to which IRBs should be judging the details of research procedures and designs (Kimmel, 2007). Researchers legitimately object to non-specialists (e.g., philosophy professors) passing judgment on methodologies they may not understand or research traditions they fail to appreciate. On the other hand, a poorly designed study has ethical implications. If it is seriously flawed methodologically, its results will be worthless, its participants could be harmed needlessly, and, at a minimum, their time will be wasted.

A second problem is that some researchers complain about IRBs being overzealous in their concern about risk, weighing it more heavily than warranted, relative to the scientific value of a study. For instance, a researcher described by Kimmel (2007) was unable to obtain IRB approval for a study in which people were asked to detect tones of varying loudness. Despite the fact that no tone was louder than conversational speech, the IRB insisted that listening to the tones "entailed a slight risk to [subjects'] welfare" (p. 283). The researcher refused to concede the point, argued with the IRB for 3 years, had no recourse for appeal, and eventually switched to animal research, stating that "the composition of animal welfare committees [was] a bit more reasonable" (p. 283). Obviously, not all IRBs are this arbitrary and inflexible, but the lack of an appeal process is a problem. Some studies have suggested that researchers, if they believe they have been treated unfairly by an IRB, might go as far as to omit from their IRB proposals some aspects of their procedure the IRB could find objectionable.

One unsettling consequence of IRBs being overly conservative, according to prominent social psychologist Roy Baumeister, is that psychology is rapidly becoming the science of self-reports and finger movements (keystrokes on a computer) instead of the science of overt behavior. After examining recent issues of the *Journal of Personality and Social Psychology*, Baumeister and his colleagues discovered that the "[d]irect observation of meaningful behavior is apparently passé"

(Baumeister, Vohs, & Funder, 2007, p. 397). Instead, it seemed that in the articles they read, subjects spent most of their time filling out surveys or describing how they or others might behave in some hypothetical situation. One explanation for the shift from overt behavior to self-report studies is efficiency; studies that ask subjects to read a scenario (e.g., encountering someone in need of help) and predict how they or others would react can be completed much more quickly than studies that actually place subjects in that scenario and record how they actually react. But another reason, Baumeister et al. argued, has to do with getting IRB approval. Measuring meaningful social behavior (as in the helping behavior example) usually means using deception, and it therefore places more of a burden on researchers to show their participants will be protected. Self-report studies are safer. Although Baumeister et al. acknowledged that important things about people can be learned from self-reports, he worried that psychology was showing signs of "abandoning its original goal of being the science of behavior" (p. 400).

A third issue that concerns psychologists is that IRBs sometimes overemphasize a biomedical research model to evaluate proposals. As a result, they might ask researchers to respond to requests that are not relevant for most psychological research. For example, they might ask that the consent form include information about procedures or alternative courses of treatment available to those who choose not to participate in the study (Azar, 2002). This makes sense for research evaluating the effectiveness of some medical treatment but makes no sense in most psychological research, where the alternative to participating is simply not to participate. Susan Fiske (2009), a prominent social psychologist and former chair of the IRB at Princeton University, recommended that universities sponsoring medical research should create separate IRBs for medical and behavioral research.

One unfortunate consequence of these three issues is a lack of consistency among IRBs. Several studies have shown that identical IRB proposals have fared differently with different IRB committee members. In one example, researchers proposed a study in which 6- to 10-year old children would view a 4-minute video in which a child actor mistakenly claimed to have been hit by a firefighter (who had in fact just told the child actor to leave his firefighter's hat alone). Children viewing the video would then be interviewed to determine their ideas about why the child actor might have lied. An IRB rejected the proposal on the grounds that "it was deemed unethical to show children public servants in a negative light" (Ceci & Bruck, 2009, p. 28). The identical IRB proposal, however, had been approved by IRBs at two other universities, had been found ethically acceptable by the National Science Foundation (which was funding the research), and was judged harmless by a panel of pediatricians and child development specialists.

Despite these issues, the primary goal of IRBs is to evaluate any ethical concerns that may arise during the course of the proposed research study. Because IRBs are comprised diverse members and may not include psychologists, they are often guided by the Nuremberg code or Belmont Report, which are broader in scope than the APA code. However, it is the responsibility of the psychology researcher to adhere to the APA code when proposing to the IRB psychological research involving humans because the APA code both encapsulates the Nuremberg code and Belmont Report as well as expands upon them.

Informed Consent and Deception in Research

A central feature of the APA code is the concept of **informed consent** (Standard 8.02), the notion that in deciding whether to participate in psychological research, human participants should be given enough information about the study's purpose and procedures to decide if they wish to volunteer. For example, the use of painful procedures in a study (e.g., electric shock and regardless of how mild it is) must be disclosed. Consent procedures evolved from the aftermath of historical abuses, most notably the medical research conducted in Germany during World War II that used concentration camp inmates as human guinea pigs. At the Nuremberg trials, the Nazi doctors defended their actions by arguing that voluntary consent didn't really exist in any medical research of the time and that the long-term importance of their research outweighed any adverse consequences to the participants. Their argument failed, they were convicted, and the presiding tribunal wrote what was called the Nuremberg Code mentioned earlier. It established the principle that consent must be informed, competent, and voluntary and that the person giving it must be able to comprehend the situation involved (Faden & Beauchamp, 1986).

Although the experiments performed on concentration camp victims are the most dramatic and appalling examples of consent violations, problems have occurred in the United States as well. See Box 2.2 for brief descriptions of cases in which (a) children with severe intellectual disabilities were infected with hepatitis in order to study the development of the illness; (b) southern Black men with syphilis were left untreated for years and misinformed about their health, also for the purpose of learning more about the time course of the disease; and (c) Americans, usually soldiers, were given LSD without their knowledge.

BOX 2.2 ETHICS—Historical Problems with Informed Consent

The research activities of doctors in the Third Reich are unprecedented in their callousness and cruelty. Nonetheless, there are cases in the United States of research projects that have provoked intensely critical reactions and have invited comparisons, albeit remote, to the Nazi doctors. Three famous examples are the Willowbrook hepatitis study, the Tuskegee syphilis study, and project MK-ULTRA.

At Willowbrook, an institution housing children with varying degrees of mental disability, an experiment began in 1956 and continued into the 1970s in which approximately 1 in 10 new admissions was purposely infected with hepatitis. The parents were told of the procedure and agreed to it, but it was later shown that they might have felt pressured into giving consent. The Willowbrook study was investigating hepatitis, not mental disability.

The study was initiated because hepatitis was rampant at Willowbrook institution, partly due to a high proportion of severely disabled children who could not be toilet-trained. At one point in the 1950s, there were 5,200 residents; of those, 3,800 had IQs lower than 20 and more than 3,000 were not toilet trained (Beauchamp & Childress, 1979). Even with the staff's best efforts, conditions were generally unsanitary and led to the spread of the disease. By deliberately infecting new admissions and placing them in a separate ward but not treating them, the researchers hoped to study the development of the disease under controlled conditions. Those in charge of the project defended it on the grounds that the children would almost certainly contract the disease anyway, so why not have them contract it in such

a way that more could be learned about it? Indeed, although the study has been legitimately criticized on ethical grounds, it did contribute to the understanding of hepatitis and improved treatment of the disease.

The Tuskegee study was designed to examine the physical deterioration of persons suffering from advanced syphilis (Jones, 1981). Beginning in the early 1930s, about 400 poor Black men from the rural South were diagnosed with the disease and deliberately left untreated. They were never informed about the nature of the disease, nor were they told its name; doctors simply informed them they had "bad blood." Also, local physicians agreed not to treat the men. Given the poverty of the participants, it was not difficult to induce (coerce?) them to visit the clinic periodically (free rides and a hot meal), where blood tests and other examinations were done. The project continued into the early 1970s, even though it was clear by the late 1940s that the subjects were dying at twice the rate of a control group and were developing significantly more medical complications (Faden & Beauchamp, 1986). Defenders of the study argued that, when it began in the 1930s, there was no effective treatment for the disease and little knowledge of it. Like Willowbrook, the Tuskegee study contributed to our understanding of a serious disease, but its value was vastly overshadowed by the consent violations.

While the chief investigators in both the Willowbrook and Tuskegee studies were misguided in their abuse of the informed consent concept, they had a strong desire to learn as much as possible about two devastating diseases,

(continued)

BOX 2.2   (CONTINUED)

hepatitis and syphilis. The third example of a consent viola-tion, unfortunately, lacked even the justification of an even-tual medical benefit. This was a project launched by the Central Intelligence Agency (CIA) to expose unknowing human participants to the drug LSD in order to gauge the drug's ability as a weapon. The project was created in the early 1950s, during the Cold War between the United States and the former Soviet Union. Prompted by an erroneous intelligence report that the Soviets were buying up the world's supply of LSD (Thomas, 1995), CIA leadership approved a program to determine if LSD could cause mental confusion or render captured spies defenseless. Over approximately 10 years, the CIA sponsored numerous stud-ies on unwitting participants, often soldiers but sometimes members of the general public. Soldiers signed consent forms, but the forms said nothing about the potential effects of the drug and were designed mostly to ensure that soldiers would not reveal their participation. That secrecy was impor-tant is clear from an internal CIA memo that read, in part,

> Precautions must be taken . . . to conceal these activities from the American public. . . . The knowledge that the Agency is engaging in unethical and illicit activities would have serious repercussions in political and diplomatic circles. (cited in Grose, 1994, p. 393)

What went on during MK-ULTRA? Projects included giv-ing soldiers LSD and then putting them in isolation, giving them the drug and then performing a lie detection task,

examining the effects of repeated doses (over 77 consecu-tive days in one case), and even surreptitiously giving the drug to men visiting prostitutes in a CIA-financed brothel, with agents observing behind two-way mirrors (Thomas, 1995). This latter study was code-named by a CIA humorist—it was called "Operation Midnight Climax."

At least two people died as part of MK-ULTRA and numerous others were adversely affected by it. Consider this case, as described in the 1994 Rockefeller Report, the results of a congressional investigation into 50 years of CIA-sponsored biological experimentation:

> In 1957, _____ volunteered for a special program to test new military protective clothing. He was offered various incentives to participate in the program, including a liberal leave policy. . . . During the 3 weeks of testing new cloth-ing, he was given two or three water-size glasses of a liquid containing LSD to drink. Thereafter, Mr. --- developed erratic behavior and even attempted suicide. He did not learn that he had received LSD . . . until 18 years later, as a result of congressional hearings in 1975. (Rockefeller Report, 1994)

The CIA did not bother to inform either Congress or the President about MK-ULTRA. The program ground to a halt in 1963, not because of any ethical misgivings on the part of the CIA, but primarily because the studies had not yielded any useful military information. Congressional investigators discovered it in the mid-1970s and eventually issued a full report (Grose, 1994).

Typical consent forms contain several features. First, potential volunteers agree to participate after learning the general purpose of the study (but not the specific hypotheses), the basic proce-dure, and the amount of time needed for the session. Second, participants understand they can leave the session at any time without penalty and with no pressure to continue. Milgram's sub-jects were encouraged to continue by the experimenter, as this was part of Milgram's procedure. In spite of subjects' lack of willingness to continue the experiment, Milgram's experimenters were trained to say thing like "The experiment requires that you continue" and "It is absolutely essential that you continue" (Milgram, 1963, p. 374). This clearly violates participants' freedom to discontinue a study at any time.[6] A third major feature of consent forms is that participants are informed that strict confidentiality and anonymity will be upheld. This feature is closely related

---

[6] For years, the Milgram study has been considered the "experiment that could never be replicated" because of the ethical issues involved. Recently, however, such a replication did occur at Santa Clara University (Burger, 2009), although substantial modifica-tions were made to Milgram's original procedure (e.g., not insisting that subjects continue, stopping the experiment earlier than Milgram did, screening subjects carefully). Despite the methodological changes designed to placate his university IRB, the study found levels of obedience similar to those observed by Milgram.

to APA General Principle E described earlier. Fourth, if questions linger about the study or if they wish to complain about their treatment as participants, there are specific people to contact, including someone from the IRB. Finally, participants are informed of any risk that might be encountered in the study, and they are given the opportunity to receive a summary of the results of the study, once it has been completed. When writing a consent form, researchers try to avoid jargon, with the aim of making the form as easy to understand as possible. Examples of a consent forms are often provided by the institution's IRB. We encourage you to explore the website for your institution's IRB to familiarize yourself with its code of ethics, committee membership, instructions for submission, and sample IRB forms. We have provided a sample of a consent form online at the Student Companion Site

A new feature of the 2002 revision of the ethics code is a more detailed set of provisions for research designed to test the effectiveness of a treatment program that might provide benefits but might also be ineffective and perhaps even harmful (Smith, 2003)—a program to treat post-traumatic stress disorder, for instance. This revision is found in Standard 8.02b, which tells researchers to be sure to inform participants that the treatment is experimental (i.e., not shown to be effective yet), that some specific services will be available to the control group at the end of the study, and that services will be available to participants who exercise their right to withdraw from the study or who choose not to participate after reading the consent form. Participants must also be informed of the method by which people have been assigned to the treatment and control groups.

Although informed consent is essential in most research in psychology, it is important to note that consent is not required for research that is exempt from full review. As Standard 8.05 indicates, consent is not needed in studies using anonymous questionnaires, for data that have already been collected for another purpose (archival data), for classroom projects in which data collection is for demonstration purposes, and for certain employment-related data collection exercises. Also, consent is not needed for observational studies that occur in certain locations; the key is whether the setting is a public one—if the study occurs in a place where anyone could be observed by anyone else, consent is not needed (Koocher & Keith-Spiegel, 1998).

Informed Consent and Special Populations

Not all research participants are capable of giving consent, due to factors as age or disability, and some persons might experience undue coercion to volunteer for research (e.g., prisoners). In these circumstances, additional procedures apply. For example, the Society for Research in Child Development (SRCD) follows a set of guidelines that expand upon some of the provisions of the code for adults. Thus, because children (anyone under age 18) might not be able to fully understand consent forms, their parents or legal guardians are the ones who give consent. Nonetheless, unless the participant is an infant or is otherwise not capable of skilled language use, researchers are obligated to inform the child about the study and to gain what is referred to as **assent**. That is, researchers give the child as much information as possible to gauge whether the child is willing to participate. According to the SRCD code, assent occurs when "the child shows some form of agreement to participate without necessarily comprehending the full significance of the research necessary to give informed consent" (SRCD, 1996, p. 337). Assent also means the researcher has a responsibility to monitor experiments with children and to stop them if it appears that undue stress is being experienced. A parent may give informed consent for a study on the effects of TV violence on children's aggressive behavior, but the parent might not be in the room when the film is shown. It is up to the researcher to be sensitive enough to remove the child from the task at hand (and repair the damage) if the stress level is too high.

In addition to the assent provision, the SRCD code requires that additional consent be obtained from others who might be involved with the study in any way. For example, this would include teachers when a study includes their students. The code also cautions researchers about incentives that might be used, either to induce a willingness to participate or as rewards for tasks completed. The rewards "must not unduly exceed the range of incentives that the child normally receives" (SRCD, 1996, p. 337). Also, researchers should not use the potential rewards as an inducement to gain the child's assent; indeed, rewards should not even be mentioned until after the parents have given full informed consent (Scott-Jones, 2000). Finally, the SRCD code mirrors the provisions of the code for adults, but warns researchers to be even more vigilant in certain areas. These include the decisions about balancing scientific gain against risk to participants, the level of deception that can be justified, and the reporting of the study's results.

Additional provisions for the protection of participants exist with other special populations. Thus, legal guardians must give truly informed consent for research with people who are confined to institutions (e.g., the Willowbrook case). Second, it is imperative to ensure that participants do not feel coerced into volunteering for a study. This problem is difficult to avoid in environments such as prisons because even with the best intentions of researchers, prisoners might believe that their failure to volunteer will cost them in the future and perhaps even affect their future parole status. In general, researchers tend to rely on simple material rewards (e.g., money) and make it clear to prisoners that their participation will not be noted in any way in their parole records (Diener & Crandall, 1978). As was the case for the SRCD code for research with children, the inducements to participate must be reasonable.

Another issue with confined populations is confidentiality (Kimmel, 2007). While normal guidelines for disguising the identity of participants apply, researchers are legally obligated to break confidentiality under circumstances that involve a clear danger (e.g., a prisoner participant reveals he is about to kill another prisoner). Finally, as illustrated in Box 2.2 in the Willowbrook case, research with confined populations should be designed for the expressed purpose of providing knowledge that will in some way benefit the members of that population.

Use of Deception

Consider the following scenario: You decide to sign up for an interesting-looking psychology experiment on problem solving. You show up at the appropriate time and place and, after being given initial instructions by an experimenter, you and another participant are left alone and given some anagrams to solve (anagrams are sets of letters that have to be unscrambled to make a word). After 5 minutes or so, the other person seems to get upset about the difficulty of the task and then storms out of the room. The experimenter returns, asks you a series of identifying questions about the person who just left (e.g., "Could you describe what she was wearing?"), and then asks you to identify this person from a set of photos. The experimenter then informs you that the real purpose of the study was eyewitness identification accuracy, not anagram problem solving. How would you react to this?

Standard 8.07 of the APA code indicates subjects might experience **deception** in a study if it is determined by the researcher, and agreed to by the IRB, that the study could not be done in any other fashion. That is, participants might not be told the complete details of a study at its outset, or they might be misled about some of the procedures or about the study's purpose, as in the eyewitness example you just read. Researchers argue that in the absence of deception in certain studies, participants would not act naturally. If you knew you were in a study on eyewitness identification and that the anagrams didn't matter, you probably wouldn't bother much with the anagrams. Instead, you'd be trying to memorize the features of the other person in the room, a behavior that would not occur in a real-world eyewitness situation. How can these apparently contradictory concepts of consent and deception be reconciled?

One could argue that truly informed consent should never result in people being deceived about the purposes of the study. Some (e.g., Baumrind, 1985) have recommended eliminating deception in all psychology experiments on the grounds that people in positions of trust (i.e., experimenters) should not be lying to others (i.e., subjects). The outcome of deceptive research, she believes, is that participants could become mistrustful of experts and perhaps even cynical about the legitimacy of psychology as a science. Others (e.g., Geller, 1982) have argued that the need for "truth in advertising" could be met by forewarning those thinking about participating in a study that involves deception. They could be given a general rationale for deception during the consent procedure, told that some form of deception would probably occur in the study, and assured that all would be revealed at the end. Forewarning has been criticized, however, on the grounds that subjects would spend more time trying to figure out the true purpose of the study than they would behaving naturally and that many would refuse to participate, thereby reducing the accuracy of the study's results (Resnick & Schwartz, 1973).

Milgram's (1963, 1974) obedience studies provide a further illustration of why psychologists sometimes withhold information about the true purpose of the study at the beginning of the experiment. We've seen that Milgram told his subjects he was investigating the effects of punishment on learning. Teachers (the real subjects) tried to teach a list of word pairs to the learner, believing they were shocking him for errors. Milgram was not really interested in learning, of course. Rather, he wanted to know whether his volunteers would (a) continue to administer apparent shocks of increasing voltage to a learner who was in discomfort and not learning much, or (b) disobey the experimenter and stop the experiment. The outcome: Few people disobeyed. In the original study, 26 out of 40 continued shocking the learner even when the voltage level seemed to reach 450 and *nobody* disobeyed until the level reached 300 volts (Milgram, 1963)! If Milgram had informed his "teachers" he was interested in seeing whether they would obey unreasonable commands, would the same results have occurred? Certainly not. Blind obedience to authority is not something people value highly, so subjects told ahead of time they are in a study of obedience would surely be less compliant than they otherwise might be. The point is that researchers want their participants to take the task seriously, to be thoroughly involved in the study, and to behave as naturally as possible. For that to happen, deception is sometimes necessary. Please keep in mind, however, that the Milgram study is an extreme example of deception. Although deception studies with elaborate cover stories are more likely to be found in social psychology than in other research areas (Korn, 1997), the level of deception is minor in most research. Typically, it involves the withholding of some information about the study rather than a cover story that creates the impression that the study concerns topic A when it really involves topic B. That is, most deception research involves omitting some information in the consent process rather than actively misleading participants about what they are to encounter (Fischman, 2000). For instance, participants in a memory study might be given a series of five word lists to study and recall, one at a time. At the end of the session, although not initially informed of it, they might be asked to recall as many words as they could from all five lists. Information about that final recall would be omitted from the original instructions to get a better measure of the memory for all of the lists, uncontaminated by extra rehearsal.

Treating Participants Well

Several portions of the ethics code are designed to ensure that volunteers are treated fairly and with respect during their participation, that they receive complete information about the study at its conclusion, that any stress they encounter is relieved, and that their participation is kept private. It is important to note this responsibility extends to everyone involved in the running of the study, from the primary researcher to the graduate students or undergraduates who might actually run the experimental sessions.

We have already seen the researcher must estimate the amount of risk to participants, with greater amounts of risk creating a greater burden to justify the study. This problem of risk and potential harm is addressed in the standards relating to informed consent and use of deception and once more in Standard 8.08, which makes it clear that responsibility does not end with the conclusion of the testing session. After the study is over, the researcher has an additional task, called **debriefing**, during which the researcher answers questions the participants might have and tells them about the purpose(s) of the study. It is not essential that participants be informed about *all* aspects of the study immediately after their participation. Standard 8.08(b) "[I]f scientific or humane values justify delaying or withholding this information, psychologists take reasonable steps to reduce the harm" makes it clear that, in some circumstances, the immediate debriefing can be incomplete. This situation occurs most frequently when some deception is involved, college students are the population under study, and the experimenter is concerned about participants talking to other potential participants (classmates). This latter problem, sometimes referred to as **participant crosstalk**, can ruin a study. Even in a study with relatively minor deception, subjects who go into the study knowing something unknown to naïve subjects will certainly be influenced by their knowledge of the study.

There is evidence that participant crosstalk occurs, especially in situations where participants (e.g., college students) can easily interact with each other (Diener, Matthews, & Smith, 1972). A recent study confirmed the problem still exists by cleverly determining the frequency of its occurrence. Edlund, Sagarin, Skowronski, Johnson, and Kutter (2009) had subjects estimate the number of beans in a jar. Those participating were then given the correct answer. The question was whether or not these subjects would pass the information along to future participants. Some clearly did just that, although the percentage doing so was small (just under 5%). The percentage was reduced in a second study, when participants were specifically asked not to reveal the number of beans to others who might participate. Aside from urging subjects not to discuss the study after their participation, a common strategy for reducing crosstalk, consistent with Standard 8.08(b), is to provide information about the *general nature* of the research during debriefing but to provide full information about the study only after the experiment has been completed.

In general, debriefing serves two related purposes, referred to by Holmes (1976a, 1976b) as dehoaxing and desensitizing. **Dehoaxing** means revealing to participants the true purpose of the study and the hypotheses being tested (or some portion of them), and **desensitizing** refers to the process of reducing stress or other negative feelings that might have been experienced during participation in the study. Subjects are also informed that, if they wish, they may have their data removed from the data set.

The amount of time spent in debriefing depends on the complexity of the study, the presence and degree of deception, and the level of potential distress. In a study involving deception, the researcher often begins a debriefing session by asking participants if they thought the study had a purpose other than the one initially described. This enables the researcher to determine if the deception was effective; it also provides a lead-in to further explication of the study. At this time, the researcher tries to justify the deception (e.g., emphasizes the importance of getting one's true reactions) and begins to alleviate stress. Participants taken in by the experiment's cover story are told their behavior reflects the effectiveness of the cover story, not any personal weakness. That is, subjects in many types of studies can be assured that the situation they experienced had powerful effects on their behavior, that their reactions don't reflect any individual inadequacies, and that others reacted similarly (Holmes, 1976b). In most cases, dehoaxing amounts to explaining the importance of eliciting natural behaviors and discussing the nature of the research topic being studied.

Several studies have shown that participants who are thoroughly debriefed evaluate the research experience positively. Smith and Richardson (1983) showed that, compared to nondeceived subjects, those in deception studies actually rated their experiences higher in both enjoyment and educational value, apparently because the debriefing was more extensive. One result of an effective debriefing is that skilled researchers can better understand their current study and improve future ones. Participants can be asked for their ideas about revising the procedure in order to learn more about the problem being studied. In many cases, their descriptions of what they were thinking about during the experiment can be helpful in interpreting the data and planning the next study.

The importance of leaving people with a good feeling about their research participation cannot be overstated. Yet it can be a difficult business, especially when deception is involved. Consider the Milgram experiment again: What must that debriefing have been like? In fairness to Milgram, he was apparently sensitive to the emotional health of his subjects. After the study was completed, he sent them a survey about their experience and a five-page report describing the results and their significance. The results of the survey indicated that 84% of participants stated they were glad to have participated (Milgram, 1964). He also completed a 1-year follow-up study in which a psychiatrist examined 40 former participants and found "no evidence . . . of any traumatic reactions" (Milgram, 1974, p. 197).

Studies surveying research volunteers have found that fears of excessive harm in psychological research might be exaggerated; participants seem to understand and accept the rationale for deception (Christensen, 1988). One survey even found that college students were considerably more lenient than professional psychologists in their judgments about the ethical appropriateness of four hypothetical studies involving such things as experimentally produced stress and alterations of self-esteem (Sullivan & Deiker, 1973). Other research shows objections by subjects to participating in psychological research seem to center more on their concern about being bored than being harmed (Coulter, 1986). On the other hand, it has been argued that post-experiment surveys of participants are biased, especially if deception has been involved. Having been misled and perhaps embarrassed in the study, deceived participants might respond positively to surveys as part of the process of convincing themselves the study was worth their time and effort (Baumrind, 1985)—another example of an *effort justification* (see Chapter 1). This phenomenon probably accounted for at least some of Milgram's survey results (the 84%). Fisher and Fyrberg (1994) avoided this post-deception survey problem by asking students who had not yet been participants in research to evaluate three published studies involving various forms of deception. They found students believed that participants would be embarrassed or made uncomfortable in the studies and that debriefing, while essential, would not completely alleviate the negative feelings. Yet, when asked to make an overall cost-benefit assessment of the three studies described, 90%, 73%, and 79% (depending on the described study) of the students judged the scientific merit of the research to be sufficient to justify the deceptions involved.

One last aspect of treating participants well concerns privacy and **confidentiality**, which is encapsulated by APA General Principle E. Research participants should be confident their identities will not be known by anyone other than the experimenter and that only group or disguised (coded) data will be reported. The only exceptions to this occur in cases when researchers might be compelled by law to report certain things disclosed by participants (e.g., child abuse, clear intent to harm oneself or another). In research that could involve such disclosure, researchers should word the consent form to make it clear that confidentiality could be limited (Folkman, 2000). The basic right to privacy also applies to research outside of the laboratory that might affect people in daily living situations. As we'll see in the next chapter, when laboratory and field research are compared, concerns over invading the privacy of people going about their daily business keeps many researchers within the protected confines of the laboratory.

In summary, in research using human participants, our ethical obligations under the APA code include the following:

* Developing a study in which the overall benefits outweigh the overall costs

* Avoiding doing anything that would harm participants

* Gaining informed consent (under most circumstances)

* Assuring volunteers they can quit the study at any time, without penalty

* Providing some form of debriefing

* Assuring participants about confidentiality and their anonymity

Research Ethics and the Internet

Because the Internet has altered life dramatically in the 21st century, you won't be surprised to learn that research in psychology has been affected by the electronic world. Online research methods of interest to psychologists falls into two broad categories (Anderson & Kanuka, 2003). First, some websites are designed to collect data from those logging into the sites. This happens most frequently in the form of online surveys and questionnaires but can involve other forms of data collection as well. For example, Amazon's Mechanical Turk (MTurk: www.mturk.com) allows researchers to generate surveys or program experiments, solicit participation, and pay subjects for their participation at very low cost. In other cases, subjects login to sites controlled by researchers on their own campus, and complete a study electronically (e.g., a survey created on software such as Survey Monkey or Qualtrics). Some research has been completed on the issue, and it appears that data collected electronically correspond reasonably well and yield similar results as data collected in a more traditional fashion (Casler, Bickel, & Hackett, 2013; McGraw, Tew, & Williams, 2000). However, it is important to also note that there are differences in the characteristics of MTurk users versus participants typically tested face-to-face. In addition to being more socially and economically diverse, MTurk users are also more likely to use the Internet to look up answers to factual questions, tend to have lower self-esteem, and be more introverted, posing challenges to research where such factors may be relevant (Goodman, Cryder, & Cheema, 2013).

The second form of online research involves a researcher studying the behavior of Internet users. This research ranges from examining the frequency of usage of selected websites to analyses of the content of web-based interactions (e.g., monitoring the activity of a Twitter feed). For both types of research, the basic principles of the ethics code apply, but research involving the Internet introduces unique ethical problems for the researcher. The problems have even resulted in the development of a code of ethics for Internet-based research, created by an organization called the Association of Internet Researchers. The American Association for the Advancement of Science has also prepared guidelines for IRBs that must decide whether to approve online research, and the APA's Board of Scientific Affairs established an advisory group on the Internet in 2001 and published its report 3 years later (Kraut, Olson, Banaji, Bruckman, Cohen, & Couper, 2004).

For online research in which computer users contribute data, problems relating to informed consent and debriefing exist. During a normal informed consent procedure, the experimenter can quickly clear up any confusion or misunderstanding on the part of participants and can be reasonably sure participants read the consent form before signing. Consent forms can be used easily enough in online studies, but there is no opportunity for researchers to answer questions (although some consent forms are accompanied by a set of frequently asked questions and their answers) and no way to know if the consent form has been read. Another consent problem concerns age: Researchers can post warnings that participants need parental consent if they are under age 18, but it is impossible to monitor compliance. Debriefing may also be problematic. A good debriefing session is interactive, with questions asked and answered, but with online research, there is no guarantee participants will even be there to read the debriefing information. One click and the participant is gone without being debriefed. Furthermore, if deception is involved, while the dehoaxing part of debriefing can be managed by presenting clear information, the desensitizing part will be difficult if not impossible to accomplish.

Online research involving the collection of information from computer users involves an additional set of problems. A major issue concerns privacy and confidentiality (Kraut et al., 2004). As you recall from the discussion of informed consent earlier in this chapter, consent is not required for studies that are purely observational and individual behavior is observed in public places. With online research, the interesting and as yet unresolved question is whether activities such as

Twitter feeds, Facebook posts, chat rooms, blogs, discussion boards, and listservs are public forums or private discussions. For the researcher, the best guideline is be faithful to the general principles of the code and to consult frequently with colleagues and the local IRB during the planning stages of online research. For users of social media, it is important to be aware that, in the absence of sophisticated encryption software, messages posted are "out there," available to anyone with an Internet connection. The best advice for users is to think of the messages they post as having about the same level of privacy as postcards.

Concerning confidentiality, researchers using Internet surveys must take steps to ensure the protection of the user's identity even if the participant used her or his own personal computer. This can mean ensuring that cookies (tools used to track information about Internet users) are not left on the participant's computer as a result of taking the survey. Also, users must be assured that if their computer's identity (e.g., an IP address) is returned with the survey, the researcher will discard the information (Pollick, 2007).

SELF TEST

2.2

1. You wish to do a study comparing two memory improvement techniques. Which category of the IRB approval process will apply in this case?
2. How does the APA define informed consent?
3. Milgram's procedure probably would not have gained IRB approval in terms of its consent procedures. What was the most obvious problem?

Ethical Guidelines for Research with Animals

As you recall from your course in introductory psychology, psychologists occasionally use animals as research subjects. Although some people have the impression that psychologists study rats more than people, the truth is that animal research involves a relatively small proportion of the total research done in psychology, about 7–9% (Gallup & Suarez, 1985a). Also, the vast majority of studies use rats and mice as subjects; dogs, cats, and nonhuman primates are used in just a tiny proportion of animal research. Despite the small proportions, many of psychology's important contributions to human welfare are based on a foundation of research with animals (Domjan & Purdy, 1995).

Animals are used in psychological research for several reasons. Methodologically, their environmental, genetic, and developmental histories can be easily controlled. Genetic and life-span developmental studies can take place quickly—female mice, for instance, produce litters after just 3 weeks of pregnancy, and 1 mouse year is the equivalent of 30 human years (Herzog, 2010). Ethically, most experimental psychologists take the position that, with certain safeguards in place, animals can be subjected to procedures that could not be used with humans. Consider Eleanor Gibson's visual cliff research again (Gibson & Walk, 1960; see Chapter 1). Thirty-six 6- to 14-month-old infants were placed in the middle of the apparatus, and although they were quite willing to crawl around on the "shallow" side, they hesitated to crawl onto the glass surface over the "deep" side. This shows that they were able to perceive depth and apparently were aware of some of its consequences. Does this mean depth perception is innate? No, because these infants had 6 to 14 months of learning experience with distance perception. To control for this experience, it would have been necessary to raise infants in complete visual isolation, a procedure that was obviously out of the question—although, as you recall from Box 2.1, Dennis (1941) had few qualms about subjecting infants to an impoverished environment. Such an isolation procedure *is* feasible with animals, however, in part because the isolation does not have to be long—animals develop the ability to move through their environments very quickly, sometimes in a matter of minutes. So Gibson and Walk tested a variety of species from rats to kittens to lambs, isolating them from birth (i.e., no specific visual experiences) until they could move around competently and then testing them on the visual cliff. They discovered that depth perception, at least as measured in the cliff apparatus, is built into the visual system, at least for those species that rely heavily on vision.

Animal Rights

The use of animals in research is an emotional and controversial issue (not a new one, though—see Box 2.3). Animal rights activists have denounced the use of animals in studies ranging from medical research to cosmetics testing. The majority of animal activists confine their activities to sincere argument and nonviolent protest, and they work hard to live a life that is consistent with their moral stance (Herzog, 1993). In some cases, however, activism has led to animal laboratories being vandalized and animals released from labs. During the 1980s, for example, animal rights extremists vandalized approximately 100 research facilities housing animals (Adler, 1992). The problem was severe enough to produce federal legislation, the Animal Enterprise Protection Act of 1992, specifically outlawing such vandalism and setting stiff penalties, and the Animal Enterprise Terrorism Act of 2006, which took an even harder line. In recent years, an alarming trend has been for some groups to target researchers directly, not just their labs. In the fall of 2008, for instance, two researchers at the University of California at Vera Cruz were the targets of firebombs (the car of one, the home of another).

BOX 2.3   ORIGINS—Antivivisection and the APA

Considering the high visibility of the animal research controversy, you might think that it is a fairly recent development. Not so; it has a long history, as documented nicely by the comparative psychologist and historian Donald Dewsbury (1990).

The term *vivisection* derives from the Latin *vivus,* or "alive," and refers to surgical procedures on live animals, historically done for scientific purposes. The antivivisection movement developed in 19th-century England, where activists' efforts contributed to the passage of England's Cruelty to Animals Act in 1876, an ethics code similar in spirit to modern APA guidelines for animals. The antivivisection movement quickly spread to the United States, where the American Antivivisection Society was founded in 1883 in Philadelphia. Antivivisectionists and animal researchers (including physiologists and early experimental psychologists) engaged in the same arguments that are heard today, with claims of unspeakable torture on the one side and justifications on scientific grounds on the other. That thoughtful scientists were torn by the issue of using animals in research is reflected in the experiences of Charles Darwin. An animal lover, surrounded by pets all his life, Darwin nonetheless argued for the importance of legitimate animal research, writing in 1871 that "it is justifiable for real investigations on physiology; but it is not for mere damnable and detestable curiosity" (quoted in Dewsbury, 1990, p. 316).

Within the field of psychology in the early years of the 20th century, one especially controversial series of animal studies concerned John B. Watson (again). In order to determine which senses were critical for maze learning, Watson conducted a series of studies in which he surgically eliminated one sense one at a time to examine the effects on rats in mazes (Watson, 1907). For instance, he learned that vision and smell did not affect the learning of a maze or the retention of an already-learned maze. Rats surgically blinded or

(continued)

From Journal of Zoophily, 1907

DREAM OF THE MEDICAL VIVISECTIONIST CRANK WHO WANTONLY AND CRUELLY OPERATED ON RATS, TO SEE THE EFFECT, FROM A "SCIENTIFIC" VIEW-POINT, OF THE LOSS OF THE DIFFERENT SENSES.

FIGURE 2.2
Antivivisectionist cartoon of Watson on the operating table. From Dewsbury (1990).

with olfactory bulbs removed performed the same as unimpaired rats. The study caused an outcry when it was reported in the *New York Times* on December 30, 1906, and Watson was vilified in the antivivisectionist *Journal of Zoophily*, which also printed the cartoon shown in Figure 2.2 (from Dewsbury, 1990).

The APA established its first code for regulating animal research in the 1920s, well before creating the code for research with humans. A committee chaired by Robert Yerkes was formed in 1924, and the following year the APA adopted its recommendations. The committee proposed that laboratories create an open-door policy in which "any accredited member of a humane society [could] be permitted to visit a laboratory to observe the care of animals and methods of experimentation" (Anderson, 1926, p. 125), that journals require authors to be clear about the use of humane procedures in their research, that psychologists defend the need for animal research, both in the classroom and publicly, and that the APA maintain a standing committee on "precautions in animal experimentation" (Anderson, 1926, p. 125).

What is the case against the use of animals as research subjects? Some argue that humans have no right to consider themselves superior to any other sentient species—that is, any species capable of experiencing pain (Singer, 1975). Sentient animals are said to have the same basic rights to privacy, autonomy, and freedom from harm as humans and therefore cannot be subjugated by humans in any way, including participation in any form of research. Others skeptical of animal research take a more moderate position, grounded in a Judeo-Christian theology. They argue that humans may have dominion over animals, but they also have a responsibility to protect them. This group recognizes the value of some research using animals, especially medical research, but rejects other types of experimentation on the grounds that researchers have inflicted needless pain and suffering when alternative approaches to the research would yield essentially the same conclusions. This argument has helped reduce unnecessary research on animals by the cosmetics industry, for instance, but it has been applied to research in psychology as well. Psychological research with animals has been described as needlessly repetitive and concerned with trivial problems that have no practical human benefit. Critics have suggested that instead of using animals in the laboratory, researchers could discover all they need to know about animal behavior by observing animals in their natural habitats, by substituting non-sentient for sentient animals, or by using computer simulations. How do research psychologists respond?

Using Animals in Psychological Research

Most psychologists simply do not agree that sentient animals have rights equal to those of humans. While granting that humans have an obligation to protect and care for nonhuman species, psychologists believe humans can be distinguished from nonhumans because of our degree of awareness, our ability to develop culture and understand history, and especially our ability to make moral judgments. Although animals are capable of complex cognition, they are "incapable of being moral subjects, of acting rightly or wrongly in the moral sense, of having, discharging, or breaching duties and obligations" (Feinberg, 1974, p. 46). Of course, differentiating between human and nonhuman species does not by itself allow the use of the latter by the former. Some psychologists (e.g., Ulrich, 1991) caution there have indeed been instances in which animals were not treated well by research psychologists and that some research has been needlessly repetitive. Most psychologists argue, however, that the use of animals in research does not constitute exploitation and that the net effect of such research is beneficial rather than costly for both humans *and* animals.

The most visible defender of animal research in psychology has been Neal Miller (1909–2002), a noted experimental psychologist. His research, on topics ranging from basic processes in conditioning and motivation to the principles underlying biofeedback, earned him the APA's Distinguished Scientific Contributions Award in 1959 and its Distinguished Professional Contributions Award in 1983. In "The Value of Behavioral Research on Animals", Miller (1985) argued that (a) animal activists sometimes overstate the harm done to animals in psychological research, (b) animal research provides clear benefits for the well-being of humans, and (c) animal research benefits animals as well. Concerning harm, Miller cited a study by Coile and Miller (1984) that examined 5 years' worth of published research in APA journals, a total of 608 studies, and found *no* instances of the forms of abuse claimed by activists. Also, examining the abuse claims shows at least some of the alleged "abuse" may not be that at all, but merely seems to be because of the inflammatory language used. For instance, Coile and Miller cited several misleading statements from activist literature, including: "[The animals] are deprived of food and water to suffer and die slowly from hunger and thirst" (p. 700). This evidently refers to the common laboratory practice in conditioning experiments of depriving animals of food or water for 24 hours. Animals then placed in a conditioning procedure are motivated to work for the food or the water (e.g., solve a maze). Is this abuse? Perhaps not, considering that veterinarians recommend most pets be fed just once a day (Gallup & Suarez, 1985b). On the other hand, some researchers argue that 6 hours without food is sufficient to create an adequate level of hunger for research purposes.

Miller (1985) argued that situations involving harm to animals during research procedures are rare, used only when less painful alternatives cannot be used, and can be justified by the ultimate good that derives from the studies. This good applies to both humans and animals, and the bulk of his 1985 article was an attempt to document the kinds of good that derive from animal studies. First, he argued that while the long history of animal conditioning research has taught us much about general principles of learning, it also has had direct application to human problems. An early example of this was a device developed and tested by Mowrer and Mowrer (1938) for treating enuresis (excessive and uncontrolled bedwetting) that was based explicitly on the classical conditioning work involving Pavlov's dogs. Teaching machines and several forms of behavior therapy (e.g., systematic desensitization) are likewise grounded in conditioning principles originally observed in research with animals. More recently, animal research has directly influenced the development of behavioral medicine—the application of behavioral principles to traditional medical practice. Disorders ranging from headaches to hypertension to the disabilities following strokes can be treated with behavioral procedures such as biofeedback, and the essential principles of biofeedback were determined using animals as subjects.

Finally, Miller (1985) argued that animal research provides direct benefits to animals themselves. Medical research with animals has improved veterinary care dramatically (e.g., developing rabies vaccine), but behavioral research has also improved the welfare of various species. The study of animal behavior by research psychologists has led to improvements in the design of zoo environments, aided in nonchemical pest control, and discouraged coyote attacks on sheep by using taste avoidance conditioning as a substitute for lethal control. Behavioral research can even help preserve endangered species. Miller used the example of imprinting, the tendency for young ducklings and other species to follow the first stimulus that moves (usually the mother). Research on imprinting led to the procedure of exposing newly hatched condors to a puppet resembling an adult condor rather than to a normal human caretaker, thereby facilitating the bonding process for the incubator-raised bird and ultimately enhancing the survival of this threatened species.

Another area of research involving animals, one that benefits both animals and humans, is **anthrozoology**—the study of human-animal interactions. The field is interdisciplinary, and includes behavioral psychologists, veterinarians, anthropologists, animal trainers, and philosophers. The topics they study include the use of pets in psychotherapy (decidedly mixed results—see Herzog, 2011), the effects of pets on the everyday lives of humans, and the training of both animals and humans to improve human–animal relationships. A good introduction, with a title that highlights the moral ambiguities of our complex relationships with animals is *Some We Love, Some We Hate, Some We Eat: Why It's So Hard to Think Straight About Animals*, by Hal Herzog (2010), a research psychologist who has become a leader in this emerging discipline.

One last point about using animals in psychological research is that most people seem to think animal research has value. Surveys of psychologists (Plous, 1996a) and psychology majors (Plous, 1996b), for instance, indicate that although they are ambivalent about research in which animals experience pain and/or must be put to death at the conclusion of the study, most psychologists and students of psychology believe that animal research in psychology is both justified and necessary. These views appear to be shared by students in general (Fulero & Kirkland, 1992; Gallup & Beckstead, 1988). Despite this general support, there are indications that animal research by psychologists is in decline. Gallup and Eddy (1990), for example, surveyed graduate programs and reported that 14.7% of them had dismantled their animal labs, mainly due to changing research interests and cost (and not because of pressure from protesters). Benedict and Stoloff (1991) found similar results among elite undergraduate colleges. The Plous surveys of psychologists and students just mentioned found general support for animal research, but his analysis also revealed stronger support among (a) older psychologists and (b) male psychologists and male psychology majors. This outcome suggests animal research among psychologists, as well as animal labs for undergraduate psychology majors (about 70% of whom are now female), may decline in the future. On the other hand, Hull (1996) surveyed 110 department chairs at schools with undergraduate psychology majors but without graduate programs and found some reason for optimism about animal research. She reported just a small drop in the use of animal labs for undergraduates over a 5-year period; 47% reported using animals (mainly rats) at the time of the survey, while 50% had used animals 5 years earlier. Hull's survey also revealed that departments using animals did not find APA and National Institutes of Health (NIH) guidelines difficult to follow and that the student response to the presence of an animal lab was mostly favorable.

The APA Code for Animal Research

Psychologists must follow federal, state, and local laws governing use of animals in research. The Animal Welfare Act (AWA) enacted in 1966 is the only federal law in the United States that regulates the treatment of animals used in research. Part of the AWA's mandate is that institutions where animal research is conducted should have an Institutional Animal Care and Use Committee (IACUC). Like an IRB, the IACUC is composed of faculty from several disciplines in addition to science, a veterinarian, and someone from outside the university.[7] Often, the IACUC will use guidelines put forth in the *Guide for the Care and Use of Laboratory Animals* (National Research Council, 2011) in its evaluation of the ethical treatment of animals in research. In addition, psychologists rely on Standard 8.09 of the 2002 APA ethics code, which describes the ethical guidelines for animal care and use (www.apa.org/science/anguide.html). The APA guidelines for using animals deal with (a) the need to justify the study when the potential for harm to the animals exists; (b) the proper acquisition and care of animals, both during and after the study; and (c) the use of animals for educational rather than research purposes. The main theme of the code is balancing the scientific justification for a particular project with the potential for harm to the animals. Here are the highlights.

Justifying the Study

Just as the researcher studying humans must weigh the scientific value of the research against the degree of risk to the participants, the animal researcher must make the case that the "scientific purpose of the research [is] of sufficient potential significance as to outweigh any harm or distress to the animals used" (APA, 1985, p. 5). The scientific purpose of the study should fall within one of four categories. The research should "(a) increase knowledge of the processes underlying the evolution, development, maintenance, alteration, control, or biological significance of behavior, (b) determine the replicability and generality of prior research, (c) increase understanding of the species under study, or (d) provide results that benefit the health or welfare of humans or other animals" (www.apa.org/science/anguide.html).

The longest section of the guidelines identifies the range of procedures that can be used. In general, researchers are told that their requirement for a strong justification increases with the degree of discomfort to be experienced by the animals. In addition, they are told that appetitive procedures (i.e., use of positive reinforcement) should be substituted for aversive procedures as much as possible, that less stressful procedures should be preferred to more stressful ones, and that surgical procedures require special care and expertise. Researchers are also encouraged to try out painful procedures on themselves first, whenever feasible. Field research procedures should disturb animals living in their natural habitat as little as possible.

Caring for the Animals

The research supervisor must be an expert in the care of the species of animals to be used, must carefully train all those who will be in contact with the animals, and must be fully aware of federal regulations about animal care. To further ensure proper care, a veterinarian must check the facilities twice annually and be on call as a general consultant. The animals should be acquired from legitimate suppliers or bred in the laboratory. If wild animals are studied in a laboratory, they must be trapped humanely.

Once an experiment is completed, alternatives to destroying the animals should be considered. However, euthanasia is sometimes necessary, "either as a requirement of the research, or because it constitutes the most humane form of disposition of an animal at the conclusion of the research" (APA, 1985, p. 8). In such cases, the process must be "accomplished in a humane

---

[7] As are IRBs, animal use committees have been controversial. One study found, for instance, that the same proposals given to different IACUCs yielded inconsistent levels of approval (Plous & Herzog, 2001).

manner, appropriate for the species, under anesthesia, or in such a way as to ensure immediate death, and in accordance with the procedures approved by the institutional animal care and use committee" (p. 8).

Using Animals for Educational Purposes

The guidelines are designed primarily to aid researchers who test animals, but animals are often used educationally to demonstrate specific behaviors, train students in animal research procedures, and give students firsthand experience in studying such well-known phenomena as classical and operant conditioning. Unlike the research situation, the educational use of animals does not result directly in new knowledge. Consequently, the educator is urged to use fewer rather than more animals to accomplish a given purpose and to consider a variety of alternative procedures. For example, instead of demonstrating the same principle (e.g., shaping) to an introductory psychology class with a new rat each semester, the instructor might do it once and make a video of the procedure for future classes.

Sometimes, computer simulations of phenomena can be substituted for live procedures; several reasonably accurate simulations of both classical and operant conditioning procedures exist. These simulations can be effective (and necessary in smaller schools that cannot keep up with federal regulations for the proper care of animals), but shaping a schematized rat to bar press is not the same as shaping a real rat. Students often experience a deep insight into the power of reinforcement contingencies when they witness the animals firsthand. Direct experiences with animals in undergraduate learning laboratories have motivated more than one student to become a research psychologist (Moses, 1991).

In summary, most psychologists defend the use of animals in behavioral research while recognizing the need to scrutinize closely the rationale for every animal study. Animal research has contributed greatly to our understanding of behavior and promises to help in the future search for solutions to AIDS, Alzheimer's disease, mental illness, and countless other human problems.

Scientific Fraud

There has been much discussion in recent years about fraud in science, with specific cases sparking debate about whether they represent the occasional bad apple or a broader, more systemic problem. Scientists in general and psychological scientists in particular are expected to be scrupulously honest in all of their scientific activities. Principle C (Integrity) of the APA ethics code unambiguously states that psychologists "seek to promote accuracy, honesty, and truthfulness in the science, teaching, and practice of psychology" (APA, 2002, p. 1062). This last section of the chapter examines the issue of scientific fraud, aiming to shed some light on the varieties of scientific misbehavior, the reasons why such behavior occasionally occurs, and the ways in which fraud can be detected.

The *American Heritage Dictionary* (1992) defines fraud as "a deception deliberately practiced in order to secure unfair or unlawful gain" (p. 722). The two major types of serious misconduct in science are (1) **plagiarism**, deliberately taking the ideas of someone else and claiming them as one's own, and (2) **falsifying data**. In the APA ethics code, plagiarism is specifically condemned in Standard 8.11 – "Psychologists do not present portions of another's work or data as their own, even if the other work or data source is cited occasionally" (APA, 2002, p. 1070); data falsification receives similar treatment in Standard 8.10a – "Psychologists do not fabricate data" (p. 1070). Plagiarism is a problem that can occur in all disciplines, and you will find further discussion of it within the context of writing APA-style lab reports (See Appendix A). Being dishonest about data, on the other hand, is a problem that happens only in science; it will be our major focus.

Data Falsification

Data are the foundation on which the entire scientific enterprise is built. If there is a mortal sin in science, it is the failure to be scrupulously honest in collecting and managing data. The most egregious sin is data falsification, which occurs when a scientist fails to collect data and simply fabricates a data set, or collects some data, but either manufactures the rest or changes some of the existing data to produce a favorable outcome. Each of these forms of data falsification occurred in a notorious recent case.

Until his 2011 resignation, Diederick Stapel was dean of the School of Social and Behavioral Sciences at Tilburg University in the Netherlands, and he was a star, one of Europe's premier social psychologists. His research was published in numerous prominent journals and frequently cited. Many of the studies involved the phenomenon of "priming," in which subjects are presented with stimuli or put in environments that lead them to think unconsciously in some fashion and then behave in certain predictable ways. In one of Stapel's better known studies, for instance, subjects placed in a trash-filled environment seemed to show racist tendencies. Specifically, White subjects were asked to choose a seat in a row of six chairs and complete a questionnaire. Sitting in the seat at the end of the row was another apparent subject, who was either Black or White. According to Stapel's data, White subjects chose to sit further away from the Black person than from the White person. According to Stapel, the dirty environment primed racist tendencies in the White subjects, leading them to avoid sitting near the Black person.

This study was published in *Science*, among the most prestigious of all scientific journals and it quickly became widely known. The only problem was that Stapel never actually conducted the study and he made up all the data. He was smart enough, however, to create data that would not raise suspicions—the results were statistically significant, but not so large as to be unbelievable. This was his typical way of committing scientific fraud—find an interesting topic, develop a simple yet creative procedure, and then manufacture results that were statistically significant but believable and simple to understand. He was even able to get away with his data falsification scheme when collaborating with other social psychologists and with graduate students. He would work closely with colleagues and students when designing a study, often helping them develop their own ideas into interesting research designs. Stapel would then tell them that the actual data collection would occur at nearby secondary schools rather than at the university, with the data collected by one of his many (fictitious, as it turned out) research friends. Stapel would then manufacture the data and give the results (not the raw data, but data coded in a way that it could be entered into a computer) to students or colleagues for analysis (Jump, 2011).

Stapel was eventually undone when he raised the suspicions of some of his more astute graduate students and colleagues. He never seemed to be able to produce raw data or the participants' completed questionnaires when asked for them (a common courtesy among scientists), his studies always seemed to work out as hypothesized (even the best researchers produce many studies that fail), and he eventually got sloppy in his data creation (one study included identical data in several places, an apparent cut-and-paste job). Stapel was investigated by his university, confessed, and resigned from Tilburg. No fewer than 55 of his scientific papers were retracted from journals (Bhattacharjee, 2013).

Explanations for why research fraud occurs range from individual (character weakness) to societal (a reflection of an alleged moral decay in modern society), with reasons relating to the academic reward system somewhere in the middle. Scientists who publish are promoted, tenured, win grants, and become influential in their fields. Sometimes, the pressure to "publish or perish" overwhelms the individual and leads the researcher (or the researcher's assistants) to cut some corners. The fraud might begin on a small scale—adding, subtracting, or altering a few pieces of data to achieve the desired outcome—but it may expand over time. Changing small amounts of data was the starting point for Stapel—long before he was manufacturing entire sets of data, he was changing individual data points to produce desired results (Crocker, 2011).

As for uncovering fraud based on falsified data, the traditional view is that it will be detected eventually because faked results won't be replicated (Hilgartner, 1990). That is, if a scientist produces a result with fraudulent data, the results won't represent some empirical truth. Hence, other scientists, intrigued or surprised by the new finding, will try to reproduce it in their own labs and may fail to do so. This will raise suspicions, and fraudulent findings eventually will be uncovered and discarded. Yet a failure to replicate is by no means a foolproof indication of fraud—results might not reproduce for several reasons. In addition, as occurred in the Stapel case, the clever fraudster can create data that will be entirely believable and may indeed replicate.

A failure to replicate may in some cases raise suspicion and subsequently lead to a request to see the raw data. However, failure to produce such data will generate even more suspicions. Scientists in psychology and other disciplines have a long history of willingness to share data and a refusal to do so would create concern about the new findings, as was the case in the Stapel fraud. Standard 8.14 of the ethics code makes it clear that data sharing is expected from researchers.

Psychological science is a collaborative activity (the concept of a "research team" will be elaborated in Chapter 3), and it is difficult to fool sharp-minded students and other research psychologists for too long. Although it took years in the Stapel case, graduate student suspicion, as we have seen, was the starting point for his downfall. Colleague suspicion was also the starting point in another well-known case of fraud that occurred in the 1980s, following a series of studies that apparently made a breakthrough in the treatment of hyperactivity in children with intellectual disabilities. Stephen Breuning of the University of Pittsburgh produced data appearing to show that stimulant drugs could be more effective than antipsychotic drugs for treating the problem (Holden, 1987). However, a colleague suspected the data were falsified, a charge that was upheld after an investigation by the National Institute of Mental Health (NIMH), which had funded some of Breuning's research. In a plea bargain, Breuning pled guilty to two counts of submitting false data to NIMH; in exchange, NIMH dropped the charge that Breuning committed perjury during the investigation (Byrne, 1988).

It is worth mentioning that some commentators (e.g., Hilgartner, 1990) believe that while falsified data may go undetected for some time because they replicate "good" data or the data just seem believable, falsified data may not be detected for two other reasons as well. First, the sheer number of studies being published today makes it easier for a bad study to slip through the cracks, especially if it isn't reporting a notable discovery that attracts widespread attention. Second, the reward system in science is structured so that new discoveries pay off, but scientists who spend their time "merely" replicating other work aren't seen as creative. However, this latter issue is currently being addressed as researchers are now undergoing various systematic replication projects; this will be discussed in more detail in Chapters 3 and 4. A third issue is that researchers are "rewarded" by publishing counterintuitive or surprising findings, which may in turn garner media attention (Shea, 2011). While it is important that we "give psychology away" as George Miller recommended (see Chapter 1), it is imperative that the information shared with the larger community is based on sound, scientific practice.

What does all this mean for you as a student researcher? At the very least, it means you must be compulsive about data. Follow procedures scrupulously and *never* succumb to the temptation to manufacture or change even a single piece of data. Likewise, never discard data from a participant unless there are clear procedures for doing so and these procedures are specified *before* the experiment begins (e.g., the participant doesn't follow instructions, the experimenter doesn't administer the procedure correctly). Finally, keep the raw data or, at the very least, the data summary sheets. Your best protection against a charge that your results seem unusual is your ability to produce the data on request. Being vigilant and truthful about your data will make you a better scientist and a better seeker of truth.

> ### SELF TEST
> ### 2.3
>
> 1. Miller argued that animal rights activists exaggerate when making claims about animal research. What were his other two arguments for the value of animal research in psychology?
> 2. What does the APA recommend about the use of animals for educational purposes?
> 3. Which facts first alerted researchers to the possibility of fraud in Stapel's research?

The importance of being aware of the ethical implications of the research you're doing cannot be overstated. It is the reason for placing this chapter early in the text, and it won't be the last you'll hear of the topic. If you glance back at the table of contents, for instance, you will notice that each of the remaining chapters includes an Ethics Box that examines such topics as maintaining privacy in field research, recruiting participants, using surveys responsibly, and being an ethically competent experimenter. On the immediate horizon, however, is a chapter that considers the problem of how to begin developing ideas for research projects.

CHAPTER SUMMARY

Developing the APA Code of Ethics

In keeping with psychology's habit of relying on data-based principles, the APA developed its initial ethics code empirically, using a critical incidents procedure. The code for research using human participants was first published in 1953 and has been revised periodically since then, most recently in 2002. It consists of general principles guiding the behavior of psychologists (e.g., concern for others' welfare) and specific standards of behavior (e.g., maintaining the confidentiality of research participants), the violation of which can lead to censure.

Ethical Guidelines for Research with Humans

The APA code for research with humans provides guidance for the researcher in planning and carrying out the study. Planning includes doing a cost-benefit analysis that weighs the degree of risk imposed on participants against the scientific value of the research. The code also requires that subjects be given sufficient information to decide whether or not to participate (i.e., informed consent). Special care must be taken with children and with people who might feel coerced into participation (e.g., prisoners). Participants must be told that they are free to withdraw from the study without penalty, and they must be assured of the confidentiality of their responses. At the conclusion of their participation, they must receive a full debriefing. Institutional Review Boards (IRBs) are responsible for ensuring research studies with human

subjects are conducted according to the ethics code and federal law. Certain forms of deception are acceptable in psychological research, but the researcher must convince an IRB the legitimate goals of the study can be met only through deception.

Ethical Guidelines for Research with Animals

APA guidelines for research with animal subjects concern the care and humane treatment of animals used for psychological research, provide guidance in choosing appropriate experimental procedures, and cover the use of animals both for research and for educational purposes. Although animal rights proponents have argued that animal research in psychology is inappropriate, most research psychologists argue that such research can benefit both humans and animals.

Scientific Fraud

Plagiarism (presenting the ideas of another as one's own) and data falsification (the manufacturing or altering of data) are the most serious forms of scientific fraud. Although data falsification is often discovered because of repeated failures to replicate unreliable findings, it may remain undetected because (a) the fraudulent findings are consistent with legitimate outcomes or (b) the sheer mass of published work precludes much replication. The academic reward system sometimes creates pressures that lead to scientific fraud.

CHAPTER REVIEW QUESTIONS

1. Distinguish between the general principles and the standards of the APA ethics code. Describe any three of the general principles, as they apply to research.

2. Describe the basic purpose of IRBs and the reasons research psychologists have criticized them.

3. What factors determine whether research proposals are exempt from IRB review, receive expedited review, or are subject to full review? How does the concept of risk relate to these judgments?

4. Distinguish between consent and assent and explain how both concepts are accomplished in research with children.

5. Describe the essential ingredients of an informed consent form to be used in research with adult participants.

6. Why is deception sometimes used in psychological research? How can the use of deception be reconciled with the concept of informed consent?

7. Describe the two main purposes of a debriefing session. When might a full debriefing be delayed until the experiment is completed?

8. Which ethical principles were violated in (a) the Willowbrook study, (b) the Tuskegee study, and (c) MK-ULTRA?

9. Use the Gibson visual cliff study to explain why psychologists sometimes use nonhuman species as research subjects.

10. Describe the arguments for and against the use of nonhuman species in psychological research.

11. Describe the kinds of research likely to be undertaken by anthrozoologists.

12. What are the essential features of the APA code for animal research?

13. What does the APA ethics code say about the use of animals for educational purposes?

14. Describe the ways in which data falsification is usually discovered. Why does this type of fraud occur?

APPLICATIONS EXERCISES

Exercise 2.1.   Thinking Scientifically About Deception

From the standpoint of a research psychologist who is thinking scientifically, how would you design a study to evaluate the following claims that are sometimes made about the use of deception in research? That is, what kinds of empirical data would you like to have in order to judge the truth of the claims?

1. Deception should never be used in psychological research because once people have been deceived in a study, they will no longer trust any psychologist.

2. Researchers could avoid deception by instructing subjects to imagine they are in a deception study and then behave as they think a typical person would.

3. Psychologists are just fooling themselves; most participants see right through their deceptions and quickly understand the true purpose of a study.

4. Deception seldom works in research with university students, because they talk to each other about the studies in which they have participated and tell each other the "true" purpose of the studies.

Exercise 2.2.   Recognizing Ethical Problems

Consider each of the following brief descriptions of actual research in social psychology. From the standpoint of the APA's code of ethics, which components could cause problems with an IRB? Explain how you might defend each study to an IRB.

1. The effect of crowding on stress was investigated in a public men's room. A member of the research team followed a subject into the bathroom and occupied either the urinal directly adjacent to the subject's or the next one down the line. Subjects were unaware they were participating in a study. On the assumption that increased stress would affect urination, the amount of time it took for the subject to begin to urinate and the total time spent urinating were recorded by another researcher hidden in one of the stalls. As predicted, subjects' urination was more disrupted when the immediately adjacent urinal was occupied (Middlemist, Knowles, & Matter, 1976).

2. In a field experiment, a woman (who was actually part of the experiment) stood by her car on the side of a road. The car had a flat tire. To determine if modeling would affect the helping behavior of passing motorists, on some trials another

woman with a flat tire was helped by a stopped motorist (all part of the staged event) about a quarter-mile before the place where the woman waited for help. As expected, motorists were more likely to stop and help if they had just witnessed another person helping (Bryan & Test, 1967).

3. In the wake of the Watergate scandal, researchers wished to determine if average people could be induced to commit a crime, especially if they thought an arm of government would give them immunity from prosecution. Subjects were recruited by the experimenter, posing as a private investigator, and asked to be part of a break-in at a local advertising agency said to be involved in tax fraud. Some subjects were told that the IRS was organizing the break-in and promised immunity from prosecution; others weren't promised immunity. A third group was told a competing advertising agency was leading the break-in, and a fourth group was not told who was behind the crime. The prediction that people would be most willing to participate for a government agency that promised immunity was confirmed; the experiment ended when participants either agreed or disagreed. No break-in actually occurred (West, Gunn, & Chernicky, 1975).

Exercise 2.3.   Replicating Milgram

Describe what changes you think could be made to Milgram's basic obedience study in order to get it approved by an IRB today. Then track down Burger's description of his replication (Burger, 2009) and describe exactly what he did. On the basis of his study, do you think it is safe to conclude that Milgram's studies have been replicated and people are just as obedient today as they were in the 1960s?

Exercise 2.4.   Decisions about Animal Research

The following exercise is based on a study by Galvin and Herzog (1992) and is used with the permission of Hal Herzog. The idea is for you to play the role of a member of an IACUC (Institutional Animal Care and Use Committee) and make decisions about whether the following studies ought to gain IACUC approval (quoting from Galvin & Herzog, p. 265):

1. *Mice.* A neurobiologist proposes to amputate the forelimbs of newborn mice to study the relative influence of heredity and environment on the development of motor patterns (grooming).

2. *Rats.* A psychologist seeks permission to conduct a classroom learning demonstration. Rats are to be deprived of food for 23 hours and taught to press a lever for food reinforcements.

3. *Monkeys.* Tissue from monkey fetuses will be implanted into the brains of adult rhesus monkeys to explore the feasibility of neural transplantation as a treatment for Alzheimer's disease.

4. *Dogs.* Stray dogs awaiting euthanasia in an animal shelter are to be used to teach surgical techniques to veterinary students.

5. *Bears.* Wild grizzly bears will be anesthetized. Collars containing radio telemetry devices will be attached to their necks for a study of their social and territorial behavior patterns.

For each of these studies, do a cost-benefit analysis, indicate whether you would approve the study, and explain the reasons why or why not. In terms of the ethics code, indicate whether some changes in procedure might switch your decision from "reject" to "approve."

ANSWERS TO SELF TESTS

✓ 2.1

1. The Hobbs committee used the procedure to collect examples of perceived ethical violations among psychologists.
2. They believed the infant has a strong constitution and would not be harmed; they also believed that the contribution to science outweighed any minor discomfort they would cause.
3. Respect for Persons, Beneficence, Justice
4. It means researchers must always weigh the benefits of their research against the potential harm to subjects, in order to achieve the greatest good.

✓ 2.2

1. Expedited review.
2. The potential subject is given enough information about the study to make a reasoned decision about whether or not to participate.
3. His procedure violated the "quit any time" proviso.

✓ 2.3

1. It benefits the well-being of humans; it also benefits animals (e.g., zoos).
2. Use live animals as sparingly as possible.
3. A failure to produce his raw data when asked and reproducing identical results across studies.

3

Developing Ideas for Research in Psychology

PREVIEW & CHAPTER OBJECTIVES

All research begins with a good question, and this chapter is designed to help you develop such questions. It begins by distinguishing among various forms of research and elaborates on a concept introduced in Chapter 1—the empirical question. You will learn how research can develop from everyday observations of behavior, from theory, and from questions left unanswered by prior research. The chapter concludes with a brief description of PsycINFO, psychology's premier information database, and advice about how to gather information for writing a literature review. When you finish this chapter, you should be able to:

- Distinguish between and identify the value of both basic and applied research.

- Distinguish between the laboratory and the field as the setting for research in psychology, and understand the advantages and disadvantages of each.

- Distinguish between qualitative and quantitative methods, and understand how they often combine.

- Be able to formulate a good empirical question.

- Understand the need for operational definitions.

- Understand how the use of several operational definitions for the same concept can strengthen conclusions about psychological phenomena (converging operations).

- Describe examples of psychological research that have developed from everyday observations and from serendipitous events.

- Describe the defining features of a theory in psychology and show how theories (a) lead to research in psychology; (b) are influenced by research outcomes; and (c) must be productive, parsimonious, and testable (i.e., capable of falsification).

- Understand the importance of the "What's next?" question and the value of research that simultaneously replicates and extends prior research.

- Distinguish between two types of replication (direct and conceptual) and explain the importance of replication in psychological science.

- Show how creative thinking occurs in science.

- Use PsycINFO and other resources to search for information about research in psychology.

As one of the requirements for your methods course, or perhaps as an independent study course, you may be asked to develop an idea for a research project, search for and read about other research that has been completed on the topic, and perhaps even complete a study yourself. You might react to this assignment with a feeling that the screen has gone blank, accompanied by a mounting sense of panic. Take heart—this chapter has come along just in time. When you finish it, you may not find ideas for research projects flowing freely into your mind, but you should at least have good ideas about where to start and how to proceed. Before looking at the sources of ideas for research, however, let us categorize the varieties of psychological research.

Varieties of Psychological Research

Research in psychology can be classified along several dimensions. Psychological scientists strive to achieve the four research goals described in Chapter 1: description, prediction, explanation, and application, but some goals may be emphasized over others. Research can be classified in terms of its goals, setting, and type of data collected. We will make the distinctions between the following varieties of research: (a) basic or applied research, (b) laboratory or field research, and (c) quantitative or qualitative research.

The Goals: Basic versus Applied Research

Some research in psychology emphasizes describing, predicting, and explaining the fundamental principles of behavior and mental processes and such research goals define **basic research**. Traditionally, those involved in basic research in psychology have studied such topics as perception, learning, cognition, and basic neurological and physiological processes as they relate to psychological phenomena. In contrast, **applied research** is so named because it has direct and immediate relevance to the solution of real-world problems. To illustrate the distinction, consider some research in the area of attention (a topic with a long history—recall the 1913 Dallenbach study in Box 1.1 in Chapter 1). A *basic* research study might investigate the ability of people to simultaneously complete two different information-processing tasks in a laboratory. The researcher might examine the effects of the similarity of the tasks, their difficulty, and so on. One well-established method involves "shadowing" in a "dichotic listening" task, a technique pioneered by Cherry (1953) and Broadbent (1958) in England. A research participant in this type of experiment wears earphones, with a different message coming into each ear simultaneously. The task is to focus attention on one message and shadow it—that is, while the message in one ear (the "attended" ear) is being heard, the subject tries to repeat out loud the message verbatim, as it is being heard. Of interest is what happens to the message coming into the other (i.e., the "unattended") ear. In general, researchers find that when people are asked about information in the unattended ear, they have a difficult time recalling any of it, unless it is especially meaningful to them (e.g., their name). The dichotic listening research has led to the development of several theories of attention, which you can learn about when you take a cognitive psychology course. For our purposes, this is a good example of basic research; it is designed to discover and better understand the basic properties of attention.

An *applied* study on attention might examine the limits of attention for a real-world task with important practical implications—using a cell phone while driving a car, for example. This activity is clearly a problem, with some surveys showing at least 85% of drivers report using their phone while driving (Hunt & Ellis, 2004) and other studies showing a substantial number of people are on their phones when they have accidents (Redelmeier & Tibshirani, 1997). An interesting series of experiments by Strayer and Johnston (2001) illustrates a combination of both basic and applied research in their study. That is, they strived to understand the role of attention in distracted driving (basic research) and to demonstrate how research can help solve the public safety concern over distracted driving (applied research). They examined how carrying on a cell phone conversation could affect simulated driving performance. In one of their experiments, college-aged participants performed a computer-tracking task involving skills analogous to those involved in driving. They either performed this task by itself ("single-task mode") or while doing a second task ("dual-task mode"). One of the second tasks was "a *shadowing* task in which the participants performed the simulated driving task while they repeated words that the experimenter read to them over a hand-held cell phone" (p. 464, italics added). The other dual task created even more of a cognitive bur-den—after hearing each word, instead of repeating it, participants had to generate a new word starting with the final letter of the word said to them. See the connection with basic research? Knowing the attention literature like the backs of their hands, Strayer and Johnston immediately thought of adapting a basic research methodology, shadowing, to an applied research study.

You might not be too surprised about the results of this study. Although "driving" performance was not much affected by the simple shadowing task, it deteriorated sharply when subjects did the more attention-demanding word-generation task. Focusing attention on word generation interfered with driving. You might be more surprised about the results of a second experiment reported by Strayer and Johnston in the same 2001 article. They compared driving simulation performance when subjects were talking on cell phones that were either hands-free or handheld. Car manufacturers that routinely include Bluetooth hands-free options in new cars base their marketing on the idea that their product is safer than a handheld phone, but Strayer and Johnston showed that *both* forms of cell phone use produced poor simulated driving performance and the two forms of cell phoning did not differ from each other. They also found that while cell phone talking adversely affected driving, listening to audio books or the radio did not affect driving performance. They concluded the problem with cell phones was not the distraction caused by physically holding the phone with one hand and driving with the other, or the act of listening to verbal material, but by the attentional demands of the conversation reducing the capacity for the driving task. Since their seminal 2001 study, Strayer and his colleagues have conducted numer-ous studies on cognitive distractions while driving. For example, texting while driving more than quadruples the number of accidents in a driving simulator (Drews, Yazdani, Godfrey, Cooper, & Strayer, 2009), and interacting with an in-vehicle speech-to-text system (including interacting with Siri on a hands-free iPhone to update Facebook and check text messages) is a more distract-ing and dangerous medium of cell phone use while driving compared to talking on the phone or with others in the car (Strayer, Cooler, Turrill, Coleman, Medeiros-Ward, & Biondi, 2013; Strayer, Turrill, Coleman, Ortiz, & Cooper, 2014).

It is sometimes believed that applied research is more valuable than basic research because an applied study seems to concern more relevant problems and to tackle them directly. It could be argued, however, that a major advantage of basic research is that the principles and procedures (e.g., shadowing) developed through basic research can potentially be used in a wide range of applied situations, even though these uses may not have been considered when the basic research was being done. Nonetheless, basic research is a frequent target of politicians who bluster about the misuse of tax dollars to fund research that doesn't seem "useful." The accusations are easy to make and tend to resonate with voters; after all, a major component of the American national character is the high value we place on the practical and the beneficial. Even those committed to a program of basic research recognize that grant funds are easier to obtain when the research appears to be useful. In an interview after being elected president of the Association for Psychological Science (APS), for instance, the noted experimental psychologist Richard F. Thompson acknowledged that "[m]any of us who have been basic scientists have come to feel that to justify our existence we, too, have really got to try to develop applications to the problems of society" (Kent, 1994, p. 10).

Another impediment to basic research is that IRBs sometimes favor applied over basic research; nonpsychologist members of an IRB in particular often fail to see the relevance of basic laboratory procedures (Kimmel, 2007). For instance, it could be difficult for an IRB member to approve a laboratory experiment on perception in which subjects see meaningless shapes that vary according to specific dimensions and then try to identify these shapes later in a recognition test. On the other hand, an experiment examining the ability to recognize people filmed on bank security cameras, their features also varying according to specific dimensions, might appear to be more important and could gain IRB approval more easily.

In some cases, what is learned from basic research can be useful in an applied project from a completely different topic area. For instance, the serial position effect, the tendency to recall words from the beginning and end of a list better than remembering words from the middle, is a well-known finding from basic research on memory. You might not think that serial position would be especially relevant for applied research on how people navigate through the environment without getting lost, yet that is exactly what happened in a study by Cornell, Heth, Kneubuhler, and Sehgal (1996). Eight- and twelve-year-olds were led on a complicated route in a campus setting and then asked to retrace their route. A serial position effect similar to the one found in basic memory research occurred; both age groups did rather well at the beginning and end of the route, and they made most of their errors in the middle of the route. Cornell et al. even converted the serial position data into probability estimates of where the children were most likely to become lost. They concluded such information could aid police searches for missing children.

If it is true that basic research often leads to applications, it is also the case that applied research outcomes frequently have relevance for basic research, providing evidence that either supports or refutes theories. Supporting a capacity theory of attention was not Strayer and Johnston's (2001) goal, but the study did just that. Similarly, the research on navigating through the environment is applied research, but its findings also increased the generality of the serial position phenomenon. More recently, researchers have labeled the merging of basic and applied research as *translational research* (see Chapter 1). We will elaborate on this form of research in Chapter 11 when we devote an entire chapter to applied research.

The Setting: Laboratory versus Field Research

Another way of classifying studies is by location. As is evident from the above labels, the distinction hinges on whether the study occurs inside or outside the controlled environment of a laboratory. **Laboratory research** allows the researcher greater control; conditions of the study can be specified more precisely, and participants can be selected and placed in the different conditions of the study more systematically. In contrast, in **field research**, the environment more closely matches the situations we encounter in daily living. Although field research is often applied research and laboratory research is often basic research, you should know that some basic research takes place in the field and some applied research takes place in the laboratory.

Laboratory research is sometimes criticized for seeming to be "artificial" and far removed from everyday life. It is clear, however, that laboratory research has yielded important knowledge about behavior, and a case can be made that there are more important considerations when judging the quality of research than mere correspondence to daily living. Social psychologist Elliot Aronson (2007), for example, made a distinction between mundane and experimental realism. **Mundane realism** refers to how closely a study mirrors real-life experiences. **Experimental realism** concerns the extent to which a research study (whether in the laboratory or in the field) "has an impact on the subjects, forces them to take the matter seriously, and involves them in the procedures" (p. 411). It is the experimental realism of the study that counts, according to Aronson. If participants are involved in the study and taking it seriously, then the researcher can draw valid conclusions about behavior. The Milgram experiments on obedience, discussed in Chapter 2, did not have much mundane realism—we are unlikely to find ourselves zapping someone who fails to learn a word list for us. Milgram's volunteers were clearly involved in the experiment, however, and his studies have strong experimental realism. Milgram's research was controversial, but it shed important light on the phenomenon of obedience to authority.

Proximity to everyday life is the strength of field research, but there are other reasons for conducting research away from the lab. On the basis of their studies of cognitive functioning in children from India infected with intestinal parasites, for instance, Sternberg and Grigorenko (1999) argued that research in the field has several strengths. First, conditions in the field often cannot be duplicated in a laboratory. Sternberg and Grigorenko studied children living in cramped quarters in 113° heat, with the smell of excrement from open sewers almost overwhelming. Such conditions can hardly be created in a laboratory, if for no other reason than an IRB almost certainly would not allow it. A second reason to do field research is to confirm the findings of laboratory studies and perhaps to correct misconceptions or oversimplifications that might be derived from the safe confines of a laboratory. A third reason is to make discoveries that could result in an immediate difference in the lives of the people being studied. Fourth, although field research is ordinarily associated with applied research, it is also a good setting in which to do basic research. Sternberg and his colleagues have studied the effects of parasitic infections in numerous locations around the globe, and one focus of their work is to test hypotheses derived from Sternberg's theories about the basic nature of intelligence. Yet the Sternberg example also points to a problem with doing field research—it can be time-consuming and expensive. For researchers in an academic environment under pressure to publish, several laboratory studies can be completed in the time it takes to set up, get IRB approval, and complete most field studies (Cialdini, 2009).

Some researchers combine both laboratory and field research within a single series of studies; a good example is a project by Bushman and Anderson (2009). They wanted to discover if exposing people to violent media would desensitize them to violence and make them less likely to be helpful to others. To do so, they completed both a laboratory study and a field study.

Research Example 1—Combining Laboratory and Field Studies

Note: This is the first of 42 descriptions of research we are calling *Research Examples*. The idea is to use examples of actual research in psychology, rather than made-up examples, to explain various methodological points and research designs to you. We believe you will find it easier to understand the concepts found in this book if you see them in action in real studies. You can find a complete listing of these Research Examples on page xv.

Bushman and Anderson's (2009) first experiment was completed in the laboratory using college students who were randomly placed into one of two groups. (You will learn in Chapter 6 that *random assignment* is an important control procedure, ensuring the different groups in an experiment are basically equivalent to each other.) In one group, students (tested one at a time) played one of four violent video games (e.g., Duke Nukem); in the second group, subjects played one of four nonviolent games (e.g., Pinball). After playing either the violent or nonviolent game for 20 minutes, subjects completed a lengthy questionnaire about the game they played and about video games and game players in general. While completing the questionnaire, they heard a professionally produced audio recording of two individuals in the next room arguing, and then fighting, with the result that one person was left with an injured ankle and the second person left the room. The question was whether the subjects, busily filling out the questionnaires, would come into the room next door and offer aid to the victim of the fight.[1] In line with the researchers' prediction,

---

[1] It might occur to you that the subjects could easily have said to themselves, "Well, OK, this person clearly needs help, but the experimenter will take care of that." To eliminate this justification for not helping, the experimenter running the study made it clear to the subject that the experimenter would be in a different part of the building while the questionnaire was being filled out, but would return after a while.

those who had played the violent game were slower to come to the victim's aid, less likely to report hearing the fight, and, if they heard the fight, less likely to consider it serious. The theoretical implication of these results is that exposure to violent video games may have desensitized subjects to aggressive or violent acts, which, in turn, decreased helping behavior.

In a second experiment, the researchers wondered if their results would generalize to a more everyday situation, so they completed a field study. Subjects were adult moviegoers who were exiting the theater after seeing either a violent (*The Ruins*) or a nonviolent (*Nim's Island*) film. Outside the theater, Bushman and Anderson (2009) staged an accident using what is known as a **confederate**—someone who appears to be part of the normal environment but is actually part of the study. In this case, it was a young woman with an apparent ankle injury who was on crutches (note the type of injury was the same in both studies). On each trial, she dropped her crutches and was trying with some difficulty to pick them up. She was helped on every trial, but those emerging from the violent movie took significantly longer to help. Again, it appeared that exposure to violence affected helping behavior.

This pair of studies has several interesting methodological aspects. First, experimenters did what is called a **manipulation check** in the first study. This procedure is often used to be sure the intended manipulations in a study have the desired effect. In this case, the researchers assumed that Duke Nuken was a more violent game than Pinball, but it was important to be sure subjects perceived them that way as well. So one of the items on the questionnaire asked subjects to rate the violence level of the game they played. Sure enough, Duke Nukem was rated considerably higher than Pinball. A second methodological point is that the two studies reported in the article were preceded by a **pilot study**. Pilot studies are often used to test aspects of the procedure to be sure the methodology is sound. In this case, in the first study Bushman and Anderson (2009) wanted to be sure the staged argument and fight were perceived as realistic by subjects. So they did a pilot study of 50 subjects, asking them simply to judge the reality of the fight—5 of the first 10 subjects thought the fight was faked, so some extra effects were added. The remaining 40 subjects thought the fight was realistic. Without the pilot study, we think you can see that experiment 1 would have been seriously flawed.

A final point is that Bushman and Anderson (2009) clearly recognized the interpretation problems that can occur in field research, which allows less control than laboratory research. In the lab, the random assignment procedure yielded two roughly equivalent groups of subjects. In the field study, however, it is possible individuals who opted to see the violent film were *different types of people* than those who chose to see the nonviolent film. And maybe those who like violent films are just less likely to be helpful to others. To deal with this problem, the researchers added a clever twist; they ran half their trials, for both types of film, during times *before* the movie started, catching people on their way in. On these trials, the amount of time taken to help the victim was the *same* for those seeing the violent film and those seeing the nonviolent film. As the authors noted, this "lack of a difference in helping before watching the movie rule[d] out the possibility that less-helpful people were more likely to attend the violent movies" (p. 277). You might recognize this ruling-out language as exactly the same as the concept of falsification thinking we introduced in Chapter 1 and will discuss later in this chapter in the discussion of theory.

Bushman and Anderson's (2009) experiments show laboratory research and field research can converge on the same conclusion. To the extent such an outcome occurs, it strengthens the argument that both types of research are important and necessary. But is the Bushman and Anderson outcome an isolated event? Can it be said in general that the results of laboratory research mirror the results of field research? Apparently so, at least in some research areas. Anderson, Lindsay, and Bushman (1999) examined several topics within social psychology and found a large collection (288 studies in all) of laboratory and field studies that investigated the same topics. For example, in the area of aggression, they matched lab and field studies investigating the effects of anonymity on aggressive behavior. They found a relatively high degree of correspondence between the results found in and outside the lab. Other studies have reached similar conclusions, although it appears that the lab-field correspondence is higher in some areas than others. For example, Mitchell (2012) reported a high degree of similarity between laboratory and field studies in industrial/organizational psychology and in personality psychology, but somewhat lesser similarity in social psychology and consumer psychology, and little similarity in developmental psychology. Nonetheless, the overall outcome of lab-field correspondence research provides aid and comfort to laboratory researchers (in most fields) who tire of hearing about the "artificiality" of their studies and to field researchers who tire of hearing about how their studies lack the controls that enable firm conclusions to be drawn.

One last point about the decision on where to locate a study concerns ethics. Besides providing increased control, researchers often prefer the laboratory to the field because of researchers' concerns with informed consent and privacy. In laboratory research, it is relatively easy to stick closely to the ethics code. In the field, however, it is difficult, and usually impossible, to provide informed consent and debriefing; in fact, in some situations, the research procedures themselves might be considered an invasion of privacy. Consequently, field studies can face a greater challenge from an IRB, and field researchers must show the importance of their study justifies the risks involved.[2] On the other hand, as seen in the Sternberg and Grigorenko (1999) example, IRBs might not allow the conditions of some field settings to be simulated in a laboratory.

The Data: Quantitative versus Qualitative Research

Recall from Chapter 1 that scientists are data driven, in that they measure psychological phenomena in some concrete way. We will begin to discuss more about data in Chapter 4, but there is an important distinction between the forms of data that help guide a researcher's approach to studying a particular phenomenon. The distinction is between quantitative methods and qualitative methods of research. Most research in psychology is quantitative in nature. That is, with **quantitative research**, the data are collected and presented in the form of numbers—average scores for different groups on some task, percentages of people who do one thing or another, graphs and tables of data, and so on. In recent years, however, a number of research psychologists have begun doing what is known as **qualitative research**, sometimes borrowing techniques from sociologists and anthropologists. Qualitative research is not easily classified, but it often includes studies that collect interview information, either from individuals or groups; it sometimes involves detailed case studies; or it might involve carefully designed observational studies. What these various forms of qualitative research have in common is that results are presented not as statistical summaries but as analytical narratives that summarize the project's main outcomes. A good illustration of a qualitative study is some research by Walker (1996), who wondered if gender differences in the control of a TV remote would affect relationships among couples. Her primary method was to conduct semi-structured interviews with 36 couples that were either married or cohabiting for at least a year. First, as is common in qualitative research, a portion of the questions resulted in responses that could be quantified—for instance, in response to a question about control over the remote when both partners were watching TV, Walker determined that women had control 20% of the time, men 80% of the time. Most of the description, however, was a qualitative analysis, a narrative based on several open-ended questions in the interview, along with quotes from the interview to illustrate conclusions.

Among other things, subjects (individually interviewed) were asked how they decided on programs to watch together, what their frustrations might be during this process, and what they

---

[2] Brad Bushman, coauthor of the study just described in Research Example 1, had greater difficulty convincing his IRB to approve the field study than the lab study. "We had to convince them that seeing a person with crutches is normal at a movie theater" (B. J. Bushman, personal communication, September 29, 2011).

would like to change about the process (Walker, 1996). Unlike descriptions of results in quantitative studies, which focus on the numerical data and the statistical analysis of it, results in qualitative studies often take longer to describe and include quotes said to represent typical responses. For example, in Walker's study, a common theme was that men seemed to take it for granted they would control the remote. As one man reported, "I should probably let her 'drive' sometimes, but [it] would bug me too much not to be able to do it" (p. 819). Another, attempting without too much success to sound fair-minded, said "I just say I want to watch something, and if she wants to watch something really bad, I will let her watch what she wants to watch" (p. 819). Walker concluded that when both partners were watching TV, men usually had control over what was being watched, and that, in general, what should be a leisure activity could be a source of stress and misunderstanding instead.

Research that is partly or wholly qualitative in nature will be described in later chapters. Most of the research you will encounter in the book, however, will be quantitative in nature.

Asking Empirical Questions

Whether a research project concerns basic or applied research, occurs in the lab or the field, or is primarily quantitative or qualitative in nature, it always begins with a question. As you recall from Chapter 1, we referred to these as *empirical questions*. They have two important features: They must be answerable with data, qualitative and/or quantitative, and their terms must be precisely defined.

We saw in Chapter 1 that questions like "Are people good or evil?" and "Is there a personal God?" are interesting and important, and individuals can reach their own conclusions about them. However, the questions are not answerable with the evidence of empirical data. Of course, some questions related to good, evil, and religion *are* empirical questions. These include:

• What is the relationship between belief in God and fear of death?

• Does belief in God influence the pain threshold of terminally ill patients?

• As people get older, are they more likely to believe in a personal God?

Notice that each of these questions allows data to be collected in some form. Before such data can be collected, however, the questions must be refined. This task can be referred to as *operationalizing* the terms in the question. Precisely defined terms are the second feature of an empirical question.

Operational Definitions

The term **operationism** originated in the 1920s in physics, with the publication of *The Logic of Modern Physics* (1927) by Harvard physicist Percy Bridgman. Bridgman argued that the terminology of science must be totally objective and precise, and that all concepts should be defined in terms of a set of "operations" or procedures to be performed. In other words, a researcher defines how the concepts to be studied "operate" in an experiment. These types of definitions came to be called **operational definitions**. The length of some object, for instance, could be defined operationally by a series of agreed-on procedures. In Bridgman's words, the "concept of length is therefore fixed when the operations by which length is measured are fixed; that is, the concept of length involves as much as and nothing more than a set of operations" (Bridgman, 1927, p. 5).

Given the tendency of experimental psychologists to emulate the older sciences, especially physics, it is not surprising that the psychological community embraced operationism when it first appeared. A strict operationism did not last long in psychology, however, in part because equating a concept with a set of operations creates an arbitrary limitation on the concept. For psychologists, the problem with operationism boiled down to how to accomplish it in practice when dealing with such complex psychological phenomena as aggression, creativity, depression, and so on. Among physicists it might not be difficult to agree on a set of operations for measuring the length of a line, but how does one operationalize a concept like "aggression"? Even if psychologists could agree that the term refers to a behavior that reflects intent to harm (Aronson, 2007), exactly what behaviors are to be measured? In the aggression literature over the years, the term has been operationalized as behaviors ranging from the delivery of electrical shocks to horn honking by car drivers to pressing a button that makes it hard for someone else to complete a task. Are these behaviors measuring the same phenomenon?

Despite this problem with the *strict* use of operational definitions, the concept has been of value to psychology by forcing researchers to clearly define the terms of their studies (Hilgard, 1987). This is especially important when you consider that most research in psychology concerns concepts that are open to numerous definitions. For instance, suppose a researcher is interested in the effects of hunger on maze learning. "Hunger" is a term that can mean several things and is not easily determined in a rat. How can you tell if a rat is hungry? The solution is to operationalize the term. You could define it operationally in terms of a procedure (e.g., not feeding the rat for 12 hours—it's reasonable to assume the operation would produce hunger) or in terms of a behavior (creating a situation in which the rat has to work hard to earn food—it's reasonable to assume a non-hungry rat wouldn't perform the task).

One important outcome of the precision resulting from operational definitions is that it allows experiments to be repeated. *Replication*, an important feature of any science, was mentioned briefly in Chapters 1 and 2 and will be elaborated later in this chapter. Research psychologists are not greatly troubled by the limitations imposed by operationally defined terms because, in the long run, the requirement for precision increases confidence in the veracity of theories about behavior. Psychologists use the concept of **converging operations**, which is the idea that our understanding of some behavioral phenomenon is increased when a series of investigations, all using slightly different operational definitions and experimental procedures, nonetheless converge on a common conclusion. Thus, if the results of several studies on the effects of hunger on maze learning reached the same conclusion, even though each used different operational definitions for hunger and for learning, then confidence would be high that a lawful relationship between hunger and maze learning had been established.

Developing fruitful empirical questions in psychology is a skill that takes practice and involves gradually narrowing a broad topic to a specific question. These questions can have several origins, as we will describe in the following sections. Empirical questions may evolve out of (a) everyday observations of behavior, (b) the need to solve a practical problem, (c) attempts to support or refute a theory, or (d) unanswered questions from a study just completed.

SELF TEST

3.1

1. Consider the psychological phenomenon of attention. Give an example of basic research on attention and one of applied research on attention.
2. Milgram's obedience study was low on mundane reality but high on experimental reality. Explain.
3. The study on male versus female control of the TV remote illustrated how two types of research can be combined in the same study. Which two types?

Developing Research from Observations of Behavior and Serendipity

All of us have had the experience of observing behavior and wondering what caused it. Why does Norma get so angry when she misses a short putt, while Jeff, who misses just as many, shrugs it off and comments on how fortunate he is to be avoiding work? Why is Aunt Ethel able to recall vivid details of her work as a nurse during the Vietnam War, yet unable to remember what she did yesterday? Why do some people eagerly volunteer to give blood, while others would not consider it? Why do some young children seem to be outgoing, while others, perhaps in the same family, seem to be painfully shy? And so on.

These same questions occur to experimental psychologists and are often the starting point for developing empirical questions. For Robert Sternberg, noted for his research on varieties of intelligence and the nature of human love, simple observations of daily life have been his principle source of inspiration:

> All of my ideas (almost) come from watching people—myself, students I work with, my kids, my relationships with people, other people's relationships, and so on. . . . The point is that in psychology, there is no better data source than the people around you. I've never found books or lectures or labs as good as real experience for getting ideas. (R. J. Sternberg, personal communication, May 18, 1993)

One famous historical example of observations leading to research comes from the social psychological research on helping behavior, which developed out of several well-publicized cases of failure to help. Most notable among them was the Kitty Genovese case in 1964, in which a woman was attacked several times and eventually murdered in New York City, in full view of at least 38 witnesses in nearby apartments, none of whom even made an anonymous call to police. As John Darley, one of the leading researchers in the area of altruism and helping behavior, recalled later:

> Certainly the precipitating event for us all was the murder of a young lady in New York, the now famous Kitty Genovese case the *New York Times* picked up. A young lady was murdered, but sadly that's a rather typical incident. What was atypical was that thirty-eight people in her apartment building watched out their windows while this happened, and none of them did much in the way of helping. Bibb [Latané, Darley's co-worker] and I were having dinner together one night shortly thereafter. Everybody was talking about it and so were we. . . . We probably sketched out the experiments on a tablecloth that day. (Krupat, 1975, p. 257)

The Kitty Genovese case led Darley and Latané (1968) to conduct a series of classic studies showing that unresponsive bystanders aren't simply uncaring; they often assume someone else will help if other people are around—they called this phenomenon the *bystander effect*. The study of helping behavior is now well established, as you can tell by looking at any modern social psychology text, which invariably includes an entire chapter on the topic of helping behavior.

Serendipitous observations can also lead to research. **Serendipity**, or discovering something while looking for something else entirely, has been a source of numerous important events in the history of science. It can happen when a scientist is wrestling with a difficult research problem and a chance event accidentally provides the key, or it might occur when something goes wrong in an experiment, such as an apparatus failure. Skinner's experience with extinction curves following an apparatus breakdown, described in Chapter 1, is a good example of a serendipitous event. Another involves the accidental discovery of feature detectors in the brain. To examine the origins of some research that led eventually to a Nobel Prize for David Hubel and Torsten Wiesel, read Box 3.1.

BOX 3.1 ORIGINS—Serendipity and Edge Detectors

Some of the most important research in the second half of the 20th century on the physiology of the visual system was triggered by a serendipitous finding in the Harvard laboratory of David Hubel and Torsten Wiesel (Hubel & Wiesel, 1959). They were investigating the behavior of single neurons at various points in the visual pathway to see if the neurons could be made to fire in response to certain stimuli. Their experimental setup consisted of a screen on which stimuli could be projected and seen by a cat with its head held stationary and an electrode implanted within a single cell of its visual system. (Even in the 1950s, procedures were precise enough to isolate the activity of single neurons.)

Hubel and Wiesel were hoping the neuron would fire in response to black or white dots projected onto the cat's retina, but their first efforts were frustrating:

> The position of the microelectrode tip, relative to the cortex, was unusually stable, so much so that we were able to listen in on one cell for a period of about nine hours. We tried everything short of standing on our heads to get it to fire. (Hubel, 1988, p. 69)

Nothing happened. Yet Hubel and Wiesel persevered, eventually concentrating on one area of the retina. Oddly, passing the dot over that area sometimes produced neuron firing, but not reliably. As they described it:

> After about five hours of struggle, we suddenly had the impression that the glass [slide] with the dot was occasionally producing a response, but the response seemed to have little to do with the dot. *Eventually we caught on: it was the sharp but faint shadow cast by the edge of the glass as we slid it into the slot that was doing the trick.* We soon convinced ourselves that the edge worked only when its shadow was swept across one small part of the retina and that the sweeping had to be done with the edge in one particular orientation. Most amazing was the contrast between the machine-gun discharge when the orientation of the stimulus was just right and the utter lack of a response if we changed the orientation or simply shined a bright flashlight into the cat's eyes. (Hubel, 1988, pp. 69–70; italics added)

Looking for neuron firing in response to a specific stimulus (a dot), Hubel and Wiesel accidentally (i.e. serendipitously) discovered that the edge of the slide was the key stimulus. The unexpected finding that cells ("edge detectors") in the visual system were specialized to respond to edges and contours set at specific orientations was just the beginning. Hubel and Wiesel went on to develop an extensive research program identifying the types of stimuli that would trigger cells at all levels of the visual system; it won them the Nobel Prize in 1981. Their work also reflects the passion for doing research that was described in Chapter 1. In discussing the years spent studying receptive fields for vision, roughly from 1950 to 1980, Hubel wrote:

> I count myself lucky to have been around in that era, a time of excitement and fun. Some of the experiments have been arduous, or so it has often seemed at 4:00 a.m., especially when everything has gone wrong. But 98 percent of the time the work is exhilarating. There is a special immediacy to neurophysiological experiments; we can see and hear a cell respond to the stimuli we use and often realize, right at the time, what the responses imply for brain function. (Hubel, 1988, p. vii)

Developing Research from Theory

Chapter 1 included a brief discussion of theory, making the point that science as a way of knowing includes the creation of theories with testable hypotheses. The chapter also described explanation as an important goal for research psychology. The process of developing explanations is, in essence, the process of theory building and theory testing. In what follows we'll take a more detailed look at the definition of a theory, the reciprocal relationship between theory development and data collection, the logical processes involved in theory development, and the criteria for determining which theories have value.

The Nature of Theory

A **theory** is a set of logically consistent statements about some phenomenon that (a) best summarizes existing empirical knowledge of the phenomenon, (b) organizes this knowledge in the form of precise statements of relationships among variables (i.e., laws), (c) proposes an explanation for the phenomenon, and (d) serves as the basis for making predictions. These predictions are then tested with research. A theory is considered to be a working truth, always subject to revision pending the outcome of empirical studies—remember from the Chapter 1 description of scientific thinking that "science produces tentative conclusions."

Theories in psychology differ in scope. Some cover broad expanses of behavior and are general theories—Erik Erikson's famous stage theory of how personality is developed and operates over the life span is an example. More often, however, a theory is more focused on a specific aspect of behavior. In social psychology, for instance, cognitive dissonance theory concerns decision making and how people resolve inconsistencies; in abnormal psychology, learned helplessness theory attempts to account for psychological depression; in developmental psychology, processing-speed theory focuses on age-related declines in cognitive processing. Theories also differ in level of precision, with some being stated in strict mathematical terms and others described more simply as a set of logically connected statements.

As an example of how theories originate and evolve, and to illustrate several of their important features, let's consider the theory of cognitive dissonance in more detail. First proposed in 1957 by the renowned social psychologist Leon Festinger, this theory is remarkably simple in conception, yet widely applicable to all sorts of phenomena. It helps explain why and how people rationalize the decisions they make, how attitudes and behaviors relate, and how people justify the contradictions in their lives. The theory was especially prominent in the 1960s and 1970s, but it remains important in social psychology even today, a regular feature of social psychology textbooks. The essence of the theory is the proposal that whenever people hold two opposing cognitions at the same time, a state of discomfort, called *cognitive dissonance*, is created. Cognitive dissonance is an example of what psychologists refer to as a **construct**. A construct is a hypothetical factor that is not observed directly; its existence is inferred from certain behaviors and assumed to follow from certain circumstances. Hence, cognitive dissonance is assumed to exist following circumstances of cognitive inconsistency and presumably leads to certain predictable behaviors.

The person experiencing dissonance is motivated to reduce the discomfort and bring the cognitions into harmony and consistency, according to the theory. Dissonance reduction can come about by several means: One or both of the cognitions could be altered, behavior could be changed, or additional cognitions could be added to bring the two dissonant cognitions into consonance. Consider smoking, for example. This is a common activity, carried on by people who frequently hear or read about the dangers of smoking. The cognitions "I am smoking" and "Smoking can kill me" do not fit together well. They create dissonance. One way to reduce the dissonance is to change the first cognition and stop smoking, and many people do, but nicotine is an addictive drug and quitting is easier said than done.[3] A second alternative is to alter the second cognition, perhaps by questioning the conclusiveness of the evidence for the ill effects of smoking (an option much harder to sustain today than it was when Festinger proposed the theory in 1957). A third option is to add cognitions that bridge the two original ones. For instance, the person might say, "OK, this smoking might be bad for me to some degree, but it helps me keep my weight down and all my friends smoke, so it helps me socially, and some really cool people in movies smoke, so it can't be all that bad." The process of reducing dissonance, then, can alter behavior (smoking stops) or shape beliefs and attitudes (smoking has benefits that offset the risks).

---

[3] The smoking example was the first one used by Festinger in his book, ironic because Festinger was a heavy smoker. Just before his death from liver cancer, he announced, reducing dissonance right to the very end, "Make sure everyone knows that it wasn't lung cancer!" (Zajonc, 1990, p. 662).

An important feature of any theory is its continual evolution in light of new research. No theory is ever complete and, as you will learn shortly, Festinger's is no exception. Its development beyond the initial formulation nicely illustrates the reciprocal relationship between theory and research and demonstrates an important attribute of a good theory: its ability to make predictions that lead to new research. This requires some elaboration.

The Relationship between Theory and Research

The move from theory to research and back again begins with the logical process of **deduction**, reasoning from a set of general statements toward the prediction of a specific event. With regard to theory, deduction takes the form of the scientist reasoning that if the theory is correct, then a specific research outcome can be predicted and should occur with some probability greater than chance. The prediction about outcomes that is derived this way is called a **hypothesis**, which in general can be considered a reasonable prediction about a research result that should occur under certain circumstances. Hypotheses lead to the design of a study, which produces results as predicted or fails to produce them. In the former case, the theory is supported, and in the latter case it is not. If the theory is supported by a large number of research outcomes, a researcher's confidence is high that the theory is a good one; to put it another way, we could say that *inductive* support for the theory increases when individual studies keep producing the results as predicted from the theory. **Induction** is the logical process of reasoning from specific events (the results of individual research studies) to the general (the theory).

Of course, research projects don't always come out as expected. The study might not be a good test of the hypothesis (e.g., the operational definitions for the variables being studied might not be the best ones), it might have methodological flaws, or it might fail for a reason that is never discovered. Also, measurements of psychological phenomena are imperfect, so a failed experiment could be the result of measurement error (more on this concept in Chapter 4). Consequently, any one study that fails to come out as one hopes seldom calls a theory into question. If results repeatedly fail to support the theory, however, especially if they occur in different laboratories, confidence in the theory begins to lessen and it may be discarded or, more likely, altered.

Note that in the above two paragraphs we have deliberately avoided statements like "a successful research outcome proves a theory to be true" and "a bad result disproves a theory." This is because scientists don't use the words *prove* and *disprove* when discussing theories and data. The use of the term *prove* implies 100% truth, but scientists can never be 100% certain their results are true. If a study comes out as expected, that outcome supports but *cannot prove* a theory, for the simple reason that future studies could potentially come out in a way that fails to support the theory. Similarly, if a study fails to come out as hoped, that outcome *cannot disprove* a theory since future research might support it. Furthermore, the study itself might be flawed or a poor test of the hypothesis. Remember that science is an ongoing endeavor; theories rise and fall over time as the result of an accumulated body of knowledge that results from lots of research. This complex relationship between theory and data is summarized in Figure 3.1.

Festinger's theory of cognitive dissonance illustrates the process nicely. For example, he used the theory to hypothesize about what happens after people make difficult decisions. What makes some decisions difficult is that both alternatives have positive and negative attributes. Deciding which house to buy would be a snap if everything about house A was good and everything about house B was bad. In reality, however, both A and B have good and bad features. Regardless of which decision is made, Festinger hypothesized, dissonance would occur immediately *after* the final choice, because the person would have chosen something with some negative attributes and rejected something with some positive attributes. The cognition "I am a good decision maker," is dissonant with the cognition "I've just chosen something with some negative features and rejected something with some positive features." To reduce dissonance, Festinger proposed the person would make cognitive changes accentuating both the positive features of the chosen alternative and the negative

Theory

A set of statements summarizing functional relationships about a phenomenon and proposed explanations; good theories are productive, precise enough for falsification, and parsimonious.

↓

From the theory, develop a research hypothesis.

Process of deduction involved here.

(If the theory is valid, then a predictable result should occur in the study.)

↓

Design a methodologically sound study to test the hypothesis.

(This will involve all the skills you've learned in your methods course.)

↓

Collect and analyze the data statistically and draw a conclusion about the study.

(This will involve all the skills you've learned in your methods and stat courses.)

↓

Determine if the research outcome is consistent with the hypotheses (or not).

↓

If it is consistent → the theory is given inductive support.

(Does not mean the theory has been "proven"—future studies might not work out so well.)

↓

If it is not consistent → the theory is not supported.

(Does not mean the theory has been "disproven"—this study might be flawed and future studies might be supportive of the theory.)

↓

If the theory is supported, be very happy, and then go on to the next logical hypothesis to test the theory further.

↓

If the theory is not supported, don't despair, and do the following:

Be sure there were no problems in running the study just completed

(e.g., instructions poorly understood by subjects).

↓

Perhaps make slight changes (e.g., better instructions, a different set of operational definitions) and do the study again.

↓

If the research repeatedly fails to support the theory, think about revising the theory or perhaps even abandoning it for a new one.

FIGURE 3.1
The continuous relationship between theory and research.

features of the rejected alternative ("Because my new house is close to the main road, I can get to work really fast; that other house was so far up the mountain it would have added 15 minutes to the commute, not to mention wear and tear on the brakes"); at the same time, the homebuyer would be expected to downplay the negative features of what was chosen and the positive features of what was not chosen ("The road noise at my new house is not bad at all and easy to get used to; I suppose the other house had a nice view, but it would have been hidden by fog half the time").

In terms of the deductive logic, Festinger's prediction might have gone like this: "If dissonance theory is correct, then, after a difficult decision, the values placed on the attributes of the selected and rejected alternatives will alter in a specific way that will reduce dissonance." This could lead to the design of a study in which individuals would choose between two attractive items; then, later, they would evaluate both the chosen and nonchosen item in some fashion. Several studies like this were completed in the early years of dissonance theory, and the outcomes supported dissonance theory. For example, Brehm (1956) asked women to rate appliances; then, as a reward for participating in the study, he let them pick an appliance from two that had been in the middle of the ratings. Later, when asked to rate all of the appliances again, the ratings shifted—for the chosen appliance, women's ratings increased, while the rating for the rejected appliance actually went down.

Now, as interesting as this supporting evidence might be, it cannot "prove" dissonance theory to be true because the ratings might have changed for some *other* reason having nothing to do with dissonance theory. What can be said—and the careful scientist will never say more than this—is that the experiment "supports" or "is consistent with" the theory. What if the appliance ratings didn't change or perhaps changed in the opposite direction? This result fails to support the theory but, as we have seen, an individual study can fail to come out as predicted for any number of reasons, and to abandon a theory after just one problematic study is an outcome that simply never happens in science. Theories are indeed discarded, but only when scientists lose confidence in them, and this takes a while, occurring only after predictions have been repeatedly disconfirmed in a number of laboratories and some competing theory arrives and begins to look more attractive.

Theories may be supported and theories may be discarded, but what happens most frequently is that they evolve as research accumulates and as challenges to the theory emerge. Festinger, reflecting on dissonance theory 30 years after its birth, had this to say about the fate of theories: "One doesn't ask about theories, can I show that they are wrong or can I show that they are right, but rather one asks, how much of the empirical realm can it handle and how must it be modified and changed as it matures" (Festinger, 1999, p. 383). Evolution is exactly what happened in the case of cognitive dissonance. For example, one of Festinger's students, Elliot Aronson (who distinguished between mundane and experimental realism earlier in this chapter), proposed that dissonance and the subsequent motivation to reduce it would be most potent when one of the cognitions related to an important aspect of the self-concept and threatened the self. For example, Aronson would argue that the dissonance involved in smoking results from an inconsistency between what a person is doing (smoking) and a part of the self-concept that says "I am smart when it comes to my health." Aronson and his students completed a number of studies supporting the importance of the self-concept in dissonance situations (e.g., Aronson & Mettee, 1968).

Attributes of Good Theories

Some theories are judged by history to be more effective than others, and those judged to be good are characterized by several features. The most obvious one is **productivity**—good theories advance knowledge by generating a great deal of research, an attribute that clearly can be applied to dissonance theory. Hundreds of studies have been done over the years. Two other attributes of good theories, falsification and parsimony, require elaboration.

Falsification

A popular misconception about theories in psychology is that the goal is to produce one so good it explains every possible outcome. In fact, however, a theory that appears to explain everything is seriously flawed. To understand why, we need to look at an approach to testing theories first advocated by the philosopher of science Karl Popper (1959), clearly implied in what you just read about supporting and failing to support theories, and mentioned briefly in the Chapter 1 discussion of scientific thinking (the section called "Science Develops Theories That Can Be Falsified").

According to Popper, science proceeds by setting up theories and then attempting to falsify them. Theories that are continually resistant to **falsification** are accepted as possibly true (with the emphasis on *possibly*). Recall our earlier comment that confidence in a theory increases as inductive support accumulates. This confidence never becomes absolute, however, because of the limits of induction. For example, 100 predictions derived from a theory could support it, but one disconfirmation could potentially call it into question. Of course, we've already seen that one disconfirmed hypothesis *never* leads to a wholesale abandonment of a theory. Nonetheless, Popper's argument suggests that disconfirmation carries greater weight than confirmation. At the least, a study that does not come out as expected requires that the disconfirmations be investigated thoroughly.

As you recall from Chapter 1, one of the attributes of pseudoscience is its tendency to sidestep falsification. Phrenology illustrates the point nicely. As you recall, by arranging the theory so it could explain (more accurately, explain away) all possible anomalies, phrenologists managed to create the appearance of an infallible theory. In fact, by explaining everything, it *failed to predict anything*. Would a large area of "acquisitiveness" mean the person would be a thief? According to phrenology, it might, but if the acquisitiveness faculty was offset by a large area of "modesty," it might not. So a large acquisitiveness area might produce a thief, but maybe it won't. This inability to predict is perhaps the greatest failing of pseudoscience.

A common criticism of Popper's falsification approach is that it fails to take into account the everyday psychology of doing research, in the sense that most researchers in the midst of their programs of research, like the phrenologists, develop a sense of ownership and tend to get more excited about supportive evidence than outcomes that question their theories. There is some truth to this, but, unlike phrenologists and other pseudoscientists, real scientists clearly recognize the importance of falsification thinking. Even though researchers might hope to find support for their own theories, they are always trying to design experiments that can rule out one explanation or another. For example, think back to the applied research study on the effects of cell phone use on a driving simulation (Strayer & Johnston, 2001), described earlier in this chapter. As you recall, one of their comparisons was between subjects using a hands-free device and others using a handheld phone. The purpose of the handheld versus hands-free comparison was to test the theory that the problem with cell phone use in a car has to do with the ability to use both hands while driving, not with the attentional demands. But because performance was poor in *both* groups, Strayer and Johnston were able to rule out (falsify) the idea that a hands-free cell phone solves the problem of using cell phones in cars. Similarly, you will recall that in Bushman and Anderson's (2009) field study, they had their confederate dropping her crutches both before *and* after the film, to rule out individual differences in the type of person going to violent or nonviolent films affecting the results. One of psychology's most famous examples of a rule-it-out approach involves the investigation of a famous horse with alleged mathematical and reading abilities. Take a moment and read Box 3.2, which chronicles the case of Clever Hans, a horse with intellectual skills more apparent than real.

BOX 3.2 CLASSIC STUDIES—Falsification and Der Kluge Hans

In Berlin at the turn of the 20th century, the best show in town, except perhaps for the just-opened subway, could be found in the courtyard adjacent to a stable on Griebenow Street. There the spectator would encounter a horse (Figure 3.2) that appeared to have remarkable intellectual powers. When asked to multiply 4 times 4, the horse would tap his front hoof 16 times and stop. Adding, subtracting, multiplying, and dividing didn't challenge the remarkable animal, known to the German public as Clever (*Kluge* in German) Hans. Even fractions and decimals were no problem. When asked to add 2/5 and 1/2, the horse would tap out 9 for the numerator and 10 for the denominator (Sanford, 1914). The horse (apparently) could also read and spell, using a system of tapping that translated letters into numbers (as you might guess, Hans was not a speed reader).

If you've been developing your scientific thinking skills, you may be a bit skeptical about this horse that read and did math better than some of your friends. Skeptics existed then

(continued)

BOX 3.2   (CONTINUED)

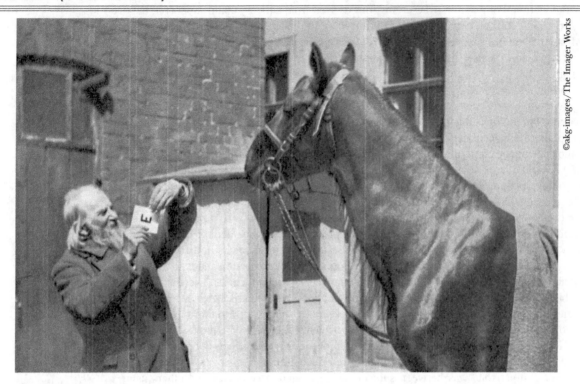

©akg-images/The Imager Works

FIGURE 3.2
Clever Hans at work.

too, and one of them, Oskar Pfungst, provides us with a wonderful example of falsification thinking. Pfungst set out to see if he could rule out higher intelligence as an explanation for the behavior of the horse, while finding a more reasonable explanation for what the horse was doing.

A special commission including scientists and animal trainers concluded that the horse's trainer, Wilhelm von Osten, was not a fraud, but Pfungst suspected the owner might be giving the animal subtle cues about how to respond. He reasoned that if this were the case, then the horse would be correct only if the questioner knew the answer.

Testing the hypothesis that the horse would not know the answer unless the questioner did was easy. Pfungst simply set up several tests in which the questioner knew the correct answer sometimes but not at other times. For example, Pfungst had questioners hold up a card with a number on it. When the questioner was allowed to see the number before holding it up, the horse tapped out the number correctly 98% of the time. However, if the questioner was not allowed to look at the card before the horse did, Hans was correct

only 8% of the time (Fernald, 1984). So much for mathematical intelligence in horses. In a series of similar tests, Pfungst was able to rule out (falsify) the idea that Hans could read.

Thus, Hans was clearly getting information about the correct answer from the person asking the question. How this occurred was still a puzzle that Pfungst eventually solved. To make a long story short, he determined the horse was responding to slight visual cues from the questioner. Whenever someone asked a question, that person would bend forward very slightly or move his or her eyes down without being aware of it (in effect, glancing down at the horse's hoof to see if it would start tapping). Hans learned the movement was a signal to begin responding. When Hans reached the correct answer, the person would straighten up or glance up, again just slightly and without awareness, but enough to signal Hans that it was time to stop. One indication that this signaling was occurring was that when Hans made errors, he was usually off by just one or two taps, just as one would expect if questioners moved their heads a little too slowly or too quickly.

The Clever Hans case illustrates two other points besides the falsification strategy of Pfungst. By showing the horse's abilities were not due to a high level of intelligence but could be explained adequately in terms of the simpler process of learning to respond to two sets of visual cues (when to start and when to stop), Pfungst provided a more *parsimonious* explanation of the horse's behavior.

Second, if von Osten was giving subtle cues that influenced behavior, then perhaps experimenters in general might subtly influence the behavior of participants when the experimenter knows what the outcome will be. We'll return to this point in Chapter 6—it is an example of what is called *experimenter bias*. As for parsimonious explanations, read on.

Parsimony

Besides being stated precisely enough to be falsified, good theories are also **parsimonious**. This means, ideally, that they include the minimum number of constructs and assumptions needed to explain the phenomenon adequately and predict future research outcomes. If two theories are equal in every way except that one is more parsimonious, then the simpler one is generally preferred.

The idea of using parsimonious explanations is essentially the same as an argument used when discussing animal behavior by the 19th-century British comparative psychologist Conwy Lloyd Morgan. He lived at a time when the theory of evolution was prompting naturalists to look for evidence of sophisticated mental processes in animals (such as mathematical ability in horses like Clever Hans), hence supporting the Darwinian notion of continuity among species. This search produced a number of excessive claims, especially by Darwin's protégée George Romanes, whose *Animal Intelligence* (1886) relied heavily on *anecdotal evidence* to support his case. (Refer back to Chapter 1 for a description of how anecdotes were an Achilles heel for phrenology). His examples were also excessively anthropomorphic, meaning that he was overly generous in assigning human attributes to animals. He argued, for instance, that moths approach candles because they are curious, that beavers show foresight and engineering ability in their dam-building activities, and that dogs were capable of logical inference. To support this latter point, he used this anecdote, sent to him by Dr. David Livingston (a famous explorer of Africa):

> A dog tracking his master along a road came to a place where three roads diverged. Scenting along two of the roads and not finding the trail, he ran off on the third without waiting to smell. Here, therefore, is a true act of inference. If the track is not on A or B, it must be on C, there being no other alternative. (p. 457)

While applauding Romanes for providing a wealth of interesting examples of animal behavior, Morgan rejected the anthropomorphic explanations. While not ruling out the idea of consciousness and mental ability in animals, Morgan argued that behavior should be explained in the simplest terms possible, yet still be sufficient to explain the behavior. His famous statement, which has come to be known as "Lloyd Morgan's Canon," was that "[i]n no case may we interpret an action as the outcome of the exercise of a higher psychical faculty, if it can be interpreted as the outcome of the exercise of one which stands lower in the psychological scale" (Morgan, 1903, p. 53). Concerning Livingstone's dog anecdote, for instance, Morgan would argue that the dog moving quickly down path C does not allow one to eliminate the sense of smell as the essential explanation for the dog's behavior. Given the exceptional olfactory capabilities of dogs, sense of smell is a more parsimonious explanation than logical inference, regardless of how quickly the dog ran down path C.

The need for parsimonious explanations also guards against one of the social cognition biases described in Chapter 1—*confirmation bias*. Hearing an interesting anecdote about a dog that appears to be using logical reasoning, the listener with a preconceived bias about dog intelligence might see this as a confirming example of dog brilliance, while ignoring other instances in which a dog's behavior did not seem so smart. The point was made nicely by another animal researcher, Edward Thorndike who stated, somewhat sarcastically,

> dogs get lost hundreds of times and no one ever notices it or sends an account of it to scientific magazines. But let one find his way from Brooklyn to Yonkers and the fact immediately becomes a circulating anecdote. Thousands of cats on thousands of occasions sit helplessly yowling, and no one takes thought of it . . .; but let one cat claw at the knob of a door supposedly as a signal to be let out, and straightaway this cat becomes representative of the cat mind. (Thorndike, 1911, p. 24).

Common Misunderstandings about Theory

One final point here is that theories are often misunderstood. For example, here are two statements that we are sure you have heard before, often from scientifically challenged politicians. Each of the statements shows a complete failure to understand the nature of theory:

- "It's not a fact; it's only a theory."
- "It's just a theory; there's no proof."

From what you now know, you should be able to see why each of these statements is meaningless. They are variations on the same theme and are often encountered in discussions about Darwin's famous theory of evolution. Both reflect a serious misunderstanding of the relationship between theory and research. You now know that theories represent "working truths" about some phenomenon, *always* subject to revision based on new data but reflecting the most reasonable current understanding of the phenomenon. "Facts" are the results of research outcomes that add inductive support for theories or fail to support theories. As you know from the discussion earlier, theories can never be *absolutely* shown to be true because of the limits of induction—that is, future studies may require that a theory be altered. So theories can be accepted only with varying degrees of confidence, depending on the strength of the empirical support. (Darwin's theory of evolution by natural and sexual selection is probably the most strongly supported theory in the history of any of the sciences.) Think of it this way—*theory never becomes fact; instead, theory serves to explain facts.*

SELF TEST

3.2

1. Research on the bystander effect is a good example of how ideas for research can come from _____.
2. When drawing conclusions from a theory about a research outcome, researchers don't use the terms *prove* or *disprove*. Explain.
3. Dogs sometimes escape from yards by lifting latches on gates. Explain why trial and error learning is a more parsimonious explanation than logical reasoning.

Developing Research from Other Research

To a large extent, this last section on developing ideas for research is an extension of what was just described about the reciprocal relationship between theory and data, but research deriving from other research occurs even when theory development is not the prime focus. Sometimes researchers simply want to investigate some phenomenon to discover regular, predictable relationships between variables (i.e., to discover laws of behavior) and are not concerned about theory building. Skinner's operant conditioning research (Chapter 12) falls into this category.

We believe the most common sources of ideas for research in psychology are unanswered questions from studies just completed. Psychologists seldom conduct individual experiments that are separate from each other; instead, they build **programs of research**, a series of inter-related studies. You won't often find someone doing a study on helping behavior and then switching to a study on aggression. Rather, researchers often become involved in a specific area of investigation and conduct a series of studies in that area that may last for years and may extend to many other researchers with an interest in the topic. The conclusion of one project invariably leads to the beginning of another because while experiments answer some empirical questions, they also typically raise new ones. The research of Festinger and his colleagues and students on cognitive dissonance is a good example of a research program, in this case, one that has lasted decades.

One unmistakable indication of how research leads to other research can be seen by scanning any issue of a typical psychology journal. Look at the authors of a specific publication; then look to see if those same names appear in the reference sections of the publication as authors of similar studies. As an illustration, the first two issues of the journal *Psychological Science* (one of experimental psychology's prominent research journals) for 2008 include 32 research articles. The authors of the articles reference other work by themselves in 25 of the 32 articles. Although some of this may be a normal human tendency to cite one's own work, for the most part it reflects the fact that researchers simply don't do single experiments—they establish systematic programs of interconnected experiments. Research always leads to more research.

Research Teams and the "What's Next?" Question

If you asked research psychologists to describe their day-to-day existence, you would get a wide variety of answers, but one general principle would emerge: Few researchers work by themselves. Rather, they assemble **research teams** within their laboratories that operate under what has been called an *apprenticeship* model (Taylor, Garner, & Hunt, 1959). Typically, the team includes a senior researcher, Dr. X, several graduate students who are working for Dr. X, and perhaps some highly motivated undergraduates who have convinced Dr. X of their interest and willingness to work odd hours and perhaps clean animal cages. The undergraduates normally work under the direction of the graduate students, who, in turn, are the apprentices of the professor. This hierarchical team may have several experiments going on at once, and team members spend long hours in the lab collecting and analyzing data. Also, they often find themselves sitting around a table in the coffee house across the street, discussing research projects in various stages of completion while consuming large amounts of caffeine.

When discussing completed projects, team members typically use what can be called *"what's-next" thinking*: Given the outcome of this study, what should we do next? At some point in the conversation, someone will get an idea and ask the single, most frequently heard question in conversations among research psychologists: "What do you think would happen if we did X?" The X refers to a rough idea for a study, and "what do you think would happen?" is a request for predictions about the outcome. Such questions lead to a lively discussion in which the group refines the idea or perhaps decides it is unworkable and instead thinks about the next what's-next question that comes up. If the idea is pursued, a procedure will be created, IRB approval will be sought, and then tested in trial runs (i.e., a pilot study), revised or refined further (additional caffeine here), and eventually shaped into a tightly designed study that is then brought to completion . . . only to spawn the next what's-next question!

The *pilot study* is a valuable way to determine whether the researchers are on the right track in developing sound procedures that will answer their empirical questions. The clarity of instructions to participants, the difficulty of the task that, the believability of a cover story (if the study involves deception), the duration of the experiment, and the adequacy of the materials are all important components of a sound research design that can be checked with a pilot study. You will recall that Bushman and Anderson (2009), in their study on media violence and helping behavior, did a pilot study to be sure their staged fight was perceived as real. Consider another example, a study by Schlagman, Schulz, and Kvavilashvili (2006); it examined the so-called positivity effect in autobiographical memory—a tendency to be more likely to recall positive experiences as we grow older. The plan was to give young and old subjects a notebook in which to record specific types of memories that occurred to them spontaneously during the course of a week. Each page of the notebook included a number of questions for subjects to answer about their memories (e.g., the mood they were in when the memory came to them). The researchers had no idea how many pages to include in the notebook, eventually settling on 20 after doing a pilot study.

> [P]articipants were provided with a diary in the form of a notebook, which contained 20 questionnaires, one to be completed for each involuntary memory experienced. This number of questionnaires was provided because, in an earlier pilot study, none of the participants who were supplied with 50 questionnaires recorded more than 20 memories in a 1-week period. (p. 164)

Once completed, a research study seldom stands by itself. Instead, its outcome almost always leads to another study, often designed to clarify some unanswered question of the first study or extend the findings in new directions. To illustrate, consider two experiments by Roediger and Karpicke (2006) on the use of testing as a study strategy to improve memory.

Research Example 2 – "What's Next?"

Roediger and Karpicke (2006) were curious about whether using a rereading study strategy or repeatedly testing students would lead to better memory for scientific texts. In their first experiment, college students read a short, scientific text one time. Then, students either reread the texts for 7 minutes (restudy group), or they were asked to write down as much as they could remember about the text (testing group). Next, students completed a final memory test 5 minutes later, 2 days later, or 1 week later. The final test was the same as the recall test used earlier by those in the testing group. The results showed that for the test given 5 minutes later, students in the restudy group recalled more information than those in the testing group (81% vs. 75%). However, after a 2-day delay, the testing group outperformed the restudy groups (68% vs. 54%), and after 1 week, the testing groups still recalled more information than the restudy group (56% vs. 42%). From this experiment, Roediger and Karpicke concluded that using testing as a study strategy leads to better memory in the long term compared to merely rereading texts.

Based on these results, Roediger and Karpicke (2006) naturally adopted a "what's-next" style of thinking in their second experiment. Specifically, they wondered what would happen if students were given more than one opportunity to reread the texts or be repeatedly tested on the texts. They also were curious about how students *thought* they would do on the final memory test 1 week later, given the study strategies they used in the experiment. Using the same types of texts as in Experiment 1, Roediger and Karpicke devised three conditions: (1) SSSS: students read and reread the text in each of four 5-minute study periods before the final test (restudy group);

(2) SSST: students read and reread the text in each of three 5-minute study periods, followed by one test (testing group); and (3) STTT: students read the text during one 5-minute study period followed by three tests before the final test (repeated testing group). After this phase of the experiment, students were asked to rate how well they thought they would remember the text after 1 week. Students took the final memory test either 5 minutes or 1 week later. All tests were identical, in that students had to write down as much as they could remember from the text they studied. The results were similar to those found in Experiment 1. For the test given 5 minutes later, those who repeatedly reread the texts remembered more than those who were tested once prior (SSSS: 83% vs. SSST: 78%) and who were repeatedly tested (STTT: 71%). But, for those who received the test 1 week later, those who were repeatedly tested performed better than those who were tested only once (STTT: 61% vs. SSST: 56%) and even better than those who repeatedly reread the texts (SSSS: 40%).

Roediger and Karpicke (2006) concluded that retesting allowed students to practice the process of retrieval which is a necessary component of any form of testing. Interestingly, students in the restudying groups thought they would perform better after 1 week than those in the retesting group. This is an important finding because it suggests that students believe that the study strategy of rereading texts will be more beneficial than practicing retrieval, but the opposite result is true! What this should tell you is that you may want to try using a testing (retrieval practice) study strategy when studying for your next test, and not fall prey to your potential misperceptions of the effectiveness of other types of study strategies, particularly rereading. Based on Roediger and Karpicke's findings, the use of testing (or retrieval practice) is an effective study strategy, and this effect has been replicated many times. What began as an interest in the effects of different types of study strategies on memory has since evolved into a prolific line of research demonstrating the power of retrieval practice for long-term learning (see Karpicke, 2012 and Karpicke & Grimaldi, 2012 for reviews).

Research in psychology (a) usually involves a continuous series of interrelated studies, each following logically from the prior one; (b) is often a communal effort, combining the efforts of several people who are immersed in the same narrowly specialized research area; and (c) is unstructured in its early, creative stages. This lack of structure was noted some time ago by a panel of distinguished experimental psychologists brought together in 1958 by the Education and Training Board of the APA and charged with making recommendations about graduate training in experimental psychology. They described "the process of doing research—that is, of creating and building a science of psychology—[as] a rather informal, often illogical and sometimes messy-looking affair. It includes a great deal of floundering around in the empirical world, sometimes dignified by names like 'pilot studies' and 'exploratory research'" (Taylor, Garner, & Hunt, 1959, p. 169).

One fairly recent development in "what's next" questioning is the extension of the concept of a research team far beyond the confines of a single laboratory. In the electronic age, it is quite common for researchers on different campuses to interact electronically. These digital conversations often include descriptions of a proposed method preceded by the famous question, "What do you think would happen if we did this?" Thus, separated by thousands of miles, researchers can nonetheless carry on the kind of informal discussion that leads to creative research and fruitful collaborations.

For you as a student, then, one strategy for getting ideas for research is to begin reading published research (Table 3.2, at the end of this chapter, gives you some guidance about how best to read a journal article). As you begin to read journal articles about research studies, be thinking in terms of "what's next?". Here are some specific tips:

- Could the next study test a suggestion made in the Discussion section of the article?

- The authors of the study will offer an explanation for their results. Could the next study test this explanation by setting up a study that compares it to some other explanation?

- The study might draw a general conclusion about some phenomenon, but you might think the conclusion more likely to apply to one type of person rather than another. Your next study could see if the conclusions of the study just read apply to certain types of persons (e.g., introverts vs. extroverts).

- Could the next study extend the findings to another age group, socioeconomic group, or culture?

- Could the procedures used in the study you just read be adapted for other kinds of research problems?

Replication

Many studies that follow on the heels of completed studies are similar enough to be considered replications but different enough so they are not exact duplicates. In other words, they include both replication and extension. As research psychologists normally use the term, **replication** refers to a study that duplicates some or all of the procedures of a prior study. There are two general types of replications. A **direct replication** is an attempted reproduction of a study's results testing the same type of sample and using the exact procedures and statistical analyses as the original study. It is an attempted exact replication of a prior study, usually done by a separate research team. A direct replication of Roediger and Karpicke's (2006) study described above would be to do the exact same study with college students as sample. In a **conceptual replication,** parts of the procedures of a prior study are purposely changed in order to test predictions similar to those in the original study. For example, one may want to replicate the effects of repeated testing on long-term learning by adapting part of Roediger's and Karpicke's procedures but use a different types of testing procedure (e.g., using multiple-choice or short-answer tests).

A good example of a case where questions were raised about a finding, which in turn led to a direct replication, is a study by Steele, Bass, and Crook (1999) with the title "The Mystery of the Mozart Effect: Failure to Replicate." The researchers were reacting to an earlier study by Rauscher, Shaw, and Key (1993) that seemed to show a short-term improvement in spatial skill following brief exposure to Mozart's music. The possibility that listening to the music could increase ability was dubbed the *Mozart effect*. There had been several (failed) attempts at replication, but the studies had not been direct replications. Steele et al., however, duplicated the Rauscher et al., study in all its essential aspects, and failed to find any evidence whatsoever for the effect. Consequently, few psychologists believe such an effect really exists. As you might guess, however, given the Chapter 1 discussion of pseudoscience, the Mozart effect lives on among the gullible, despite the absence of any convincing evidence for its existence. There is even a website where you can purchase Mozart CDs designed to make you think your child will be smarter as a result. *Caveat emptor*.

With successful replications, researchers can be more confident that the results from their research are accurate and reliable. Replication is also important in that if results are accurate, they can better inform public policy makers in developing effective policy at the societal level. In contrast, failures to replicate can lead to less confidence in one's research results and sometimes can lead to the discovery of scientific fraud, as described in Chapter 2. Before reading further, please read Box 3.3 which describes a survey of psychologists' research practices and serves as a discussion point for the importance of replication in science.

BOX 3.3   ETHICS—Questionable Research Practices and Replication Remedies

Given recently noted cases of blatant scientific fraud in psychology, such as that by Diederik Stapel discussed in Chapter 2, it is important to also notice that there are other forms of scientific misconduct that may go unnoticed, referred to as Questionable Research Practices (QRPs) by John, Loewenstein, and Prelec (2012). In the wake of cases of scientific fraud, concerns about QRPs are mounting across disciplines, including medical and psychological research. John et al. conducted a study in which they anonymously surveyed over 2,000 psychologists about ten different types of QRPs ranging in severity from not reporting all measures used in a study, to "selectively reporting studies that 'worked,'" to outright falsifying data (see Table 3.1 for all ten QRPs). Psychologists responded if they admitted to committing any of the QRPs and they also estimated how many other psychologists they knew who committed such QRPs. From these two measures, John et al. calculated an estimate of how often QRPs occur in the practice of research, also known as a prevalence estimate. They found that some

QRPs are estimated to occur upwards as high as 78% of the time on average, but blatant data falsification was estimated to occur on average of 9% of the time. Table 3.1 shows all of the average estimates for each QRP. It is important to note that although data falsification was estimated to occur only about 9% of the time, other QRPs, such as excluding data after checking to see how it impacts the results (estimated to occur about 62% of the time) actually results in very similar situations. That is, the data are altered to "fit" a certain researcher's expectation about what the results of the study should be. As a consequence, the research results may not be easily replicated. Other QRPs, such as "selectively reporting studies that 'worked'" and "stopping data collection after achieving the desired result" also may result in failures to replicate. With an inability to replicate prior results, many studies may go unpublished and unnoticed only to be 'filed away' as unsuccessful studies. We will return to this issue of what is known as a *file drawer effect* in Chapter 4 when we discuss hypothesis testing.

Table 3.1   **Questionable Research Practices (QRPs) and their Average Estimated Prevalence Rates (from Figure 1 of John, Loewenstein, & Prelec, 2012, p. 527)**

QRP Item	Prevalence Estimate
Failing to report all dependent measures	78%
Collecting more data after seeing whether results were significant	72%
Failing to report all conditions	42%
Stopping data collection after achieving the desired result	36%
Rounding down *p*-values	39%
Selectively reporting studies that "worked"	67%
Excluding data after looking at the impact of doing so	62%
Claiming to have predicted an unexpected finding	54%
Falsely claiming that results are unaffected by demographics	13%
Falsifying data	9%

Note: Estimated prevalence rates were calculated as the self-admission rate divided by the reported prevalence rate of others who committed QRPs. The self-admission rate, the others-admission rate, and the estimated rate were then averaged and are reported above.

As noted earlier, it is important that any results you obtain in a research study are accurate. Furthermore, the data should speak for themselves, without the bias of the researcher. Although replication is an important part of giving increased

credibility to a science, very few direct replications of research studies seem to have occurred. In an extensive review of 100 of the top psychology journals in our science dating back to 1900, Makel, Plucker, Hegarty in 2012 estimated that less than

(continued)

BOX 3.2   (CONTINUED)

2% of studies in those journals included direct replications. They suggested that if scientists replicated their studies, and journals published those direct replications, then this "would help avoid flawed or fraudulent findings going unquestioned over an extended period of time" (p. 541).

In an effort to combat growing concerns among psychologists about the reproducibility of research results, several researchers have spearheaded efforts to create research repositories, such as Open Science Framework (OSF), where researchers can archive study materials and data for others to use for replication purposes. PsychFileDrawer.org allows users to upload and view attempted replications of studies in psychology, and the Open Science Collaboration (OSC) is systematically replicating experiments published in leading psychology journals. Its first effort involved replicating studies from the year 2008 in three influential journals: *Psychological Science*, the *Journal of Personality and Social Psychology*, and the *Journal of Experimental Psychology: Learning, Memory, and Cognition*. The Association for Psychological Science, a leading psychological organization in our field, has now created a venue for large-scale replication projects in their journal *Perspectives on Psychological Science*. You will read about their first "registered replication report" in Chapter 10.

Creative Thinking in Science

One element of the research-generating process that has been implied several times in this chapter, but not dealt with directly, is scientific creativity. It is one thing to say research can be generated from simple observations, from theory, or from the outcomes of other studies, but the jump from these sources of research ideas to the actual research study does not occur automatically. At some point, the experiment must be *created*. Sometimes the study follows logically from what preceded it and becomes a conceptual replication. At other times, a creative leap occurs.

Creative thinking in research design involves a process of recognizing meaningful connections between apparently unrelated ideas and seeing those connections as the key to developing the study. Such thinking does not occur in a vacuum, however, but rather in the context of some problem to be solved by a scientist with considerable knowledge of the problem. As the famous biologist Louis Pasteur put it, "chance favors the prepared mind" (cited in Myers, 1992, p. 335). Thus, serendipity does not by itself produce an idea for a research study; the serendipitous event must be seen by the scientist immersed in a topic as the missing piece that solves the problem at hand. This is one reason why researchers work in teams: The presence of several minds increases the chances someone will have an idea another team member will see as the missing piece to the puzzle.

To examine a specific example of scientific creativity, consider maze learning. Ask a psychologist to name famous pieces of research equipment, and mazes will be at or near the top of the list. Although the maze reached its peak of popularity between 1920 and 1940, it is still an important tool used to study such topics as spatial memory and as an instrument to examine the effects of drugs on learning. Credit for the first maze learning study with rats belongs to Willard Small of Clark University, who completed his research over 100 years ago (Small, 1901).

How did Small get the idea of putting rats in mazes? Along with his laboratory colleague, Linus Kline, he was interested in rat behavior, in particular the rat's "home-finding tendencies." In a discussion with Edmund Sanford, director of Clark's lab, Kline described some tunnels he had observed "made by large feral rats to their nests under the porch of an old cabin. . . . These runways were from three to six inches below the surface of the ground and when exposed during excavation presented a veritable maze" (Miles, 1930, p. 331). The term *maze* apparently made a connection for Sanford, and he suggested that Kline build a maze himself. In particular, Sanford proposed using as a model the well-known Hampton Court maze, England's popular people-size labyrinth.

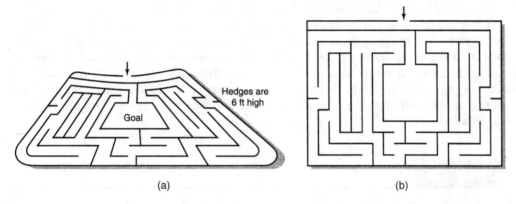

FIGURE 3.3
(a) Design of England's Hampton Court maze; (b) Small's readjustment of the Hampton Court maze design to a rectangular configuration. Drawn by Dr. C. James Goodwin.

With other projects under way, Kline passed along the idea to Small, who built a 6 × 8-foot wire mesh maze, changing the Hampton Court maze's trapezoidal shape (Figure 3.3a) to rectangular (Figure 3.3b), but keeping the design the same. Small ran several studies examining how rats learned the maze; the Hampton design became common in the early decades of the 20th century, and thus began a rats-in-mazes tradition that continues to the present day.[4]

The story is a good illustration of scientific creativity. Scientists (Kline and Small) knowledgeable in some research area (animal behavior) were wrestling with a difficult problem (how to study home finding in the rat). An offhand comment (Kline's recollection of rats tunneling under a porch) combined serendipitously with Sanford's familiarity with the Hampton Court maze produced a link between seemingly unrelated events, and the problem was solved—the way to study a rat's home-finding tendencies was to create an apparatus modeled on a famous maze in England.

It is worth noting that a thorough knowledge of one's field may be a prerequisite to creative thinking in science, but the blade is double-edged. Such knowledge can also create rigid patterns of thinking that inhibit creativity. Scientists occasionally become so accustomed to a particular method or so comfortable with a particular theory that they fail to consider alternatives, thereby reducing the chances of making new discoveries. Consider maze learning again.

The maze has contributed a great deal to our understanding of basic learning processes; however, the apparatus has also led to many dead ends, so to speak. Once established as a standard apparatus, the maze occasionally hindered creativity, leading researchers to narrow the focus of their work to situations that were relevant to mazes but to little else. The phenomenon of "centrifugal swing" is an example. Investigated heavily in the 1920s and 1930s, it was said to be a tendency for an animal to emerge from one turn in a maze (presumably at high speed) and swing by centrifugal force to the far wall. This would then influence the direction of its next turn. This swing was contrasted with a "forward-moving tendency." Dozens of studies attempted to tease out the factors that would produce either a swing or a forward move (e.g., Schneirla, 1929). The studies were elegantly designed and they no doubt helped develop the research skills of a number of experimental psychologists, but the research had no importance beyond the maze apparatus itself and shed no light on basic learning processes.

---

[4] Incidentally, although critics sometimes refer to the maze as an example of the "artificiality" of laboratory research in psychology (i.e., no mundane reality for the rat), it is worth noting that Small's original intent in using the maze was not to create a sterile environment but one close to the rat's world, or, as Small (1901) put it, to create "as little difference as possible between the conditions of experiment and of ordinary experience" (p. 209).

Perhaps the famous behaviorist E. C. Tolman was only half serious when he closed his 1937 APA presidential address by professing that "everything important in psychology . . . . can be investigated in essence through the . . . . analysis of the determiners of rat behavior at a choice-point in a maze" (cited in Hilgard, 1978, p. 364). His comment, however, shows how focus on an existing apparatus can limit creative thinking in science. The origins of scientific equipment such as mazes may reveal creative thinking at its best (e.g., Sanford's idea to use the Hampton Court maze), but innovation can be dampened once an apparatus or a research procedure becomes established.

SELF TEST

3.3

1. What is the goal of a "what's next?" question?
2. What is the difference between a direct replication and a conceptual replication?
3. What is the point of Pasteur's comment that "chance favors the prepared mind?"

Reviewing the Literature

Research projects do not develop in a vacuum. The psychologists involved in a program of research are thoroughly familiar not only with the work of their own lab but also with the work done in other labs conducting similar research. Those researchers deriving experiments from theory are likewise familiar with the research concerning the theory in question. Even the experimenter who gets an idea for a study after making a casual observation often makes that observation within the context of related knowledge or a problem at hand. How is one's knowledge of the literature acquired?

Computerized Database Searches

Chances are you have already used an electronic database to search for information. Some common ones are EBSCO, JSTOR, Science Direct, and Academic Search Premier. And you have undoubtedly started many of your searches by simply relying on Google (what you might not know is that you can search for scientific literature on a subset of Google called Google Scholar). In psychology, the APA's PsycINFO Services provides a variety of electronic search tools. The primary database, from which all of the others are derived, is called PsycINFO. It includes references to journal articles, doctoral dissertations, technical reports, books, and book chapters. It includes journal articles dating back to 1887, the year American psychology's first successful journal, the *American Journal of Psychology*, was founded. It includes more than 3 million abstracts, covers literature published in more than 2,500 journals, and is updated weekly. The features of PsycINFO are constantly being improved, so for the most up-to-date information, you should check out PsycINFO's website at www.apa.org/psycinfo.

Although PsycINFO is the primary database for psychologists, other databases may also be useful, depending on your research interests. For example, if you are interested in education and ↑ psychology, then ERIC may be a useful database; if you are interested in neuroscience, MedLine may be pertinent. Most likely, your school's library has an online search capability in which you can use multiple databases for a single search. For instance, EBSCO allows you to select both ERIC and PsycINFO databases to search simultaneously.

You should be able to find PsycINFO among the list of electronic databases on your library's website. It can appear in any of several formats, depending on how your library subscribes. Regardless of which service is used, the basic features of PsycINFO are the same. So how do you use PsycINFO to find the sources you need?

Search Tips

Experience is the best teacher of PsycINFO, but guidelines can help you become a proficient user. Because PsycINFO contains so much information, you must narrow your search strategy to find the sources most important for your topic. To begin, recall your *empirical question* and hone in on your *operational definitions*. In PsycINFO, you should always use an Advanced Search, which allows you to enter multiple search terms. For example, if you type in "memory" as a search term, you will end up with 210,349 results (as of the time of this printing; if you try it as you read this, there will certainly be more!). You can be more specific and type in "eyewitness memory," thus narrowing your search to 828 items. This is still way too many for you to sift through, so you should include multiple terms in the Advanced Search option. If you try "eyewitness memory" AND "individual differences," for instance, your search now yields a much more manageable 52 results. We strongly recommend that you keep track of your search terms and the combinations of search terms you use, so when you enter PsycINFO again, you are familiar with the searches that did and did not work so well.

In the Advanced Search, you can search by such fields as author, article title, journal name, and/or year of publication. You can also choose various search limiters. Thus, you could choose a publication type search, a neat device for focusing on specific types of articles. For example, you can limit the search to longitudinal studies, experimental replications, literature reviews, or meta-analyses. These last two types of searches can be especially useful because they yield articles that summarize the results of many other articles. The reference sections of these literature reviews and meta-analyses alone will have great value in your research.

Another potentially useful feature of PsycINFO is a truncated search. To illustrate, suppose you performed an Advanced Search on "altruism" AND "evolutionary psychology" and got 136 results. However, there are likely more than 136 sources on this popular topic. By asking for "evolutionary psychology," you eliminated records that included just the terms "evolution" or "evolutionary." To solve the problem, the evolutionary psychology term could be "truncated" (i.e., shortened). This is done by using only the first few key letters and adding an asterisk. For example, using "evol*" retrieves all of the terms that begin with those four letters, including *evolutionary*, *evolution*, *evolved*, and *evolving*. If you search for "altruism and evol*," 736 records appear. This is more than 136, but too many to manage, so it may be necessary to add a third search term based on your empirical question and/or operational definitions, or limit your search in other ways as described earlier. The truncated search was what Makel et al., (2014) did when they searched 100 psychology journals for replication studies in the ISI Web of Knowledge Citation Reports database; they used the truncated term *replicat** to be sure to capture the terms *replication, replicate*, and *replicated* in their search.

In sum, the best way to learn the mechanics of using PsycINFO is to sit at your computer and experiment, perhaps starting by working your way through the help screens. The APA also publishes various downloadable guides (e.g., www.apa.org/databases/training/searchguides.html), and reference librarians are always happy to assist you as well.

Search Results

Your search will produce specific results, and you will notice that relevant sources are listed by title in the order of the most recently published to the oldest. If you click on the active link for the source (usually the title of the work), you should be able to read the abstract (or summary) of the article, book chapter, etc., as well as obtain many other relevant details about the source. Figure 3.4 shows you what a typical PsycINFO record for a journal article looks like (you should recognize the article as one featured earlier in this chapter concerning cell phones and driving—Strayer & Johnston, 2001). As you can see, each record includes several important categories of information. These categories are called *fields*, and they include, among other things, the article's title and its author(s), all of the needed reference information (journal name, volume number, and page numbers), an abstract of the article, and descriptors (terms that can be used to search further). Reading the abstracts will tell you whether the article is especially relevant. If so, depending on your library's subscription to the database, you can probably download, e-mail, and/or print a copy of the article itself. An important note here: It may be tempting to limit your search to results with available online copies, but this may cause you to miss important articles. Such full-text versions of articles may be found in other databases, or your library can get you these articles through interlibrary loan, usually within a few days.

As you are searching, pay special attention to articles in the journals *Psychological Bulletin*, *Psychological Review*, and *Perspectives on Psychological Science* as well as chapters in the book series *Annual Review of Psychology*. All publish long literature reviews and theoretical articles that are potential gold mines because they contain extensive reference lists. Once you begin finding good articles on your topic of choice, you can use the reference sections of the actual articles as a means of further search. From these references you might pick up new search terms, and you can identify names of researchers who seem to publish a lot on the topic, enabling additional searches by author. Also, because PsycINFO lists the items by most recent date, it is always a

Title:	Driven to distraction: Dual-task studies of simulated driving and conversing on a cellular telephone.
Pub. Yr.:	2001
Author(s):	Strayer, David L.; Johnston, William A.
Affiliation:	U Utah, Department of Psychology
Source:	Psychological Science. Vol. 12(6), Nov. 2001, 462-466.
Abstract:	Dual-task studies assessed the effects of cellular-phone conversations on performance of 48 Ss (aged 18-30 yr) on a simulated driving task. Performance was not disrupted by listening to radio broadcasts or listening to a book on tape. Nor was it disturbed by a continuous shadowing task using a handheld phone, ruling out, in this case, dual-task interpretations associated with holding the phone, listening, or speaking. However, significant interference was observed in a word-generation variant of the shadowing task, and this deficit increased with the difficulty of driving. Moreover, unconstrained conversations using either a handheld or a hands-free phone resulted in a twofold increase in the failure to detect simulated traffic signals and slower reactions to those signals that were detected. The authors suggest that cellular phone use disrupts performance by diverting attention to cognitive context other than the one immediately associated with driving.
Subjects:	Attention; Distractibility; Driving Behavior; Reaction Time; Telephone Systems; Distraction; Task Analysis; Task Complexity
Classification:	Attention; Transportation
Age Group:	Adulthood (18 yrs and older); Young Adulthood (18-29 yrs); Thirties (30-39 yrs)
Digital Object Identifier:	10.1111/1467-9280.00386

FIGURE 3.4

The PsycINFO record for the study by Strayer and Johnston (2001) on the effects of cell phone use on driving.

good idea to look at the most recent articles first; they represent what is most current in the field and their reference sections will tell you the most important earlier articles. Thus, if you yield a search of many records, reviewing the most recent ones will give you a good start.

Once you have sources in hand, you have to read them. You should carefully examine Table 3.2 at the end of this chapter for tips on how to read a psychology research article effectively.

Table 3.2   Getting the Most Out of Reading Journal Articles

At some point in your research methods course (and other psychology courses as well), perhaps as part of an assignment to complete a literature review, you will find yourself reading empirical research articles in one of the many psychology journals. It is important to keep in mind that journal articles were not written for an undergraduate audience; rather, they are aimed at other professional researchers. So they can be hard to read. Most empirical research articles follow a certain structure—an introduction, followed by descriptions of method and results, and ending with a discussion of the results. These sections of the paper are described in more detail in Appendix A, which will teach you how to write one of these reports. As for reading an empirical research article, here are some good tips:

- Get as much as you can out of the abstract. This is a summary of the research and probably the easiest section of the paper to read and understand. Read it several times.

- In the opening paragraph or two of the introduction, look for a general statement of the problem being studied. By the way, this part of the paper will not be labeled "Introduction," but it will include everything between the abstract and the section labeled "Method."

- Throughout the introduction, take note of any theories that are described and if a particular theory is being tested. Keep in mind that the introduction may provide other relevant sources for your literature review. You can find all the citations in the text of the introduction at the end of the article in the references list.

- Near the end of the introduction, probably in the final paragraph, look for statements of the hypothesis or hypotheses being tested in the study. These will emerge from the problem statement and the research questions raised by the studies described in the middle part of the introduction (the literature review portion). Write down the hypotheses and keep them in mind as you continue reading. Don't be concerned if the word *hypothesis* does not appear. Instead, you might see words like *prediction* and *expectation*.

- In the method section, take note of the participants tested, particularly if the type of participant is a factor being explored in the study (e.g., individuals with bipolar disorder versus those with major depression).

- Also in the method section, review the materials used for the study; these often include the tests used (e.g., Beck Depression Inventory, or BDI). It is important to keep track of this information to see how it compares with tests used in other articles. For example, depression might be measured with the BDI in one study, but by some other test in a second article.

- Pay careful attention to the description of the procedure used and the experimental design. Try to place yourself in the role of a participant in the study and develop a clear idea of what the participants did. If the study is experimental, identify and write down the independent and dependent variables (you've encountered these terms in your general psychology course and you'll learn much more about them in Chapter 5).

- The results section might be especially difficult because it will include statistical information and symbols that might seem incomprehensible. Statistics is considered a language of its own, one that provides the reader with the exact evidence of the conclusions drawn on the basis of the study data. A good results section presents a clear description of the results. You should be able to understand the gist of what happened in the study without looking at a single number. You should also find graphs and tables helpful; they are often visually compelling and make the basic results easy to grasp.

- The last main part of the article is the discussion section. It often begins with a paragraph that summarizes the main results, so if the results section is Greek to you, there's still hope. The main purpose of the discussion section is to explain the results with reference to the original hypotheses, so the writer makes connections to the introduction. The researcher also addresses any weaknesses that might have existed in the study, or alternative explanations of the results. Finally, look for a description of what research should be done next (the "what's-next?" question). This part points toward future research and is a great source of ideas. If your assignment involves doing a literature search and then developing a research proposal, this "what's-next?" portion of the discussion is where you'll get excellent ideas.

The knowledge you gain from effectively reviewing the literature puts you in a better position to develop more ideas for research, formulate them as empirical questions, and develop them into testable hypotheses. With a good research hypothesis, you are ready to design a study that will provide answers to your empirical question. The problem of design will be dealt with shortly. First, however, it is necessary to introduce you to the basics about the data that you will be collecting and how to think about testing your hypotheses. In other words, it is important to familiarize yourself with how psychologists measure and analyze the data they collect in order to answer their empirical questions.

CHAPTER SUMMARY

Varieties of Psychological Research

Basic research in psychology aims to discover fundamental principles of behavior, while applied research is undertaken with specific practical problems in mind. Both basic and applied research can take place in either the laboratory or a field setting. Laboratory research allows greater control, but field research more closely approximates real-life situations. Research that involves participants in the procedures (i.e., has experimental reality), even if it places people in situations far removed from everyday living, can yield important information about behavior. Most research in psychology is quantitative in nature, involving numerical data subjected to statistical analysis, but recent years have seen an increase in qualitative research (e.g., content analysis of structured interviews, observational research).

Asking Empirical Questions

The initial step in any research project is to formulate an empirical question—one that can be answered with the evidence of objective data. Empirical questions include terms that are defined precisely enough (i.e., operationally) to allow replication to occur. Several studies on the same topic might use different operational definitions of terms, yet converge (converging operations) on the same general conclusion about behavior (e.g., frustration leads to aggression).

Developing Research from Observations of Behavior and Serendipity

Some research ideas derive from reflection on everyday observations, especially of events unusual enough to attract one's attention. Specific problems to be solved also lead to research; much of applied research in general and program evaluation research in particular develops this way. Sometimes we observe events that occur unexpectedly or accidentally. Serendipity is the act of discovering something by accident; serendipitous events often yield ideas for further research. The discovery of edge detectors in vision is an example.

Developing Research from Theory

Theories summarize and organize existing knowledge, provide a basis for making predictions, and provide a working explanation about some phenomenon. The relationship between theory building and research is reciprocal. Empirical questions can be deduced from theory and lead to specific hypotheses and then to the design of experiments. The conclusions of the completed experiments either support or fail to support the theory. A theory can be discarded, but only after a consensus develops that it is consistently failing to make good predictions. In most cases, theories evolve to take into account the accumulating knowledge about some phenomenon. Theories in psychology are useful to the extent they generate research that increases our understanding of behavior. Also, good theories are parsimonious and stated precisely enough to be falsified by well-designed research.

Developing Research from Other Research

Researchers in psychology seldom think in terms of isolated experiments. Instead, they produce programs of research, series of interrelated experiments within a specific area. They continually use the results of experiments as starting points for the next experiment. Research programs often include studies that involve direct and conceptual replications of existing findings, along with new ideas into new areas of research.

Creative Thinking in Science

Scientific creativity occurs when researchers make connections among ideas or events that other people perceive as unrelated. The creative scientist must be knowledgeable in a particular research area and prepared to notice the relevance of events apparently unrelated to the problem at hand.

Reviewing the Literature

Empirical questions occur more frequently to the investigator who knows the research literature in a particular area. Most searching is done electronically using such tools as PsycINFO.

CHAPTER REVIEW QUESTIONS

1. What is the essential difference between basic and applied research? Use the basic shadowing and applied cell phone studies to illustrate.

2. What are the comparative advantages and disadvantages of research completed in and out of the laboratory?

3. In the Bushman and Anderson (2009) study of the effects of media violence on helping, why did the researchers believe it necessary to complete the field study, given the results of their laboratory study?

4. What are pilot studies, and what purpose do they serve? What is a manipulation check?

5. Give three operational definitions of hunger and explain why research using all three could result in converging operations.

6. What is a theory in psychology? What are the attributes of good theories?

7. Use cognitive dissonance theory to illustrate the reciprocal relationship between theory and research. Be sure to work the terms deduction, induction, and hypothesis into your answer.

8. Explain why you are unlikely to hear scientists say that a theory has been *proven* or *disproven*.

9. Explain how the Clever Hans study illustrates the importance of (a) a falsification strategy, and (b) the use of parsimonious explanations.

10. Explain why both direct and conceptual replications are important for psychology science.

11. Use the origins of maze learning to illustrate the process of creative thinking in science.

12. Describe any three tips that facilitate searches in PsycINFO.

APPLICATIONS EXERCISES

Exercise 3.1.   What's Next?

Consider each of the following research outcomes. If you were a part of the research team, (a) what might you suggest as the next study to do, and (b) what do you predict would happen (i.e., what would the hypothesis be)?

1. College students are shown a video of a male college-age student driving an expensive car while talking on a cell phone. Asked to give their impressions of the driver, the students rate him high on the following attributes: egotistical, extroverted, and unconcerned for others.

2. In a study of aggression, some preschool boys see cartoons with violent themes, while other boys see interesting but nonviolent cartoons. Later, given a chance to be aggressive, children in the first group hit a punching bag more frequently and with greater force than children in the second group.

3. In a direction-finding study that takes place at a central point on campus, college students are asked to point as accurately as they can in the direction of four major cities, two of them more than 200 miles from campus and two less than 20 miles from campus. The students are more accurate for the closer cities.

4. In a memory experiment in which a list of 30 words is to be memorized, college students recall more words if they study while listening to a violin concerto than when they listen to bluegrass.

Exercise 3.2.   Replicating and Extending Milgram's Obedience Research

Consider Milgram's obedience study, highlighted in Chapter 2 in the context of ethics. As you recall, subjects playing the role of teachers thought they were in a study of the effect of punishment on learning. A learner, who was in on the deception and in the adjacent room, pretended to make numerous errors, and the teacher's job was to shock the learner for each error and increase the voltage by 15 volts for each successive error. Milgram was interested in discovering the point, from 15 to 450 volts, at which the teacher/subject would stop the experiment, thereby showing disobedience. Describe how you might conceptually replicate Milgram's study to test these hypotheses:

1. Because of their greater compassion, women teachers would be more likely to disobey the male experimenter, especially if the learner was also a woman.

2. The more the experimenter is perceived as a genuine and legitimate authority, the greater the level of obedience.

3. Subjects delivered lots of shocks because they simply enjoyed doing it—after all, everyone is a bit sadistic.

4. Disobedience will be greater if the learner has a noticeable health problem (e.g., complains of cardiac symptoms).

Exercise 3.3.   Creating Operational Definitions

Create two operational definitions for each of the following psychological constructs.

1. frustration

2. cognitive dissonance

3. anxiety

4. sense of direction

5. memory

6. self-esteem

Exercise 3.4.   —Searching PsycINFO

Using PsycINFO, find records for any five of the articles referenced in this chapter. For each of the five articles, (a) find another article by the same author, and (b) find another article on the same topic published within the last 3 years.

ANSWERS TO SELF TESTS

✓ 3.1

1. Basic → a dichotic listening experiment that varied the message in the nonattended ear.
   Applied → an experiment on how cell phone use while driving affects driving.
2. The experimental setting would not be encountered in real life (mundane reality), but subjects were deeply involved in the procedure and took it seriously (experimental reality).
3. Qualitative and quantitative.

✓ 3.2

1. Everyday observations of behavior.
2. A study that comes out as predicted cannot prove a theory because future research might not come out as predicted; studies not coming out as expected don't disprove a theory for similar reasons and because the study in question could be flawed in some way.
3. Trial-and-error learning is a simpler but still adequate explanation.

✓ 3.3

1. It gets researchers thinking about the next logical experiment, following up on a recently completed study.
2. A direct replication exactly duplicates a study's procedures, and a conceptual replication changes some part or parts of an original study's procedures.
3. Serendipity by itself won't produce scientific creativity; the scientist also must have a certain degree of knowledge about the phenomenon in question.

Sampling, Measurement, and Hypothesis Testing

4

PREVIEW & CHAPTER OBJECTIVES

In this chapter, we focus on data produced by research in psychology. First, we examine the sampling procedures used to obtain data from participants. Next, we explore the range of behaviors measured in research, the factors determining whether these measures are of any value, and a system for classifying scales of measurement. The chapter also introduces (and, for most of you, we hope, reviews) the important distinction between descriptive and inferential statistics, and describes the process of hypothesis testing. When you finish this chapter, you should be able to:

- Distinguish between probability and nonprobability sampling.

- Describe three varieties of probability sampling, and know when each is used.

- Recognize the variety of behavioral measures used when conducting research in psychology.

- Understand what psychologists mean by a construct (e.g., visual imagery) and how measurable behaviors (e.g., reaction time) are developed and used to study constructs.

- Explain how a behavioral measure is reliable and relatively free from measurement error.

- Explain how a behavioral measure is valid, and distinguish several forms of validity (content validity, criterion validity, and construct validity).

- Identify the defining features of data in terms of nominal, ordinal, interval, and ratio scales of measurement, and know when each should be used.

- Summarize data using measures of central tendency (e.g., mean), measures of variability (e.g., standard deviation), and visual displays (e.g., histograms).

- Understand the logic of hypothesis testing and what is involved in making an inferential analysis of data.

- Describe the criticisms of hypothesis testing and the suggested alternatives (e.g., confidence intervals).

- Understand what is meant by (a) effect size and (b) the power of a statistical test, and know the factors that enhance power.

You know from Chapter 1 that research psychologists are data-driven, insisting that conclusions about behavior be based on data collected via scientific methods. Deciding precisely which behaviors to measure, how to take the measurements, and how to make sense of the resulting collection of numbers are no simple tasks. This chapter begins the discussion of the relationship between data and psychological knowledge.

Who to Measure—Sampling Procedures

At the start of any research project, an important consideration will be the attributes of those participating in the study. Those participants constitute a **sample**, which may be considered a subset of some general group, called the **population**. The eventual goal of research in psychology is to draw conclusions that apply to some general population. For example, your goal might be to discover something about the memory abilities of adults in their 70s. In that case the population would be "adults in their 70s," and the sample would be those adults in their 70s participating in your study. On rare occasions, a sample can be the same as the population. For example, if you wanted to learn the attitudes of all of the people in your experimental psychology class about the issue of animal experimentation and did not wish to generalize beyond that class, you could survey everyone in the class. In this case, the size of the population would be the size of your class. As you might guess, however, the population of interest to a researcher is usually much too large for every member in it to be tested. Hence, a subset of that population, a sample, must be selected. The general process of sampling refers to the manner by which you get individuals to participate. There are two broad categories—probability sampling and nonprobability sampling.

Probability Sampling

In probability sampling, each member of the population has a definable probability of being selected for the sample. Probability sampling is commonly used in survey research when researchers have better access to their target population of interest from which they want to take a sample. We will discuss survey research methods in more depth in Chapter 9. Even though an entire population is seldom tested in a study, the researcher hopes to draw conclusions about this broader group, not just about the sample. Thus, it is important for the sample to reflect the attributes of the target population as a whole. When this happens, the sample is **representative**; if it doesn't happen, the sample is **biased**. For instance, if you wanted to investigate student perceptions of college life, it would be a serious mistake to select people from a list that included only students living in college residence halls. Because off-campus residents and commuter students might have different attitudes from on-campus residents, the results of your study would be biased, because the sample is not representative of the entire student body.

As a scientific thinker, you should be skeptical about claims made on the basis of biased samples. The lesson, of course, is that if you want to make an accurate statement about a specific population, you should use a sample that represents that population, and you must select the sample using a clearly defined sampling procedure. If you have no choice but to use data from a self-selected sample, and this happens sometimes, you should at least try to determine if the attributes of the sample (e.g., average age, income) match the attributes of the population you have in mind. Even then you need to be cautious in the conclusions you draw.

Random Sampling

The simplest form of probability sampling is to take a **simple random sample**. In essence, this means each member of the population has an equal chance of being selected as a member of the sample. To select a random sample of 100 students from your school, for instance, you could place all of their names in a large hat and pick out 100. In actual practice, the procedure is a bit more sophisticated than this, usually involving software that uses a random number generator or table.

Simple random sampling is often an effective, practical way to create a representative sample. It is sometimes the method of choice for ethical reasons as well. In situations in which only a small group can receive some benefit or must incur some cost, and there is no other reasonable basis for decision-making, random sampling is the fairest method to use. A famous example occurred in 1969 in the midst of the Vietnam War, when a lottery system was established to see who would be drafted in the army. For obvious reasons of fairness, birthdays for each of the 365 days of the year were supposed to have an equal probability of being selected first, second, third, and so on. Unfortunately, the actual procedure had some bias (Kolata, 1986). Capsules, one for every day of the year, were placed in a large drum one month at a time. The January capsules went in first, then the February ones, and so on. The drum was rotated to mix the capsules, but apparently this did not succeed completely because when the dates were drawn, those capsules entering the drum last tended to be the first to be picked. This was not a good time to have a birthday in December.

There are two problems with simple random sampling. First, there may be systematic features of the population you might like to have reflected in your sample. Second, the procedure may not be practical if the population is extremely large. How could you get a list of everyone in the United States in order to select a simple random sample of Americans? The first problem is solved by using stratified sampling; cluster sampling solves the second difficulty.

Stratified Sampling

Suppose you wanted to measure students' attitudes about abortion on your campus, and the school's population is 5,000 students, of whom 3,000 are women. You decide to sample 100 students. If you take a simple random sample, there will probably be more women than men in your sample, but the proportions in the sample may not match those in the population precisely. Your goal is to make the sample truly representative of the population and, on a question like abortion, there might be important differences of opinion between women and men. Therefore, if your sample happens to be overrepresented with men, it might not truly portray campus attitudes. In a situation like this, it would be a good idea to decide ahead of time that if 60% of the population is female, then exactly 60% of the sample will also be female. Just as the population has two layers (or strata), so should the sample.

In a **stratified sample**, the proportions of important subgroups in the population are represented precisely. In the previous example, with a goal of a sample of 100, 60 women would be randomly sampled from the list of female students, and 40 men would be randomly selected from the list of male students. Note that some judgment is required here; the researcher must decide how many layers (or strata) to use. In the case of abortion, women and men were sampled in proportion to their overall numbers. Should each of the four undergraduate classes be proportionately represented also? What about Protestants and Catholics and Muslims? What about left- and right-handers? Obviously, the researcher has to draw the line somewhere. Some characteristics (religion) may be more relevant than others (class standing, handedness) in deciding how to stratify the sample. It is up to the researcher to use good sense based on prior research or the goals of the current study.

Cluster Sampling

Stratified sampling is effective, but it still doesn't solve the problem of trying to sample from a large population, when it is often impossible to acquire a complete list of individuals. **Cluster sampling**, a procedure frequently used by national polling organizations, solves the problem. With this approach, the researcher randomly selects a cluster of people all having some feature in common. A campus survey at a large university might be done this way. If a researcher wanted a cross section of students and stratified sampling was not feasible, an alternative would be to get a list of required "core" classes. Each class would be a cluster and would include students from a variety of majors. If 40 core classes were being offered, the researcher might randomly select 10 of them and then administer the survey to all students in each of the selected classes.

If the selected clusters are too large, the researcher can sample a smaller cluster within the larger one. Suppose you wanted to find out how students liked living in the high-rise dorms on your campus, which you've defined operationally as any dorm with eight floors or more. Further suppose that 15 of these buildings exist on your campus, housing a total of 9,000 students. Using cluster sampling, you could first select six of the buildings (each building = one cluster), and then, for each building, randomly select three floors and sample all of the residents (about 40 per floor, let's say) of the selected floors in the selected dorms. This would give you an overall sample size of 720 (40 × 3 × 6). Notice you also could combine elements of stratified sampling here. If 10 of the dorms house women, and men live in the remaining five, you might select your first clusters to reflect these proportions: four female dorms and two male dorms.

Nonprobability Sampling

Probability sampling might be the best strategy for doing survey research, but it is not essential for most research in psychology. Rather, it is sufficient to choose, as participants, a **convenience sample**. This is a group of individuals who meet the general requirements of the study and are recruited in a variety of nonrandom ways. Often they are from the "subject pool"—often psychology students being asked to participate in research. You will learn about some of the ethical issues related to these pools in Chapter 5. Sometimes a specific type of person is recruited for the study, a convenience sampling strategy called **purposive sampling**. For instance, when Stanley Milgram first recruited participants for his obedience studies, he placed ads in the local newspaper asking for volunteers. He deliberately (i.e., purposely) avoided using college students because he was concerned they might be "too homogeneous a group. . . . [He] wanted a wide range of individuals drawn from a broad spectrum of class backgrounds" (Milgram, 1974, p. 14).

Two other forms of convenience sampling are quota sampling and snowball sampling. In **quota sampling**, the researcher attempts to accomplish the same goal as stratified sampling—representing subgroups proportionally—but does so in a nonrandom fashion. Using the example of a survey on abortion again, in a quota sample the researcher hoping for a sample of 100 would still aim for the 60/40 split but would simply recruit subjects, perhaps using the subject pool, until 60 women and 40 men had been surveyed. In **snowball sampling**, once a member of a particular group has been surveyed, the researcher asks that person to help recruit additional subjects through a network of friends. This sometimes occurs when a survey is designed to measure attitudes and beliefs of a relatively small group (e.g., triathlon runners) or a group that generally wishes to remain hidden (e.g., prostitutes). It is also easy to use snowball sampling if your study is conducted online and you provide participants with the opportunity to share the study with others via a weblink or use of social media. Researchers using quota or snowball sampling recognize their results will have a degree of bias, so they will be properly cautious in the conclusions they make from their sample to the population as a whole.

What to Measure—Varieties of Behavior

The variety of behaviors measured by research psychologists is virtually unlimited. What is measured ranges from overt behavior (e.g., rats running through a maze) to self-report (e.g., college students completing an attitude survey) to recordings of physiological activity (e.g., blood pressure readings). To illustrate the rich variety of behaviors measured in psychological research, consider these examples:

1. Elkins, Cromwell, and Asarnow (1992) investigated attention-span limitations in patients diagnosed with schizophrenia. The behavior measured was whether or not the participants could accurately name target letters embedded in an array of distracting letters. Compared with control subjects (individuals who did not have schizophrenia), those with the disorder did poorly when asked to identify target letters.

2. Westman and Eden (1997) examined the effects of a vacation on perceived stress and degree of burnout for clerical workers in an electronics firm. On three occasions—before, during, and after a vacation—researchers measured (a) perceptions of job stress with eight items from a survey instrument called the Job Characteristics Questionnaire, and (b) job burnout with a 21-item Burnout Index. Participants also completed a Vacation Satisfaction Scale. Initially, high stress and burnout scores dropped precipitously during the vacation, but the effect was short-lived. By 3 weeks after the vacation, stress and burnout levels were back at the pre-vacation level.

3. Diener, Fraser, Beaman, and Kelem (1976) observed the candy- and money-taking behavior of children on Halloween night. The behavior observed (from behind a screen by an experimenter) was whether children took extra amounts of candy, and/or took money from a nearby bowl, when the woman answering the door briefly left the room. When given an opportunity to steal, the children were most likely to succumb to temptation when (a) they were in groups rather than alone, and (b) anonymous (i.e., not asked their name) rather than known.

4. Holmes, McGilley, and Houston (1984) compared people with Type A or Type B personalities on a digit span task (listen to a list of numbers, then repeat them accurately) that varied in difficulty. While performing the task, several physiological measures of arousal were taken, including systolic and diastolic blood pressure. Compared with more laid-back Type B subjects, hard-driving Type A subjects showed elevated blood pressure, especially when the task increased in difficulty.

Developing Measures from Constructs

From these examples, you can see that researchers measure behavior in many ways. But how do they decide *what* to measure? Where do they get the idea to measure attention by seeing which letters can be selected accurately from an array, job burnout by giving a specific survey, moral behavior by observing candy taking, or arousal by measuring blood pressure?

In part, they know what to measure because they know the literature in their area of expertise, and so they know what measures are used by other investigators. They also develop ideas for new measures by modifying commonly used measures, or perhaps by creatively seeing a new use for an old measure. Finally, they develop measures out of the process of refining the constructs of interest in the study in hopes of answering their empirical question. Let us elaborate.

Recall that researchers generate empirical questions that propose relationships between psychological constructs. When a researcher is planning a study, one of the first decisions is to define the constructs to be used in the project as precisely as possible. Sound familiar? It should, because we are talking about *operational definitions* again. Part of any study involves deciding which behaviors will adequately reflect the constructs, which by definition are not directly observable. In the previous examples, each researcher faced the task of turning some empirical question into a manageable experiment by carefully defining the constructs in terms of measurable behaviors. Table 4.1 summarizes those four examples in terms of the constructs studied and how they were operationalized into specific behaviors.

Table 4.1   Sample Constructs and How They Are Measured

Construct	Behavior to Measure the Construct
Attention span	Letter identification accuracy
Burnout	Score on self-reported Burnout Index
Honesty	Amount of candy or money taken
Arousal	Systolic and diastolic blood pressure

One thing you may notice is that none of these constructs (attention, burnout, honesty, and arousal) is directly observable; each must be inferred from the measures used to investigate it. This process is repeated over and over in psychology and allows the research psychologist to ask empirical questions that might seem impossible to answer at first glance. Let's consider in greater detail two examples of procedures frequently used to investigate questions that might seem difficult, if not impossible, to answer empirically:

- Do preverbal infants understand the concept of gravity?

- Can you demonstrate that people use visual images?

The following two Research Examples explore measures used to study these seemingly nonempirical questions. They can be as simple as recording (a) how long an infant looks at something, and (b) how long it takes people to make decisions.

Research Example 3—Testing Constructs Using Habituation

Do infants have a concept of gravity? How could you ever find out? You cannot ask them directly, of course, but the question can be asked indirectly via a technique in which the amount of time a baby spends looking at different stimuli is measured. This habituation procedure involves showing an infant the same stimulus repeatedly and then changing to a new stimulus. From other research on "preferential looking," it is known that infants prefer to look at events that are new to them (Spelke, 1985), so if the same stimulus is presented repeatedly, they lose interest (i.e., they look less or stop looking altogether). The term *habituation* is defined as a gradual decrease in responding to repeated stimuli. If a new stimulus is presented *and* it is recognized as something new or unusual, the infant will increase the time spent looking at it. So if looking time in response to stimuli decreases and then suddenly increases, you can infer that the infant has noticed something new.

With this in mind, consider a creative study by Kim and Spelke (1992). They compared 5- and 7-month-olds and concluded that some type of basic understanding of gravity develops during that 2-month period of infancy. To produce habituation, infants were first shown repeated film clips of balls speeding up while rolling down inclined planes, as depicted in the first frame of Figure 4.1.[1] This event reflects the natural effect of gravity on a ball rolling down a hill. After habituation occurred (i.e., looking time decreased after repeated trials), the infants encountered either a "natural test event" (middle frame), a ball slowing down while going up a hill, or an "unnatural test event" (third frame), a ball speeding up while going up the hill. Notice the natural test event differs from the habituation event in two ways, direction and speed, while the unnatural event differs only in one way, direction. It seems reasonable to expect the infants to perceive the natural event as novel (direction and speed changed) and to look longer at it than at the unnatural one (speed changed). Indeed, the 5-month-old infants did just that. The 7-month-olds, however, looked at the *unnatural* event more, presumably because it violated what gravity dictates, whereas the natural event continued to be consistent with the law of gravity displayed in the habituation events.

---

[1] For control purposes, Kim and Spelke (1992) also included a second set of trials, starting with the habituation event of a ball slowing down while going up the incline.

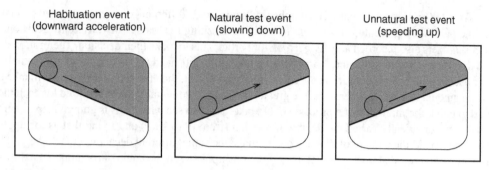

FIGURE 4.1
Stimulus items from Kim and Spelke's (1992) habituation study.

Hence, the younger infants noticed changes in the total number of stimulus dimensions, while the older ones noticed changes violating the law of gravity. From the measures of preferential looking, then, Kim and Spelke concluded that the infants, at least the 7-month-olds, possessed some form of understanding of the concept of gravity.

The behavior being measured here was the amount of time spent looking at the visual display. This means human experimenters were doing the timing, introducing the possibility of error. To reduce that possibility, Kim and Spelke (1992) carefully defined all aspects of a "looking" event. For example, infants were thought to have stopped looking whenever they "looked away from the screen for 2 [seconds] continuously" (p.387)—that is, they created clear *operational definitions* of the behaviors they measured. Also, two different experimenters timed each event to ensure consistency. One other aspect of this study connects with a concept you learned about in Chapter 3—*manipulation check*. Kim and Spelke wanted to be sure the videos of the balls rolling up and down inclines would truly be perceived as either natural or unnatural by the average observer. To test this, they showed the videos to a sample of adults and asked for "naturalness" ratings. The videos successfully passed the test.

Research Example 4—Testing Constructs Using Reaction Time

Do we use visual images as part of our cognitive processing? How could you find out? Of course, you could ask, but if someone says, "Yes, I'm using images," how could you be sure what the person was doing? You would be confronting the same problem that brought about the demise of introspection as a method: its lack of objectivity. You could, however, ask people to perform a task that would produce one type of behavior if images were being used and a different type of behavior if images weren't being used. That was the strategy behind a well-known series of studies by Shepard and his colleagues of what is termed *mental rotation*.

Look at the two pairs of geometric objects in Figure 4.2. Could the right-hand object of each pair be the same as the left-hand object, but rotated to a different orientation? Or is it a different object altogether? How did you decide? Shepard and Metzler (1971) asked each of their eight participants

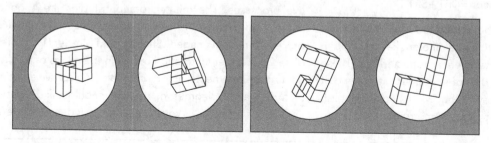

FIGURE 4.2
Stimulus items from Shepard and Metzler's (1971) mental rotation studies.

to make 1,600 of these decisions. The number of "same" and "different" correct answers was equal, and the pairs were presented randomly.[2] In addition to asking for "same" or "different" decisions, the researchers also recorded *how long it took* for participants to make their decision. Their rationale was that if participants solve these problems by taking the left-hand object and turning it mentally (i.e., use a visual image) until it overlaps the right-hand object, then the rotation process will take a certain amount of time. Furthermore, the greater the degree of mental rotation required to reach the overlap point, the more time the process should take. You can see where this is going. Shepard and Metzler systematically varied the degree of rotation (from 0° to 180°) and found that as the angle increased, so did the amount of time needed to make the same/different decision; in fact, the graph of the results showed almost a perfect linear relationship between the angle of rotation in the drawings and the amount of time needed for a decision. From these measures of reaction time, then, they inferred that mental imagery was being used to solve the problems.

Reaction time is one of psychology's oldest and most enduring methods, but the rationale for its use has changed over the years. For more on its origins and evolution as a tried-and-true method in experimental psychology, see Box 4.1.

BOX 4.1   ORIGINS—Reaction Time: From Mental Chronometry to Mental Rotation

The use of reaction time in psychology can be traced to the work of F. C. Donders (1818–1889), a Dutch physiologist, who argued that times for mental events could be determined by calculating the differences between the reaction times for different kinds of tasks (Boring, 1950). His idea ushered in a flood of research on what became known as *mental chronometry* or the *complication experiment*. Researchers measured the time for a simple reaction (SRT): a single response made as quickly as possible after perceiving a single stimulus, a red light, for instance. The task could then be "complicated" by displaying one of two stimuli and telling the person to respond to only one of them. This was called discrimination reaction time (DRT) because the person first had to discriminate between the two stimuli, such as a red and a green light, and then respond. DRT includes all of SRT plus the mental event of "discrimination," so subtracting SRT from DRT yields the time taken for the mental event of discrimination:

$$DRT = SRT + discrimination$$
$$therefore,$$
$$discrimination = DRT - SRT$$

The procedure could be elaborated even more (e.g., press one key for a red light and a different key for a green light), with additional mental events subtracted out. These studies generated a great deal of excitement at the end of the 19th century because psychology was trying to establish itself as a science, and what could be more scientific than to

have mental events measured to the fraction of a second? The procedure was especially popular in Wundt's laboratory at Leipzig and was quickly imported to the United States, as you can see from Figure 4.3, which shows a reaction time experiment in progress at Clark University in 1892.

Unfortunately, it soon became apparent that problems existed with the procedure. In particular, some reaction times were faster than predicted, others slower. Oswald Külpe, one of Wundt's students, pointed out the fatal flaw: Mental events don't combine in a simple additive fashion to form more complicated events. Rather, a complex mental event has a quality all its own that is more than the sum of simpler events.

Although Külpe's arguments effectively ended mental chronometry, and reaction time as a method declined in use during the heyday of behaviorism (roughly 1930–1950), the method has enjoyed a resurgence in several areas of cognitive psychology. The idea is no longer to measure the precise times of mental events but to test predictions and make inferences (more on this later in this chapter) about cognitive processes. The mental rotation studies are a good example of the use of reaction time to test the cognitive process of mental imagery. Shepard and Metzler (1971) predicted that if mental rotation occurs in the minds of participants, then this mental activity should take a certain amount of time. Larger degrees of rotation should take greater amounts of time and, as you have seen, this indeed occurred.

---

[2] You are probably thankful you didn't have to participate in this study, given the time commitment. Shepard and Metzler (1971) recognized that fatigue would be an issue, so each subject completed the 1,600 trials by spending an hour in the lab for 8 to 10 separate 1-hour sessions.

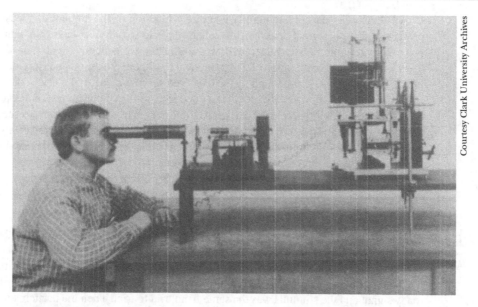

FIGURE 4.3
Reaction time study in progress at Clark University, circa 1892. The response is made by releasing a telegraph key with the right hand as quickly as possible when the stimulus is seen through the tube.

Courtesy Clark University Archives

Evaluating Measures

How can you tell if a procedure for measuring behavior is any good? What accounts for the confidence psychologists have for using measures of preferential looking and reaction time, tests of intelligence and blood pressure, and surveys of burnout, for example? Determining if a measure is any good requires a discussion of two key factors: reliability and validity.

Reliability

In general, a measure of behavior is said to be **reliable** if its results are repeatable when the behaviors are remeasured. Reaction time is a good example; its high reliability is one reason for its popularity over the years. Someone responding to a red light in 0.18 seconds (18 hundredths of a second, or about one-fifth of a second) on one trial will almost certainly respond with just about the same speed on other trials, and practically all of that person's trials will be in the general vicinity of 0.18 seconds. Similarly, scores on the SAT are reasonably reliable. Someone with a combined score of 1,100 would probably score close to that a second time and would be unlikely to reach a score like 1,800.

From these two examples, you can see why reliability is essential in any measure. Without it, there is no way to determine what a score on any one particular measure *means*. Presumably, in reaction time you are trying to determine how fast someone is. If the reaction times vary wildly, there is no way to determine whether the person is fast or slow. Likewise, if SAT scores bounced 400 or 500 points from one testing session to another, the numbers would be of no use whatsoever to colleges and universities because they would have no way of estimating the student's true score.

A behavioral measure's reliability is a direct function of the amount of **measurement error** present. If there is a great deal of error, reliability is low, and vice versa. No behavioral measure is perfectly reliable, so some degree of measurement error occurs with all measurement. That is, every measure is a combination of a hypothetical true score plus some measurement error. Ideally, measurement error is low enough so the observed score is close to the true score.

The reaction time procedure provides a good illustration of how measurement error works and how it affects reliability. As in the earlier example, suppose a person takes 0.18 seconds on a reaction time trial. Is this the *true* measure of speed? Probably not—a conclusion easily reached when you notice that for the following five hypothetical trials this same person's reaction times are:

Person A: 0.16 sec 0.17 sec 0.19 sec 0.17 sec 0.19 sec

These scores vary (slightly) because some degree of measurement error contributes to each trial. This error is caused by several possible factors, some of which operate randomly from trial to trial. For example, on a particular trial the person might respond faster than the true score by guessing the stimulus was about to be presented or slower because of a momentary lapse of attention. Also, a systematic amount of error could occur if, for example, the experimenter signaled the participants to get ready just before turning on the stimulus, and the amount of time between the ready signal and the stimulus was the same from trial to trial. Then the participants could learn to anticipate the stimulus and produce reaction times systematically faster than true ones.

Despite the presence of a small degree of measurement error, the above scores do cluster together pretty well, and the reaction times certainly would be judged more reliable than if the scores following the 0.18 seconds were these:

Person B: 0.11 sec 0.21 sec 0.19 sec 0.08 sec 0.33 sec

With scores ranging from less than one-tenth of a second to one-third of a second, it is difficult to say with any confidence what the person's real speed is.

When scores are reliable, therefore, the researcher can assign some meaning to their magnitude. Reliability also allows the researcher to make more meaningful comparisons with other sets of scores. For example, comparing the first set of scores above (0.16, 0.17, etc.) with the ones below reveals a clear difference in basic speed of response:

Person C: .23 sec .25 sec .21 sec .22 sec .24 sec

It is fair to say the true reaction time of Person C is slower than that of Person A.

There are ways of calculating reliability, but this is seldom done in experimental research. Rather, confidence in the reliability of a measure develops over time, a benefit of the replication process. For example, the habituation and reaction time procedures have been used often enough and yielded consistent enough results for researchers to be highly confident about their reliability.

Reliability *is* assessed more formally in research that evaluates the adequacy of any type of psychological test. These are instruments designed to measure such constructs as personality factors (e.g., extroversion), abilities (e.g., intelligence), and attitudes (e.g., political beliefs). They are usually paper-and-pencil tests in which a person responds to questions or statements. In the study mentioned earlier on burnout and vacations, participants filled out several self-report measures, including one called the BI, or Burnout Index (Westman & Eden, 1997). Analyses designed to establish the reliability of this kind of test require correlational statistical procedures. For example, the test could be given on two occasions and the similarity of the two sets of results could be determined. Unless dramatic changes are taking place in the participant's life, the scores on two measurements with the BI should be similar. The degree of similarity is expressed in terms of a correlation (high similarity = strong positive correlation). The specifics of this kind of statistical analysis, especially as it relates to psychological testing, will be explained more fully in Chapter 9.

Validity

A behavioral measure is said to be **valid** if it measures what it is designed to measure. A measure of burnout should truly measure the phenomenon of burnout and not some other construct. A test of intelligence should measure intelligence and not something else.

Conceptually, the simplest level of validity is called **content validity**. This type of validity concerns whether or not the actual content of the items on a test makes sense in terms of the construct being measured. It comes into play at the start of the process of creating a test, because it concerns the precise wording of the test items. A measure of burnout, for example, is more likely to be reflected by a measure of perceived job stress than of vocabulary, and the opposite is true of a measure of intelligence. With a complex construct of many attributes, such as intelligence, content validity also concerns whether the measure includes items that assess each of the attributes. Content validity is sometimes confused with **face validity**, which is not actually a "valid" form of validity at all (Anastasi & Urbina, 1997). Face validity concerns whether the measure seems valid to those who are taking it, and it is important only in the sense that we want those taking our tests and filling out our surveys to treat the task seriously. Of course, a test can seem to make sense to those taking it and still not be a valid test. Most of the surveys found in popular magazines ("What's Your Sex Appeal Index?") fit into this category.

A more critical test of validity is called **criterion validity**, or whether the measure is related to some behavioral outcome or criterion that has been established by prior research. Criterion validity is further subdivided into two additional forms of validity: **predictive validity** and **concurrent validity**. Predictive validity is whether the measure can accurately forecast some future behavior, and concurrent validity is whether the measure is meaningfully related to some other measure of behavior. For example, for a test to be a useful intelligence test, it should (a) do a reasonably good job of predicting how well a child will do in school and (b) produce results similar to those produced by other known measures of intelligent behavior. In the examples above, the criterion variables are (a) future grades in school (predictive) and (b) scores on an already established test for intelligence (concurrent). As with reliability estimates, criterion validity research is correlational in nature and occurs primarily in research on psychological testing.

A third form of validity, **construct validity**, concerns whether a test adequately measures some construct, and it connects directly with what is now a familiar concept to you—the *operational definition*. As you recall from Chapter 3, a construct (e.g., cognitive dissonance) is a hypothetical factor developed as part of a theory to help explain a phenomenon (e.g., decision making) or created as a shorthand term for a cluster of related behaviors (e.g., self-esteem). Constructs are never observed directly, so we develop operational definitions for them as a way of investigating them empirically, and then develop measures for them. For example, aggression is a construct that in a particular study might be operationally defined as the number of shocks subjects believe they are delivering to another subject. Another example: Emotional intelligence is a construct operationally defined as a score on a paper-and-pencil test with items designed to identify people skilled at reading the emotions of others. Construct validity relates to whether a particular measurement truly measures the construct as a whole; it is similar to theory in the sense that it is never established or destroyed with a single study, and it is never proven for the same reason theories are never proven. Rather, confidence in construct validity accumulates gradually and inductively as research produces supportive results.

Research establishing criterion validity helps establish construct validity, but construct validity research includes two additional procedures: convergent and discriminant validity. Scores on a test measuring some construct should relate to scores on other tests that are theoretically related to the construct (**convergent validity**), but not to scores on other tests that are theoretically unrelated to the construct (**discriminant validity**). Consider, for example, the construct of self-efficacy. This construct, first developed by Bandura (1986), refers to "judgments of [our] capabilities to organize and execute courses of action required to attain designated types of performances" (p. 391). Students with a high degree of self-efficacy about their schoolwork, for instance, believe they have good academic skills, know what to do to get good grades, and tend to get good grades. To increase confidence in the construct validity of a test designed to measure self-efficacy, one might compare self-efficacy scores with those on already established tests of locus of control and self-confidence. Locus of control (LOC) concerns our personal beliefs about the causes of what happens to us. Those with an internal LOC believe they control what happens to them (by working hard, for instance), while those with an external LOC believe outside forces (luck, for instance) determine what happens to them. You can see that someone with a high level of self-efficacy should also be someone with an internal LOC. Thus, research showing a strong relationship between the two would strengthen the construct validity of the self-efficacy measure because *convergent validity* would have been demonstrated. On the other hand, self-confidence is not necessarily related to self-efficacy. Someone with high self-efficacy might indeed be self-confident, but lots of people with high self-confidence might be confident for the wrong reasons and not be high in self-efficacy. You have probably met people who put on a display of self-confidence, but don't have much substance to back it up. So research showing that measures of self-efficacy and self-confidence are not related or only weakly related would establish *discriminant validity* for the measure of self-efficacy.

Research Example 5—Construct Validity

As a concrete example of construct validity research, consider this study by Mayer and Frantz (2004). They developed a test called the Connectedness to Nature Scale (CNS), designed to measure individual differences in "levels of feeling emotionally connected with the natural world" (p. 503). They hoped the scale would be useful in predicting environmentally friendly behavior (e.g., recycling, not littering). Here are a few items from the scale:

- I think of the natural world as a community to which I belong.

- I have a deep understanding of how my actions affect the natural world.

- Like a tree can be part of a forest, I feel embedded within the broader natural world.

- My personal welfare is independent of the welfare of the natural world.

Those scoring high and therefore having a large amount of the construct connectedness to nature would agree with the first three statements and disagree with the fourth one.

Mayer and Frantz (2004) completed a series of studies to establish the validity and reliability of their new scale. To evaluate the construct validity of the CNS, they gave the test to a wide range of adults (i.e., not just college students), along with another test called the New Ecological Paradigm (NEP) scale, a survey about "their lifestyle patterns and time spent outdoors" (p. 505). The NEP scale (Dunlap, Van Liere, Mertig, & Jones, 2000) measures cognitive beliefs about ecological issues (sample item—"We are approaching the limit of the number of people the earth can support."). Mayer and Frantz also gathered data on participants' ecological behaviors (e.g., how often they turned off the lights in vacant rooms), scholastic aptitude (this part of the research used college students and collected SAT data), and a measure of social desirability (those scoring high on this test want to look good to others). They expected the CNS and NEP to be related, and they were; people scoring high on one were likely to score high on the other. This outcome supported *convergent validity*, as did the finding that high CNS scores predicted ecological behavior and outdoor lifestyle patterns. They also expected CNS scores would *not* be related to SAT scores or to the measure of social desirability and this also happened (*discriminant validity*).

This brief description only scratches the surface of Mayer and Frantz's (2004) article, which included five different studies, but it should give you a sense of what is involved in trying to establish the construct validity of a new measuring tool, in this case the Connectedness to Nature Scale.

Reliability and Validity

For a measure to be of value in psychological research, it must be sufficiently reliable and valid. Reliability is important because it enables one to have confidence that the measure taken is close to the true measure. Validity is important because it tells you if the measure actually measures what it is supposed to measure, and not something else. Note that validity assumes reliability, but the converse is not true. Measures can be reliable but not valid; valid measures must be reliable.

A simple example illustrates this. In Chapter 1, you learned something about 19th-century phrenology, a popular theory claiming you could measure a person's "faculties" by examining skull contour. From the discussion of reliability, you should recognize that phrenological measures of the skull were highly reliable—the distance between a point 2 inches above your left ear and 2 inches above your right ear will not change very much if measured on two separate occasions. However, to say the measure is an indication of the faculty of "destructiveness" is quite another matter. We know skull contour measurement is not a valid measure of destructiveness because it doesn't make much sense to us today in light of what we know about the brain (content validity), fails to predict aggressive behavior (criterion validity), and does not fit well with other research on constructs relating to destructiveness, such as impulsiveness, or with research on brain function (construct validity).

The issues of reliability and validity have ethical implications, especially when measures are used to make decisions affecting the lives of others. Students are accepted or not accepted into college or graduate school, job applicants are hired or not hired, and people are given a psychiatric diagnosis and treatment, all on the basis of measurements of ability or behavior. If those measures fail the tests of reliability and validity, then the decisions will not be made in a fair and just fashion. If you were applying for a job and your score on some test was to be the determining factor, you would be justifiably upset to learn the test was neither reliable nor valid.

One final and important point: The concept of validity has been discussed here in the context of measurement. As you will see in the next chapter, measures of psychological constructs are not the only things judged valid or not. Validity also extends more broadly to the entire research project being undertaken. Strictly in the context of measurement, validity concerns whether the tool being used measures what it is supposed to measure. Over the entire research project, validity concerns whether the study has been properly conducted and whether the hypothesis in question has been properly tested. This point will be elaborated in Chapter 5.

Scales of Measurement

Once we have established a measure to use and have confidence that our measure is valid and reliable, we also need to be aware of the type of data that will emerge from the measure. Whenever a behavior is measured, numbers are assigned to it in some fashion. We say someone responded in 3.5 seconds, scored 120 on an intelligence test, finished third in a crossword puzzle test, or determine the guilt or innocence of an individual. These examples illustrate four ways of assigning numbers to events, that is, four different **measurement scales**. An understanding of these

DILBERT ©1995 Scott Adams. Used by permission of UNIVERSAL UCLICK.

FIGURE 4.4
Problems with scales of measurement.

scales is an important prelude to a discussion of statistics (this chapter's next main topic), because the type of measurement scale being used helps determine the appropriate statistical analysis to be completed. Confusion over measurement scales is behind the problem experienced by Dilbert in Figure 4.4.

Nominal Scales

Sometimes the number we assign to events serves only to classify them into one group or another. When this happens, we are using what is called a **nominal scale** of measurement. Studies using these scales typically assign people to names of categories (e.g., those who are guilty, those who are innocent) and count the number of people falling into each category. We use nominal scales when we ask empirical questions like these:

- Are people more likely to help in an emergency situation when there are few people versus many people around?

- What verdict will individuals make in a legal case involving either a man or a woman accused of murder?

- Is a woman more likely to give her phone number to a man if the man is accompanied by a dog?

The unfortunate answer to the last question is "quite possibly," according to research by French psychologists Guéguen and Ciccotti (2008). They did a simple but clever field study in which an attractive man ("attractiveness" determined with a *pilot study*) approached a woman in a "pedestrian zone" (p. 345) of a city and said:

> Hello. My name's Antoine. I just want to say that I think you're really pretty. I have to go to work this afternoon, but I was wondering if you would give me your phone number. I'll phone you later and we can have a drink together someplace. (p. 345)

On half the trials, Antoine had a dog with him; on the remaining trials Antoine was on his own. The medium-sized, mixed-breed dog had been judged in pilot testing to be "kind, dynamic, and pleasant" (p. 341). Results? Overall, the majority of women sensibly told Antoine to get lost. The dog, however, mattered. With the dog by his side, Antoine acquired phone numbers on 28 of 80 trials (35%); without the dog, Antoine was successful on just 9 of 80 trials (11%).

For our purposes, the nominal scale of measurement was whether or phone number was given or refused (two categories of response). For this research study, the response depended upon whether the dog was present or absent. The data can then be organized by the number of women falling into one of four conditions, which are illustrated in the table below:

	Phone number given	Phone number refused
Dog present	28	52
Dog absent	9	71

It is important to note that the measure used is whether the phone number was given or refused, not whether the dog was present or absent. The researchers in this case were wondering if the presence (or absence) of the dog affected women's behavior (giving or refusing a phone number).

Ordinal Scales

Ordinal scales of measurement are sets of rankings, showing the relative standing of objects or individuals. College transcripts, for example, often list a student's general class rank: 1st, 2nd, 3rd, 50th, and so on. From these rankings, you can infer that one student had higher grades than another. Relative standing is the *only* thing you know, however. Dan, Fran, and Jan would be ranked 1, 2, and 3 in each of the following cases, even though Dan is clearly superior to Fran and Jan as a student only in the second case:

Case 1		Case 2	
Dan's GPA	4.0	Dan's GPA	4.0
Fran's GPA	3.9	Fran's GPA	3.2
Jan's GPA	3.8	Jan's GPA	3.0

Studies using ordinal scales ask empirical questions like these:

- If a child ranks five toys and is given the one ranked third, will the ranking for that toy go up or down after the child has played with it for a week?

- Do students rank order textbook authors in the sciences and in the humanities differently when they are told the gender of the writers?

- How do young versus old people rank 10 movies that vary the amount of sex and aggression they contain?

A good example of an ordinal scale is from a study by Korn, Davis, and Davis (1991). Historians of psychology and department chairpersons were asked to list, in rank order from 1 to 10, the psychologists they considered to have made the most important contributions to the field. Two sets of rankings were solicited—one for the top 10 of "all time" and the second for a "contemporary" top 10. The returns were then summarized to yield a picture of eminence in psychology. Who topped the chart? B. F. Skinner was considered the most eminent contemporary psychologist by both historians and chairpersons. Department chairs also ranked Skinner first for all time; historians, who tended to select psychologists from earlier periods for their all-time list, dropped Skinner to eighth place and put Wundt on top. One important point about ordinal scales of measurement is that often rank order data are derived from other data. For example, Haggbloom et al. (2002) also provided a rank order of the top 100 psychologists of the 20th century by creating a composite score from journal citations, textbook citations, survey data, and other measures. Skinner still topped the list in the final rank order.

Interval Scales

Most research in psychology uses interval or ratio scales of measurement. **Interval scales** extend the idea of rank order to include the concept of equal intervals between the ordered events. Research using psychological tests of personality, attitude, and ability are the most common examples of studies typically considered to involve interval scales. Scores on intelligence tests, for example, are usually assumed to be arranged this way. Someone with an IQ of 120 is believed to be more intelligent (granting, for the sake of illustration, that IQ measures intelligence) than someone with an IQ of 110. Furthermore, and this is the defining feature of an interval scale, the difference in intelligence between people with IQs of 120 and 110 is assumed to involve the same quantity of intelligence as the difference between people with IQs of 110 and 100. In other words, each single point of increase in an IQ score is believed to represent the same amount of increase in intelligence—the intervals are equal. Note the word *assumed*, however; some psychologists consider IQ (and scores on most personality tests as well) an example of an ordinal scale, arguing that it is difficult, if not impossible, to be sure about the equal-interval assumption in this case. Most accept the inclusion of IQ as an example of an interval scale, though, partly for a practical reason: Psychologists prefer to use interval and ratio scales generally because data on those scales allow more sophisticated statistical analyses and a wider range of them.

The brief description earlier of the study of burnout used several measures (e.g., Vacation Satisfaction Scale) that illustrate interval scales. Take a look at Box 4.2, which describes a classic set of studies in which interval scales were used in an attempt to show that our body type influences the kind of person we are.

BOX 4.2   CLASSIC STUDIES—Measuring Somatotypes on an Interval Scale: Hoping for 4-4-4

You have already learned that phrenologists speculated about the relationship between a physical characteristic (skull contour) and what a person was like. Phrenology seems almost quaint to us today, but the idea of a relationship between physical characteristics and personality has endured. A 20th century attempt to explore the connection was made by William Sheldon (1940, 1942).

Sheldon tried to define human physique in terms of a scale of measurement that went beyond prior attempts that produced a set of discrete "body types." After examining about 4,000 photos of naked college men, he developed a system of classifying physiques in terms of three 7-point interval scales. Each scale reflected the degree to which the men displayed three ideal body types: endomorphy (fat), mesomorphy (muscular), and ectomorphy (thin). Everyone was assumed to have some degree of each of the physiques, with one of them

usually predominant. Thus, an extremely round person might be labeled a 7–1–1, while a very thin person would be a 1–1–7, and Arnold Schwarzenegger (when he was in shape) would be a 1–7–1. A 4–4–4 would be a perfectly balanced person (Sheldon assessed himself as a 3.5–3.5–5). The set of numbers applied to a particular man was called his *somatotype*.

After measuring somatotypes, Sheldon set out to measure personality types. These, he believed, also fell into three categories that could be measured on 7-point interval scales that summarized the results of several personality tests. He labeled the categories *viscerotonia*, *somatotonia*, and *cerebrotonia*. Generally, viscerotonics were sociable, fun-loving, slow-moving, even-tempered, and interested in food. Somatotonics were aggressive, self-centered, and risk-taking, and cerebrotonics were shy and secretive, preferred to be alone, and tended to pursue intellectual tasks.

Sheldon's final step was to see if somatotypes related to personality types. You will not be surprised to learn that these pairs occurred together most often:

endomorph—viscerotonia

mesomorph—somatotonia

ectomorph—cerebrotonics

Sheldon believed body type led the individual to develop a certain personality, but critics pointed out the relationships were not strong and could be accounted for in different ways. Being an endomorph could cause someone to like food, but couldn't a strong liking for food create an endomorph?

The issues surrounding Sheldon's work were complex, and his theory has been discredited for a number of reasons. For example, stereotypical biases influenced the measurements, all of which were made by Sheldon (i.e., both the somatotype and the temperament measurements). For our purposes, Sheldon's research is a classic example of trying to quantify human personality and relate it to a person's physical attributes on a measurable scale of physique, in this case an interval scale of measurement.

It is important to note that with interval scales, a score of zero is simply another point on the scale—it does not mean the absence of the quantity being measured. The standard example is temperature. Zero degrees Celsius or Fahrenheit does not mean an absence of heat; it is simply a point on the scale that means, "put your sweater on." Likewise, if a test of anxiety has scores ranging from 0 to 20, a score of 0 is simply the lowest point on the scale and does not mean the complete absence of anxiety, just a very low score.

Ratio Scales

With a **ratio scale**, the concepts of order and equal interval are carried over from ordinal and interval scales, but, in addition, the ratio scale has a true zero point—that is, for ratio scores, a score of zero means the complete absence of the attribute being measured. For instance, an error score of zero attained by a rat running a maze means the absence of wrong turns. Ratio scales are typically found in studies using physical measures such as height, weight, and time. The research examples described earlier on habituation (measured by time spent looking at arrays) and reaction time both illustrate the use of a ratio scale (Kim & Spelke, 1992; Shepard & Metzler, 1971). Ratio scales are also used when one wants to measure a countable quantity of some sort – such as the number of errors or the number of items correctly recalled.

SELF TEST

4.1

1. Suppose the average discrimination reaction time is 0.28 sec. If the average simple reaction time is 0.19 sec, how long would the mental event of "discrimination" take, according to Donders' method?
2. Suppose I claim that head size is a good measure of IQ and my measure is head circumference. Is the measure reliable? Valid? Explain.
3. In the Dilbert cartoon, which measurement scale was Dilbert using? What about Liz?

Statistical Analysis

The first sentence in a self-help book called *The Road Less Traveled* (Peck, 1978) is "Life is difficult" (p. 15). This belief is shared by many students taking a course in statistics, who readily identify with the confused character in Figure 4.5. We won't try to convince you that doing statistics compares with lying on a Florida beach in February, but we hope you'll come to see that part of the excitement of doing research in psychology is analyzing the data you have painstakingly collected and finding out what *actually* happened in the study. We've seen mature, responsible adults hold their breath, wide-eyed like kids in a candy store, while waiting for the results of a statistical analysis, then slump in anguish or leap in ecstasy when the magic numbers appear on the screen. So, if you develop a passion for doing research in psychology, much of your emotion will be invested in the subtleties of statistical analysis.

Our goal here is to introduce you to statistical thinking and the types of statistical analysis that you are most likely to encounter when doing research in psychology. Ideally, you have already taken a course in statistics. If not, you should take one as soon as possible, especially if you have any desire to go to graduate school in psychology. Believe it or not, when graduate schools in psychology list the courses they especially look for in applicants to their programs, the statistics course is number 1, just ahead of research methods (refer to the 1996 survey by Norcross, Hanych, & Terranova, described in Chapter 1). This book covers some of the essentials of statistical analysis, but there is no substitute for a complete course (or two).

You will find information about statistics popping up throughout the rest of the book, for the simple reason that designing research in psychology cannot be separated from the statistical analysis of that research. In this chapter, you will learn about (a) the difference between descriptive and inferential statistics, (b) the logic of null hypothesis significance testing (NHST), and (c) recent recommendations about statistical analysis beyond NHST.

FIGURE 4.5
A common perception of statistics.

Descriptive and Inferential Statistics

The most fundamental distinction among types of statistics is between those called *descriptive* and those referred to as *inferential*. The difference parallels the distinction between samples and populations. Recall that a *population* consists of all members of a defined group, whereas a *sample* is a subset of that group. Simply put, **descriptive statistics** summarize the data collected from the sample of participants in your study, and **inferential statistics** allow you to draw conclusions about your data that can be applied to the wider population.

Descriptive Statistics

In essence, descriptive statistical procedures enable you to turn a large set of numbers that cannot be comprehended at a glance into a small set of numbers that can be more easily understood. Descriptive statistics include measures of central tendency, variability, and association, presented both numerically and visually (e.g., in graphs). In this chapter, we will consider the more common procedures for measuring central tendency and variability. Measures of association (e.g., coefficients of correlation) will be covered in Chapter 9. It is also important for researchers to view the distribution of the data they have collected, because many statistical tests have assumptions embedded within them that the data is "normally distributed." Let us explore the measures of central tendency, variability, and the distribution of data in turn.

To illustrate measures of central tendency and variability, consider these sample data from a hypothetical memory study in which 20 people study and then try to recall a list of 25 words. Each number in the data set below represents the number of words recalled by each of the 20 participants.

16	18	19	19
18	19	15	21
14	16	15	17
17	20	17	15
18	17	18	18

You can easily see that communicating the results of this study requires more than showing someone this list of 20 numbers. Instead, you could try to identify a *typical* score, or *measure of central tendency*. The most common measure of central tendency used by research psychologists is the **mean**, or arithmetic average, found by adding the scores together and dividing by the total number of scores. The mean for the memory scores above is 347/20 or 17.35.

Two other measures of central tendency are the median and the mode. The **median** is the score in the exact middle of a set of scores. Half the scores are higher and half lower than the median. To determine the median by hand, the first step is to arrange the scores in sequential order, from the lowest to the highest score. For the memory data, this produces:

14 15 15 15 16 16 17 17 17 17   18 18 18 18 18 19 19 19 20 21

⇑

The next step is to determine the **median location**, the place in the sequence of scores where the median will lie (Witte & Witte, 2014). It is determined by the formula:

$$\text{Median location} = \frac{N+1}{2}, \text{where } N = \text{the total number of scores in the sample}$$

For the memory data, the median location is $(20 + 1) / 2 = 10.5$, which means it falls midway between the 10th and the 11th numbers in the sequence. Counting from left to right, you can see the 10th number is a 17 and the 11th number is an 18 (this point in the sequence above is marked with an arrow). The median is the average of the two numbers immediately adjacent to the median location (17 and 18), 17.5 in this case. It is the exact middle of the set of scores—there are 10 scores on either side of this median.

The median is sometimes used when a set of scores includes some scores that are very different from the rest; when this outcome occurs, the mean gives a distorted view of the typical score. Scores that are far removed from other scores in a data set are known as **outliers**. For instance, suppose the IQ scores of the five teachers in your psychology department were 93, 105, 105, 122, and 200 (the outlier is probably the IQ of the person teaching the research methods course). The mean IQ score, which happens to be 125 (you should check this), gives a false impression that the psychology faculty as a whole is above average (average IQ is 100). The median gives a better estimate of a typical IQ in this case. Thus, the median location is equal to $(5 + 1) / 2 = 3$, and with the scores lined up in sequence, the third number is 105:

$$93 \quad 105 \quad \textbf{105} \quad 122 \quad 200$$
$$\Uparrow$$

Clearly, the median IQ of 105 is a much better indication of the typical intellectual capacity found in this hypothetical psychology department. In general, the presence of outliers makes the median a better choice than the mean when describing central tendency.

The **mode** is the score occurring most frequently in a set of scores. It is 105 in the psychology department IQ example. The mode for the hypothetical memory scores is slightly higher than the median—a score of 18 occurs five times, more often than any other score. Because there are no unusually high or low scores in the memory data set, the mean (17.35), median (17.5), and mode (18) are quite close to each other, and each is a good measure of central tendency.

Measures of central tendency are obviously needed to summarize data. Less obvious but equally important, the amount of variability in any set of scores must be described. Suppose you are the golf pro at a local country club, ready to give lessons to one group of five golfers at 8:00 and another group at 9:00. You measure their skill by determining their normal score (i.e., number of strokes) for nine holes. Here are the data:

8:00 group:	50	52	58	46	54
9:00 group:	36	62	50	72	40

Notice the mean is the same for both sets of golfers: $260 / 5 = 52$ strokes. The pro will have plenty to say to both groups. The second group, however, creates much more of a problem. The scores there go from 36 (quite good) to 72 (might consider bowling instead). In other words, there is a lot of *variability* in the scores for the 9:00 group. In the 8:00 group, however, the scores are generally close to each other—all five are at about the same skill level. Clearly, before starting the lessons, the pro would like to know more than the mean score for the group.

The simplest measure of variability is the **range**—the difference between the high and low scores of a group. For the memory data presented earlier, the range is 7 $(21 - 14)$. For the golf lesson example, the 8:00 group has a range of 12 $(58 - 46)$, whereas the range for the 9:00 class is a whopping 36 $(72 - 36)$. The range provides a rough estimate of variability, but it doesn't tell you any more than the difference between the most extreme scores.

Under some circumstances, researchers will calculate an **interquartile range**. It is useful for exactly the reason a median is sometimes useful: when there are outliers. The interquartile range is the range of scores between the bottom 25 percent of scores (25th percentile) and the top 25 percent of scores (75th percentile). The procedure is simple. First, divide the data set in two at the median. Then, find the midpoint for the data below the median (call it Q1—it's the 25th percentile) and the midpoint for the data above the median (Q3, or the 75th percentile). The interquartile range (IQR) is equal to Q3 − Q1. Consider the memory data again:

14 15 15 15 16   16 17 17 17 17   18 18 18 18 18   19 19 19 20 21

⇑   ⇑   ⇑

Q1   median   Q3

$Q1 = 16$ $Q3 = 18.5$ $IQR = Q3 - Q1 = 18.5 - 16 = 2.5$

Notice the IQR would not change if outliers were present. For example, if the first two memory scores were 3 and 4 instead of 14 and 15, the IQR would still be 2.5 (and the median would still be 17.5).

In addition to describing the set of data obtained in a study, the use of the median and the interquartile range can be useful for researchers who want to test groups of individuals who score differently on a psychological test. For example, suppose a researcher wants to examine the relationship between self-esteem and academic performance. First, a researcher needs to determine participants' self-esteem levels and may do so by giving them a valid and reliable self-esteem test. The scores obtained can then be organized in sequential order and a median can be calculated. The researcher may do what is called a "median split" where the researcher will use the median as the point in the distribution where all scores below the median would be grouped into the low self-esteem group and all scores above the median would be grouped into the high self-esteem group. This works well if scores are regularly distributed across a wide range of scores (like the 9:00 golf group) and not all clumped together, say, around the mean (like the 8:00 golf group). If the scores are all hovering around the mean (and median), then this tells you that the self-esteem scores are mostly in the middle-ground between low and high self-esteem. Instead, an astute research may use the interquartile range to establish low (Q1) and high (Q4) self-esteem groups that may better reflect lower and higher levels of self-esteem, rather than moderate levels of self-esteem.

A third measure of variability is the **variance**, which represents how distributed the scores are, relative to the mean. The Student Statistics Guide on the Student Companion Site shows you how to calculate variance, using what is called the definition formula. Variance is seldom reported when listing descriptive statistics because it represents the units of measurement squared (e.g., "words recalled squared"). Variance is a central feature of a common inferential procedure found in psychology, the *analysis of variance*, which allows one to use sample to data to make inferences about the variance in the population. We will describe the analysis of variance statistical technique in more detail in Chapters 7 and 8 of this text.

The **standard deviation** for a set of sample scores is an estimate of the average amount by which the scores in the sample deviate from the mean score. The Student Statistics Guide on the Student Companion Site shows you how to calculate, which is easy enough after you have calculated variance—standard deviation is the square-root of the variance! For the scores in the hypothetical memory study, one standard deviation is equal to 1.81 words. For the golf lesson example, the standard deviation for the 8:00 class is 4.47 strokes, whereas for the 9:00 group it is 15.03 strokes. Compared to the range and interquartile range, the variance and standard deviation are a more fine-grained measures of variability of scores in a set of data, but because of their reliance on the mean in its calculation should be used only when the data is fairly normally distributed. Finally, a very important distinction between variance and standard deviation is that the variance is reported when the data represent the entire *population* of scores; the standard deviation is reported when the data represent a *sample* of scores from the population.

Measures of central tendency and variability are universal features of any description of data, but researchers also like to examine the entire set of scores at one time. Just looking at the data set doesn't usually help, but there are other ways to organize the scores so they present a meaningful visual image. One way to accomplish this is by creating a **histogram**. This is a graph showing the number of times each score occurs, or, if there is a large number of scores, how often scores within a defined range occur. The first step is to create a **frequency distribution**, a table that records the number of times each score occurs. The frequency distribution of scores for the memory study looks like this:

Score	Frequency	Frequencies as Asterisks
14	1	*
15	3	***
16	2	**
17	4	****
18	5	*****
19	3	***
20	1	*
21	1	*

Plotting the histogram is easy once a table of frequencies is created. Simply place the actual score values on the *X*-axis (horizontal axis) of a graph and the frequency of occurrence on the *Y*-axis (vertical axis); then draw the bars appropriately. The result should look like Figure 4.6.

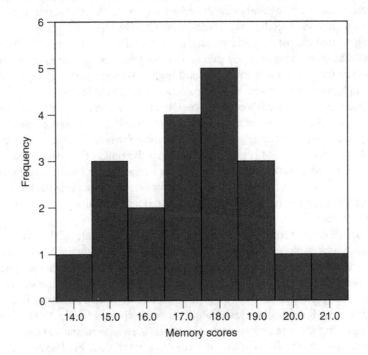

FIGURE 4.6

A histogram of scores on a memory test.

Notice that taking the pattern of asterisks from the frequency distribution and rotating it 90° results in the equivalent of Figure 4.6.

Another point to note about the histogram is that it bulges near the middle and is relatively flat at each end. This is a distribution of scores that roughly approximates what would happen if you created a histogram for the entire population, not just for the 20 people in the memory study described here. Such a population distribution is the familiar bell-shaped curve known as the **normal curve** or normal distribution—see Figure 4.7.

The normal curve is a frequency distribution just like one for the memory scores, except instead of being an *actual* (or "empirical") distribution of sample scores, it is a *hypothetical* (or "theoretical") distribution of what all the scores in the population would be if everyone was tested on a particular measure. The mean score, as well as the median and the mode, are all at the center of a normal distribution. This is exactly why the mean, median, and mode are referred to as measures of central tendency; they tend to be in the center of normal distribution of scores. A key assumption in several common statistical analyses is that if the empirical distributions of scores resemble the normal distribution, then the mathematical properties of the normal distribution can be used to draw conclusions about the empirical distribution.

In the normal curve in Figure 4.7, notice that we have marked two standard deviations on either side of the mean. From the mathematical properties of the curve, it is possible to know that about two-thirds or 68% of all the scores in a population of scores fall within a single standard deviation on either side of the mean. Furthermore, about 95% of all scores fall within two standard deviations on either side of the mean. Obviously, scores that fall beyond two standard deviations are rare; they occur only 5% of the time. You might even describe such rare events as *significant*, as in "statistically significant." Keep this concept in mind; we'll return to it shortly.

In articles describing research outcomes, descriptive statistics are reported three ways. First, if there are just a few numbers to report (e.g., means and standard deviations for the groups in an experiment), they are sometimes worked into the narrative description of the results. Second, the means and standard deviations might be presented in a table; third, they might be reported in the visual form of a graph. Descriptions of how to construct tables and graphs that conform to APA guidelines can be found in the sample research report in Appendix A, and Chapters 7 and 8 include information on graph making. Also, look at Box 4.3, which makes it clear that statistical analysis and graph making have an ethical dimension.

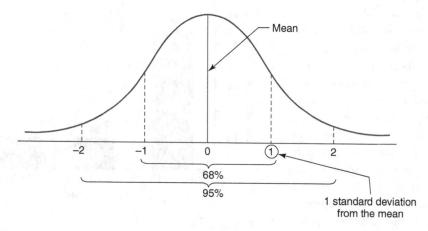

FIGURE 4.7
The normal curve.

BOX 4.3   ETHICS—Statistics that Mislead

We have all been exposed to the deceptive use of statistical information. Although politicians might be the worst offenders, with writers of advertising copy perhaps a close second, statistics are abused frequently enough that many people are skeptical about them, and you often hear them say things like "Statistics don't really tell you anything useful; you can make them do anything you'd like." Is this really true?

Certainly decisions must be made about how to present data and what conclusions to draw from them. You can be reasonably confident that articles published in reputable journals, having gone through a tough peer review process, are reporting statistical analyses that lead to defensible conclusions. What you must be careful about are the uses of statistics in the broader public arena or by people determined to convince you they know the truth or to get you to buy something.

Being informed about the proper use of statistics will enable you to identify these questionable statistical practices. Some points to be careful about were first described in Darrell Huff's famous *How to Lie with Statistics* (1954). The book begins with a well-known quote attributed to the British politician Benjamin Disraeli that sums up a common perception of statistics: "There are lies, damned lies, and statistics" (p. 2). Here are two examples of how the presentation of descriptive statistics can mislead. The first occurs frequently in the descriptions of medical research; the second involves the visual portrayal of data—graphs.

In the first case, we frequently learn of medical research concerning factors that influence our chances of contracting some disease or other. For example, a 2007 report in the *British Journal of Cancer* reported that grapefruit consumption increased the risk of breast cancer by 30%(!). According to Tavris and Bluming (2008), fear of cancer vastly exceeds fears of other diseases in women, so this news was received with some alarm. It is easy to imagine large piles of unsold grapefruit in grocery stores. Yet the 30% number is what is called *relative risk* and, by itself, virtually meaningless as a statistic. What one must know is the absolute number of grapefruit-eating and non-grapefruit-eating women. Suppose you compared 1,000 women in each of these two groups and discovered that 2 women in the non-grapefruit-eating group had breast cancer. In the grapefruit group, suppose you find 3 women out of 1,000 with breast cancer. That shift, from 2 to 3 women out of 1,000, represents a 50%

increase. If you found 4 out of 1,000 in the grapefruit group, that's a 100% increase. But notice that the absolute numbers are very small—2 and 3 women or 2 and 4 women out of a total of 2,000. So merely reporting a percentage increase is meaningless in the absence of the actual numbers of cases. Thus, studies showing that using antibiotics increases the breast cancer risk by 207%, using an electric blanket increases the risk by 630%, or being an Icelandic flight attendant increases the risk by 410% (examples reported by Tavris and Bluming) can be seriously misleading.

As for graphs that mislead, consider Figure 4.8, a graph that appeared briefly on the CNN website, reporting the results of a poll in 2005. At issue was a heartbreaking case in which a young Florida woman, Terry Schiavo, had fallen into a persistent vegetative state and was essentially brain-dead. A battle was being fought between her husband, who wished to remove her feeding tube, and her parents, who believed she could recover. National politicians with axes to grind even became involved, never a good sign. The dispute eventually reached the Supreme Court, which decided the feeding tube could be removed (Schiavo died shortly thereafter). The subsequent CNN poll about the case included this question: "Based on what you have heard or read about the case, do you agree with the court's decision to have the feeding tube removed?" Figure 4.8 was used to compare the results for Democrat, Republican, and Independent voters who responded. As you can see, a quick look makes it appear that Democrats were much more likely to agree with the

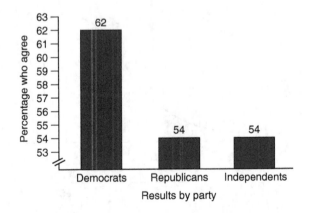

FIGURE 4.8
Graph as it appeared in the original reporting of the CNN/USA/Gallup poll.

decision than were Republicans or Independents. In fact the differences among them were quite small (8 percentage points) and happened to be within the margin of error for the survey.

Huff (1954) called this type of graph a "gee-whiz" graph, for obvious reasons: When you first look at it, you find yourself saying, "Gee whiz, what a huge difference!" Democrats reading the graph might be inclined to think they are more reasonable than the other groups, while the other groups might think Democrats value life less than they do. The problem, however, is that the percentages are grossly exaggerated by using just a small range of numbers on the vertical or Y-axis, and by not starting the Y-axis at a percentage of zero.

This graph-making strategy exaggerates small differences. A more reasonable labeling of the Y-axis yields the graph in Figure 4.9, which gives you a more truthful picture of the outcome—that no substantial differences among the groups occurred and that for all three groups, the majority agreed with the court's decision. (*Note*: To their credit, CNN quickly recognized the problem and replaced the graph in Figure 4.8 with the more accurate one in Figure 4.9.)

The moral here is obvious: Beware the Y-axis. Be especially skeptical about graphs that seem to show large differences on a Y-axis that is not labeled, labeled ambiguously, labeled in tiny gradations from top to bottom, and/or does not start at zero.

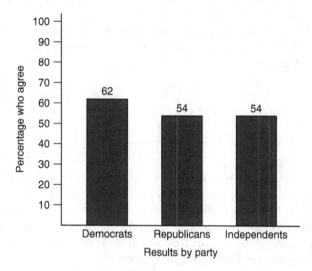

FIGURE 4.9
CNN's corrected graph that more accurately reflects the data.

Inferential Statistics

Like most people, researchers need to believe their work is important. One way to accomplish this goal is to produce interesting research outcomes, results that apply beyond the data collected in one study. That is, although a study looks at merely a small *sample* (a subset of the members of a defined group—50 college students, for instance) of all the data that could be collected, the researcher's hope is to arrive at a conclusion that will apply to the wider *population* (all the members of a defined group—all college students, for instance). After all, the idea of the whole research enterprise is to arrive at general laws of behavior. Inferential statistics allow the researcher to make inferences about the population based on the sample data and to do so with a certain degree of certainty or confidence.

To illustrate what an inferential analysis tries to accomplish, let's consider a hypothetical maze-learning study comparing rats fed immediately after reaching the end of a maze with rats fed 10 seconds after reaching the end of the maze. Thus, the empirical question is whether immediate reinforcement results in faster maze learning than delayed reinforcement. Suppose the following results occurred for five rats in each group. Each score is the total number of trials the rat takes to learn the maze; learning is operationally defined as two consecutive errorless runs through the maze.

Rat #	Immediate Food	Rat #	Delayed Food
1	12	6	19
2	13	7	20
3	16	8	16
4	11	9	18
5	14	10	15

Notice the scores within each column are not all the same, a result of *measurement error*: slight differences between the five rats in each group and perhaps other random factors. Despite the lack of absolute uniformity, however, it appears the rats given immediate reinforcement learned the maze faster (i.e., require fewer trials).

Of course, we need more than a general impression resulting from a quick glance at the numbers. The first step is to calculate descriptive statistics, such as the mean and standard deviation. Here they are:

	Immediate	Delayed
Mean	13.20	17.60
Standard deviation	1.92	2.07

On average, at least for this sample, maze learning required more trials when the food reward was delayed. Also, the variability of the scores within each set, as reflected in the standard deviations, is fairly low and about the same for both groups. Can we conclude *in general* (i.e., with reference to the population of all rats) that immediate reinforcement speeds maze learning? Not yet. What is needed is an inferential analysis of the data, which in this case involves a procedure called *null hypothesis significance testing*.[3]

SELF TEST

4.2

1. If the data include significant outliers, what is the best measure of (a) central tendency and (b) variability?
2. When reporting a mean, why is it also important to report a standard deviation?
3. Why is it difficult to interpret a graph if the Y-axis is not labeled?

Null Hypothesis Significance Testing

Recall from Chapter 1, the assumptions of discoverability and determinism. We wish to discover relationships between psychological constructs and ultimately to determine the causes of behavior. Because the research enterprise tends to test samples selected from a target population, we can never be 100% certain about conclusions drawn from research testing samples. But, we can

---

[3] A second category of inferential analysis is called *estimation*, which involves estimating population values from individual sample scores.

estimate the likelihood, or probability, that our results are not due to chance. Thus, we use *statistical determinism* to establish laws about behavior and make predications with probabilities greater than chance. Null hypothesis significance testing (NHST) yields these probabilities.

The first step in significance testing is to assume there is *no difference* in performance between the conditions that you are studying, in this case between immediate and delayed rewards. This assumption is called the **null hypothesis** (null = nothing), symbolized H_0. The research hypothesis, the outcome you as a researcher are *hoping* to find (fewer learning trials for rats receiving immediate reward), is called the **alternative hypothesis** (or sometimes *research hypothesis*) or H_1. The logic of NHST is that we only can test the null hypothesis. Why? Because the only "given" we know is that all participants in the study begin the study being relatively equal (assuming good sampling procedures), regardless of what they later do as participants in the study. It may seem strange that you are testing the null hypothesis, when as a researcher you have developed a research hypothesis you want to test. However, statistical determinism begins with what is known or given (you don't know what will happen with your participants as a result of doing your study yet!), and therefore the only given is the null hypothesis. Thus, in your study, you test the null hypothesis, and you hope to be able to reject H_0 with a degree of confidence, thereby supporting (but not proving) H_1, the hypothesis closer to your heart.

If this language sounds odd to you, think of it as analogous to what happens in a court of law. There, the accused person initially is presumed innocent. The assumption is that the defendant has done nothing (null-thing) wrong. The job of the prosecution is to convince the jury of its alternative hypothesis, namely, the defendant committed the crime. Like the prosecutor, the researcher must show that something indeed happened, namely, the reinforcement delay influenced learning in our maze-learning example.

An inferential analysis with NHST can have only two outcomes: reject H_0 or fail to reject H_0. If you reject H_0, you are saying that you reject the idea that there is no difference (or no relationship) between conditions. Yes, in grammatical terms, this is a double-negative—which translates into "there is a statistically significant difference between conditions." The differences you find between the two groups of rats could be due to a genuine, real, honest-to-goodness effect (e.g., reinforcement delay). If you fail to reject H_0, you are saying that you fail to reject that there is no difference between conditions. Translated, this means "there is no statistically significant difference between conditions," and that the results you discovered were due to chance. The important point here is to think about what numbers are being compared when determining with what probability there is a difference between conditions. In the rat example, there is a numerical difference between the means of each group. The statistical test is whether that numerical difference is a real difference or a difference due to chance. In the maze example, rejecting H_0—that is, finding a statistically significant difference—means it really does seem that immediate reinforcement aids maze learning.

The researcher's hypothesis (H_1) is never proven true in an absolute sense, just as defendants are never *absolutely* proven guilty: Guilt is said to be proven only beyond a reasonable doubt. Thus, H_0 can only be rejected with some degree of confidence, which is set by what is called the **alpha (α) level**. Technically, alpha refers to the probability of obtaining your particular results if H_0 (no difference) is really true. By convention, alpha is set at .05 ($\alpha = .05$), but it can be set at other, more stringent, levels as well (e.g., $\alpha = .01$). If H_0 is rejected when alpha equals .05, it means you believe the probability is very low (5 out of 100) that your research outcome is the result of chance factors. Another way to think of the alpha level is to think that you want to be pretty confident that your results are NOT due to chance if your study is replicated, say, 100 times. With an alpha of .05, you are hoping that only 5% of the time (or less) your results are due to chance. You want to be at least 95% confident that your results are NOT due to chance, or that if your study replicated 100 times, you should get the same results 95% of the time (or 95 times of 100). When running various statistical tests, you can calculate (or let software calculate) the probability based on your sample that your results are due to chance. This calculated probability is called a *p*-value. You can compare the calculated *p*-value to the alpha to determine the probability that your results are due to chance is less than 5% ($\alpha = .05$). If your *p* is less than α, then you can reject null hypothesis (which predicts no difference – or your results are due to chance). Then, you conclude there is a statistically significant difference between your conditions. If your result is not due to chance, then it must be due to something else—namely (you hope), the phenomenon you are studying, immediacy of reinforcement in this case.

The choice of .05 as the alpha level relates to the earlier discussion of the characteristics of the normal curve. Remember, for a normal distribution of scores, the probability that a given score will be more than two standard deviations from the mean is rare, 5% or less. Similarly, when comparing two sets of scores, as in the maze study, one asks about the probability of the obtained difference between the means occurring if the truth was that no real difference existed (i.e., if H_0 is true). If that probability is low enough, we reject H_0 and decide some real difference must be occurring. The "low enough" is the probability of 5%, or .05. Another way to put it is to say the obtained difference between the sample means would be so unexpected (i.e., rare) if H_0 were true that we just cannot believe H_0 is really true. We believe something else happened (i.e., reinforcement delay really does slow learning), so we reject H_0 and conclude a "statistically significant" difference exists between the groups.

Type I and Type II Errors

Clear from the previous discussion is that when you decide whether or not to reject H_0, you could be wrong. Actually, you could make two kinds of errors. First, you might reject H_0 and support H_1, get all excited about making a breakthrough discovery, but be wrong. Rejecting H_0 when it is in fact true is called a **Type I error**. The chance of this happening is equal to the value of alpha, normally .05. That is, setting alpha at .05 and rejecting H_0 means you have a 5% chance of making a Type I error—a 5% chance of thinking you have a real effect but are wrong. Type I errors are sometimes suspected when a research outcome fails several attempts at replication.

The other kind of mistake you could make is called a **Type II error**. This happens when you fail to reject H_0 but you are wrong—that is, you don't find a significant effect in your study, naturally feel depressed about it, but are in fact in error. There really is a true effect in the population; you just haven't found it in the sample you tested. Type II errors sometimes occur when the measurements used aren't reliable or aren't sensitive enough to detect true differences between groups, or that you have a small sample size. As you will see in Chapter 11, this sometimes happens in program evaluation research. A program might indeed have a significant but small effect on those in it, but the measures used are too weak to detect it with any degree of certainty.

Table 4.2 summarizes the four possible outcomes of an inferential statistical analysis comparing two conditions of an experiment. As you can see, correct decisions result from rejecting H_0 when it is false and failing to reject H_0 when it is true. Erroneously rejecting H_0 produces a Type I error; a failure to reject H_0 when H_0 is false is a Type II error. If it makes it easier to understand the terminology, you can make the following substitutions in Table 4.2:

For "Fail to Reject H_0," substitute:

> —"You did the study, you went through all of the proper analyses, and what you came up with was zilch, nothing, nada, no significant differences, and yes, you have good reason to be distraught, especially if this is your senior thesis project!"

For "Reject H_0," substitute:

> —"You did the study, you went through all of the proper analyses, and the difference came out significant at the .05 level, and yes, your life now has meaning and you'll be able to impress your friends and especially your thesis director because you went through all of this work and you *actually found something!*"

Table 4.2 **Statistical Decision Making: Four Possible Outcomes of a Study Comparing Two Conditions, X and Y**

		The True State of Affairs	
		H_0 **is true:** There is no difference between X and Y	H_0 **is false:** There really is a difference between X and Y
Your Statistical Decision	**Fail to reject H_0:** In my study, I found no significant difference between X and Y, so I cannot reject H_0	**Correct decision**	**Type II error**
	Reject H_0: In my study, I found a significant difference between X and Y, so I reject H_0	**Type I error**	**Correct decision** (experimenter heaven)

For "H_0 is true," substitute:

—"Regardless of what might have occurred in your study, no true difference exists."

For "H_0 is false," substitute:

—"Regardless of what might have occurred in your study, a true difference does exist."

With these substitutions in mind, correct decisions mean either (a) no real difference exists, which is OK because you didn't find one anyway or (b) a real difference exists and you found it (experimenter heaven). A Type I error means there's no real difference but you think there is because of the results of your particular study. A Type II error means there really is a difference but you failed to find it in your study.

One final point. You will not necessarily know if you have committed a Type I or Type II error in your study until further research is done to (hopefully) rule out the likelihood of having committed a Type I or Type II error. As we will discuss in future chapters, through sound research design, we can minimize the likelihood of committing these errors. For example, having strong methodological control can reduce the chances of making a Type I error, and we will explore this more deeply in Chapters 5 and 6. Having a large enough sample size and using valid, reliable measures can mitigate against committing a Type II error, issues we will discuss in Chapters 9–11.

Interpreting Failures to Reject H_0

For academic researchers, the road to tenure and promotion passes through what we have called "experimenter heaven" (rejecting null hypotheses when there is indeed a true effect) but, of course, sometimes the result of a study is a failure to reject H_0 (no significant differences occur). The typical reaction of a researcher to this second type of outcome result is unprintable in this family-oriented research methods textbook. However, there *are* circumstances when a failure to reject H_0 is not such a bad outcome. In general, it is important to note that interpreting failures to reject H_0 must be done with great caution. There might indeed be no difference to be found, or it could be there is one, but you have failed to find it in your study (a Type II error). So if you are comparing, say, those who get a drug and those who don't, hoping to find the drug improves memory, but you fail to find a significant difference between the two groups, you're not allowed to say, "OK that settles it—there's no effect of this drug." On the other hand, and this is where replication once again comes into play, consistent failures to find differences can indeed be important outcomes. For example, as you will learn in the Chapter 7 discussion of *yoked control groups*, those who develop a new therapy (to cure extreme anxiety in that case) are obligated to provide evidence of its effectiveness. Several findings of no difference between the new therapy and a group given no therapy would raise questions about the usefulness of the new approach.

For an example relevant to your life as students, consider a study by Vandehey, Marsh, and Diekhoff (2005). They examined the question of whether instructors should provide a full set of their lecture notes (typically on an instructor website) to students. Some argue that if students already have all the notes, they don't have to worry about writing furiously in class, thereby missing important points. But others argue that if students have all of the notes, they won't come to class (why bother if the notes are posted online?). Over the course of a semester, Vandehey and his colleagues compared classes that provided full instructor notes online, partial notes, or no notes. They found *no* significant differences in class attendance among any of the groups and no differences in course grades either. If this result holds up to replication (and some other studies have found slightly different results), it means instructors providing all of their notes don't need to worry about teaching to empty classrooms.

Another implication of the failure-to-reject issue is that often (but not always) nonsignificant findings do not get published. The notion that only "statistically significant" results get published is referred to as a **publication bias**, and is a topic of much current discussion in psychological science. Recently, de Bruin, Treccani, and Della Sala (2015) challenged the belief that bilingual individuals have a cognitive advantage over their monolingual counterparts on various tasks of controlled attention and working memory. They demonstrated that this widely held belief is based primarily on a publication bias of results that demonstrate the bilingual advantage. They then analyzed conference abstracts from 1999 to 2012 to see which resulted in peer-reviewed publications. Want to guess what they found? Those studies that demonstrated a bilingual advantage were most likely to be published, and those that challenged the view (i.e., those that found mixed or opposite results, or no effect) were least likely to be published. Clearly, as demonstrated by de Bruin et al. it could very well be that important research outcomes aren't becoming known. Studies finding no differences are less likely to be published, and wind up stored away in someone's files—a phenomenon called the **file drawer effect** (Rosenthal, 1979). A big problem occurs, however, if only a few published studies show an effect, no published studies show the opposite or no effect, but many studies languish in file drawers because no differences were found and the studies couldn't get published. de Bruin et al. showed that 63% (34 out of 54) of studies from the conferences showing a bilingual advantage were published, whereas only 36% (18 out of 50) that challenged the effect or found no effect were published. Someone looking at the literature (i.e., the published research) would think a genuine bilingual advantage has been found when, in fact, the evidence might be quite weak.

There are also ethical issues related to the failure-to-reject issue. Social psychologist Brain Nosek suggests that questionable research practices, like those described in Chapter 3 may occur in part because nonsignificant results are rarely published in psychological journals (Carpenter, 2012). As noted in Chapter 3, there is a strong movement in psychological science to replicate prior results and also to share failures to replicate. Online repositories like PsychFileDrawer.org allow users to attempt to replicate listed studies, and the site reports successful and unsuccessful replication attempts. Both exact and conceptual replications are also distinguished on this website. As a new scientist to psychological science, you may learn quite a lot from being a part of a replication project. You will not only learn the importance of replication, but also you will very clearly see how studies are designed, implemented, and tested statistically. Ask your professor for advice on how to become involved in replication!

Beyond Null Hypothesis Significance Testing

Although NHST has a long history and is the backbone of statistical decision making among many psychologists, it has also been a focus of criticism. A major point of contention has been the all-or-none character of null hypothesis decision making, with the alpha level of .05 taking on seemingly magical properties (Cohen, 1994). Why, it is sometimes asked, is a difference between two means "significant" at the .05 level and another difference between another pair of means not significant at the .06 level? Studies producing these two outcomes are essentially identical in terms of the result, but one meets the magical .05 cutoff (and gets published) while the other one falls short (and gets stuffed into the file drawer labeled "nonsignificant results"). Defenders of NHST argue that providing a strong test before drawing a conclusion is not necessarily a bad thing; they also ask, if not .05 as a cutoff, then what should it be? .10? .15?

A beneficial effect of the argument has been an elaboration of the kinds of statistical analyses being used by research psychologists today. Based on recommendations from a special task force created by the APA (Wilkinson et al., 1999), researchers have begun to include several new features in their descriptions of statistical analyses, including calculations of effect sizes, confidence intervals, and estimates of power. In most journals that publish research articles that include NHST, the authors are often also required to include reports of effect sizes and confidence intervals. The journal *Basic and Applied Social Psychology* has gone so far as to ban reports of NHST; instead, authors are asked to support their research findings with reports of other statistical metrics, including effect sizes and confidence intervals (Trafimow & Marks, 2015).[4] In addition, researchers are beginning to realize that even beyond statistical analysis, confidence in the validity of research outcomes requires a greater value being placed on the replication process. Kline (2004), for example, argued that it

> would make a very strong statement if journals and granting agencies required replication. This would increase the demands on the researcher and result in fewer published studies. The quality of what would be published might improve, however. A requirement for replication would also filter out some of the fad social science research topics that bloom for a short time but then quickly disappear. (p. 89)

Effect Size

The result of a null hypothesis significance test could be that a statistically significant difference between two groups or among multiple groups exists. But this outcome does not inform the researcher about the *size* of the difference(s). An effect size index is designed to do just that. **Effect size** provides an estimate of the magnitude of the difference among sets of scores, while taking into account the amount of variability in the scores. Different types of effect size calculations are used for different kinds of research designs. All yield a statistic that enables the researcher to decide if the study produced a small, medium, or large effect. One common measure of effect size between two conditions is Cohen's *d*. A Google search for it will yield several sites that will automatically calculate effect size if you plug in the means and standard deviations for two groups. In the Student Statistics Guide on the Student Companion site, we show you how to calculate the effect size for the maze example earlier using a specific formula for Cohen's *d* for independent groups with equal *n*'s in each group. Depending on the type of research design you have, there are certain calculations of effect size. We will revisit effect sizes in later chapters when we discuss specific research designs, but examples of calculations of other effect sizes and how to interpret them are found on the Student Companion site.

One major advantage of calculating effect sizes is that it enables researchers to arrive at a common metric for evaluating a diverse array of experiments. That is, if you examine 20 studies designed to test the frustration-aggression hypothesis, each using different operational definitions of terms, different procedures, and different types of participants, an effect size can be calculated

---

[4] One alternative to NHST that researchers may favor is called a Bayesian approach, which allows researchers to better quantify the certainty in one's results based on making inferences about different models of the data from calculations of probability. The Bayesian approach is one that you would likely learn more about in a more specialized statistics course at the advanced undergraduate or graduate level.

for each study and these effect sizes can be combined to yield an overall statistical conclusion about the generality of the relationship between frustration and aggression, across all the studies. This is precisely what is done in a type of study called a **meta-analysis**. A meta-analysis uses effect-size analyses to combine the results from several (often, many) experiments that use the same variables, even though these variables are likely to have different operational definitions. For example, Anderson and Bushman (2001) combined the effect sizes from 35 studies using more than 4,000 total participants to argue that playing violent video games increases levels of aggressiveness in children and young adults. The outcome of a meta-analysis relates to the concept of *converging operations*, introduced in Chapter 3. Meta-analyses are also related to replication of results, and specifically the generality of a phenomenon based on mostly *conceptual replications*. However, meta-analysis can be used with *direct replications* and is used in many of the on-going replication projects occurring in the science of psychology. We will explore meta-analysis in more depth in Chapter 10 when we review how such a replication project was conducted and what the results revealed. In general, confidence in the generality of a conclusion increases when similar results occur, even though a variety of methods and definitions of terms have been used.

Confidence Intervals

Calculating confidence intervals for specific means adds to the quality of the information provided in a description of results. In particular, a confidence interval is an inferential statistic that enables the researcher to draw a conclusion about the population as a whole based on the sample data. As you recall from our opening remarks about inferential statistics, drawing general conclusions is the name of the game for an inferential analysis. Using the hypothetical maze data again, the means and standard deviations can be supplemented with confidence intervals as follows:

	Immediate	Delayed
Mean	13.20	17.60
Standard deviation	1.92	2.07
Confidence interval	(10.81, 15.56)	(15.03, 20.16)

A **confidence interval** is a range of values expected to include a population value with a certain degree of confidence. What a confidence interval tells us is that, based on the data for a sample, we can be 95% confident the calculated interval captures the population mean.[5] Hence, there is a very good chance (95 out of 100) the population mean for the immediately reinforced group is somewhere between 10.81 trials and 15.56 trials and the population mean for the delayed group falls somewhere between 15.03 trials and 20.16 trials. We describe how to calculate confidence intervals in the Student Statistics Guide on the Student Companion site. As for the use of confidence intervals in drawing conclusions about an experiment, note very little overlap in the intervals for the two groups in the maze study. The upper limit of the immediate group overlaps the lower limit for the delayed group, but just slightly. In general, non-overlapping confidence intervals indicate a meaningful difference between the two conditions of the study. In our hypothetical study, delaying reinforcement seems to have an effect in slowing down maze learning (i.e., increasing the number of trials it takes to learn the maze).[6]

---

[5] Although the term *confidence interval* is seldom used when reporting the results of polls, it is in fact the key statistic yielding the "margin of error," as in "The president currently has a 56% approval rating, with a margin of error of $\pm$4%."

[6] A second type of confidence interval also can be calculated, one that produces a range of mean differences for a study that compares two means. For more details on how to calculate and interpret a confidence interval around a mean difference, consult a statistics textbook (e.g., Witte & Witte, 2014).

In contrast to NHST, which encourages dichotomous statistical decision making—that is, is there a significant effect or not—the combination of effect size and confidence intervals can better explain your results. Effect size allows you to answer the question about how big the effect is, and confidence intervals allow you to answer whether the population mean would be included in the range of scores around the mean, taking into account error variance. While NHST may show a "significant effect," say in the maze example above, with a closer examination of the effect size and confidence interval, you can better explain the result, in that the effect is large (Cohens $d = 2.20$) and there is a good chance the population mean for each condition would not be overlapping across conditions. Researchers are often encouraged to report both effect sizes and confidence intervals for various journals, including all of the journals published by the American Psychological Association, which includes some the top journals in our field.

Power

When completing a null hypothesis significance test, one hopes to be able to reject H_0 when it is, in fact, false (the "experimenter heaven" cell of Table 4.2). The chance of this happening is referred to as the **power** of the statistical test. That is, a test is said to have high power if it results in a high probability that a real difference will be found in a particular study. Note the inverse relationship between power and a Type II error. This type of error, you will recall, occurs when a true effect exists, but the experiment fails to find a significant difference. As power increases, the chance of a Type II error decreases, and vice versa. The probability of a Type II error occurring is sometimes referred to as β (*beta*). Power, then, is $1-\beta$.

Power is affected by the alpha level (e.g., $\alpha = .05$), by the effect size, and, especially, by the size of the sample. This latter attribute is directly under the experimenter's control, and researchers sometimes perform a *power analysis* at the outset of a study to help them choose the best sample size for their study. G*Power is a free online software tool used for calculating power, or you can consult a statistics text for more details on completing a power analysis.

Students are often frustrated when their study "doesn't come out" (i.e., no significant differences occur), an outcome that often results from a small sample size. That is, power was low and the chances of a Type II error were high, so some effect might indeed have occurred in their study, but they failed to detect it with either NHST or an evaluation of effect size and confidence intervals. Increasing sample size, in a study that is well designed, is usually the best way to increase power. However, the other side of the power coin is that a huge sample size might produce a result that is statistically significant, but meaningless in a practical sense—that is, a small effect size between groups might have little importance in a study with huge numbers of participants. For instance, suppose that, in a study evaluating the effects of orange juice on IQ, you include 5,000 people in each of two groups (orange juice versus no orange juice), find a 2-point improvement in average IQ for the orange juice group and no change for the other group, and determine the difference is significant at the .05 level. This is a test with very high power. Such a difference, however, would be of no real practical value. Two IQ points? Who cares? Part of the skill of becoming an accomplished researcher involves balancing considerations of power, effect size, significance level, and sample size.

SELF TEST

4.3

1. A researcher believes wild rats will learn to escape from a puzzle box more quickly than tame rats. What is H_0 in this study?
2. In the same study with rats, what kind of result would be considered a Type I error? Type II?
3. What is a meta-analysis and how does it relate to effect size?

Armed with some of the basic tools psychologists use to think about data, you are now ready to tackle the first of three chapters dealing with the experimental method, psychology's most powerful tool for trying to understand the intricacies of behavior and mental processes. We'll begin with a general introduction to the experimental method and then consider some control problems that occur with such research; third, we'll examine the features of the most common types of experimental designs.

CHAPTER SUMMARY

Who to Measure—Sampling Procedures

Participants in a research study are a sample, which is a subset of a general group, or population. Probability sampling is designed to create good samples, and there are three common forms: a simple random sample, a stratified sample, and a cluster sample. In simple random sampling, every member of the population has an equal chance of being selected. Stratified sampling ensures that important subgroups in the population are represented proportionally in the sample. Cluster sampling is used when it is impossible to know all of the members of the population. Quota sampling is a nonprobability sampling technique that has a goal similar to that of stratified sampling (proportionality). Two other nonprobability convenience sampling methods are purposive sampling, in which a specific group is targeted, and snowball sampling, in which subjects recommend others known to them as additional subjects in the study.

What to Measure—Varieties of Behavior

The behaviors measured in psychological research range from overt actions to self-reports to physiological recordings; the measures chosen for a particular study depend on the manner in which the study's constructs are operationally defined. In many areas of psychological research, standard measures have developed over the years (e.g., preferential looking, reaction time).

Evaluating Measures

High-quality measures of behavior are both reliable and valid. To be reliable is to be repeatable and low in measurement error. Measures are valid if they actually measure what they are supposed to measure. Confidence in validity increases if a measure makes sense (content validity) and predicts future outcomes well (criterion validity). Construct validity means the measurement being used is a good measure of the construct being studied (e.g., "connectedness to nature") and the construct itself is useful for understanding some behavior. Valid constructs also show convergent and discriminant validity. Construct validity develops over time, when a research program investigating relationships between the construct being measured and related phenomena results in consistent, predictable outcomes.

Scales of Measurement

Data for psychological research can be classified into four scales of measurement: nominal, ordinal, interval, and ratio. In a nominal scale, categories (e.g., receptive female when male has dog, receptive female when male does not have dog) are identified and the frequency of occurrences per category is the main research interest. Ordinal scales occur when events are placed in rank order. Interval and ratio scales both assume equal intervals between quantitatively increasing scores; only ratio scales have a true zero point, however. Traditionally, psychologists have preferred to rely on interval and ratio scales because of the wider range of statistical analyses available when these scales are used.

Statistical Analysis

Statistical analysis in psychology is an essential tool for understanding the meaning of research outcomes. Descriptive statistics are calculated for the sample of participants in a particular study. They provide a summary of results and include measures of central tendency (e.g., mean, median, and mode) and variability (e.g., range, standard deviation, variance, interquartile range). For data with outliers, medians and interquartile ranges substitute for means and standard deviations. Data can be presented visually via graphical representation (e.g., histogram). Inferential statistics allow decisions about whether the results of a study are due to chance factors or appear to reflect a genuine relationship that can be applied to the larger population. The goal of null hypothesis significance testing is to reject the hypothesis of no difference (i.e., the null hypothesis) when a true difference indeed occurs. A Type I error is when the null hypothesis is rejected but should not have been, and a Type II error is when a true effect exists but no statistically significant difference is found in the study. Another form of inferential analysis involves calculating effect sizes and confidence intervals. Finally, a statistical test has high power if the chances are high it will detect a true effect.

CHAPTER REVIEW QUESTIONS

1. Describe the three forms of probability sampling described in the chapter.

2. Define nonprobability sampling and describe three forms of it.

3. Describe the logic behind Donders's "mental chronometry" research. What was the basic flaw?

4. Define reliability and explain why phrenological measurements would have been highly reliable.

5. Define validity and explain why phrenological measurements would have failed a validity test.

6. Explain why it is more important that a measure be both reliable and valid rather than be merely reliable (but not valid).

7. Use the Connectedness to Nature Scale as an example to show how construct validity can be determined. Be sure to work convergent and discriminant validity into your answer.

8. Describe the essential difference between descriptive and inferential statistics.

9. Distinguish between a mean, a median, and a mode, and explain when a median is a better descriptor of central tendency than a mean.

10. Why is the standard deviation a better measure of variability than the range?

11. When describing variability, what is interquartile range and when is it most likely to be used?

12. Describe the basic logic of hypothesis testing and distinguish between Type I and Type II errors.

13. What are confidence intervals and how are they interpreted?

14. What is effect size and how does its calculation complement hypothesis testing?

15. What is meant by the power of a statistical test? How might power be enhanced?

APPLICATIONS EXERCISES

Exercise 4.1. Scales of Measurement

For each of the following studies, indicate which scale of measurement (nominal, ordinal, interval, and ratio) is being used for the behavior being measured.

1. Sally wishes to discover whether the children of Republicans and Democrats are more likely to major in the sciences, humanities, or business.

2. Jack decides to investigate whether rats that have learned one maze will learn a second one more quickly (i.e., show fewer errors) than naïve rats.

3. Jim hypothesizes that children will rank TV movies higher if they are in color but that adults' rankings won't be affected by color.

4. Nancy believes somatotype changes with age, so she proposes to use Sheldon's scale to measure somatotypes for a group of people on their tenth, fifteenth, and twentieth birthdays.

5. Susan is interested in the phenomenon of helping behavior and believes whether or not someone helps will be influenced by weather—the chances of someone helping will be greater on sunny than on cloudy days.

6. Dave wishes to determine which of five new varieties of beer will be liked best (i.e., recognized as number 1) by the patrons of his bar.

7. Ellen is interested in how students perceive the safety of various campus buildings. She asks a sample of students to arrange a deck of cards in a pile, each containing the name of a campus building, with the safest building on top and the least safe building on the bottom.

8. Pat believes people with an obsessive-compulsive disorder will make fewer formatting errors on APA-style lab reports than those without the disorder.

9. Jesse is interested in gender differences in shyness and gives a 15-item shyness test to groups of men and women. Each item is a statement (e.g., I have difficulty talking to strangers) that responders rate on a scale from 1 (*strongly disagree*) through 5 (*strongly agree*).

10. Francis wishes to know whether age differences (comparing people in their twenties with those in their fifties) exist for those who consider themselves either morning people (best able to perform cognitive tasks then) or evening people.

Exercise 4.2. H_0, H_1, Type I Errors, and Type II Errors

For each of the following studies, (a) identify the null hypothesis, (b) make your best guess about the alternative hypothesis—that is, what you would expect to happen in this study, (c) describe a research outcome that would be a Type I error, and (d) describe an outcome that would be a Type II error.

1. In a study of how well people can detect lying, female and male participants will try to detect deception in films of women lying in some parts of the film and telling the truth in other parts.

2. In a perception study, infants will view slides of normal faces and faces with slight irregularities to examine which type of face infants will look at longer.

3. Patients with and without a diagnosis of depression will be asked to predict how they will do in negotiating a human maze.

4. Some athletes will be given training in a new imaging procedure they are to use just prior to shooting foul shots; they will be compared with other athletes not given any special training.

Exercise 4.3. Practicing Statistical Analysis

Suppose you did a study comparing the critical thinking skills of psychology majors and philosophy majors. You collect the data found in the following table. Each number is a score on a test of critical and logical thinking. Scores can range from a low of 5 to a high of 80. Calculate a complete set of descriptive statistics, 95% confidence intervals, a *t* test, and an effect size index. On the basis of what you have calculated, what would you conclude from the study?

Here are the scores on the critical thinking test:

Psychology Majors	Philosophy Majors
67	58
53	62
74	44
60	51
49	51
55	47
65	43
72	55
60	61
63	67

Note: For calculations, you can go to the Student Companion site and follow the instructions in the Student Statistics Guide.

ANSWERS TO SELF TESTS

✓ 4.1

1. 0.09 sec (0.28 − 0.19 = 0.09).
2. The measure would be reliable—same circumference tomorrow as today; it would not be valid—for example, head size would not predict GPA (students with larger heads would probably not have higher GPAs).
3. Dilbert is using an interval scale, probably ranging from 1 to10; Liz is using a ratio scale (time).

✓ 4.2

1. (a) median; (b) interquartile range.
2. Two sets of scores can have the same mean but different amounts of variability.
3. Small and meaningless differences in the data can be grossly exaggerated, resulting in a misleading interpretation of the data.

✓ 4.3

1. Wild and tame rats will be equal in their ability to escape.
2. Type I → wild rats are found to escape significantly faster than tame rats, but, in reality, the two types of rats are equal in their ability to escape.
   Type II → no significant difference in ability to escape is found in the study, but, in reality, wild rats are superior to tame rats.
3. Meta-analysis is a statistical tool for combining the results of multiple studies: What is taken from the various studies are the effects sizes, which are combined.

Introduction to Experimental Research

5

PREVIEW & CHAPTER OBJECTIVES

The middle four chapters of this text, Chapters 5 through 8, concern the design of experiments. The first half of Chapter 5 outlines the essential features of an experiment: varying factors of interest (the independent variables), controlling all other factors (extraneous variables), and measuring outcomes (dependent variables). In the second part of this chapter, you will learn how the validity of a study can be affected by how well it is designed. When you finish this chapter, you should be able to:

- Describe the impact of Robert Woodworth's 1938 *Experimental Psychology* on the way psychologists define an experiment.

- Define a manipulated independent variable, and identify examples of situational, task, and instructional variables.

- Distinguish between experimental and control groups.

- Describe John Stuart Mill's rules of inductive logic, and apply them to the concepts of experimental and control groups.

- Recognize the presence of confounding variables in an experiment, and understand why cofounds create serious problems for interpreting the results of an experiment.

- Identify independent and dependent variables, given a brief description of any experiment.

- Distinguish between independent variables that are manipulated variables and those that are subject variables, and understand the interpretation problems that accompany the use of subject variables.

- Recognize the factors that can reduce the statistical conclusion validity of an experiment.

- Describe how construct validity applies to the design of an experiment.

- Distinguish between the internal and external validity of a study.

- Describe the various factors affecting an experiment's external validity.

- Describe and be able to recognize the various threats to an experiment's internal validity.

- Recognize that external validity might not be important for all research but that internal validity is essential.

- Understand the ethical guidelines for running a subject pool.

When Robert Sessions Woodworth published his *Experimental Psychology* in 1938, the book's contents were already well known among psychologists. As early as 1909, Woodworth was giving his Columbia University students copies of a mimeographed handout called "Problems and Methods in Psychology," and a companion handout called "Laboratory Manual: Experiments in Memory, etc." appeared in 1912. By 1920, the manuscript filled 285 pages and was called "A Textbook of Experimental Psychology." After a 1932 revision, still in mimeograph form, the book finally was published in 1938. By then Woodworth's students were using it to teach their own students, and it was so widely known that the publisher's announcement of its publication said simply, "The Bible Is Out" (Winston, 1990).

The so-called Columbia bible was encyclopedic, with more than 823 pages of text and another 36 pages of references. After an introductory chapter, it was organized into 29 research topics such as memory, maze learning, reaction time, association, hearing, the perception of color, and thinking. Students wading through the text would learn about the methods used in each content area, and they would also learn virtually everything there was to know in 1938 about each topic.

The impact of the Columbia bible on the teaching of experimental psychology has been incalculable. Indeed, the teaching of experimental psychology today, and to some degree the structure of the book you are now reading, is largely cast in the mold set by Woodworth. In particular, he took the term *experiment*, until then loosely defined as virtually any type of empirical research, and gave it the definition it has in psychology today. In particular, he contrasted experimental with correlational research, a distinction now well known by research psychologists.

The defining feature of the experimental method was the manipulation of what Woodworth (1938) called an "independent variable," which affected what he called the "dependent variable." In his words, the experimenter "holds all the conditions constant except for one factor which is his 'experimental factor' or his 'independent variable.' The observed effect is the 'dependent variable' which in a psychological experiment is some characteristic of behavior or reported experience" (p. 2). Although Woodworth did not invent these terms, he was the first to use them as they are used routinely today.

While the experimental method manipulates independent variables, the correlational method, according to Woodworth (1938), "[m]easures two or more characteristics of the same individuals [and] computes the correlation of these characteristics. This method . . . has no 'independent variable' but treats all the measured variables alike" (p. 3). You will learn more about correlational research in later chapters. In this and the next three chapters, however, the focus will be on the experimental method, the researcher's most powerful tool for identifying cause-and-effect relationships. After all, as psychologists we seek to discover the causes of behavior; thus, the experimental method is the best tool to help up understand those causes and what effects they have on behavior.

Essential Features of Experimental Research

Since Woodworth's time, psychologists have thought of an **experiment** as a systematic research study in which the investigator directly varies some factor (or factors), holds all other factors constant, and observes the results of the variation. The factors under the control of the experimenter are called *independent variables*, the factors being held constant are the *extraneous variables*, and the behaviors measured are called *dependent variables*. Before we examine these concepts more closely, however, you should read Box 5.1, which describes the logical foundations of the experimental method in a set of rules proposed by the British philosopher John Stuart Mill in 1843.

BOX 5.1   ORIGINS—John Stuart Mill and the Rules of Inductive Logic

John Stuart Mill (1805–1873) was England's preeminent 19th century philosopher. Although he was known primarily as a political philosopher, much of his work has direct relevance for psychology. For example, his book on *The Subjection of Women* (1869) argued forcefully and well ahead of its time that women had abilities equal to those of men and ought to be treated equally with men. Of importance for our focus on methodology, in 1843, he published *A System of Logic, Ratiocinative and Inductive, Being a Connected View of the Principles of Evidence, and the Methods of Scientific Investigation* (in those days, they liked to pack all they could into a title!). In his *Logic*, Mill argued for the creation of a science of psychology (he called it *ethology*) on the grounds that while it might not reach the level of precision found in physics, it could do just as well as some other disciplines that were considered scientific at the time (meteorology was the example he used). He also laid out a set of methods that form the logical basis for what you will learn in this chapter and in the later discussion of correlation. The methods were those of "Agreement" and "Difference" (relevant for this chapter), and of "Concomitant Variation" (relevant for correlation, covered in Chapter 9).

Taken together, the methods of Agreement and Difference enable us to conclude, with a high degree of confidence (but not absolute certainty), that some factor, X, causes some result, Y. The Method of Agreement states that if X is regularly followed by Y, then X is *sufficient* for Y to occur, and could be a cause of Y—that is, "if X, then Y." The Method of Difference states that if X does not occur and Y also does not occur, then X is *necessary* for Y to occur— "if no X, then no Y." Taken together (what Mill called the Joint Method), the methods of Agreement and Difference provide the necessary and sufficient conditions (i.e., the immediate cause) for Y to happen.

To make this more concrete, suppose we are trying to determine if watching violent TV causes children to become aggressive. "Watching violent TV" is X, and "aggression" is Y. If we can determine that every time a child watches violent TV (X), the result is some act of aggression (Y), then we have satisfied the method of Agreement, and we can say that watching violent TV is enough (sufficient) to produce aggression. If the child watches violent TV (X), then aggression (Y) occurs ("If X, then Y"). If we can also show that whenever violent TV is not watched (not X), the child is not aggressive (not Y), then we can say that watching violent TV is necessary in order for aggression to occur. This satisfies the Method of Difference. If the child does not watch violent TV, aggression does not occur ("If no X, then no Y"). This combined outcome (Joint Method) would establish that watching TV causes aggression in children.

It is important to note that in the real world of research, the conditions described in these methods are never fully met. It is impossible to identify and measure what happens every time a child watches TV. Rather, the best one can do is to observe systematically as many examples as possible, under controlled conditions, and then draw conclusions with a certain amount of confidence, based on some form of statistical analysis. That is precisely what research psychologists do and, as you recall from the Chapter 1 discussion of scientific thinking, the reason why researchers regard all knowledge based on science to be tentative, pending additional research. As findings are replicated, confidence in them increases.

As you work through this chapter, especially at the point where you learn about studies with experimental and control groups, you will see that an experimental group (e.g., some children shown violent TV shows) accomplishes Mill's Method of Agreement, whereas a control group (e.g., other children not shown violent films) accomplishes the Method of Difference. Studies with both experimental and control groups meet the conditions of Mill's Joint Method.

Establishing Independent Variables

Any experiment can be described as a study investigating the effect of *X* on *Y*. The *X* is what Woodworth called the **independent variable**: It is the factor of interest to the experimenter, the one being studied to see if it will influence behavior (the "watching violent TV" in the John Stuart Mill example). It is sometimes called a *manipulated* variable or factor because the experimenter has complete control over it and is creating the situations research participants will encounter in the study. As you will see, the concept of an independent variable can also be stretched to cover *non-manipulated* or *subject variables*, but, for now, let us consider only those independent variables that are under the experimenter's total control. We will refer to them as *manipulated independent variables*.

All manipulated independent variables must have a minimum of two *levels*—that is, at the very least, an experiment involves a comparison between two situations (or *conditions*). For example, suppose a researcher is interested in the effects of caffeine on reaction time. Such a study requires at least two dosage levels of caffeine in order to make a comparison. This study would be described as an experiment with "amount of caffeine consumed" as the manipulated independent variable and two different dosages as the two levels of the independent variable. You could also say the study has two conditions: the two dosages. Of course, independent variables can have more than two levels. In fact, there are distinct advantages to adding levels beyond the minimum of two, as you will learn in Chapter 7.

As you recall from Chapter 3, experimental research can be either basic or applied, and it can be conducted either in the laboratory or in the field. Experiments that take place in the field are sometimes called **field experiments**. The term *field research* is a broader term for any empirical research outside the laboratory, including both experimental studies and studies using non-experimental methods.

Varieties of Manipulated Independent Variables

The range of factors that can be used as manipulated independent variables is limited only by the creative thinking of the researcher. However, independent variables that are manipulated in a study tend to fall into three somewhat overlapping categories: situational, task, and instructional variables.

Situational variables are features in the environment that participants might encounter. For example, in a helping behavior study, the researcher interested in studying the effect of the number of bystanders on the chances of help being offered might create a situation in which subjects encounter a person in need of help. Sometimes, the participant is alone with the person needing aid; at other times, the participant and the victim are accompanied by a group of either three or six bystanders. In this case, the independent variable is the number of potential helpers on the scene besides the participant, and the levels are zero, three, and six bystanders. Thus the experimenter has created three situations.

Sometimes, experimenters vary the type of task performed by subjects. One way to manipulate **task variables** is to give participants different kinds of problems to solve. For instance, research on the psychology of reasoning often involves giving people different kinds of logic problems to determine the kinds of errors people tend to make. Similarly, mazes can differ in degree of complexity, different types of illusions could be presented in a perception study, and so on.

Instructional variables are manipulated by telling different groups to perform a particular task in different ways. For example, students in a memory task who are all shown the same list of words might be given different instructions about how to memorize the list. Some might be told to form visual images of the words, others might be told to form associations between adjacent pairs of words, and still others might be told simply to repeat each word three times as it is presented.

It is possible to combine several types of independent variables in a single study. A study of the effects of crowding, task difficulty, and motivation on problem-solving ability could have participants placed in either a large or a small room, thereby manipulating crowding through the situational variable of room size. Some participants in each type of room could be given difficult crossword puzzles to solve and others less difficult ones—a task variable. Finally, an instructional variable could manipulate motivation by telling participants they will earn either $1 or $5 for completing the puzzles.

Control Groups

In some experiments, the independent variable is whether or not some experimental condition occurs. Some subjects get the treatment condition, and others do not. In a study of the effects of TV violence on children's aggressive behavior, for instance, some children might be shown a violent TV program, while others don't get to see it (they will probably be shown a non-violent TV program). The term **experimental group** is used as a label for the first situation, in which the treatment is present. Those in the second type of condition, in which treatment is withheld, are said to be in the **control group**. Ideally, the participants in a control group are identical to those in the experimental group in all ways except the control group participants do not get the experimental treatment. As you recall from Box 5.1, the conditions of the experimental group (shown violent TV) satisfy Mill's Method of Agreement (if violent TV, then aggression) and the control group (not shown violent TV) can satisfy the Method of Difference (if no violent TV, then no aggression). Thus, a simple experiment with an experimental and a control group is an example of Mill's Joint Method. In essence, the control group provides a baseline measure against which the experimental group's behavior can be compared. Think of it this way: control group = comparison group.

Please don't think control groups are necessary in all research, however. It is indeed important to *control* extraneous variables, as you are about to learn, but control *groups* occur only in research when it is important to have a comparison with some baseline level of performance. For example, suppose you were interested in the construct "sense of direction" and wanted to know whether a training program would help people avoid getting lost in new environments. In that study, a reasonable comparison would be between a training group and a control group that did not get any training. On the other hand, if your empirical question concerns gender differences in sense of direction, the comparison will be between a group of male subjects and a group of female subjects; neither would be considered a control group. You will learn about several specialized types of control groups in Chapter 7, the first of two chapters dealing with experimental design. For an example of a study comparing simple experimental and a control groups, consider this interesting study about superstition.

Research Example 6—Experimental and Control Groups

Is there such a thing as good luck? As a golfer, will you putt better if you think you're using a lucky ball? In a manual dexterity game, will you do better if others say they have their fingers crossed for you? Will you do better on a memory or an anagram task if you have your lucky charm with you? The answer to all these questions appears to be *yes*, according to a simple yet clever set of studies by Damisch, Stoberock, and Mussweiler (2010). In each of four studies, subjects in an experimental group were given reason to think they might be lucky; those in a control group were not given any reason to think that luck would occur. In the first study, subjects were asked to make 10 putts of 100 cm (just over 3 feet). Experimental group subjects were handed a golf ball and told, "Here is your ball. So far, it has turned out to be a lucky ball" (p. 1015); control group subjects were told, "This is the ball everyone has used so far" (p. 1015).

Here are the means (*M*) (average number of putts made) and standard deviations (*SD*) for the two groups:

$$\text{Experimental group}\left(\text{lucky ball}\right): \quad M = 6.42 \quad SD = 1.88$$
$$\text{Control group}\left(\text{no mention of luck}\right): \quad M = 4.75 \quad SD = 2.15$$

Recall from Chapter 4 that to achieve a significant difference between two groups in null hypothesis significance testing, there should be a noticeable difference between the mean scores for the groups and a relatively small amount of variability within each group. That happened in this case—the experimental group holed significantly more putts than the control group and the standard deviations are small; in addition, the effect size was determined to be large (Cohen's *d* equaled an impressive .83).

Damisch et al. (2010) reacted to the putting outcome as we suspect you might have—they weren't quite sure they believed such a minor thing ("you have a lucky ball") could make such a big difference. So they did three more experiments, all using the same basic design—experimental group subjects being given some indication they would have luck on their side, control group subjects given no such indication. Manipulating "luck" as the independent variable worked in all the experiments. Subjects believing luck would be with them outperformed controls on a manual dexterity task, a memory task, and a problem-solving task. In the dexterity task, the experimenter simply told subjects in the experimental group "I'll have my fingers crossed for you." In the memory and problem-solving tasks, experimental subjects were allowed to keep a "lucky charm" with them as they did the experiment. All three of these subsequent studies replicated the results of the one that measured putting performance. Of course, Damisch and her colleagues did not conclude that luck existed as an explanation for the results. Rather, based on some other measures they took, they concluded that those in the experimental group simply believed they would do well and, as a result of their enhanced "self-efficacy," did the kinds of things that might be expected to improve performance (e.g., concentrate harder than those in the control groups).

The concept of a control group has a long history. As just one example, Francis Galton had it in mind for his famous study on the efficacy of prayer that you learned about in Chapter 1. As you recall, he concluded that prayers had no measurable effect. When planning the study, Galton (1872) argued that for the study to be of any value, "prudent pious people must be compared with prudent materialistic people and not with the imprudent nor the vicious" (p. 126). That is, those who prayed (i.e., the pious, an experimental group) were to be compared with those who did not pray (i.e., the materialistic, a control group), but it was important that the two groups be alike in all other ways (e.g., prudent). You will learn in Chapter 6 that Galton was advocating the idea of creating comparable groups through a procedure of *matching*—selecting two groups carefully so that they are alike in all important ways except for the conditions being compared.

Controlling Extraneous Variables

After manipulating independent variables, the second feature of the experimental method is that the researcher tries to control **extraneous variables**. These are variables that are not of interest to the researcher but that might influence the behavior being studied if not controlled properly. As long as these are held constant, they present no danger to the study. In the "putt your lucky ball" study, for instance, putts attempted by subjects in both groups were always of the same length. In Galton's prayer study, it was important for both the pious and the non-pious to be equally "prudent." If a researcher fails to control extraneous variables, they can systematically influence the behavior being measured. The result is called *confounding*. A **confound** is any uncontrolled extraneous variable that co-varies with the independent variable and could provide an alternative explanation of the results. That is, a confounding variable changes in the same way that an independent variable changes (i.e., they co-vary) and, consequently, its effect cannot be distinguished from the effect of the independent variable. Hence, when a study has a confound, the results could be due to the effects of *either* the confounding variable or the independent variable, or some combination of the two, and there is no way to know which variable explains the results. Thus, results from studies with confounds are uninterpretable.

To illustrate confounding, consider a verbal learning experiment in which a researcher wants to show that students who try to learn a large amount of course material all at once don't do as well as those who spread their studying over several sessions—that is, massed practice (e.g., cramming the night before an exam) is predicted to be inferior to distributed practice. Three groups of students are selected, and each group is given the same chapter in a general psychology text to learn. Participants in the first group are given 3 hours on Monday to study the material. Participants in the second group are given 3 hours on Monday and 3 hours on Tuesday, and those in the final group get 3 hours each on Monday, Tuesday, and Wednesday. On Friday, all the groups are tested on the material. Table 5.1 shows the design. The results show that subjects in Group 3 score the highest, followed by those in Group 2; Group 1 subjects do not do well at all. On the basis of this outcome, the researcher concludes that distributed practice is superior to massed practice. Do you agree with this conclusion?

Table 5.1 **Confounding in a Hypothetical Distribution of Practice Experiment**

	Monday	Tuesday	Wednesday	Thursday	Friday
Group 1	3	—	—	—	Exam
Group 2	3	3	—	—	Exam
Group 3	3	3	3	—	Exam

Note: The 3s in each column equal the number of hours spent studying a chapter of a psychology text.

You probably don't (we hope) because there are two serious confounds in this study, and both should be easy for you to spot. The participants certainly differ in how their practice is distributed (1, 2, or 3 days), but they *also* differ in how much total practice they get during the week (3, 6, or 9 hours). This is a perfect example of a confound: it is impossible to tell if the results are due to one factor (distribution of practice) or the other (total practice hours). In other words, the two factors co-vary perfectly. The way to describe this situation is to say "the distribution of practice is confounded with total study hours." A second confound is perhaps less obvious but is equally problematic. It concerns the retention interval. The test is on Friday for everyone, but different amounts of time have elapsed between study and test for each group. Perhaps Group 3 did the best because they studied the material most recently and forgot the least amount. In this experiment, the distribution of practice is confounded both with total study hours and with retention interval. Each confound by itself could account for the results.

Table 5.2 gives you a convenient way to identify confounds. In the first column are the levels of the independent variable and in the final column are the results. The middle columns are extraneous variables that should be held constant through the use of appropriate methodological controls. If they are not kept constant, then confounding may occur. As you can see for the distributed practice example, the results could be explained by the variation in any of the first three columns, either individually or in combination. To correct the confound problem in this case, you must ensure the middle two columns each have the same terms in them. Thus, instead of 3, 6, or 9 hours for the first extraneous variable (EV#1), the total number of hours spent studying should be the same. Likewise, instead of 1, 2, or 3 days for EV#2, the number of days in the retention interval should be the same. Table 5.3 shows you one way to control for what is confounded in Table 5.1. As you can see, total study time and retention interval are held constant.

Table 5.2   **Identifying Confounds**

Levels of IV Distribution of Practice	EV 1 Study Hours	EV 2 Retention Interval	DV Retention Test Performance
1 day	3 hours	3 days	Lousy
2 days	6 hours	2 days	Average
3 days	9 hours	1 day	Great

IV = independent variable.
EV = extraneous variable.
DV = dependent variable.

Table 5.3   **Eliminating Confounds in a Hypothetical Distribution of Practice Experiment**

	Monday	Tuesday	Wednesday	Thursday	Friday
Group 1	—	—	—	3	Exam
Group 1	—	—	1.5	1.5	Exam
Group 1	—	1	1	1	Exam

A problem students sometimes have with understanding confounds is that they tend to use the term whenever they spot something in a study that might appear to be a flaw. For example, suppose the distribution of practice study included the statement that all the subjects in the study were between 60 and 65 years old. Some students reading the description might think there's a confound here that concerns age. What they really mean is they believe a wider range of ages ought to be used. They could be right, but age in this case is not a confound. Age would be a confound *only* if subjects in the three groups were of three *different* age ranges. If those in Group 1 were aged 60–65, those in Group 2 were 30–35, and those in Group 3 were 18–22, then a confound would exist. Group differences in the results could be due to the independent variable or to age; those in Group 3 might do better because their studying has be spread out, but they might do better simply because they are younger.

Learning to be aware of potential confounding factors and building appropriate ways to control for them is a scientific thinking skill that is difficult to develop. Not all confounds are as obvious as the massed/distributed practice example. We'll encounter the problem occasionally in the remaining chapters and address it again shortly when we discuss the *internal validity* of a study.

Measuring Dependent Variables

The third part of any experiment is measuring some behavior that is presumably being influenced by the independent variable. The term **dependent variable** is used to describe the behavior that is the measured outcome of a study. If, as mentioned earlier, an experiment can be described as the effect of X on Y and X is the independent variable, then Y is the dependent variable. In a study of the effects of TV violence on children's aggressiveness (the example from Box 5.1 on Mill's Joint Method), the dependent variable would be some measure of aggressiveness. In the distribution of practice study, it would be a measure of exam performance.

The credibility of any experiment and its chances of discovering anything of value depend partly on the decisions made about what behaviors to measure as dependent variables. In Chapter 3's discussion of operational definitions, we have already seen that empirical questions cannot be answered unless the terms are defined with some precision. When an experiment is designed, therefore, one key component concerns the operational definitions for the behaviors to be measured as dependent variables. Unless the behaviors are defined precisely in terms of their measurement, direct replication is impossible.

Deciding on dependent variables can be tricky. A useful guide is to know the prior research and use already-established dependent measures—those that have been shown to be valid and reliable. Sometimes, you have to develop a new measure, however, and when you do, a brief pilot study might help you avoid two major problems that can occur with poorly chosen dependent variables: ceiling and floor effects. A **ceiling effect** occurs when the average scores for the groups in the study are so high that no difference can be determined between conditions. For example, this can happen when your dependent measure is so easy that everyone gets a high score. Conversely, a **floor effect** happens when all the scores are extremely low, usually because the task is too difficult for everyone, once again producing a failure to find any differences between conditions.

One final point about variables: It is important to realize that a particular construct could be an independent, an extraneous, *or* a dependent variable, depending on the research problem at hand. An experimenter might manipulate a particular construct as an independent variable, try to control it as an extraneous factor, or measure it as a dependent variable. Consider the construct of anxiety, for instance. It could be a manipulated independent variable by telling participants (instructional independent variable) that they will experience shocks, either mild or painful, when they make errors on a simulated driving task. Anxiety could also be a factor that must be held constant in some experiments. For instance, if you wanted to evaluate the effects of a public speaking workshop on the ability of students to deliver a brief speech, you wouldn't want to video the students in one group without doing so in the other group as well. If everyone is videoed, then the level of anxiety created by that factor (video recording) is held constant for everyone. Finally, anxiety could be a dependent variable in a study of the effects of different types of exams (e.g., multiple choice versus essay) on the perceived test anxiety of students during final exam week. Some physiological measures of anxiety might be used in this case. Anxiety could also be considered a personality characteristic, with some people characteristically having more of it than others. This last possibility leads to our next topic.

SELF TEST

5.1

1. In a study of the effects of problem difficulty (easy or hard) and reward size ($1 or $5 for each solution) on an anagram problem-solving task, what are the independent and dependent variables?
2. What are extraneous variables and what happens if they are not controlled properly?
3. Explain how frustration could be an independent, extraneous, or dependent variable, depending on the study.

Subject Variables

Up to this point, the term *independent variable* has meant a factor directly manipulated by the researcher. An experiment compares one condition created by and under the control of the experimenter with another. However, in many studies, comparisons are made between groups of people who differ from each other in ways other than those directly manipulated by the researcher. Factors that are not directly manipulated by an experimenter are referred to variously as ex post facto variables, natural group variables, participant variables, or **subject variables**, which will be our focus here. Subject variables are already existing characteristics of the individuals participating in the study, such as gender, age, socioeconomic class, cultural group, intelligence, physical or psychiatric disorder, and any personality attribute you can name. When using subject variables in a study, the researcher cannot manipulate them directly but must *select* people for the conditions of the experiment by virtue of the characteristics they already have.

To see the differences between manipulated and subject variables, consider a hypothetical study of the effects of anxiety on maze learning in humans. You could *manipulate* anxiety directly by creating a situation in which one group is made anxious (told they'll be performing in front of a large audience, perhaps), while a second group is not (no audience). In that study, any person who volunteers could potentially wind up in one group or the other. To do the study using a *subject* variable, on the other hand, you would select two groups differing in their characteristic levels of anxiety and ask each to try the maze. The first group would be people who tend to be anxious all the time (as determined ahead of time, perhaps, by a personality test for anxiety proneness). The second group would include more relaxed people. Notice the major difference between this situation and one involving a manipulated variable. With anxiety as a subject variable, volunteers coming into the study cannot be placed into either of the conditions (anxious-all-the-time-Fred cannot be put into the low-anxiety group) but must be in one group or the other, depending on attributes they *already possess* upon entering the study.

Some researchers, true to Woodworth's original use of the term, prefer to reserve the term *independent variable* for variables directly manipulated by the experimenter. Others are willing to include subject variables as examples of a particular type of independent variable because the experimenter has some degree of control over them by virtue of the decisions involved in selecting them in the first place and because the statistical analyses will be the same in both cases. We take this latter position and will use the term *independent variable* in the broader sense. However, whether the term is used broadly (manipulated or subject) or narrowly (manipulated only), it is important that you understand the difference between a manipulated variable and a non-manipulated, subject variable both in terms of how the groups are formed in the study, and the kinds of conclusions that can be drawn from them.

Research Example 7—Using Subject Variables

One common type of research using subject variables examines differences between cultures. Ji, Peng, and Nisbett (2000) provide a nice example. They examined the implications of the differences between people raised in Asian cultures and those raised in Western cultures. In general, they pointed out that Asian-Americans, especially those with families from China, Korea, and Japan, have a "relatively holistic orientation, emphasizing relationships and connectedness" (p. 943) among objects, rather than on the individual properties of the objects themselves. Those from Western cultures, especially those deriving from the Greek "analytic" tradition, are "prone to focus more exclusively on the object, searching for those attributes of the object that would help explain and control its behavior" (p. 943).

This cultural difference led Ji et al. (2000) to make several predictions, including one that produced a study with two subject variables: culture and gender. For their dependent measure, they chose performance on a cognitive task that has a long history, the rod and frame test (RFT). While sitting in a darkened room, participants in an RFT study see an illuminated square frame projected on a screen in front of them, along with a separate illuminated straight line (rod) inside the frame. The frame can be oriented to various angles by the experimenter, and the participant's task is to move a device that changes the orientation of the rod. The goal is to make the rod perfectly vertical regardless of the frame's orientation. The classic finding (Witkin & Goodenough, 1977) is that some people (field independent) are quite able to bring the rod into a true vertical position, disregarding the distraction of the frame, while others (field dependent) adjust the rod with reference to the frame and not with reference to true vertical. Can you guess the hypothesis? The researchers predicted that participants from Asian cultures would be more likely to be field dependent than those from Western cultures. They also hypothesized greater field dependence for women, a prediction based on a typical finding in RFT studies. The standard RFT procedure was used in the same way it was used in past studies. So, in the replication terms you learned about in Chapter 3, part of this study (gender) involved direct replication and part (culture) involved conceptual replication.

Because the undergraduate population of the University of Michigan (where the research was conducted) included a large number of people originally from East Asia, Ji et al. (2000) were able to complete their study using students enrolled in general psychology classes there (in a few pages you'll be learning about university "subject pools"). They compared 56 European-Americans with 42 East Asian-Americans (most from China, Korea, and Japan) who had been living in the United States for an average of about 2.5 years. Students in the two cultural groups were matched in terms of SAT math scores, and each group had about an equal number of male and female participants.

As you can see from Figure 5.1, the results supported both hypotheses (larger error scores on the Y-axis indicated a greater degree of field dependence). The finding about women being more field dependent than men was replicated and that difference occurred in both cultures. In addition, the main finding was the difference between the cultures: Those from East Asian cultures were more field dependent than the European Americans. As Ji et al. (2000) described the outcome, the relative field independence of the Americans reflected their tendency to be "more attentive to the object and its relation to the self than to the field" (p. 951), while the field dependence of those from Asian cultures tended to be "more attentive to the field and to the relationship between the object and the field" (p. 952). One statistical point worth noting relates to the concept of an *outlier*, introduced in Chapter 4. Each subject did the RFT task 16 times

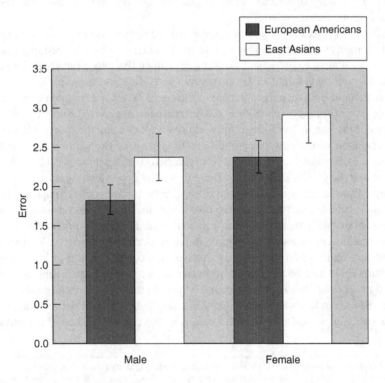

FIGURE 5.1
Gender and cultural differences in the rod and frame test, from Ji, Peng, and Nisbett's (2000) cross-cultural study.

and, on average, 1.2 of the scores were omitted from the analysis because they were significantly beyond the normal range of scores. Their operational definition of outlier was somewhat technical, but related to the distance from the interquartile range, another concept you recall from Chapter 4.

Only a study using manipulated independent variables can be called an experiment in the strictest sense of the term; it is sometimes called a true experiment (which sounds a bit pretentious and carries the unfortunate implication that other studies are somehow false). Studies using independent variables that are *subject* variables are occasionally called *ex post facto studies*, *natural groups studies*, or *quasi experiments* (*quasi* meaning "to some degree" here).[1] Studies often include both manipulated and subject independent variables, as you will learn in Chapter 8. Being aware of subject variables is important because they affect the kinds of conclusions that can be drawn.

Drawing Conclusions When Using Subject Variables

Put a little asterisk next to this section—it is extremely important. Recall from Chapter 1 that one of the goals of research in psychology is to discover explanations for behavior—that is, we wish to know what caused some behavior to occur. Simply put, with manipulated variables, conclusions about the causes of behavior can be made with some degree of confidence; with subject variables, causal conclusions cannot be drawn. The reason has to do with the amount of control held by the experimenter.

With manipulated variables, the experiment can meet the criteria listed in Chapter 1 for demonstrating causality. The independent variable precedes the dependent variable and can be considered the most reasonable explanation for the results, assuming no confounds are present. In other words, if you vary one factor and successfully hold all else constant, the results can be attributed *only* to the factor varied.

When using subject variables, however, the experimenter can vary a factor (i.e., select participants having certain characteristics) but cannot hold all else constant. Selecting participants who are high or low on anxiety proneness does not guarantee the two groups will be equivalent in other ways. In fact, they might differ in several ways (e.g., self-confidence, tendency to be depressed) that could influence the outcome of the study. When a difference between the groups occurs in this type of study, we cannot say the differences were *caused* solely by the subject variable. In terms of the conditions for causality, although we can say the independent variable precedes the dependent variable, we cannot eliminate alternative explanations for the relationship because certain extraneous factors cannot be controlled. When subject variables are present, all we can say is that the groups performed differently on the dependent measure.

An example from social psychology might help clarify the distinction. Suppose you were interested in altruistic behavior and wanted to see how it was affected by the construct of "self-esteem." The study could be done in two ways. First, you could manipulate self-esteem directly by first giving subjects an achievement test. By providing different kinds of false feedback about their performance on the test, either positive or negative, self-esteem could be raised or lowered temporarily. The participants could then be asked to do volunteer work to see if those feeling good about themselves would be more likely to help.[2] A second way to do this study is to give participants a valid and reliable self-esteem test and select those who score high or low on the measure as the participants for the two groups. Self-esteem in this case is a subject variable; half of the participants will

---

[1] The term *quasi-experimental design* is actually a broader designation referring to any type of design in which participants cannot be randomly assigned to the groups being studied (Cook & Campbell, 1979). These designs are often found in applied research and will be elaborated in Chapter 11.

[2] Manipulating self-esteem raises ethical questions that were considered in a study described in Chapter 2 by Sullivan and Deiker (1973).

naturally have low self-esteem, while the other half will naturally have high self-esteem. As in the first study, these two groups of people then could be asked about volunteering.

In the first study, differences in volunteering can be traced *directly* to the self-esteem manipulation. If all other factors are properly controlled, the temporary feeling of increased or decreased self-esteem is the *only* thing that could have produced the differences in helping. In the second study, however, you cannot say high self-esteem is the direct cause of the helping behavior; all you can say is that people with high self-esteem are more likely to help than those with low self-esteem. Your conclusion would then be limited to making educated guesses about the reasons why this might be true because these participants may differ from each other in other ways unknown to you. For instance, people with high self-esteem might have had prior experience in volunteering, and this experience might have had the joint effect of raising or strengthening their characteristic self-esteem and increasing the chances they would volunteer in the future. Or they might have greater expertise in the specific volunteering tasks (e.g., public speaking skills). As you will see in Chapters 9 and 10, this difficulty in interpreting research with subject variables is exactly the same problem encountered when trying to draw conclusions from correlational research (Chapter 9) and quasi-experimental research (Chapter 10).

Returning for a moment to the Ji et al. (2000) study, which featured the subject variables of culture and gender, the authors were careful to avoid drawing conclusions about causality. The word *cause* never appears in their article, and the descriptions of results are always in the form "this group scored higher than this other group." In their words, "European Americans made fewer mistakes on the RFT than East Asians, . . . [and] men made fewer mistakes than women" (p. 950).

Before moving on to the discussion of the validity of experimental research, read Box 5.2. It identifies the variables in a classic study you probably recall from your general psychology course—one of the so-called Bobo doll experiments that first investigated imitative aggression. Working through the example will help you apply your knowledge of independent, extraneous, and dependent variables and will allow you to see how manipulated and subject variables are often encountered in the same study.

BOX 5.2   CLASSIC STUDIES—Bobo Dolls and Aggression

Ask any student who has just completed a course in child, social, or personality psychology (perhaps even general psychology) to tell you about the Bobo doll studies (see Figure 5.2). The response will be immediate recognition and a brief description along the lines of "Oh, yes, the studies showing that children will punch an inflated doll if they see an adult doing it." A description of one of these studies is a good way to clarify the differences between independent, extraneous, and dependent variables. The study was published by Albert Bandura and his colleagues in 1963 and is entitled "Imitation of Film-Mediated Aggressive Models" (Bandura, Ross, & Ross, 1963).

Establishing Independent Variables

The study included both manipulated and subject variables. The major manipulated variable was the type of experience that preceded the opportunity for aggression. There

were four levels, including three experimental groups and one control group.

Experimental Group 1: real-life aggression (children directly observed an adult model aggressing against a 5-foot-tall Bobo doll)

Experimental Group 2: human film aggression (children observed a film of an adult model aggressing against Bobo)

Experimental Group 3: cartoon film aggression (children observed a cartoon of "Herman the Cat" aggressing against a cartoon Bobo)

Control Group: no exposure to aggressive models

The non-manipulated independent variable (subject variable) was gender. Male and female children from the Stanford University Nursery School (mean age = 52 months) were the participants in the study. (Actually, there was also

(continued)

BOX 5.2   (CONTINUED)

The Drs. Nicholas and Dorothy Cummings Center for the History of Psychology, The University of Akron.

FIGURE 5.2
One of Bandura's Bobo dolls, donated by Bandura to the Center for the History of Psychology at the University of Akron.

another manipulated variable; participants in Groups 1 and 2 were exposed to either a same-sex or opposite-sex model.) The basic procedure of the experiment was to expose the children to some type of aggressive model (or not, for the control group) and then put them into a room full of toys, including a 3-foot-tall Bobo doll,* thereby giving the children the opportunity to be aggressive themselves.

Controlling Extraneous Variables

Several possible confounds were avoided. First, whenever a child was put into the room with the toys to see if aggressive

behavior would occur, the toys were always arranged in exactly the same way "in order to eliminate any variation in behavior due to mere placement of the toys in the room" (Bandura et al., 1963, p. 5). Second, participants in all four groups were mildly frustrated before being given a chance to aggress. They were allowed to play for a few minutes with some very attractive toys and then were told by the experimenter that the toys were special and were being reserved for some other children. Thus, *all* of the children had an approximately equivalent increase in their degree of emotional arousal just prior to the time they were given the opportunity to act aggressively. In other words, any differences in aggressiveness could be attributed to the imitative effects and not to any emotional differences between the groups.

---

* Notice that the adults hit a *5-foot tall* Bobo, but the children were given the opportunity to hit a smaller doll, a *3-foot* Bobo. This is a nice design feature in the study. Can you see why?

Measuring Dependent Variables

Several measures of aggression were used in this study. Aggressive responses were categorized as imitative, partially imitative, or non-imitative, depending on how closely they matched the model's behavior. For example, the operational definition of imitative aggressive behaviors included striking the doll with a wooden mallet, punching it in the nose, and kicking it. Partially imitative behaviors included hitting something else with the mallet and sitting on the doll but not hitting it. Non-imitative aggression included shooting darts from an available dart gun at targets other than Bobo and acting aggressively toward other objects in the room.

Briefly, the results of the study were that children in Groups 1, 2, and 3 showed significantly more aggressive behavior than those in the control group, but the same amount of overall aggression occurred regardless of the type of modeling. Also, boys were more aggressive than girls in all conditions; some gender differences also occurred in the form of the aggression: girls "were more inclined than boys to sit on the Bobo doll but [unlike the boys] refrained from punching it" (Bandura et al., 1963, p. 9). Figure 5.3 summarizes the results.

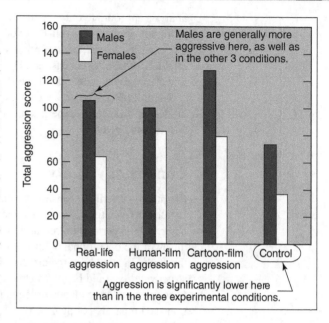

FIGURE 5.3

Data from Bandura, Ross, and Ross's Bobo study (1963) of the effects of imitation on aggression.

The Validity of Experimental Research

Chapter 4 introduced the concept of validity in the context of measurement. The term also applies to research methodology as a whole. Just as a measure is valid if it measures what it is supposed to measure, psychological research is said to be valid if it provides the understanding about behavior it is supposed to provide. This section of the chapter introduces four types of validity, following the scheme first outlined by Cook and Campbell (1979) for research in field settings but applicable to any research in psychology. The four types of validity are statistical conclusion validity, construct validity (again), external validity, and, of major importance, internal validity.

Statistical Conclusion Validity

The previous chapter introduced you to the use of statistics in psychology. In particular, you learned about measurement scales, the distinction between descriptive and inferential statistics, and the basics of hypothesis testing. **Statistical conclusion validity** concerns the extent to which the researcher uses statistics properly and draws the appropriate conclusions from the statistical analysis.

The statistical conclusion validity of a study can be reduced in several ways. First, researchers might do the wrong analysis or violate some of the assumptions required for performing a particular analysis. For instance, the data for a study might be measured using an ordinal scale, thereby requiring the use of a particular type of statistical procedure, but the researcher mistakenly uses an analysis appropriate only for interval or ratio data. Another factor reducing the statistical validity of a study concerns the reliability of the measures used. If the dependent measures are not reliable, there will be a great deal of error variability, which reduces the chances of finding a significant effect. If a true effect exists (i.e., H_0 should be rejected) but low reliability results in a failure to find that effect, the outcome is a Type II error, which reduces the statistical conclusion validity.

Careful researchers decide on the statistical analysis at the same time they plan the experimental design. In fact, no experiment should ever be designed without thought given to how the data will be analyzed.

Construct Validity

Chapter 4 described construct validity in the context of measuring psychological constructs: It refers to whether a test truly measures some construct (e.g., self-efficacy, connectedness to nature). In experimental research, *construct validity* has a related meaning, referring to the adequacy of the operational definitions for *both* the independent and the dependent variables used in the study. In a study of the effects of TV violence on children's aggression, questions about construct validity could be (a) whether the programs chosen by the experimenter are the best choices to contrast violent with nonviolent television programming, and (b) whether the operational definitions and measures of aggression used are the best that could be chosen. If the study used violent cartoon characters (e.g., Tom and Jerry) compared to nonviolent characters (e.g., Winnie the Pooh), someone might argue that children's aggressive behavior is unaffected by fantasy; hence, a more *valid* manipulation of the independent variable, called "level of filmed violence," would involve showing children realistic films of people that varied in the amount of violence portrayed.

Similarly, someone might criticize the appropriateness of a measure of aggression used in a particular study. This, in fact, has been a problem in research on aggression. For rather obvious ethical reasons, you cannot design a study that results in subjects pounding each other into submission. Instead, aggression has been defined operationally in a variety of ways, some of which might seem to you to be more valid (e.g., angered participants led to believe they are delivering electric shocks to another person) than others (e.g., horn honking by frustrated drivers). As was true in our earlier discussion of construct validity, when the emphasis was on measurement, the validity of the choices about exactly how to define independent and dependent variables develops over time as accumulated research fits into a coherent and theoretically meaningful pattern.

External Validity

Experimental psychologists have been criticized for knowing a great deal about undergraduate students and white rats and very little about anything else. This is, in essence, a criticism of **external validity**, the degree to which research findings generalize beyond the specific context of the experiment being conducted. For research to achieve the highest degree of external validity, it is argued, its results should generalize in three ways: to other populations, to other environments, and to other times.

Other Populations

The comment about rats and undergraduates fits here. As we saw in Chapter 2, part of the debate about the appropriateness of animal research has to do with how well this research provides explanations relevant for human behavior. Concerning undergraduates, recall that Milgram deliberately avoided using college students, selecting adults from the general population as subjects for his obedience studies. The same cannot be said of most psychologists, however. In an analysis of all empirical papers in six top-tier psychology journals published between 2003 and 2007,

Arnett (2008) reported that 68% of participants were from the United States alone, and, including the U.S., 96% of participants were from Western industrialized countries. Furthermore, 67% of U.S. study participants and 80% of participants in other countries were undergraduate students. Henrich, Heine, and Norenzayan (2010) suggested that undergraduate students are "a truly unusual group" (p. 61) and "outliers within an outlier population" (p. 78) referring to them as WEIRD – or "people from Western, Educated, Industrialized, Rich, and Democratic societies" (p. 61). They argued that researchers must be extremely careful when generalizing their results to human beings in general when their sample (i.e., likely college undergraduates) represents a very small subset of the global population. However, Sears (1986) pointed out that many research areas (e.g., perception, memory, and attention) produce outcomes relatively unaffected by the special characteristics of college students, and there is no question that students exist in large numbers and are readily available. One prominent memory researcher (Roediger, 2004) went so far as to argue that college students were the *ideal* subjects for his research: "Millions of years of evolution have designed a creature that is a learning and memorizing marvel. Students in my experiments have also been carefully selected through 12 or more years of education before they get to my lab. The world could not have arranged a more ideal subject" (p. 46). Some special ethical considerations apply when using college students, especially when recruiting them from introductory psychology courses. Box 5.3 lists some guidelines for using a "subject pool" ethically.

BOX 5.3   ETHICS—Recruiting Participants: Everyone's in the Pool

Most research psychologists are employed by colleges and universities and consequently are surrounded by an available supply of participants for their research. Because students may not readily volunteer to participate in research, most university psychology departments establish what is called a **subject pool** or participant pool. The term refers to a group of students, typically those enrolled in introductory psychology classes, who are asked to participate in research as part of a course requirement. If you are a student at a large university, you probably had this experience when you took your introductory psychology course. At a large university, if 800 students take the intro course each semester and each student signs up for three studies, 2,400 participants are available to researchers.

Subject pools are convenient for researchers, and they are defended on the grounds that research participation is part of the educational process (Kimmel, 2007). Ideally, students acquire insight into the research process by being in the middle of experiments and learning something about the psychological phenomena being investigated. To maintain the "voluntary" nature, students are given the opportunity to complete the requirement with alternatives other than direct research participation. Problems exist, however. A study by Sieber and Saks (1989), for example, found

evidence that 89% of 366 departments surveyed had pools that failed to meet at least one of the APA's recommendations (below). Critics sometimes argue that the pools are not really voluntary, that alternative activities (e.g., writing papers) are often so onerous and time-consuming that students are effectively compelled to sign up for the research. On the other hand, a study by Trafimow, Madson, and Gwizdowski (2006) found that, when given a choice between research participation and a brief paper that was described as requiring the same amount of effort as participation, most students opted for participation, and a substantial number (43.5% of those surveyed) indicated that participation in research while in introductory psychology had increased their interest in psychology.

Although there is potential for abuse, many psychology departments try to make the research experience educational for students. For example, during debriefing for a memory experiment, the participant/student could be told how the study relates to the information in the memory chapter of the text being used in the introductory course. Many departments also include creative alternative activities. These include having nonparticipating students (a) observe ongoing studies and record their observations, (b) participate in community volunteer work, or (c) attend

(continued)

BOX 5.3   (CONTINUED)

a research presentation by a visiting scholar and write a brief summary of it (Kimmel, 2007; McCord, 1991). Some studies have shown that students generally find research participation valuable, especially if researchers make an attempt to tie the participation to the content of the introductory psychology course (e.g., Landrum & Chastain, 1999; Leak, 1981).

The APA (1982, pp. 47–48) has provided guidelines for recruiting students as research participants, the main points being these:

- Students should be aware of the requirement before signing up for the course.

- Students should get a thorough description of the requirement on the first day of class, including a clear description of alternative activities if they opt not to serve as research subjects.

- Alternative activities must equal research participation in time and effort and, like participation, must have educational value.

- All proposals for research using subject pools must have prior IRB approval.

- Special effort must be made to treat students courteously.

- There must be a clear and simple procedure for students to complain about mistreatment without their course grade being affected.

- All other aspects of the APA ethics code must be rigorously followed.

- The psychology department must have a mechanism in place to provide periodic review of subject pool policies.

Testing only undergraduate students is only one example of the concern about generalizing to other groups. Another has to do with gender. Some of psychology's most famous research has been limited by studying only males (or, less frequently, only females) but drawing conclusions as if they apply to everyone. Perhaps the best-known example is Lawrence Kohlberg's research on children's moral development. Kohlberg (1964) asked adolescent boys (aged 10–16) to read and respond to brief accounts of various moral dilemmas. On the basis of the boys' responses, Kohlberg developed a six-stage theory of moral development that became a fixture in developmental psychology texts. At the most advanced stage, the person acts according to a set of universal principles based on preserving justice and individual rights.

Kohlberg's theory has been criticized on external validity grounds. For example, Gilligan (1982) argued that Kohlberg's model overlooked important gender differences in thinking patterns and in how moral decisions are made. Males may place the highest value on individual rights, but females tend to value the preservation of individual relationships. Hence, girls responding to some of Kohlberg's moral dilemmas might not seem to be as morally "advanced" as boys, but this is due to the bias of the entire model because Kohlberg sampled only boys, according to Gilligan.

Research psychologists also are careful about generalizing results from one culture to another. For example, "individualist" cultures are said to emphasize the unique person over the group, and personal responsibility and initiative are valued. On the other hand, the group is more important than the individual in "collectivist" cultures (Triandis, 1995). Hence, research conclusions based on just one culture might not be universally applicable. Again, Henrich et al. (2010) reviewed many differences between WEIRD (Western, Educated, Industrialized, Rich, and Democratic) people compared to other populations, and many psychological theories are less clear when one considers other cultures or populations. For example, Research Example 7 found a cultural difference in field dependence. As another example, most children in the United States are taught to place great value on personal achievement. In Japan, on the other hand, children learn that if they stand out from the crowd, they might diminish the value of others in the group; individual achievement is not as valuable. One study found that personal achievement was associated with positive emotions for American students but with *negative* emotions for Japanese students (Kitayama,

Markus, Matsumoto, & Norasakkunkit, 1997). To conclude that feeling good about individual achievement is a universal human trait would be a mistake. Does this mean all research in psychology should make cross-cultural comparisons? No. It just means conclusions must be drawn cautiously and with reference to the group studied in the research project.

Other Environments

Besides generalizing to other types of individuals, externally valid results are applicable to other settings. This problem is the basis for the occasional criticism of laboratory research mentioned in Chapter 3: It is sometimes said to be artificial and too far removed from real life. Recall from the discussion of basic and applied research (Chapter 3) that the laboratory researcher's response to criticisms about artificiality is to use Aronson's concept of experimental reality. The important thing is that people are involved in the study; mundane reality is secondary. In addition, laboratory researchers argue that some research is designed purely for theory testing and, as such, whether the results apply to real-life settings is less relevant than whether the results provide a good test of the theory (Mook, 1983).

Nonetheless, important developments in many areas of psychology have resulted from attempts to study psychological phenomena in real-life settings. A good example concerns the history of research on human memory. For much of the 20th century, memory research occurred largely in the laboratory, where countless undergraduate students memorized seemingly endless lists of words, nonsense syllables, strings of digits, and so on. The research created a comprehensive body of knowledge about basic memory processes that has value for the development of theories about memory and cognition, but whether principles discovered in the lab generalized to real-life memory situations was not clear. Change occurred in the 1970s, led by Cornell's Ulric Neisser. In *Cognition and Reality* (1976), he argued that the laboratory tradition in cognitive psychology, while producing important results, nonetheless had failed to yield enough useful information about information processing in real-world contexts. He called for more research concerning what he referred to as **ecological validity**—research with relevance for the everyday cognitive activities of people trying to adapt to their environment. Experimental psychologists, Neisser urged, "must make a greater effort to understand cognition as it occurs in the ordinary environment and in the context of natural purposeful activity. This would not mean an end to laboratory experiments, but a commitment to the study of variables that are ecologically important rather than those that are easily manageable" (p. 7).

Neisser's call to arms was embraced by many cognitive researchers, and the 1980s and 1990s saw increased study of such topics as eyewitness memory (e.g., Loftus, 1979) and the long-term recall of subjects learned in school, such as Spanish (e.g., Bahrick, 1984). And as you might guess, the concept of ecological validity found its way into many areas of psychology, not just cognitive psychology. In social psychology, the topic of interpersonal attraction, for instance, Finkel and Eastwick (2008) hit on the creative idea of using a speed-dating format for their research. As you probably know, in speed dating, couples pair off for a brief period of time and introduce themselves to each other and then move on to subsequent pairings. If the event includes 10 men and 10 women, for instance, the men and women will be paired together randomly, interact for perhaps 5 minutes, and then a new pairing will occur, leading to another 5-minute event, and so on, until each man has interacted with each woman. Then (or sometimes after each pairing, to avoid memory problems) all 20 people complete a survey indicating how they perceived each of the other persons they met, and organizers arrange for pairs that seem attracted to each other to meet again on their own. Finkel and Eastwick argued that the procedure is ideal for research—there is a high degree of control over the interactions (e.g., each lasts a fixed amount of time), there is a great opportunity to collect mountains of data (e.g., eye contact data can be matched to attractiveness judgments), and the procedure has a high degree of ecological validity. It is a real-life event populated with people who are genuinely interested in meeting others and perhaps developing a continuing relationship, and it resembles other kinds of circumstances where couples meet for the first time (e.g., a blind date).

Other Times

The third way in which external validity is sometimes questioned has to do with the longevity of results or the historical era during which a particular experiment was completed. An example is the study used to illustrate an ordinal scale in Chapter 4. Korn, Davis, and Davis (1991) found that department chairpersons ranked B. F. Skinner first on a list of top 10 contemporary psychologists. But Skinner had died just the year before and his lifetime achievements were highly visible at the time. Replicating that study 25 years later might very well produce a different outcome. As an older example, some of the most famous experiments in the history of psychology are the conformity studies done by Solomon Asch in the 1950s (e.g., Asch, 1956). These experiments were completed at a time when conservative values were dominant in the United States, the "red menace" of the Soviet Union was a force to be concerned about, and conformity and obedience to authority were valued in American society. In that context, Asch found that college students were remarkably susceptible to conformity pressures. Would the same be true today? Would the factors Asch found to influence conformity (e.g., group consensus) operate in the same way now? In general, research concerned with more fundamental processes (e.g., cognition) stands the test of time better than research involving social factors that may be embedded in historical context.

A Note of Caution about External Validity

Although external validity has value under many circumstances, it is important to point out that it is not often a major concern in the design of a research project. Some (e.g., Mook, 1983) have even criticized the use of the term because it carries the implication that research low in external validity is therefore "invalid." Yet there are many examples of research, completed in the laboratory under the so-called artificial conditions, which have great value for the understanding of human behavior. Consider research on "false memory," for example (Roediger & McDermott, 1995). The typical laboratory strategy is to give people a list of words to memorize, including a number of words from the same category—"sleep," for instance. The list might include the words dream, bed, pillow, nap, and so on, but not the broader term sleep. When recalling the list, many people recall the word *sleep* and they are often confident the word was on the list. That is, a laboratory paradigm exists demonstrating that people can sometimes remember something with confidence that they did not experience. The phenomenon has relevance for eyewitness memory (jurors pay more attention to confident eyewitnesses, even if they are wrong), but the procedure is far removed from an eyewitness context. It might be judged by some to be low in external validity. Yet there is much research that continues to explore the theoretical basis for false memory, determining, for instance, the limits of the phenomenon and exactly how it occurs. Eventually, that research will produce a body of knowledge that comprehensively explains the false memory phenomenon.

In summary, the external validity of a research finding increases as it applies to other people, places, and times. But must researchers design a study that includes many groups of people, takes place in several settings, including "realistic" ones, and is repeated every decade? Of course not. External validity is not determined by an individual research project; it accumulates over time as research is replicated in various contexts. Indeed, for the researcher designing a study, considerations of external validity pale compared to the importance of our next topic.

Internal Validity

The final type of experimental validity described by Cook and Campbell (1979) is called **internal validity**—the degree to which an experiment is methodologically sound and confound-free. In an internally valid study, the researcher feels confident that the results, as measured by the dependent variable, are directly associated with the independent variable and are not the result of some other, uncontrolled factor. In a study with confounding factors, as we've already seen in the massed/distributed practice example, the results are uninterpretable. The outcome could be the result of the independent variable, the confounding variable(s), or some combination of both, and there is no clear way to decide. Such a study would be quite low in internal validity.

SELF TEST

5.2

1. Explain how anxiety could be both a manipulated variable and a subject variable.
2. In the famous Bobo doll study, what were the manipulated and the subject variables?
3. What is the basic difference between internal and external validity?
4. The study on interpersonal attraction during speed dating was used to illustrate which form of validity?

Threats to Internal Validity

Any uncontrolled extraneous factor (i.e., the confounds you learned about earlier in the chapter) can reduce a study's internal validity, but a number of problems require special notice (Cook & Campbell, 1979). These problems or threats to internal validity are notably dangerous when control groups are absent, an issue that sometimes occurs in an applied form of research called *program evaluation* (see Chapter 11). Many of these threats occur in studies that extend over a period during which several measures are taken. For example, participants might receive a pretest, an experimental treatment of some kind, and then a posttest, and maybe even a follow-up test. Ideally, the treatment should produce a positive effect that can be assessed by observing changes from the pretest to the posttest, changes that are maintained in the follow-up. A second general type of threat occurs when comparisons are made between groups said to be "nonequivalent." These so-called subject selection problems can interact with the other threats to internal validity.

Studies Extending Over Time

Do students learn general psychology better if the course is self-paced and computerized? If a college institutes a program to reduce test anxiety, can it be shown that it works? If you train people in various mnemonic strategies, will it improve their memories? These are all empirical questions that ask whether people will change over time as the result of some experience (a course, a program, and memory training). To judge whether change occurred, one procedure is to evaluate people prior to the experience with a **pretest**. Then, after the experience, a **posttest** measure is taken. Please note that although we will be using pretests and posttests to illustrate several threats to internal validity, these threats can occur in any study extending over time when participants are tested multiple times, whether or not pretests are used.

The ideal outcome for the examples we've just described is that, at the end of the period for the study, people (a) know general psychology better than they did at the outset, (b) are less anxious in test taking than they were before, or (c) show improvement in their memory. A typical research design includes pretests and posttests and compares experimental and control groups:

Experimental :   pretest   → *treatment* →   posttest

Control :   pretest   →   posttest

If this type of procedure occurs without a control group, there are several threats to internal validity. For example, suppose we are trying to evaluate the effectiveness of a college's program to help incoming students who suffer from test anxiety—that is, they have decent study skills and seem to know the material, but they are so anxious during exams they don't perform well on them. During freshman orientation, first-year students complete several questionnaires, including one that serves as a pretest for test anxiety. Let's assume that the scores can range from 20 to 100, with higher scores indicating greater anxiety. Some incoming students who score very high (i.e., they have the greatest need for the program) are asked to participate in the college's test anxiety program, which includes relaxation training, study skills training, and other techniques. Three months later, these students are assessed again for test anxiety, and the results look like this:

pretest *treatment* posttest
90 70

Thus, the average pretest score of those selected for the program is 90, and the average posttest score is 70. Assuming that the difference is statistically significant, what would you conclude? Did the treatment program work? Was the change due to the treatment, or could other factors have been involved? We hope you can see several ways of interpreting this outcome and that it is not at all certain the program worked.

History and Maturation

Sometimes, an event outside of the study occurs between pre- and post-testing that produces large changes unrelated to the treatment program itself; when this happens, the study is confounded by the threat of **history**. For example, suppose the college in the above example decided that grades are counterproductive to learning and that all courses will henceforth be graded on a pass/fail basis. Furthermore, suppose that this decision came after the pretest for test anxiety and in the middle of the treatment program for reducing anxiety. The posttest might show a huge drop in anxiety, but this result could very likely be due to the historical event of the college's change in grading policy rather than to the program. Wouldn't you be a little more relaxed about this research methods course if grades weren't an issue?

In a similar fashion, the program for test anxiety involves students at the very start of their college careers, so changes in scores could also be the result of a general **maturation** of these students as they become accustomed to college life. As you probably recall, the first semester of college was a time of real change in your life. Maturation, or developmental changes that occur with the passage of time, is always a concern whenever a study extends over time.

Notice that if a control group is used, the experimenter can account for the effects of both history and maturation. These potential threats could be ruled out and the test anxiety program deemed effective if these results occurred:

Experimental : pretest *treatment* posttest
90 70
Control : pretest posttest
90 90

On the other hand, history or maturation or both would have to be considered as explanations for the changes in the experimental group if the control group scores also dropped to 70 on the posttest.

Regression to the Mean

To regress is to go back, in this case in the direction of a mean (average) score. Hence, the phenomenon described here is sometimes called **regression to the mean**. In essence, it refers to the fact that if the first score from a subject is an extreme score, then the second or third score from the same person will be closer to whatever the mean is for the larger set of scores. This is because, for a large set of scores, most will cluster around the mean and only a few will be far removed from the mean (i.e., extreme scores). Imagine you are selecting some score randomly from the normal distribution in Figure 5.4. Most of the scores center around the mean, so, if you make a random selection, you'll most likely choose a score near the mean (*X* on the left-hand graph of Figure 5.4). However, suppose you happen to select one that is far removed from the mean (i.e., an extreme score: *Y*). If you then choose again, are you most likely to pick

   a. the same extreme score again?

   b. a score even more extreme than the first one?

   c. a score less extreme (i.e., closer to the mean) than the first one?

Our guess is you've chosen alternative "c," which means you understand the basic concept of regression to the mean. To take a more concrete example (refer to the right-hand graph of Figure 5.4), suppose you know that on the average (based on several hundred throws), Ted can throw a baseball 300 feet. Then he throws one 380 feet. If you were betting on his *next* throw, where would you put your money?

   a. 380 feet

   b. 420 feet

   c. 330 feet

Again, you've probably chosen *c*, further convincing yourself that you get the idea of the regression phenomenon. But what does this have to do with our study about test anxiety?

In a number of pre-post studies, people are selected for some treatment because they've made an *extreme* score on the pretest. Thus, in the test anxiety study, participants were selected because on the pretest they scored very high for anxiety. On the posttest, their anxiety scores might be lower than on the pretest, but the change in scores could be due to regression to the mean, at least in part, rather than the result of the anxiety improvement program. Once again, a control group of equivalent high-anxiety participants would enable the researcher to control for regression to the mean. For instance, the following outcome would suggest regression to the

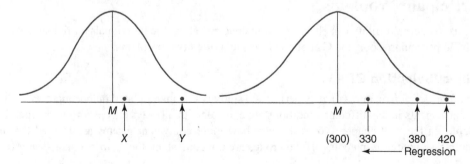

FIGURE 5.4
Regression to the mean.

mean might be involved,[3] but the program nonetheless seemed to have an effect. Can you see why this is so?

Experimental :	pretest	*treatment*	posttest	
	90		70	
Control :	pretest		posttest	
	90		80	

Regression to the mean can cause a number of problems and were probably the culprit in some early studies that erroneously questioned the effectiveness of the well-known Head Start program. That particular example will be taken up in Chapter 11 as an example of problems involved in assessing large-scale, federally supported programs.

Testing and Instrumentation

Testing is considered a threat to internal validity when the mere fact of taking a pretest has an effect on posttest scores. There could be a practice effect of repeated testing, or aspects of the pretest could sensitize participants to something about the program. For example, if the treatment program is a self-paced, computerized psychology course, the pretest would be a test of knowledge. Participants might be sensitized by the pretest to topics about which they seem to know nothing; they could then pay more attention to those topics during the course and do better on the posttest as a result.

Instrumentation is a problem when the measurement instrument changes from pretest to posttest. In the self-paced psychology course mentioned earlier, the pretest and posttest wouldn't be the same but would presumably be equivalent in level of difficulty. However, if the posttest happened to be easier, it would produce improvement that was more apparent than real. Instrumentation is sometimes a problem when the measurement tool involves observations. Those doing the observing might get better at it with practice, making the posttest instrument essentially different (more accurate in this case) from the pretest instrument.

Like the problems of history, maturation, and regression to the mean, the possible confounds of testing and instrumentation can be accounted for by including a control group. The only exception is that in the case of pretest sensitization, the experimental group might have a slight advantage over the control group on the posttest because the knowledge gained from the pretest might enable the experimental participants to focus on specific weaknesses during the treatment phase, whereas the control participants would be less likely to have that opportunity.

Participant Problems

Threats to internal validity can also arise from concerns about the individuals participating in the study. In particular, Cook and Campbell (1979) identified two problems.

Subject Selection Effects

One of the defining features of an experimental study with a manipulated independent variable is that participants in the different conditions are equivalent in all ways except for the independent variable. In the next chapter, you will learn how these equivalent groups are formed through random assignment or matching. If the groups are not equivalent, then **subject selection effects**

---

[3] Notice that the sentence reads, "might be involved," not "must be involved." This is because it is also possible that the control group's change from 90 to 80 could be due to one of the other threats. Regression would be suspected if these other threats could be ruled out.

might occur. For example, suppose two sections of a psychology course are being offered and a researcher wants to compare a traditional lecture course with the one combining lecture and discussion groups. School policy (a) prevents the researcher from randomly assigning students to the two courses and (b) requires full disclosure of the nature of the courses. Thus, students can sign up for either section. You can see the difficulty here. If students in the lecture plus discussion course outperform students in the straight lecture course, what caused the difference? Was it the nature of the course (the discussion element), or was it something about the students who *chose* that course? Maybe they were more articulate (hence, interested in discussion, and perhaps better students) than those in the straight lecture course. In short, there is a confound due to the selection of subjects for the two groups being compared.

Selection effects can also interact with other threats to internal validity. For example, in a study with two groups, some historical event might affect one group but not the other. This would be referred to as a *history x selection confound* (read as "history by selection"). Similarly, two groups might mature at different rates, respond to testing at different rates, be influenced by instrumentation in different ways, or show different degrees of regression.

One of psychology's most famous studies is (unfortunately) a good example of a subject selection effect. Known as the "ulcers in executive monkeys" study, it was a pioneering investigation by Joseph Brady in the area of health psychology. Brady and his colleagues investigated the relationship between stress and its physical consequences by placing pairs of rhesus monkeys in adjoining restraint chairs (Brady, Porter, Conrad, & Mason, 1958). One monkey, the "executive" (note the allusion to the stereotype of the hard-driving, stressed-out, responsible-for-everything business executive), could avoid mild shocks to its feet that were programmed to occur every 20 seconds by pressing a lever at any time during the interval. For the control monkey (stereotype of the worker with no control over anything), the lever didn't work, and it was shocked every time the executive monkey let the 20 seconds go by and was shocked. Thus, both monkeys were shocked equally often, but only one monkey had the ability to control the shocks. The outcome was a stomach ulcer for the executive monkey, but none for the control monkey. Brady et al. then replicated the experiment with a second pair of monkeys and found the same result. They eventually reported data on four pairs of animals, concluding the psychological stress of being in command, not just of one's own fate but also of that of a subordinate, could lead to health problems (ulcers in this case).

The Brady research was widely reported in introductory psychology texts, and its publication in *Scientific American* (Brady, 1958) gave it an even broader audience. However, a close examination of Brady's procedure showed a subject selection confound. Specifically, Brady did not place the monkeys randomly in the two groups. Rather, all eight of them started out as executives in the sense that they were pretested on how quickly they would learn the avoidance conditioning procedure. Those learning most quickly were placed in the executive condition for the experiment proper. Although Brady didn't know it at the time, animals differ in their characteristic levels of emotionality, and the more emotional ones respond most quickly to shock. Thus, he unwittingly placed highly emotional (and therefore ulcer-prone) animals in the executive condition and more laid-back animals in the control condition. The first to point out the selection confound was Weiss (1968), whose better-controlled studies with rats produced results the *opposite* of Brady's. Weiss found that those with control over the shock, in fact, developed *fewer* ulcers than those with no control over the shocks.

Attrition

Participants do not always complete the experiment they begin. Some studies may last for a relatively long period, and people move away, lose interest, and even die. In some studies, participants may become uncomfortable and exercise their right to be released from further testing. Hence, for any number of reasons, there may be 100 participants at the start of the study and only 60 at the end. This problem sometimes is called *subject mortality*, or **attrition**. Attrition is a problem because, if particular types of people are more likely to drop out than others, then the group finishing the study is on average made up of different types of people than is the group that started the study, which affects the external validity of the study. It is a particular problem when one condition in the study has a higher attrition rate than another condition. Now you have a confound and a clear threat to internal validity. In either case, in the final analysis, the group beginning the study is not equivalent to the group completing the study. Note that one way to test for differences between those continuing a study and those leaving it is to look at the pretest scores or other attributes at the outset of the study for both groups. If "attriters" and "continuers" are indistinguishable at the start of the study, then overall conclusions at the end of the study are strengthened, even with the loss through attrition.

A Final Note on Internal Validity, Confounding, and External Validity

As you recall from Chapter 1, one of the goals of this text is to make you critical consumers of psychological research—that is, we hope you will be able to read research and spot any flaws. Sometimes, students have a tendency to overuse the term *confound*, reporting that a study is "confounded" when they spot a flaw that is, in fact, not a confound. Specifically, they tend to confuse the issues of internal and external validity. Remember, *internal validity* refers to the methodological soundness of a study—it is free from confounds. *External validity* concerns whether or not the results of the study generalize beyond the specific features of the study. Sometimes, students think they have identified a confound when, in fact, external validity is at issue. For example, suppose you read about a problem-solving study using anagrams in which the independent variable is problem difficulty (two levels—easy and hard) and the dependent variable is the number of problems solved in 15 minutes. You learn the subjects in the study are students in the college's honors program. Thinking critically, you believe the study is flawed and would be better if it tested students with a wider range of ability—you might say the study is confounded by using only honors students. You might be right about who should be in the study, but you would be wrong to call it confounding. You have confused internal and external validity. There would only be a confound in this case if honors students were in one group (e.g., the easy problems) and non-honors students were in the other group (e.g., the hard problems). Then, any differences could be due to the type of problem encountered or the type of student doing the problem solving—a classic confound. Criticizing the use of honors students is therefore not a problem with internal validity but a problem with external validity; the results might not generalize to other types of students. Keep this distinction in mind as you work through Applications Exercise 5.2; we have deliberately put in some external validity issues, in addition to the confounds you will be identifying.

SELF TEST

5.3

1. Determined to get into graduate school, Jan takes the GRE nine times. In her first 7 attempts, she scored between 1050 and 1100, averaging 1075. On her eighth try, she gets a 1250. What do you expect her score to be like on her ninth try? Why?
2. What is the best way to control for the effects of history, maturation, and regression?
3. How can attrition produce an effect similar to a subject selection effect?

This concludes our introduction to the experimental method. The next three chapters will elaborate. In Chapter 6, we distinguish between-subjects designs from within-subjects (or repeated measures) designs, and we also describe a number of control problems in experimental research. In particular, we explore the problems of creating equivalent groups in between-subjects designs, controlling for order effects in within-subjects designs, and the biasing effects that result from the fact that both experimenters and participants are humans. Chapters 7 and 8 describe research designs ranging from those with a single independent variable (Chapter 7) to those with multiple independent variables, which are known as *factorial designs* (Chapter 8).

CHAPTER SUMMARY

Essential Features of Experimental Research

An experiment in psychology involves establishing independent variables, controlling extraneous variables, and measuring dependent variables. Independent variables are the experimental conditions or comparisons under the direct control of the researcher. Manipulated independent variables can involve placing participants in different situations, assigning them different tasks, or giving them different instructions. Extraneous variables are factors that are not of interest to the researcher, and failure to control them leads to a problem called confounding. When a confound exists, the results could be due to the independent variable or the confounding variable. Dependent variables are the behaviors measured in the study; they must be defined precisely (operationally).

Subject Variables

Some research in psychology compares groups of participants who differ from each other in some way before the study begins (e.g., gender, age, shyness). When this occurs, the independent variable of interest is said to be selected by the experimenter rather than manipulated directly, and it is called a subject variable. Research in psychology frequently includes both manipulated and subject variables (e.g., Bandura's Bobo doll study). In a well-controlled study, conclusions about cause and effect can be drawn for manipulated variables but not for subject variables.

The Validity of Experimental Research

There are four ways in which psychological research can be considered valid. Valid research uses statistical analysis properly (statistical conclusion validity), defines independent and dependent variables meaningfully and precisely (construct validity), and is free of confounding variables (internal validity). External validity refers to whether the study's results generalize beyond the particular experiment just completed.

Threats to Internal Validity

The internal validity of an experiment can be threatened by a number of factors. History, maturation, regression, testing, and instrumentation are confounding factors especially likely to occur in poorly controlled studies that include comparisons between pretests and posttests. Selection problems can occur when comparisons are made between groups of individuals that are nonequivalent before the study begins. Selection problems also can interact with the other threats to internal validity. In experiments extending over time, attrition can result in a type of selection problem—the small group remaining at the conclusion of the study could be systematically different from the larger group that started the study.

CHAPTER REVIEW QUESTIONS

1. What was Robert Woodworth's definition of an experiment in psychology?

2. With anxiety as an example, illustrate the difference between independent variables that are (a) manipulated variables and (b) subject variables.

3. Distinguish between Mill's methods of Agreement and Difference, and apply them to a study with an experimental and a control group.

4. Use examples to show the differences between situational, task, and instructional independent variables.

5. What is a confound and why does the presence of one make it impossible to interpret the results of a study?

6. When a study uses subject variables, it is said that causal conclusions cannot be drawn. Why not?

7. Describe the circumstances that could reduce the statistical conclusion validity of an experiment.

8. Describe the three types of circumstances in which external validity can be reduced.

9. Explain why using speed dating is a good illustration of ecological validity.

10. Explain how the presence of a control group can help reduce threats to internal validity. Use history, maturation, and regression to the mean as specific examples.

11. As threats to internal validity, distinguish between testing and instrumentation.

12. Use Brady et al.'s (1958) study of "ulcers in executive monkeys" to illustrate subject selection effects.

13. What is attrition, when is it likely to occur, and why is it a problem?

14. Explain how internal and external validity are sometimes confused when students critically examine a research report.

APPLICATIONS EXERCISES

Exercise 5.1. Identifying Variables

For each of the following, identify the independent variable(s), the levels of the independent variable(s), and the dependent variable(s). For independent variables, identify whether they are manipulated variables or non-manipulated subject variables. For the manipulated variables, indicate whether they are situational, task, or instructional variables. For dependent variables, indicate the scale of measurement being used.

1. In a cognitive mapping study, first-year students are compared with seniors in their ability to point accurately to campus buildings. Half the students are told to visually imagine the campus buildings before they point; the remaining students are not given any specific strategy to use. Participants are asked to indicate (on a scale of 1 to 10) how confident they are about their pointing accuracy; the amount of error (in degrees) in their pointing is also recorded.

2. In a study of the effectiveness of a new drug in treating depression, some patients receive the drug while others only think they are receiving it. A third group is not treated at all. After the program is completed, participants complete the Beck Depression Inventory and are rated on depression (10-point scale) by trained observers.

3. In a Pavlovian conditioning study, hungry dogs (i.e., 12 hours without food) and not-so-hungry dogs (i.e., 6 hours without food) are conditioned to salivate to the sound of a tone by pairing the tone with food. For some animals, the tone is turned on and then off before the food is presented. For others, the tone remains on until the food is presented. For still others, the food precedes the tone. Experimenters record when salivation first begins and how much saliva accumulates for a fixed time interval.

4. In a study of developmental psycholinguistics, 2-, 3-, and 4-year-old children are shown dolls and told to act out several scenes to determine if they can use certain grammatical rules. Sometimes, each child is asked to act out a scene in the active voice ("Ernie hit Bert"); at other times, each child acts out a scene in the passive voice ("Ernie was hit by Bert"). Children are judged by whether or not they act out the scene accurately (two possible scores) and by how quickly they begin acting out the scene.

5. In a study of maze learning, some rats are given an elevated maze to learn (no side walls); others have to learn a more traditional alley maze (with side walls). The maze pattern is the same in both cases. Half the rats in each condition are wild rats; the remaining rats were bred in the laboratory. The researcher makes note of any errors (wrong turns) made and how long it takes the animal to reach the goal.

6. In a helping behavior study, passersby in a mall are approached by a student who is either well dressed or shabbily dressed. The student asks for directions to either the public restroom or the Wal-Mart. Nearby, an experimenter records whether or not people provide any help.

7. In a memory study, a researcher wishes to know how well people can recall the locations of items in an environment. Girls and boys (ages 8–10) are compared. Each is shown a sheet of paper containing line drawings of 30 objects. For half the subjects, the items on the sheet are stereotypically male-oriented (e.g., a football); the remaining subjects get stereotypically female-oriented items (e.g., a measuring cup). After studying the objects on the first sheet for 3 minutes, all subjects are then shown a second sheet in which some of the items have moved to a new location on the page. Subjects are told to circle the objects that have moved to a new location.

8. In a study of cell phone use and driving, some participants try to perform as accurately as they can in a driving simulator (i.e., keep the car on a narrow road) while talking on a hand-held cell phone, others while talking on a

hands-free phone, and yet others without talking on a phone at all. Half the subjects have 2 years of driving experience. The remaining participants have 4 years of driving experience.

Exercise 5.2. Spot the Confound(s)

For each of the following, identify the independent and dependent variables and the levels of each independent variable, and find at least one extraneous variable that has not been adequately controlled (i.e., that is creating a confound). Be sure not to confuse internal and external validity. Use the format illustrated in Table 5.2.

1. A testing company is trying to determine if a new type of driver (club 1) will drive a golf ball greater distances than three competing brands (clubs 2–4). Twenty male golf pros are recruited. Each golfer hits 50 balls with club 1, then 50 more with 2, then 50 with 3, then 50 with 4. To add realism, the experiment takes place over the first four holes of an actual golf course—the first set of 50 balls is hit from the first tee, the second 50 from the second tee, and so on. The first four holes are all 380–400 yards in length, and each is a par 4 hole.

2. A researcher is interested in the ability of patients with schizophrenia to judge time durations. It is hypothesized that loud noise will adversely affect their judgment. Participants are tested two ways. In the "quiet" condition, some participants are tested in a small soundproof room used for hearing tests. Those in the "noisy" condition are tested in a nurse's office where a stereo is playing music at a constant (and loud) volume. Because of scheduling problems, locked-ward (i.e., slightly more dangerous) patients are available for testing *only* on Monday, and open-ward (i.e., slightly less dangerous) patients are available for testing *only* on Thursday. Furthermore, hearing tests are scheduled for Thursdays, so the soundproof room is available only on Monday.

3. An experimenter is interested in whether memory can be improved in older adults if they use visual imagery. Participants (all women over the age of 65) are placed in one of two groups; some are trained in imagery techniques, and others are trained to use rote repetition. The imagery group is given a list of 20 concrete nouns (for which it is easier to form images than abstract nouns) to study, and the other group is given 20 abstract words (ones that are especially easy to pronounce, so repetition will be easy), matched with the concrete words for frequency of general usage. To match the method of presentation with the method of study, participants in the imagery group are shown the words visually (on a computer screen). To control for any "computer-phobia," rote participants also sit at the computer terminal, but the computer is programmed to read the lists to them. After the word lists have been presented, participants have a minute to recall as many words as they can in any order that occurs to them.

4. A social psychologist is interested in helping behavior and happens to know two male graduate students who would be happy to assist. The first (Felix) is generally well dressed, but the second (Oscar) doesn't care much about appearances. An experiment is designed in which passersby in a mall will be approached by a student who is either well-dressed Felix or shabbily-dressed Oscar. All of the testing sessions occur between 8 and 9 o'clock in the evening, with Felix working on Monday and Oscar working on Friday. The student will approach a shopper and ask for a dollar for a cup of coffee. Nearby, the experimenter will record whether or not people give money.

Exercise 5.3. Operational Definitions (Again)

In Chapter 3, you first learned about operational definitions and completed an exercise on the operational definitions of some familiar constructs used in psychological research. In this exercise, you are to play the role of an experimenter designing a study. For each of the four hypotheses:

a. Identify the independent variable(s), decide how many levels of the independent variable(s) you would like to use, and identify the levels.

b. Identify the dependent variable in each study (one dependent variable per item).

c. Create operational definitions for your independent and dependent variables.

1. People are more likely to offer help to someone in need if the situation unambiguously calls for help.

2. Ability to concentrate on a task deteriorates when people feel crowded.

3. Good bowlers improve their performance in the presence of an audience, whereas average bowlers do worse when an audience is watching.

4. Animals learn a difficult maze best when they are moderately aroused. They do poorly in difficult mazes when their arousal is high or low. When the maze is easy, performance improves steadily from low to moderate to high arousal.

5. Caffeine improves memory, but only for older people.

6. In a bratwurst eating contest, those scoring high on a "sensation-seeking" scale will consume more, and this is especially true for fans of the Pittsburgh Steelers, compared with Baltimore Ravens fans.

ANSWERS TO SELF TESTS

✓ 5.1

1. IVs = problem difficulty and reward size.
   DV = number of anagrams solved.
2. Extraneous variables are all of the factors that must be controlled or kept constant from one group to another in an experiment; failure to control these variables results in a confound.
3. Frustration could be manipulated as an IV by having two groups, one allowed to complete a maze, and the other prevented from doing so. It could also be an extraneous variable being controlled in a study in which frustration was avoided completely. It could also be what is measured in a study that looked at whether self-reported frustration levels differed for those given impossible problems to solve, compared to others given solvable problems.

✓ 5.2

1. As a manipulated variable, some people in a study could be made anxious ("you will be shocked if you make errors"), and others not; as a subject variable, people who are generally anxious would be in one group, and low anxious people would be in a second group.
2. Manipulated → the viewing experience shown to children.
   Subject → gender.
3. Internal → the study is free from confounds.
   External → results generalize beyond the confines of the study.
4. Ecological.

✓ 5.3

1. Somewhere around 1075 to 1100; regression to the mean.
2. Add a control group.
3. If those who drop out are systematically different from those who stay, then the group of subjects who started the study will be quite different from those who finished.

Methodological Control in Experimental Research

6

PREVIEW & CHAPTER OBJECTIVES

In Chapter 5, you learned the essentials of the experimental method—manipulating an independent variable, controlling extraneous variables, and measuring the dependent variable. In this chapter, we examine two general types of experimental designs, one in which different groups of subjects contribute data to different levels of the independent variable (between-subjects design) and one in which the same subjects contribute data to all levels of the independent variable (within-subjects design). As you are about to learn, each approach has advantages, but each has a problem that must be carefully controlled: the problem of equivalent groups for between-subjects designs and problem of order effects for within-subjects designs. The last third of the chapter addresses the issue of experimenter and participant biases and ways of controlling them. When you finish this chapter, you should be able to:

- Distinguish between-subjects designs from within-subjects designs.

- Understand how random assignment solves the equivalent groups problem in between-subjects designs.

- Understand when matching, followed by random assignment, should be used instead of simple random assignment when attempting to create equivalent groups.

- Understand why counterbalancing is needed to control for order effects in within-subjects designs.

- Distinguish between progressive and carry-over effects in within-subjects designs, and understand why counterbalancing usually works better with the former than with the latter.

- Describe the various forms of counterbalancing for situations in which participants are tested once per condition and more than once per condition.

- Describe the specific types of between- and within-subjects designs that occur in research in developmental psychology, and understand the methodological problems associated with each.

- Describe how experimenter bias can occur and how it can be controlled.

- Describe how participant bias can occur and how it can be controlled.

- Describe the origins of the biasing phenomenon known as the Hawthorne effect.

In his landmark experimental psychology text, just after introducing his now famous distinction between independent and dependent variables, R. S. Woodworth emphasized the importance of *control* in experimental research. As Woodworth (1938) put it, "Whether one or more independent variables are used, it remains essential that all other conditions be constant. Otherwise you cannot connect the effect observed with any definite cause. The psychologist must expect to encounter difficulties in meeting this requirement." (p. 3). Some of these difficulties we have already seen. The general problem of confounding and the specific threats to internal validity, discussed in the previous chapter, are basically problems of controlling extraneous factors. In this chapter, we will describe other aspects of maintaining control: the problem of creating equivalent groups in experiments involving separate groups of subjects, the problem of order effects in experiments in which subjects are tested several times, and problems resulting from biases held by both experimenters and research participants.

Recall that any independent variable must have a minimum of two levels. At the very least, an experiment will compare level A with level B. Those who participate in the study might be placed in level A, level B, or both. If they receive either A *or* B but not both, the design is a **between-subjects design**, so named because the comparison of conditions A and B will be a contrast *between* two groups of individuals. On the other hand, if each participant receives both levels A *and* B, you could say both levels exist *within* each individual participating in the study; hence, this design is called a **within-subjects design** (or, sometimes, a *repeated-measures design*). Let's examine each approach.

Between-Subjects Designs

Between-subjects designs are sometimes used because they must be used. If the independent variable is a subject variable, for instance, there is usually no choice. A study comparing introverts with extroverts requires two different groups of people, some shy, some outgoing; a study on gender differences in children requires a group of girls and a group of boys.

Using a between-subjects design is also unavoidable in studies that use certain types of manipulated independent variables. That is, sometimes when people participate in one level of an independent variable, the experience gained there will make it impossible for them to participate in other levels. This often happens in social psychological research and most research involving deception. Consider an experiment on the effects of the physical attractiveness of a defendant on recommended sentence length by Sigall and Ostrove (1975). They gave college students descriptions of a crime and asked them to recommend a jail sentence for the woman convicted. There were two separate between-subjects, manipulated independent variables. One variable was the type of crime—either a burglary in which "Barbara Helm" broke into a neighbor's apartment and stole $2,200 (a fair amount of money in 1975) or a swindle in which Barbara "ingratiated herself to a middle-aged bachelor and induced him to invest $2,200 in a nonexistent corporation" (p. 412). The other manipulated variable was Barbara's attractiveness. Some participants saw a photo of her in which she was very attractive, others saw a photo of a Barbara made up to be unattractive (the same woman posed for both photos), and a control group did not see any photo. The interesting result was that when the crime was burglary, attractiveness paid. Attractive Barbara got a lighter sentence on average (2.80 years) than unattractive (5.20) or control (5.10) Barbara. However, the opposite happened when the crime was a swindle. Apparently thinking Barbara was using her good looks to commit the crime, participants gave attractive Barbara a harsher sentence (5.45 years) than they gave the unattractive (4.35) or control (4.35) Barbara. (Notice we are reporting the *means* for each condition here; we will do this when we describe many studies in this textbook.)

Can you see why it was necessary to run this study with between-subjects independent variables? For those participating in the Attractive-Barbara-Swindle condition, for example, the experience would certainly affect them and make it impossible for them to start fresh in, say, the Unattractive-Barbara-Burglary condition. In some studies, participating in one condition makes it impossible for the same person to be in a second condition. Sometimes, it is essential that each condition include uninformed participants.

While the advantage of a between-subjects design is that each subject enters the study fresh, and naïve with respect to the hypotheses to be tested, the prime disadvantage is that large numbers of people may need to be recruited, tested, and debriefed during the course of the experiment. Hence, the researcher invests a great deal of energy in this type of design. The Barbara Helm study used six groups with 20 subjects in each group for a total of 120 people.

Another disadvantage of between-subjects designs is that differences between the conditions might be due to the independent variables, but they might also be due to differences between the individuals in the different groups. Perhaps the subjects in one group are smarter than those in another group. To deal with this potential confound, deliberate steps must be taken to create **equivalent groups**. These groups are equal to each other in every important way except for the levels of the independent variable.

Creating Equivalent Groups

There are two common techniques for creating equivalent groups in a between-subjects experiment. One approach is to use simple random assignment. A second strategy is to use a matching procedure, followed by random assignment.

Random Assignment

First, be sure you understand that *random assignment* and *random selection* are not the same procedures. Random selection is a sampling procedure designed to obtain a *random sample* as described in Chapter 4. It is a process designed to produce a sample of individuals that reflects the broader population, and it is a common strategy used in survey research. Random assignment, in contrast, is a method for placing participants, once already selected for a study, into the different conditions. When **random assignment** is used, every person volunteering for the study has an equal chance of being placed in any of the conditions being formed.

The goal of random assignment is to take individual difference factors that could influence the study and spread them evenly throughout the different groups. For instance, suppose you are comparing two presentation rates in a simple memory study. Further suppose anxious participants don't do as well on your memory task as non-anxious participants, but you as the researcher are unaware of that at the outset of the study (or it just doesn't occur to you). Some subjects are shown a word list at a rate of 2 seconds per word; others at 4 seconds per word. The prediction is that recall will be better with a longer presentation rate or for the 4-second condition. You randomly assign participants to one condition or the other. Here are some hypothetical data that such a study might produce. Each number refers to the number of words recalled out of a list of 30. After each subject number, we placed an *A* or an *R* in parentheses to indicate which participants are anxious (A) and which are relaxed (R). Data for the anxious people are shaded.

Participant	2-Second Rate	Participant	4-Second Rate
S1(R)	16	S9 (R)	23
S2(R)	15	S10 (R)	19
S3(R)	16	S11 (R)	19
S4(R)	18	S12 (R)	20
S5(R)	20	S13 (R)	25
S6(A)	10	S14 (A)	16
S7(A)	12	S15 (A)	14
S8(A)	13	S16 (A)	16
M	15.00	M	19.00
SD	3.25	SD	3.70

If you look carefully at these data, you'll see the three anxious participants in each group did worse than their five relaxed peers. Because the number of anxious participants in each group is equal, however, the dampening effect of anxiety on recall is about the same for both groups. Thus, the main comparison of interest, the difference in presentation rates, is preserved—a mean of 15 words for the 2-second group and 19 for the 4-second group.

Random assignment won't guarantee placing an equal number of anxious participants in each group, but in general, the procedure has the effect of spreading potential confounds evenly among the groups. This is especially true when large numbers of individuals are assigned to each group. In fact, the greater the number of subjects involved, the greater the chance that random assignment will work to create equivalent groups. If groups are equivalent and everything else is adequately controlled, then you are in the enviable position of being able to say your independent variable likely caused differences between your groups.

You might think the process of random assignment would be fairly simple, but the result of such a procedure is that your groups will almost certainly contain different numbers of people. In the worst-case scenario, imagine you are doing a study using 20 participants divided into two groups of 10. You decide to flip a coin as each volunteer arrives: heads, they're in group A; tails, group B. But what if the coin comes up heads all 20 times? Unlikely, but possible.

To complete the assignment of participants to conditions in a way that guarantees an equal number of subjects per group, a researcher can use **blocked random assignment**, a procedure ensuring that each condition of the study has a participant randomly assigned to it before any condition is repeated a second time. Each block contains all of the conditions of the study in a randomized order. This can be done by hand, using a table of random numbers, but researchers typically rely on a simple computer application to generate a sequence of conditions meeting the requirements of block randomization; you can find one at www.randomizer.org that will accomplish both random sampling and random assignment.

One final point about random assignment is that the process is normally associated with laboratory research. That environment allows a high degree of control, so it is not difficult to ensure that each person signing up for the study has an equal chance of being assigned to any of the conditions. Although it is not always feasible, random assignment is also possible in some field research. For example, some universities use random assignment to assign roommates, thereby providing an opportunity to study a number of factors affecting college students. For example,

Shook and Fazio (2008) examined the so-called contact hypothesis, the idea that racial prejudice can be reduced when members of different races are in frequent contact with each other (and other factors, such as equal status, are in play). They found a university where roommates were randomly assigned and designed an experiment to compare two groups of white first-year students—those randomly assigned to another white student and those randomly assigned to an African-American student. Over the course of a fall quarter, the researchers examined whether the close proximity of having a different-race roommate would reduce prejudice. In line with the contact hypothesis, it did.

Matching

When only a small number of subjects are available for your experiment, random assignment can, by chance, fail to create equivalent groups. The following example shows how this might happen. Let's take the same study of the effect of presentation rate on memory, used earlier, and assume the data you just examined reflect an outcome in which random assignment happened to work—that is, there was an exact balance of five relaxed and three anxious people in each group. However, it is *possible* that random assignment could place all six of the anxious participants in *one* of the groups. This is unlikely, but it could occur (just as it's remotely possible for a perfectly fair coin to come up heads 10 times in a row). If it did, this might happen:

Participant	2-Second Rate	Participant	4-Second Rate
S1(R)	15	S9 (R)	23
S2(R)	17	S10 (R)	20
S3(R)	16	S11 (A)	16
S4(R)	18	S12 (A)	14
S5(R)	20	S13 (A)	16
S6(R)	17	S14 (A)	16
S7(R)	18	S15 (A)	14
S8(R)	15	S16 (A)	17
M	17.00	*M*	17.00
SD	1.69	*SD*	3.07

This outcome, of course, is totally different from the first example. Instead of concluding that recall was better for a slower presentation rate (as in the earlier example), the researcher in this case could not reject the null hypothesis (that is, the groups are equal: 17 = 17). Participants were randomly assigned, and the researcher's prediction about better recall for a slower presentation rate certainly makes sense. So what went wrong?

Random assignment, in this case, inadvertently created two decidedly nonequivalent groups—one made up entirely of relaxed people and one mostly including anxious folks. A 4-second rate probably does produce better recall, but the true difference was not found in this study because the mean for the 2-second group was inflated by the relatively high scores of the relaxed participants and the 4-second group's mean was suppressed because of anxiety. Another way of saying this is that the failure of random assignment to create equivalent groups probably led to a Type II error (presentation rate really does affect recall but this study failed to find the effect). To repeat what was mentioned earlier, a critical point is that the chance of random assignment working to create equivalent groups increases as sample size increases. Our example only had 16 participants, so there is a good chance of creating non-equivalent groups even using random assignment.

Note the exact same outcome just described could also occur if you failed to make any effort to create equivalent groups. For example, suppose you tested people as they signed up for your study, starting with the 2-second/item condition and then finishing with the 4-second/item condition. It is conceivable that anxious subjects would be slower to sign up than relaxed subjects, resulting in the second group being composed mostly of anxious subjects.

A second general strategy for deliberately trying to create equivalent groups is to use a matching procedure. In **matching**, participants are grouped together on some *subject variable* such as their characteristic level of anxiety and then distributed randomly to the different groups in the experiment. In the memory study, "anxiety level" would be called a **matching variable**. Individuals in the memory experiment would be given a valid and reliable measure of anxiety, those with similar scores would be paired, and one person in each pair would be randomly assigned to the group getting the 2-second rate and the other the group with the 4-second rate. As an illustration of exactly how to accomplish matching in our hypothetical two-group experiment on memory, with anxiety as a matching variable, you should work through the example in Table 6.1

Matching sometimes is used when the number of subjects is small and random assignment alone is therefore risky and might not yield equivalent groups. Fung and Leung (2014), for instance, attempted to increase the social responsiveness of children with autism by exposing them to therapy dogs (i.e., golden retrievers in this case, dogs known be calm and friendly to children). They only had 10 children with autism in their study, however, so they used matching to create a therapy group and a non-therapy control group, with 5 children in each group. Their matching variables were intellectual ability and verbal fluency. Even with matching, however, their small sample size prevented them from finding much evidence for the effectiveness of the therapy.

In order to undertake matching, regardless of whether sample size is an issue, two important conditions must be met. First, you must have good reason to believe the matching variable will have a predictable effect on the outcome of the study—that is, you must be confident that the matching variable would be correlated with the dependent variable. Because you haven't run your study yet to know if your matching variable correlates with your dependent variable, you would usually determine this by closely reading and evaluating previous, related research. When the correlation between the matching variable and the dependent variable is high, the statistical techniques for evaluating matched-groups designs are sensitive to differences between the groups. On the other hand, if matching is done when the correlation between the matching variable and the dependent variable is low, the chance of finding a true difference between the groups declines. So it is important to be careful when selecting matching variables.

A second important condition for matching is that there must be a reasonable way of measuring or identifying participants on the matching variable. In some studies, participants must be tested on the matching variable first, then assigned to groups, and then put through the experimental procedure. Depending on the circumstances, this might require bringing participants into the lab on two separate occasions, which can create logistical problems. Also, the initial testing on the matching variable might give participants an indication of the study's purpose, thereby introducing bias into the study. The simplest matching situations occur when the matching variables are constructs that can be determined without directly testing the

Table 6.1   How to Use a Matching Procedure

In our hypothetical study on the effect of presentation rate on memory, suppose that the researcher believes that matching is needed. That is, the researcher thinks that anxiety might correlate with memory performance. While screening subjects for the experiment, then, the researcher gives potential subjects a reliable and valid test designed to measure someone's characteristic levels of anxiety. For the sake of illustration, assume that scores on this test range from 10 to 50, with higher scores indicating greater levels of typical anxiety felt by people. Thus, a matching procedure is chosen, in order to ensure that the two groups of subjects in the memory experiment are equivalent to each other in terms of typical anxiety levels.

Step 1.   Get a score for each person on the matching variable. This will be their score on the anxiety test (ranging from 10 to 50). Suppose there will be 10 subjects ("Ss") in the study, 5 per group. Here are their anxiety scores:

S1: 32	S6: 45
S2: 18	S7: 26
S3: 43	S8: 29
S4: 39	S9: 31
S5: 19	S10: 41

Step 2.   Arrange the anxiety scores in ascending order.

S2: 18	S1: 32
S5: 19	S4: 39
S7: 26	S10: 41
S8: 29	S3: 43
S9: 31	S6: 45

Step 3.   Create five pairs of scores, with each pair consisting of quantitatively adjacent anxiety scores:

Pair 1:	18 and 19
Pair 2:	26 and 29
Pair 3:	31 and 32
Pair 4:	39 and 41
Pair 5:	43 and 45

Step 4.   For each pair, randomly assign one subject to group 1 (2-sec/item) and one to group 2 (4-sec/item). Here's one possible outcome:

	2-Sec/Item Group	4-Sec/Item Group
	18	19
	29	26
	31	32
	39	41
	45	43
Mean anxiety	**32.4**	**32.2**

Now the study can proceed with some assurance that the two groups are equivalent (32.4 is virtually the same as 32.2) in terms of anxiety.

Note: If more than two groups are being tested in the experiment, the matching procedure is the same up to and including step 2. In step 3, instead of creating pairs of scores, the researcher creates clusters equal to the number of groups needed. Then in step 4, the subjects in each cluster are randomly assigned to the multiple groups.

participants (e.g., intellectual ability and verbal fluency for the children with autism, based on already-available information), or by matching on the dependent variable itself. For instance, in a memory study, participants could be given an initial memory test, then matched on their performance, and then randomly assigned to groups. Their preexisting memory ability would thereby be under control, and the differences in performance could be attributed to the independent variable.

A nice example of a study using a matching procedure examined the "testing effect" that you learned about in Research Example 2 in the Chapter 3 discussion of "what's next" thinking. Goosens, Camp, Verkoeijen, Tabbers, and Zwann (2014) completed a conceptual replication of the testing effect to see if it would apply to 9-year-old school children (as it had with college-aged students). Children learned vocabulary words either by a simple study procedure (similar to a typical laboratory procedure), an elaborative study procedure (similar to the kinds of classroom exercises used with school children), or a "retrieval practice" procedure that involved repeated testing. Sample size was not a concern, but the researchers believed that it was important to assign children to the three groups after matching them on their pre-existing vocabulary capability. That is, in terms of the two critical conditions we just described that make matching a good idea, (a) there was good reason to believe that children with advanced vocabulary skills would perform better in the study than those with weaker skills, and (b) it was not difficult to determine the vocabulary competence of the children before the study began. With the matching procedure insuring equivalent groups, the research continued, and the general finding was that retrieval practice was superior to the other two forms of studying, thus providing more evidence for the validity of the testing effect. You might also note that because the study was completed in a school environment instead of a laboratory, it enhanced the *ecological validity* of the testing effect.

One final point about matching is the practical difficulty of deciding how many matching variables to use and which are the best to use. In a testing effect study, should the children have also been matched on general intelligence? What about anxiety level? You can see that some judgment is required here, for matching is difficult to accomplish with more than one matching variable and sometimes results in eliminating participants because close matches cannot be made. The problem of deciding on and measuring matching variables is one reason research psychologists generally prefer to make the effort to recruit enough volunteers to use random assignment even when they might suspect that some extraneous variable correlates with the dependent variable. In memory research, for instance, researchers are seldom concerned about such extraneous factors as anxiety level, intelligence, or education level. They simply make the groups large enough and assume that random assignment will distribute these extraneous (and potentially confounding) factors evenly throughout the conditions of the study.

SELF TEST

6.1

1. What is the defining feature of a between-subjects design? What is the main control problem that must be solved with this type of design?
2. It is sometimes the case that a study using deception requires a between-subjects design. Why?
3. Sal wishes to see if the font used when printing a document will influence comprehension of the material in the document. He thinks about matching on verbal fluency. What two conditions must be in effect before this matching can occur?

Within-Subjects Designs

As mentioned at the start of this chapter, each participant is exposed to each level of the independent variable in a within-subjects design. Because everyone in this type of study is measured several times, this procedure is sometimes described as a *repeated-measures* design. One practical advantage of this design should be obvious: Fewer people need to be recruited. If you have a study comparing two experimental conditions and you want to test 20 people in Condition 1, you'll need to recruit 40 people for a between-subjects study, but only 20 for a within-subjects study.

Within-subjects designs are sometimes the only reasonable choice. In experiments in areas such as physiological psychology and sensation and perception, comparisons often are made between conditions that require just a brief time to test but might demand extensive preparation. For example, a perceptual study using the Müller-Lyer illusion might vary the orientations of the lines to see if the illusion is especially strong when presented vertically (see Figure 6.1). The task might involve showing the illusion on a computer screen and asking the participant to tap a key that gradually changes the length of one of the lines. Participants are told to adjust the line until both lines are perceived to be the same length. Any one trial might take no more than 5 seconds, so it would be absurd to make the illusion orientation variable a between-subjects factor and use one person for a fraction of a minute. Instead, it makes more sense to make the orientation variable a within-subjects factor and give each participant a sequence of trials to cover all levels of the variable and probably duplicate each level several times (to get consistent measurements). And unlike the attractive/unattractive Barbara Helm study, serving in one condition in this perception study would not make it impossible to serve in another.

A within-subjects design might also be necessary when volunteers are scarce because the entire population of interest is small. Studying astronauts or people with special expertise (e.g., world-class chess players, to use an example you will see shortly) are just two examples. Of course, there are times when, even with a limited population, the design may require a between-subjects manipulation. Fung and Leung (2014), mentioned earlier, evaluated the effects of a pet-assisted therapy for children with autism in an experiment that required comparing those in therapy with others in a control group not being exposed to the therapy.

Besides convenience, another advantage of within-subjects designs is that they eliminate problems associated with creating equivalent groups associated with between-subjects designs. Having different individuals in each condition in a between-subjects design introduces more *variability* in each condition of your study. Even with random assignment, a portion of the *variance* in a between-subjects design can result from individual differences between subjects in the different groups. But in a within-subjects design, any between-condition individual difference variance disappears. Let's look at a simple example.

Suppose you are comparing two golf balls for distance. You recruit 10 professional golfers and randomly assign them to two groups of 5. After loosening up, each golfer hits one ball or the other. Here are the results (each number refers to the number of yards a ball has been hit).

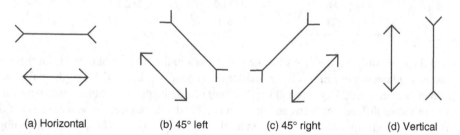

| (a) Horizontal | (b) 45° left | (c) 45° right | (d) Vertical |

FIGURE 6.1

Set of four Müller-Lyer illusions: horizontal, 45° left, 45° right, vertical.

Pros in the First Group	Golf ball 1	Pros in the Second Group	Golf ball 2
Pro 1	255	Pro 6	269
Pro 2	261	Pro 7	266
Pro 3	248	Pro 8	260
Pro 4	256	Pro 9	273
Pro 5	245	Pro 10	257
M	253.00	M	265.00
SD	6.44	SD	6.52

Note several points here. First, there is variability within each group, as reflected in the standard deviation for each (6.44 yards and 6.52 yards). Second, there is apparently an overall difference between the groups (253 yards and 265 yards). The pros in the second group hit their ball farther than the pros in the first group. Why? Three possibilities:

a. *The golf ball:* Perhaps the brand of golf ball hit by the second group simply goes farther (this, of course, is the research hypothesis).

b. *Individual differences:* Maybe the golfers in the second group are stronger or more skilled than those in the first group.

c. *Chance:* Perhaps this is not a statistically significant difference, and even if it is, there's a 5% chance it is a Type I error if the null hypothesis (i.e., no real difference) is actually true.

The chances that the second possibility is a major problem are reduced by the procedures for creating equivalent groups described earlier. Using random assignment or matching allows you to be reasonably sure the second group of golfers is approximately equal to the first group in ability, strength, and so on. Despite that, however, it is still possible that *some* of the difference between these groups can be traced to the individual differences between the groups. This problem simply does not occur in a within-subjects design, however. Suppose you repeated the study but used just the first five golfers, and each pro hit ball 1, and then ball 2. Now the table looks like this.

Pros in the First Group	Golf ball 1	Golf ball 2
Pro 1	255	269
Pro 2	261	266
Pro 3	248	260
Pro 4	256	273
Pro 5	245	257
M	253.00	265.00
SD	6.44	6.52

Of the three possible explanations for the differences in the first set of data, when there were two groups, explanation b. can be eliminated for the second set. In the first set, the difference in the first row between the 255 yards and the 269 yards could be due to the difference between the balls, or individual differences between pros 1 and 6, 2 and 7 or chance. In the second set of data, there is no second group of golfers, so the second possibility is gone. Thus, in a within-subjects design, individual differences are eliminated from the estimate of the variability between conditions. Statistically, this means that, in a within-subjects design, an *inferential analysis* will be more sensitive to small differences between means than it would in a between-subjects design. We will describe in more depth inferential analysis in Chapter 7 when we describe our first inferential statistic, the *t*-test.

But wait. Are you completely satisfied that in the second case, the differences between the first set of scores and the second set could be due *only* to chance factors and/or the superiority of the second ball? Are you thinking that perhaps pro 1 actually changed in some way between hitting ball 1 and hitting ball 2? Although it's unlikely that the golfer will add 10 pounds of muscle between swings, what if some kind of practice or warm-up effect was operating? Or perhaps the pro detected a slight malfunction in his swing at ball 1 and corrected it for ball 2. Or perhaps the wind changed. In short, with a within-subjects design, a major problem is that once a participant has completed the first part of a study, the experience or altered circumstances could influence performance in later parts of the study. The problem is referred to as a sequence or **order effect**, and it can operate in several ways.

First, Trial 1 might affect the participant so performance on Trial 2 is steadily improved, as in the example of a practice effect. On the other hand, sometimes repeated trials produce gradual fatigue or boredom, and performance steadily declines from trial to trial. These two effects can both be referred to as **progressive effects** because it is assumed that performance changes steadily (progressively) from trial to trial. Second, some sequences might produce effects different from those of other sequences, what could be called a **carry-over effect**. Thus, in a study with two basic conditions, experiencing the first condition before the second might affect the person much differently than experiencing the second before the first. For example, suppose you are studying the effects of noise on a problem-solving task using a within-subjects design. Let's say participants will be trying to solve anagram problems (rearrange letters to form words). In condition UPN (UnPredictable Noise), they have to solve the anagrams while distracting noises come from the next room, and these noises are presented randomly and therefore are unpredictable. In condition PN (Predictable Noise), the same total amount of noise occurs; however, it is not randomly presented but instead occurs in predictable patterns (e.g., every 30 seconds). If you put the people in condition UPN first, and then in PN, they will probably do poorly in UPN (most people do). This poor performance might discourage them and *carry over* to condition PN. They should do better in PN, but as soon as the noise begins, they might say to themselves, "Here we go again," and perhaps not try as hard. On the other hand, if you run condition PN first, the predictable noise, your subjects might do reasonably well (most people do), and some of the confidence might carry over to the second part of the study—UPN. ("Here comes the noise again, but I handled it before, I can handle it again.") When they encounter condition UPN in the second part of the study, they might do better than you would ordinarily expect. Thus, performance in condition UPN might be much worse in the sequence UPN–PN than in the sequence PN–UPN. Furthermore, a similar problem would occur for condition PN. In short, the order in which the conditions are presented, independently of practice or fatigue effects, might influence the study's outcome. In studies where carryover effects might be suspected, researchers usually decide to use a between-subjects rather than a within-subjects design. Indeed, studies comparing predictable and unpredictable noise typically put people in two different groups precisely because of this carryover issue.

Controlling Order Effects

The typical way to control order effects in a within-subjects design is to use more than one sequence, a strategy known as **counterbalancing**. As is clear from the predictable versus unpredictable noise example, the procedure works better for progressive effects than for carryover effects. There are two general categories of counterbalancing, depending on whether participants are tested in each experimental condition just one time or are tested more than once per condition.

Testing Once per Condition

In some experiments, participants are tested in each of the conditions but only once per condition. Consider, for example, an interesting study by Reynolds (1992) on the ability of chess players to recognize the level of expertise in other chess players. He recruited 15 chess players with different degrees of expertise from various clubs in New York City and asked them to look at 6 chess games that were said to be in progress (i.e., about 20 moves into the game). On each trial, the players examined the board of an in-progress game (they were told to assume the two players in each game were of equal ability) and estimated the skill level of the players according to a standard rating system. The games were deliberately set up to reflect different levels of player expertise. Reynolds found the more highly skilled of the 15 chess players made more accurate estimates of the ability reflected in the board setups they examined than did the less skilled players.

Can you see that the Reynolds study used within-subjects design? Each of the 15 participants examined all six games. Also, you can see it made sense for each game to be evaluated just one time by each player. Hence, Reynolds was faced with the question of how to control for order effects that might be present. He certainly didn't want all 15 participants to see the 6 games in exactly the same order. How might he have proceeded?

Complete Counterbalancing

Whenever participants are tested once per condition in a within-subjects design, one solution to the order problem is to use **complete counterbalancing**. This means every possible sequence will be used at least once. The total number of sequences needed can be determined by calculating $X!$, where X is the number of conditions, and ! stands for the mathematical calculation of a factorial. For example, if a study has three conditions, there are six possible orders that can be used:

$$3! = 3 \times 2 \times 1 = 6$$

The six sequences in a study with conditions A, B, and C would be:

A B C	B A C
A C B	C A B
B C A	C B A

Then, subjects in this study would be randomly assigned to one of the six orders.

The problem with complete counterbalancing is that as the number of levels of the independent variable increases, and the possible orders needed increase dramatically. Six orders are needed for three conditions, but look what happens if you add a fourth condition:

$$4! = 4 \times 3 \times 2 \times 1 = 24$$

By adding just one more condition, the number of possible orders increases from 6 to 24. As you can guess, complete counterbalancing was not possible in the Reynolds study unless he recruited many more than 15 chess players. In fact, with 6 different games (i.e., conditions), he would need to find 6! or 720 players to cover all of the possible orders. Clearly, Reynolds used a different strategy.

Partial Counterbalancing

Whenever a subset of the total number of orders is used, the result is called **partial counterbalancing** or, sometimes, *incomplete counterbalancing* This can be accomplished by taking a random sample of orders from the complete set of all possible orders or, more simply, by randomizing the order of conditions for each subject.[1] The latter was Reynolds's solution—"the order of presentation [was] randomized for each subject" (Reynolds, 1992, p. 411). Sampling from the population of orders is a common strategy whenever there are fewer participants available than possible orders or when there is a fairly large number of conditions.

Reynolds (1992) sampled from the total number of orders, but he could have chosen another approach that is used sometimes: the balanced **Latin square**. This device gets its name from an ancient Roman puzzle about arranging Latin letters in a matrix so each letter appears only once in each row and once in each column (Kirk, 1968). The Latin square strategy is more sophisticated than choosing a random subset of the whole. With a perfectly balanced Latin square, you are assured that (a) every condition of the study occurs equally often in every sequential position, and (b) every condition precedes and follows every other condition exactly once. Also, the number of rows in a Latin square is exactly equal to the number of elements in the study that are in need of counterbalancing. Here is an example of a 6x6 square.[2] Think of each letter as one of the six games inspected by Reynolds's chess players.

A	B	F	C	E	D
B	C	A	D	F	E
C	D	B	E	A	F
D	E	C	F	B	A
E	F	D	A	C	B
F	A	E	B	D	C

We've boldfaced condition **A** (representing chess game setup #1) to show you how the square meets the two requirements listed in the preceding paragraph. First, condition A occurs in each of the six sequential positions (first in the first row, third in the second row, etc.). Second, A is followed by each of the other letters exactly once. From the top to the bottom rows, (1) A is followed by B, D, F, nothing, C, and E, and (2) A is preceded by nothing, C, E, B, D, and F. The same is true for each of the other letters. Once you have generated a balanced Latin square, you can then randomly assign participants to one of the orders (rows). In our example, participants would be randomly assigned to one of the six orders, represented as rows in the Latin square.

When using Latin squares, it is important for the number of subjects in the study to be equal to or a multiple of the number of rows in the square. That Reynolds had 15 subjects in his study tells you he didn't use a Latin square. If he had added three more chess players, giving him an N of 18, he could have randomly assigned three players to each of the 6 rows of the square (3 x 6 = 18).

Testing More than Once per Condition

In the Reynolds (1992) study, it made no sense to ask the chess players to look at any of the six games more than once. Similarly, if participants in a memory experiment are asked to study and recall four lists of words, with the order of the lists determined by a 4 x 4 Latin square, they are seldom asked to study and recall any particular list a second time unless the researcher is specifically interested in the effects of repeated trials on memory. However, in many studies, it is reasonable, even necessary, for participants to experience each condition more than once. This often happens in research in perception and attention, for instance. A look back at the Müller-Lyer illusions in Figure 6.1 provides an example.

---

[1] Strictly speaking, these two procedures are not the same. Sampling from all possible orders guarantees that no one order will ever be repeated; randomizing the order for each subject does not carry that guarantee.

[2] There are easy-to-use formulas available for building Latin squares; instructions on how to build them and examples of Latin squares can be found quickly with a Google search.

Suppose you were conducting a study in which you wanted to see if participants would be more affected by the Müller-Lyer illusion when it was presented vertically than when shown horizontally or at a 45° angle. Four conditions of the study shown in Figure 6.1, when assigned to the letters A, B, C, and D, are as follows:

A = horizontal

B = 45° to the left

C = 45° to the right

D = vertical

Participants in the study are shown the illusion on a computer screen and make adjustments to the lengths of the parallel lines until they perceive the lines to be equal. A researcher would probably want to test participants in each of the four conditions (A, B, C, and D) more than once to get a more reliable measure of perception and to reduce any chances of measurement error. The four conditions could be presented multiple times to people according to one of two basic procedures.

Reverse Counterbalancing

When using **reverse counterbalancing**, the experimenter simply presents the conditions in one order and then presents them again in the reverse order. In the illusion case, the order would be A–B–C–D, then D–C–B–A. If the researcher wants the participant to perform the task more than twice per condition, and this is common in perception research, this sequence of orders could be repeated as many times as necessary. Hence, if you wanted each participant to adjust each of the four illusions of Figure 6.1 six separate times, and you decided to use reverse counterbalancing, half the participants would be randomly assigned to see the illusions in this order:

A-B-C-D – D-C-B-A – A-B-C-D – D-C-B-A – A-B-C-D – D-C-B-A

while the remaining would see this order:

D-C-B-A – A-B-C-D – D-C-B-A – A-B-C-D – D-C-B-A – A-B-C-D

Reverse counterbalancing was used in one of psychology's most famous studies, completed in the 1930s by J. Ridley Stroop. You've probably tried the Stroop task yourself—when shown color names printed in the wrong colors, you were asked to name the color rather than read the word. That is, when shown the word *red* printed in blue ink, the correct response is "blue," not "red." Stroop's study is a classic example of a particular type of design described in the next chapter, so you will be learning more about his work when you encounter Box 7.1 in Chapter 7.[3]

Block Randomization

A second way to present a sequence of conditions when each condition is presented more than once is to use **block randomization**, where the basic rule is that every condition must occur once before any condition can be repeated. Within each block, the order of conditions is randomized. This strategy eliminates the possibility that participants can predict what is coming next, a problem that can occur with reverse counterbalancing, especially if the reversals occur

---

[3] Although reverse counterbalancing normally occurs when participants are tested more than once per condition, the principle can also be applied in a within-subjects design in which participants see each condition only once. Thus, if a within-subjects study has six conditions, each tested only once per person, half of the participants could get the sequence A-B-C-D-E-F, while the remaining participants experience the reverse order (F-E-D-C-B-A).

several times. In principle, this is the same procedure outlined earlier in the context of how to assign subjects randomly to groups in a between-subjects experiment. Given the ease of obtaining computer-generated randomized orders, this procedure is used more frequently than reverse counterbalancing.

Using the illusions example again (Figure 6.1), participants would encounter all four conditions in a randomized order, then all four again but in a block with a new randomized order, and so on, for as many blocks of four as needed. A reverse counterbalancing would look like this:

A-B-C-D – D-C-B-A

A block randomization procedure might produce either of these two sequences (among others):

B-C-D-A – C-A-D-B   or   C-A-B-D – A-B-D-C

To give you a sense of how block randomization works in an actual within-subjects experiment employing many trials, consider the following study, which suggests that wearing red in an aggressive sport might help you win.

Research Example 8—Counterbalancing with Block Randomization

An interesting study by Hagemann, Strauss, and Leißing (2008) suggests that those who referee combative forms of athletics (e.g., wrestling, judo) can be influenced in their scoring by the colors worn by combatants. They asked 42 experienced tae kwon do referees to examine video segments of matches between two males of equal ability and to assign scoring points that followed their standard set of rules. Each of the combatants wore a white tae kwon do uniform, but each also wore "trunk and head protectors" (p. 769) that were either red or blue.

Each video segment lasted 4.4 seconds and 11 different videos were made. Each referee saw all of the videos, making this a within-subjects design requiring counterbalancing. Block randomization was set up this way: Each referee saw a block of the 11 videos in a random order, and then saw a second block of the same 11 videos, also in a random order. Why two blocks? In one of the blocks of 11 videos, one of the fighters wore red protective gear while the other wore blue. In the second block, the same 11 clips were seen, but the researchers digitally switched the colors of the protective gear. The two blocks were also counterbalanced, so half the refs saw each block first. Thus, referees saw the same tae kwon do event twice, with players dressed in different colors. By creating this design, Hagemann et al. (2008) could determine it was more likely their independent variable (color of the protectors) that would cause differences in referees' judgments rather than the fighters themselves or the fight events themselves.

For experienced and highly competent referees, the color of protective gear should make no difference in judging the quality of the fighting performance, but it did. Figure 6.2 shows the results. The two bars on the left show that in the first block of 11 videos, those wearing red protective gear scored higher than those wearing blue. When the colors were reversed (two bars on the right), even though the *same events* were seen, red protective gear still gave a perceived advantage.

This outcome, of course, makes little sense if you believe referees are objective, and Hagemann et al. (2008) did not provide much of an explanation for their results. Other studies have proposed that red suggests aggressiveness and blue projects calmness, though, so it is conceivable those associations played a role in the biased judgments.

One final point: Notice that Figure 6.2 includes vertical lines at the top of each bar (they also appear in Figure 5.1 in Chapter 5). These are called **error bars**, and they indicate the amount of variability that occurred within each condition. In this case, the distance between the top of a bar and the end of the vertical line represents standard errors, a concept related to the standard

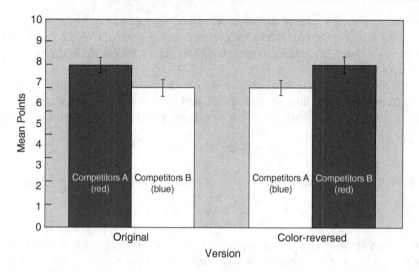

FIGURE 6.2
The effects of color bias on referee judgment of tae kwon do matches (from Hagemann, Strauss, & Leißing (2008).

deviation (error bars can sometimes mean other things, such as confidence intervals). Including error bars in graphs enables the researcher to show the reader both central tendency *and* variability; these bars are now standard features of graphical displays of data.

SELF TEST

6.2

1. What is the defining feature of a within-subjects design? What is the main control problem that must be solved with this type of design?
2. If your IV has six levels, each tested just once per subject, why are you more likely to use partial counterbalancing than complete counterbalancing?
3. If participants are going to be tested more than one time for each level of the IV, what two forms of counterbalancing may be used?

Methodological Control in Developmental Research

As you have learned, the researcher must weigh several factors when deciding whether to use a between-subjects design or a within-subjects design. Additional considerations affect researchers in developmental psychology, where two specific versions of these designs occur. These methods are known as *cross-sectional* and *longitudinal designs*.

You've seen these terms before if you have taken a course in developmental or child psychology. Research in these areas includes age as the prime independent variable; after all, the name of the game in developmental psychology is to discover how we change as we grow older. A **cross-sectional study** takes a between-subjects approach. A cross-sectional study comparing the language performance of 3-, 4-, and 5-year-old children would use three groups of children. A **longitudinal study**, on the other hand, takes a within-subjects or repeated measures approach in which a single group of subjects is studied over time. The same language study would measure language behavior in a group of 3-year-olds and then study these same children when they turned 4, and again at age 5.

The obvious advantage of the cross-sectional approach to the experiment on language is time; data collection for a study comparing 3-, 4-, and 5-year-olds might take a month. If done as a longitudinal study, data collection would take at least 2 years. However, a potentially serious difficulty with some cross-sectional studies is a special form of the problem of non-equivalent groups and involves **cohort effects**. A cohort is a group of people born at about the same time. If you are studying three age groups, they differ not only in chronological age but also in terms of the environments in which they were raised. The problem is not especially noticeable when comparing 3-, 4-, and 5-year-olds, but what if you're interested in whether intelligence declines with age and decide to compare groups aged 45, 65, and 85? You might indeed find a decline with age but does it mean that intelligence decreases with age, or might the differences relate to the very different life histories of the three groups? For example, the 85-year-olds went to school during the Great Depression, the 65-year-olds were educated during the post–World War II boom, and the 45-year-olds were raised on TV. These factors could bias the results. Indeed, this outcome has occurred. Early research on the effects of age on IQ suggested that significant declines occurred, but these studies were cross sectional (e.g., Miles, 1933). Subsequent longitudinal studies revealed a different pattern, however (Schaie, 1988). For example, verbal abilities show minimal decline, especially if the person remains verbally active (moral: for some skills at least, use it or lose it).

While cohort effects can plague cross-sectional studies, longitudinal studies also have problems, most notably with *attrition* (Chapter 5). If a large number of participants drop out of the study, the group completing it may be different from the group starting it. Referring to the age and IQ example, if people stay healthy, they may remain more active intellectually than if they are sick all of the time. If they are chronically ill, they may die before a study is completed, leaving a group that may be generally more intelligent than the group starting the study. Longitudinal studies also pose potential ethical problems. As people develop and mature, they might change their attitudes about their willingness to participate. Most researchers doing longitudinal research recognize that informed consent is an ongoing process, not a one-time event. Ethically sensitive researchers will periodically renew the consent process in long-term studies, perhaps every few years (Fischman, 2000).

In trying to balance cohort and attrition problems, many developmental researchers use a strategy that combines cross sectional with longitudinal studies; one such design is called a **cohort sequential design**. In such a study, a group of subjects is selected and retested every few years, and additional cohorts are selected every few years and also retested over time. So different cohorts are continually being retested. To take a simple example, suppose you wished to examine the effects of aging on memory, comparing ages 55, 60, and 65. In the study's first year, you would recruit a group of 55 year olds. Then, every 5 years after that, you would recruit new groups of 55-year-olds *and* retest those who had been recruited earlier. Schematically, the design for a study that began in the year 2010 and lasted for 30 years would look like this (the numbers in the matrix refer to the age of the subjects at any given testing point):

Cohort #	Year of the Study						
	2010	2015	2020	2025	2030	2035	2040
1	55	60	65				
2		55	60	65			
3			55	60	65		
4				55	60	65	
5					55	60	65

So in 2010, you test a group of 55 year olds. In 2015, you retest these same people (now 60 years old), along with a new group of 55-year-olds. By year three (2020), you have cohorts for all three age groups. By 2040, combining the data in each of the diagonals will give you an overall comparison of those aged 55, 60, and 65. Comparing the data in the rows gives you longitudinal designs, while comparing data in columns (especially 2020, 2025, and 2030) gives you cross-sectional comparisons. Comparing the rows enables a comparison of overall differences among cohorts. In actual practice, these designs are more complicated because researchers will typically start the first year of the study with a fuller range of ages. But the diagram gives you the basic idea.

Perhaps the best-known example of this type of sequential design is a long series of studies by K. Warner Schaie (2005), known as the Seattle Longitudinal Study. Begun in 1956, it was designed to examine age-related changes in various mental abilities. The initial cohort had 500 people, ranging in age from their early 20's to their late 60's (as of 2005, 38 of these subjects were still in the study, 49 years later!). The study has added a new cohort at 7-year intervals ever since 1956 and has recently reached the 50-year mark. About 6,000 in all people have participated. In general, Schaie and his team have found that performance on mental ability tasks declines slightly with age, but with no serious losses before age 60, and the losses can be reduced by good physical health and lots of crossword puzzles. Concerning cohort effects, they have found that overall performance has been progressively better for those born more recently. Presumably, those born later in the 20th century have had the advantages of better education, better nutrition, and so on.

The length of Schaie's (2005) Seattle project is impressive, but the world record for perseverance in a repeated-measures study occurred in what is arguably the most famous longitudinal study of all time. Before continuing, read Box 6.1, which chronicles the epic tale of Lewis Terman's study of gifted children.

BOX 6.1   CLASSIC STUDIES—The Record for Repeated Measures

In 1921, the psychologist Lewis Terman (1877–1956) began what became the longest-running repeated-measures design in the history of psychology. A precocious child himself, Terman developed an interest in studying gifted children as a graduate student. His doctoral dissertation, supervised by Edmund Sanford at Clark University in 1905, was his first serious investigation of giftedness; in it, he compared what he labeled "bright" and "dull" local school children to see which tests might best distinguish between them (Minton, 1987). This early interest in giftedness and mental testing foreshadowed Terman's two main contributions to psychology. First, he transformed the intelligence test created by Alfred Binet of France into the popular Stanford-Binet IQ test. Second, he began a longitudinal study of gifted children that continued long after he died.

Terman was motivated by the belief, shared by most mental testers of his day, that the United States should become a meritocracy—that is, he believed that positions of leadership should be held by those most *able* to lead. You can see how this belief led to his interests in IQ and giftedness. To bring about a meritocracy, there must be ways to recognize (i.e., measure) and nurture talent.

Unlike his dissertation, which studied just 14 children, Terman's longitudinal study of gifted children was a mammoth undertaking. Through a variety of screening procedures, he recruited 1,470 children (824 boys and 646 girls). Most were in elementary school, but a group of 444 were in junior or senior high school (sample numbers from Minton, 1988). Their average IQ score was 150, which put the group roughly in the top 1 percent of the population. (Despite the large sample size it is worth noting that the sample was severely biased—heavily weighted with White, middle- and upper-class children.) Each child selected was given an extensive battery of tests and questionnaires by the team of graduate students assembled by Terman. By the time the initial testing was complete, each child had a file of about 100 pages long (Minton, 1988)! The results of the first analysis of the group were published in more than 600 pages as the *Mental and Physical Traits of a Thousand Gifted Children* (Terman, 1925).

Terman intended to do just a single brief follow-up study, but the project took on a life of its own. The sample was retested in the late 1920s (Burks, Jensen, & Terman, 1930), and additional follow-up studies during Terman's lifetime were published 25 (Terman & Oden, 1947) and 35 (Terman & Oden, 1959) years after the initial testing. Following Terman's death, the project was taken over by Robert Sears, a member of the gifted group and a well-known psychologist in his own right. In the foreword to the 35-year follow-up, Sears wrote: "On actuarial grounds, there is considerable likelihood that the last of Terman's Gifted Children will not have yielded his last report to the files before the year 2010!" (Terman & Oden, 1959, p. 9). Between 1960 and 1986, Sears produced five additional follow-up studies of the group, and he was working on a book-length study of the group as they aged when he died in 1989 (Cronbach, Hastorf, Hilgard, & Maccoby, 1990). The book was eventually published as *The Gifted Group in Later Maturity* (Holahan, Sears, & Cronbach, 1995).

Three points are worth making about this mega-longitudinal study. First, Terman's work questioned the stereotype of the gifted child as someone who was brilliant but socially inept and prone to burnout early in life. Rather, the members of his group as a whole were both brilliant and well-adjusted, and they became successful as they matured. By the time they reached maturity, "the group had produced thousands of scientific papers, 60 nonfiction books,

33 novels, 375 short stories, 230 patents, and numerous radio and television shows, works of art, and musical compositions" (Hothersall, 1990, p. 353). Second, the data collected by Terman's team continues to be a source of rich archival information for modern researchers (look ahead to Chapter 10 for more on archival research methodology). For instance, studies have been published on the careers of the gifted females in Terman's group (Tomlinson-Keasy, 1990) and on the predictors of longevity in the group (Friedman et al., 1995). Third, Terman's follow-up studies are incredible from the methodological standpoint of a longitudinal study's typical nemesis: *attrition*. The following figures (taken from Minton, 1988) are the percentage of living participants who participated in the first three follow-ups:

After 10 years: 92%

After 25 years: 98%

After 35 years: 93%

These are remarkably high numbers and reflect the intense loyalty Terman and his group had for each other. Members of the group referred to themselves as "Termites," and some even wore termite jewelry (Hothersall, 1990). Terman corresponded with hundreds of his participants and genuinely cared for them. After all, the group represented the type of person Terman believed held the key to America's future.

Controlling for the Effects of Bias

Because humans are always the experimenters and usually the participants in psychology research, there is the chance the results of a study could be influenced by some human bias, a preconceived expectation about what is to happen in an experiment. These biases take several forms but fall into two broad categories: those affecting experimenters and those affecting research participants. These two forms of bias often interact.

Experimenter Bias

As well as illustrating falsification and parsimony, the Clever Hans case (Box 3.2 in Chapter 3) is often used to show the effects of **experimenter bias** on the outcome of some study. Hans's questioner, knowing the outcome to the question "What is 3 times 3?" sent subtle head movement cues that were read by the apparently intelligent horse. Similarly, experimenters testing hypotheses sometimes may inadvertently do something that leads participants to behave in ways that confirm the hypothesis. Although the stereotype of the scientist is that of an objective, dispassionate, even mechanical person, the truth is that researchers can become emotionally involved in their research. It's not difficult to see how a desire to confirm a strongly held hypothesis might lead an unwary but emotionally involved experimenter to behave (without awareness) in such a way as to influence the outcome of the study.

For one thing, biased experimenters might treat the research participants in the various conditions differently. Rosenthal developed one procedure demonstrating this. Participants in one of his studies (e.g., Rosenthal & Fode, 1963a) were shown a set of photographs of faces and asked to make judgments about the people pictured in them. For example, they might be asked to rate each photo on how successful the person seemed to be, with the interval scale ranging from −10 (*total failure*) to +10 (*total success*). All participants saw the same photos and made the same judgments. The independent variable was experimenter expectancy. Some experimenters were led to believe most subjects would give people the benefit of the doubt and rate the pictures positively; other experimenters were told to expect negative ratings. Interestingly, the experimenter's expectancies typically produced effects on the subjects' rating behavior, even though the pictures were identical for both groups. How can this be?

According to Rosenthal (1966), experimenters can innocently communicate their expectancies in a number of subtle ways. For instance, on the person perception task, the experimenter holds up a picture while the participant rates it. If the experimenter is expecting a +8 and the person says −3, how might the experimenter act—with a slight frown perhaps? How might the participant read the frown? Might he or she try a +7 on the next trial to see if this could elicit a smile or a nod from the experimenter? In general, could it be that experimenters in this situation, without being aware of it, subtly shape the response of their participants? Does this remind you of Clever Hans?

Rosenthal has even shown that experimenter expectancies can be communicated to subjects in animal research. For instance, he found that rats learned mazes faster for experimenters who *thought* their animals had been bred for maze-running ability than for those who expected their rats to be "maze-dull" (Rosenthal & Fode, 1963b). The rats, of course, were randomly assigned to the experimenters and equal in ability. The determining factor seemed to be that experimenters expecting their rats to be "maze-bright" treated them better; for example, they handled them more, a behavior known to affect learning.

Rosenthal's research has been criticized (e.g., Barber, 1976) on statistical (omitting some data, a *QRP* – see Chapter 3) and methodological grounds (real studies never have such large numbers of experimenters), but the experimenter expectancy effect cannot be ignored; it has been replicated in a variety of situations and by many researchers other than Rosenthal and his colleagues (e.g., Word, Zanna, & Cooper, 1974). Furthermore, experimenters can be shown to influence the outcomes of studies in ways other than through their expectations. The behavior of participants can be affected by the experimenter's race and gender, as well as by demeanor, friendliness, and overall attitude (Adair, 1973). An example of the latter is a study by Fraysse and Desprels-Fraysse (1990), who found that preschoolers' performance on a cognitive task could be influenced by experimenter attitude. The children performed significantly better with "caring" than with "indifferent" experimenters.

Controlling for Experimenter Bias

It is probably impossible to eliminate experimenter effects completely. Experimenters cannot be turned into machines. However, one strategy to reduce bias is to mechanize procedures as much as possible. For instance, it's not hard to remove a frowning or smiling experimenter from the person perception task. Instead, subjects can be shown photos on a screen and asked to make their responses with a key press while the experimenter is out of sight or in a different room entirely.

Similarly, procedures for testing animals automatically have been available since the 1920s, even to the extent of eliminating human handling completely. E. C. Tolman didn't wait for computers to come along before inventing "a self-recording maze with an automatic delivery table" (Tolman, Tryon, & Jeffries, 1929). The delivery table was so-called because it "automatically delivers each rat into the entrance of the maze and 'collects' him at the end without the mediation of the experimenter. Objectivity of scoring is insured by the use of a device which automatically records his path through the maze" (Tryon, 1929, p. 73). Today such automation is routine. Furthermore, computers make it easy to present instructions and stimuli to participants while keeping track of data.

Experimenters can mechanize many procedures, to some degree at least, but the experimenter interacts with every participant nonetheless (e.g., during the consent process). Hence, it is important for experimenters to be trained in how to be experimenters and for the experiments to have highly detailed descriptions of the sequence of steps that experimenters should follow in every research session. These descriptions are called research **protocols**.

A common strategy for controlling for experimenter bias is to use what is called a **double blind** procedure. This means that experimenters are kept unaware, or "in the dark" (blind), about what to expect of participants in a particular testing session; in addition, subjects do not know what to expect. Specifically, neither the experimenters nor the participants know which condition is being tested on any particular trial—hence the designation *double*. (A **single blind** procedure is one in which subjects are unaware but the experimenters know the condition in which each subject is being tested.) A double blind procedure can be accomplished when the principal investigator sets up the experiment but a colleague (usually a graduate student) actually collects the data. Double blind studies are not always easy to create but can be more easily managed, as illustrated in a study by Williams and Bargh (2008). They wondered whether "experiences of physical warmth (or coldness) would increase feelings of interpersonal warmth (or coldness), without the person's being aware of this influence" (p. 606). In their procedure, experimenters handed subjects a cup of either hot or iced coffee. Those whose hands had been warmed subsequently judged a neutral third person as warmer in personality than those given cold hands. The researchers recognized the possibility for bias; the experimenters obviously knew who had received the warm coffee and who had received the iced coffee (i.e., a single blind procedure was in effect). To eliminate the chance that experimenters had "inadvertently treated participants in the two conditions differently" (p. 607), Williams and Bargh ran a second study using a double blind procedure; they created physical warmth and coldness in subjects in a way that kept experimenters uninformed about which condition was being tested. In essence, they replicated their results using single- and double-blind procedures—warm or cold hands influenced participants' behavior. This indicated that the effects of physical warmth on personality judgments was not due to experimenter bias but likely do to a real relationship between warmth and personality.

Research Example 9, which has a practical take-home message for senior citizens (have some coffee around 4:00 in the afternoon) illustrates the effective use of a double blind procedure.

Research Example 9—Using a Double Blind Procedure

There is considerable evidence that as we age, we become less efficient cognitively in the afternoon. Also, older adults are more likely to describe themselves as "morning persons." Ryan, Hatfield, and Hofstetter (2002) wondered if the cognitive decline, as the day wears on, could be neutralized by America's favorite drug—caffeine. They recruited 40 seniors, all 65 or older and self-described as (a) morning types and (b) moderate users of caffeine, and placed them in either a caffeine group or a decaf group (using Starbucks house blend). At each testing session, participants drank a 12-ounce cup of coffee, either caffeinated or not; 30 minutes later, they were given a standardized memory test. The second independent variable was time of testing—either 8:00 A.M. or 4:00 P.M. Subjects were tested twice, once at each time, with a 5- to 11-day interval between sessions. Thus, "time of testing" was a within-subjects manipulated independent variable; whether the seniors drank caffeine or decaf was a between-subjects manipulated independent variable.

The procedure was a double blind one because the experimenters administering the memory tests did not know which participants had ingested caffeine and the seniors did not know which type of coffee they were drinking. And to test for the adequacy of the control procedures, the researchers completed a clever *manipulation check* (a concept you learned about in Chapter 3). At the end of the study, during debriefing, they asked the participants to guess whether they had been drinking the real stuff or the decaf. The accuracy of the seniors' responses was at chance level; they had no idea what they had been drinking. In fact, most guessed incorrectly that they had been given regular coffee during one testing session and decaf at the other. In fact, all subjects had been given either caffeinated coffee at both sessions or decaf at both sessions.

The researchers also did a nice job of incorporating some of the other control procedures you learned about in this chapter. For instance, the seniors were randomly assigned to the two groups, and this *random assignment* seemed to produce the desired equivalence; the groups were indistinguishable in terms of age, education level, and average daily intake of caffeine.[4] Also, *counterbalancing* was used to ensure half of the seniors were tested first in the morning, then the afternoon, while the other half were tested in the afternoon-then-morning sequence.

The results? Time of day did not seem to affect an immediate short-term memory task, but it had a significant effect on a more difficult longer-term memory task. For this second task, seniors studied some information, waited 20 minutes, tried to recall the information, and then completed a recognition test for that same information. Caffeine prevented the decline for this more demanding task. On both the delayed recall and the delayed recognition tasks, seniors scored equally well in the morning sessions. In the afternoon sessions, however, those ingesting caffeine still did well, but the performance of those taking decaf declined. On the delayed recall task, for instance, here are the means of the total number of words recalled (out of 16). Also, remember from Chapter 4 that, when reporting descriptive statistics, it is important to report not just a measure of central tendency (mean) but also an indication of variability. So, in parentheses after each mean below, we have included the standard deviations (*SD*).

Morning with caffeine ➔ 11.8 ($SD = 2.9$)

Morning with decaf ➔ 11.8 ($SD = 2.7$)

Afternoon with caffeine ➔ 11.7 ($SD = 2.8$)

Afternoon with decaf ➔ 8.9 ($SD = 3.0$)

So, if the word gets out about this study, the average age of Starbucks' clients might start to go up, starting around 4:00 in the afternoon. Of course, they will need to avoid the decaf.

Participant Bias

People participating in psychological research cannot be expected to respond like machines. They are humans who *know* they are in an experiment. Presumably, they have been told about the general nature of the research during the informed consent process, but in deception studies, they also know (or at least suspect) they haven't been told everything. Furthermore, even if there is no deception in a study, participants may not believe it—after all, they are in a psychology experiment and aren't psychologists always trying to psychoanalyze or manipulate people? In short, **participant bias** can occur in several ways, depending on what participants are expecting and what they believe their role should be in the study. The forms of participant bias often interact.

---

[4] Note that when researchers use random assignment, they assume the procedure will produce equivalent groups, especially if the groups are large enough. But, they often check to see if random assignment has done its job. In this case, they collected data from the seniors on such factors as their education level and average caffeine consumption. In Chapter 9, you will learn that this kind of information is called *demographic* data, and it is a common feature of most research in psychology. After collecting these demographic data, the experimenters determined no differences between the groups existed, which meant their random assignment procedure worked.

When behavior is affected by the knowledge that one is in an experiment and is therefore important to the study's success, the phenomenon is sometimes called the **Hawthorne effect**, after a famous series of studies of worker productivity. To understand the origins of this term, you should read Box 6.2 before continuing. You may be surprised to learn that most historians believe the Hawthorne effect has been misnamed and that the data of the original study might have been distorted for political reasons.

BOX 6.2 ORIGINS—Productivity at Western Electric

The research that led to naming the so-called Hawthorne effect took place at the Western Electric Plant in Hawthorne, Illinois, over a period of about 10 years, from 1924 to 1933. According to the traditional account, the purpose of the study was to investigate factors influencing worker productivity. Numerous experiments were completed, but the most famous series became known as the Relay Assembly Test Room study.

In the Relay Assembly experiment, six female workers were selected from a larger group in the plant. Their job was to assemble relays for the phone company. Five workers did the actual assembly, and the sixth supplied them with parts. The assembly was a time-consuming, labor-intensive, repetitive job requiring the construction of some 35 parts per relay. Western Electric produced about seven million relays a year (Gillespie, 1988), so naturally they were interested in making workers as productive as possible.

The first series of relay studies extended from May 1927 through September 1928 (Gillespie, 1988). During that time, several workplace variables were studied (and confounded with each other, actually). At various times, there were changes in the scheduling of rest periods, total hours of work, and bonuses paid for certain levels of production. The standard account has it that productivity for this small group quickly reached high levels and stayed there even when working conditions deteriorated. The example always mentioned concerned the infamous "12th test period" when workers were informed the work week would increase from 42 to 48 hours and that rest periods and free lunches would be discontinued. Virtually all textbooks describe the results somewhat like this:

> With few exceptions, no matter what changes were made— whether there were many or few rest periods, whether the workday was made longer or shorter, and so on—the women tended to produce more and more telephone relays.

> (Elmes, Kantowitz, & Roediger, 2006, p. 150)

Supposedly, the workers remained productive because they believed they were a special group and the focus of attention—they were part of an experiment. This is the origin of the concept called the *Hawthorne effect*, the tendency for performance to be affected because people know they are being studied in an experiment. The effect may be genuine, but whether it truly happened at Western Electric is uncertain.

A close look at what actually happened reveals interesting alternative explanations. First, although accounts of the study typically emphasize how delighted the women were to be in this special testing room, the fact is that of the five original assemblers, two had to be removed from the room for insubordination and low output. One was said to have "gone Bolshevik" (Bramel & Friend, 1981). (Remember, the Soviet Union was brand new in the 1920s, and the "red menace" was a threat to industrial America, resulting in, among other things, a fear of labor unions.) Of the two replacements, one was especially talented and enthusiastic and quickly became the group leader. She apparently was selected because she "held the record as the fastest relay-assembler in the regular department" (Gillespie, 1988, p. 122). As you might suspect, her efforts contributed substantially to the high level of productivity.

A second problem with interpreting the relay data is a simple statistical conclusion validity issue. In the famous 12th period, productivity was recorded as output per week rather than output per hour, yet workers were putting in an extra six hours per week compared to the previous test period. If the more appropriate output per hour is used, productivity actually *declined* slightly (Bramel & Friend, 1981). Also, the women were apparently angry about the change, but afraid to complain lest they be removed from the test room, thereby losing potential bonus money. Lastly, in some of the Hawthorne experiments, increased worker productivity could have been simply the result of feedback about performance, along with rewards for productivity (Parsons, 1974).

(continued)

BOX 6.2 (CONTINUED)

Historians argue that events must be understood within their entire political/economic/institutional context, and the Hawthorne studies are no exception. Painting a glossy picture of workers unaffected by specific working conditions and more concerned with being considered special ushered in the human relations movement in industry and led corporations to emphasize the humane management of employees in order to create one big happy family of labor and management. However, this picture also helps maintain power at the level of management and impede efforts at unionization (considered by managers in the 1930s to be a step toward Communism), which some historians (e.g., Bramel & Friend, 1981) believe were the true motives behind the studies completed at Western Electric.

Most research participants, in the spirit of trying to help the experimenter and contribute meaningful results, perhaps part of their Hawthorne feeling of being special, take on the role of the **good subject**, first described by Orne (1962). There are exceptions, of course, but, in general, participants tend to be cooperative, to the point of persevering through repetitive and boring tasks, all in the name of psychological science. Besides being good subjects (and maybe trying to confirm what they think is the hypothesis), research participants also wish to be perceived as competent, creative, emotionally stable, and so on. The belief that they are being evaluated in the experiment produces what Rosenberg (1969) called **evaluation apprehension**. Participants want to be evaluated positively, so they may behave as they think the ideal person should behave. This concern over how one is going to look and the desire to help the experimenter often leads to the same behavior among participants, but sometimes the desire to create a favorable impression and the desire to be a good subject conflict. For example, in a helping behavior study, astute participants might guess they are in the condition of the study designed to reduce the chances that help will be offered—the experimenter doesn't want them to help. On the other hand, altruism is a valued, even heroic, behavior in society. The pressure to be a good subject and support the hypothesis pulls the participant toward non-helping, but evaluation apprehension makes the individual want to help. At least one study has suggested that when participants are faced with the option of confirming the hypothesis and being evaluated positively, the latter is the more powerful motivator (Rosnow, Goodstadt, Suls, & Gitter, 1973).

Furthermore, if participants can figure out the hypothesis, they may try to behave in a way that confirms it. Orne (1962) used the term **demand characteristics** to refer to those aspects of the study that reveal the hypotheses being tested. If these features are too obvious to participants, participants may no longer act naturally; instead, they may behave the way they think they are supposed to behave, making it difficult to interpret the results. Did participants behave as they normally would or did they come to understand the hypothesis and behave so as to make it come true or even to defy it? The presence of demand characteristics can severely reduce a study's internal validity. The possibility that demand characteristics are operating can affect the choice of between- or within-subject designs. Participants serving in all of the conditions of a study have a greater opportunity to figure out the hypothesis. Hence, demand characteristics are potentially more troublesome in within-subject designs than in between-subjects designs. For both types, demand characteristics are especially devastating if they affect some conditions but not others, thereby introducing a confound.

Demand characteristics can operate in many subtle ways. Here is an example of a study showing how they might operate in a research area that has become an important one for human well-being.

Research Example 10—Demand Characteristics

With obesity a major health risk, psychologists for some time have been interested in studying the factors that affect eating behavior. The result has been a long list of reasons why people often eat even if they are not especially hungry, ranging from emotional factors such as depression to situational cues such as the visual attractiveness of food. A common procedure is to give subjects the opportunity to evaluate food in some form of taste test, while giving them the opportunity to eat as much of the sample food as they would like. The researcher will be more interesting in measuring how much is eaten rather than the taste evaluations. Robinson, Kersbergen, Brunstrom, and Field (2014) wondered if demand characteristics could be operating in these eating behavior studies. In particular, they were concerned that if subjects detected that "amount of food eaten" was the dependent measure of interest, they might eat less than they normally would eat.

After conducting an online survey showing that people reported that they would be likely to reduce their eating behavior if they suspected their eating was being monitored, Robinson et al. (2014) designed a study to see if cues about the experimenter monitoring food consumption would in fact reduce eating behavior. Subjects were randomly assigned to three groups in a study using a standard taste-test procedure. Thus, all participants were told that they would be evaluating the taste of a batch of cookies, that "they were free to eat as many cookies as they liked, and that any remaining food would be thrown away" (p. 22). This is all that subjects in a control condition were told; those assigned to a "monitored" condition were also told that the researcher would be recording how many cookies were eaten; those in an "unmonitored" condition were told to dispose of remaining cookies in a waste bin after they finished their taste ratings. This third condition was included in an attempt "to convince the participants that their food consumption was not being monitored" (p. 22).

The results clearly indicated that eating behavior was affected by knowledge of food monitoring—subjects ate significantly less when they knew the number of cookies they were eating would be counted. Here are the means and standard deviations (the dependent variable was the number of grams of cookie eaten):

Control condition	M = 45.8	SD = 21.9
Monitored condition	M = 29.3	SD = 12.4
Unmonitored condition	M = 47.7	SD = 25.3

As a *manipulation check*, Robinson et al. (2014) asked subjects at the end of the study to indicate on a 5-point scale whether they believed their eating behavior was being monitored (regardless of what their instructions had been). These data were

Control condition	M = 3.7	SD = 1.1
Monitored condition	M = 4.0	SD = 0.8
Unmonitored condition	M = 3.3	SD = 0.9

These means were not significantly different from each other.

Taken together, these results indicate that if subjects in eating behavior studies suspect the amount of their food consumption is being measured, they will significantly reduce their eating behavior. This is the classic instance of a demand characteristic – knowledge of a researcher's purpose affecting participant behavior. One particular danger that Robinson et al. (2014) pointed out was that this demand characteristic could result in some eating behavior studies finding no significant results because of a *floor effect*. That is, in a study designed to show that some factor reduces eating, the demand characteristic might reduce eating to low levels in all the conditions of the study, making it impossible to detect differences among conditions.

Controlling for Participant Bias

The primary strategy for controlling participant bias is to reduce demand characteristics to the minimum. One way of accomplishing this, of course, is through deception. As we've seen in Chapter 2, the primary purpose of deception is to induce participants to behave more naturally than they otherwise might. A second strategy, normally found in drug studies, is to use a placebo control group (elaborated in Chapter 7). This procedure allows for comparison of those actually getting some treatment (e.g., a drug) and those who *think* they are getting the treatment but aren't. If the people in both groups behave identically, the effects can be attributed to participant expectations of the treatment's effects. You have probably already recognized that the caffeine study you read about (Research Example 9) used this form of logic.

A second way to check for the presence of demand characteristics is to do a *manipulation check.* This can be accomplished during debriefing by asking participants in a deception study to indicate what they believe the true hypothesis to be (the "good subject" might feign ignorance, though). You recall that this was the strategy used in Research Example 9 by asking participants to guess whether they had been given caffeine in their coffee or not. Manipulation checks can also be performed during an experiment. Sometimes, a random subset of participants in each condition will be stopped in the middle of a procedure and asked about the clarity of the instructions, what they think is going on, and so on. In the study on violent video games, desensitization, and helping that you read about in Chapter 3 (Research Example 1), the manipulation check was built directly into the procedure in the form of a survey asking subjects to rate the violence level of the video games. Manipulation checks are also used to see if some procedure is producing the effect it is supposed to produce. For example, if a procedure is supposed to make people feel anxious (e.g., telling participants to expect shock), a sample of participants might be stopped in the middle of the study and assessed for level of anxiety.

A final way of avoiding demand characteristics is to conduct field research. If participants are unaware they are in a study, they are unlikely to spend any time thinking about research hypotheses and reacting to demand characteristics. Of course, field studies have problems of their own, as you recall from the discussion of informed consent in Chapter 2.

Although we stated earlier that most research participants play the role of "good subjects," this is not uniformly true, and differences exist between those who truly volunteer and are interested in the experiment and those who are more reluctant and less interested. For instance, true volunteers tend to be slightly more intelligent and have a higher need for social approval (Adair, 1973). Differences between volunteers and non-volunteers can be a problem when college students are asked to serve as participants as part of a course requirement; some students are more enthusiastic volunteers than others. Furthermore, a semester effect can operate. The true volunteers, those really interested in participating, sign up earlier in the semester than the reluctant volunteers. Therefore, if you ran a study with two groups, and one group was tested in the first half of the semester and the other group in the second half, the differences found could be due to the independent variable, but they also could be due to differences between the true volunteers who signed up first and the reluctant volunteers who waited as long as they could to sign up. Can you think of a way to control for this problem? If "blocked random assignment" occurs to you, and you say to yourself "This will distribute the conditions of the study equally throughout the duration of the semester," then you've accomplished something in this chapter. Well done!

SELF TEST

6.3

1. Unlike most longitudinal studies, Terman's study of gifted children did not experience which control problem?
2. Why does a double blind procedure control for experimenter bias?
3. How can a demand characteristic influence the outcome of a study?

To close this chapter, read Box 6.3, which concerns the ethical obligations of participants in psychological research. The list of responsibilities you'll find there is based on the assumption that research should be a collaborative effort between experimenters and participants. We've seen that experimenters must follow the APA ethics code. In Box 6.3 you'll learn that participants have responsibilities too.

In the last two chapters, you have learned about the essential features of experimental research and some of the control problems faced by those who wish to do research in psychology. We've now completed the necessary groundwork for introducing the various experimental designs used to test the effects of independent variables. So, let the designs begin!

BOX 6.3   ETHICS—Research Participants Have Responsibilities Too

The APA ethics code spells out the responsibilities researchers have to those who participate in their experiments. Participants have a right to expect that the guidelines will be followed, and the process for registering complaints should be a clear if they are not. But what about the participants? What are their obligations?

An article by Korn in the journal *Teaching of Psychology* (1988) outlines the basic rights that college students have when they participate in research, but it also lists the responsibilities of those who volunteer. These include:

- Be responsible about scheduling by showing up on time for appointments with researchers.

- Be cooperative and acting professionally by giving their best and most honest effort.

- Listen carefully to the experimenter during the informed consent and instructions phases and asking questions if they are not sure what to do.

- Respect any request by the researcher to avoid discussing the research with others until all the data are collected.

- Be active during the debriefing process by helping the researcher understand the phenomenon being studied.

The assumption underlying this list is that research should be a collaborative effort between researchers and participants. Korn's (1988) suggestion that subjects take a more assertive role in making research collaborative is a welcome one. This assertiveness, however, must be accompanied by enlightened experimentation that values and probes for the insights participants have about what might be going on in a study. An experimenter who simply runs a subject and records the data is ignoring valuable information.

CHAPTER SUMMARY

Between-Subjects Designs

In between-subjects designs, individuals participate in just one of the experiment's conditions; hence, each condition in the study involves a different group of participants. Such a design is usually necessary when subject variables (e.g., gender) are being studied or when being in one condition of the experiment changes participants in ways that make it impossible for them to participate in another condition. With between-subjects designs, the main difficulty is creating groups that are essentially equivalent on all factors except for the independent variable.

Creating Equivalent Groups

The preferred method of creating equivalent groups in between-subjects designs is random assignment. Random assignment has the effect of spreading unforeseen confounding factors evenly throughout the different groups, thereby eliminating their damaging influence. The chance of random assignment working to produce equivalent groups increases as the number of participants per group increases. If few participants are available, if some factor (e.g., intelligence) correlates highly with the dependent variable, and if that factor can be assessed without difficulty before the experiment begins, then equivalent groups can be formed by using a matching procedure. Subjects are matched on some matching variable and then randomly assigned to groups.

Within-Subjects Designs

When each individual participates in all of the study's conditions, the study is using a within-subjects (or repeated-measures) design. For these designs, participating in one condition might affect how participants behave in other conditions—that is, sequence or order effects can occur, both of which can produce confounded results if not controlled. Order effects include progressive effects (they gradually accumulate, as in fatigue or boredom) and carryover effects (one sequence of conditions might produce effects different from another sequence). When substantial carryover effects are suspected, researchers usually switch to a between-subjects design.

Controlling Order Effects

Order effects are controlled by counterbalancing procedures that ensure the conditions are tested in more than one sequence. When participants serve in every condition of the study just once, complete (all possible orders of conditions used) or partial (a sample of different orders or a Latin square) counterbalancing is used. When participants serve in every condition more than once, reverse counterbalancing or blocked randomization can be used.

Methodological Control in Developmental Research

In developmental psychology, the major independent variable is age, a subject variable. If age is studied between subjects, the design is cross sectional. It has the advantage of efficiency, but cohort effects can occur, a special form of the problem of non-equivalent groups. If age is a within-subjects variable, the design is longitudinal and attrition can be a problem. The two strategies can be combined in a cohort sequential design: selecting new cohorts every few years and testing each cohort longitudinally.

Controlling for the Effects of Bias

The results of research in psychology can be biased by experimenter expectancy effects. These can lead the experimenter to treat participants in different conditions in various ways, making the results difficult to interpret. Such effects can be reduced by automating the procedures and/or using double blind control procedures. Participant bias also occurs. Participants might behave in unusual ways simply because they know they are in an experiment or they might confirm the researcher's hypothesis if demand characteristics suggest to them the true purpose of a study. Demand characteristics are usually controlled through varying degrees of deception; the extent of participant bias can be evaluated by using a manipulation check.

CHAPTER REVIEW QUESTIONS

1. Under what circumstances would a between-subjects design be preferred over a within-subjects design?

2. Under what circumstances would a within-subjects design be preferred over a between-subjects design?

3. How does random selection differ from random assignment, and what is the purpose of each?

4. As a means of creating equivalent groups, when is matching more likely to be used than random assignment?

5. Distinguish between progressive effects and carryover effects, and explain why counterbalancing might be more successful with the former than the latter.

6. In a taste test, Joan is asked to evaluate four dry white wines for taste: wines A, B, C, and D. In what sequence would they be tasted if (a) reverse counterbalancing or (b) blocked randomization were being used? How many orders would be required if the researcher used complete counterbalancing?

7. What are the defining features of a Latin square, and when is one likely to be used?

8. What specific control problems exist in developmental psychology with (a) cross-sectional studies and (b) longitudinal studies?

9. What is a cohort sequential design, and why is it an improvement on cross-sectional and longitudinal designs?

10. Describe an example of a study that illustrates experimenter bias. How might such bias be controlled?

11. What are demand characteristics and how might they be controlled?

12. What is a Hawthorne effect? What is the origin of the term?

APPLICATIONS EXERCISES

Exercise 6.1. Between-Subject or Within-Subject?

Think of a study that might test each of the following hypotheses. For each, indicate whether you think the independent variable should be a between- or a within-subjects variable or whether either approach would be reasonable. Explain your decision in each case.

1. A neuroscientist hypothesizes that damage to the primary visual cortex is permanent in older animals.

2. A sensory psychologist predicts that it is easier to distinguish slightly different shades of gray under daylight than under fluorescent light.

3. A clinical psychologist thinks that phobias can be cured by repeatedly exposing the person to the feared object and not allowing the person to escape until the person realizes the object really is harmless.

4. A developmental psychologist predicts cultural differences in moral development.

5. A social psychologist believes people will solve problems more creatively when in groups than when alone.

6. A cognitive psychologist hypothesizes that giving subjects repeated tests of verbal information will lead to greater retention than asking subjects to study the verbal information repeatedly.

7. A clinician hypothesizes that people with obsessive-compulsive disorder will be easier to hypnotize than people with a phobic disorder.

8. An industrial psychologist predicts that worker productivity will increase if the company introduces flextime scheduling (i.e., work eight hours, but start and end at different times).

Exercise 6.2. Fixing Confounds

Return to Exercise 5.2 in Chapter 5 and fix the confounds in those studies by designing a well-controlled study for each scenario. For each study, be sure to explain how you would use the methodological controls you learned about in Chapter 6.

Exercise 6.3. Random Assignment and Matching

A researcher investigates the effectiveness of an experimental weight-loss program. Sixteen volunteers will participate, half assigned to the experimental program and half placed in a control group. In a study such as this, it would be good if the average weights of the subjects in the two groups were approximately equal at the start of the experiment. Here are the weights, in pounds, for the 16 subjects before the study begins.

168	210	182	238	198	175	205	215
186	178	185	191	221	226	188	184

First, use a matching procedure as the method to form the two groups (experimental and control) and then calculate the average weight per group. Second, assign participants to the groups again, this time using random assignment (cut out 20 small pieces of paper, write one of the weights on each, and then draw them out of a hat to form the two groups). Again, calculate the average weight per group after the random assignment has occurred. Compare your results to those of the rest of the class. Are the average weights for the groups closer to each other with matching or with random assignment? In a situation such as this, what do you conclude about the relative merits of matching and random assignment?

ANSWERS TO SELF TESTS

✓ 6.1

1. A minimum of two groups of subjects is tested in the study, one group for each level of the IV; the problem of equivalent groups.
2. As in the Barbara Helm study, it is sometimes essential that subjects not be aware of what occurs in other conditions of the study.
3. Sal must have a reason to expect verbal fluency to correlate with his dependent variable; he must also have a good way to measure verbal fluency.

✓ 6.2

1. Each subject participates in each level of the IV; order effects
2. With six levels of the IV, complete counterbalancing requires a minimum of 720 subjects (6 x 5 x 4 x 3 x 2 x 1), which could be impractical.
3. Reverse counterbalancing or block randomization.

✓ 6.3

1. Attrition.
2. If the experimenter does not know which subjects are in each of the groups in the study, the experimenter cannot behave in a biased fashion.
3. If subjects know what is expected of them, they might be "good subjects" and not behave naturally.

Experimental Design I: Single-Factor Designs

7

PREVIEW & CHAPTER OBJECTIVES

Chapters 5 and 6 have set the stage for this and the following chapter. In Chapter 5, we introduced you to the experimental method; distinguished between independent, extraneous, and dependent variables; considered the problem of confounding; and discussed several factors relating to the validity of psychology experiments. Chapter 6 compared between-subjects and within-subjects designs, described the basic techniques of control associated with each (e.g., random assignment, counterbalancing), and dealt with the problems of experimenter and subject bias in psychological research. With the stage now ready, this and the next chapter can be considered a playbill—a listing and description of the research designs that constitute experimental research in psychology. This chapter considers designs that feature single independent variables with two or more levels. Adding independent variables creates factorial designs, the main topic of Chapter 8. When you finish this chapter, you should be able to:

- Identify and understand the defining features of the four varieties of single-factor designs: independent groups, matched groups, ex post facto, and repeated measures.

- Describe two reasons for using more than two levels of an independent variable.

- Decide when to use a bar graph to present data and when to use a line graph.

- Describe the goals of the Ebbinghaus memory research, his methodology, and the results he obtained.

- Understand the logic behind the use of three types of control groups: placebo, wait list, and yoked.

- Understand the ethical issues involved when using certain types of control groups.

- Know when to use an independent samples *t*-test and when to use a dependent samples *t*-test, when doing an inferential analysis of a single-factor, two-level design.

- Understand why a one-way ANOVA, rather than multiple *t*-tests, is the appropriate analysis when examining data from single-factor, multilevel studies.

- Understand why post hoc statistical analyses typically accompany one-way ANOVAs for single-factor, multilevel studies.

In Chapter 3's discussion of scientific creativity we used the origins of maze-learning research as an example. Willard Small's research, using a modified version of the Hampton Court maze, was the first of a flood of studies on maze learning that appeared in the first two decades of the 20th century. Most of the early research aimed to determine which of the rat's senses was critical to the learning process. You might recall from Box 2.3 of Chapter 2 that John Watson ran into trouble with "antivivisectionists" for doing a series of studies in which he surgically eliminated one sense after another and discovered that maze learning was not hampered even if rats were deprived of most of their senses. He concluded that rats rely on their muscle (kinesthetic) sense to learn and recall the maze. In effect, he argued that the rat learns to take so many steps, and turn right, and so on.

To test his kinesthesis idea directly, he completed a simple yet elegant study with his University of Chicago colleague Harvey Carr. After one group of rats learned a complicated maze, Carr and Watson (1908) removed a middle section of the maze structure, thereby making certain portions of the maze shorter than before, while maintaining the same overall maze design. They predicted that rats trained on the longer maze might literally run into the walls when the maze was shortened. Sure enough, in a description of one of the rats, the researchers noted that it "ran into [the wall] with all her strength. Was badly staggered and did not recover normal conduct until she had gone [another] 9 feet" (p. 39). A second group of rats was trained on the shorter maze and then tested on the longer one. These rats behaved similarly, often turning too soon and running into the sidewall of an alley, apparently expecting to find a turn there. Long after he left academia, John Watson remembered this study as one of his most important. Subsequent research on maze learning questioned the kinesthesis conclusion, but the important point here is that good research does not require immensely complex research designs. In some cases, comparing two groups will do just fine.

Single Factor—Two Levels

As you can see from the decision tree in Figure 7.1, four basic research designs can be called **single-factor designs**, with the term *factor* meaning "independent variable" here. Thus, single-factor designs have one independent variable. We will start with the simplest ones, those with two levels of the independent variable. The four designs result from decisions about the independent variable under investigation. First, the independent variable can be tested either between- or within-subjects. If it is tested between-subjects, it could be either a manipulated or a subject variable. If the independent variable is manipulated, the design will be called either an **independent groups design**, if simple random assignment is used to create equivalent groups, or a **matched groups design**, if a matching procedure followed by random assignment is used. As you recall from Chapter 6, decisions about whether to use random assignment or matching have to do with sample size and the need to be wary about extraneous variables that are highly correlated with the dependent variable.

If a subject variable is being investigated, the groups are composed of different types of individuals (e.g., male or female, introverted or extroverted, liberal or conservative, living in Pittsburgh or living in Cleveland). This design is called an **ex post facto design** because the subjects in the study are placed into the groups "after the fact" of their already existing subject characteristics. Researchers using ex post facto designs typically attempt to make the groups as similar as possible with reference to other variables. For instance, a study comparing males and females might select participants for each group that are about the same age and from the same socioeconomic class. Note that this type of matching, in which males are recruited so they are comparable in age and class to females, is a bit different from the kind of matching that occurs in the matched group design. In the latter, after matched pairs have been formed, they are randomly assigned to groups. In ex post facto designs, random assignment is not possible; subjects are already in one group or another by virtue of the subject variable being investigated (e.g., gender). You will see these two forms of matching in Research Examples 12 and 13 below.

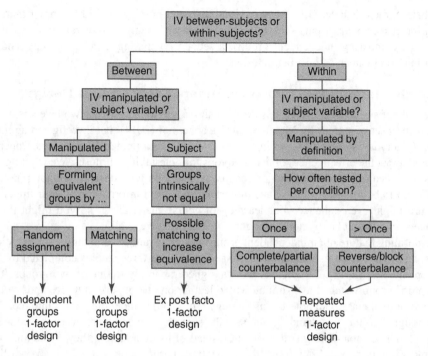

Figure 7.1
Decision tree—single-factor designs.

Table 7.1   **Attributes of Four Single-Factor Designs**

Types of Design	Minimum Levels of Independent Variable?	Independent Variable Between or Within?	Independent Variable Type?	Creating Equivalent Groups
Independent groups	2	between	manipulated	random assignment
Matched groups	2	between	manipulated	matching
Ex post facto	2	between	subject	matching may increase equivalence
Repeated measures	2	within	manipulated	n/a

The fourth type of single-factor design is a **repeated-measures design**, used when the independent variable is tested within-subjects—that is, each participant in the study experiences each level of the independent variable (i.e., is measured repeatedly). The major attributes of each of the four main types of designs are summarized in Table 7.1. Let's look at specific examples.

Between-Subjects, Single-Factor Designs

Single-factor studies using only two levels are not as common as you might think. Most researchers prefer to use more complex designs, which often produce more elaborate and more intriguing outcomes. Also, journal editors are often unimpressed with single-factor, two-level designs.

Nonetheless, there is a certain beauty in simplicity, and nothing could be simpler than a study comparing just two conditions. The following Research Examples illustrate three such experiments, one comparing independent groups, a second comparing matched groups, and a third comparing groups in an ex post facto design.

Research Example 11—Two-Level Independent Groups Design

An example of an independent groups design using a single factor with two levels is the first of an interesting set of studies by Mueller and Oppenheimer (2014) that investigated an important aspect of everyday student life—taking notes in class. In particular, Mueller and Oppenheimer wondered about the effectiveness of using laptops for note-taking purposes. We would guess that you like the idea of having information readily available on your devices, so laptop note-taking would seem to be a useful way to have important classroom information at your fingertips; the procedure might even enhance your learning of course material. Or so you might think—the evidence suggests that laptop note-taking is not very effective at all.

The defining feature of an independent groups design is random assignment of participants to groups, and that is what happened in the first of a series of three studies completed by Mueller and Oppenheimer (2014). Participants were assigned randomly to one of two groups. Those in the "laptop" group watched a 15-minute video lecture on one of several topics and were told to "use their normal classroom note-taking strategy" (p. 1160) while typing notes into their laptops. Those assigned to the "longhand" group saw the same lecture and were given the same instructions (i.e., normal note-taking strategy), but instead of using a laptop, they wrote their notes in longhand on note paper. After finishing the lecture, participants completed several distractor tasks lasting 30 minutes and then had their memory for the lecture tested. Questions (quoted from p. 1160) were both factual (e.g., "Approximately how many years ago did the Indus civilization exist?") and conceptual (e.g., "How do Japan and Sweden differ in their approaches to equality within their societies?").

On the factual questions, no differences occurred between the two groups. So, there was no advantage to taking notes on a laptop versus taking notes by hand when being tested on factual questions. On the conceptual questions however, there was a clear advantage for those taking notes by longhand over those typing notes into the laptop. This was true regardless of the topic of the lecture that participants listened to, and despite the fact that laptop note takers wrote significantly more words in their notes than did longhand note takers.

In Chapter 3 you learned that research outcomes often lead naturally to follow-up studies and that was exactly what happened with Mueller and Oppenheimer (2014). Using good *"what's next"* thinking and *conceptual replication* of their first experiment, they wondered what might account for the group differences. They had noticed in Study 1 that the laptop note takers seemed to transcribe the lectures verbatim, so they wondered if the advantages of longhand note taking might disappear if all subjects were explicitly instructed *not* to take down the lecture content in verbatim terms. What they found in Study 2 was that asking laptop subjects *not* to take notes verbatim did not improve memory performance and that these subjects still, despite the instructions, tended to write down content word for word. This outcome led to Study 3, in which they reasoned that perhaps the longhand note advantage would disappear if subjects were allowed to study their notes before taking the memory test (you can detect some *ecological validity* thinking here, creating a situation close to what students typically do—take notes, study notes, take a test). In this third study, longhand note takers still prevailed. Taken together, this set of experiments have clear implications for students in class—take notes by hand, and don't copy down what the professor is saying word for word. Translating lecture content into your own words produces a deeper level of information processing and improves memory for the lecture.

One final methodological point about this study is worth mentioning here. Especially on the conceptual questions, scoring was to some extent subjective, opening the door for some potential bias. To control for this, the study's first author scored all the responses while not knowing which group was being scored; furthermore, a second scorer was used, and the results of the two scorers were compared. You might recognize this as a form of reliability (Chapter 4); in this case it is called **inter-rater reliability** and it was quite high in the study, giving the authors confidence that the test scoring was accurate.

Research Example 12— Two-Level Matched Groups Design

As you recall from Chapter 6, researchers often use a matching procedure, followed by random assignment, when (a) they have a small number of subjects, (b) they are concerned that some attribute of these subjects could affect the outcome, and (c) they have a good way of measuring that attribute. All three of those factors occurred in an interesting study on autism by Kroeger, Schultz, and Newsom (2007). They developed a video peer-modeling program designed to improve the social skills of young children (ages 4 to 6) with autism.

During 15 hour-long sessions over a 5-week period, some children with autism participated in a "Direct Teaching" group, spending part of their sessions seeing a brief video of other 4- to 6-year-old children modeling social skills that are typically absent in children with autism (e.g., taking turns with another child in a puzzle completion task). They then were given the opportunity to imitate those skills during a play period, with reinforcement for doing so. Children in a second ("Play Activities") group did not see the videos; they spent the time in play sessions that equaled the time the video-modeling group spent watching the video and then playing. Everything else was the same for both groups—for instance, children in the second group were also reinforced for displaying such social skills as taking turns in a puzzle task.

There were only 25 children in the study, and children with autism can display a wide range in their general level of functioning. Hence, a simple random assignment procedure might run the risk of producing two groups with different average levels of functioning. To avoid the problem, Kroeger et al. (2007) used a matching procedure followed by random assignment. Using a standard scale for measuring autism, the Gilliam Autism Rating Scale (a checklist completed by parents that lists a range of behaviors), Kroeger and her colleagues created pairs of children with matching levels of functioning (an "Autism Quotient"), and then randomly assigned one of each pair to each group.[1] The procedure worked; the average Autism Quotient scores for the two groups were essentially identical (92.15 and 92.58). Because it is necessary to have close supervision and small groups when working with children with autism, there were actually three Direct Teaching groups and three Play Activities groups, and a child-adult ratio of 2:1 was maintained in all groups.

In a study like this one, given the range of behaviors that can occur in a free play situation, it is important to have good *operational definitions* for the behaviors being measured. In this case, Kroeger et al. (2007) had a standardized measure available to them, the Social Interaction Observation Code. It measures "the prosocial behaviors of initiating a social interaction, responding to an initiation or invitation to socialize, and maintaining that social interaction" (p. 814). Even with such a tool, however, observations were made by fallible human observers, who did their scoring while watching video of the sessions. Three important control procedures were used to minimize human error and bias. First, observers were given extensive training. Second, researchers used the *double blind* procedure you learned about in Chapter 6; observers scoring a particular session did not know if the children were in the modeling group or not. Third, because any one observer might make errors, pairs of observers were used for each video segment, and the extent to which their coding results agreed was assessed. As in Mueller and Oppenheimer's

---

[1] Good for you if you wondered how the matching procedure worked with an odd number of subjects ($N = 25$). The senior author of the study (it was her doctoral dissertation) recalls that after 12 pairs had been formed, the parents of the remaining subject were given the choice of which group their child would join. Naturally, researchers don't like to turn away willing participants. Even with this slight deviation from a normal matching procedure, children in the two groups were equivalent on the matching variable, the Autism Quotient scores (K. A. Kroeger-Geoppinger, personal communication, November 8, 2011).

(2014) note-taking study, *inter-rater reliability* was assessed for observers who scored the video. After undergoing training, the observers in this autism study were quite good; they agreed 98.4% of the time. As for the results, the video modeling procedure worked. The children in the Direct Teaching group showed dramatic improvement in their social interaction skills, while those in the Play Activities group did not change.

Research Example 13— Two-Level Ex Post Facto Design

One type of research that calls for an ex post facto design examines the effects of brain damage that results from an accident. For obvious ethical reasons, an independent groups design with human subjects is out of the question (any volunteers for the experimental group, those randomly assigned to the group receiving the brain damage?). Although most research studies comparing those with traumatic brain injuries (TBI) look at cognitive factors (e.g., effects on memory or language), an interesting study by McDonald and Flanagan (2004) investigated the abilities of 34 subjects with TBI to process and understand social exchanges. As with many ex post facto studies, the researchers tried to select subjects so the two groups would be as similar as possible, except for the brain damage; in this case they selected control group subjects (without TBI) that were "matched on the basis of age, education, and gender" (p. 574). Note again that this is matching "after the fact" and different from the situation in Research Example 12, when matching was followed by random assignment. Matching followed by random assignment creates equivalent groups; matching in an ex post facto design makes the groups more similar to each other, but we cannot say equivalent groups are the result because random assignment is not possible with the subject variables that define the ex post facto design.

In the McDonald and Flanagan (2004) study, both groups viewed brief videos from The Awareness of Social Inference Test (TASIT). The videos portrayed people having various kinds of social interactions and displaying a range of emotions. For instance, one TASIT video includes an exchange in which one person is displaying sarcasm, while another video has one person lying to another. McDonald and Flanagan were interested in determining if those with TBI were impaired in their ability to (a) accurately detect the basic emotions being felt by those in the videos (e.g., the anger of someone who was being sarcastic), (b) distinguish sincere from sarcastic comments, and (c) distinguish "diplomatic" lies (told to avoid hurting someone's feelings) from lies told in a sarcastic fashion. The results? Compared to controls, those with TBI were significantly impaired in their abilities to recognize emotions and to recognize a lack of sincerity. For example, because they had problems detecting anger, they found it hard to distinguish sarcasm from sincerity.

In studies like this, one methodological concern is *external validity* (Chapter 5). To what extent did the 34 experimental subjects in the McDonald and Flanagan (2004) study represent a typical TBI patient? The researchers were aware of the issue and took pains to select participants who would, as a group, reflect the usual attributes of TBI patients. For example, they compared the number of days of posttraumatic amnesia (76) for their TBI subjects with the number of amnesia days reported "in a consecutive series of 100 people with TBI who were discharged from a comparable brain-injury unit in an independent study" (p. 573), and found no significant difference. From this and other factors, McDonald and Flanagan concluded their "group was representative of the severity of injury typically seen in this population" (p. 573).

Within-Subjects, Single-Factor Designs

As you already know, any within-subjects design (a) requires fewer participants, (b) is more sensitive to small differences between means, and (c) typically uses counterbalancing to control for order effects. A within-subjects design with a single independent variable and two levels will counterbalance in one of two ways. If subjects participate in each condition just once, complete counterbalancing will be used. Half of the participants will experience condition A and then B, and the rest will get B and then A. If participants are tested more than once per condition, reverse counterbalancing (ABBA) could be used. This route was taken by J. Ridley Stroop in the first two of three studies he reported in 1935. This study is high on anyone's "Top 10 Classic Studies" list. For a close look at it, read Box 7.1 before continuing.

BOX 7.1   CLASSIC STUDIES—Psychology's Most Widely Replicated Finding?

Reverse counterbalancing was the strategy used in a study first published in 1935 by J. Ridley Stroop. The study is so well known that the phenomenon it demonstrated is now called the "Stroop effect." In an article accompanying a 1992 reprinting of the original paper, Colin MacLeod called the Stroop effect the "gold standard" of measures of attention, and opened his essay by writing that

> it would be virtually impossible to find anyone in cognitive psychology who does not have at least a passing acquaintance with the Stroop effect. Indeed, this generalization could probably be extended to all those who have taken a standard introductory course, where the Stroop task is an almost inevitable demonstration. (MacLeod, 1992, p. 12)

MacLeod went on to state that the Stroop effect is one of psychology's most widely replicated and most frequently cited findings—a PsycINFO search for "Stroop effect OR Stroop test OR Stroop interference" yields more than 4,000 hits. So what did J. Ridley Stroop do?

The original 1935 publication summarized three experiments completed by Stroop as his doctoral dissertation at George Peabody College (now part of Vanderbilt University). We'll focus on the first two experiments because they each illustrate a within-subjects design with one independent variable, tested at two levels, and using reverse counterbalancing. In the first experiment, 14 males and 56 females performed two tasks. Both involved reading the names of color words. Stroop (1992, p. 16) called one of the conditions RCNb ("**R**eading **C**olor **N**ames printed in **b**lack"). Participants read 100 color names (e.g., GREEN) printed in black ink as quickly and accurately as they could. The second condition Stroop (1992, p. 16) called RCNd ("**R**eading **C**olor **N**ames where the color of the print and the word are **d**ifferent"). In this case, the 100 color names were printed in colored ink, but the colors of the ink did not match the color name (e.g., the word GREEN was printed in red ink). The subjects' task was to read the word (e.g., the correct response is "green").

As a good researcher, Stroop (1935) was aware of the problems with *order effects*, so he used reverse counterbalancing (ABBA) to deal with the problem. After subdividing each of the stimulus lists into two sets of 50 items, Stroop gave some participants the sequence RCNb–RCNd–RCNd–RCNb, and an equal number of participants the sequence RCNd–RCNb–RCNb–RCNd. Thus, each subject read a total of 200 color names.

In Experiment 1, Stroop (1935) found *no difference* in performance between the RCNb and RCNd conditions. The average amount of time to read 100 words of each type was 41.0 seconds and 43.3 seconds, respectively. Reading the color names in the RCNd condition was unaffected by having the words printed in contrasting colors. It was in Experiment 2 that Stroop found the huge difference that eventually made his name so well known. Using the same basic design, this time the response was *naming the colors* rather than reading color names. In one condition, NC ("**N**aming **C**olor test"), participants named the colors of square color patches. In the second and key condition, NCWd ("**N**aming **C**olor of **W**ord test, where the color of the print and the word are **d**ifferent"), participants saw the same material as in the RCNd condition of Experiment 1, but this time, instead of reading the color name, they were to name the color in which the word was printed. If the letters of the word GREEN were printed in red ink, the correct response this time would be "red," not "green." Stroop's subjects had the same difficulty experienced by people trying this task today. Because reading is such an overlearned and automatic process, it interferes with the color naming, resulting in errors and slower reading times. Stroop found the average color naming times were 63.3 seconds for condition NC and a whopping 110.3 seconds for the NCWd condition. We've taken the four outcomes, reported by Stroop in the form of tables, and drawn a bar graph of them in Figure 7.2. As you can see, the Stroop effect is a robust phenomenon.

(continued)

BOX 7.1 (CONTINUED)

We mentioned earlier that Stroop actually completed three experiments for his dissertation. The third demonstrated that participants could improve on the NCWd task (the classic Stroop task) if given practice. An unusual aspect of this final study was that in the place of square color patches on the NC test, Stroop, for control purposes, substituted color patches in the shape of swastikas. This "made it possible to print the NC test in shades which more nearly match[ed] those in the NCWd test" (Stroop, 1992, p. 18). The choice probably reflected Stroop's religiosity—he regularly taught Bible classes and was well-known in the South for writing a series of instructional books called *God's Plan and Me* (MacLeod, 1991). He would have known the swastika originated as an ancient religious symbol, formed by bending the arms of a traditional Greek cross (+). Ironically, Stroop's study was published the same year (1935) the swastika was officially adopted as the symbol for the National Socialist (or "Nazi" for short) party in Germany.

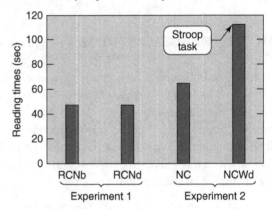

Figure 7.2
Combined data from the first two experiments of the original Stroop study (1935).

Two other counterbalancing strategies for a study with two conditions, when each condition is being tested many times, are simply to alternate the conditions (ABAB . . .) or to just present the sequences randomly. The latter approach was taken in the following experiment.

Research Example 14—Two-Level Repeated Measures Design

If you taste a nice piece of chocolate, do you think your experience will be influenced by having someone sitting next to you also eating the same kind of chocolate? Based on a long history of research in social psychology showing that people can influence others in a wide variety of ways, Boothby, Clark, and Bargh (2014) hypothesized that if two people share the same experience, their reactions to that experience might be amplified. They designed a clever within-subjects experiment with two conditions—shared experience and unshared experience. The experience to be measured involved tasting and then rating chocolate. A within-subjects design was chosen because this is a typical design in experiments involving a series of perceptual judgments.

The basic task was for participants (all female) to taste a piece of chocolate and then rate the experience along several dimensions (e.g., liking, how flavorful it was). They completed the task in the same room with a woman who appeared to be another subject, but was actually an experimental *confederate*, a term you recall from Chapter 3. In the shared experience condition, both women (participant and confederate) tasted and rated chocolate; in the unshared condition, the participant rated the chocolate while the confederate rated several paintings. In both conditions, the two "subjects" were told not to talk to each other.

You might suspect that subjects would be a little suspicious about having to rate chocolate two times in a row. In studies involving some level of deception, researchers always try to create a believable script, what they refer to as a *cover story*. In this case, subjects were led to believe they would be completing four tasks—rating two different varieties of chocolate and rating two different sets of paintings. In fact, the subjects only completed two tasks. They rated what they thought were two different types of chocolate (but were in fact from the same chocolate bar)—one with

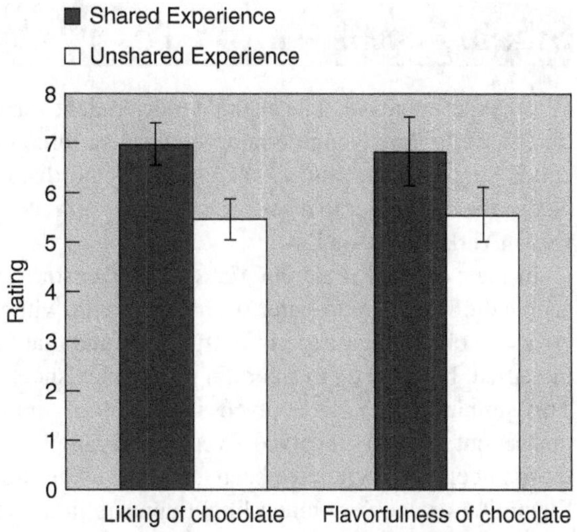

Figure 7.3
Judgments of how much chocolate was liked (left-hand bars) and how flavorful it seemed to be (right-hand bars) for those sharing or not sharing the chocolate-eating experience. From Boothby, Clark, and Bargh (2014).

the confederate also tasting chocolate (shared condition) and one with the confederate rating a booklet of artwork (unshared condition) with the counterbalanced order determined randomly. To enhance the cover story, the researchers also arranged for what seemed to be random drawings to determine who would be doing each task—the subjects believed they would always rate chocolates before the confederates would.

Figure 7.3 shows the results for the ratings of how much the subjects liked the chocolate and how flavorful they judged the chocolate to be. As you can see, in the shared experience condition, participants liked the chocolate better and judged it to have more flavor than in the unshared condition. Hence, sharing an experience seems to amplify the perception of that experience, even in the absence of any discussion about the experience.

Boothby et al.'s (2014) experiment involved a pleasant experience, and they wondered (*what's next thinking*) if the shared experiences truly intensified a perception or whether the sharing just made experiences more pleasant. As they put it, perhaps "Tootsie Rolls and fried tarantulas alike could be more palatable if tasted with another person" (p. 2212). This led them to replicate the study with bitter tasting chocolate. In this case the shared experience led subjects to a greater level of *dislike* for the chocolate; that is, sharing experiences intensifies whatever the initial experience, positive or negative, might be. The authors concluded that "every day, people spend time together in the absence of explicit communication. . . . Yet even in silence, people often share experiences, and the mental space inhabited together is a place where good experiences get better and bad experiences get worse" (p. 2215).

SELF TEST

7.1

1. There are two groups in a study, and participants are randomly assigned to one group or the other. What's the design?
2. Ellen signs up for a study in which she completes the Stroop test. Then she is asked to do the task again, but this time the words are turned upside down. What's the design?
3. What is the name of the design used when a subject variable is the independent variable?

Single Factor—More Than Two Levels

When experiments include a single independent variable, using two levels is the exception rather than the rule. Most single-factor studies use three or more levels and, for that reason, they are called **single-factor multilevel designs**. One distinct advantage of multilevel designs is they enable the researcher to discover **nonlinear effects**. To take a simple example, consider the well-known Yerkes-Dodson Law.

In their original research, Yerkes and Dodson (1908) taught mice a simple two-choice discrimination (choose to enter a chamber with white walls or black walls), shocking them for errors. In one of their experiments, they found that the mice learned faster as the shock intensity increased, but only up to a certain point; once shock reached high levels, performance declined. This simple finding has evolved over the years into a general "law" about arousal and performance, but the study involved a very small sample of mice, had a great deal of variability among those mice, and might have been analyzed using the wrong dependent variable (Teigen, 1994).[2] Figure 7.4 or one very much like it appears in a wide range of textbooks, showing that performance (athletic performance is the typical example) will be poor with low arousal, improves as arousal increases, and then declines when arousal becomes too high. Notice the value of having more than two levels of some "arousal" independent variable. If you only used low and moderate arousal (i.e., just two levels), you would conclude simply that performance increases as arousal increases. If you only used moderate and high arousal, you would conclude that performance decreases as arousal increases. And if you happened to use only very low and very high arousal, you would conclude that arousal does not affect performance at all. Using all three levels, resulting in the nonlinear effect, gives you a better overall picture of the effect of arousal – performance is best at moderate levels of arousal, and poor at either high or low levels of arousal.

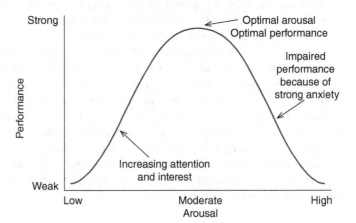

Figure 7.4
A typical presentation of the
Yerkes–Dodson Law.

In addition to identifying nonlinear relationships, single-factor multilevel designs can also test for specific alternative hypotheses and perhaps rule them out while supporting the researcher's hypothesis. This is a strategy you will recognize from the discussions in Chapters 1 and 3 on the merits of *falsification* thinking. For example, from the literature on memory, consider a well-known series of studies by Bransford and Johnson (1972). In one of their procedures, subjects tried to memorize a paragraph that, in the absence of a topic, made little sense, as you can judge for yourself:

> The procedure is actually quite simple. First you arrange things into different groups. Of course, one pile may be sufficient depending on how much there is to do. If you

---

[2] Despite the apparent disconnect between the original study by Yerkes and Dodson and the subsequent "law" relating general arousal to motor performance, there is a long history of research showing that the Yerkes-Dodson principle works reasonably well, at least under certain circumstances (e.g., moderately difficult tasks).

have to go somewhere else due to lack of facilities that is the next step, otherwise you are pretty well set. It is important not to overdo things. That is, it is better to do too few things at once than too many. In the short run this may not seem important but complications can easily arise. A mistake can be expensive as well. At first the whole procedure will seem complicated. Soon, however, it will become just another facet of life. It is difficult to foresee any end to the necessity for this task in the immediate future, but then one never can tell. After the procedure is completed one arranges the materials into different groups again. Then they can be put into their appropriate places. Eventually they will be used once more and the whole cycle will then have to be repeated. However, that is part of life. (p. 722).

In an *independent groups design*, Bransford and Johnson (1972) assigned participants to one of three groups. Those in Group 1 ("No Topic") had the paragraph read to them by the experimenter and then (after answering some questions about how well they understood the paragraph) tried to recall as much of it as they could. Those in Group 2 ("Topic Before") were told before they read the paragraph that "The paragraph you will hear will be about washing clothes" (p. 722). After the paragraph was read, and before recall occurred, group 3 participants ("Topic After") were told that "It may help you to know that the paragraph was about washing clothes" (p. 723). Bransford and Johnson identified 18 possible idea units that could be recalled and here are the average idea units recalled by each group[3]:

No Topic	$M = 2.82$	$SD = 2.47$
Topic Before	$M = 5.83$	$SD = 2.02$
Topic After	$M = 2.65$	$SD = 2.18$

Bransford and Johnson were interested in finding out if memory would be better if participants were giving an overall framework (or context) for the information being read to them. So they could have done a study with two levels, No Topic and Topic Before, and they would indeed have found evidence that providing a context ("the paragraph is about washing clothes") led to better memory performance (5.83 > 2.82). By adding the third level of the independent variable, however, they were able to evaluate if memory is better during the time when the information was being stored in memory (Topic Before) or at the time when the information was recalled from memory (Topic After). Their results showed them that providing a framework helps memory, but *only* if the framework is provided before the material to be learned. That is, they were able to *rule out* the hypothesis that providing a framework helps memory, regardless of when the framework is given.

Between-Subjects, Multilevel Designs

As with the two-level designs, the multilevel designs include both between- and within-subjects designs of the same four types: independent groups designs, matched groups designs, ex post facto designs, and within-subjects or repeated measures designs. Here is clever example of a between-subjects multilevel independent groups design.

Research Example 15—Multilevel Independent Groups Design

In Chapter 3 you read about the origins of Latane and Darley's (1968) groundbreaking research on helping behavior. Based on media reports of a real case (the murder of Kitty Genovese), they discovered and named the *bystander effect*—the tendency of people to fail to help if there are other bystanders witnessing the event. A considerable amount of subsequent research examined this effect and all the conditions enhancing or inhibiting it, but virtually no studies had used

---

[3] Bransford and Johnson (1972) reported standard error of the mean as their measure of variability within the sample. We converted standard errors to standard deviations.

young children as participants. Whether young children would show a bystander effect was the empirical question asked by Plötner, Over, Carpenter, and Tomasello (2015).

The experiment included three groups with random assignment used to place subjects into groups. In the "alone" condition, there was a single 5-year-old child in a room with a teacher who was in need of help. In the "bystander" condition, the child was joined by two other children of the same age, and in the "bystander-unavailable" condition, there were also two other children, but they were unable to help when the time came for help to be given. The situation requiring help was the teacher spilling a cup of colored water while painting at her desk, and helping was *operationally defined* as the child participant leaving his or her (half the participants were male, half female) chair and bringing the teacher some conveniently placed paper towels within 90 seconds. In the two bystander conditions, the other two children were 5-year-old *confederates*, and their use created a methodological issue seldom seen with confederates. Because of their age, they could not always be relied upon to stick to the script, so Plötner et al. (2015) had to eliminate some data due to "confederate error" (e.g., hinting about what was to happen). To be sure that trials for confederate error were not being deleted in some biased fashion, the researchers went as far as to calculate *inter-rater reliability* on the decision to exclude data, and reliability was high.

The results are pretty clear from Figure 7.5. When alone and when bystanders were unable to help (a barrier prevented them from getting to paper towels) almost all the children helped; when bystanders were present and able to help, however, the children helped just over half the time. Notice the advantage of going beyond just two IV levels and adding the third group. Had the study only included the alone and bystander groups, a bystander effect would have been demonstrated, but adding the bystander-unavailable condition allowed Plötner et al. (2015) to rule out two of the reasons typically given for the bystander effect (shyness, social referencing) while supporting a third reason (diffusion of responsibility, the idea that with several bystanders present,

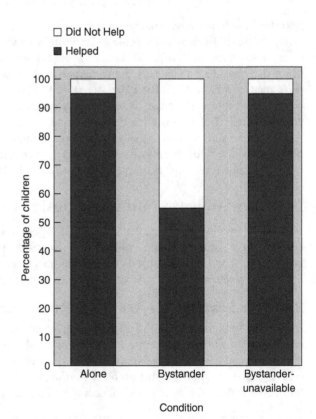

Figure 7.5
Percentage of children helping a teacher in a study of the bystander effect. From Plötner, Over, Carpenter, and Tomasello (2015).

the responsibility to help is shared and any one individual feels less responsible to help). As Plötner et al. described it,

> When bystanders were present but confined behind a barrier and therefore unavailable to help, children helped just as often as they did when they were alone. Thus, it was not simply the mere presence of bystanders that caused the effect (e.g., through shyness to act in front of others). Nor was it social referencing of the bystanders' passivity, as participants looked toward the bystanders equally often irrespective of their availability to help. . . . Rather, it appears that the effect was driven by diffusion of responsibility, which existed only in the bystander condition. (p. 504)

One final point about the study is that it could be considered an example of a *conceptual replication*. That is, Plötner et al. (2015) took a phenomenon (the bystander effect) that normally has been studied with adult subjects, and extended it to a different population, very young children.

Within-Subjects, Multilevel Designs

Whereas a single-factor, repeated-measures design with two levels has limited counterbalancing options, going beyond two levels makes all the counterbalancing options available. If each condition is tested once per subject, then both full and partial counterbalancing procedures are available. And when each condition is tested several times per subject, both reverse and blocked randomization procedures can be used. In the following study, each condition was tested just once, and partial counterbalancing (a Latin square) was used.

Research Example 16—Multilevel Repeated Measures Design

In the Chapter 3 discussion of replication, we briefly mentioned a study by Steele, Bass, and Crook (1999) that failed to replicate a controversial study by Rauscher, Shaw, and Key (1993). The Rauscher et al. study apparently discovered that small but significant improvements in spatial skills could follow from listening to music by Mozart. News of the research reached the popular press, which often distorts accounts of scientific research, and soon stories appeared urging parents to play Mozart to their infants to improve their cognitive abilities. Yet as we saw in Chapter 3, several replication efforts failed. Another study by Steele and his colleagues further questioned the viability of this alleged "Mozart effect."

Steele, Ball, and Runk (1997) included three conditions in their experiment: listening to Mozart for 10 minutes, listening to a recording of soothing environmental sounds (a gentle rainstorm) for 10 minutes, and not listening to anything (sitting quietly for 10 minutes and trying to relax). All 36 participants in the study were tested in each of the three conditions, making this a single-factor, multilevel, repeated-measures design. Although complete counterbalancing would have been easy to implement ($3! = 3 \times 2 \times 1$, or six orders of conditions, with six subjects randomly assigned to each order), the authors chose to use a 3×3 *Latin square*, with 12 participants randomly assigned to each row of the square. To avoid the bias that might result if participants thought they were evaluating the Mozart effect, the study's *cover story* was that "the experiment concerned the effect of relaxation on recall" (Steele et al., 1997, p. 1181). Instead of using a spatial skills task, Steele et al., used a difficult memory task, a backward digit span procedure where subjects must repeat the sequence of digits in backward order from which it was provided. For example, given a stimulus such as "6-8-3-1-7," the correct response would be "7-1-3-8-6." On a given trial, participants would listen to Mozart, listen to gentle rainfall, or sit quietly, and then be given three consecutive digit span trials. Each digit span included nine numbers, presented in a random order. Thus, a score from 0 to 27 could be earned for the three trials combined.

The study produced statistically significant findings, but none that would comfort those advocating for the Mozart effect. The average number of digits correctly recalled was virtually identical for all three conditions: 18.53 ($SD = 4.14$) for Mozart, 18.50 ($SD = 6.07$) for the gentle rain, and 18.72 ($SD = 5.09$) for the control condition. There was a significant practice effect, however. Regardless of the order in which the conditions were presented, participants improved from the first set of digit span tests to the third set. From the first to the third, the averages were 15.64, 19.14, and 20.97 (SDs of 4.70, 4.87, and 4.29, respectively). So, should parents play Mozart tapes for their children? Sure, why not? Will it make them smarter? Apparently not, although it could make them enjoy classical music, an outcome of value by itself.

Analyzing Data From Single-Factor Designs

As we described in Chapter 4, researchers use both descriptive and inferential statistics to evaluate data from their studies. In this section, we discuss ways to visually depict descriptive data, then we turn to inferential analysis of data.

Presenting the Data

One decision to be made when reporting the results of any research study is how to present the data. There are three choices. First, the numbers can be presented in sentence form, an approach that might be fine for reporting the results of experimental studies with two or three levels (e.g., the Mozart example) but makes for tedious reading as the amount of data increases. A second approach is to construct a table of results. Usually, means and standard deviations for each condition are presented in tables. A table for the Bransford and Johnson (1972) study, using APA format, would look like Table 7.2.

A third way to present the data is in the form of a graph. Note that in an experimental study (e.g., Figure 7.5), a graph always places the dependent variable on the vertical (Y) axis and the independent variable on the horizontal (X) axis. The situation becomes a bit more complicated when more than one independent variable is used, as you will see in the next chapter. Regardless of the number of independent variables, the dependent variable *always* goes on the vertical axis.

Deciding between tables and figures is often a matter of the researcher's preference. Graphs can be especially striking if there are large differences to report or (especially) if nonlinear effects (e.g., the Yerkes-Dodson Law) occur or if the result is an *interaction* between two factors (coming in Chapter 8). Tables are often preferred when data points are so numerous that a graph would be uninterpretable or when the researcher wishes to inform the reader of the precise values of the means and standard deviations. One rule you can certainly apply is to never present the same data in both table and graph form. In general, you should present data in such a way that the results you have worked so hard to obtain are shown most clearly.

Table 7.2   Bransford and Johnson's (1972) Data in Table Format Mean Number of Idea Units Recalled as a Function of Different Learning and Recall Contexts

Condition	Mean Score	Standard Deviation
No Topic	2.82	2.47
Topic Before	5.83	2.02
Topic After	2.65	2.18

Note. The maximum score was 18.

Types of Graphs

When we first described the data from Bransford and Johnson's (1972) study on memory for doing laundry, we simply listed the means and standard deviations for the three groups. An alternative would have been to present the data in the form of a bar graph, as in Figure 7.6.

The graph clearly shows the advantage of context on memory. But could we also have shown these data in the form of a line graph, as in Figure 7.7?

The answer is no. The problem concerns the nature of the construct used as the independent variable and whether the independent variable is a between-subjects factor or a within-subjects factor. If the independent variable is manipulated between-subjects or is a subject variable, then the type of graph to use is a bar graph. (Remember B: between-subjects = bar graph). The reason for this is because the levels of the independent variable represent separate groups of individuals, so the data in the graph should best reflect separate groups, or separate bars in this case.[4] The top

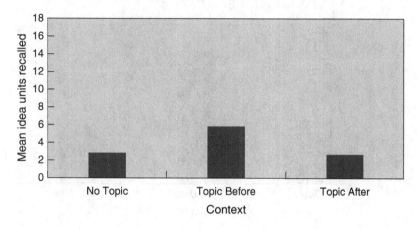

Figure 7.6
The Bransford and Johnson (1972) "laundry" study presented as a bar graph.

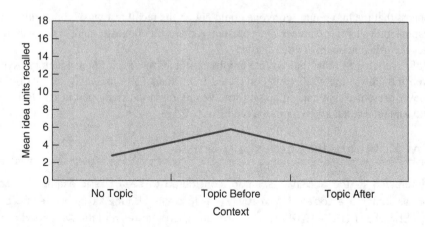

Figure 7.7
The Bransford and Johnson (1972) "laundry" study presented inappropriately as a line graph.

---

[4] Generally speaking, bar graphs are used with between-subjects designs, but if the independent variable represents a continuous-type variable, then a line graph can be used. For example, in a study that manipulates drug dosage levels (3 mg, 5 mg, and 7 mg) between different groups of rats, the dosage level is a continuous variable, in which the variable exists on a continuum. In such cases, the researcher may opt to represent the means of each dosage level as points on a continuous line (i.e., a line graph).

of each bar represents the mean for each condition in the study. Often, researchers will also place *error bars* on the tops of the graphs which can reflect standard deviations or *confidence intervals* for each condition. If the independent variable is a within-subjects manipulated or subject variable, then it is appropriate to use a line graph. The reason for this is because participants are experiencing all levels of that independent variable, so the data should "connect" in a more continuous way. Thus, a line graph shows participants going through the levels of the independent variable. On a line graph, the points usually represent the means of each condition, and error bars are typically placed on each point on the graph.

In general then, bar graphs can be used for between-subjects designs, and line graphs should be used for within-subjects designs. Be sure to review Box 4.3 in Chapter 4 for a reminder about the ethics of presenting the data. It is easy to mislead the uninformed consumer of research by, for example, altering the distances on the *Y*-axis. Figure 7.8 is a "gee whiz" graph illustrating Bransford and Johnson's (1972) data after altering the *Y*-axis.

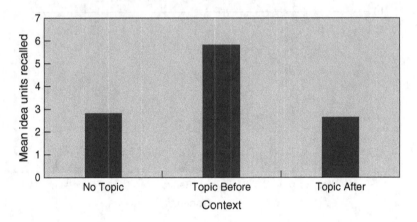

Figure 7.8
The Bransford and Johnson (1972) "laundry" study presented inappropriately as "Gee whiz!" graph.

It appears that the maximum score one could get on the recall test was 7, but really it was 18. Your responsibility as a researcher is to present your results honestly and in the way that best illustrates the true outcomes of your study.

One of psychology's most famous line graphs continues to appear in introductory psychology texts even though (a) the study was completed more than 130 years ago and (b) the study's author never presented that data in graph form. For more on the study that is said to have originated experimental research on memory, read Box 7.2.

BOX 7.2   ORIGINS—The Ebbinghaus Forgetting Curve

Trained as a philosopher and interested in the ancient philosophical problem of how ideas become associated together in the mind, Hermann Ebbinghaus (1850–1909) completed the first systematic study of memory in psychology's history. The work was summarized in his brief (123 pages in a 1964 reprinting) *Memory: A Contribution to Experimental Psychology* (Ebbinghaus, 1885/1964).

The first task for Ebbinghaus was to find materials that would not normally be associated with each other. His solution, considered to be a classic example of scientific creativity, was to create about 2300 stimuli, each consisting of a consonant, then a vowel, and then a second consonant (e.g., ZEK, KIG). These "CVCs" (or "nonsense syllables" as they later came to be called) were not necessarily meaningless in themselves, but sequences of them were unlikely to bring old associations to mind, Hence, memorizing a list of them would constitute, as far as Ebbinghaus was concerned, the creation of a brand new set of associations. For several years, showing great perseverance and/or a complete lack of social life, Ebbinghaus spent several hours a day memorizing and recalling lists of CVCs, Yes, he was the *only* subject in the research. He carefully studied such factors as the number of CVCs per list, the number of study trials per list, and whether the study trials were crammed together or spread out.

Ebbinghaus's most famous study examined the time course of forgetting; his empirical question was "Once some material has been memorized, how much of that memory persists after varying amounts of time?" His outcome illustrates two ideas you have learned about in this chapter—the appearance of nonlinear effects when there are more than two levels of an independent variable, and the effective use of a line graph with a within-subjects, manipulated variable (time). The famous Ebbinghaus forgetting curve is shown in Figure 7.9. Although Ebbinghaus presented his data in table form, most subsequent descriptions of the study have used a line graph like the one shown here.

In his study of forgetting, Ebbinghaus memorized lists of 13 CVCs and then tried to recall them after various amounts of time—from the *X*-axis, you can see that the levels of his independent variable (retention interval) were 20 minutes, 1 hour, 8.8 hours, 1 day, 2 days, 6 days, and 31 days. His dependent variable used what he called the method of savings. He would learn a list, wait for the retention interval to pass, and then try to relearn the list again. If it took him 20 minutes to learn the list at first, and 5 minutes to relearn it, he determined that he had "saved" 15 minutes. His *Y*-axis, "% saved" was calculated this way: [(original learning time–relearning time)/original learning time]. For this example, the savings would be 75%. Ebbinghaus's method of savings has an interesting implication for you as a student. You might think that you don't remember anything about your introductory psychology course, but the fact that you would relearn the material more quickly than you learned it originally means that some memory is still there to help you in your relearning of the material.

As you can see from the graph, recall declined as the retention interval increased, but the decline was not a steady or linear one. Instead, a nonlinear effect occurred. Forgetting occurred very rapidly at first, but then the rate of forgetting slowed. Thus, after a mere 20 minutes, only about 60% (58.2 actually) of the original learning had been saved. At the other end of the curve, there wasn't much difference between an interval of a week (25.4% saved) and a month (21.1% saved).

From the standpoint of methodological control, there are several other interesting points about the Ebbinghaus research. To ensure a constant presentation rate, for example, he set a metronome to 150 beats per minute and read each CVC on one of the beats. He also tried to study the lists in the same environment and at about the same time of day, and to use no memorization technique except simple repetition. Also, Ebbinghaus worked only when sufficiently motivated so that he could "keep the attention concentrated on the tiresome task" (Ebbinghaus, 1885/1964, p. 25). Finally, he understood the importance of *replication*. He completed one set of studies in 1879–1880 and then replicated all his work three years later, in 1883–1884.

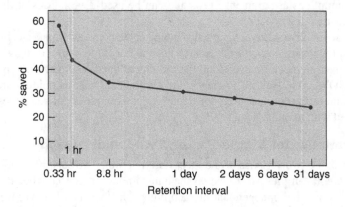

Figure 7.9
The Ebbinghaus forgetting curve—appropriately drawn as a line graph and a good illustration of a nonlinear effect.

Analyzing the Data

To determine whether the differences found between the conditions of a single-factor design are significant or due to chance, inferential statistical analysis is required. An inferential statistical decision to reject or not reject the null hypothesis in a study depends on analyzing two types of variability in the data. The first refers to the differences between groups, which are caused by a combination of (a) systematic variance and (b) error variance. **Systematic variance** is the result of an identifiable factor, either the variable of interest or some factor that you've failed to control adequately (such as confounds). **Error variance** is nonsystematic variability due to individual differences between subjects in the groups and any number of random, unpredictable effects that might have occurred during the study. Error variance also occurs within each group, also as a result of individual differences and other random effects, and accounts for the differences found there. Mathematically, many inferential analyses calculate a ratio that takes this form:

$$\text{Inferential statistic} = \frac{\text{Variability between conditions}\,(\text{systematic} + \text{error})}{\text{Variability within each condition}\,(\text{error})}$$

The ideal outcome is to find that variability between conditions is large and variability within each condition is small. An inferential statistic will then test to see if the researcher can reject the null hypothesis and conclude with a certain degree of confidence that there is a significant difference between the levels of the independent variable.

Recall from Chapter 4 that *inferential statistics* are used to infer from a sample what might occur in the population of interest. Inferential statistical tests can be either parametric tests or nonparametric tests. Parametric tests are tests which have certain assumptions (or parameters) that are required to best estimate the population. For example, some tests assume your data in level of the independent variable approximates a normal distribution. For this reason, it is important to examine the distributions of data so you can select the appropriate statistical test. Another assumption is called **homogeneity of variance**, which means the variability of each set of scores being compared ought to be similar. So, if the standard deviation for one group is significantly larger than the standard deviation for the other group, there may be a violation of the assumption of homogeneity of variance. Tests for homogeneity of variance exist, and if these tests indicate a violation, nonparametric tests can be used. These tests that do not have the same assumptions as parametric tests and can be used if violations of the parameters for your ideal statistical tests occur.

Scales of measurement are also important to consider when selecting the appropriate statistical test for a particular type of research design. For single-factor designs when interval or ratio scales of measurement are used (and the aforementioned parameters are met), then *t*-tests or one-way ANOVA (ANalysis Of VAriance) are calculated. Other techniques are required when nominal or ordinal scales of measurement are used. For example, a chi-square test of independence could be used with nominal data.

Statistics for Single-Factor, Two-Level Designs

There are two varieties of the *t*-test for comparing two sets of scores. The first is called an **independent samples *t*-test**, and, as the name implies, it is used when the two groups of participants are completely independent of each other. This occurs whenever we use random assignment to create equivalent groups, or if the variable being studied is a subject variable involving two different groups (e.g., males versus females). If the independent variable is a within-subjects factor, or if two groups of people are formed in such a way that some relationship exists between them (e.g., participants in Group A are matched on intelligence with participants in Group B), a

dependent samples or paired *t*-test is used. For the four single-factor designs just considered, the following *t*-tests would be appropriate:

- independent samples *t*-test
  - independent groups design
  - ex post facto design

- dependent samples *t*-test
  - matched groups design[5]
  - repeated-measures design

In essence, the *t*-test examines the difference between the mean scores for the two samples and determines (with some probability) whether this difference is larger than would be expected by chance factors alone. If the difference is indeed sufficiently large, and if potential confounds can be ruled out, then the researcher can conclude with a high probability that the differences between the means reflect a real effect. Be mindful, though, that the *t*-test is a parametric statistic with the assumptions of normal distributions of data and homogeneity of variance. So, if your data don't meet these assumptions, then an alternate nonparametric test can be used, such as the Mann-Whitney *U*-test.

As you recall from Chapter 4, in addition to determining if differences are statistically significant, it is also possible to determine the magnitude of the difference by calculating *effect size*, usually Cohen's *d* for two-sample tests. To learn (or, I hope, review) the exact procedures involved, both in calculating the two forms of *t*-test and in determining effect size, please review the Student Statistics Guide on the Student Companion site or consult any introductory statistics text (e.g., Witte & Witte, 2014). Also in that guide, if your school uses SPSS (a common statistical software package), you can use learn how to perform both types of *t*-tests in SPSS.

Statistics for Single-Factor, Two-Level Designs

For single-factor, multilevel designs such as Bransford and Johnson's (1972) laundry study, you might think the analysis would be a simple matter of completing a series of *t*-tests between all of the possible pairs of conditions (i.e., No Topic versus Topic Before; No Topic versus Topic After; Topic Before versus Topic After). Unfortunately, matters aren't quite that simple. The difficulty is that completing multiple *t*-tests increases the risks of making a Type I error—that is, the more *t*-tests you calculate, the greater the chances that one of them will accidentally yield significant differences between conditions. In a study with five levels of the independent variable, for example, you would have to complete 10 *t*-tests to cover all of the pairs of levels of the independent variable.

The chances of making at least one Type I error when doing multiple *t*-tests can be estimated by using this formula:

$$1-(1-\text{alpha})^{c}$$

where *c* = the number of comparisons being made.

---

[5] You may be wondering why a matched group design, which involves random assignment of participants to separate groups, would require a dependent samples *t*-test. The reason is that before random assignment to condition, participants are matched on at least one variable, and conceptually, this makes the individuals that are paired together with similar scores essentially one "person." Thus, when the pair is split and participants with similar scores are assigned to different, independent groups, you essentially have the same "person" in each level of the independent variable. Therefore, you are treating the data like within-subjects data, which requires (in this case) a dependent samples *t*-test.

Thus, if all the possible t-tests are completed in a study with five levels, there is a very good chance (4 out of 10) of making at least one Type I error:

$$1-(1-0.05)^{10} = 1-(0.95)^{10} = 1-0.60 = 0.40 \text{ or } 40\%$$

To avoid the problem of multiple t-tests in single-factor designs, researchers typically use a procedure called a *one-way* (sometimes *one-factor*) *analysis of variance* or one-way **ANOVA** (**AN**alysis **O**f **VA**riance). The *one* in the "one-way" means one independent variable. In essence, a one-way ANOVA tests for the presence of an overall significant effect that could exist somewhere between the levels of the independent variable. Hence, in a study with three levels, the null hypothesis is "level 1 = level 2 = level 3." Rejecting the null hypothesis does not identify which condition differs from which, however. To determine precisely which condition is significantly different from another requires subsequent testing or post hoc (after the fact) analyses. In a study with three levels, subsequent testing would analyze each of the three pairs of comparisons, but only after the overall ANOVA has indicated some significance exists. Selecting one of the types of post hoc analyses depends on sample size and how conservative the researcher wishes to be when testing for differences between conditions. For example, Tukey's HSD test, with the HSD standing for "honestly significant difference," is one of the most popular of the post hoc choices (Sprinthall, 2000), but it requires that there are equal numbers of participants in each level of the independent variable. A more conservative test for comparisons of groups with unequal sample sizes per condition is the Bonferroni correction. SPSS provides many options for different post hoc tests, or you can consult a statistics textbook for more information. Importantly, if the ANOVA does not find any significance, subsequent testing is normally not done, unless specific predictions about particular pairs of levels of the independent variable have been made ahead of time. In this latter case, the testing is not post hoc tests, but referred to as *planned comparisons*.

The one-way ANOVA yields an F score or an F ratio. Like the calculated outcome of a t-test, the F ratio examines the extent to which the obtained mean differences could be due to chance or are the result of some other factor (presumably the independent variable). For a one-way ANOVA the inferential statistic is the F ratio. It is typically portrayed in a table called an **ANOVA source table**. An example of how one of these could be constructed for a one-way ANOVA for an independent groups design with three levels of the independent variable is in the Student Statistics Guide on the Student Companion Site. The complete calculations for this analysis, as well as a follow-up analysis for effect size, can also be practiced there, and the guide also shows you how to use SPSS to complete a one-way ANOVA as well as a Tukey's HSD test.

Recall that the independent samples t-test is used with independent groups and ex post facto designs, and the dependent samples t-test is used with matched groups and repeated measures designs. The same thing occurs for the one-way ANOVA. In addition to the one-way ANOVA for independent groups, there is also a one-way ANOVA for repeated measures. Parallel to the t-tests, these ANOVAs are used in these situations:

- one-way ANOVA for independent groups
  - multilevel independent groups design
  - multilevel ex post facto design

- one-way ANOVA for repeated measures
  - multilevel matched groups design
  - multilevel repeated-measures design

Again, be mindful of the parameters required for the use of the one-way ANOVA, which like the t-test, requires normal distributions of data and homogeneity of variance. If either or both are violated, alternate nonparametric tests should be used.

1. Why must a study like the Bransford and Johnson study (effect of context on memory) be portrayed with a bar graph and not a line graph?

2. Suppose a researcher wanted to test the difference between women and men on the number of items answered correctly on a cognitive reasoning task. What statistical test(s) would be appropriate to use for this design?

3. Suppose a researcher wanted to test children at the beginning, middle, and end of the school year to see their progress on standardized math tests. What statistical test(s) would be appropriate to use for this design?

Special-Purpose Control Group Designs

We introduced the basic distinction between experimental groups and control groups in Chapter 5. As you recall, although control groups are not always needed, they are especially useful when the research calls for a comparison of a treatment of some kind (e.g., a drug effect) with a baseline level of behavior. Experimental groups receive the treatment, while those in the control group do not. In repeated-measures designs, a parallel distinction can be made between experimental conditions and control *conditions*, with both conditions experienced by each of the study's participants. Besides the typical control group situation in which a group is untreated, three other special-purpose control group designs are worth describing: placebo controls, wait list controls, and yoked controls. These types of control groups are most informative when used in the context of multilevel experimental designs.

Placebo Control Group Designs

A **placebo** (from Latin, meaning "I shall please") is a substance or treatment given to a participant in a form suggesting a specific effect when, in fact, the substance or treatment has no genuine effect. In drug research, for example, patients will sometimes show improvement when given a placebo but told it is a real drug, simply because they *believe* the drug will make them better. In research, members of a **placebo control group** are led to believe they are receiving a particular treatment when, in fact, they aren't. Can you see why this would be necessary? Suppose you wished to determine if alcohol slows reaction time. If you used a simple experimental group that was given alcohol and a second group that received nothing to drink, then gave both groups a reaction time test, the reactions indeed might be slower for the first group. Can you conclude that alcohol slows reaction time? No—participants might hold the general belief that alcohol will slow them down, and their reactions might be influenced by that knowledge. To solve the problem, you must include a group given a drink that seems to be alcoholic (and cannot be distinguished in taste from the true alcoholic drink) but is not. This group is the placebo control group. Should you eliminate the straight control group (no drinks at all)? Probably not, for these individuals yield a simple baseline measure of reaction time. If you include all three groups and get these average reaction times:

Experimental group:	0.32 second
Placebo control:	0.22 second
Straight control:	0.16 second

You could conclude that what people expect about the effects of alcohol slowed reaction time somewhat (from 0.16 to 0.22) but that alcohol by itself also had an effect beyond people's expectations (0.22 to 0.32). By the way, in terms of the designs introduced earlier in this chapter, this study would be an independent groups, single-factor, multilevel design, assuming subjects would be randomly assigned to groups. If subjects were first matched on some variable (e.g., matched for weight), the study would be a matched groups, single-factor, multilevel design. Can you think why an ex post facto design or a repeated-measures design would not be appropriate here?

Wait List Control Group Designs

Wait list control groups are often used in research designed to assess the effectiveness of a program (Chapter 11) or in studies on the effects of psychotherapy. In this design, the participants in the experimental group are in a program because they are experiencing a problem the program is designed to alleviate; wait list controls are also experiencing the problem. For instance, a study by Miller and DiPilato (1983) evaluated the effectiveness of two forms of therapy (relaxation and desensitization) to treat clients who suffered from nightmares. They wanted to include a no-treatment control, but to ensure clients in all three groups (relaxation, desensitization, and control) were generally equivalent, the control group subjects also had to be nightmare sufferers. From an identified pool of nightmare sufferers, participants were randomly assigned to one of the three groups, making this an independent groups, single-factor, multilevel design. For ethical reasons, those assigned to the wait list were assured they would be helped, and after the study ended they were given treatment equivalent to that experienced by the experimental groups.

Giving the wait list participants an opportunity to benefit from some therapy procedure provides an important protection for subject welfare, but it also creates pressures on the researcher to use this control procedure only for therapies or programs of relatively brief duration. In Miller and DiPilato's (1983) study, for example, the subjects in the two experimental groups were in relaxation or desensitization therapy for 15 weeks, and both forms of therapy produced a reduction in nightmares compared to the wait list control subjects. At the end of 15 weeks, those in the wait list control group began treatment (randomly assigned to either relaxation or desensitization, because both procedures had worked equally well).

Some might argue it is unethical to put people into a wait list control group because they won't receive the program's benefits right away and might be harmed while waiting. This issue can be especially problematic when research evaluates life-influencing programs. Read Box 7.3 for an examination of this issue and a defense of the use of control groups, including wait lists, in research.

BOX 7.3 ETHICS—Who's in the Control Group?

In a study on human memory in which an experimental group gets special instructions to use visual imagery, while a control group is told to learn the word lists any way they can, the question of who is assigned to the control group does not create an ethical dilemma. However, things are not so simple when an experiment is designed to evaluate a program or treatment that, if effective, would clearly benefit people, perhaps even by prolonging their lives. For example, in a well-known study of the effects of personal control on health (Langer & Rodin, 1976),

some nursing home residents were given increased control over their daily planning, while control group residents had their daily planning done for them (for the most part) by the nursing staff. On the average, residents in the first group were healthier, mentally and physically, and were more likely to be alive when the authors came back and did an 18-month follow-up study (Rodin & Langer, 1977). If you discovered one of your relatives (now dead) had been assigned to the control group, do you think you would be upset?

In a similar vein, there has been controversy over the assignment of participants to control groups in studies with cancer patients (Adler, 1992). The research concerned the effects of support groups on the psychological well-being and physical health of women with breast cancer. The findings indicated that women in support groups recovered more quickly and even lived longer than women not placed in these groups (i.e., those in the control group). Some researchers argued the results did not reflect the benefits of support groups as much as the harm done to those in the control group who might feel left out or rejected. This could create stress, and it is known that stress can harm the immune system, leading to a host of health-related problems. So is there some truth to Figure 7.10? At the extreme, can being in a control group kill you?

Defenders of the control group approach to evaluating programs make three strong arguments. First, they point out that hindsight is usually perfect. It is easy to say after the fact that "a program as effective as this one ought to be available to everyone." The problem is that *before* the fact, it is not so obvious that a program will be effective. The only way to tell is to do the study. Prior to Langer and Rodin's (1977) nursing home study, for example, one easily could have predicted that the experimental group subjects would be unnecessarily stressed by the added responsibility of caring for themselves and drop like flies. Similarly, those defending the cancer studies point out that, when these studies began, few women expressed any preference about their assignment to either an experimental or a control group, and some actually preferred to avoid the support groups (Adler, 1992). Hence, it was not necessarily the case that control group participants would feel left out or overly stressed.

Second, researchers point out that in research evaluating a new treatment or program, the comparison is not between the new treatment and no treatment; it is between the new treatment and the most favored *current* treatment. So, for control group members, available services are not being withheld; they are receiving normal, well-established services. Furthermore, once the study has demonstrated a positive effect of the experimental treatment, members of the control groups are typically given the opportunity to be treated with the new approach.

Third, treatments cost money, and it is certainly worthwhile to spend the bucks on the best treatment. That cannot be determined without well-designed research on program effectiveness, however. In the long run, programs with empirically demonstrated effectiveness serve the general good and may save or prolong lives.

©The New Yorker Collection 1993 Donald Reilly from cartoonbank.com. All Rights Reserved.

Figure 7.10
Potential consequences of being assigned to the control group.

Remember the Chapter 1 discussion of pseudoscience as illustrated by handwriting analysis. Another common example of pseudoscience involves the use of the so-called subliminal self-help. The idea is that while you listen to what appears to be the soothing sounds of ocean waves, subliminal messages (i.e., below the threshold of normal hearing) are sent that will be detected by your unconscious mind and lead you to make changes that will improve your life in some fashion. In fact, there is ample research indicating that any positive effects of these tapes are the result of what people *expect* to happen. Testing expectancy often involves the use of placebo controls, but consider the following Research Example, which effectively combines both placebos and wait lists to yield a different interpretation of what these self-help programs accomplish.

Research Example 17—Using Both Placebo and Wait List Control Groups

One of the favorite markets for the subliminal self-help business is in the area of weight loss. Americans in particular try to lose weight by attempting an unending variety of techniques, from fad diets to surgery. People are especially willing to try something when minimal effort is involved, and this is a defining feature of the subliminal approach; just open a file on your iPhone and pretty soon your unconscious will be directing your behavior so that weight loss will be inevitable. In a study that creatively combined a placebo control and a wait list control, Merikle and Skanes (1992) evaluated the effectiveness of self-help weight loss audiotapes (no iPhones in 1992). Forty-seven adult females were recruited through newspaper ads and randomly assigned to one of three groups. The experimental group participants ($n = 15$) were given a commercially produced subliminal self-help audiotape that was supposed to help listeners lose weight. Those in the placebo control group ($n = 15$) thought they were getting a subliminal tape designed for weight loss, but in fact they were given one designed to relieve dental anxiety (the researchers had a sense of humor). Based on *pilot study* results, the two tapes were indistinguishable to ordinary listeners. A third group, the wait list control ($n = 17$), was told "that the maximum number of subjects was currently participating in the study and that. . .they had to be placed on a waiting list" (p. 774). Those in the experimental and placebo groups were told to listen to their tapes for one to three hours per day and participants in all three groups were weighed weekly for five weeks.

The results? As you can see in Figure 7.11, those in the experimental group lost a modest amount of weight (very modest—check out the *Y*-axis), but the *same* amount was also lost by those in the placebo control group. This is the outcome typical with this type of study, indicating

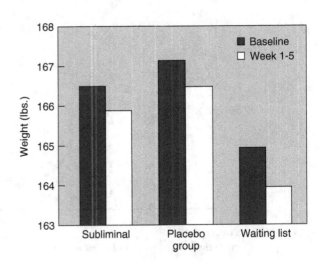

Figure 7.11
Results of the Merikle and Skanes (1992) study using placebo and wait list control groups to evaluate a subliminal self-help program for weight loss.

the subliminal tapes have no effect by themselves. The interesting outcome, however, was that the wait list group also lost weight—about the same amount as the other two groups. This result led Merikle and Skanes to conclude that subliminal tapes do not produce their results simply because of a placebo effect. If this had been true, the placebo group participants, believing their mind was being altered, would have lost more weight than the wait list group folks, who, not yet in possession of the tapes, would not have lost any weight. That subjects in all three groups lost weight led the authors to argue that simply being in an experiment on weight led subjects in all the groups to think about the problem they were experiencing. Subjects in the three groups "may have lost weight simply because participation in the study increased the likelihood that they would attend to and think about weight-related issues during the course of the study" (p. 776).

In this study, the wait list control group had the effect of evaluating the strength of the placebo effect and providing an alternative explanation for the apparent success of subliminal tapes. Also, although the authors didn't mention the term, the study's outcome sounds suspiciously like a *Hawthorne effect*, which you learned about in Chapter 6. And you might have noticed the rationale for adding the wait list control group is another example, like Bransford and Johnson's (1972) memory study described earlier, of adding more than two levels to an independent variable in order to directly test (and potentially rule out) certain hypotheses. The Merikle and Skanes study raises serious questions about the placebo effect hypothesis as an explanation for the effects of subliminal self-help recordings. It also provides additional evidence that there is no validity to the claim that subliminal recordings work.

One final point worth mentioning about this study is that the second author, Heather Skanes, was the experimenter throughout the study, and the first author, Philip Merikle, arranged the subliminal tape labels. Thus, he was the only one who knew who was getting the weight loss tape (experimental group) and who was getting the dental anxiety tape (placebo group). The authors thus built a nice *double blind* control into their study.

Yoked Control Group Designs

A third type of control group is the **yoked control group**. It is used when each subject in the experimental group, for one reason or another, participates for varying amounts of time or is subjected to different types of events in the study. Each member of the control group is then matched, or "yoked," to a member of the experimental group so that, for the groups as a whole, the time spent participating or the types of events encountered is kept constant. A specific example will clarify.

Research Example 18—A Yoked Control Group

A nice example of a yoked control group is a study by Dunn, Schwartz, Hatfield, and Wiegele (1996). The study was designed to evaluate the effectiveness of a psychotherapy technique that was popular (but controversial) in the 1990s. The therapy is called "eye movement desensitization and reprocessing," or EMDR. It is said to be effective as a treatment for anxiety disorders, especially posttraumatic stress disorder. The essence of the therapy is that the client brings to mind and concentrates on a personal traumatic event. While thinking about this event, the client follows a series of hand movements made by the therapist by moving the eyes rapidly from side to side. During the session, the client continuously rates the level of stress being experienced, and when it reaches a certain low point, the eye movement tracking stops. This might sound a bit fishy to you, as it did to Dunn and his colleagues. They wondered if a placebo effect might be operating— clients think the procedure will work and their expectations and faith in the therapist make them feel better. Most of the support for EMDR has been anecdotal (and you know from Chapter 1 to be skeptical about testimonials), so Dunn decided to use a stronger experimental test.

Dunn et al. (1996) identified 28 college students who had experienced mildly traumatic events (those found with more serious trauma were referred to the university counseling center), and after using a matching procedure to create equivalent groups (matching them for age, gender, and the type of traumatic event they reported), randomly assigned them to an experimental and a yoked control group. In the experimental group, participants underwent EMDR. As they thought about their traumatic event and tracked the experimenter's finger with their eyes, they periodically reported their level of stress on a 10-point "SUD" (Subjective Units of Discomfort) scale. Some physiological measures (e.g., pulse) were also recorded. This procedure continued until they reached a SUD level of 0–1 or until 45 minutes had elapsed. Hence, the therapy lasted for varying amounts of time for those in the experimental group, making this study a good candidate for a yoked control group procedure.

Participants in the control group were yoked in terms of how long the session lasted, so if a subject in the EMDR group took 25 minutes to reach a SUD level of 0–1, a subject in the yoked control group would participate in the control procedures for 25 minutes. The control group did everything the experimental group did (i.e., thought about the trauma, reported SUD), but instead of the eye movements, they focused their visual attention on a nonmoving red dot in the middle of a yellow card. By using the yoked control procedure, Dunn et al., (1996) guaranteed the average amount of time spent in a session would be identical for the experimental and control group subjects and that the two groups would do everything the same, except for the eye movements. They also began testing a third yoked group that would only think about the trauma but not get any form of therapeutic treatment during the session. After just a few subjects were tested, however, this third group was cancelled on ethical grounds—the subjects found the procedure too stressful.

The results? The EMDR group showed a significant reduction in the SUD score, as you can see in Figure 7.12.[6] Unfortunately for advocates of EMDR, the yoked control group also showed a drop and, while the reduction seems to be slightly larger for the EMDR group, differences between the two groups were not significant. That both groups showed essentially the same degree of improvement led Dunn et al. (1996) to conclude that a placebo effect is probably lurking behind any alleged success of EMDR.

One final point about this EMDR study is that it demonstrates that a finding of "no difference" between groups can be important. Recall from Chapter 4 that finding a significant difference

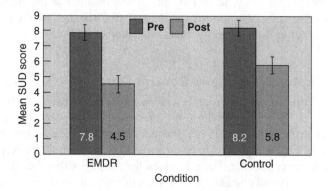

Figure 7.12
Results of the Dunn et al. (1996) study evaluating the effectiveness of EMDR therapy.

---

[6] You encountered *error bars* in Figures 5.1 in Chapter 5 and 6.2 in Chapter 6 and learned they have become standard features of graphs. They were not often used in the 1990s; Merikle and Skanes (1992) did not include them in their subliminal self-help graph (Figure 7.11), but Dunn et al., (1996) did in their EMDR graph (Figure 7.12).

when the null hypothesis is indeed false can be experimenter heaven. Failing to reject a null hypothesis is usually disappointing and can be a difficult finding to interpret, but such an outcome can be useful in a study like the EMDR one. Any time someone advocates a new treatment program, that person is obligated to show the program works. This means finding a significant difference between those getting the treatment and those not getting it, and a failure to find such a difference invites skepticism. Recall from Chapter 1 that researchers are skeptical optimists. They are prepared to accept new ideas supported by good research but are skeptical about claims not supported by empirical evidence.

SELF TEST

7.3

1. Look back at the hypothetical reaction time data in the "placebo control groups" section of the chapter. Suppose nothing but a placebo effect was operating. How would the reaction time numbers change?
2. In the Research Example evaluating EMDR, why is it that a finding of "no difference" between the experimental and control groups can be a useful outcome?

The designs in this chapter have in common the presence of a single independent variable. Some had two levels; some were multilevel. In Chapter 8, you will encounter the next logical step—designs with more than one independent variable. These are called *factorial designs*.

CHAPTER SUMMARY

Single Factor—Two Levels

The simplest experimental designs have a single independent variable (or factor) with two levels of that variable. These designs can include between-subjects factors or within-subjects factors. Between-subjects factors can be directly manipulated or they can be selected as subject factors. If manipulated, participants can be randomly assigned to groups (independent groups design) or matched on a potentially confounding variable, and then randomly assigned (matched groups design). If a subject variable is used, the between-subjects design is called an ex post facto design. Single-factor designs using a within-subjects factor are usually called repeated-measures designs (e.g., the famous Stroop studies). Studies using two levels of the independent variable are normally evaluated statistically with *t*-tests (assuming interval or ratio data, normal distributions, and homogeneity of variance).

Single Factor—More Than Two Levels

When only two levels of an experimental variable are compared, the results will always appear linear because a graph of the results will have only two points. Some relationships are nonlinear, however

(e.g., the Yerkes-Dodson law; the Ebbinghaus forgetting curve), and they can be discovered by adding more than two levels to an independent variable. Adding levels can also function as a way to test and perhaps rule out (falsify) alternative explanations of the main result. Like the two-level case, multilevel designs can be either between- or within-subjects designs.

Analyzing Data from Single-Factor Designs

Results can be presented visually in a bar graph when the independent variable is a discrete variable, or in a line graph if the variable is continuous. Studies using more than two levels of an independent variable are normally evaluated statistically with a one-way analysis of variance or ANOVA (assuming interval or ratio data, normal distributions, and homogeneity of variance). A significant F ratio results in subsequent post hoc testing (e.g., Tukey's HSD test) to identify precisely which means differ. Independent groups and ex post facto designs are evaluated with a one-way ANOVA for independent groups; matched groups and repeated-measures designs are evaluated with a one-way ANOVA for repeated measures.

Special-Purpose Control Group Designs

In control group designs, the experimental treatment is absent for at least one condition. Varieties of control groups include placebo controls, often found in drug research; wait list controls, found in research on the effectiveness of a program or therapy; and yoked controls, in which the procedural experiences of the control group participants correspond exactly to those of the treatment group participants.

CHAPTER REVIEW QUESTIONS

1. Consider independent groups designs, matched groups designs, and ex post facto designs. What do they all have in common and how do they differ?

2. In the Research Example that examined a peer modeling program to help children with autism (Kroeger et al., 2007), why was a matched groups design used, instead of an independent groups design, and what was the matching variable?

3. Describe the Stroop effect, the experimental design used by Stroop (1935), and his method for controlling order effects.

4. Use the hypothetical caffeine and reaction time study to illustrate how multilevel designs can produce nonlinear effects.

5. Assuming for the moment the Yerkes-Dodson law is valid, explain why testing three levels of "arousal" yields a totally different result than testing just two levels.

6. Use the Bransford and Johnson (1972) experiment on the effects of context on memory to illustrate how a design with more than two levels of an independent variable can serve the purpose of falsification.

7. Describe when it is best to use a line graph and when to use a bar graph. Explain why a line graph would be inappropriate in a study comparing the reaction times of men and women, but was a good choice for the Ebbinghaus forgetting curve.

8. Describe the two varieties of two-sample t-tests and, with reference to the four designs in the first part of the chapter (single factor–two levels), explain when each type of test is used.

9. For an independent groups study with one independent variable and three levels, what is the proper inferential statistical analysis, and why is this approach better than doing multiple t-tests? How does post hoc testing come into play?

10. Use the example of the effects of alcohol on reaction time to explain the usefulness of a placebo control group.

11. Use the subliminal self-help study (Merikle & Skanes, 1992) to illustrate the usefulness of a wait list control group.

12. Use the study of the effectiveness of EMDR therapy (Dunn et al., 1996) to explain how a yoked control group works.

APPLICATIONS EXERCISES

Exercise 7.1. Identifying Variables

As a review, look back at each of the Research Examples in this chapter and identify: (a) the independent variable; (b) the levels of the independent variable; (c) the type of independent variable (situational, instructional, task, and subject); (d) the dependent variable; and (e) the scale of measurement of the dependent variable (nominal, ordinal, interval, or ratio).

1. Research Example 11—Two-Level Independent Groups Design

2. Research Example 12—Two-Level Matched Groups Design

3. Research Example 13—Two-Level Ex Post Facto Design

4. Research Example 14—Two-Level Repeated Measures Design

5. Research Example 15—Multilevel Independent Groups Design

6. Research Example 16—Multilevel Repeated Measures Design

7. Research Example 17—Using Both Placebo and Wait List Control Groups

8. Research Example 18—A Yoked Control Group

Exercise 7.2. Identifying Designs

For each of the following descriptions of studies, identify the independent and dependent variables involved and the nature of the independent variable (between-subjects or within-subjects; manipulated or subject variable), name the experimental design being used, identify the measurement scale (nominal, ordinal, interval, or ratio) for the dependent variable(s), and indicate which inferential analysis ought to be done (which type of t-test or ANOVA).

1. In a study of how bulimia affects the perception of body size, a group of woman with bulimia and a group of same-age women without bulimia are asked to examine a precisely graded series of 10 drawings of women of different sizes and to indicate which size best matches the way they think they look.

2. College students in a cognitive mapping study are asked to use a direction finder to point accurately to three unseen locations that differ in distance from the laboratory. One is a nearby campus location, one is a nearby city, and the other one is a distant city.

3. Three groups of preschoolers (50 per group, assigned randomly) are in a study of task perseverance in which the size of the delay of reward is varied. The children in all three groups are given a difficult puzzle and told to work on it as long as they would like. One group is told that as payment they will be given $5 at the end of the session. The second group will get the $5 after two days from the end of the session, and the third will get the money after four days.

4. To examine whether crowding affects problem-solving performance, participants are placed in either a large or a small room while attempting to solve a set of word puzzles. Before assigning participants to the two conditions, the researcher takes a measure of their verbal intelligence to ensure the average verbal IQ of the groups is equivalent.

5. In a study of first impressions, students examine three consecutive photos of a young woman whose arms are covered with varying amounts of tattoos. In one photo, the woman has no tattoos; in the second photo, she has one tattoo on each arm; in the third photo, she has three tattoos per arm. From a checklist, students indicate which of five majors the woman is likely to be enrolled in and rate her on 10 different 7-point scales (e.g., one scale has 1 = emotionally insecure and 7 = emotionally secure).

6. In an attempt to identify the personality characteristics of cell phone users, three groups of college students are identified: those who do not have a cell phone; those who own a cell phone, but report using it less than 10 hours per week; and those who own a cell phone and report using it more than 10 hours per week. They are given a personality test that identifies whether they have an outgoing or a shy personality.

7. A researcher studies a group of 20 men, each with the same type of brain injury. They are divided into two groups in such a way that their ages and educational levels are kept constant.

All are given anagram problems to solve; first group is given 2 minutes to solve each anagram and the second group is given 4 minutes per anagram.

8. To determine if maze learning is affected by the type of maze used, 20 rats are randomly assigned to learn a standard alley maze (i.e., includes side walls; located on the lab floor); another 20 learn an elevated maze (no side walls; raised above floor level). Learning is assumed to occur when the rats run through the maze without making any wrong turns.

Exercise 7.3. Outcomes

For each of the following studies, decide whether to illustrate the described outcomes with a line graph or a bar graph; then create graphs that accurately portray the outcomes.

1. In a study of the effects of marijuana on immediate memory for a 30-item word list, participants are randomly assigned to an experimental group, a placebo control group, or a straight control group.

   Outcome A. Marijuana impairs recall, while expectations about marijuana have no effect on recall.

   Outcome B. Marijuana impairs recall, but expectations about marijuana also reduce recall performance.

   Outcome C. The apparently adverse affect of marijuana on recall can be attributed entirely to placebo effects.

2. A researcher uses a reliable and valid test to assess the autonomy levels of three groups of first-year female college students after they have been in college for two months. Someone with a high level of autonomy has the ability to function well without help from others—that is, to be independent. Tests scores range from 0 to 50, with higher scores indicating greater autonomy. One group (R300) is made up of resident students whose homes are 300 miles or more from campus; the second group includes resident students whose homes are less than 100 miles from campus (R100); the third group includes commuter students (C).

   Outcome A. Commuter students are more autonomous than resident students.

   Outcome B. The farther one's home is from the campus, the more autonomous that person is likely to be.

   Outcome C. Commuters and R300 students are both autonomous, while R100 students are not.

3. Animals learn a maze and, as they do, errors (i.e., wrong turns) are recorded. When they reach the goal box on each trial, they are rewarded with food. For one group of rats, the food is delivered immediately after they reach the goal (0 delay). For a second group, the food appears 5 seconds after they reach the goal (5-second delay).

Outcome A. Reinforcement delay hinders learning.

Outcome B. Reinforcement delay has no effect on learning.

4. Basketball players shoot three sets of 20 foul shots under three levels of arousal: low, moderate, and high. Under low arousal, every missed free throw means they have to run a lap around the court (i.e., it is a minimal penalty, not likely to cause arousal). Moderate arousal means two laps per miss and high arousal means four laps per miss (i.e., enough of a penalty to create high arousal, perhaps in the form of anxiety). It is a repeated-measures design; assume proper counterbalancing.

Outcome A. There is a linear relationship between arousal and performance; as arousal increases, performance declines.

Outcome B. There is a nonlinear relationship between arousal and performance; performance is good only for moderate arousal.

ANSWERS TO SELF TESTS

✓7.1

1. Single factor, two-level independent groups design.
2. Single factor, two-level repeated-measures design.
3. An ex post facto design.

✓7.2

1. Independent samples *t*-test.
2. The IV is a discrete variable, with no intermediate points that would allow for extrapolation in a line graph.
3. Repeated measures one-way ANOVA, with a post-hoc test if F-test is statistically significant.

✓7.3

1. Instead of 0.32 sec, the RT for the experimental group would be 0.22 sec (same as placebo group).
2. It raises questions about the validity of the new therapy being proposed. Those making claims about therapy are obligated to show that it works (i.e., produces results significantly better than a control group).

Experimental Design II: Factorial Designs

PREVIEW & CHAPTER OBJECTIVES

Chapter 7 introduced you to some basic experimental designs—those involving a single independent variable, with two or more levels of that variable being compared. The beauty of these designs is their simplicity, but human behavior is immensely complex. Thus, researchers often prefer to examine more than a single factor in their studies. To do this methodologically, the next logical step is to increase the number of independent variables being examined. When a study includes more than a single independent variable, the result is called a *factorial design*, the focus of this chapter. When you complete this chapter, you should be able to:

- Describe factorial designs using a standardized notation system (2 × 2, 3 × 5, etc.).

- Place data accurately into a factorial matrix, and calculate row and column means.

- Understand what is meant by a main effect, and know how to determine if one exists.

- Understand what is meant by an interaction effect, and know how to determine if one exists.

- Know how to interpret interactions and know the presence of an interaction sometimes lessens or eliminates the relevance of a main effect.

- Describe the research design of Jenkins and Dallenbach's (1924) famous study on sleep and memory and explain why their results could be considered an interaction.

- Identify the varieties of factorials corresponding to the single-factor designs of Chapter 7 (independent groups, matched groups, ex post facto, repeated measures).

- Identify a mixed factorial design, and understand why counterbalancing is not always used in such a design.

- Identify a P × E factorial design and understand what is meant when such a design produces main effects and interactions.

- Distinguish mixed P × E factorial from simple P × E factorial designs.

- Calculate the number of subjects needed to complete each type of factorial design.

- Know how to be an ethically responsible experimenter.

As you have worked your way through this research methods course, you have probably noticed that experimental psychologists seem to have a language of their own. They talk about operationalizing constructs, rejecting null hypotheses, and eliminating confounds, and when they talk about regression, they are not discussing Freud. You haven't seen anything yet. After mastering this chapter, you will be able to say things like this: "It was a two by three mixed factorial that produced one main effect for the repeated measures variable plus an interaction." Let's start with the basics.

Essentials of Factorial Designs

Suppose you are interested in memory and wish to find out if recall can be improved by training people to use visual imagery while memorizing a list of words. You could create a simple two-group experiment in which some people are trained to use visual imagery techniques while memorizing the words ("create a mental image of each word") and others are told to use rote repetition ("just repeat the words over and over to yourself"). Suppose you also wonder about how memory is affected by how quickly words are presented, that is, a word list's presentation rate. Again, you could do a simple two-group study in which some participants see the lists at the rate of 2 seconds per word, others at 4 seconds per word. With a factorial design, *both* of these studies can be done as part of the same experiment, allowing the researcher to examine the effects of both repetition and presentation rate, and to determine if these factors combine to affect memory.

By definition, a **factorial design** involves any study with more than one independent variable (recall from Chapter 7 that the terms *independent variable* and *factor* mean the same thing). In principle, factorial designs could involve dozens of independent variables, but in practice these designs usually involve two or three factors, sometimes four.

Identifying Factorial Designs

A factorial design is described with a numbering system that simultaneously identifies the number of independent variables and the number of levels of each variable. Each digit in the system represents an independent variable, and the numerical value of each digit indicates the number of levels of each independent variable. Thus, a 2 × 3 (read this as "two by three") factorial design has two independent variables; the first has two levels and the second has three. A more complex design, a 3 × 4 × 5 factorial, has three independent variables with three, four, and five levels, respectively. The hypothetical memory study we just described would be a 2 × 2 design, with two levels of the "type of training" independent variable (imagery and rote repetition) and two levels of the "presentation rate" independent variable (2 and 4 seconds per item).

The total number of conditions to be tested in a factorial study can be identified by looking at all possible combinations of the levels of each independent variable. In our hypothetical memory study, this produces a display called a **factorial matrix**, which looks like this:

| | Presentation rate | |
	2-sec/word	4-sec/word
Imagery		
Rote		

Type of training

Before going on, note this carefully: Up to this point in the book, we have been using the concepts "conditions of the experiment" and "levels of the independent variable" as if they meant the same thing. These concepts indeed are interchangeable in single-factor experiments (i.e., one independent variable). In factorial designs, however, this is no longer the case. In all experimental designs, the term *levels* refers to the number of levels of any one independent variable. In factorial designs, the term *conditions* equals the number of cells in a matrix like the one you just examined. Hence, the 2 × 2 memory study has *two* independent variables, each with *two* levels. It has *four* conditions, however, one for each of the four cells. The number of conditions in any factorial design can be determined by multiplying the numbers in the notation system. Thus, a 3 × 3 design has nine conditions; a 2 × 5 has ten conditions, and a 2 × 2 × 2 has eight conditions. Incidentally, although the use of a factorial matrix is a bit awkward when there are three independent variables, as in the 2 × 2 × 2 just mentioned, a matrix can be drawn. Suppose our memory study added gender as a third factor, in addition to presentation rate and type of training. The factorial matrix could look like this:

| | Men | | Women | |
	2-sec/item	4-sec/item	2-sec/item	4-sec/item
Imagery				
Rote				

Outcomes—Main Effects and Interactions

In factorial studies, two kinds of results occur: main effects and interactions. *Main effects* refer to the overall influence of each of the independent variables, and *interactions* examine whether the variables combine to form a more complex result. Let's look at each in more detail.

Main Effects

In the memory experiment we've been using as a model, the researcher is interested in the effects of two independent variables: type of training and presentation rate. In factorial designs, the term **main effect** is used to describe the overall effect of a single independent variable. Specifically, a main effect is the difference between the means of the levels of any one independent variable. So, in a study with two independent variables, such as a 2 × 2 factorial, there can be at most two significant main effects. Determining the main effect of one factor involves combining all of the data for each of the levels of that factor. In our hypothetical memory study, this can be illustrated as follows. The main effect of type of training is determined by combining the data for participants trained to use imagery (for both presentation rates combined) and comparing it to all of the data for participants using rote repetition. Hence, all of the information in the lightly shaded cells (imagery) of the following matrix would be combined and compared with the combined data in the more heavily shaded cells (rote):

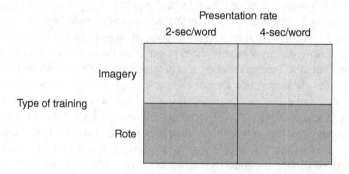

Similarly, the main effect of presentation rate is determined by combining the data for everyone presented the words at a 2-second rate and comparing that with the data from those presented the words at a 4-second rate. In the following matrix, the effect of presentation rate would be evaluated by comparing all of the information in the lightly shaded cells (2-sec/item) with all of the data in the more heavily shaded cells (4-sec/item):

	Presentation rate	
	2-sec/word	4-sec/word
Imagery		
Type of training		
Rote		

Let's consider hypothetical data for a memory experiment like the example we've been using. Assume 25 subjects in each condition (i.e., each cell of the matrix). Their task is to memorize a list of 30 words. The average number of words recalled for each of the four conditions might look like this:

	Presentation rate	
	2-sec/word	4-sec/word
Imagery	17	23
Type of training		
Rote	12	18

Does imagery training produce better recall than rote repetition? That is, is there a main effect of type of training? The way to find out is to compare all of the "imagery" data with all of the "rote" data. Specifically, this involves calculating *row means*. The "imagery" row mean is **20** words [(17 + 23)/2 = 40/2 = 20], and the "rote" row mean is **15** words [(12 + 18)/2 = 30/2 = 15]. When asking if training type is a main effect, the question is: "Is the difference between the row means of 20 and 15 statistically significant or due to chance?"

In the same fashion, calculating *column means* allows us to see if presentation rate is a main effect. For the 2 sec/item column, the mean is **14.5** words; it is **20.5** words for the 4 sec/item row (you should check this). Putting all of this together yields this outcome:

	Presentation rate		
	2-sec/word	4-sec/word	**Row means**
Imagery	17	23	**20.0**
Rote	12	18	**15.0**
Column means	**14.5**	**20.5**	

(Type of training labels the rows; Imagery and Rote.)

For these data, it appears that imagery improves memory (20 > 15) and that recall is higher if the words are presented at a slower rate (20.5 > 14.5). That is, there seem to be two main effects here (of course, it takes an analysis of variance (ANOVA) to make a judgment about whether the differences are significant statistically or due to chance—more on *factorial ANOVAs* later in this chapter). For a real example of a study that produced two main effects, consider this example of the so-called closing time effect.

Research Example 19—Main Effects

We don't know how often country music produces empirical questions that intrigue research psychologists, but one example is a song produced by Mickey Gilley in 1975, "The Girls All Get Prettier at Closing Time," which includes the lyrics: "Ain't it funny, ain't it strange, the way a man's opinion changes, when he starts to face that lonely night." The song suggests that, as the night wears on, men in bars, desperate to find a companion for the night, lower their "attractiveness" threshold—the same woman who only seemed moderately attractive at 10:00 p.m. becomes more eye-catching as closing time looms. Yes, pathetic. Nonetheless, several researchers have ventured courageously into bars and clubs on the edges of campuses to test this "closing time" concept, and to determine whether it applies to both men *and* women who are searching for. . .whatever. One interesting example is a study by Gladue and Delaney (1990). In addition to resulting in two main effects (gender and time), the study also illustrates several other methodological points.

Gladue and Delaney's (1990) study took place over a 3-month period at a large bar that included a dance floor and had the reputation as being a place where "one had a high probability of meeting someone for subsequent romantic. . .activities" (p. 380). The researchers recruited 58 male and 43 female patrons, who made attractiveness ratings of a set of photographs of men and women and also made global ratings of the overall attractiveness of the people who happened to be at the bar—"Overall, how attractive would you rate the men/women in the bar right now?" (p. 381). The ratings, made at 9:00 p.m., 10:30 p.m., and 12:00 midnight, were on a 10-point scale, with 10 being the most attractive. For the global ratings, here is the factorial matrix for the results (means estimated from the graph in Figure 8.1):

	Time period			
	9:00	**10:30**	**12:00**	**Row means**
Men rating women	5.6	6.4	6.6	**6.2**
Women rating men	4.8	5.2	5.6	**5.2**
Column means	**5.2**	**5.8**	**6.1**	

Both main effects were significant (remember that main effects are determined by examining row and column means). In this case, the average ratings increased for both men *and* women as the night wore on (column means → 5.2 < 5.8 < 6.1). Also, women were generally more discerning—they rated men lower than men rated women during all three periods combined (row means → 5.2 < 6.2). Figure 8.1 is Gladue and Delaney's (1990) bar graph of the same data. Note the use of error bars.

You might be thinking that one potential confound in the study was alcohol use. As one drinks more during the course of an evening, others might come to be seen as more attractive. So alcohol consumption could be confounded with the time of the attractiveness rating. Gladue and Delaney (1990) dealt with this by measuring alcohol intake and eliminated the problem by finding no over-all relationship between intake amount and the attractiveness ratings. Another problem was that the global ratings of attractiveness were relatively crude measures, open to a number of interpreta-tions. For instance, the actual people in the bar at the three times were probably different (people come and go during the evening), so the ratings at the three times might reflect actual attractive-ness differences in those at the bar. To account for this problem, Gladue and Delaney also asked their subjects to rate photos of college-age female and male students. The same photos were used for all three periods. These photos had been pretested for levels of attractiveness, and photos with

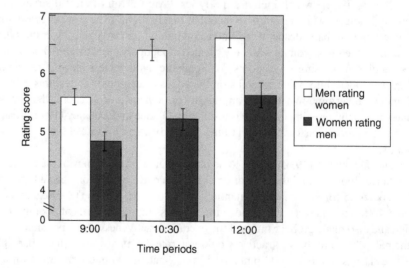

FIGURE 8.1
Main Effects—attractiveness ratings over the course of an evening for men and women rating each other, from the "closing time" study by Gladue and Delaney (1990).

moderate degrees of attractiveness had been chosen by the researchers. Why moderate? The researchers wished to avoid a problem first mentioned in Chapter 5—*ceiling effects* and *floor effects*. That is, they wanted to use photos for which changes in ratings, either up or down, would be likely to occur during the three periods. The ratings of the photos produced a more subtle effect than the global ratings. As the time passed, a closing time effect occurred for men (confirming Mickey Gilley, perhaps), but it did *not* occur for women; their ratings stayed about the same across all three time periods. This outcome is known as an *interaction*, our next topic.

SELF TEST

8.1

1. A $2 \times 3 \times 4$ factorial design has (a) how many IVs, (b) how many levels of each IV, and (c) how many total conditions?
2. What is the basic definition of a main effect?
3. A memory study with a 2 (type of instruction) $\times$ 2 (presentation rate) factorial, like the example used at the start of the chapter, has these results (DV = words recalled):

   Imagery/2-sec rate = 20 words
   Imagery/4-sec rate = 20 words
   Rote/2-sec rate = 12 words
   Rote/4-sec rate = 12 words

   Are there any apparent main effects here? If so, for which factor? or both? Calculate the row and column means.

Interactions

Main effects are important outcomes in factorial designs, but the distinct advantage of factorials over single-factor designs lies in their potential to show interactive effects. In a factorial design, an **interaction** is said to occur when the effect of one independent variable depends on the level of another independent variable. This is a moderately difficult concept to grasp, but it is of immense importance because interactions often provide the most interesting results in a factorial study. In fact, interactions sometimes render main effects irrelevant. To start, consider a simple example. Suppose we hypothesize that an introductory psychology course is best taught as a laboratory self-discovery course rather than as a straight lecture course, but we also wonder if this is generally true or true only for certain kinds of students. Perhaps science majors would especially benefit from the laboratory approach. To test the idea, we need to compare a lab with a lecture version of introductory psychology, but we also need to compare types of students, perhaps science majors and humanities majors. This calls for a 2×2 design that looks like this:

Course type

	Lab emphasis	Lecture emphasis
Science		
Humanities		

Student's major

In a study like this, the dependent variable would be some measure of learning; let's use a score from 1 to 100 on a standardized test of knowledge of general psychology, given during final exam week. Suppose these results occurred:

		Course type	
		Lab emphasis	Lecture emphasis
Student's major	Science	80	70
	Humanities	70	80

Are there any main effects here? No—all of the row and column means are the same: 75. So did anything at all happen in this study? Yes—something clearly happened. Specifically, the science students did better in the lab course than in the lecture course, but the humanities students did better in the lecture course than in the lab course. Or, to put it in terms of the definition of an interaction, the effect of one variable (course type) depended on the level of the other variable (major). Hence, even if no main effects occur, an interaction can occur and produce an interesting outcome.

This teaching example also highlights the distinct advantage of factorial designs over single-factor designs. Suppose you completed the study as a single-factor, two-level design, comparing lab with lecture versions of introductory psychology. You would probably use a matched group design, with student GPA and perhaps major as matching variables. In effect, you might end up with the same people who were in the factorial example. However, by running it as a single-factor design, your results would be:

$$\text{Lab course}: 75 \quad \text{Lecture course}: 75$$

and you might conclude it doesn't matter whether introductory psychology includes a lab or not. With the factorial design, however, you know the lab indeed matters, *but only for certain types of students*. In short, factorial designs can be more informative than single-factor designs. To further illustrate the concept of interactions, in this case one that also failed to find main effects, consider the outcome of the following study.

Research Example 20—An Interaction with No Main Effects

Considerable research indicates that people remember information best if they are in the same general environment or context where they learned the information in the first place. A typical design is a 2×2 factorial, with the independent variables being the situation when the material is studied and the situation when the material is recalled. A nice example, and one that has clear relevance for students, is a study conducted by Veronica Dark and a group of her undergraduate students (Grant et al., 1998).

Grant et al.'s (1998) study originated from a concern that students often study under conditions quite different from the test-taking environment: They often study in a noisy environment but then take their tests in a quiet room. So, in the experiment, participants were asked to study a two-page article on psychoimmunology. Half of the participants studied the article while listening (over headphones) to background noise from a tape made during a busy lunchtime in a cafeteria (no distinct voices, but a "general conversational hum that was intermixed with the sounds produced by movement of chairs and dishes"—p. 619); the remaining participants studied the same article without any background noise (but with the headphones on—can you see why they used headphones in this second group?). After a short break, all of the participants were tested on the material (with short answer and multiple-choice questions), also in either a noisy or quiet environment. This 2 × 2 independent groups design yielded the following four conditions:

1. silent study — silent recall

2. noisy study — noisy recall

3. silent study — noisy recall

4. noisy study — silent recall

The results for both the short answer and the multiple-choice tests showed the same general pattern; here are the mean scores for the multiple-choice results (max score = 16):

	Study condition		
	Silent	Noisy	**Row means**
Silent during recall	14.3	12.7	**12.8**
Noisy during recall	12.7	14.3	**13.5**
Column means	**12.8**	**13.5**	

This outcome is similar to the pattern found in the hypothetical study about ways of teaching introductory psychology to science and humanities students. Row and column means were close (12.8 and 13.5), and they were not significantly different from each other. So there were no main effects. But examining the four individual cell means shows an interaction clearly occurred. When the students studied the essay in peace and quiet, they recalled well in the quiet context (14.3) but not so well in the noisy context (12.7); when they studied in noisy conditions, they recalled poorly in a quiet context (12.7) but did well when recalling when it was noisy (14.3). That is, learning was best when the study context matched the recall context. To put it in interaction language, the effect of one factor (where they recalled) depended on the level of the other factor (where they studied). Figure 8.2 presents the data in bar graph form.

This study had important limitations. First, there were few subjects (total of 39). Second, there were several experimenters, all undergraduate students of uncertain training and consistency as experimenters. Nonetheless, the predicted interaction occurred, one that is similar to the results of other studies with the same basic design (e.g., Godden & Baddeley, 1975), perhaps an indication of an effect strong enough to overcome methodological weaknesses.

Can you see the relevance of this for your life as a student? First, unlike much of the research on this context effect, which typically uses lists of words for study, Grant et al. (1998) used study material similar to the kind you would encounter as a student—text information to be comprehended. So the study has a certain amount of *ecological validity* (Chapter 5). Second, although you might conclude from these data that it doesn't matter whether you study in a quiet or noisy environment (just be sure to take the test in the same kind of environment), a fact of academic life is that tests are taken in quiet rooms. Unless you can convince your professors to let you take tests with your iPod going full blast (don't count on it), this study suggests it is clearly to your advantage to study for exams in a quiet place.

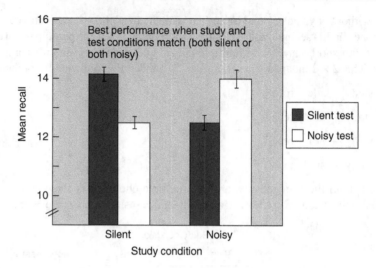

FIGURE 8.2
Bar graph showing an interaction between study and recall conditions (constructed from data in Grant et al., 1998).

Interactions Sometimes Trump Main Effects

In the opening paragraph describing interactions, you might have noticed a comment about interactions sometimes making main effects irrelevant. This frequently occurs in factorial designs for a specific type of interaction. A good example will make the point. Research Example 9 (Chapter 6) was designed to illustrate the use of a double blind procedure, but it also produced a significant interaction and two significant but irrelevant main effects. As you recall, the study examined the effect of caffeine on the memory of elderly subjects who were self-described "morning people." When tested in the morning, they did equally well whether taking caffeine in their coffee or having decaf. In the late afternoon, however, they did well with caffeine, but poorly with decaf. Here are the data in factorial matrix form:

	Time of day		
	Morning	Afternoon	**Row means**
Caffeinated coffee	11.8	11.7	**11.8**
Decaffeinated coffee	11.0	8.9	**10.0**
Column means	**11.4**	**10.3**	

In this experiment, both main effects were statistically significant. Overall, recall was better for caffeine than for decaf (11.8 > 10.0) and recall was also better for morning sessions than afternoon sessions (11.4 > 10.3). If you carefully examine the four cell means, however, you can see performance was about the same for three of the cells, and declined only for the cell with the 8.9 in it—decaf in the afternoon. You can see this effect even more clearly in Figure 8.3: Three of the bars are essentially the same height, while the fourth is much lower.

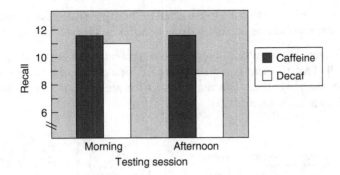

FIGURE 8.3
When an interaction renders main effects meaningless (from Ryan, Hatfield, & Hofstetter, 2002).

The only really important finding here is that recall declined in the afternoon for elderly adults drinking decaf—if they drank caffeinated coffee in the afternoon, they did as well as they had in the morning. Thus, you do not get a true picture of the key result if you report that, overall, caffeine produced better memory than decaf (11.8 > 10.0). In fact, caffeine's only advantage was in the afternoon; in the morning, whether subjects drank caffeine or decaf did not matter. Similarly, emphasizing the second main effect, that recall was generally better in the morning than in the afternoon (11.4 > 10.3), also gives a false impression of the key result. Recall was only better in the morning when decaf was consumed; when caffeine was used, morning or afternoon didn't matter. In short, for this kind of outcome, the interaction is the only important result. The tip-off that you are dealing with the kind of interaction where main effects do not matter is a graph like Figure 8.3, where three of the bars (or points on a line graph) are essentially the same, and a fourth bar (or point) is very different in height.

Combinations of Main Effects and Interactions

The experiment on studying and recalling with or without background noise (Research Example 20) illustrates one type of outcome in a factorial design (an interaction, but no main effects), but many patterns of results could occur. In a simple 2 × 2 design, for instance, there are eight possibilities:

1. a main effect for the first factor only

2. a main effect for the second factor only

3. main effects for both factors; no interaction

4. a main effect for the first factor plus an interaction

5. a main effect for the second factor plus an interaction

6. main effects for both factors plus an interaction

7. an interaction only, no main effects

8. no main effects, no interaction

Let's briefly consider several of these outcomes in the context of the earlier hypothetical experiment on imagery training and presentation rate. For each of the following examples, we have created data that might result from the study on the effects of imagery instructions and presentation rate on memory for a 30-word list, translated the data into a line graph, and verbally described the results. We haven't tried to create all of the eight possibilities listed above; rather, the following examples illustrate outcomes likely to occur in this type of study.

1. Imagery training improves recall, regardless of presentation rate; presentation rate doesn't affect recall. That is, there is a main effect for type of training factor—imagery (22) is better than rote (14). There is no main effect for presentation rate, however—the 2-sec rate (18) equals the 4-sec rate (18).

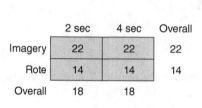

	2 sec	4 sec	Overall
Imagery	22	22	22
Rote	14	14	14
Overall	18	18	

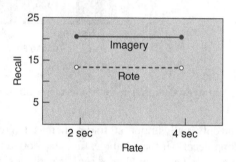

2. Recall is better with slower rates of presentation, but the imagery training was not effective in improving recall. That is, there is a main effect for the presentation rate factor—recall was better at 4-sec/item (22) than at 2-sec/item (14). But there was no main effect for type of training—imagery (18) was the same as rote (18).

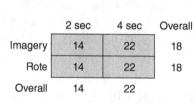

	2 sec	4 sec	Overall
Imagery	14	22	18
Rote	14	22	18
Overall	14	22	

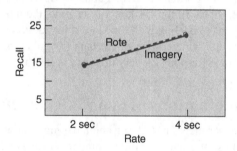

3. Recall is better with slower rates of presentation (20 > 16); in addition, the imagery training was effective in improving recall (20 > 16). In this case, main effects for both factors occur. This is the outcome most likely to occur if you actually completed this study.

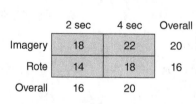

	2 sec	4 sec	Overall
Imagery	18	22	20
Rote	14	18	16
Overall	16	20	

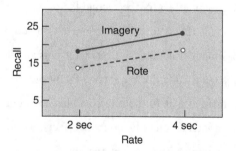

4. At the 2-sec presentation rate, imagery training clearly improves recall (i.e., from 12 to 28); however, at the 4-sec rate, recall is almost perfect (28 = 28), regardless of how subjects are trained. Another way to say this is that when using imagery, presentation rate doesn't matter, but it does matter when using rote repetition. In short, there is an interaction between type of training and presentation rate. In this case, the interaction may have been influenced

by a *ceiling effect*, a result in which the scores for different conditions are all so close to the maximum (30 words in this example) that no difference could occur. Here, the imagery group recalls nearly all the words, regardless of presentation rate. To test for the presence of a ceiling effect, you could replicate the study with 50-item word lists and see if performance improves for the imagery/4-sec group.

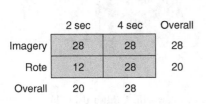

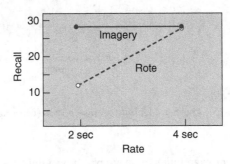

You may be wondering about the obvious main effects that occur in this example. Surely the row (20 and 28) and column (also 20 and 28) means indicate significant overall effects for both factors. Technically, yes, the analysis probably would yield statistically significant main effects in this example, but this just illustrates again that interactions can trump main effects when the results are interpreted—the same point just made about the decaf-in-the-afternoon study. For the hypothetical memory study, the main effects are not meaningful; the statement that imagery yields a general improvement in recall is not really accurate. Rather, it only seems to improve recall at the faster presentation rate. Likewise, concluding that 4 seconds per item produces better recall than 2 seconds per item is misleading—it is only true for the rote groups. Hence, the interaction is the key finding here.

5. This is not to say that main effects never matter when an interaction exists, however. Consider this last example:

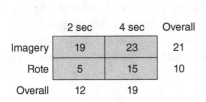

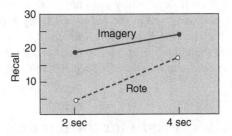

In this case, imagery training generally improves recall (i.e., there's a main effect for type of training: 21 > 10). Also, a slower presentation rate improves recall for both groups (i.e., a main effect for presentation rate also: 19 > 12). Both of these outcomes are worth reporting. Imagery works better than rote at *both* presentation rates (19 > 5 and 23 > 15), and the 4-sec rate works better than the 2-sec rate for *both* types of training (23 > 19 and 15 > 5). What the interaction shows is that slowing the presentation rate improves recall somewhat for the imagery group (23 is a bit better than 19), but slowing the rate improves recall considerably for the rote rehearsal group (15 is a lot better than 5). Another way of describing the interaction is to say that at the fast rate, the imagery training is especially effective (19 is a lot better than 5—a difference of 14 items on the memory test). At the slower rate, imagery training still yields better recall, but not by as much as at the fast rate (23 is somewhat better than 15—a difference of just 8 items on the memory test).

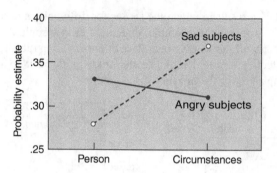

FIGURE 8.4
Using a line graph to highlight an interaction (from Keltner, Ellsworth, & Edwards, 1993).

From examining these graphs, you might have noticed a standard feature of interactions. In general, if the lines on the graph are parallel, then no interaction is present. If the lines are nonparallel, however, an interaction probably exists. Of course, this is only a general guideline. Whether an interaction exists (in essence, whether the lines are sufficiently nonparallel) is a statistical decision, to be determined by an ANOVA.

Identifying interactions by examining whether lines are parallel or not is easier with line graphs than with bar graphs. Hence, the guideline mentioned in Chapter 7 about line graphs being used only with within-subjects factors is sometimes ignored by researchers if the key finding is an interaction. For example, a study by Keltner, Ellsworth, and Edwards (1993) showed that when participants were asked to estimate the likelihood of a bad event (e.g., a car accident) occurring, there was an interaction between the emotion they experienced during the experiment and whether the hypothetical event was said to be caused by a person or by circumstances. When participants were feeling sad, they believed events produced by circumstances (e.g., wet roads) were more likely to occur than events produced by individual actions (e.g., poor driving). When participants were angry, however, the opposite happened—they believed events caused by individuals were more likely. As you can see from Figure 8.4, a line graph was used in the published study even though the X-axis uses a discrete variable. Keltner et al. (1993) probably wanted to show the interaction as clearly as possible, so they ignored the guideline about discrete variables. To repeat a point made earlier, when presenting any data, the overriding concern is to make one's hard-earned results as clear as possible to the reader.

Creating Graphs for the Results of Factorial Designs

Whether it's the line or the bar version, students sometimes find it difficult to create graphs when studies use factorial designs. In single-factor designs, the process is easy; there is only a single independent variable, so there is no question about what will appear on the X-axis. With factorials, however, the situation is more complicated. A 2 × 2, for example, has two independent variables, but a graph has only one X-axis. How does one proceed?

This problem can be solved in a number of ways, but here is a simple and fool-proof system. Let's use Example 5 of the hypothetical imagery training and presentation rate study we have just worked through—the one with two main effects and an interaction. Creating the graph on the right from the matrix on the left can be accomplished as follows:

Step 1. Make the independent variable in the columns of the matrix the label for the *X*-axis. Think of this visually. The "2 sec" and "4 sec" are horizontal on the matrix—keep them horizontal on the graph and just slide them down to the *X*-axis. Label the *Y*-axis with the dependent variable.

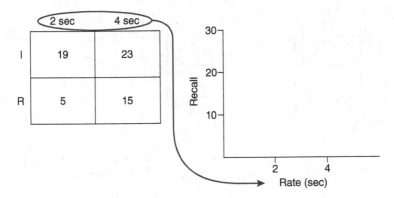

Step 2. Move the means from the top row of the matrix directly to the graph. Just as the "19" is on the left and the "23" is on the right side of the matrix, they wind up on the same left and right sides of the graph.

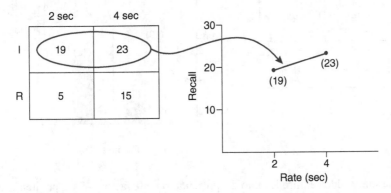

Step 3. Do the same with the means from the bottom row of the matrix ("5" and "15").

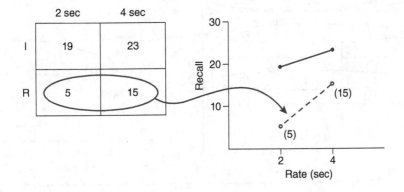

Step 4.   Create a legend that identifies the second independent variable. Again think visually— "imagery" is above "rote" in the matrix and in the legend.

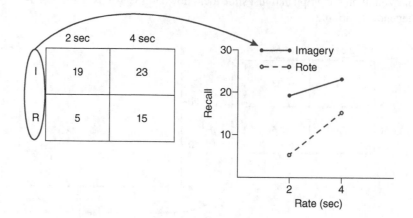

Note that if you wish to create a bar graph, the same basic process applies. Each of the points in the line graph turns into the top line of a bar.

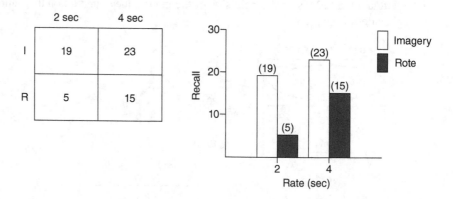

Suppose the study added a third level to the presentation rate factor—6 sec per item, for instance. Here's how the graph building process would proceed:

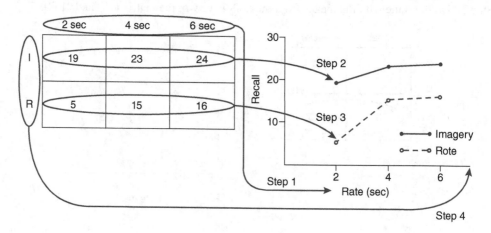

You learned in Chapter 6 that in recent years it has become standard practice to include *error bars* on graphs. The points on a line graph and the tops of the bars on a bar graph are the mean scores; error bars tell you about the amount of variability in a set of scores. Error bars can be in the form of standard deviations, standard errors (an estimate of the population standard deviation, based on sample data), or confidence intervals (when SPSS does a graph, this is the default choice). Suppose you had a set of scores for which the mean was 20 and the standard deviation was 3. Here's how the error bars would look on both a bar graph and a line graph (for real examples in this chapter, look at Figures 8.8 and 8.10).

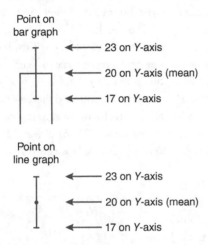

Before we turn to a system for categorizing types of factorial designs, you should read Box 8.1. It describes one of psychology's most famous experiments, a classic study supporting the idea that between the time you last study for an exam and the time you take the exam, you should be sleeping. It was completed in the early 1920s, when the term *factorial design* had not yet been invented and when analysis of variance, the statistical tool most frequently used to analyze factorials, was just starting to be conceptualized. Yet the study illustrates the kind of thinking that leads to factorial designs: the desire to examine more than one independent variable at the same time.

BOX 8.1   CLASSIC STUDIES—To Sleep, Perchance to Recall

Although the term *factorial design* and the statistical tools to analyze factorials were not used widely until after World War II, attempts to study more than one variable at a time occurred well before then. A classic example is a study by Jenkins and Dallenbach (1924) that still appears in many general psychology books as the standard example of retroactive interference (RI), or the tendency for memory to be hindered if other mental activities intervene between the time of study and the time of recall. In essence, the study was a 2 × 4 repeated-measures factorial design. The "2" was whether or not activities intervened between learning and a recall test, and the "4" referred to four retention intervals; recall was tested 1, 2, 4, or 8 hours after initial learning. What made the study interesting (and, eventually, famous) was the first factor. Participants spent the time between study and recall either awake and doing normal student behaviors, or asleep in Cornell's psychology lab. The prediction, that being asleep would produce less RI, and therefore better recall, was supported.

(continued)

BOX 8.1 (CONTINUED)

A close examination of the study illustrates some of the attributes of typical 1920s-era research and also shows that experimenters were just as careful about issues of methodological control then as they are now. As you will learn in Chapter 12, research in psychology's early years often featured very few participants. Compared with modern memory research, which uses many participants and summarizes data statistically, early studies were more likely to include just one, two, or three participants and report extensive data for each—additional participants served the purpose of replication. This happened in Jenkins and Dallenbach's (1924) study; there were just two subjects (referred to as *Observers* or *Os*, another typical convention of the time), both seniors at Cornell. When using small numbers of participants, researchers tried to get as much out of them as they could, and the result in this case was what we would call a repeated-measures study today. That is, both students contributed data to all eight cells of the 2 × 4 design, with each student learning and recalling lists eight times in each of the eight conditions—a total of 64 trials. If you are beginning to think the study was a major undertaking for the two Cornell seniors, you're right. During the study, the two students and Jenkins, who served as experimenter, "lived in the laboratory during the course of the experiments" (p. 606) in a simulated dorm room, and the study lasted from April 14, 1923, to June 7. Imagine giving up your last month and a half of college to science!

As good researchers, Jenkins and Dallenbach (1924) were concerned about control, and they used many of the procedures you've been learning about. For instance, they used 10-item lists of nonsense syllables, and the subjects read them aloud during the study trials until one perfect recitation occurred (i.e., their operational definition of learning). They took measures to ensure a consistent pronunciation of the syllables, and they used counterbalancing to avoid sequence effects in the presentation of the different retention intervals—"[t]he time-intervals between learning and reproduction were varied at haphazard" (p. 607). For the "awake" condition, the students learned their lists between 8 and 10 in the morning, then went about their normal business as students, and then returned to the lab for recall after 1, 2, 4, or 8 hours. For the "asleep" condition, lists were studied between 11:30 at night and 1:00 in the morning. Students then went to bed, and were awakened for recall by

Jenkins 1, 2, 4, or 8 hours later. There was one potential confound in the study: On the awake trials, the students were told when to return to the lab for recall (i.e., they knew the retention interval), but during the asleep trials, students did not know when they would be awakened. Jenkins and Dallenbach were aware of the problem, considered alternatives, but decided their procedure was adequate.

The results? Figure 8.5 reproduces their original graph showing the data for each student. Each data point is an average of the eight trials for each condition of the study. Several things are clear. First, both students ("H" and "Mc") behaved similarly. Second, and this was the big finding, there was a big advantage for recall after sleeping, compared with recall after being awake. Third, there is the hint of an interaction. As Jenkins and Dallenbach (1924) described it: "The curves of

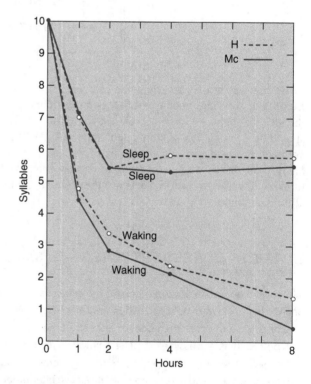

FIGURE 8.5

The Jenkins and Dallenbach study on retroactive interference, showing data for both of the Cornell students who participated, L. R. Hodell (H) and J. S. McGrew (Mc). Keep in mind that the study was completed long before an ethics code would have deleted the participants' names (from Jenkins & Dallenbach, 1924).

the waking experiments take the familiar form: a sharp decline which becomes progressively flatter. The form of the curves of the sleep experiments, however, is very different: after a small initial decline, the curves flatten and a high and constant level is thenceforth maintained" (p. 610).

One other intriguing outcome of the study is never reported in textbook accounts. As the experiment progressed, it became increasingly difficult for Jenkins to wake up the students. It was also hard for Jenkins to "know when they were awake. The Os would leave their beds, go into the next room, give their reproductions, and the next morning say that they remembered nothing of it" (Jenkins & Dallenbach, 1924, p. 607)! At the time, a semi-asleep state was thought to be similar to hypnosis, so Jenkins and Dallenbach rounded up another student and replicated part of the study, but instead of having the student sleep for varying amounts of time, they had the student learn and recall the lists at different retention intervals while hypnotized (during both learning and recall). They found recall to be virtually perfect for all of the intervals, an early hint at what later came to be called *state-dependent learning* by cognitive psychologists (and similar to Research Example 20, regarding noisy or quiet study environments and exam performance).

SELF TEST

8.2

1. A maze learning study with a 2 (type of maze: alley maze or elevated maze) × 2 (type of rat: wild or bred in the lab) factorial has these results (DV = number of trials until performance is perfect):

   Alley maze / wild rats = 12 trials
   Alley maze / tame rats = 20 trials
   Elevated maze / wild rats = 20 trials
   Elevated maze / tame rats = 12 trials

   Summarize the results in terms of main effects and interactions.

2. In terms of main effects and interactions, describe the results of the Research Example about studying and taking exams (Research Example 20).

Varieties of Factorial Designs

Like the decision tree in Figure 7.1 for single-factor designs, Figure 8.6 shows the decisions involved in arriving at one of seven factorial designs. You'll recognize that four of the designs mirror those in Figure 7.1, but the other designs are unique to factorials. First, factorial designs can be completely between-subjects, meaning all the independent variables are between-subjects factors. Also, factorial designs can be completely within-subjects, in which all the independent variables are within-subjects factors. When a mixture of between- and within-subjects factors exist in the same experiment, the design is called a **mixed factorial design.** In a mixed design, at least one variable must be tested between subjects, and at least one must be tested within subjects. Second, some between-subjects factorials include both a subject variable and a manipulated independent variable. Because these designs can yield an interaction between the type of person (P) in the study and the situation or environment (E) created in the study, they can be called **P × E factorial designs** ("P by E"), or Person by Environment designs, with Person defined as some subject variable and Environment defined broadly to include any manipulated independent variable. A further distinction can be made

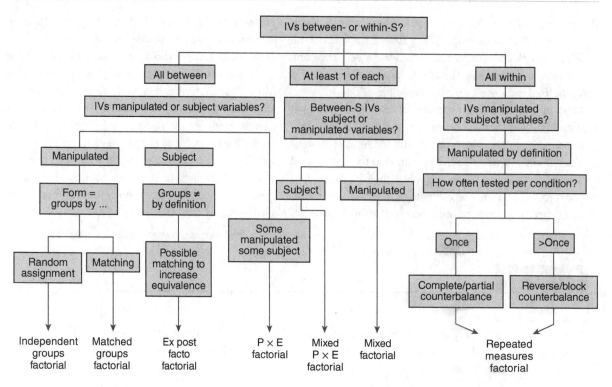

FIGURE 8.6
A decision tree for factorial designs.

within P × E designs, depending on whether the variables are between-subjects or within-subjects factors. In most cases the P variable is a between-subjects factor because it is a subject variable. However, it could be a within-subjects factor if the participants are tested over time, as in a developmental design. The E variable can also be manipulated as either a between- or within-subjects factor. If the P factor is between-subjects, and the E factor is within-subjects, then the P × E is a **mixed P × E factorial**. Let's examine mixed factorials and then P × E factorials in more detail.

Mixed Factorial Designs

In Chapter 6, you learned that when independent variables are between-subjects factors, creating equivalent groups can be a problem, and procedures like random assignment and matching are used to solve the problem. Similarly, when independent variables are within-subjects variables, a difficulty arises because of potential order effects, and counterbalancing is the normal solution. Thus, in a mixed design, the researcher usually gets to deal with both the problems of equivalent groups *and* the problems of order effects. Not always, though—there is one variety of mixed design where counterbalancing is not used because order effects themselves are the outcome of interest. For example, in learning and memory research, "trials" is frequently encountered as a within-subjects factor. Counterbalancing makes no sense in this case because one purpose of the study is to show regular changes from trial to trial. The following two Research Examples show two types of mixed designs, one requiring normal counterbalancing and one in which trials is the repeated measure.

Research Example 21—A Mixed Factorial with Counterbalancing

Terror Management Theory (TMT; Greenberg, Pyszcznski, & Solomon, 1986) is based on the idea that, as a species, we humans have the unique ability to know that our lives will, without a doubt, someday end. This awareness, according to the theory, scares the heck out of us, leading us to develop various coping mechanisms. Concern with death makes it easy for us to believe in some form of afterlife, for example. Research on TMT has focused on seeing what happens if people are reminded of their future death, and these reminders have had a number of interesting effects. For example, Kasser and Sheldon (2000) found that subjects asked to write essays about their future demise developed feelings of insecurity that led them to predict (hope for?) higher estimates of their future financial worth than subjects writing essays about their music preferences.

Cohen, Solomon, Maxfield, Pyszcznski, and Greenberg (2004) examined the relationship between TMT and leadership style. They made the interesting prediction that reminders of death would enhance the appeal of charismatic leaders, leaders whose vision can help overcome feelings of personal insecurity. They designed a 2 × 3 mixed factorial to test the idea. The between-subjects factor, as is typical in TMT studies, randomly assigned participants to one of two groups. One (mortality salient) wrote essays about "the emotions that the thought of your own death arouses in you" (p. 848), while the other (exam salient) wrote essays about the emotions aroused by thoughts of a forthcoming important exam. The within-subjects factor was leadership style. Participants evaluated hypothetical candidates for governor who were described as charismatic (the description emphasized being visionary, creative, and willing to take risks), task-oriented (the description emphasized setting realistic goals and developing clear plans), or relationship-oriented (the description emphasized being friendly and respectful of citizens). You can see why leadership style was tested as a repeated measure—Cohen et al., wanted each participant to evaluate each candidate. With just three levels of the within-subject factor, complete counterbalancing was feasible and was implemented (only six different orders of the three leader descriptions were needed).

The outcome was a significant main effect and an interaction. Although we have seen that interactions sometimes qualify main effects, in this case both outcomes told an important part of the story. The main effect was that task-oriented leaders were generally favored over the other leadership styles, a finding that is fairly typical in research on leadership. The interaction was in line with Cohen et al.'s (2004) TMT prediction. The task-oriented leader was rated highly regardless of mortality or exam salience (middle bars in Figure 8.7); however, reminding participants of their mortality led them to increase their evaluations of charismatic leaders (bars on the left) and decrease their evaluations of relationship-oriented leaders (bars on the right). Apparently, anxiety about the future can lead people to value leaders who promise a secure and optimistic future, and be skeptical about leaders who focus on interpersonal communication.

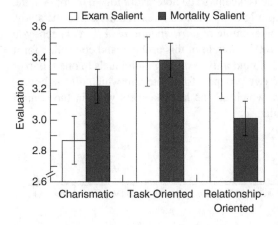

FIGURE 8.7

Mean evaluations of candidates who were described as charismatic, task-oriented, or relationship-oriented (from Cohen, Solomon, Maxfield, Pyszcznski, & Greenberg, 2004)

Research Example 22—A Mixed Factorial without Counterbalancing

In some mixed designs, the within-subjects factor examines changes in behavior with the passage of time—a trials effect—so counterbalancing does not come into play. This was the case in a fascinating study by Crum and Langer (2007); it showed that those doing physical labor for a living might achieve positive health benefits if they did nothing more than redefine their working activities as "exercise." It is no surprise that research shows a relationship between exercise and good health. What you might be surprised to learn is that improvements in health can occur if people merely *think* that what they do in the normal course of a day could be called "exercise."

Crum and Langer (2007) created a 2 × 2 mixed factorial design to examine the extent to which beliefs can affect health. The subjects in the study were 84 women who worked housekeeping jobs in hotels. They work hard, and most of what they do clearly involves exercise (climbing stairs, pushing a heavy cart, lifting mattresses, etc.); Crum and Langer estimated they easily exceed the Surgeon General's recommendation to get 30 minutes of exercise per day to enhance health. Housekeepers don't usually think of their work as exercise, however; they just think of it as work. To alter that perception, Crum and Langer randomly assigned some housekeepers ($n = 44$) to an "informed" group in which they were explicitly told that the work they did exceeded the Surgeon General's recommendations for daily exercise. They were also given specific details about how many calories were burned when doing their tasks (e.g., 15 minutes of vacuuming burns 50 calories). The remaining housekeepers ($n = 40$) were not told anything about their work being considered healthful exercise.[1] The within-subjects factor was time; measures were taken at the start of the study and again four weeks later. There were several dependent variables, both self-report measures (e.g., self-reported levels of exercise when not working) and physiological measures (e.g., blood pressure, body mass index).

Think about this for a minute. Over the course of four weeks, two groups of women did the same amount of physical labor (this was verified independently); the only difference between them was *how they thought about what they were doing*. It is hard to believe that just calling your work "exercise" can have any beneficial physical effect, but that is exactly what happened. After four weeks of thinking their work could also be considered exercise (and therefore healthy), the informed housekeepers showed small but significant decreases in weight, body mass index, body-fat percentage, waist-to-hip ratio, and systolic blood pressure (but not diastolic blood pressure), compared to those in the control group. Mind affects body. Figure 8.8 shows these changes (note the use of error bars in line graphs). In terms of the factorial language we have been using, five of the six graphs (diastolic blood pressure being the exception), showed an interaction between the group (informed or not) and the passage of time. Although it appears there are also main effects for the group factor, at least in the first four graphs, none of these effects were statistically significant.

It might have occurred to you that because housekeepers at a hotel work together, some in the informed group and some in the control group might have talked to each other about the study, thereby muddying the results. This would be an example of *participant crosstalk*, a concept you encountered in Chapter 2. Crum and Langer (2007) thought of this problem and controlled for it in their random assignment procedure. Instead of randomly assigning individuals to one group or another, they randomly assigned *hotels* to the two groups—four hotels in which all the housekeepers were in the informed group, three in which all the housekeepers were in the control group. The hotels in the two groups were similar.

---

[1] All the subjects in the study knew they were in a study and were told that the purpose was "to find ways to improve the health and happiness of women in a hotel workplace" (p. 167).

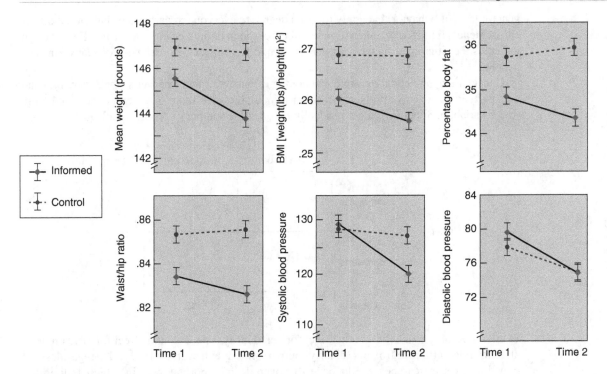

FIGURE 8.8
The health benefits of relabeling work as exercise (from Crum & Langer, 2007).

The final point is an ethical one. After the study was over and it was discovered that the mere relabeling of work as exercise had beneficial health effects for those in the informed group, Crum and Langer (2007) arranged it so all the housekeepers in the control group were given the same information about how their work could be considered healthy exercise.

Factorials with Subject and Manipulated Variables: P × E Designs

Chapter 5 introduced the concept of a subject variable—an existing attribute of an individual such as age, gender, or some personality characteristic. You also learned to be cautious about drawing conclusions when subject variables are involved. Assuming proper control, causal conclusions can be drawn with manipulated independent variables, but with subject variables such conclusions cannot be drawn. P × E designs include both subject and manipulated variables in the same study. Causal conclusions can be drawn if a significant main effect occurs for the manipulated Environment factor, but they cannot be drawn when a main effect occurs for the subject variable or Person factor, and they also cannot be drawn if an interaction occurs. Despite these limitations, designs including both subject and manipulated variables are popular, in part because they combine the two research traditions identified by Woodworth in his famous "Columbia bible" (see the opening paragraphs of Chapter 5). The correlational tradition is associated with the study of individual differences, and the subject variable or *P* factor in the P × E design looks specifically at these differences. A significant main effect for this factor shows two different *types* of individuals perform differently on whatever behavior is being measured as the dependent variable. The experimental tradition, on the other hand, is concerned with identifying general laws of behavior that apply to some degree to everyone, regardless of individual differences. Hence, finding a significant main effect for the manipulated or E factor in a $P \times E$ design indicates the situational factor is powerful enough to influence the behavior of many kinds of persons.

Consider a hypothetical example that compares introverts and extroverts (the P variable) and asks participants to solve problems in either a small, crowded room or a large, uncrowded room (the E variable). Suppose you get results like this (DV = number of problems solved):

		E factor		
		Small room	Large room	**Row means**
	Introverts	18	18	**18**
P factor				
	Extroverts	12	12	**12**
Column means		**15**	**15**	

In this case, there would be a main effect for personality type, no main effect for environment, and no interaction. Introverts clearly outperformed extroverts (18 > 12) regardless of crowding. The researcher would have discovered an important way in which individuals differ, and the differences extend to more than one kind of environment (i.e., both small and large rooms).

A very different conclusion would be drawn from this outcome:

		E factor		
		Small room	Large room	**Row means**
	Introverts	12	18	**15**
P factor				
	Extroverts	12	18	**15**
Column means		**12**	**18**	

This yields a main effect for the environmental factor, no main effect for personality type, and no interaction. Here the environment (room size) produced the powerful effect (18 > 12), and this effect extended beyond a single type of individual; regardless of personality type, introverted or extroverted, performance deteriorated under crowded conditions. Thus, finding a significant main effect for the P factor indicates that powerful personality differences occur, while finding a significant main effect for the E factor shows the power of some environmental influence to go beyond just one type of person. Of course, another result could be two main effects, indicating that each factor is important.

The most interesting outcome of a $P \times E$ design, however, is an interaction. When this occurs, it shows that for one type of individual, changes in the environment have one kind of effect, while for another type of individual, the same environmental changes have a different effect. Staying with the introvert/extrovert example, suppose this happened:

E factor

	Small room	Large room	**Row means**
Introverts	18	12	**15**
Extroverts	12	18	**15**
Column means	**15**	**15**	

P factor

In this case, neither main effect would be significant, but an interaction clearly occurred. One effect happened for introverts, but something different occurred for extroverts. Specifically, introverts performed much better in the small than in the large room, while extroverts did much better in the large room than in the small one.

Factorial designs that include both subject variables and manipulated variables are popular in educational research and in research on the effectiveness of psychotherapy (Smith & Sechrest, 1991). In both areas, the importance of finding significant interactions is indicated by the fact that such designs are sometimes called **ATI designs**, or "Aptitude-Treatment Interaction designs." As you might guess, the "aptitude" refers to the subject (person) variable and the "treatment" refers to the manipulated, environmental variable. An example from psychotherapy research is a study by Abramovitz, Abramovitz, Roback, and Jackson (1974). Their *P* variable was locus of control. Those with an external locus of control generally believe external events exert control over their lives, while individuals with an internal locus believe what happens to them is a consequence of their own decisions and actions. In the study, externals did well in therapy that was more directive in providing guidance for them, but they did poorly in nondirective therapy, which places more responsibility for progress on the client. For internals, the opposite was true: They did better in the nondirective therapy and not too well in directive therapy.

ATIs in educational research usually occur when the aptitude or person factor is a learning style variable and the treatment or environmental factor is some aspect of instruction. For example, Figure 8.9 shows the outcome of educational research reported by Valerie Shute, a leading authority on ATI designs (Shute, 1994). The study compared two educational strategies for teaching basic principles of electricity: rule induction and rule application. Participants were

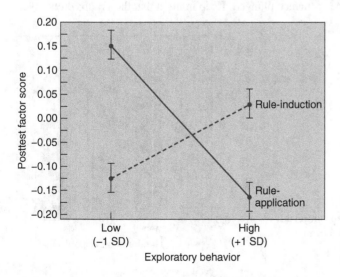

FIGURE 8.9

An ATI interaction between level of exploratory behavior and type of learning environment (from Shute, 1994).

randomly assigned to one strategy or the other. The subject variable was whether learners scored high or low on a measure of "exploratory" behavior. The graph shows those scoring high on exploratory behavior performed better in a rule induction setting, where they were asked to do more work on their own, whereas those scoring low on exploratory behavior performed better in a rule application environment, where the educational procedures were more structured for them.

P × E factorial designs are also popular in research in personality psychology, abnormal psychology, developmental psychology, and any research area interested in gender differences. In personality research, the subject variable or *P* factor will involve comparing personality types; in abnormal psychology, the *P* factor often will be groups of people with different types of mental disorders, and in cross-sectional studies in developmental psychology, the *P* factor will be age. Gender cuts across all of psychology's subdisciplines. The following experiment uses gender as the subject factor and illustrates an unfortunate effect of stereotyping.

Research Example 23—A Factorial Design with a P × E Interaction

Stereotypes are oversimplified and biased beliefs about identifiable groups. They assume that all members of a particular group share particular traits. These traits are usually negative. Stereotypes are dangerous because they result in people being judged with reference to the group they belong to rather than as individuals. The term *stereotype threat* refers to any situation that reminds people of a stereotype. A stereotype that interested Inzlicht and Ben-Zeev (2000) concerns math and the bias that women are not as talented mathematically as men. Their somewhat distressing study shows that stereotypes about women not being suited for math can affect their actual math performance if they are placed in a situation that reminds them of the bias. Experiment 2 of their study was a 2 × 2 P × E factorial. The first factor, the subject variable, was gender; participants were male and female college students at Brown University. The manipulated or environmental factor was the composition of a three-person group given the task of completing a series of math problems. In the "same-sex" condition, all three students taking the test together were either males or females. In the "minority" condition, either women or men were in the minority; that is, the groups included either two men and one woman or two women and one man. The three-person groups had 20 minutes to solve the math problems. They were informed that, after the session was over, their scores would be made public. Figure 8.10 shows the rather startling interaction.

Notice that, for men, performance was unaffected by who was taking the test with them; they did about the same, regardless of whether they took the test with two other men or with two women. It was a different story for women, however. They did quite well when they were in a group of other women (slightly better than the men, in fact), but when they took the test with two other men (the stereotype threat condition), their performance plunged. Keep in mind that the groups didn't even

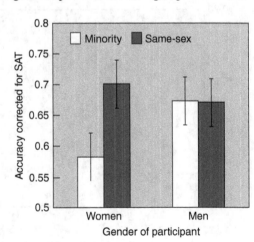

FIGURE 8.10

A P × E interaction: Gender and group composition when solving math problems (adapted from Inzlicht & Ben-Zeev, 2002).

interact; they were just in the same room, taking the test together. Simply being in the room with other men, in the context of a math test, created a perceived stereotype threat and led to a serious drop in performance for women, even women who were highly intelligent (i.e., good enough for admission to a highly selective university). Inzlicht and Ben-Zeev (2000) concluded that the widely held stereotype of men being better at math was evidently sufficient to disrupt the performance of women when they found themselves in the presence of and outnumbered by men. Although they correctly recognized that their study did not directly address the issue of single-sex math classes, Inzlicht and Ben-Zeev argued that "females may in fact benefit from being placed in single-sex math classrooms" (p. 370). On an encouraging note, a more recent study by Johns, Schmader, and Martens (2005) showed that educating women about these stereotype threats, or describing the task as "problem solving" rather than a "math test," substantially reduced the problem.

From the standpoint of the concepts you've been learning about in your methods course, one other point about the Inzlicht and Ben-Zeev (2000) study is worth noting. Remember the concept of *falsification* (Chapters 1, 3, and 5), the process of ruling out alternative hypotheses? The study we just described was actually Experiment 2 of a pair of studies. In Experiment 1, Inzlicht and Ben-Zeev found the drop in women's performance happened when a math test was used, but it did *not* happen with a test of verbal abilities. They contrasted two hypotheses, a "stereotype threat" hypothesis and a "tokenism" hypothesis. The tokenism hypothesis proposes that a person included in a group, but in the minority, perceives herself or himself as a mere token, placed there to give the appearance of inclusiveness. The tokenism hypothesis predicts a decline in female performance *regardless* of the type of test given. Yet the performance decline did not occur with the verbal test, leading Inzlicht and Ben-Zeev to argue that the tokenism hypothesis could be ruled out (falsified), in favor of the alternative, which proposed that performance would decline only in a situation that activated a specific stereotype (i.e., the idea that men and boys are better than women and girls at math).

In this stereotype threat P × E study, the E factor (group composition) was tested as a between-subjects factor. If this factor is tested within-subjects, then a P × E design meets the criterion for a mixed design, and can be called a *mixed P × E factorial*. Such is the case in Research Example 24, which includes a rather unsettling conclusion about older drivers.

Research Example 24—A Mixed P × E Factorial with Two Main Effects

Research on the divided attention that results from cell phone use and driving, done by Strayer and his colleagues (Strayer & Johnston, 2001), was mentioned in Chapter 3 as an example of applied research, on attention. Another study by this research team (Strayer & Drews, 2004) compared young and old drivers, a subject variable, and also included two types of tasks: driving while using a cell phone, and driving without using one. This second factor was tested within-subjects—both young and old drivers completed both types of tasks. Hence, the design is a mixed P × E factorial—mixed because it includes both between- (driver age) and within-subjects (cell phone use) factors, and P × E because it includes both a subject (driver age) variable and a manipulated (cell phone use) variable.

Strayer and Drews (2004) operationally defined their subject variable this way: The 20 younger drivers ranged in age from 18 to 25, while the 20 older drivers were between 65 and 74 years old. All the participants were healthy and had normal vision. In a desire to create a procedure with some degree of *ecological validity*, the researchers used a state-of-the-art driving simulator and a "car-following paradigm" (p. 641), in which drivers followed a pace car while other cars passed them periodically. Subjects had to maintain proper distance from the pace car, which would hit the brakes frequently (32 times in a 10-minute trial). The dependent variables were driving speed, distance from the pace car, and reaction time (hitting the brakes when the pace car did). There were four 10-minute trials, two with subjects simply driving ("single-task") and two with the subjects driving while carrying on a cell phone conversation (hands-free phone) with an experimenter ("dual-task"). The cell phone conversations were on topics known from a pre-testing survey to be of interest to subjects. Because the cell phone factor was a repeated measure, the four trials were counterbalanced "with the constraint that both single- and dual-task conditions were performed in the first half of the experiment and both. . .were performed in the last half of the experiment" (p. 642). You might recognize this as a form of *block randomization* (Chapter 6).

Given the variety of dependent measures, there were several results, but they fell into a general pattern that is best illustrated by the reaction time data. As the factorial matrix here shows, there were main effects for both factors—age and driving condition.

| | Driving condition | | |
	Single-task	Dual-task	Row means
Young drivers	780	912	846
Old drivers	912	1086	999
Column means	846	999	

Note: DV = reaction time in ms

Thus, younger drivers (846 ms, or 0.846 seconds) had quicker reactions overall than older drivers (999 ms), and those driving undistracted in the single-task condition (also 846 ms) were quicker overall than those driving while on the cell phone (also 999 ms). There was no interaction. But a look at the cell means yields another result, one with interesting implications: The reaction time for older drivers in the single-task condition is identical to the reaction time for younger drivers in the dual-task condition (912 ms). Reaction time for the young people who were using a cell phone was the *same* as for the old folks not using the phone (!). The outcome is sobering for older drivers (who still think they have it), while at the same time, perhaps of concern to younger drivers. When this study was discussed in class, one creative 20-year-old student asked, "Does this mean that if I talk on my cell while driving, I'll be just like an old person?"

One final point about P × E designs: The label pays homage to the work of Kurt Lewin (1890–1947), a pioneer in social and child psychology. The central theme guiding Lewin's work was that a full understanding of behavior required studying both the person's individual characteristics and the environment in which the person operated. He expressed this idea in terms of a famous formula, $B = f(P, E)$—Behavior is a joint *function* of the *Person* and the *Environment* (Goodwin, 2012). P × E factorial designs, named for Lewin's formula, are perfectly suited for discovering the kinds of interactive relationships Lewin believed characterized human behavior.[2]

Recruiting Participants for Factorial Designs

It should be evident from the definitions of factorial design types that the number of subjects needed to complete a study could vary considerably. If you need 5 participants to fill one of the cells in the 2 × 2 factorial, for example, the total number of people to be recruited for the study as a whole could be 5, 10 or 20. Figure 8.11 shows you why. In Figure 8.11a, both variables are tested between subjects, and 5 participants are needed per cell, for a total of 20. In Figure 8.11b, both variables are tested within subjects, making the design a repeated-measures factorial. The same 5 individuals will

---

[2] One unfortunate implication of Lewin's choice of the label *P* is that a P × E design implies that only human participants are being used. Yet it is quite common for such a design to be used with animal subjects (a study in which the subject variable is the species of the primates being tested, for instance).

(a) For a 2 × 2 design with 4 different groups and 5 participants per cell—20 subjects needed

S1	S11
S2	S12
S3	S13
S4	S14
S5	S15
S6	S16
S7	S17
S8	S18
S9	S19
S10	S20

(b) For a 2 × 2 repeated-measures design with 5 participants per cell—5 subjects needed

S1	S1
S2	S2
S3	S3
S4	S4
S5	S5
S1	S1
S2	S2
S3	S3
S4	S4
S5	S5

(c) For a 2 × 2 mixed design with 5 participants per cell—10 subjects needed

S1	S1
S2	S2
S3	S3
S4	S4
S5	S5
S6	S6
S7	S7
S8	S8
S9	S9
S10	S10

FIGURE 8.11
Participant requirements in factorial designs.

contribute data to each of the four cells. In a mixed design, Figure 8.11c, one of the variables is tested between subjects and the other is tested within subjects. Thus, 5 participants will participate in two cells and 5 will participate in the other two cells, for a total of 10 participants.[3]

Knowing how many participants to recruit for an experiment leads naturally to the question of how to treat the people who arrive at your experiment. Box 8.2 provides a hands-on, practical guide to being an ethically competent researcher.

BOX 8.2   ETHICS—On Being a Competent and Ethical Researcher

You learned about the APA code of ethics in Chapter 2, and you have encountered Ethics boxes in each chapter since then. Although you should have a pretty good sense of the ethical requirements of a study (consent, confidentiality, debriefing, etc.), you might not be sure how to put this into practice. Hence, this might be a good time to give you a list of practical tips for being an ethically responsible experimenter.

- Get to your session early enough to have all of the materials organized and ready to go when your participants arrive.

- Always treat the people who volunteer for your study with the same courtesy and respect you would hope to receive if the roles were reversed. Greet them when they show up at the lab and thank them for signing up and coming to the session. They might be apprehensive about what will happen to them in a psychology experiment, so your first task is to put them at ease, at the same time maintaining your professional role as the person in charge of the session. Always remember that they are doing you a favor—the reverse is not true. Smile often.

- Start the session with the informed consent form. Don't convey the attitude that this is a time-consuming technicality that must be completed before the important part starts. Instead, make it clear you want your participants to have a good idea of what they are being asked to do. If they don't ask questions while reading the consent form, be sure to ask them if they have any when they finish reading. Make sure there are two copies of the signed consent form, one for them to take and one for your records.

- Prepare a written *protocol* (see Chapter 6) ahead of time. This is a detailed sequence of steps you must complete in order to run the session successfully from start to finish.

It helps ensure each subject has a standardized experience. The protocol might include explicit instructions to be read to the subjects, or it might indicate the point where subjects are given a sheet of paper with written instructions on it.

- Before you test any "real" participants, practice playing the role of experimenter a few times with friends or lab partners. Go through the whole experimental procedure. Think of it as a dress rehearsal and an opportunity to iron out any problems with the procedure.

- Be alert to signs of distress in your subjects during the session. Depending on the constraints of the procedure, this could mean halting the study and discarding their data, but their welfare is more important than your data. Also, you are not a professional counselor; if they seem disturbed by their participation, gently refer them to your course instructor or the school's counseling center.

- Prepare the debriefing carefully. As a student experimenter, you probably won't be running studies involving elaborate deception or producing high levels of stress, but you will be responsible for making this an educational experience for your participants. Hence, you should work hard on a simplified description of what the study hopes to discover, and you should give participants the chance to suggest improvements in the procedure or ideas for the next study. So don't rush the debriefing or give a cursory description that implies you hope they will just leave. And if they seem to want to leave without any debriefing (some will), try not to let them. Debriefing is an important part of your responsibility as a researcher and an educator. (Of course, if they say, "I thought you said we could leave any time," there's not much you can do!)

---

[3] These small sample sizes are used merely to illustrate the subject needs for the types of factorial designs. In actual practice, sample sizes are typically much larger, determined either through a power analysis (Chapter 4) or with reference to standard practice in some research area. In a recent article that made several proposals for avoiding false positives (Type I errors) in research, Simmons, Nelson, and Simonsohn (2011) recommended that studies "collect a minimum of 20 observations per cell or else provide a compelling cost-of-data-collection justification" (p. 1363).

- Before they go, remind participants that the information on the consent form includes names of people to contact about the study if questions occur to them later. Give them a rough idea of when the study will be completed and when they can expect to hear about the overall results (if they indicate they would like to receive this information). To avoid *participant crosstalk* (Chapter 2), ask them not to discuss the experiment with others who might be participants. Participant crosstalk can be a serious problem, especially at small schools (refer to Box 6.3 in Chapter 6, for more on the responsibilities of research subjects). If you are good to your participants throughout the session, however, you increase the chances of their cooperation in this regard. Also, remember from Chapter 2 that if you have special reasons to be concerned about crosstalk (e.g., substantial deception in a study), the ethics code allows you to make the debriefing more cursory, as long as you give them the opportunity to receive complete results once the study is completed.

- As they are leaving, be sure to thank them for their time and effort, and be sure you are smiling as they go out the door. Remember that some of the students you test will be undecided about a major and perhaps thinking about psychology. Their participation in your study could enhance their interest.

Analyzing Data from Factorial Designs

We have already seen that multilevel, single-factor designs using interval or ratio data are analyzed using an analysis of variance (ANOVA) procedure. ANOVAs are also the analysis of choice for factorial designs. When doing a one-way ANOVA, just one F ratio is calculated. Then subsequent testing may be done if the F is significant. For a factorial design, however, more than one F ratio will be calculated. Specifically, there will be an F for each possible main effect and for each possible interaction. For example, in the 2×2 design investigating the effects of imagery training and presentation rate on memory, an F ratio will be calculated to examine the possibility of a main effect for type of training, another for the main effect of presentation rate, and a third for the potential interaction between the two. In an $A \times B \times C$ factorial, *seven F ratios* will be calculated: three for each of the main effects of A, B, and C; three more for the two-way interaction effects of $A \times B$, $B \times C$, and $A \times C$; plus one for the three-way interaction, $A \times B \times C$.

As you recall from Chapter 7, the type of design dictates whether the one-way ANOVA will be an ANOVA for independent groups or a repeated measures ANOVA. In the same way, the design also determines if a factorial ANOVA will be one of these two types, or a third type: A mixed ANOVA is called for when a mixed factorial design is used. Also, as was the case for one-way ANOVAs, subsequent (post hoc) testing may occur with factorial ANOVAs. For example, in a 2×3 ANOVA, a significant main effect for the factor with three levels would trigger a subsequent analysis (e.g., Tukey's HSD) that compared the overall performance of levels 1 and 2, 1 and 3, and 2 and 3. Following a significant interaction, one common procedure is to complete a **simple effects analysis**. This involves comparing each of the levels of one factor with each level of the other factor. A concrete example will make this clear. Refer to the point in the chapter where we introduced interactions by discussing a 2×2 factorial with type of course (lab versus lecture) and type of student (science versus humanities major) as the factors. As you recall, no main effects occurred (row and column means were all 75). A simple effects analysis would make these comparisons:

1. For science majors, compare lab emphasis (mean of 80) with lecture emphasis (70)

2. For humanities majors, compare lab emphasis (70) with lecture emphasis (80)

3. For the lab emphasis, compare science (80) with humanities majors (70)

4. For the lecture emphasis, compare science (70) with humanities majors (80)

For details on how to complete a simple effects analysis, consult any good statistics text (e.g., Witte & Witte, 2010).

For information on how to create and ANOVA source table for a 2 × 2 factorial ANOVA for independent groups, consult the Student Statistics Guide on the Student Companion Site. A good statistics text will explain how to create source tables for other forms of ANOVA. In addition, see the guide to learn how to perform various factorial ANOVAs using SPSS.

SELF TEST

8.3

1. What is the defining feature of a mixed design? In a 3 × 3 mixed design with 20 subjects in the first cell, how many subjects are needed to complete the study?
2. Distinguish a P × E design from an ATI design.
3. If you need a total of 25 participants in a 4 × 4 factorial study and there are 25 participants in one of the cells, what kind of design is this?

Before closing this chapter, here is one final point about factorial designs and the analysis of variance. You've been looking at many factorial matrices in this chapter. They might vaguely remind you of aerial views of farms in Kansas. If so, it's no accident, as you can discover by reading Box 8.3, which tells you a bit about Sir Ronald Fisher, who invented the analysis of variance.

BOX 8.3   ORIGINS—Factorials Down on the Farm

Imagine you're in a small plane flying over Kansas. Looking out the window, you see mile after mile of farms, their fields laid out in blocks. The pattern might remind you of the factorial matrices you've just encountered in this chapter. This is probably a coincidence, but factorial designs and the ANOVA procedures for analyzing them were first developed in the context of agricultural research by Sir Ronald Fisher. The empirical question was, "What are the best possible conditions or combinations of conditions for raising crop X?"

Ronald Aylmer Fisher (1890–1962) was one of Great Britain's best-known statisticians, equal in rank to the great Karl Pearson, who invented the correlation measure we now call Pearson's r (next chapter). Fisher created statistical procedures useful in testing predictions about genetics, but he is perhaps best known among research psychologists for creating the ANOVA, which yielded F ratios that allowed decisions about the null hypothesis in experimental agricultural research. You can easily guess what the F represents.

For about 15 years beginning in 1920, Fisher worked at an experimental agricultural station at Rothamsted, England.

While there, he was involved in research investigating the effects on crop yield of such variables as fertilizer type, rainfall level, planting sequence, and genetic strain of various crops. He published articles with titles like "Studies in Crop Variation: VI. Experiments on the Response of the Potato to Potash and Nitrogen" (Kendall, 1970, p. 447). In the process, he invented ANOVA as a way of analyzing the data. He especially emphasized the importance of using factorial designs, "for with separate [single-factor] experiments we should obtain no light whatever on the possible *interactions* of the different ingredients" (Fisher, 1935/1951, p. 95, italics added). In the real world of agriculture, crop yields resulted from complex combinations of factors, and studying one factor at a time wouldn't allow a thorough evaluation of those interactive effects. As you have seen in this chapter, the interaction is often the most intriguing result in a factorial study.

A simple 2 × 2 design for one of Fisher's experiments, with each block representing how a small square of land was treated, might look like Figure 8.12. As with any factorial, this design allows one to evaluate main effects (of fertilizer and type of wheat in this case), as well as the interaction of the two factors. In the example in Figure 8.12, if we assume the shaded field produces significantly more wheat than the other three (which equal each other), then we would say an interaction clearly occurred: The fertilizer was effective, but for only one specific strain of wheat.

Fisher first published his work on ANOVA in book form in 1925 (a year after Jenkins and Dallenbach published their classic sleep and memory study), as part of a larger text on statistics (Fisher, 1925). His most famous work on ANOVA, which combined a discussion of statistics and research methodology, appeared 10 years later as *The Design of Experiments* (Fisher, 1935/1951). ANOVA techniques and factorial designs were slow to catch on in the United States,

but by the early 1950s, they had become institutionalized as a dominant statistical tool for experimental psychologists (Rucci & Tweney, 1980).

	Experimental fertilizer	No experimental fertilizer
Wheat: genetic strain I	Wheat field A	Wheat field B
Wheat: genetic strain II	Wheat field C	Wheat field D

FIGURE 8.12
An agricultural interaction.

This completes our two-chapter sequence about experimental design. The material (along with Chapters 5 and 6) is sure to require more than one reading and a fair amount of practice with designs before you'll feel confident about your ability to use experimental psychologist language fluently and to create a methodologically sound experiment that is a good test of your hypothesis. Next up is a closer look at a research tradition in which the emphasis is not on examining differences but degrees of association between measured variables.

CHAPTER SUMMARY

Essentials of Factorial Designs

Factorial designs examine the effects of more than one independent variable. Factorial designs are identified with a notation system that identifies the number of independent variables, the number of levels of each independent variable, and the total number of conditions in the study. For example, a 2 × 3 ("2 by 3") factorial design has two independent variables, the first with two levels and the second with three levels, and six different conditions (2 times 3).

Outcomes—Main Effects and Interactions

The overall influence of an independent variable in a factorial study is called a main effect. There are two possible main effects in a 2 × 3 design, one for the factor with two levels and one for the factor with three levels. The main advantage of a factorial design over studies with a single independent variable is that factorials allow the discovery of interactions between the factors. In an interaction, the influence of one independent variable differs for the levels of the other independent variable. The outcomes of factorial studies can include significant main effects, interactions, both, or neither. When a study yields both main effects and interactions, the interactions should be interpreted first; sometimes an interaction is the important result, while the main effects in the study are irrelevant.

Varieties of Factorial Designs

All of the independent variables in a factorial design can be between-subjects factors or all can be within-subjects factors. Completely between-subjects factorial designs can include independent groups, matched groups, or ex post facto designs. Completely within-subjects factorial designs are also called repeated-measures factorial designs. A mixed factorial design includes at least one factor of each type (between and within). Factorial designs with at least one subject variable and at least one manipulated variable allow for the discovery of Person × Environment (P × E) interactions. When these interactions occur, they show how stimulus situations affect one type of person one way and a second type of person another way. A main effect for the *P* factor (i.e., subject variable) indicates important differences between types of individuals that exist in several environments. A main effect for the *E* factor (i.e., manipulated variable) indicates important environmental influences that exist for several types of persons. In educational research and research on the effectiveness of psychotherapy, these interactions between persons and environments are sometimes called Aptitude-Treatment-Interactions (ATIs). In a mixed P × E design, the *E* factor is a within-subjects variable.

CHAPTER REVIEW QUESTIONS

1. For a factorial design, distinguish between "levels" and "conditions."

2. What is meant by a main effect? In terms of the contents of a factorial matrix, how does one go about determining if a main effect has occurred?

3. Use the "closing time" study by Gladue and Delaney (1990) to show that an experiment can result in two important outcomes— two main effects.

4. Use the Grant et al. (1998) experiment (studying in noisy or quiet environments) to show that important results can occur in a study, even if no main effects occur.

5. In a study with both main effects and an interaction, explain why the interaction must be interpreted first and how the statistically significant main effects might have little meaning for the overall outcome of the study. Use the caffeine study to illustrate.

6. Distinguish between a mixed factorial design and a P × E design. How can a design be both a mixed design and a P × E design?

7. Use the introvert/extrovert and room size example to show how P × E designs can discover important ways in which (a) individuals differ, and (b) situations can be more powerful than individual differences.

8. Mixed factorial designs may or may not involve counterbalancing. Explain.

9. Describe the basic research design and the general outcome of Jenkins and Dallenbach's (1924) famous study on sleep and memory. What interaction might have occurred in their study?

10. What is a simple effects analysis and when are these analyses done?

APPLICATIONS EXERCISES

Exercise 8.1.   Identifying Designs

For each of the following descriptions of studies, identify the independent and dependent variables involved, the levels of the independent variable, and the nature of each independent variable (between-subjects or within-subjects; manipulated or subject variables). Also, describe the number of independent variables and levels of each by using the factorial notation system (e.g., 2 × 3), and use Figure 8.6 to identify the design.

1. On the basis of scores on the Jenkins Activity Survey, three groups of subjects are identified: Type A, Type B, and intermediate. An equal number of subjects in each group are given one of two tasks to perform. One of the tasks is to sit quietly in a small room and estimate, in the absence of a clock, when 2 full minutes have elapsed. The second task is to make the same estimate, except that while in the small room, the subject will be playing a hand-held video game.

2. College students in a cognitive mapping study are asked to use a direction finder to point accurately to three unseen locations that vary in distance from the lab. One is a nearby campus location, one is a nearby city, and the third is a distant city. Half of the participants perform the task in a windowless room with a compass indicating the direction of north. The remaining participants perform the task in the same room without a compass.

3. In a study of touch sensitivity, two-point thresholds are measured on 10 skin locations for an equal number of blind and sighted adults. Half of the participants perform the task in the morning and half in the evening.

4. Three groups of preschoolers are put into a study of delay of gratification in which the length of the delay is varied. Children in all three groups complete a puzzle task. One group is told that as payment they can have $1 now or $3 tomorrow. The second group chooses between $1 now and $3 two days from now, and the third group chooses between $1 now and $3 three days from now. For each of the three groups, half of the children solve an easy puzzle and half solve a difficult puzzle. The groups are formed in such a way that the average parents' income is the same for children in each group.

5. In a study of visual illusions and size perception, participants adjust a dial that alters one of two stimuli. The goal is to make the two stimuli appear equal in size, and the size of the error in this judgment is measured on each trial. Each participant completes 40 trials. On half of the trials, the pairs of stimuli are in color; on the other half, they are in black and white. For both the colored and the black-and-white stimuli, half are presented at a distance of 10 feet from the participant and half are presented at 20 feet.

6. In a study of reading comprehension, sixth-grade students read a short story about baseball. The students are divided into two groups based on their knowledge of baseball. Within each group, half of the students are high scorers on a test of verbal IQ, while the remaining students are low scorers.

7. In a study on stereotyping, students are asked to read an essay said to be written by either a psychiatric patient or a mental health professional. Half of the subjects given each essay are told the writer is a male and half are told the writer is a female. Subjects are randomly assigned to the four groups and asked to judge the quality of the essay.

8. In a maze learning study, the performance (number of trials to learn the maze) of wild and lab-reared albino rats is compared. Half of each group of rats is randomly assigned to an alley maze; others learn an elevated maze.

Exercise 8.2.   Main Effects and Interactions

For each of the following studies:

a. Identify the independent variables, the levels of each, and the dependent variable.

b. Place the data into the correct cells of a factorial matrix and draw a graph of the results.

c. Determine if main effects and/or interactions exist and give a verbal description of the study's outcome.

For the purposes of the exercise, assume that a difference of *more than 2* between any of the row, column, or cell means is a statistically significant difference.

1. A researcher is interested in the effects of ambiguity and number of bystanders on helping behavior. Participants complete a questionnaire in a room with zero or two other people (i.e., bystanders) who appear to be other subjects but are actors in the study. The experimenter distributes the questionnaire and then goes into the room next door. After 5 minutes, there is a loud crash, possibly caused by the experimenter falling. For half of the participants, the experimenter unambiguously calls out that he has fallen, is hurt, and needs help. For the remaining participants, the situation is more ambiguous; the experimenter says nothing after the apparent fall. In all cases, the actors (bystanders) do not get up to help. The experimenter records how long it takes (in seconds) before a participant offers help. Here are the four conditions and the data:

0 bystanders, ambiguous	24 sec
2 bystanders, ambiguous	38 sec
0 bystanders, unambiguous	14 sec
2 bystanders, unambiguous	14 sec

2. In a maze learning study, a researcher is interested in the effects of reinforcement size and reinforcement delay. Half of the rats in the study are given a 1 cm square block of cheese upon completing the maze; the other half gets a 2 cm square block. Within each reinforcement size group, half of the rats are given the cheese on arrival at the goal box and half waits for the cheese for 15 seconds after their arrival.

Hence, there are four groups and the data (dependent variable is number of errors during 10 trials):

small reward, 0 sec delay	17 errors
large reward, 0 sec delay	15 errors
small reward, 15 sec delay	25 errors
large reward, 15 sec delay	23 errors

3. A cognitive psychologist interested in gender and spatial ability decides to examine whether gender differences in a mental rotation task (see Chapter 4 for a reminder of this task) can be influenced by instructions. One set of instructions emphasizes the spatial nature of the task and relates it to working as a carpenter (male-oriented instructions); a second set of instructions emphasizes the problem-solving nature of the task and relates it to working as an interior decorator (female-oriented instructions); the third set of instructions is neutral. An equal number of men and women participate in each instructional condition. Here are the six conditions and the data:

men with male-oriented instructions	26 problems correct
men with female-oriented instructions	23 problems correct
men with normal instructions	26 problems correct
women with male-oriented instructions	18 problems correct
women with female-oriented instructions	24 problems correct
women with normal instructions	18 problems correct

4. A forensic psychologist wishes to determine if prison sentence length can be affected by defendant attractiveness and facial expression. Subjects read a detailed crime description (a felony breaking and entering) and are asked to recommend a sentence for the criminal, who has been arrested and found guilty. A photo of the defendant accompanies the description. Half the time the photo is of a woman made up to look attractive, and half the time the woman is made up to look unattractive. For each type of photo, the woman is smiling, scowling, or showing a neutral expression. Here are the conditions and the data:

attractive, smiling	8 years
attractive, scowling	14 years
attractive, neutral	9 years
unattractive, smiling	12 years
unattractive, scowling	18 years
unattractive, neutral	13 years

Exercise 8.3.   Estimating Participant Needs

For each of the following, use the available information to determine how many research subjects are needed to complete the study (*Hint*: One of these is unanswerable without more information):

1. a 3 × 3 mixed factorial; each cell needs 10 participants

2. a 2 × 3 repeated-measures factorial; each cell needs 20 participants

3. a 2 × 4 mixed factorial; each cell needs 8 participants

4. a 2 × 2 × 2 independent groups factorial; each cell needs 5 participants

5. a 2 × 2 matched groups factorial; each cell needs 8 participants

6. a 4 × 4 ex post facto factorial; each cell needs 8 participants

---

ANSWERS TO SELF TESTS

✓ 8.1

1. (a) 3; (b) 2, 3, and 4; (c) 24
2. A main effect concerns whether a significant difference exists among the levels of an independent variable.
3. A main effect for the type of instruction factor (row means of 20 for imagery and 12 for rote), but no main effect for presentation rate (both column means are 16).

✓ 8.2

1. There are no main effects (row and column means all equal 16), but there is an interaction. Wild rats performed better (fewer trials to learn) in the alley maze, while tame rats performed better in the elevated maze.
2. No overall main effect for whether studying took place in a noisy or a quiet environment; also, no overall main effect for whether recall took place in noisy or quiet environment; there was an interaction—recall was good when study and test conditions matched, and poor when study and test conditions did not match.

✓ 8.3

1. There is at least one between-subjects factor and at least one within-subjects factor; 60.
2. A P × E design has at least one subject factor (P) and one manipulated (E) factor; an ATI design is a type of P × E design in which the "P" factor refers to some kind of ability or aptitude; these ATI designs are frequently seen in educational research.
3. It must be a repeated-measure factorial design.

Non-Experimental Design I: Survey Methods

9

PREVIEW & CHAPTER OBJECTIVES

You have just finished a four-chapter sequence that concentrated on the experimental method in psychology. Four chapters remain, each dealing with a slightly different research tradition. In this chapter, we will examine survey methods for doing research in psychology that are primarily descriptive in nature. The major purpose of interview and survey research is to provide accurate descriptions of behavior and mental processes and of the interrelationships among individuals and their environments. We will also describe how different statistical techniques, including correlation and regression, examine relationships among variables, and can be used with survey and interview methods. You will see that caution is needed to interpret the results of correlational analyses and that regression techniques can be useful when psychologists try to make predictions about behavior. Interview and survey methods can be a rich source of ideas for further research using other methods, including experimental methods. When you finish this chapter, you should be able to:

- Explain why sampling issues are more relevant for interview and survey methods than for most other research methods in psychology.

- Articulate the principles of good survey construction.

- Explain the problems (e.g., social desirability bias, item wording) that can make it difficult to interpret survey data.

- Describe four ways to collect survey data and list the advantages and disadvantages of each.

- Distinguish between positive and negative bivariate correlations and create scatterplots to illustrate them.

- Calculate a coefficient of determination (r^2), and interpret its meaning.

- Understand how a regression analysis accomplishes the goal of prediction, and distinguish between simple linear regression and multiple regression techniques.

- Understand how directionality can make it difficult to interpret correlations and how a cross-lagged panel design can help with the directionality problem.

- Understand the third variable problem and how such variables can be evaluated and controlled through a partial correlation procedure.

- Distinguish between mediators and moderators within the context of understanding third variables in a correlation.

Remember Robert Woodworth and the "Columbia bible," his precedent-setting text in experimental psychology (Chapter 5's opening paragraphs)? The book institutionalized the distinction we routinely make today between independent and dependent variables in experimental research. The second distinction made by Woodworth, between experimental and correlational methods, likewise has had a profound effect on research in psychology. The experimental method manipulates independent variables, according to Woodworth, while the correlational method "[m]easur[es] two or more characteristics of the same individual [and] computes the correlation of these characteristics" (Woodworth, 1938, p. 3). Woodworth took pains to assure the reader that these two research strategies were of equal value. The correlational method was "[t]o be distinguished from the experimental method, [but] standing on a par with it in value, rather than above or below" (Woodworth, 1938, p. 3). After making this assertion, however, Woodworth referred the reader elsewhere for information about correlational research and devoted the remaining 820 pages of his text to research illustrating the experimental method. The reader could be excused for thinking that correlational research was not quite as important as experimental research. However, correlational research has much value in psychological science. The types of designs described in this and subsequent chapters can be referred to as non-experimental, correlational, or descriptive research designs. We will explore the nuts and bolts of correlation and regression later in this chapter. First, let's examine survey and interview methods in some detail.

Survey Research

Survey research is based on the simple idea that if you want to find out what people think about some topic, you just ask them. A **survey** is a structured set of questions or statements given to a group of people to measure their attitudes, beliefs, values, or tendencies to act. Over the years, people have responded to surveys assessing everything from their political preferences to their favorite leisure activities. The method has been around for some time, as you can tell from Box 9.1.

BOX 9.1 ORIGINS—Creating the "Questionary"

In one of psychology's most famous books *Principles of Psychology*, William James (1890/1950) included a chapter on methodology, in which his comments on survey research were less than complimentary:

> Messrs. Darwin and Galton have set the example of circulars of questions sent out by the hundreds to those supposed able to reply. The custom has spread, and it will be well for us in the next generation if such circulars be not ranked among the common pests of life. (p. 194)

Sir Francis Galton (1822–1911) is normally credited with originating the survey method, although a case can be made that his cousin, Charles Darwin (1809-1882), preceded him. Darwin developed a series of questions on emotional expressions that he distributed to colleagues in several

countries (he met many of them during his around-the-world voyage in the 1830s). In what might be the first cross-cultural study, he attempted to determine if facial expressions of emotion were universal, an outcome that would strengthen his belief in the power of evolution. Here are two of the questions he included:

> Is astonishment expressed by the eyes and mouth being opened wide, and by the eyebrows being raised?
> Is contempt expressed by a slight protrusion of the lips and by turning up the nose, and with a slight expiration? (Darwin, 1872, pp. 15–16)

Darwin's correspondents answered "yes" to these and other questions, perhaps not surprising in light of the way they were worded. (You'll soon be reading about "leading" questions—these are good examples.) On the basis of this and other research, Darwin developed an evolutionary theory of facial expressions of emotion. The emotional expression when we feel contempt, for instance, was said to have evolved from the fundamental reaction to bad smells (e.g., turning up the nose).

Galton used the same question-asking strategy, and he employed it more often than his cousin. Through survey data, for example, he accumulated information from scientists about the origins of their interests in science, asking them, for instance, "How far do your scientific tastes appear innate?" (quoted from Forrest, 1974, p. 126). Their answers were generally "quite far"—they reported being interested in science for as long as they could recall. Ignoring the possibility that environmental influences (e.g., parental encouragement) could have contributed to their love of science, Galton used the replies to support his strong belief that intellectual ability was primarily innate. He summarized his work in *English Men of Science: Their Nature and Nurture* (Galton, 1874), notable for giving a label (nature-nurture) to an issue that continues to be debated today.

In the United States, the undisputed champion of the survey, which he called the "Questionary," was G. Stanley Hall, known in psychology's history as Mr. First (e.g., created the first true experimental lab in America at Johns Hopkins in 1883, began the first psychology journal in the United States in 1887, the *American Journal of Psychology*, founded the American Psychological Association in 1892, and claimed to have earned the first Ph.D. in psychology in the United States). Hall developed what was called the "child study movement" in the 1880s, an educational effort to study children systematically and find the best ways to educate them. Part of his effort was to develop "questionaries" designed to uncover as much as possible about children. These were distributed to teachers, who, in turn, administered them to children.

Hall's first study, completed in the early 1880s, was designed to explore "The Contents of Children's Minds" (Hall, 1883). Data were collected from 200 urban (Boston) children just beginning school, and the result was that the children didn't seem to know very much. For instance, 75.5% could not identify what season of the year it was, 87.5% didn't know what an island was, and 90.5% couldn't locate their ribs. Hall also found that children who had been reared in the country and then moved to Boston knew more than those reared in the city. This did not surprise Hall, a farm boy himself. Although today we might think that an urban environment would provide a richer variety of experiences and therefore an enhanced knowledge base, few people believed that in the 1880s and Hall was not alone in thinking urban life stunted intellectual development. With his penchant for overstatement, Hall commented that a "few days in the country at this age has raised the level of many a city child's intelligence more than a term or two of school training could do without it" (pp. 261–262).

Survey methodology did not immediately gain respect in psychology. The attitude of William James is pretty clear from this box's opening quote, and his opinion was shared by others. E. B. Titchener, for example, a leading experimental psychologist, said this about Hall and his methods, in a letter to a colleague of Hall's:

> [Y]ou probably have no idea of the sort of contempt in which Hall's methods and the men trained solely by him are in general held in psychology. . . . Whenever his questionary papers get reviewed, they get slightingly reviewed. (Titchener, 1906)

Now Titchener tended to be critical of just about everyone, but his attitude, like James's, illustrates why survey research was slow to be accepted as a legitimate methodological tool.

Sampling Issues in Survey Research

Unlike most of the methods described in this text, surveying usually requires careful attention to sampling procedures. This point requires elaboration. For most of the research methods you've read about, the emphasis has been on establishing relationships between and among variables. From some of the research you have read about in this text, for instance, you know researchers have been interested in such topics as the effects of (a) infants' understanding of gravity, (b) closing time on perceived attractiveness, (c) laptop note-taking on exam performance, and (d) cell phone use while driving. For studies such as these, researchers naturally hope the results will generalize beyond the people participating in them, but they assume that if the relationship studied is powerful, it will occur for most individuals, regardless of how they are chosen to participate in the study.

Of course, whether this assumption turns out to be true depends on the normal processes of replication and extension. Recall from Chapter 5 that *external validity* is established only after many studies have been done on different populations, in different environments, and replicated during different time periods. So, in a study on the capacity limits of short-term memory in adults, it is not necessary to select a random sample; virtually any group of reasonably fluent adults will do. Because samples in many studies are not chosen using a random procedure, the selection procedure is referred to as *nonprobability sampling*. However, *probability sampling* is most likely to be used in survey research. As you recall from Chapter 4, although an entire population is seldom tested in a study, the researcher hopes to draw conclusions about the population based on the sample. Thus, in survey research, it is important for the sample to reflect the attributes of the target population as a whole. If the sample is not *representative* of the population, then the sample is potentially *biased*.

Perhaps the most famous historical example of biased sampling occurred during political polling in the presidential election of 1936. As it had been doing with reasonable success for several previous elections, the magazine *Literary Digest* tried to predict the election outcome by sending out about 10 million simulated ballots to subscribers, to others selected from a sample of phone books from around the country, and to others from motor vehicle registration information (Sprinthall, 2000). Close to 25% (almost 2.5 million) of the ballots were returned to the magazine; of these respondents, 57% preferred the Republican candidate, Alf Landon, and 40% chose the incumbent president, Franklin Roosevelt. In the actual election, Roosevelt won in a landslide with more than 60% of the vote. Can you guess why the sample was biased?

Although the editors of *Literary Digest* were aware that their own subscribers tended to be upper middle class and Republican, they thought they were broadening the sample and making it more representative by adding people chosen from phone books and car registration data. In fact, they were selecting more Republicans. In the midst of the Great Depression, practically the only people who could afford phones and cars were members of the upper-middle and upper classes, and these were more likely to be Republicans than Democrats. So, in the survey the magazine actually was asking Republicans how they were going to cast their votes.

You might have noticed another flaw in the *Literary Digest* survey. A large number of ballots was returned, and the magazine was quite confident in its prediction of a Landon victory because the data reflected the views of a substantial number of people—about 2.5 million. Note, however, that not only does the total represent only one-fourth of the ballots originally sent out but also the returns were from those who *chose* to send them back. So, those responding to the survey tended to be not just Republicans, but Republicans who wished to make their views known (in light of which, the 57% preferring Landon actually looks rather small, don't you think?).

This **self-selection** bias is typical in surveys that appear in popular magazines and newspapers. A survey will appear, along with an appeal to readers to reply (usually online). Then the results of those who reply are reported, usually implying that the results are valid. The person reporting the survey will try to impress you with the total number of returns rather than the representativeness of the sample. An example of this ploy is a well-known report on female sexuality (Hite, 1987). It claimed, among other things, that more than 90% of married women felt emotionally abused in their relationships, and a substantial majority reported dissatisfaction in marriage. When criticized because the survey was sent only to a select group of women's organizations and only 4.5% of 100,000 people returned the survey, the author simply pointed out that 4,500 people were enough for her (just as 2.5 million people were enough for *Literary Digest*). But research that uses appropriate probability sampling techniques generally shows that satisfaction/happiness in marriage is actually quite high. The Hite data were misleading, to say the least.

As a critical thinker, you should be skeptical about results from surveys based on biased samples. In order to obtain a representative sample of the population, scientists use various probability sampling procedures. You should review Chapter 4 about these procedures, which include random sampling, stratified sampling, and cluster sampling.

Surveys versus Psychological Assessment

Most surveys include various questions (in the form of a questionnaire) that are delivered online, through the mail, or administered in some more direct fashion (e.g., to a class of students). It is important to note that surveys tend to assess attitudes, beliefs, opinions, and projected behaviors. In contrast, *psychological tests* can include questionnaires, but such tests are used in more formal assessments of psychological functioning, usually in a clinical setting. Psychological tests usually have undergone rigorous tests of *reliability* and *validity* in order to establish a measure that accurately reflects some psychological construct, such as personality, depression, or self-esteem. For example, a questionnaire such as the Beck Depression Inventory-II (Beck, Steer, & Brown, 1996) is a psychological test that may be used as a tool by clinical researchers to study and/or to help diagnose depression. Our focus in this chapter is not on the development of psychological measures to assess broader psychological constructs like personality or depression, but on the development of survey items that assess individuals' attitudes, beliefs, and opinions at a given moments in time. There are various ways to collect survey data, and each method has its strengths and weaknesses.

Creating an Effective Survey

What constitutes a good survey can differ slightly depending on the format (interview, written, etc.). This section addresses the construction of written questionnaire surveys, which can be delivered in-person in an interview, mailed to potential survey-takers, conducted over the telephone, or done online – but more on administering surveys later. When designing a survey, the researcher must create items that effectively answer the empirical question(s) at hand and must be very careful with the structure and the wording of items.

As with any research in psychology, survey research begins with empirical questions that develop into hypotheses to be tested by collecting data. For example, in a college or university environment, such questions might include focused, single-issue ones:

- Do students feel safe when crossing the campus at night?

- Do students eat balanced, nutritious meals?

- Are faculty more politically liberal than students?

Or they might be more broad-based:

- Are students satisfied with their education at the university?

- Considering college student behavior as a whole, can it be characterized as health-enhancing or health-inhibiting?

Types of Survey Questions or Statements

Once an empirical question is framed and its terms operationally defined, the researcher decides on the type of items to use and the wording of those items. Survey items can take a variety of forms. Survey items can be phrased as a question or as a statement. When questions are asked, they can be either open-ended or closed. An **open-ended question** requires a response beyond a yes or no; participants must provide narrative information. A **closed question** can be answered with a yes or a no or by choosing a single response from among several alternatives. To illustrate the difference, consider these two ways of asking about school financing:

Open: How do you think we should finance public education?
Closed: Do you think state lottery money should be used to finance public education?

Open-ended questions can be useful for eliciting a wide range of responses, including some not even conceived of by the researchers. They can also increase the respondent's sense of control while completing the survey. Because they can produce such a wide range of responses, however, open-ended questions are difficult to score and can add considerably to the time required to complete the survey. Hence, they should be used sparingly (most phone interviews, which must be completed quickly, use closed questions). One good method is to give respondents an opportunity to elaborate on their responses to closed questions. For example, at the end of a set of closed questions, the survey might provide space for the respondents to comment on their answers to any of the items, especially those for which they gave extreme ratings. Another good use of open-ended questions is in a pilot study as a way of identifying alternatives for a subsequent questionnaire to be composed of closed items. For example, a common open-ended question is sometimes referred to as the "most important problem" item (Schuman & Presser, 1996). An example might be:

In your judgment, what are the most important problems facing this university today?

This question is likely to elicit a variety of responses in a pilot test, and these responses could become the alternatives in a final item that could ask:

Which of the following is the most important problem facing this university today?

____ overall quality of teaching

____ inadequate computer facilities

____ lack of diversity in the student body

____ poor quality of dormitory rooms

____ inadequate career advising

Finally, some survey items can be "partially" open by including a specific checklist, ending it with an "Other" category and allowing respondents to write in their responses. Using the example above, a partially open item could be:

Which of the following is an important problem facing this university today? Check all that apply.

____ overall quality of teaching

____ inadequate computer facilities

____ lack of diversity in the student body

____ poor quality of dormitory rooms

____ inadequate career advising

____ other (please state):

Surveys with closed questions require a specific response, such as a Yes-No response. For example, on a survey of attitudes about televised coverage of news, a sample item might look like this:

Should a person anchoring a news show have at least 5 years of experience as a professional journalist?

Yes   No

Here, the respondent merely needs to select a Yes or No as their answer. Often, survey items are phrased in terms of statements, and respondents are asked to indicate their level of agreement with the statement. Surveys with closed questions often use an interval scale for measuring the responses. As you recall from Chapter 4, with an interval scale, there is no true zero point, but the intervals between points on the scale are assumed to be equal. Rather than simply asking a question that requires a Yes or No response (and therefore a nominal scale of measurement), using an interval scale can help the researcher better ascertain the intensity of one's attitude or opinion about a particular item. The most common type of interval scale used in surveys is the Likert scale (after the person who invented it, Rensis Likert). A typical Likert scale has from five to nine distinct points on it (always an odd number—there must be a midpoint that is a "neutral" choice in order for it to be a Likert scale), with each point reflecting a score on the continuum. For example, in a similar survey item about televised new coverage, participants might be asked to indicate how much they agree with a series of statements according to a 5-point scale. A sample item might look like this:

The person anchoring a news show should have at least 5 years of experience as a professional journalist.

1	2	3	4	5
strongly disagree	somewhat disagree	neutral	somewhat agree	strongly agree

Respondents circle or state the number or label on the scale that indicates what they believe. Because numbers correspond to particular response options, responses from all of the participants can be summarized with means and standard deviations. For instance, if the mean score on the news anchor question was 4.5, the researcher would conclude that respondents are midway between "agree" and "strongly agree" on the item. Also, scores from several items designed to measure the same issue could be combined into a single mean score.

The above Likert item could be made into a 7-point scale by adding "very strongly agree" and "very strongly disagree." There is no clear advantage to either a 5- or a 7- (or more) point scale. A 5-point scale normally provides sufficient discrimination among levels of agreement but might become a de facto 3-point scale in practice, given the tendency for some people to avoid the ends of the scale. On the other hand, a 7-point scale yields 5 points even if people avoid the extremes, but adding the extra level of discrimination can increase the time it takes to complete the survey. One general rule is to avoid mixing formats. If you decide to use a 5-point Likert scale, use it throughout; don't mix 5- and 7-point scales in the same survey.

One other point about a Likert scale is that when using one, it is normally a good idea to word some of the statements favorably and others unfavorably. In a survey that evaluates teaching, for example, consecutive statements might be phrased like this:

The instructor held my attention during class lectures.

The instructor wrote exams that fairly tested the material covered.

The instructor seemed to be well prepared for class.

The instructor was available for extra help outside of class.

These items are all worded *favorably*, so if a student liked the instructor, that student might race through the survey without reading the items carefully and simply agree with everything. Also, some students might have a response bias called **response acquiescence**—a tendency to agree with statements. To avoid these problems, surveys with Likert scales typically balance favorable and unfavorable statements. This forces respondents to read each item carefully and make item-by-item decisions (Patten, 1998). For example, the above statements could be presented like this, with two items worded favorably and two unfavorably:

> The instructor was seldom able to hold my attention during class lectures.
>
> The instructor wrote exams that fairly tested the material covered.
>
> The instructor often appeared unprepared for class.
>
> The instructor was available for extra help outside of class.

When items are balanced like this, it is a good idea to emphasize this fact in the instructions.

It is also important to be concerned about the sequencing of the items on your survey. For example, if your research requires that you include questions some respondents might find sensitive (e.g., frequency of alcohol or drug use, sexual activities), put them near the end of the survey. If you start with them, respondents might stop right away; if they are at the end, respondents have already invested some time and may be more willing to finish the survey. Start the survey with questions that are not especially personal and are both easy to answer and interesting. Also, cluster items on the same general topic in the same place on the survey. For example, if your survey is about satisfaction with college, group the items about courses together, and separate them from items about student activities.

Assessing Memory and Knowledge

In addition to asking about attitudes and opinions, surveys sometimes attempt to assess the respondent's memory or what they know. In this case, there are two important guidelines: Don't overburden memory, and use DK ("don't know") alternatives sparingly.

When asking how often respondents have done certain things in the past requires one to remember past events, and making the interval too long increases the chances of memory errors. For example, on a survey about drinking behavior (assume the definition of a "drink" has been made clear to the respondent), it is better to ask participants to specify exactly what they have had to drink in the past week than in the past month. Of course, the proper interval will depend on the question being asked. If the activity is a relatively infrequent one (e.g., visiting zoos), a short interval will yield too many scores of zero. One way to aid memory is to provide lists. In a survey about leisure-time activities, for instance, respondents might be asked to examine the past month and indicate how frequently they have rented a movie, gone on a hike, attended the symphony, and so on.

When inquiring about what a person knows, there is always the chance the honest answer will be "I don't know." Hence, survey items that deal with knowledge often include what is called a **DK alternative** ("don't know"). Some experts discourage the use of DK alternatives because respondents might overuse them, conservatively choosing DK even if they have some knowledge of the issue. Survey results with a lot of DK answers are not useful. On the other hand, omitting DK as a choice might force respondents to mentally flip a coin on items about which they are truly ignorant (Schuman & Presser, 1996). One way to include DK choices, while encouraging respondents to avoid overusing them, is to disguise knowledge questions by prefacing them with such statements as "Using your best guess . . ." or "Have you heard or have you read that . . ." (examples from Fink, 1995, p. 76). Also, DK alternatives should be used only when it is reasonable to expect that some respondents will have no idea what the answer might be (Patten, 1998).

Adding Demographic Information

Demographic information is the basic data that identifies the characteristics of survey respondent. These data can include age, gender, socioeconomic status, marital status, and so on. Sometimes, the empirical question at hand will determine the type of demographic information needed. In a survey about attitudes toward animal experimentation, for example, it might be useful for the researcher to know whether or not the respondent is a pet owner. Including this demographic information enables the survey researcher to group the results by demographic categories, in this case comparing pet owners and non-owners on attitudes toward animal research.

In general, it is a good idea to put questions about demographic information at the end of a survey. If you start the survey with them, participants might become bored and not attend to the key items as well as you would like. Also, you should include only demographic categories that are important for the empirical questions that interest you. The more demographic information you include, the longer the survey and the greater the risk that respondents will tune out. And respondents might become irritated; some requests for demographic information (e.g., income) can be perceived as invasions of privacy, even when respondents are assured about confidentiality (Patten, 1998). Here are guidelines for requesting demographic information:

- When asking about age, ask for date of birth.

- When asking for annual income, provide ranges to reduce privacy concerns (e.g., $50,000 or less; $50,001–$100,000).

- Don't let the alternatives overlap (e.g., as in the income ranges above).

- If making comparisons to other surveys, ask for identical demographic information.

- Let the pros do the work: Borrow items from the U.S. Census Bureau (www.census.gov). For example, whereas a novice might include "married, single, divorced, and widowed" under marital status, a pro would recognize the ambiguity in "single" and use the census categories "married, separated, widowed, divorced, never married" (Patten, 1998, p. 27).

A Key Problem: Survey Wording

A major problem in survey construction concerns the wording of the items. Although it is impossible for the survey writer to ensure that all respondents interpret each question or statement the same way, some guidelines can help in the construction of a good survey. The most important one is to conduct a *pilot study* (Chapter 3) to test the instrument on several groups of friends, colleagues, and even people you don't like. You will be surprised at how often you think you have a perfect item and then three friends interpret it three different ways. One tip is to define any terms you think could be interpreted in more than one way.

Avoid these three specific problems: linguistic ambiguity, asking two questions in one item, and asking leading questions. First, questions can be ambiguous, as when people are asked whether they agree with statements like this:

Visiting relatives can be fun.

What's fun? The relatives who are visiting or the act of visiting the relatives?

Second, survey writers sometimes include too much in an item, resulting in one that actually asks for two responses at once. This is sometimes referred to as a **double-barreled question**. Here's an example:

It is wrong for women in bars to curse and to buy drinks for men who are unknown to them.

The responder who agrees with the cursing part but disagrees with the drink-buying part would not know how to answer this question.

Third, what lawyers call a **leading question** is one that is structured so that it is likely to produce an answer desired by the asker. Here are two ways of asking about the Clean Air Act that would almost certainly yield different responses:

> Given the importance to future generations of preserving the environment, do you believe the Clean Air Act should be strengthened, weakened, or left alone?
>
> Given the fact that installing scrubbers at utility plants could increase electricity bills by 25%, do you believe the Clean Air Act should be strengthened, weakened, or left alone?

This type of survey bias, the leading question, occurs frequently in the worlds of business or politics, where the intent is to sell a product or candidate, or to promote an opinion. In politics, for example, it is common for both Republican and Democratic National Committees (RNC and DNC) to send out surveys that always include leading questions. For instance, in the 2008 Presidential campaign, Republican candidate John McCain, while trying to make the point that getting out of Iraq would not be easy and the U.S. might always have some military presence there, made the mistake of mentioning (not "pledging") "100 years" in one of his speeches. In a subsequent survey sent to Democrats by the DNC, this item appeared:

> Do you believe that John McCain's pledge to keep troops in Iraq for another 100 years will be a liability in the General Election?

We never saw the results of this survey, but the outcome for this item would not be hard to guess. Surveys sent to Republicans by the RNC are just as biased.

Consider this example from the world of business. In an attempt to outsell McDonald's, Burger King once reported a survey claiming about 75% of people surveyed preferred their Whoppers to Big Macs. The key question was phrased this way (Kimmel, 2007, p. 208):

> Do you prefer your hamburgers flame-broiled or fried?

Do you see the problem? Burger King's "flame-broiled" method sounds more natural and appetizing than McDonald's "fried" method, so perhaps the outcome was not a surprise. However, another surveyor asked the same question a different way (Kimmel, 2007, p. 208):

> Do you prefer a hamburger that is grilled on a hot stainless steel grill or cooked by passing the raw meat through an open gas flame?

In this case, McDonald's method (the steel grill) was preferred by more than half of the respondents, a figure that rose to 85% when the researcher indicated that after encountering the gas flame, the Burger King burgers were reheated in a microwave oven before being served. The moral of the story: It is probably fair to say that skepticism is the best response when businesses report survey results in their advertising. Unfortunately, this situation lends credence to the widely held belief that surveys can be created and manipulated to produce virtually any outcome.

Here are more tips about wording (most examples from Fink, 1995):

- Always opt for simplicity over complexity.
    - *Poor:* Doctors should be intelligible when explaining a diagnosis to a patient.
    - *Better:* Doctors should use simple and clear language when explaining a diagnosis to a patient.

- Use complete sentences.

  Poor: Place of residence?

  Better: What is the name of the city where you currently live?

- Avoid negatively phrased questions; negative statements are more difficult to process than positive ones.

  Poor: Do you believe the university should not have the right to search your dorm room?

  Better: Should the university have the right to search your dorm room?

- Use balanced items, not those favoring one position or another.

  Poor: Do you support the use of animals in undergraduate laboratory courses?

  Better: Do you support or oppose the use of animals in undergraduate laboratory courses?

- Avoid most abbreviations.

  USC could be University of Southern California, but it could also be the University of South Carolina.

- Avoid slang and colloquial expressions.

  They go out of fashion; "information superhighway," for example, is an outdated expression.

- Avoid jargon.

  As a program evaluator, you might know the difference between "formative" and "summative" evaluations, but most survey respondents won't.

Another important consideration in creating a survey is to avoid creating any *carry-over effects* (see Chapter 6) across items on a survey that may bias survey responses. Carry-over effects within surveys occur when earlier items may influence responses on later items. For example, compared to prior CNN/ORC polls, a December 2015 CNN/ORC poll of registered Republican voters in the U.S., revealed that real estate mogul and reality TV star Donald Trump received one of his highest poll numbers in support of the Republican nominee for president among other Republican contenders.[1] The poll, however, was inherently biased, according to a December 4 report by *U.S. News & World Report.* Just before the survey asked choices for Republican nominees, it asked several questions about illegal immigration about which Trump had been most vocal since his entry into the Presidential race. Because respondents may have been thinking about illegal immigration, they may have also been thinking about Trump prior to the questions about selecting a nominee, potentially biasing their response selections in favor of Trump.

SELF TEST

9.1

1. What is the term used to describe a poorly constructed survey item that asks for two or more responses from one question or statement?
2. On a written survey, what is demographic information and where should it be placed in the survey?
3. Describe an advantage and a disadvantage of including DK alternatives.

---

[1] The CNN/ORC poll was reported on December 4, 2015. It should be noted that the poll itself was conducted on November 27 through December 1, which may also be problematic in terms of representativeness of historical time—it was Thanksgiving weekend in the United States. http://i2.cdn.turner.com/cnn/2015/images/12/04/cnnorc12042015gopprimarypoll.pdf

These are just some examples of the issues involved when creating survey items. For more detailed guidance on the construction of reliable and valid survey items, several excellent guides exist (e.g., Converse & Presser, 1986; Fink, 1995; Fowler, 1998; Patten, 1998; Dillman, Smyth, & Christian, 2009).

Collecting Survey Data

All data collection for survey data begins with some form of written survey that is delivered in-person in the form of an interview, through the mail, on the phone, or online. In-person surveys may be done in the form of an interview, which we will discuss later. Of course, all surveys begin with well-written survey items that can effectively engage the participant. Each mode of delivery of a survey (i.e., mail, on the phone, and online) have their own unique considerations which we describe here.

In-Person Interviews

You have undoubtedly heard of the Kinsey Report, perhaps the most famous sex survey of all time. Completed in the years just following World War II, it resulted from detailed, face-to-face interviews with thousands of men and women, and it yielded two large books on sexual behavior in America, one for men (Kinsey, Pomeroy, & Martin, 1948) and one for women (Kinsey, Pomeroy, Martin, & Gebhard, 1953).[2] Although you might think Kinsey's **interview survey** format might have prevented people from describing the intimate details of their sexual attitudes and behaviors, especially considering the historical era in which the studies were done, this apparently did not occur. In fact, conservative postwar America was shocked by the frequency of the reported levels of premarital sex, masturbation, and adultery. The books, although written in dry academic prose and loaded with tables and bar graphs, nonetheless reached best-seller status and made Kinsey a celebrated yet controversial figure. Accused by some of contributing to a moral decline and even of being a Communist, he was regarded by others as a pioneer in the scientific study of an important aspect of human behavior (Christenson, 1971).

The interview format for surveying individuals about attitudes, opinions, beliefs, and the like has the advantages of being comprehensive and highly detailed.[3] Even though the interviewer typically asks a standard set of questions, the skilled interviewer is able to elicit considerable information through follow-up questions or probes. Having an interviewer present also reduces the problem of unclear questions; the interviewer can clarify information on the spot. Sampling is sometimes a problem because, in many cases, sizable segments of the population may not be included if they refuse to be interviewed, cannot be located, or live in an area the interviewer would prefer to avoid. For example, the poor and homeless are usually underrepresented in national surveys using the interview format. Interviews can occur in a group format; the *focus group* procedure described in Chapter 11 is an example.

Besides sampling issues, other major problems with the interview approach are cost, logistics, and interviewer bias. Interviewers must be hired and trained, travel expenses can be substantial, and interviews might be restricted to a fairly small geographic area because of the logistical problems of sending interviewers long distances. And despite training, there is always the possibility that interviewer bias can affect the responses given in the face-to-face setting. For example, cross-race bias may exist, resulting in systematic differences between interviews with members of the interviewer's own race and members of other races.

---

[2] Kinsey's life and research were also portrayed in the movie *Kinsey*, starring Liam Neeson, which appeared in 2004.
[3] The interview survey method must be distinguished from the clinical interview, which is a diagnostic procedure used by clinical psychologists and requires a high degree of training in diagnosing psychological disorders.

The careful researcher using interviews will develop a training program to standardize the interview process as much as possible. Certain types of interviewers may be trained for specific purposes. For example, middle-aged female interviewers may elicit more cooperation in an interview survey of retired women than young male interviewers, who may not get past the door (van Kammen & Stouthamer-Loeber, 1998).

Mailed Written Surveys

Written surveys sent through the mail may have problems with how many people actually return a completed survey (as you know, because you've probably thrown a few away). Return rates of 85% or higher are considered excellent (and rare), 70–85% very good, and 60–70% more or less acceptable (Mangione, 1998). Anything below 60% makes researchers nervous about whether the data are representative. Another problem with rate of return occurs when people who return surveys differ in some important way from those who don't return them, a problem called **nonresponse bias** (Rogelberg & Luong, 1998). When this happens, drawing a conclusion about a population is risky at best. The profile of the typical non-responder is an older, unmarried male without a lot of education (Mangione, 1998); nonresponse also occurs when people have some attribute that makes the survey irrelevant for them (e.g., vegetarians surveyed about meat preferences).

The best chance for a decent return rate for a mailed written survey is when (a) the survey is brief and easy to fill out; (b) the form starts with relatively interesting questions and leaves the boring items (i.e., demographic information) until the end; (c) before the survey is sent out, participants are notified that a survey is on the way and that their help will be greatly appreciated; (d) nonresponse triggers follow-up reminders, a second mailing of the survey, and perhaps even a phone request to fill out the form; (e) the entire package is highly professional in appearance, with a cover letter signed by a real person instead of a machine; (f) return postage is included; and (g) the recipient has no reason to think the survey is merely the first step in a sales pitch (Fowler, 1993; Rogelberg & Luong, 1998). Return rates can also be improved by including a small gift or token amount of money. For example, Dillman et al., (2009) reported a study that increased response rate from 52% to 64% by adding a token gift of a dollar in the survey mailing.

One important problem that exists with all forms of survey research is a **social desirability bias**. Sometimes, people respond to a survey question in a way that reflects not how they truly feel or what they truly believe, but how they think they *should* respond—that is, they attempt to create a positive picture of themselves, one that is socially desirable. For instance, people are likely to distort their voting record, reporting they vote more often than they actually do (Anderson, Silver, & Abramson, 1988). And you might not be surprised to learn that people do not wash their hands after using restrooms as often as they say they do. A study by Zezima (2010) found a discrepancy between the percentage of those who reported they always washed their hands after using a public bathroom and those who actually did wash their hands. Close to 100% reported on a survey that they always washed, but the observed percentages (yes, researchers sometimes show up in bathrooms) were much lower in such places as Grand Central Station in New York (80%) and in major league ballparks. For men, Turner Field in Atlanta had the poorest "washing rate" (67%).[4]

Ensuring survey participants of anonymity can help reduce the social desirability bias, but the problem is persistent and it is hard to gauge its extent. The social psychology literature has a long history of research showing the attitudes people express on some issue do not always match their behavior. Thus, the results of survey research must be interpreted with this response bias in mind, and conclusions drawn from surveys can be strengthened to the extent that other research provides converging results.

---

[4] The women at Turner Field washed their hands at a very high rate (98%), a sign either of greater conscientiousness than males or less interest in returning quickly to the game.

Phone Surveys

A second way to conduct a survey is to pick up the phone and call people. According to Dillman et al. (2009), **phone surveying** had its peak of popularity in the 1980s; virtually every home had a telephone, households could be selected randomly through a procedure called *random-digit-dialing*, and people were generally open to being surveyed. And then two developments created serious difficulties for the phone surveying business: telemarketing and cell phones. Telemarketing produced a level of annoyance sufficient to lead to the creation of national do-not-call lists, and the marketing strategy also had the effect of creating high levels of suspicion and distrust in the general public, especially when telemarketers begin the call by pretending they are conducting a survey, when in fact they are selling a product (a ploy known in marketing research as **sugging**— *S*elling *U*nder the *G*uise of a survey).[5] As for cell phones, they have changed the dynamic of phone surveying. When the only phones in the house were landlines, surveyors would call and the unit of measurement typically would be the "household." With cell phones, however, the unit is the individual, thereby changing the nature of the population.

Nonetheless, phone surveying does have positive aspects. Unlike a mailed written survey, there is more human contact when one is speaking over the phone than when one is reading a paper survey. The method combines the efficiency of a mailed survey with the personal contact of an interview. To increase the chances of people responding, one technique used by legitimate phone surveyors is to precede the call with a brief letter, post card, or e-mail alerting the respondent that a phone call is on the way ("and please cooperate, we could really use your help; and we promise it will be brief"). This is an example of the mixed-mode approach (mixing mail and phone) advocated by Dillman et al., (2009).

Online Surveys

As you recall from the ethics chapter, researchers are increasingly turning to the Internet for data collection. One of the most common forms of Internet data collection involves **online surveys**, which is accomplished in several ways. First, online surveys can be sent as Internet url's via e-mail to a selected sample of individuals. E-mail lists can be purchased or, following the ethically dubious lead of spammers, obtained by using "search spiders" that search the Internet for posted e-mails and accumulate e-mail addresses. A second form of online survey is one that can be posted on a listserv or social media site, collecting data from those who choose to respond. A third procedure is to follow a probability sampling procedure with incentives for participating in online surveys. For example, some companies create national samples by randomly sampling addresses rather than phone numbers. They then recruit subjects by regular mail to participate in multiple online surveys by providing the incentive of free Internet access (e.g., Wirth & Bodenhausen, 2009). Several technologies have emerged that allow survey developers to use software to create online surveys and even experiments. For example, SurveyMonkey and Qualtrics are two popular types of software for developing online surveys. Amazon's Mechanical Turk (MTurk) is a platform that allows researchers to place their surveys and program experiments that can be conducted online. Further, MTurk participants can be paid for their participation for very small amounts of money (e.g., a dollar or two per participant).

The main advantage of online surveying is that a large amount of data can be collected in a relatively short time for minimal cost. There are costs for researcher time and surveying software, but usually no postage, phone, or employee costs. And with the Internet open 24 hours a day, online surveying can be completed in less time than other forms of surveys.

Problems exist, however. Although Internet use is widespread, the sample tends to be biased; for instance, responders are unlikely to be representative of all income and education levels. With e-mail surveys, the researcher runs the risk of having the survey appear to be just another piece

---

[5] Another marketing strategy is called *frugging*, for *F*und *R*aising *U*nder the *G*uise of surveying

of spam or, worse, a potential entryway for a virus. By one estimate (Anderson & Kanuka, 2003), 85% of e-mail users delete messages without reading them, at least some of the time. So, at the least, the e-mail survey must have a subject line that will catch the reader's attention. With web-based surveys, the problem (which you probably have already recognized) is that the sample is bound to be self-selected, resulting in bias. Furthermore, it could be that a teenager out there has little else to do but respond to your survey several hundred times a day for a week or two. Despite the difficulties, however, online surveying occupies a large niche in the 21st-century survey business. As with phone surveying, savvy researchers can use a mixed mode approach—sending a letter in the mail that appeals to the reader to complete the survey, perhaps including in the letter a website address with a password to enter the survey. Or, as mentioned earlier, survey companies sometimes provide incentives for participation.

SELF TEST

9.2

1. Compared to written surveys sent through the mail, what is one advantage and one dis-advantage of an interview survey?
2. What is meant by a "mixed mode" approach to administering surveys?
3. What methods might one use to distribute a survey online?

Ethical Considerations

One point worth noting about survey research is that in some cases, the APA does not require informed consent. In Standard 8.05, the APA excuses "anonymous questionnaires [assuming that] disclosure of responses would not place participants at risk of criminal or civil liability or damage their financial standing, employability, or reputation, and confidentiality is protected" (APA, 2002, p.1069–1070). Despite this, it is customary for researchers to include consent language in a cover letter that precedes the survey or in the opening screens of an online survey.

A second point about survey research and ethics is that decisions affecting people's lives are sometimes made with the help of survey data, and if the surveys are flawed and biased, or poorly constructed, people can be hurt or, at the least, have their time wasted. Although professional psychologists operating within the APA's ethics code are unlikely to use surveys inappropriately, abuses nonetheless can occur. The problem is recognized by the judicial system, which has

BOX 9.2 ETHICS—Using and Abusing Surveys

In early 1981, television station KMBC of Kansas City hired Christine Craft, a news journalist from California, to co-anchor its evening news. Less than a year later, she was demoted from that position. The station claimed incompetence, but Craft sued, arguing she was hired for her journalistic talent, not her youthful good looks, yet was fired for the latter reason. She won.

On the surface, the station appeared to act prudently, basing its decision not merely on whim but on data collected

in a professional phone survey of 400 viewers. However, this case illustrates not the use of survey research but its misuse. According to Beisecker (1988), the study had several major flaws.

First, although the use of a survey conveys the impression of objectivity, the research was hopelessly biased from the start. One major problem was that the firm doing the research also served as a paid consultant to the station, and those doing the research already knew what decision the

(continued)

BOX 9.2   (CONTINUED)

station wanted. The resulting bias was reflected in the wording of a phone survey that was used. One purpose of the survey was to compare Craft with other local news anchors, yet the questions were stacked against her. For example, she did poorly compared to other anchors on a question regarding which news anchor "knows Kansas City best" (p. 23), which is not surprising when one considers that (a) at the time of the survey Craft had been with the station for all of 6 months and the other anchors had all been at their stations at least a year and (b) in her early months with KMBC, Craft had been vigorously promoted as "a fresh new face from California" (p. 23). Also, few survey items assessed journalistic ability; rather, much of the survey dealt with questions about attractiveness and appearance (e.g., "Her good looks are a big plus for the newscast she's on," p. 23).

In addition to the bias that characterized the project from the start, its statistical problems were serious enough for Beisecker (1988) to conclude that "the research firm did not employ any recognizable statistical tests or principles of statistical inference to justify its generalizations from the sample data" (p. 25). In other words, while the consultant firm reported simple *descriptive* statistics summarizing the survey results, they did not conduct the proper *inferential* statistics that would allow conclusions about the significance of the results. For example, it was reported that among 25- to 34-year-olds asked which channel's news had declined in quality, 30% said KMBC and 16% said a competing channel, KCMO. Much was made of this "2-1 margin," and it was attributed to the allegedly detrimental effects of Craft's presence. However, the year before (1980), when Craft was still in California, the *same* question on another survey by the *same* firm yielded 26% for KMBC and 15% for KCMO. An inferential analysis surely would have shown no difference in the ratings between the 2 years. Not only was the analysis not done, the consultant/researchers conveniently omitted the 1980 data from the 1981 results.

Clearly, survey research can be done well and its results interpreted meaningfully. In the case of Christine Craft, though, the "survey research" basis for her firing had no credibility.

established a set of standards for the use of survey data in courts of law (Morgan, 1990). The standards amount to this: If you are going to collect and use survey data, behave like a professional psychologist—that is, be careful about sampling, survey construction, and data analysis. For an interesting and rather disturbing example of how survey methods can be badly misused, read Ethics Box 12.3, which examines the case of a female journalist who was fired from her news anchor job, partly on the basis of a rigged survey.

We close the discussion of survey methods with a specific Research Example. As you recall from Chapter 3, an important part of doing research is considering the *"what's next"* question. We described a study about how students who engaged in self-testing as a study strategy outperformed those who merely reread the study material (Research Example 2; Roediger & Karpicke, 2006). This was also an example of an experimental design in which students were randomly assigned to a type of study strategy and taught how to use the self-testing strategy. However, what types of study strategies to students naturally use in an academic setting, and how are the strategies used by students related to academic achievement? These empirical questions were addressed by Hartwig and Dunlosky (2012) in their survey research.

Research Example 25—A Survey of College Students' Study Strategies

Researchers including Roediger and Karpicke (2006) have established that a study strategy of self-testing leads to better test performance, but do students use this type of study strategy in the real-world setting of studying for their classes? To answer this question, Hartwig and Dunlosky (2012) used a survey method to assess different types of study strategies that college students report using. In addition, they tested the relationship between study strategies and academic achievement. To do so, they began by creating a survey that was in part a *direct replication* of a survey used by Kornell and Bjork (2007). To assess the types of study strategies students use, they used seven items from Kornell and Bjork's original survey. All of these items were *closed questions*, with specific response options that students could select. For example, when asked "If you quiz yourself while you study (either using a quiz at the end of the chapter or a practice quiz, or flashcards, or something else), why do you do so?" the response options were:

- I learn more that way than I would through rereading
- To figure out how well I have learned the information I'm studying
- I find quizzing more enjoyable than reading
- I usually do not quiz myself (Kornell & Bjork, p. 223).

Hartwig and Dunlosky asked another question about the types of study strategies students regularly used, a question that asked students to check all strategies that applied to them. The response options included strategies of self-testing, using flashcards, rereading, making outlines, underlining or highlighting, and studying with friends (among other options). In addition, Hartwig and Dunlosky also included questions on their survey to ascertain how students schedule their study time, including time of day and whether students tend to cram or space out their study over several days or weeks. Because the researchers added their own survey questions to answer their own empirical questions, their study was also *conceptual replication* of the work by Kornell and Bjork. For their measure of academic achievement, Hartwig and Dunlosky asked students to report their GPA from options that included *ranges* of GPA. Recall that providing ranges can reduce privacy concerns in participants; it can also help alleviate concerns with memory accuracy if one's exact GPA is not readily available at the time of taking the survey. In total, the written survey included 12 items, all of which were closed questions.

Hartwig and Dunlosky (2012) tested 324 students from introductory psychology courses, as such a sample taps into a more diverse population of students in large part because the course is very popular and is a required course for many students. Students completed the written survey within 10 minutes. First, they found that they replicated Kornell and Bjork's results in the first seven survey items. For example, in response to the question above about quizzing yourself, in both studies, most students reported that they quiz themselves when they are trying to figure out if they have learned the material (second option above). In terms of the types of strategies students use, most students reported underlining or highlighting when reading (72%), testing themselves (71%), rereading the material (66%), "cram[ming] lots of material the night before the test" (66%), and using flashcards (62%) (p. 128–129). As for when students report studying, you may not be surprised to learn that most students reported studying in the evening. Also, 53% of students reported that they most often cram their studying into one session, whereas 47% of students report spacing their study out over a multiple days or weeks. OK, so how are these related to academic success, as measured by GPA?

When you look at the two self-testing strategies of "test yourself with questions or practice problems" and "use flashcards" (p. 130), Hartwig and Dunlosky (2012) found that using practice tests was related to GPA, but using flashcards was not. In other words, students who reported using practice tests also had higher GPAs, but using flashcards was not related to higher GPAs. With regard to scheduling, those with the lowest GPAs reported that when deciding on what to study next, they would study whatever was due soonest or was already overdue. Students with the highest GPAs planned a study schedule and used the schedule to determine what to study next. Interestingly, despite much research on the ill-effects of cramming on test performance, Hartwig and Dunlosky did not find a significant relationship between cramming or spacing their study and GPA. This is not to say that a null result means it is OK to cram or OK to space your study, but rather that there is not sufficient evidence in this study to suggest that one is better than the other. That said, there is overwhelming evidence by many researchers showing that spaced study is superior to cramming (see Delaney, Verkoeijen, & Spirgel, 2010 for a review).

Analyzing Data from Non-Experimental Methods

Survey and interview methods are examples of non-experimental research designs. You will read about more non-experimental designs in the next few chapters of this textbook. Because researchers do not experimentally manipulate variables in such designs, the statistical techniques and the conclusions drawn from such techniques reflect a description of the relationships between variables in the study. Researchers seek to discover relationships between variables, and they often wish to make predictions about future behavior from the data collected by using various statistical techniques. In this section, we describe correlational techniques to evaluate quantitative data derived from surveys but is also relevant for areas of study in psychology. Then, we discuss how to make predictions from the data using regression analyses. Finally, we conclude with a discussion of other statistical techniques you may encounter when reading articles using non-experimental research methods. Data derived from interviews in particular may be qualitative in nature, and researchers may try to convert qualitative information (e.g., answers to open-ended questions) to coded, quantitative data. We will explore this in more depth in Chapter 10.

Correlation: Describing Relationships

A correlation exists whenever two variables are associated or related. This idea is implied by the term itself: *co* for two and *relation* for, well, relation. Correlations can occur for data of all different types of scales of measurement, but we will focus here on interval and ratio data. In a **positive correlation**, the relationship is such that a high score on one variable is associated with a high score on the second variable; similarly, a low score on one relates to a low score on the other. A **negative correlation**, on the other hand, is an inverse relationship. High scores on one variable are associated with low scores on the second variable, and vice versa.

The relationship between study time and grades is a simple example of a positive correlation. If study time, operationalized as the total number of hours per week spent studying, is one variable and grade point average (GPA) ranging from 0.0 to 4.0 is the second, you can easily see the positive correlation between the two in these hypothetical data from eight students:

	Study Hours	GPA
Student 1:	42	3.3
Student 2:	23	2.9
Student 3:	31	3.2
Student 4:	35	3.2
Student 5:	16	1.9
Student 6:	26	2.4
Student 7:	39	3.7
Student 8:	19	2.5

Spending a significant amount of time studying (e.g., 42 hours) is associated with a high GPA (3.3), whereas minimal study time (e.g., 16 hours) is paired with a low GPA (1.9).

An example of negative correlation might be the relationship between goof-off time and GPA. Goof-off time could be operationally defined as the number of hours per week spent in a specific list of activities that might include video game playing, TV watching, and playing golf (of course, these same activities could be called therapy time). Here are hypothetical data for another eight students. This time, examine the inverse relationship between the number of hours per week spent goofing off and GPA:

	Goof-Off Hours	GPA
Student 1:	42	1.8
Student 2:	23	3.0
Student 3:	31	2.2
Student 4:	35	2.9
Student 5:	16	3.7
Student 6:	26	3.0
Student 7:	39	2.4
Student 8:	19	3.4

Notice that in a negative correlation, the variables go in opposite directions. Large amounts of goof-off time (e.g., 42 hours) accompany a low GPA (1.8); small amounts of goof-off time (e.g., 16 hours) relate to a higher GPA (3.7).

Scatterplots

An indication of the strength of a relationship between two variables can be discerned by examining a **scatterplot**, which is a visual representation of the relationship between the two measured variables. Generally speaking, the stronger the relationship between the two variables, the closer the points on the scatterplot will be a straight line. If there is more variability in the scores for the two variables, then the points on the scatterplot will be more spread out, that is, more scattered. As shown in the examples in Figure 9.1, perfect positive (9.1a) and perfect negative (9.1b) correlations produce points falling on a straight line, whereas a correlation of zero yields a scatterplot (9.1c) in which the points appear to be randomly distributed on the surface of the graph. Compared to those for relatively weak correlations (9.1d and 9.1e), the points bunch closer together for relatively strong ones (9.1f and 9.1g). In general, as any correlation weakens, the points on a scatterplot move farther away from the diagonal lines that would connect the points in a perfect correlation. Note the dotted line ovals in Figure 9.1 are not a normal feature of scatterplots; we put them there just to show you how the points are more tightly bunched as a correlation strengthens.

Figure 9.2 shows you how a scatterplot is created from a set of data; each point on the scatterplot represents a participant's score on each of two measures, one plotted from the X-axis and one plotted from the Y-axis. Therefore, each point represents two scores per participant. Figure 9.3 displays the scatterplots for the hypothetical GPA examples. They indicate a strong positive correlation between study time and GPA and a strong negative one between goof-off time and GPA.

The scatterplots we've seen contain points that vary to some degree from the straight line of a perfect correlation. Some relationships are not linear, however, and applying statistical procedures that assume linearity will fail to identify the true nature of the relationship. Figure 7.4 shows a hypothetical example, the famous (yet perhaps misnamed) Yerkes-Dodson Law you learned about in Chapter 7. On tasks that are somewhat difficult, performance is good at moderate levels

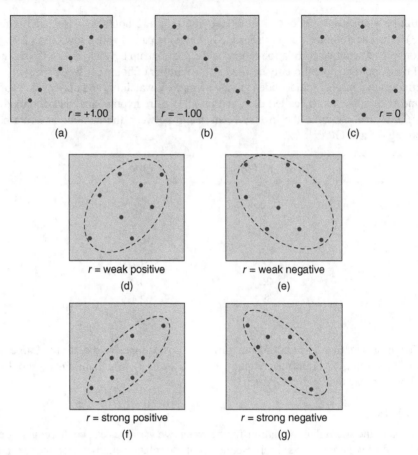

FIGURE 9.1
Varieties of scatterplots.

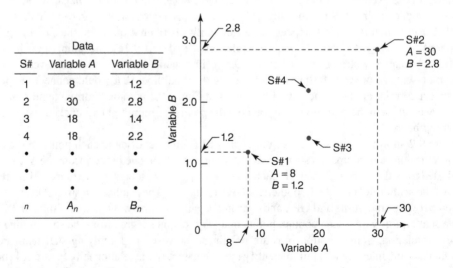

FIGURE 9.2
Creating a scatterplot from a data set.

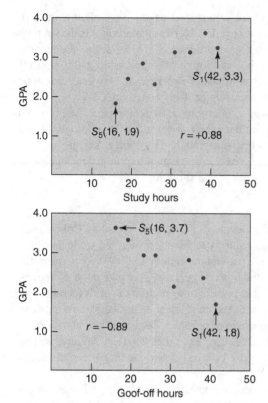

FIGURE 9.3
Scatterplots for some hypothetical GPA data.

of arousal but suffers if arousal is very low or very high. At very low levels of arousal, the person presumably doesn't have the energy to perform the task, and at very high levels, the intense arousal interferes with the efficient processing of information necessary to complete the task. You can see from the scatterplot that points would fall consistently along this curved line, but trying to apply a linear correlational procedure would yield zero correlation.

Correlation Coefficients

The strength and direction of a correlation is indicated by the size of a statistic called the *coefficient of correlation*. The most common coefficient is the **Pearson's** *r*, named for Karl Pearson, the British statistician who rivals Sir Ronald Fisher (the ANOVA guy) in stature.[6] Pearson's *r* is calculated for data measured on either an interval or a ratio scale of measurement. Other kinds of correlations can be calculated for data measured on other scales. For instance, a correlation coefficient called *Spearman's rho* (reads "row") is calculated for ordinal (i.e., rankings) data and a chi-square test of independence (also invented by Pearson) or the phi coefficient works for nominal data.[7] The Students Statistics Guide on the Student Companion Site provides examples of how to calculate a Pearson's *r* by hand and how to do a correlational analysis with SPSS.

---

[6] Sir Francis Galton, mentioned in Box 9.1 as a pioneer in the use of survey data, is also known as the creator of the correlation as a statistical tool, writing a paper in 1888 entitled "Co-relations and their measurement, chiefly from anthropometric data" (Galton, 1888). The concept was refined by a protégée of Galton's, mathematician Karl Pearson, and the correlation calculated today for interval and ratio data is known as Pearson's *r*.

[7] The Student Statistics Guide, part of the Student Companion Site, shows you how to calculate and interpret two forms of chi-square (chi-square goodness of fit test; chi-square test of independence). Because researchers often collect frequency data (i.e., nominal scale data), chi-square is a popular test. For example, it would be used to analyze the data reported in Chapter 4 example of nominal scale data, in which females were responsive to males when males had a dog with them (Guéguen & Ciccotti, 2008).

The correlation coefficient itself ranges from −1.00 for a perfect negative correlation, through 0.00 for no relationship, to +1.00 for a perfect positive correlation. The digit represents the strength of the relationship between two variables: the closer the coefficient is to 1 or −1, the stronger the relationship. The sign of the coefficient represents the direction of the relationship, either positive or negative. The GPA examples above illustrate a strong positive correlation between study time and GPA ($r = +.88$) and a strong negative one between goof-off time and GPA ($r = −.89$). Remember effect size from Chapter 4? Another way to interpret the correlation coefficient is in a form of *effect size* of the strength of the relationship between two variables. Psychologists often use Cohen's (1988) conventions of .10 for a small effect size, .30 for a medium effect size, and .50 for a large effect size. So, if one obtains a Pearson's r of .23, one may interpret the correlation as having a small-to-medium-sized relationship between the two variables.

Coefficient of Determination

It is easy to misinterpret the meaning of a particular Pearson's r or its corresponding Cohen interpretation of effect size. If it equals +.70, the relationship is relatively strong, but students sometimes look at such a correlation and think the +.70 somehow relates to 70% and perhaps the correlation means the relationship is true 70% of the time. This is *not* what a Pearson's r means. A better interpretation of a correlation is to use what is called the **coefficient of determination** (r^2). It is found by squaring the Pearson's r—hence, the coefficient will always be a positive number, regardless of whether the correlation is positive or negative. Technically, r^2 is defined as the percent of variance in one variable that is explained by the other variable. Another way to think of this is how much variability is shared across both variables, a concept called *shared variance*. An example should make this clear.

Suppose you complete a study involving 100 people and you measure an SAT score and a grade point average (GPA) for each person. You correlate the two variables and find a positive correlation. The higher the SAT score, the higher the GPA; conversely, low SAT scores tend to be accompanied by a low GPA. Consider two hypothetical correlations that might result from this study, a perfect +1.00 and +.50. The coefficients of determination for these cases will be 1.00 and .25, respectively. To understand what this means, first recognize that the GPAs for the 100 people in the study probably vary quite a bit, possibly from 0.0 to 4.0. As researchers, we would like to know what produces this variability—why one person gets a 3.8, another gets a 2.4, and so on. That is, what accounts for individual differences in GPA? Probably, a number of factors lead to different levels of GPA: study habits, general intelligence, motivation, emotional stability, ability to avoid taking physics courses, and so on.

Our hypothetical study has examined one of those factors, a measure of academic ability, as reflected in scores on the SAT. The r^2 indicates how much the variability in GPA can be associated with the SAT scores. In the first outcome, with an r of +1.00 and an r^2 of 1.00, we could conclude that 100% of the variability in GPA can be explained with reference to SAT scores. That is, we could say that 100% of the difference between the GPAs of 3.8 and 2.4 (and others) could be attributed to whatever SAT measures. (This, of course, would never happen in a real study; human behavior is much too complex.) In the second case, with an r of +.50 and an r^2 of .25, only a quarter (25%) of the variability in GPA scores can be associated with SAT scores. Presumably, the remaining 75% would be related to other factors, such as the ones listed previously (study habits, etc.). As mentioned earlier, actual research indicates the correlation between SAT and GPA is in the vicinity of +.30 to +.40. Thus, SAT accounts for about 9% to 16% of the variability in GPA, which might seem rather small to you, and probably accounts for some of the controversy over the value of the SAT.

One final point: Notice, for example, that for a correlation of +.70, the coefficient of determination is .49, while a correlation of +.50 has an r^2 of .25. We might be tempted to think the relationships are both "strong" correlations, according to Cohen's (1988) conventions. However, the reality is the amount of shared variance is almost twice as much in the first case as in the second. That is, a correlation of +.70 is *much* stronger than a correlation of +.50.

Be Aware of Outliers

An *outlier* is a score that is dramatically different from the remaining scores in a data set. As you recall from Chapter 4, when a data set has an outlier or two, central tendency is best represented with a median instead of a mean, and interquartile range is a better indication of variability than a standard deviation. With correlational research, an outlier can seriously distort the calculated value of a Pearson's r and the coefficient of determination (r^2). For example, consider a class exercise completed by Nolan and Heinzen (2012). They asked a group of students to estimate (a) how many hours a week they studied, and (b) the size of their monthly cell phone bill in dollars. Almost all the students had similar phone bills of $100 or less; their study hours were a little more variable. For most of the scatterplot, there does not appear to be much of a correlation. One student had a $500 phone bill, however. Nolan and Heinzen calculated a correlation for all the students and the result was a Pearson's r of +.39, a medium-sized correlation. When they recalculated the correlation without the $500 student, however, the Pearson's r changed to −.14, essentially no relationship. Thus, including the outlier gives the impression, there is indeed a relationship between studying and cell phone use, but that impression is false. Removing the $500 student yielded a more accurate picture—no substantial association between studying and cell phone use. Another way of saying this is that including the outlier would lead one to make a *Type I error* (you think there is a relationship, based on rejecting the null hypothesis, but there really is no relationship). The best way to spot an outlier in a correlational study is to examine a scatterplot. As mentioned in Chapter 4, general guidelines, usually based on standard deviation information, are used to eliminate outliers, but these must be established prior to data collection.

Regression: Making Predictions

Psychologists are often in the business of predicting behavior from a variety of factors or variables. With an experimental design, the independent variable serves as a predictor of some measured outcome variable (the dependent variable). In non-experimental designs, researchers can use regression techniques to predict behaviors, based on the correlations between variables. Making predictions on the basis of correlations is referred to as doing a **regression analysis**. If you know a statistically significant correlation exists between two variables, then knowing a score on one of the variables enables you to predict a score on the other (if the correlation is not significant, regression analyses should not be done). You can see how this would work with the GPA example. Knowing of the strong relationship between study time and GPA for a sample of students, if we tell you a student (not in the study's sample) studies 45 hours per week, you could safely predict a relatively high GPA for that person. Similarly, a high GPA allows a prediction about study time. As you'll see later in the chapter, correlational and regression analyses provide the foundation for using various psychological surveys and tests to make predictions.

Figure 9.4 reproduces the scatterplots for (a) study time and GPA and (b) goof-off time and GPA, but this time each includes what is called a **regression line**. This line is used for making the predictions and is also called the *line of best fit*; it provides the best possible way of summarizing the points on the scatterplot. More precisely, if you took the absolute values of the shortest distances between each point and the line, those distances would be at a minimum.

In a regression analysis, a regression equation is used to predict a value for Y (e.g., GPA) based on a given value of X (e.g., study time). Y is sometimes referred to as the **criterion variable** and X as the **predictor variable**. In order to predict with confidence, however, the correlation must be significantly greater than zero. The higher the correlation, the closer the points on the scatterplot will be to the regression line and the more confident you can be in your prediction. And that confidence can be expressed mathematically in the form of a confidence interval, a concept introduced in Chapter 4 as a way of determining a range of scores within which the true mean of

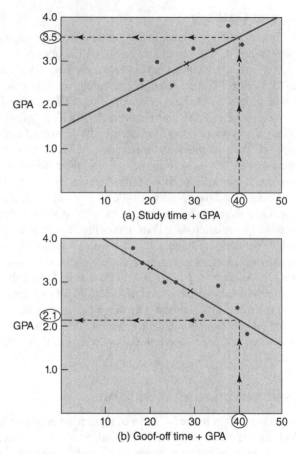

FIGURE 9.4
Scatterplots with regression lines.

a population is likely to be found. When making a prediction in a regression analysis, it is possible to establish a range of scores for the prediction (i.e., the confidence interval), within which the true prediction is likely to occur a high percentage of times (95% or 99%). In general, as the correlation gets stronger (i.e., closer to either +1.00 or −1.00), one can be more confident of the prediction. This will be reflected in a narrower range of scores when the confidence interval is calculated. To see how to calculate confidence intervals for a regression prediction, consult a statistics textbook (e.g., Sprinthall, 2000).

From Figure 9.5, you can also see how a regression line aids in making predictions. Given the relationship between study time and GPA, for example, one could ask what GPA could be expected from someone with 40 study hours. The process can be visualized by drawing vertical dotted lines up from the X-axis to the regression line and then taking a 90° left turn until the Y-axis is encountered. The value on the Y-axis is the prediction. Thus, a study time (the predictor variable) of 40 hours predicts a GPA (the criterion variable) of about 3.5, while 40 hours of goof-off time predicts a GPA of just under 2.1. The exact predictions, 3.48 and 2.13, respectively, can be calculated using the regression formula on the Student Companion Site. And because the correlations are both strong (+.88 for study time and −.89 for goof-off time), the confidence intervals for each will have a fairly narrow range. The 95% confidence interval for GPA is 2.94 to 4.02 for the study time prediction; hence, we can be 95% confident that the calculated range of GPAs will include the true prediction. Sprinthall (2000) provides a good description of how to calculate the confidence intervals for regression predictions.

The actual regression analysis will yield standardized estimates of the strength of the predictor variable's ability to predict changes in the outcome or criterion variable; this is estimate is usually a beta coefficient, represented as β. Technically, beta is the slope of the regression line, as represented in the formula for creating a straight line on a graph with X and Y coordinates, where X would be the predictor variable and Y would be the criterion variable:

$$Y = a + bX$$

Beta can be interpreted in a similar fashion as a correlation coefficient, but a regression analysis also yields information about how strong those predictors are. Statistical tests of whether the predictor variable is a statistically significant predictor are calculated in a regression analysis and may be reported as F- or t-tests (not to be confused by the tests described in Chapters 7 and 8). In Research Example 25 on student study strategies, Hartwig and Dunlosky (2012) discovered that testing yourself ($\beta = .18$) and rereading ($\beta = .12$) were significant positive predictors of GPA, meaning that students report using either of these strategies, they will likely have higher GPAs. In contrast, making outlines ($\beta = -.12$) and studying with friends ($\beta = -.11$) were significant negative predictors, meaning that if students report using either of these strategies, they will likely have lower GPAs.

Thus far, we have described what is known as a **bivariate** approach to data analysis, which investigates the relationships between any two variables. A **multivariate** approach, on the other hand, examines the relationships among more than two variables (often many more than two). In the case of simple, linear regression, two variables are involved: the predictor variable and the outcome variable. If SAT scores correlate with freshman year GPA, then the SAT can be used as a predictor of academic success. However, as you know from firsthand experience, phenomena like "success in college" are more complicated than this. SAT scores might predict success, but what about the influence of other factors like "motivation" and "high school grades" and "study time"?

Multiple regression solves the problem of having more than one predictor of some outcome. A **multiple regression** analysis has one criterion variable and a minimum of two predictor variables. The analysis enables you to determine not just that these two or more variables combine to predict some criterion but also how they uniquely predict some criterion variable. Multiple regression allows the researcher to estimate the relative strengths of the predictors. These strengths are reflected in the multiple regression formula for raw scores, which is an extension of the formula for simple regression:

$$Y = a + b_1 X_1 + b_2 X_2 + \ldots + b_n X_n$$

where each X is a different predictor score; Y is the criterion, or the score being predicted; and the size of the b's are the beta coefficients that reflect the relative importance of each predictor— they are also known as *beta weights* in multiple regression (Licht, 1995). A multiple regression analysis also yields a multiple correlation coefficient (R) and a multiple coefficient of determination (R^2). R is a correlation between the combined predictors and the criterion, and R^2 provides an index of the variation in the criterion variable that can be accounted for by the combined predictors. Note the use of upper case letters to differentiate the multivariate R and R^2 from the bivariate Pearson's r and r^2. Their interpretations are similar, however. Both R and r tell you about the strength of a correlation, and both R^2 and r^2 tell you about the amount of shared, explained variation.

The advantage of a multiple regression analysis is that when the influences of several predictor variables are combined (especially if the predictors are not highly correlated with each other), prediction improves compared to the single regression case. For instance, high school grades by themselves predict college success, as do SAT scores. Together, however, they predict better than either one by itself (Sprinthall, 2000). As students, you might find the following Research Example interesting. It is a good example of both simple, linear regression and multiple regression and it might give you some insight into how the passion and motivation you may feel for studying psychology can predict how engaged or overwhelmed you feel.

Research Example 26 – Regression and Multiple Regression

Stoeber, Childs, Hayward, and Feast (2011) used several different questionnaires to examine the relationships between passion for studying, academic engagement, and burnout in college students. First, using simple, linear regression, they wanted to see if degrees of passion could predict scores on the measures of engagement and burnout. Thus, passion was their *predictor variable*, and engagement and burnout were *criterion variables*. They used two separate linear regression analyses for each criterion variable. Passion was conceptualized as two different types: harmonious passion and obsessive passion. Harmonious passion is characterized as the passion one feels when an individual engages in activities freely and thus controls the passion. Unlike harmonious passion, obsessive passion occurs when the individual feels personal pressure to engage in activities and thus feels less control of the passion. As you might guess, unlike harmonious passion, obsessive passion tends to create conflict with other life domains (such as life with family and friends). It seems easy to imagine situations in which students may feel either harmonious passion or obsessive passion about studying for psychology. For example, harmonious passion might be thought of as loving psychology and wanting to study it freely, without pressure to do so – studying psychology for the pure love it. Obsessive passion might be thought of as still loving psychology, but feeling internal pressure to get good grades or go to graduate school or the like – studying psychology to be the best student possible, at whatever cost.

Stoeber et al. (2011) wanted to predict students' feelings of engagement in their studies and academic burnout from their passion. To do so, they asked 105 college students to complete three questionnaires that measured passion, engagement, and burnout. Items on the surveys asked students to rate their level of agreement on various items on 7-point Likert scales from 1 (*strongly disagree*) to 7 (*strongly agree*). For the criterion variables of engagement and burnout, the surveys allowed Stoeber et al., to subdivide academic engagement into three components: how dedicated one was to their work (dedication), how vigorously one worked (vigor), and how absorbed one became in one's work (absorption). Burnout was also subdivided into three components: feeling exhausted about studying (exhaustion), feeling pessimistic or skeptical about studying (cynicism), and feeling unable to produce the effects they want from their efforts (inefficacy). They first ran correlations between all their measures and after finding significant correlations between passion and academic engagement and burnout, they ran two separate simple, linear regression models, one for each criterion variable, engagement and burnout. They also found some degree of correlations between harmonious and obsessive passion, as their overall measure of passion tapped into both forms of passion. The regression analysis, however, enables researchers to examine the unique contributions (i.e., unique variance) of a variable by controlling for shared variance across variables. Thus, by using regression, Stoeber et al. controlled for *shared variance* (remember r^2?) across the two types of passion and tested if harmonious and obsessive passion would uniquely predict academic engagement and burnout. And, they did! Harmonious passion uniquely predicted all three measured aspects of academic engagement: dedication, vigor, and absorption. Obsessive passion uniquely predicted only vigor and absorption but not dedication. For academic burnout, harmonious passion was a unique negative predictor of all three aspects of burnout, where higher levels of harmonious passion predicted lower levels of exhaustion, cynicism, and inefficacy. In contrast, obsessive passion did not predict exhaustion and cynicism features of burnout, but it did predict inefficacy, in which higher levels obsessive passion predicted lower levels of inefficacy.

You might be wondering if motivation played some sort of role in students' passion for studying. Maybe students who are more motivated also felt more passionate about studying. Well, Stoeber et al., (2011) also controlled for motivation using multiple regression. Thus, passion and motivation were *predictor variables* and engagement and burnout were *criterion variables*. Like the linear regression analyses, they had to run separate multiple regression analyses – one for each criterion variable.[8] To measure motivation, students wrote down two personal goals they wished to achieve when studying. They then rated on a 7-point Likert scale their level of agreement of the reason for each goal. For example, students rated to how much they agreed that their goal was intrinsically motivated or extrinsically motivated, which was then coded by Stoeber et al. as autonomous or controlled motivation, respectively. The results from the multiple regression analyses were virtually identical to the linear regression analyses, meaning that neither type of motivation factored into the relationships between passion, achievement, and burnout demonstrated by the first set of regression analyses.

Stoeber et al.'s (2011) results were the first that demonstrated the relationships between passion, engagement, and burnout in a college setting, and their work serves as an extension of *applied research* in the field of industrial-organizational psychology on employee burnout. The *external validity* of the study should be considered, as the authors caution that their results should not be generalized to all college students, in large part because they tested a lot more women ($n = 93$) than men ($n = 12$). Such research certainly opens the door for more "*what's next*" type of thinking, including asking empirical questions about gender differences in passion and motivation, and whether passion and engagement are related to academic success. For you as students, harmonious passion is probably a healthier form of passion than obsessive passion. Obsessive passion relates to more pressures to perform and burnout, which may sour you on studying psychology. Harmonious passion for psychology can be better for you in terms of feeling more involved and in control your love of psychology.

One final point about a regression analysis is both procedural and ethical. In general, predictions should be made only for people who fall within the range of scores on which the correlation is based. For example, if a regression equation predicting college success is based on a study using middle-class suburban Caucasians with SAT scores ranging from 1000 to 1400, then the equation should not be used to predict success for any future applicant not part of that population.

SELF TEST

9.3

1. Consider the relationship between depression and exercise. Do you think it is a positive or a negative correlation? Explain.
2. Suppose you wish to predict academic success in college by looking at high school grades. Which is the criterion variable and which is the predictor variable?
3. How does simple, linear regression differ from multiple regression?

---

[8] Stoeber et al. (2011) actually ran what is called a hierarchical linear regression model, which is a form of multiple regression which allows the researcher to enter multiple predictors in a step-wise fashion, rather than adding all predictors into the model at once. Technically, the hierarchical regression allows the research to statistically control for one predictor before another predictor is entered into the model. In Stoeber et al.'s case, they controlled for the unique contributions of motivation *before* testing the passion predictor.

Interpreting Correlational Results

Both correlation and regression are statistical techniques that are used in non-experimental methods, including survey research. Such techniques are also used in many other types of non-experimental methods, which you will encounter in Chapters 10 and 11. For now, it is important to keep some things in mind when interpreting data from research that uses correlations and regression analyses. In an experimental study with a manipulated independent variable, we've already seen that cause-and-effect conclusions can be drawn with some degree of confidence. The independent variable of interest is manipulated and, if all else is held constant (i.e., no confounds), the results can be attributed directly to the independent variable. With non-experimental research using correlations, the "all else held constant" feature is missing, however, and this lack of control makes it impossible to conclude anything about cause and effect from a simple correlation. Let's consider two specific ways in which interpretation problems can occur with correlations. These are the *directionality problem* and the *third variable problem* (Neale & Liebert, 1973).

Directionality

If there is a correlation between two variables, A and B, it is possible that A is causing B to occur (A → B), but it also could be that B is causing A to occur (B → A). That the causal relation could occur in either direction is known as the **directionality problem**. The existence of the correlation *by itself* does not allow one to decide about the direction of causality. For instance, consider a study described in the *New York Times* in 2008, in which researchers examined the research productivity and beer consumption of ornithologists in the Czech Republic. They found a negative correlation: The more beer consumed by ornithologists, the less productive they were as scientists, a finding not likely to be taken well by those scientists who often claim that their best ideas occur to them in bars or pubs. The *Times* article emphasized the interpretation that probably occurred to you, that spending too much time drinking beer might cause the scientists to have little time left for research. But one researcher, thinking in terms of directionality, suggested that perhaps "those with poor publication records are drowning their sorrows" (For Scientists, 2008). So it is conceivable that drinking lots of beer causes Czech ornithologists to fail in their publishing efforts (A → B), but it is also possible that failing to publish causes Czech ornithologists to drink more beer (B → A). It is also worth noting the article also illustrated *external validity*, a concept you learned about in Chapter 5. One non-ornithologist critic of the study suggested that perhaps the results were limited to scientists who studied birds. Another suggested the results were limited individuals from the Czech Republic, which, the article claimed, has the highest rate of beer consumption on Earth.

Research on the relationship between TV watching and children's aggression typifies the directionality problem. Some of these studies are correlational and take the following general form. Some measure (variable A) of TV watching is made, the number of hours per week perhaps. For the same children, a second measure (variable B) of aggressive behavior is taken. It might be a combined score of teacher ratings of the aggressiveness of those in the study. Suppose this study yields a correlation of +.58, which is found to be significantly greater than zero. What can be concluded?

One possibility, of course, is that watching large amounts of TV inevitably exposes the child to a great deal of violence, and we know children learn by observation; thus, it would follow that a large dose of TV watching causes children to become aggressive—that is, A → B. Even if a regression analysis is conducted and watching TV (A) is a significant predictor of aggression (B), this still doesn't mean that watching TV causes aggression. Why? Because the regression itself is based on a correlation, and the research design is non-experimental. But could causality be working in the reverse direction? Could it be that children who are already aggressive for some other reason simply like to watch more TV than their nonaggressive peers? Knowing that much of television involves violent programming, perhaps aggressive children choose to watch more of the things that really interest them. In short, perhaps being aggressive causes children to watch more TV—that is, B → A.

Choosing the correct causal direction is not possible based on an existing correlation. However, the directionality problem can be addressed to some extent. The approach derives from the criteria for determining causality first described in Chapter 1. As you recall, research psychologists are generally satisfied with attributing causality between A and B when they occur together with some regularity, when A precedes B in time, when A causing B makes sense in relation to some theory, and when other explanations for their co-occurrence can be ruled out.

For the TV and aggressiveness study, all we have is A and B occurring together and the fact that A causing B makes some sense from what is known about observational learning theory (remember Bandura's Bobo doll study from Chapter 5—Box 5.2?). However, using a procedure called a **cross-lagged panel correlation**, it is possible to increase one's confidence about directionality. In essence, this procedure investigates correlations between variables at several points in time. Hence, it is a type of *longitudinal design*, adding the causal element of A preceding B. The following Research Example illustrates the procedure.

Research Example 27—Correlations and Directionality

In a famous study, Eron, Huesman, Lefkowitz, and Walder (1972) looked at the same relationship between TV watching and aggression that we've been using as a hypothetical example.[9] In particular, they measured (a) preference for watching violent television programs and (b) peer ratings of aggressiveness. The participants were 875 third graders from a rural area of New York State, first studied in 1960; a modest but significant correlation of +.21 between preference for violent TV and aggressiveness was found. What made the study interesting, however, was that Eron's team returned 10 years later, found 427 of the same students (now arbitrarily labeled "thirteenth graders"), and reassessed the same two variables. By measuring the two variables at two points in time, six correlations could be calculated. These correlations, as they occurred in the Eron et al. study, are displayed in Figure 9.5.

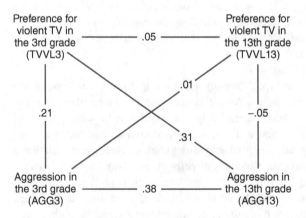

FIGURE 9.5
Results of a cross-lagged panel study of the effects of preference for violent TV programs on later aggression (from Eron et al., 1972).

---

[9] Actually, the study began with another purpose: to see if parental child rearing practices led to aggressiveness in children. But in a questionnaire for parents, Eron et al. included "filler" questions, items designed to disguise the study's true purpose. One asked parents to list their child's three favorite TV programs. When looking at the data, Eron et al. were surprised to see a relationship emerge: Children who preferred violent programs tended to be more aggressive. The entire focus of the study then changed (Huesman & Dubow, 2008). You might recognize this as an example of how *serendipity* (Chapter 3) can alter the direction of research.

Of special interest are the diagonal or cross-lagged correlations because they measure the relationships between two main variables but separated in time. If third-grade aggressiveness caused a later preference for watching violent TV (B → A), then we would expect a fair-sized correlation between aggressiveness at time 1 and preference at time 2; in fact, the correlation is virtually zero (+.01). On the other hand, if an early preference for viewing violent TV programs led to a later pattern of aggressiveness (A → B), then the correlation between preference at time 1 and aggressiveness at time 2 should be substantial. As you can see, this correlation is + .31, not terribly large but significant. Based on this finding, as well as on other indications in their study, Eron and his colleagues concluded that an early preference for watching violent TV is at least partially the cause of later aggressiveness.

Cross-lagged panel correlations must be interpreted cautiously, however (Rogosa, 1980). For one thing, if you examine the overall pattern of correlations in Figure 9.8, you will notice the correlation of +.31 may be partially accounted for by the correlations of +.21 and +.38—that is, rather than a direct path leading from 3rd-grade preference to 13th-grade aggression, perhaps the path is an indirect result of the relationship between preference for violent TV and aggression in the 3rd grade and between the two measures of aggression. A child scoring high on preference for violent TV in 3rd grade might also be aggressive in 3rd grade and still be aggressive (or even more so) in 13th grade. Alternatively, it could be that aggressiveness in third grade produced both (a) a preference for watching violent TV in third grade and (b) later aggressiveness. Thus, cross-lagged panel correlations help with the directionality dilemma, but problems of interpretation remain. More generally, interpretation difficulties take the form of the third variable problem.

Third Variables

The June 4, 2000, issue of the *New York Times Magazine,* contained a playful article entitled "Greens Peace" (Plotz, 2000). In it the author addressed the weighty issue of why some countries seem to be always at war, while others remain relatively peaceful. His answer was golf: Countries where a substantial portion of the population plays golf are less belligerent than countries without golf. As Plotz put it:

> Every peaceful European nation loves golf. But Russia, at war in Chechnya, doesn't hit the links. Non-golf Greece and non-golf Turkey have long warred over non-golf Cyprus. The former Yugoslavia has fragmented into five states. Only peaceful Slovenia swings the sticks. Do India or Pakistan golf? Of course not. Algerians shoot one another; Moroccans next door shoot par. (p. 32)

Although the slogan "make par, not war" (p. 37) might have merit, I think you can see the absurdity of the argument that golf causes peace. And it is only slightly more likely that the reverse is true—that peace causes golf. Rather, if there really is a correlation between peace and golf on a national level, and Plotz doesn't present a Pearson's *r*, of course, its existence is an exaggerated example of what researchers call the **third variable problem**. Because correlational research may not attempt to control extraneous variables directly, these variables often provide an explanation for the correlation found—that is, rather than A causing B or B causing A, an unknown third variable, C, might be causing both A and B to happen. C is an uncontrolled third variable (or variables—it is often the case that more than one uncontrolled variable lies behind a correlation). Can you think of third variables that could produce the alleged golf-peace correlation? Economic prosperity perhaps? Highly prosperous countries might be more likely to be peaceful and also have more time for leisure, including golf.

The relationship between watching violent TV programming and children's aggressiveness provides a clear example of the third variable problem. As we've already seen, it is possible that watching TV violence increases aggression (A → B) but that causality in the opposite direction could also occur (B → A). Children who are already aggressive might seek out and watch violent programs. The third possibility is that both A and B result from a third variable, C (C → A and B). For instance, perhaps the parents are violent people. They cause their children to be violent by modeling aggressive behavior, which the children imitate, and they also cause their children to watch a lot of TV. The children might watch TV in order to lie low and avoid contact with parents who are always physically punishing them. Another third variable might be a lack of verbal fluency. Perhaps children are aggressive because they don't argue effectively, and they also watch a lot of TV as a way of avoiding verbal contact with others.

Sometimes, trying to identify third variables is a purely speculative affair. On other occasions, however, one might have reason to suspect a particular third variable is operating. If so, and if it is possible to measure this third variable, its effects can be evaluated using a procedure called **partial correlation**, which attempts to control for third variables statistically. For example, suppose you know that the correlation between reading speed and reading comprehension is high, +.55 perhaps (example from Sprinthall, 2000). Furthermore, you suspect that a third variable, IQ, might be producing this correlation—that is, high IQ might yield both rapid reading and strong comprehension. To complete a partial correlation, you would correlate (a) IQ and reading speed and (b) IQ and reading comprehension.

Let's suppose these correlations turn out to be +.70 and +.72, respectively, high enough for you to suspect that IQ might be an influential third variable. Calculating a partial correlation involves incorporating all three of these correlations (see Sprinthall [2000] for the exact procedure). What results is a partial correlation that measures the remaining relationship between reading speed and reading comprehension, with IQ *partialed out* or *controlled*. In this case, the partial correlation turns out to be +.10. Thus, when IQ is statistically controlled ("partialed out"), the correlation between speed and comprehension virtually disappears, which means that IQ is indeed an important third variable making a major contribution to the original +.55 correlation between speed and comprehension. On the other hand, if you complete a partial correlation procedure and the original correlation does not change much, then you can rule out a third variable. That is exactly what happened in the Eron et al. (1972) study.

Several partial correlations were calculated by Eron and his colleagues (1972) to see if any important third variables might be responsible for the significant correlation (+.31) between 3rd-grade preference for violence and 13th-grade aggressiveness. Eron et al. identified 12 potential third variables, including peer-rated aggression, father's occupational status, and child's IQ. But, the partial correlations ranged from +.25 to +.31, indicating that *none* of the 12 factors were very different from the original correlation of +.31. Even taking into account these other factors, the correlation between early preference for violent TV programs and later aggressiveness remained close to +.31. The analysis strengthened their conclusion "that there is a probable causative influence of watching violent television programs in [the] early formative years on later aggression" (p. 263).

There are two different types of third variables that may help explain a correlation: a mediator and a moderator. Each is accompanied by advanced statistical analyses to test to see whether the variable is a factor in a correlation between two variables (Baron & Kenny, 1986). A **mediating variable** (or mediator) is one that explains how or why a relationship exists between two variables. For example, there is a wealth of research out there that demonstrates a correlation between alcohol consumption and engaging in risky sexual behavior (see Cooper, 2006 for a brief review). Keep in mind that because of the issue of directionality, we don't know if consuming more alcohol causes risky sexual behavior, or vice versa. But, much research that has been gathered seems to suggest directionality in the relationship. What factors might be creating this correlation between alcohol use and sex? One factor that helps explain this correlation is poor impulse control. Figure 9.6a depicts the mediating role that poor impulse control has on the relationship between alcohol use and sexual behavior. Consuming alcohol can reduce controlling one's impulses, which

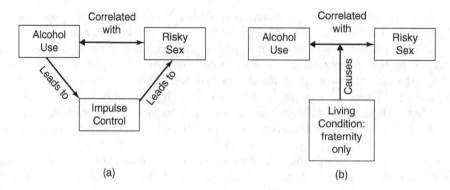

FIGURE 9.6

Mediating (a) and Moderating (b) effects on the correlation between alcohol consumption and risky sexual behavior.

in turn leads to engaging in risky sexual behavior. Here, impulse control explains *why* the relationship exists between alcohol and sex. If impulse control is statistically tested as a mediator, then the original correlation between alcohol use and sex is reduced, much like what occurs with partial correlation techniques described above. This gives you a clearer indication that impulse control is a driving force behind the correlation between alcohol use and engaging in risky sex.

A **moderating variable** (or moderator) is one that explains under what conditions does the relationship between two variables exist; this can include for what types of people or when does the correlation exist. It is similar to what we described as independent variables in Chapter 5, but importantly here, these factors are not experimentally manipulated. One factor that might be important in explaining the relationship between alcohol use and sex is one's living condition, such as whether one is living alone or in a fraternity house. A moderating variable might be that the correlation between alcohol use and having risky sex is because of those living in a fraternity, but the relationship does not exist for those who live alone. Figure 9.6b shows the moderating role that living conditions have on the correlation between alcohol use and sex. Here, it is living in a fraternity house (in contrast to living alone) that explains (or causes) the relationship between alcohol use and having sex. A fraternity house may be place where more alcohol is consumed, which may also be related to partaking in risky sexual behavior.

Combining Non-Experimental and Experimental Methods

We have seen that causal conclusions cannot be drawn from studies reporting simple correlations between two variables. We have also seen, as in the Eron et al. (1972) study, that strategies exist to mitigate the directionality (cross-lagged panel correlations) and third variable interpretation problems (partial correlations). Another common strategy for increasing confidence in causality is to do a correlational study, use it to create causal hypotheses, and then follow the correlational study with experimental studies. This was the strategy used in the following Research Example, which first showed a relationship between loneliness and a tendency to anthropomorphize, and then showed that feelings of loneliness could directly cause this anthropomorphizing tendency.

Research Example 28—Combining Methods

To be anthropomorphic is to assign human characteristics to non-human objects. We anthropomorphize when we think our dog is smiling and therefore pleased with us, when we think of the deity as an old guy with a white beard, when we think that ants have a really impressive work ethic, and so on. Epley, Akalis, Waytz, and Cacioppo (2008) wondered if the tendency to anthropomorphize could be related to loneliness, whether there was a connection between "loneliness and perceived agency in gadgets, Gods, and greyhounds" (p. 114). They started with the assumption that people generally value congenial relationships with others and that people who are lonely have, by definition, an insufficient supply of these relationships. It occurred to them that one way for lonely people to create a feeling of social connection might be to anthropomorphize objects.

Epley et al.'s (2008) first of three studies ("gadgets") was a simple correlational one, designed to see if a relationship between loneliness and anthropomorphism existed. It did. Twenty subjects completed a brief personality test for loneliness. Their tendency to anthropomorphize was assessed with a clever set of surveys. They read descriptions of four creative gadgets—for instance, one was called "Clocky," and was described as "a wheeled alarm clock that 'runs away' so that you must get up to turn it off" (p. 115). After reading the description of each gadget, subjects rated the gadget on five attributes that assessed anthropomorphism (e.g., the extent to which the gadget had a mind of its own) and three attributes that were non-anthropomorphic (e.g., the gadget was efficient). What they found was a correlation of +.53 between loneliness and the tendency to agree with the anthropomorphic attributes. Subjects who scored high on loneliness were more likely to think Clocky had a mind of its own.

After establishing that correlation between loneliness and anthropomorphism, Epley et al. (2008) recognized they had to go further. As they put it, "a correlational study using a dispositional measure of social disconnection cannot demonstrate that social disconnection caused the observed results. We therefore adopted an experimental approach in the next two studies in order to manipulate social connection directly" (p. 115). Directly manipulating social disconnection (i.e., to create feelings of loneliness) means random assignment, of course, and that is exactly what the researchers did. In their second study ("Gods"), they gave subjects a standardized personality inventory said to yield a personality description and a description of "future life predictions" (p. 116). What subjects did not know was that the future life prediction was bogus; subjects were randomly assigned to be given one of two types of false feedback. Those assigned to the "disconnected" condition were given a paragraph that summarized their so-called personality inventory, indicating they would probably spend their lives being alone; those in the "connected" condition were led to believe they would have many future satisfying social relationships. After being given the false feedback, all subjects were asked to indicate how much they believed in the reality of supernatural objects (i.e., ghosts, the Devil, miracles, curses, God). As Epley et al. predicted, those in the disconnected condition reported a significantly higher level of anthropomorphic belief in the supernatural.[10]

In a third study ("greyhounds"), Epley et al., (2008) manipulated a feeling of connectedness by randomly assigning subjects to groups that would see brief video clips designed to elicit feelings of disconnection (from *Cast Away*, in which a FedEx worker finds himself alone on an island) or connection (from *Major League*, in which a group of teammates celebrate). After viewing the films, subjects rated pets (either their own pet or the pet of a friend) on a series of scales, including some that rated clearly anthropomorphic traits (e.g., thoughtful, considerate). To reduce *demand characteristics* (Chapter 6), Epley et al. told subjects the pet ratings were "ostensibly . . . part of an unrelated experiment" (p. 117). At this point you can guess the results: Those who watched the video designed to produce feelings of disconnection showed more anthropomorphism than those in the other group. In sum, Epley et al., believed they had demonstrated not just a correlation between loneliness and anthropomorphism but a causal connection between the two. Make someone feel disconnected from others and that person might start to see human intentions in gadgets, might increase their beliefs in God, and might consider greyhounds thoughtful.

---

[10] Epley et al., (2008) also included a subject variable in their study—50 of the subjects in the study were self-described as believers in God; 49 were non-believers. The study was thus a 2 (believer or not) x 2 (connected or not) factorial. Unsurprisingly, believers scored higher than non-believers. There was no interaction; the connection manipulation increased the level of reported belief for both believers and nonbelievers.

As you can tell from this chapter, survey research and correlational procedures contribute substantially to modern research in psychology. Correlations are often necessary when experimental procedures cannot possibly be used, and with the development of highly sophisticated statistical procedures, questions of cause and effect can be addressed more directly than in the past.

Much non-experimental research takes place outside the laboratory. In the next chapter, we'll look more closely at observational research and archival research, and in Chapter 11, we will explore applied research by outlining the details of several so-called quasi-experimental designs. We'll also look at program evaluation research as a specific example of applied research that is becoming increasingly important for the social service industry and for education.

CHAPTER SUMMARY

Survey Research

The primary purpose of survey research is to gather descriptive information about people's self-described attitudes, opinions, feelings, and behaviors. Unlike most research in psychology, which typically relies on convenience samples, surveys are most effective when administered to a representative sample. Conclusions drawn from survey research can be erroneous if the group sampled does not reflect the population targeted by the survey. Researchers must have clear empirical questions in mind and must exercise great care in the wording and organization of survey items. Survey data can be affected by such respondent biases as social desirability and response acquiescence. Surveys can be administered in face-to-face interviews, by means of written questionnaires, over the phone, or online.

Analyzing Data from Non-Experimental Designs

Two variables are correlated when a reliable relationship exists between them. The relationship is a direct one in a positive correlation and an inverse one in a negative correlation. The strength of the relationship can be inferred from a scatterplot, from the absolute value of the correlation coefficient (e.g., Pearson's r for interval and ratio data), and from the coefficient of determination, found by squaring the correlation coefficient. Knowing a correlation allows predictions to be made through a process called regression analysis. If there is a significant correlation between two variables, A and B, then knowing the value of A enables the prediction of B with greater than chance probability.

Interpreting Correlational Results

A significant correlation between variables A and B does not, by itself, allow us to conclude that A causes B. The directionality problem is that causality can be in either of two directions—A causing B or B causing A. The directionality problem can be reduced if there is a time lag between the measurement of A and B, as in a cross-lagged panel correlation study. The third variable problem is that, for many correlations, the relationship results from one or a combination of variables that naturally covary with the variables being measured. That is, some third variable might cause changes in both variables A and B. The influence of third variables can be evaluated using a partial correlations or mediation-moderation analyses.

Combining Non-Experimental and Experimental Methods

Surveys can serve as a basis for extracting a large amount of information about individuals' attitudes, beliefs, opinions, and behaviors. Surveys and interviews can provide a wealth of information and can provide a basis for describing behavior. They can also serve as the first step in a more comprehensive understanding of human behavior by providing a basis upon which experimental designs can be built. Non-experimental designs can provide good descriptive information without causal effects, whereas experimental designs all researchers to derive causal conclusions from the data.

CHAPTER REVIEW QUESTIONS

1. If you are conducting a mail-in written survey, what can you do to increase the return rate? What is meant by a nonresponse bias?

2. Use the hamburger example to illustrate the dangers of using leading questions in survey research.

3. Use the case of the news journalist Christine Craft to illustrate how survey research can be misused.

4. What is response acquiescence, and how can it be avoided?

5. Describe the advantages and disadvantages of face-to-face interviews as a way of doing survey research.

6. Describe two varieties of online surveys. What are the advantages and disadvantages of online surveying?

7. Describe how the shape of a scatterplot changes when comparing (a) positive and negative correlation and (b) strong and weak correlations.

8. What is the coefficient of determination, and what does it tell you? Use the example of SAT scores and GPA to illustrate.

9. A researcher finds that people with high self-esteem tend to exercise more than people with low self-esteem.

Explain the directionality problem and how it could influence the interpretation of this correlation.

10. A researcher finds that children who play lots of video games also tend to be aggressive with their peers at school. Explain the third variable problem and how it could influence the interpretation of this correlation

11. Use the Eron et al. (1972) study, which found a significant relationship between 3rd-grade TV preferences and "13th-grade" aggression, to explain why you would use a partial correlation procedure.

12. Distinguish between bivariate and multivariate analysis and describe the logic behind the use of a multiple regression procedure.

APPLICATIONS EXERCISES

Exercise 9.1.   Deciding on a Survey Method

For each of the hypotheses listed below, identify the best methodological approach from among the following possibilities. Indicate the reason(s) for your choice. Some items have more than one correct answer.

mail-in survey	interview survey
phone survey	online survey

1. When respondents are given the opportunity and encouragement to explain their opinions on controversial issues, their beliefs are usually determined to be based on anecdotal evidence.

2. There is a correlation between online shopping and attitudes about risk-taking: Those who shop online regularly tend to be willing to take risks.

3. A national sample of 2,000 people is chosen for a consumer survey on preferred cable TV shows.

4. College students who major in the physical sciences tend to hold more rigid stereotypes than students who major in the social sciences.

5. Facebook users present more positive information about themselves than negative information.

6. Attitudes about transgender identity differ among members of the LGBTQ community.

Exercise 9.2.   Improving Poor Survey Items

The following are several examples of items that could be found on surveys. Some are in the form of closed questions, others in the form of agree/disagree statements. For each item, (a) identify what is wrong and (b) rewrite it so as to solve the problem.

1. Have you had an upset stomach lately?

2. Highly prejudiced people are usually hostile and not very smart.

3. In your opinion, how young is the average smoker?

4. Do you agree with most people that violations of seat-belt laws should result in harsh penalties?

5. Most doctors have a superior attitude.

6. People who are overweight lack willpower and are usually unhappy.

Exercise 9.3.   Interpreting Correlations

Each of the following describes the outcome of a hypothetical bivariate correlational study. State whether you believe the correlation is a positive or a negative one. With both the directionality problem and the third variable problem in mind, describe at least two ways of interpreting each.

1. There is a correlation between the level of dominance shown by mothers and the level of shyness shown by children.

2. There is a correlation between depression and aerobic fitness level.

3. There is a correlation between the number of books found in the home and the college GPAs of the students living in those homes.

4. There is a correlation between seating location in class and grades—the closer to the front, the higher the grade.

5. There is a correlation between grades and test anxiety.

6. There is a correlation between a student's college grades and the number of text messages sent per month.

7. There is a correlation between milk drinking and cancer—the more milk one drinks, the greater the chances of getting cancer.

ANSWERS TO SELF TESTS

✓9.1

1. Double-barreled question.
2. This is basic information that identifies respondents (e.g., age and gender); it is best to put it at the end of a survey.
3. Advantage: doesn't force a choice when the respondent truly does not know. Disadvantage: may be chosen too often.

✓9.2

1. Advantages: follow-up questions, ambiguous questions can be clarified. Disadvantages: cost, logistics, representativeness. It means that the sample is a good reflection of the wider population; survey results from a representative sample can be generalized to the population.
2. Combining methods of survey delivery, such as sending an email or mailing a letter prior to a phone survey.
3. Email, listservs, social media sites, and MTurk.

✓9.3

1. Negative; high scores on some measure of depression would be associated with low scores on a measure of exercise, and vice versa.
2. Predictor = high school grades; criterion = college grades.
3. In simple, linear regression there is one predictor variable, whereas in multiple regression, there is more than one predictor variable; in both, there will be just one criterion variable.

Non-Experimental Design II: Observational and Archival Methods

10

PREVIEW & CHAPTER OBJECTIVES

In this chapter, we will examine two methods for doing research in psychology that are primarily descriptive in nature: observational research and archival research. Observational methods are certainly involved in other methods, but here they serve as methods designed to provide accurate descriptions of observed behaviors that occur in specific environments. With archival methods, observations, surveys, interviews, or psychological testing have already been completed by other researchers, and the data are available to be used by other researchers to evaluate relationships between variables. Both observational and archival methods may rely on qualitative analysis of the phenomena being studied, but they can include sophisticated quantitative analysis as well. Both methods can be a rich source of ideas for further research. When you finish this chapter, you should be able to:

- Distinguish between naturalistic and participant observation methods.

- Articulate the problems that can occur in observational research (control, bias, reactivity, and ethics) and how researchers address those problems.

- Explain how thematic analysis can be a tool for evaluating qualitative data.

- Define archival research and explain why archival research is non-experimental.

- Describe the advantages and limitations of archival research.

- Describe methods of analyzing data from observational and archival research.

- Explain how meta-analysis can be used to evaluate replication of research results.

   In Chapter 3, we discussed creativity in science. In the context of how researchers develop ideas for research, we pointed out that creative thinkers in science recognize connections between ideas that might seem at first glance to be unrelated to each other. It is also true that creative scientists can see connections between methods that might not ordinarily be thought of together. In this chapter, you will learn about observational methods, which involve carefully examining what happens as it happens, and archival methods, which involve carefully examining what has already happened in the past. Combining methodologies also requires creativity. In Chapter 9, we described a study by Eply et al. (2008) who used both survey and experimental methods to answer empirical questions about loneliness and anthropomorphism. In this chapter, we will see how a series of studies by Rozin, Kablick, Pete, Fischler, and Shields (2003) used both observational and archival methods to investigate what has been called the French paradox, the fact that the French tend to have a calorie-rich diet, yet seem to be, on average, skinnier and less prone to heart disease than Americans. Rozin and his colleagues wondered if portion size might be the culprit. Perhaps Americans just eat more per serving than the French. Two of their studies were observational—they observed and measured portion size differences in comparable restaurants in Philadelphia and Paris (e.g., chains such as McDonald's and Pizza Hut) and they went to restaurants and observed people eating. Also, two of their studies were archival—they examined portion sizes in Zagat restaurant guides and in a variety of cookbook menus. Together, this interesting combination of studies demonstrated that Americans indeed tend to eat larger portions than the French and that Americans also tend to eat these portions more quickly.

As you can see, both observational and archival research can produce really interesting results, even though both are non-experimental in nature (e.g., no random assignment, so there's caution needed about drawing cause-and-effect conclusions). Let us now examine these methods in more detail.

Observational Research

As you recall from Chapter 1, one of the main goals of research in psychology is to provide clear and accurate descriptions of behavior. The major purpose of observational research is to produce this descriptive information. All of us observe human (and animal) behavior all the time, and we use these observations in our attempt to understand and predict what humans (and animals) will do. Psychological scientists make the same kinds of observations for the same basic reasons (understanding and predicting), but, as we shall see, they make their observations in a highly systematic fashion.

Varieties of Observational Research

Observational research with the goal of describing behavior can be divided into two broad categories, depending on the degree of experimenter involvement with participants in the study. Sometimes, the researcher does not interact in any substantial way with the group being observed, while at other times the researcher is directly involved with the group being studied and might even become a member of it. These types of studies are called *naturalistic observation* and *participant observation*, respectively, and we will elaborate on them shortly.

Observational research can vary in other ways. First, some observational studies are more global, observing a variety of behaviors, while others are narrower, focusing on a specific behavior. The wide-ranging studies of primate behavior by Jane Goodall (1990) illustrate the former strategy; over a number of years, she studied virtually every aspect of chimpanzee behavior in the wild. An example of the latter strategy is a study by O'Brien, Walley, Anderson-Smith, and Drabman (1982), who observed the specific behavior of "snack selection" by obese and non-obese children at a movie theater (they were surprised to find no difference). Second, researchers impose varying degrees of structure on the setting being observed. This can range from zero, when the researcher simply enters some environment and observes behavior without trying to influence it in any way, to quite a bit, when the researcher creates a structured setting and observes what occurs in it. As an example of the former, a study with minimal imposed structure, Forsyth and Lennox (2010) examined "gender differences in the choreography of alcohol-related violence" (p. 75) by spending lots of time in bars observing fights between pairs of men or pairs of women. Most bar fights featured men, but almost 40% involved women, and the form of the aggression differed: more punching for men fighting other men and more hair-pulling for women fighting other women. Men also had a more predictable pre-fight ritual or "choreography" (facing each other, expanding chest muscles, etc.). Fights involving women were less ritualized (making it more difficult for staff to see a fight coming and intervene), and other women often intervened to stop the fight but got caught up in the action. This would often "result in intervening [women] being pulled in, to produce an entangled melee" (p. 84).

An example of more highly structured observation research is a study by Peterson, Ridley-Johnson, and Carter (1984), who studied helping behavior in a preschool setting. Because this behavior did not often occur naturally, the researchers created a situation that increased the chances that helping would occur. Children took turns wearing a "supersuit" that enhanced their status in the class. The supersuit was a smock that was difficult for students to put on by themselves—help was needed. Hence, the researchers were able to add structure to a setting to increase the frequency of otherwise rare events (helping). One surprising result of the study was the way in which recipients responded to being helped—children rarely reinforced others for helping. In fact, "more child recipients actually gave negative consequences (e.g., 'go away' and a shove in response to another child's attempt to help fasten the suit) than positive consequences for helping" (p. 238).

Studies with a very high degree of structure often take place in a laboratory environment and are sometimes called *laboratory observation studies*. One famous set of laboratory observation studies featured a procedure called the "strange situation" (Ainsworth, Blehar, Waters, & Wall, 1978), designed to investigate parent–child attachment patterns. The strange situation incorporates a sequence of events in which a parent, a child, and a stranger interact in a laboratory environment with observation occurring via two-way mirrors (the observers can see through the mirror, but to the child, it appears to be a regular mirror).

In what follows, we will examine the two main forms of observational research (naturalistic and participant) more closely, describe challenges posed by observational research in general, and provide in-depth examples of (a) a naturalistic observation study of parent–child interaction in a science museum and (b) a participant observation study in a homeless shelter.

Naturalistic Observation

In a **naturalistic observation** study, the goal is to study the behaviors of people or animals as they act in their everyday environments. Settings for naturalistic observation studies range from preschools to malls to the Amazon rainforest, and the individuals observed have included humans of all ages and animals of virtually every species. In some cases, semi-artificial environments are sufficiently "natural" for the research to be considered a naturalistic observation. Studying animal behavior in modern zoos, which often simulate the animals' normal environment to a considerable degree, is an example.[1]

In order for the researcher to feel confident the behavior being observed is typical in the observed environment, it is important that it not be affected by the experimenter's presence. There are two strategies for accomplishing this. First, in some naturalistic studies, the observer is hidden from those being observed. In a study of sharing behavior among preschoolers, for example, observers may be in the next room, viewing the children through a two-way mirror. In a mall, an observer studying the mating rituals of the suburban adolescent could simply sit on a bench in

---

[1] The question of what constitutes a "natural" environment for observation has been a matter of debate for some time. At the turn of the 20th century, for example, the Canadian comparative psychologist Wesley Mills criticized E. L. Thorndike's puzzle box studies (see Box 12.1 in Chapter 12) because of the "artificiality" of the puzzle box environment. Mills (1899) argued that trying to understand everyday cat behavior from such studies would be like trying to understand human behavior by "enclose[ing] a living man in a coffin, lower[ing] him . . . into the earth, and attempt[ing] to deduce normal psychology from his conduct" (p. 266). Mills went on to report how much he had learned about his cat's remarkable motor coordination by watching it climb on bookcases. In his reply, Thorndike (1899) countered that bookcases were no more "natural" for cats than puzzle boxes and that cats constantly face new situations. He asked, Who is to say whether one is more "natural" than another?

a strategic location and appear to be reading. In other studies, the observer may not be present at all; some naturalistic observation studies (including Research Example 29, described later in this chapter) use video recorders. The videos are viewed later and scored for the behaviors being investigated.

In some naturalistic observations, especially those involving animals, it can be impossible for the observer to remain hidden; the subjects quickly sense the presence of an outsider. Under these circumstances, the observer typically makes no attempt to hide. Rather, it is hoped that after time, the animals will become so habituated to the observer that they will behave normally. With some species, the process can take quite a bit of time. When she first went to study chimpanzees in the East African country of Tanganyika (now Tanzania), for instance, Jane Goodall had to wait 3 months before the chimps would let her observe them from a distance of 60 feet (Morell, 1995). After a few more months, they became even more accustomed to her. Louis Leakey, her mentor, wrote proudly to a colleague that she "has now had a Chimpanzee family sitting within ten feet of her, behaving in a normal fashion as though she was not there" (quoted in Morell, 1995, p. 249). This habituation strategy is also common in anthropology, in which field workers spend long periods living among native members of remote cultures.

Participant Observation

Occasionally, researchers will join a group being observed, or at least make their presence known to the group, thus making the study a **participant observation**. The chief virtue of this strategy is its power to get the investigator as close to the action as possible. Being a participating member of the group can give the researcher firsthand insights that remain hidden to a more remote observer. In some cases, perhaps because a group is closed to outsiders and therefore not available for naturalistic observation (e.g., a college fraternity), participant observation might be the only option. Participant observation is a common technique of qualitative research because the descriptions usually involve a narrative analysis of the group being studied.

One of psychology's classic studies involved participant observation. In it, a small group of social psychologists joined a religious cult in order to examine the thinking that characterized its members. In particular, they examined this empirical question: If you publicly prophesize the end of the world and the world fails to end, how do you deal with your failed prophecy? The answer was surprising enough to contribute to the development of one of social psychology's best-known theories: the theory of cognitive dissonance that you learned about in Chapter 3. To learn more about this study of what happens when prophecy fails, read Box 10.1.

BOX 10.1   CLASSIC STUDIES—When Prophecy Fails

One of social psychology's dominant theories in the second half of the 20th century was that of cognitive dissonance, developed by Leon Festinger. As you recall from Chapter 3, this theory proposed that when we experience thoughts that contradict each other, we will be uncomfortable (i.e., we will experience cognitive dissonance). We then will be motivated to reduce the dissonance in order to return to a state of cognitive balance. One prediction derived from the theory is that if we exert a tremendous effort and the outcome is not what we had expected, we will need to convince ourselves the effort was worthwhile anyway. Festinger got

the chance to test the prediction after encountering a news story with the following headline (Festinger, Riecken, & Schachter, 1956, p. 30):

Prophecy from Planet. Clarion Call to City: Flee That Flood. It'll Swamp Us on Dec. 21, Outer Space Tells Suburbanite

The story described how a certain Mrs. Keetch had predicted a flood that would destroy most of North America in late December. How did she know? She was in direct contact with aliens from a planet called Clarion who had been visiting Earth in their flying saucers and had seen fault lines that were about to rupture and open the floodgates. Mrs. Keetch gathered a small group of followers, in effect a religious cult, and they became devoted to convincing the world to repent of their sins before it was too late. And time was running out; the story appeared just 4 months before the predicted catastrophe.

Festinger guessed the flood would not occur, so he became interested in how Mrs. Keetch and the group would react during the aftermath of a failed prophecy. He decided to see firsthand. Over the next several weeks, along with two colleagues and five hired observers, Festinger joined the group as a participant observer. What transpired is described in a delightful book (Festinger et al., 1956) with the same title as this box. From a methodological standpoint, there are several points worth noting.

First, recording the data created a number of problems. The observers did not want to reveal their true purpose, so they could hardly take notes during the meetings at Mrs. Keetch's house. Hence, they found it necessary to rely on memory more than they would have liked. The problem was overcome to some degree when they hit on the idea of using the bathroom as a place to write down as much of their narrative data as they could. A second problem was a concern about how the group's behavior might be influenced by the observers' presence. At no point did they believe the group knew their true purpose, but the researchers were concerned that their presence strengthened certain of the group's beliefs. Because so many new people seemed to be joining the group over a short period,

Mrs. Keetch believed (and therefore the group believed) the mass joining was a "sign from above" that the flood prophecy was correct. Two of Festinger's observers were believed by the group to have been "'sent' by the Guardians" (Festinger et al., 1956, p. 242), the residents of Clarion, and one observer was actually believed to be *from* Clarion. Hence, the participant observers probably strengthened the convictions of Mrs. Keetch's small group, the effects of which were difficult to assess. This factor also posed an ethical dilemma. By strengthening the group's convictions, it could be argued that Festinger and his colleagues contributed to their "pathology."

As you know, because you're reading this now, the world didn't end that December 21 in the 1950s. This was not the only failed prophecy. Mrs. Keetch also told the group the Guardians would send a space ship that would land in her backyard on December 17 to carry them to safety. Of course, the ship didn't arrive and the world didn't end 4 days later. Did the group become discouraged, give up, call Mrs. Keetch insane, and return to their normal lives? No. In fact, most of them became even *more* vigorous in their proselytizing, at least for a time. Apparently, in order to justify their efforts, they convinced themselves their work had *prevented* the catastrophe; the group "spread so much light that God had saved the world from destruction" (p. 169). Hence, rather than quitting after a prophecy fails, one may find that his or her commitment can actually be strengthened. More generally, Festinger concluded that when we expend great effort, dissonance is produced, and we feel internal pressure to convince ourselves the effort was worthwhile.

Challenges Facing Observational Methods

The researcher using observational methods must be prepared to counter several problems, including the absence of control and the possibilities of observer bias and subject reactivity. There are also ethical dilemmas to be resolved.

Absence of Control

Some degree of control occurs in observational studies (e.g., operational definitions of behaviors to be observed), but, in general, the observational researcher must take what circumstances provide. Because of this lack of direct control, the conclusions from observational studies must be drawn very carefully. If an observer records that child A picks up a toy and shortly thereafter child B picks up a duplicate of the same toy, does it mean B is imitating A? Perhaps, but other interpretations are possible, the most obvious one being that the toy is simply attractive.

Despite the lack of control, observational research can be a rich source of ideas for further study and it can sometimes serve the purpose of falsification, an important strategy for theory testing.

An observation consistent with theoretical expectations provides useful inductive support, but an observation that contradicts a theory is perhaps even more informative. For example, an influential theory of animal aggression in the 1960s (Lorenz, 1966) held that fighting between members of the same species was hardly ever fatal to the combatants, except for humans. For years, those studying aggression argued over the reasons why human aggression seemed so different from and so much worse than animal aggression. However, explaining the difference presupposes the difference truly exists. Goodall's research, however, raised serious questions about the alleged non-fatality of animal aggression. In conflicts over territory among chimpanzees, for example, something analogous to "border wars" occurs (Goodall, 1978). If a lone chimp from one group encounters several chimps from another group, the lone chimp will almost certainly be attacked and is likely to be killed. This finding raised serious questions about Lorenz's claim that non-human aggression is seldom if ever fatal.

In a more recent example, Boesch-Achermann and Boesch (1993) observed several instances of parent chimpanzees teaching their offspring how to use tools (a hammer/anvil operation) to open several varieties of nuts. This is an important finding that questioned earlier beliefs. As the researchers put it:

> Recent critical reviews of animal learning processes have denied that animals have the ability to imitate, but the teaching instances we observed would have no functional role if the chimpanzees did not have an imitative capacity. Many people still consider pedagogy one of the uniquely human attributes; our observations of chimpanzees indicate otherwise. (p. 20)

Despite control difficulties, observational research can provide important and useful information. It can call ideas into question, and it can also suggest hypotheses for further study. Hence, the Boesch-Achermann and Boesch study questioned prior claims about the teaching abilities of chimps, but the study could also lead to further research on the teaching capacities of nonhuman primates. For instance, could chimpanzees in captivity that have learned an operant task teach it to their offspring?

Observer Bias

A second problem for those doing observational research is experimenter bias. In Chapter 6, you learned that when experimenters expect certain outcomes to occur, they might act in ways that could bring about such a result. In observational research, **observer bias** means having preconceived ideas about what will be observed and having those ideas color one's observations. For example, consider what might happen if someone is studying aggression in pre-schoolers and believes from the outset that little boys will be more aggressive than little girls. For that observer, the exact same ambiguous behavior could be scored as aggressive if a boy did it but not aggressive if performed by a girl. Similarly, in an animal study, observers with different beliefs about whether animals can be altruistic might interpret ambiguous behaviors differently. Bias can also occur because observational studies may collect huge amounts of information. Deciding which observations to report involves reducing this information to a manageable size, and the choices about what to select as relevant and what to omit can be affected by preconceived beliefs.

Biasing effects can be reduced by using good operational definitions and by training observers to identify the precisely defined target behaviors. When actually making the observations, **behavior checklists** are normally used. These are lists of predefined behaviors that observers are trained to spot. Consider, for example, the care taken in a study that observed the behavior of pizza deliverers, whose driving accident rate is three times the national average. Ludwig and Geller (1997) used a checklist "developed over a decade of driver observations and over 2 years of observing pizza deliverers" (p. 254). Part of the list included observations of driver behavior while turning onto a main road from an intersection near the pizza shop. There was a stop sign there, and the behaviors were placed into three categories: a complete stop, a "slow rolling advance," and a "fast rolling advance." Each had its own definition; for instance, the slow rolling advance was defined as when the vehicle moved through the stop sign at "approximately the walking speed of an adult" (p. 255). Observers also recorded oncoming traffic conditions, whether the driver used a directional signal, and whether the driver wore a seat belt.

In addition to defining behaviors with precision, another way to control for observer bias is to have several observers present and see if their records match. This is *inter-rater reliability*, a concept you encountered in Research Example 12 in Chapter 7. Within the context of observational studies, this type of reliability is also called inter-observer reliability and is usually measured in terms of the percentage of times that observers agree. Of course, both observers could be biased in exactly the same way, but a combination of checklists, observer training, and agreement among several observers generally controls bias. Bias also can be reduced to the extent that procedures are mechanized. For example, a video recording increases objectivity by making it possible for the same event to be observed multiple times.

Finally, bias can be reduced by introducing sampling procedures for systematically selecting a subset of the available information for observation and analysis. For example, a procedure called **time sampling** is sometimes used in observational studies. Rather than trying to maintain a continuous record of everything occurring, behavior is sampled at predefined times and only at those times. These times can be selected according to some rule, or they may be randomly selected. Similarly, **event sampling** selects a specific set of events for observation; others are ignored.

Participant Reactivity

Think about all the things you do in a typical day. Would you do them all in exactly the same way if you knew you were being observed? Probably not. In all likelihood, you would show **reactivity**—that is, your behavior would be influenced by the knowledge that you were being observed and recorded. Obviously, this problem can occur in observational research and is the reason for the popularity of devices like two-way mirrors. The problem also exists when animals are the subjects of observation and the observers cannot hide. As mentioned earlier, researchers assume that after time the animals will become accustomed to the presence of outsiders, but it is difficult to evaluate the extent to which this occurs. Reactivity can be a special problem for participant observation, in which the observers are involved in the group activities. As you recall from the Festinger prophecy study, the researchers were quite concerned about how their presence might affect the group's behavior.

Reactivity can be reduced by using **unobtrusive measures**. These are measures taken of behavior, either directly or indirectly, when the subject is unaware of the measurement being made. Direct unobtrusive measures include hidden video or audio recordings or behavior samples. Indirect unobtrusive measures record events and outcomes one assumes resulted from certain behaviors even though the behaviors themselves were not observed. Webb, Campbell, Schwartz, Sechrest, and Grove (1981) describe a number of indirect measures, some quite creative. Here's a sample:

- contents of trash to study eating and drinking habits

- accumulation of dust on library books as an indication of usage

- degree of wear on floor coverings placed in strategic locations to study foot traffic

- analysis of political bumper stickers in an election year

Ethics

As you surely recognize by now, reducing reactivity raises the ethical problems of invading privacy and lack of informed consent, particularly if children or members of some other special population (refer to Chapter 2 for more on special populations) are being observed. Wouldn't you be a bit disturbed to discover that researchers were hiding under the bed in your dorm, keeping track of everything you said and did? Believe it or not, that study has already been done, although quite clearly it would not gain IRB approval today. In a 1938 study by Henle and Hubbell, designed to classify conservational speech into "ego-related, social, and object-related" categories (p. 228), the researchers "concealed themselves under beds in students' rooms where tea parties were being held, eavesdropped in dormitory smoking-rooms and dormitory wash-rooms and listened to telephone conversation" (p. 230). One finding: These 1938 college students had a high enough percentage of ego-related talk that Henle and Hubbell thought they were just as self-centered as children. Before you read further, consider Silverman's (1975) study of the potential legal ramifications of doing research outside the friendly confines of the laboratory.

BOX 10.2   ETHICS—A Matter of Privacy

Unlike laboratory research, field research sometimes causes problems with informed consent, freedom to leave the study, debriefing, and invasion of privacy. An interesting study by Silverman (1975) illustrates why researchers are sometimes hesitant about doing field studies. He gave descriptions of 10 published field studies to two lawyers and asked them to judge whether the procedures might violate any laws or lead to any invasion of privacy. The procedures, based on actual studies in social psychology, included having a confederate fall down in a subway car to see if anyone would help, leaving cars in different places to see if they would be vandalized, going to shoe stores and trying on many pairs of shoes, and asking for small amounts of money from passersby.

The two lawyers gave almost *opposite* responses. Lawyer 1 believed intent and a concern for the greater good were the key factors. The studies were designed for the ultimate good of increasing knowledge of human behavior and not for the personal gain of the scientist. He believed that if charges were brought against the psychologist (e.g., laws against panhandling), the judge would "seek a balance between degree of annoyance and degree of legitimate purpose" (Silverman, 1975, p. 766). Lawyer 2, however, felt several of the studies contained grounds not only for a civil suit on the part of individuals not wanting to be subjects of research (i.e., invasion of privacy) but also for criminal action in the form of harassment, fraud, criminal trespass, and even disorderly conduct! Note that even with psychologist-friendly Lawyer 1, the researcher could still wind up in court.

Silverman was disconcerted enough by the responses to bring the description of the subway helping behavior study to a judge for his considered opinion about whether civil or criminal charges could be brought. In general, the judge sided with Lawyer 1, at least on the issue of criminal charges, but also pointed out that experiments in the field might have unforeseen consequences that could result in a negligence suit. In short, the psychologist doing field research faces serious risks that do not occur in the laboratory.

By the way, you might be interested to know that Lawyer 1, who didn't think the researcher would be in great jeopardy, was a successful criminal defense lawyer accustomed to seeing his clients charged but then acquitted. Lawyer 2's specialty was in medical law; he usually "defended the legal rights of patients and subjects in medical practice and research" (Silverman, 1975, p. 767). In his mind, "research psychologists invading privacy" fell into the same category as "doctors harming patients."

As you might guess, some researchers are hesitant to conduct research in the field because of concerns over privacy rights, informed consent, and even the possibility that researchers could be charged with a misdemeanor crime (e.g., disorderly conduct) or be sued. However, the APA ethics code (see Standard 8.05 of the APA code of ethics) condones the use of naturalistic observation and does not require informed consent or debriefing, provided certain safeguards are in place. For example, informed consent of participants is not considered essential if behavior is studied in public environments (as opposed to the privacy of one's dorm room), people are not interfered with in any way, and strict confidentiality and anonymity are maintained. Of course, the researcher planning a naturalistic observation study must convince an IRB that the scientific value of the study is sufficiently high.

But what about participant observation? You might have been concerned about the lack of consent in Festinger's failed prophecy study (Box 10.1). With good reason, Festinger believed he and his colleagues would never have been able to join the group if normal consent procedures had been followed. Participant observation is a fairly common form of qualitative research today, and the issue of consent is a matter of some debate. Informed consent of the group being observed from within is now common and its absence requires a strong justification (Taylor & Bogdan, 1998). Analogous to the habituation rationale for naturalistic observation, it is assumed that even if group members know they are being observed, they will eventually get used to the participant observer and behave naturally. On the other hand, in some cases, the group being studied would be unlikely to consent to a participant observer. The first author in a participant observation study by Brotsky and Giles (2007), for example, joined several online "pro-ana" groups (i.e., for "pro-anorexia"—these groups support people with eating disorders and in some cases encourage them to think of anorexia or bulimia as lifestyles and not disorders). Because these groups are highly suspicious of outsiders, the researchers were quite certain their study would never get off the ground if Brotsky identified herself as a scientist and tried to obtain informed consent. Instead, she created a profile of herself as a young woman with anorexia, was accepted by the pro-ana community, and joined in numerous chat room conversations.

Before we describe how we analyze data from observational research, consider two thought-provoking Research Examples—a naturalistic observation and a participant observation.

Research Example 29—A Naturalistic Observation

School-aged boys generally outperform girls in science, and there is evidence that part of the reason is how they are treated by teachers. Many teachers (there are exceptions, of course) seem to expect boys to do better and consequently they tend to encourage boys in a number of subtle ways (e.g., by responding more completely to science questions from boys than from girls). This is disturbing enough, but a study by Crowley, Callahan, Tenenbaum, and Allen (2001) suggests the differential treatment can begin earlier than the school years and can be a part of normal family life. They observed the behavior of parents and their children (both boys and girls) in a science museum and a quick look at Figure 10.1 tells you that big differences occurred. The study also reveals some of the methodological decisions that must be made when doing observational research.

Crowley et al. (2001) set up video cameras and microphones at 18 interactive science exhibits in a California science museum. To assure a wide representation of families, they did the study over a 30-month period, included weekdays and weekends, and tested both during the school year and in the summer. Because the museum was a fairly controlled environment, the researchers were able to accomplish one task that is normally not feasible in naturalistic observation: They were able to obtain a degree of informed consent. As families entered the museum, they were told that researchers were videotaping activity in the museum (families weren't told that

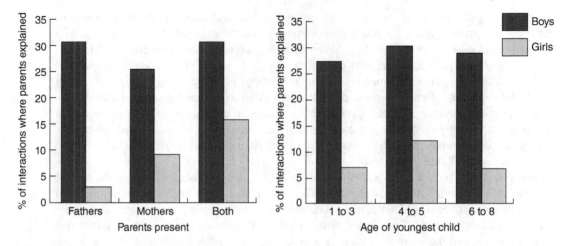

FIGURE 10.1

Differences in how young boys and girls are treated by their parents in science museums, from Crowley et al. (2001).

gender differences were being investigated). Almost all families (90%) agreed to be recorded; the children in these families were given a sticker to wear that indicated their age and enabled researchers to identify them easily on the videos. All of the children were younger than 8, and most were under 5.

Crowley et al. (2001) used a form of event sampling in their study, operationally defining the start of a trial whenever

> the first child from a family—the *target child*—engaged an exhibit and ending when he or she disengaged. The next target child was the first child from a new family who engaged the exhibit after all members of the previous target child's family had disengaged. Thus, each interaction was a unique [event] capturing the complete engagement of a particular child at an exhibit" (p. 259, italics in the original).

Trials occurred only if the child engaged the exhibit in the presence of at least one parent. The study included a total of 351 independent trials (i.e., observations made of 351 different children).

In addition to defining trials, the researchers also developed a scheme to code the verbal interactions. They decided on three categories of parental comment: "explanations," "giving directions," and "talking about evidence" (Crowley et al., 2001, p. 259). For example, a comment that would be coded as an explanation might be something like this: "'When you turn that fast, it makes more electricity' at an exhibit including a hand-cranked generator" (p. 259). *Inter-rater reliability* was assessed by having more than one rater code the interactions on 20% of the trials; agreement occurred 86% of the time.

As for the results, boys and girls did not differ in terms of how much time they spent at exhibits or in the extent to which they actively engaged the exhibits (e.g., turned the crank at the electricity exhibit). What was very different, however, was the behavior of the parents. Figure 10.1 shows the interactions during which parents gave explanation-type comments. Clearly, boys were much more likely to be given explanations than girls. From the left-hand panel, you can see that both dads *and* moms favored boys when giving explanations. The right-hand panel shows the same pattern existed regardless of the age of the child.

As in any good study, Crowley et al. (2001) considered more than one explanation for their results and they were able to rule out some alternatives (falsification again). For example, perhaps the differences resulted from boys asking more questions of their parents than girls did. Not so. In fact, very few of the explanations from parents were triggered by children's questions, and no gender differences occurred in the number of questions asked. In the 60-second intervals prior to any parental explanation, only 15% of boys and 13% of girls asked questions. Hence, although the parents brought both boys and girls to the museum, they treated their children differently once there. That differences occurred for children as young as 1 to 3 years suggests "that parents may be involved in creating gender bias in science learning years before children's first classroom science instruction" (p. 260). This study might be worth remembering, especially if you hope to raise a woman scientist someday.

Research Example 30—A Covert Participant Observation

Farrington and Robinson (1999) gained some insight into the phenomenon of homelessness by using a participant observation methodology. As in the pro-ana study mentioned earlier, they convinced their IRB that getting informed consent would render the study meaningless; any attempt by the observer "to adopt a researcher role would . . . almost certainly have led to uncooperative and/or distorted comments from the homeless" (p. 181). Hence, participants were unaware they were being observed. This situation, when subjects are not told they are in a study, is sometimes called a *covert participant observation study*.

The purpose of the study was to discover the "identity maintenance strategies" (Farrington & Robinson, p. 176) used by people who came regularly to a homeless shelter. In other words, given that people who are homeless are generally perceived as a low-status group, the researchers wished to determine how those in this group maintained a positive identity and some sense of self-esteem. For example, one strategy might be for homeless people to do social comparisons and decide that their situations are more promising than those of other homeless persons. Furthermore, the researchers hypothesized that the specific maintenance strategies would change as a function of how long the subjects had been homeless. The first author was the participant observer; she had been serving for 2 years as a volunteer helper at the homeless shelter and that was her cover story during the 3-month long study. Her duties as a volunteer included "serving and clearing drinks and meals, preparing beds, giving out clothing and toiletries, and chatting with residents" (p. 181). She kept her observations of behavior and her recall of conversations (among those in the shelter and between her and individual subjects) in a journal that was later content analyzed. There were 21 subjects (20 were male) in the study; their average age was 36.3 years, and the average amount of time they had been homeless was 5.9 years.

Farrington and Robinson (1999) analyzed their data first by categorizing subjects in terms of the amount of time they had been homeless. Then, for each subgroup, they examined the journal for evidence of identity maintenance strategies. One substantial difference they found was between those who had been homeless for less than a year and those who had been homeless for some time (more than 5 years). The first group ($N = 3$) used the strategies of "intragroup comparison" and "distancing"—they compared themselves favorably with others in the shelter "by stressing their skills, travel experience, and coping abilities" (p. 183), and they "distanced themselves both behaviorally and cognitively" (p. 183) from others at the shelter, mainly by interacting among themselves only. Those who had been homeless for more than 5 years ($N = 10$) were more difficult to summarize, but they did much less comparison and distancing; indeed, many of them thought of their group of "veterans" as a type of family. Compared to those in the first group, the veterans were much less optimistic about changing their lives for the better.

Farrington and Robinson (1999) were properly cautious about their conclusions, noting the sample size was small and mostly male and that the study was cross-sectional (in the sense of comparing groups differing in their length of time being homeless). They recommended that future research have a larger sample and be longitudinal in design, following people over a longer period. They recognized that *attrition* would be a difficulty with a longitudinal study, however. Even in the brief period of their study, 5 of the 22 subjects dropped out (one left town, one was jailed, one died, and two were banned from the shelter).

Analyzing Qualitative Data from Non-Experimental Designs

As you might have noticed, we have already touched upon methods for data collection and analysis for observational studies. Researchers need to have clear operational definitions, may use behavior checklists, and likely must concern themselves with inter-observer reliability. Some behaviors, like verbal behaviors described in the museum study above, are considered *qualitative* data. Depending upon the research questions involved, some qualitative data may be transformed into *quantitative* data with techniques like coding; Crowley et al. (2001) did that with parental comments as described above. It is important to note that although we are discussing qualitative data within the context of observational studies, qualitative data analysis can be done with other methods too, such as with open-ended survey or interview responses.

One technique used for analyzing qualitative data is **thematic analysis**, which is a method of identifying and analyzing patterns of responses (or themes) within qualitative data (Braun & Clarke, 2006). One way to think of thematic analysis is that the researcher is discovering recurring themes emerging from the data; this approach would be an inductive thematic analysis because you are allowing the data to guide the discoveries of themes. In contrast, researchers doing a more theoretical thematic analysis may predict certain themes prior to data analysis, based on their deductive reasoning rooted in theories about the phenomenon they are studying. Recall from Chapter 3 that the logical process of *induction* is the process of reasoning from specific events (data) to develop a theory, whereas the process of *deduction* is reasoning from theories to predictions specific events. A researcher using thematic analysis may easily use both approaches in their analysis of qualitative data in order to more fully capture the phenomenon being studied.

Braun and Clarke (2006, 2013) provide a useful explanation and guide for conducting a thematic analysis.[2] In Table 10.1, we summarize the six phases of thematic analysis, which, according to Braun and Clarke, can be done in almost any order, depending on whether you are taking an inductive or deductive approach to thematic analysis.

Several researchers have effectively utilized thematic analysis and their results have led to more in-depth understanding of various phenomena. For example, Frith and Gleeson (2004) used thematic analysis of men's feelings about whether their own body image is related to how they dress. They used a combination of survey and interview methods and their thematic analysis revealed four main themes: (1) men emphasized the importance of practical rather than aesthetic aspects of clothing; (2) men reported a lack of concern about their appearance, but their clothing practices indicated concern with body appearance; (3) men's concerns about their appearance were strongly related to comments about using clothing to conceal their bodies; and (4) men tended to use clothes to conform to a cultural ideal of male body image as being tall, slim, and muscular. Frith and Gleeson concluded that despite the belief that men care little about their appearance and that they even report so, their behaviors related to outward appearance and clothing practices demonstrate otherwise.

---

[2] Thematic analysis is more thoroughly explained in Braun and Clarke's (2013) book entitled *Successful Qualitative Research: A Practical Guide for Beginners*, and is a recommended resource for anyone interested in qualitative data analysis in psychology.

Table 10.1   **Six Phases of Thematic Analysis (Braun & Clarke, 2006, 2013)**

Phase	Description
1. Get familiar with the data	Immerse oneself in the data. Read and re-read the data, noting any initial ideas about the data.
2. Code	Generate codes for interesting features of the data, being mindful that codes should capture both sematic and conceptual reading of the data. Code data systematically across the entire data set.
3. Search for themes	Identify similarities and patterns in the coded data to extract themes. Collate coded data construct coherent theme related to one's empirical question.
4. Review themes	Review all coded information for each theme to see if a coherent pattern has emerged. Themes may be modified or discarded if the data do not support a coherent theme, or coding may need to be refined to better capture patterns in the data.
5. Define and name themes	Detail the specifics of each theme, including telling the overall story of the data analysis, generating clear definitions and names for each theme.
6. Write report	Write an analytic narrative that tells the story of the data, providing specific data extracted from the data set to contextualize and support the story.

As you can see, data from non-experimental studies can be qualitative in nature, and psychologists are developing interesting approaches to analyzing such data. Qualitative data can be found in observational studies, surveys, and interviews, as well as in archival research, which we will now explore.

SELF TEST

10.1

1. In naturalistic observations of animals, it is usually impossible for observers to be hidden from the animals. What is the strategy for reducing reactivity for this type of research?
2. What is inter-observer reliability and what is its purpose?
3. Which ethical problem, typical in observational research, was not a problem in the science museum study?

Archival Research

Up to this point, we have described research that occurs in the laboratory or in the field, whether the designs are experimental designs, like those in Chapters 7 and 8, or non-experimental designs, like surveys, interviews, or observational studies. There is another entire realm of research out there where data is already collected and is awaiting curious researchers who can use it to answer empirical questions. **Archival research** involves use of information already collected for some other purpose, rather than by collecting new data. It often includes independent variables, but because these variables are non-manipulated (i.e., no random assignment), archival research can be considered non-experimental research. Data from archival studies can be subjected to a wide range of statistical analyses including techniques we have already considered (e.g., correlation and regression), as well as two techniques we will describe in a few pages, *factor analysis* and *meta-analysis*.

Archival Data

Archival research uses **archival data**, which refers to information already gathered for some reason aside from the research project at hand. These data range from public information such as census data, court records (e.g., felonies and misdemeanors), genealogical data, corporate annual reports, and patent office records to more private information such as credit histories, health history data, educational records, personal correspondence, and diaries. The term *archives* refers both to the records themselves and to the places where the records are stored. Archives are located in places such as university libraries, government offices, and computerized databases. Below is a list of a few public databases with large amounts of archival data available for scholarly use.

Inter-University Consortium for Political and Social Research (ICPSR)
www.icpsr.umich.edu

The United States Census Bureau
www.census.gov

National Institute on Drug Abuse Data Share (via National Institutes of Health)
https://datashare.nida.nih.gov

Psychiatric Genomics Consortium
www.med.unc.edu/pgc

APA Links to Data Sets and Repositories
www.apa.org/research/responsible/data-links.aspx

Internet-based technology is transforming the way scientists conduct research, as psychologists can use the Internet to collect and analyze large datasets. The term **big data** is used to describe the vast amount of data available in electronic databases that can be extracted and analyzed with the use of advanced data analytic tools. Sources of information vary and include databases like those listed above, cell phone records, social media sites like Facebook and Twitter, and other data stored "in the cloud" from Smartphone apps or electronic monitoring devices like a Fitbit or a Google watch. Once extracted, data can be used to answer psychological scientists' empirical questions about numerous topics. For example, Eichstaedt et al. (2015) found that language used on Twitter predicted heart disease rates within communities. Negative tweets, which included expressions of negative emotions like anger, were related to a higher risk of heart disease. Positive tweets, which included expressions of positive emotions, were related to lower risk of heart disease and were seen as protective factors in the development of heart disease. In 2009, researchers at Google found that Google searches about the flu could be used to track variation the prevalence of flu symptoms at various locations and was reported instantly to the United States Center for Disease Control. Such research on world health and well-being is being tapped by researchers like Eichstaedt in the World Well-Being Project, launched in 2011 with the goal of measuring the psychological well-being and physical health of large populations by analyzing language used in large datasets from social media sites (http://www.wwbp.org/). Clearly, there is a world of data out there waiting to be explored to allow us to better understand each other and perhaps better the world.

The data extracted from archival sources sometimes stand on their own, ready for analysis. For example, Reifman and Larrick's (1991) archival study on heat and aggression in baseball involved examining box scores of major-league baseball games over several years. The researchers (a) tabulated where batters were hit by a pitch and (b) examined weather records to determine the air temperature during games. The idea was to test a notion that as temperatures increase, people get irritable and aggressive behavior becomes more likely. Assuming that a hit batter implies some degree of aggression on the part of the pitcher (arguable), Reifman and Larrick were curious about a correlation between hit batters and heat. They found one: Games played in hotter weather produced more hit batters than games in cooler weather.

Sometimes, the archival information must undergo a **content analysis** before statistical procedures can be applied. Content analysis can be defined as any systematic examination of qualitative information in terms of predefined categories. For example, in the Rozin et al. (2003) portion size studies mentioned at the beginning of the chapter, they content analyzed restaurant guides, menus, and cookbooks in the United States and France. When they compared restaurant guides in Philadelphia and Paris, for instance, an emphasis on large portions was more likely to be found in Philadelphia guides (88%) than for those in Paris (52%); in addition, buffet or all-you-can-eat options were found in 18 descriptions of Philadelphia restaurants, but not in a single Paris restaurant.

Although content analysis normally occurs with verbal materials, that is not always the case. In a study by Brantjes and Bouma (1991), for instance, the drawings by patients with Alzheimer's disease were content analyzed and scored in terms of degree of mental deterioration and then compared to the drawings by those not suffering from the disease. Because content analysis involves a degree of subjectivity, these procedures also typically include multiple coders and *inter-rater reliability* estimates.

The most obvious strength of archival research is that the amount of information available is virtually unlimited, and the possibilities for archival research are restricted only by the creativity of the investigator. Yet archival data can create problems for researchers. Despite the vast amount of data available, some information vital to a researcher may be missing, or the available data may not be representative of some population. In a study that examined the content of advice columns, for example, Schoeneman and Rubanowitz (1985) had to contend with the fact that what eventually is printed in an advice column is a small proportion of the letters written to advice columnists. Who can say what factors determine the selection of letters for publication?

Another problem with archival research is *experimenter bias* (Chapter 6). In archival research, this bias can take the form of attending more closely to records that support one's hypothesis or interpreting the content of records in a way that is biased by one's expectations. The problem can be difficult to avoid completely because the researcher doing archival research typically is faced with much more information than can be used, and the information can often be open to several interpretations. But the problem can also be managed most of the time by using the control procedures described in Chapter 6 (e.g., not disclosing the hypothesis to those responsible for coding or classifying the archival data—in effect, a *double blind* procedure).

One problem often faced by researchers that does *not* occur with archival research is participant *reactivity*. For those participating directly in a research study, the knowledge that their behavior is being observed can influence that behavior in ways that yield a distorted result. For instance, if you are a male runner, have you ever noticed your running form is better and that you run just a little bit faster during that part of the route that takes you by the women's dorm? With archival research, the information for analysis already exists, collected for reasons other than your research project, so reactivity can be ruled out as a factor affecting behavior.

By its nature, archival research does not allow for random assignment in between-subject designs, which makes it non-experimental. Like other non-experimental research, however, these studies often involve sophisticated attempts to control for potential threats to internal validity. A clever example is an often-cited study by Ulrich (1984), who demonstrated that recovery from surgery could be influenced by having a room with a view.

Research Example 31—A Non-Experimental Design Using Archival Data

One of the more interesting areas of research that has developed in psychology within the past 30 years concerns the relationship between psychological and physical well-being. In Chapter 1, we introduced you to the term *translational research*, where researchers study various topics in order to promote physical and psychological well-being. Health psychologists study topics such as the link between stress and illness, the doctor–patient relationship, and, in the case of the Ulrich study, whether such a seemingly minor factor as hospital architecture can affect patient health.

Ulrich (1984) examined patient records for approximately 10 years in a suburban Pennsylvania hospital. He was interested in whether recovery from surgery could be affected by the type of room in which the patient spent postoperative time. In particular, he compared rooms that had windows overlooking a brick wall with rooms having windows that provided a pleasant view of a small group of trees (see Figure 10.2 for a floor diagram). All of the rooms were the same size, and in each room, the beds were arranged so that patients could easily look out of the window.

Because the study was archival, Ulrich (1984) could not randomly assign patients to the rooms. He did everything possible to make the two groups of patients comparable, though. First, he only used patients recovering from a common type of gallbladder surgery and omitted those under the age of 20 and over 69. Second, he created two similar groups using *matching* variables including age, gender, smoking history, and weight. Thus, he examined records for two generally similar groups of patients that still were, by definition, nonequivalent. The independent variable was the type of view they had out of their windows: trees (experimental group) or bricks (control group). And to ensure a similar experience for all those in the experimental group, Ulrich used only records for patients hospitalized between May 1 and October 20 in each of the study's 10 years. Why were those months selected? Because during the rest of the year, the trees lacked foliage, and the goal was to compare patients who were looking at brick walls with those looking at a fully leafed trees and, presumably, a more aesthetically pleasing environment. Ulrich controlled for experimenter bias by having a nurse decide which records were selected for the study. When making those decisions, the nurse had no way of knowing which room the patients had occupied (another *double blind* procedure).

From the archival records, Ulrich (1984) examined the length of postoperative hospitalization, whether and in what amounts patients requested medication for pain and/or anxiety, the frequency of minor complications such as headache or nausea, and nurses' notes about the patients. What he found was a clear advantage for those recovering in a room with a view. Those patients spent an average of almost one full day less in the hospital after surgery (7.96 versus 8.70), they requested less pain medication, and when they did request it, they asked for lower doses than patients staring at the bricks. An analysis of nursing records determined that those looking out on the park-like setting were more likely to be perceived as having a positive attitude than the others (but maybe the nurses were affected by the trees too!).

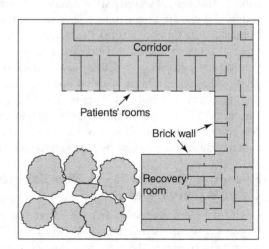

FIGURE 10.2
Floor plan of a hospital used in archival study of recovery from surgery, showing rooms facing either a group of trees or a brick wall (from Ulrich, 1984).

The groups did not differ in their requests for antianxiety medication, nor were there differences in minor postoperative complications.

Ulrich's (1984) study is one of a growing number that show how physical health can be influenced by any number of nonmedical factors. The study also illustrates how health psychology has become a multidisciplinary field; at the time of the study's publication, Ulrich taught in the Department of *Geography* at the University of Delaware. His research can be considered an early example of translational research, which will explore in more depth in Chapter 11.

In sum, studies employing archival data are an effective way to use information about events that have already occurred and therefore enable the researcher to test hypotheses when variables aren't available for direct experimental manipulation. Researchers are tapping into *big data* from data pooled from various resources, often housed online. Considering the vast amount of information out there and its increased availability (Internet), archival research is an approach that promises to become even more visible in the years ahead.

Analyzing Archival Data

Archival research can provide you with a lot of data. So how do you organize it in a way that makes sense and can test your hypotheses? Thus far, you have already learned about some basic tools researchers use to organize and analyze their data. Because archival research is non-experimental, researchers often use various types of *multiple regression* analyses to test the strengths of certain predictors on various outcome (criterion) variables. Another approach to handling a large amount of data, including data from *survey research* and archival research, is to use an approach called **factor analysis**. Factor analysis is a *multivariate* technique in which a large number of measured variables are correlated with each other. It is then determined whether groups of these variables cluster together to form *factors*. A simple example will clarify the idea. Suppose you had access to a database of school-age children's test scores on the following tasks:

- a vocabulary test (VOC)

- a reading comprehension test (COM)

- an analogy test (e.g., doctor is to patient as lawyer is to ???) (ANA)

- a geometry test (GEO)

- a puzzle completion test (PUZ)

- a rotated figures test (ROT)

Pearson's *r*'s could be calculated for all possible pairs of tests, yielding a *correlation* matrix. It might look like this:

	VOC	COM	ANA	GEO	PUZ	ROT
VOC	—	+.76	+.65	−.09	+.02	−.08
COM		—	+.55	+.04	+.01	−.02
ANA			—	−.07	−.08	+.09
GEO				—	+.78	+.49
PUZ					—	+.68
ROT						—

Notice how some of the correlations cluster together (we've circled two clusters). Correlations between vocabulary, reading comprehension, and analogies are all high, as are those between geometry, puzzles, and rotation. Correlations between tests from one cluster and tests from the second cluster are essentially zero. This pattern suggests the tests are measuring two fundamentally different mental abilities or factors. We could label them "verbal fluency" and "spatial skills."

Factor analysis is a multivariate statistical tool that identifies factors from sets of inter-correlations among variables. It would most likely yield the same two factors we just arrived at by scanning the matrix. The analysis also determines what are called *factor loadings*. These, in essence, are correlations between each of the measures and each of the identified factors. In the previous example, the first three measures would be heavily loaded on Factor 1 (verbal fluency), and the second three would be heavily loaded on Factor 2 (spatial skills). Of course, in real research, the correlations never cluster together as clearly as in the example, and researchers often debate whether the factors identified are truly distinct from other factors. Also, they occasionally disagree over the proper labels for the factors. Factor analysis itself only identifies factors; what they should be called is left to the researcher's judgment. Once such factors may be identified by a researcher, then decisions can be made on whether to use those factors as predictors in a regression model.

Meta-Analysis—A Special Case of Archival Research

In Chapter 4, we introduced you to a type of study called a *meta-analysis*, where a researcher statistically analyzes the *effect sizes* from various completed studies on a particular topic. Recall that effect size is an estimate of how large an effect is in a study, taking into account measures of variability. Because a meta-analysis uses data from pre-existing sources (that is, completed research studies), it can be considered a form of archival research. Depending upon the research designs, different effect sizes can be calculated. Although the specifics behind how to conduct a meta-analysis are probably beyond the scope of this research methods course, it is an interesting approach to learn.[3]

The primary goal of a meta-analysis is to systematically synthesize the scientific literature on some phenomenon and combine the results across studies to better understand the phenomenon. Two main questions can be answered with a meta-analysis. First, is the effect consistent across many other studies that test the same effect? And second, if the effect is consistent, then what is the size of the overall effect across studies? There are many examples of meta-analyses in the psychological literature and many are done to better estimate an effect from many studies that may vary in the conditions used and methodological procedures employed. For instance,

- Across 14 studies (with a combined total of 1,506 participants) that used randomized controlled trials testing different types of interventions for individuals with both post-traumatic stress disorder (PTSD) and substance use disorder (SUD), it was found that individual (rather than group)-trauma-focused, cognitive-behavioral treatments combined with SUD intervention were most effective at reducing PTSD severity and alcohol/drug use over time. (Roberts, Roberts, Jones, & Bisson, 2015)

- In an examination of the relationship between childhood maltreatment and depression across 12 studies (with a combined total of 4,372 participants), meta-analytic results revealed that psychological abuse and neglect were more closely associated with depression than was physical or sexual abuse. (Infurna et al., 2016)

---

[3] We recommend Rosenthal's (1991) new-classic textbook entitled *Meta-Analytic Procedures for Social Research* as a foundational textbook on meta-analysis. His *Psychological Bulletin* article from 1995 guides the reader on how to write-up a meta-analysis for publication. Also very useful is Cooper, Hedges, and Valentine's (2009) *Handbook of Research Synthesis and Meta-Analysis*.

- Across 22 studies using brain imaging from fMRI and PET scans to examine brain areas related to language, researchers compared children with autism spectrum disorder (ASD, $n = 328$) and typically developing children (TD, $n = 324$). Typically, language areas are specialized in the left hemisphere in normal brain development. The meta-analysis showed that compared to TD children, children with ASD consistently showed more right hemisphere activity in core language areas of the brain, especially on tasks where they performed poorly. (Herringshaw, Ammons, DeRamus, & Kana, 2016)

Meta-analyses can demonstrate the overall strength and reproducibility of the effect across many studies. In Research Example 32 below, we revisit the topic of replication and show how the field of psychology is handling replication reports by using the tools of meta-analysis.

Research Example 32—Meta-analysis and Psychology's First Registered Replication Report (RRR)

Recall from Chapter 3 the crucial role of replication in psychological science. *Direct replications* are exact reproductions of research studies, using similar samples and essentially the same procedures. *Conceptual replications* change some procedures and/or samples to confirm a finding but also to extend it in some fashion (e.g., show that the original finding also applies to a different population). In general, successful replication allows researchers to be more confident in their results. Furthermore, failures to replicate can signal the possibility of scientific fraud or the kinds of questionable research practices (QRP's) described in Chapter 3. Recognizing that direct replications are not always popular with researchers—new findings have a better chance of being published—the Association for Psychological Science (APS) began an initiative in 2013 to support and fund direct replications of well-known findings. These replications would then be combined, using meta-analysis, with the final product to be known as a Registered Replication Report (RRR).

APS's first RRR was based on a 1990 finding by Schooler and Engstler-Schooler that examined accuracy in eyewitness identification. Imagine you witness a crime, and police then ask you to provide a verbal description of the perpetrator. Later, you try to identify the perpetrator from a lineup. Your chances of making the correct identification will depend on a number of factors, but the fact that you first described the perpetrator verbally can actually reduce the accuracy of identifying that person in a lineup. This phenomenon was discovered by Schooler and Engstler-Schooler and is known as the *verbal overshadowing effect*. The basic idea is that when individuals first verbally describe a face, they then relied on their recollection of their verbal description, rather than their visual memory for the face. Thus, the verbal description overshadowed their visual memory. In their initial study, Schooler and Engstler-Schooler reported that individuals were 25% worse at identifying the culprit from a lineup if they first verbally described him than if they did not. The finding was a surprise and has some obvious practical implications for police procedures. However, given that the result was unexpected, combined with the fact that sample sizes were small in the original research, Schooler and others recognized the need for replication, which indeed occurred over the next several years.

About a decade later after the original publication, Meissner and Brigham (2001) published a meta-analysis of 29 studies on verbal overshadowing. The effect was replicated, but it did not seem to be as strong as originally thought (i.e., an estimated 12% impairment in lineup identification instead of 25%). The studies included in Meissner and Brigham's meta-analysis, however, varied in the procedures used in testing the verbal overshadowing effect. That is, Meissner and Brigham conducted a meta-analysis of *conceptual replications* of overshadowing. But what would happen to the overshadowing effect if *direct replications* were attempted? Enter APS and its first RRR.

Starting in 2013, APS funded direct replications of the original Schooler and Engstler-Schooler (1990) research. There were two replication projects, RRR1 and RRR2, which varied slightly in the timing of the procedures (Alonso et al., 2014). Our focus will be on RRR2, which duplicated

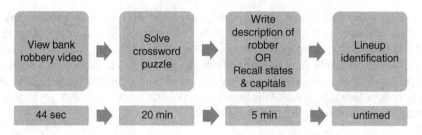

FIGURE 10.3
Procedure of Schooler and Engstler-Schooler's (1990) verbal overshadowing experiment.

the methodology of the first of six experiments completed by Schooler and Engstler-Schooler the experiment that yielded the 25% drop in accuracy. Figure 10.3 outlines the sequence of events in the procedure. As you can see, participants viewed the crime, had a 20-minute filler task, spent 5 minutes writing a verbal description of the criminal, and then tried to identify the criminal out of an 8-person lineup. For both replication projects, samples sizes were greater than those used by Schooler and Engstler-Schooler.

A total of 22 different labs conducted direct replications of the original Schooler and Engstler-Schooler experiments. The results of the 22 different studies were subjected to a meta-analysis, and the overall outcome was that the verbal overshadowing effect did indeed occur, although it was not quite as robust as in the original Schooler and Engstler-Schooler (1990) study. Instead of a 25% reduction in accuracy, the reduction for all the studies combined was 16% (Alonga et al., 2014). Although the effect was not as large in the replication, given that the effect still consistently occurred across multiple replications, it can be concluded that the verbal overshadowing effect has strong empirical support.

One final point about the APS replication project is that it addresses a problem that we described in Chapter 4, the *file drawer effect*. As you recall, there is a publication bias such that studies failing to find significant effects often wind up in researchers' filing cabinets instead of in print. To repeat the Chapter 4 example, if there are 10 published studies showing a gender difference on some phenomenon, but 90 studies showing no difference but failing to be published, one gets the impression of a strong effect (10 studies show it) that might not really exist (90 studies failed to find it). One unique attribute of the APS replication effort was that all the participating labs were told their studies would be published *regardless* of the outcome. Hence, file drawer effects cannot occur in the published RRRs.

Psychology's first RRR project used meta-analytic techniques to estimate effect sizes of direct replications from multiple, independent labs. As should be clear by now, replication is imperative for science to proceed, as it allows us to be more confident in our results. With more confidence, we can better achieve three of the four goals of research in psychology, discussed in Chapter 1; with replication, we can be more confident in describing, explaining, and predicting various psychological phenomena. In the next chapter, we will turn to the fourth goal of research in psychology: application.

SELF TEST

10.2

1. Archival research does not have to deal with the problem of reactivity. Explain.
2. How are correlations used in a factor analysis?
3. What two questions can be answered with a meta-analysis?

CHAPTER SUMMARY

Observational Research

The goal of providing accurate qualitative and quantitative descriptions of behavior can be accomplished by using basic observational methods. In naturalistic observation, the observer is separate from those being observed, and the subjects of study are either unaware of the observer's presence or habituated to it. The observer becomes an active member of the group being studied in participant observation studies. Observation studies vary in the amount of structure imposed by the researcher. Lack of control, observer bias, and subject reactivity are three methodological problems that accompany observational research. The researcher also must confront the ethical dilemmas of informed consent and invasion of privacy. Observational research, as well as the other forms of descriptive research described in this chapter, can be used to falsify claims about behavior and is often a useful source of hypotheses for further investigation.

Archival Research

Archival research relies on data (e.g., hospital records) collected for another purpose and then reanalyzed to answer some empirical question (e.g., can environmental factors affect postoperative recovery?). A major advantage of archival research is the absence of participant reactivity, but experimenter bias may be a disadvantage. Factor analysis is a multivariate technique that might be used in archival research; it identifies clusters of factors underlying a large number of relationships. Meta-analysis can be considered a special type of archival research – one that tests effect sizes across already completed research studies.

CHAPTER REVIEW QUESTIONS

1. Distinguish between naturalistic and participant observational procedures in terms of both method and ethics.

2. What is meant by the problem of reactivity, and how can it be overcome?

3. Describe some methodological control issues in observational research.

4. Give an example to show how observer bias can influence observational research, and describe how such bias can be reduced.

5. Describe an example that shows how observational research can serve the purpose of falsification.

6. Explain how qualitative data from non-experimental designs can be analyzed using thematic analysis.

7. What are archival data, and why is archival research with independent variables considered non-experimental research?

8. Explain how qualitative data from archival research would go through a content analysis before statistical procedures are applied to the data.

9. Describe factor analysis as multivariate method is used as a tool to examine large amounts of data.

10. Describe the goals of meta-analysis and explain how effect sizes are an important part of a meta-analysis.

11. Explain how meta-analysis can be used as a tool for replication of psychological research.

12. Explain how the APS's replication project eliminates the file drawer effect?

APPLICATIONS EXERCISES

Exercise 10.1. Defining Behaviors for Observational Research

Imagine that you are in the beginning stages of an observational research study and must arrive at operational definitions for the behaviors you'll be observing. For each of the following hypotheses, operationally define the behaviors to be recorded and describe how you would set up the study (i.e., where you would conduct the study, whether you would create some level of structure, etc.).

1. In the college library, most students spend less than half of their time actually studying.

2. Men interrupt women more than women interrupt men.

3. In a free play situation, older children play cooperatively but younger children engage in parallel play.

4. Teenagers patrolling malls follow clearly defined routes that they repeat at regular intervals.

5. Couples look at each other more when they are dating than when they are married.

6. Dogs are more aggressive within their own territories than outside of them.

Exercise 10.2.   Deciding on a Method

For each of the hypotheses listed below, identify the best methodological approach from among the following possibilities. Indicate the reason(s) for your choice. Some items have more than one correct answer.

naturalistic observation	participant observation	archival research

1. After altering the content of bird feeders, the proportions of two species of birds at the feeder will change within a few days.

2. In the United States, Black adolescent males receive longer jail sentences than White adolescent males for similar crimes.

3. Men and women are less likely to hold open a door for a woman on a cell phone than for a woman not on a cell phone.

4. When college students enter the cafeteria, men are more likely to be unaccompanied by other students than are women; this is especially true for the dinner meal.

5. Mental health records that include psychological tests of individuals suffering from depression and anxiety are factor analyzed to evaluate clusters of information relevant for clinical treatment.

6. The Mozart effect is not a strong and reliable effect, as originally reported.

ANSWERS TO SELF TESTS

✓ **10.1**

1. Researchers stay in the open and assume that, over time, animals will habituate to their presence and act normally.
2. It refers to the extent of agreement among observers about what is being observed; its purpose is to reduce observer bias.
3. Informed consent.

✓ **10.2**

1. The data were already collected for some other purpose, so subjects could not react in any way to their research participation.
2. Strong correlations between variables may cluster together to form factors in a factor analysis.
3. Is the effect consistent across many other studies that test the same effect? If consistent, what is the size of the overall effect across studies?

Quasi-Experimental Designs and Applied Research

11

PREVIEW & CHAPTER OBJECTIVES

In this chapter, we consider a type of research design that, like an experiment, includes independent and dependent variables but involves a situation in which research participants cannot be randomly assigned to groups. Because the absence of random assignment means causal conclusions cannot be made, whereas they can be made with some degree of confidence in a purely experimental study, this design is called quasi-experimental ("almost" experimental). One type of design you have already encountered (in Chapter 5) is an example of a quasi-experimental design—any study having subject variables. The inability to randomly assign often (but not always) occurs in applied research that takes place outside of the lab, so one focus of the chapter will be applied research, a strategy you first encountered in Chapter 3, when it was contrasted with basic research. You will learn that applied research represents a strong tradition in American experimental psychology and reflects the core American value of pragmatism. Program evaluation is a form of applied research that uses a variety of strategies to examine the effectiveness of programs designed to help people. Program evaluation is especially likely to use qualitative analysis. When you finish this chapter, you should be able to:

- Identify the dual functions of applied research.

- Understand why applied psychology has always been an important element in American psychology.

- Define translational research and explain how psychological research can translate into applied settings.

- Identify the design and ethical problems associated with applied research, especially if that research occurs outside of the laboratory.

- Identify the defining feature of a quasi-experimental design, and recognize which designs appearing in earlier chapters were quasi-experimental.

- Describe the features of a nonequivalent control group design, and understand why this design is necessarily confounded.

- Understand why matching nonequivalent groups on pretest scores can introduce a regression artifact.

- Describe the features of interrupted time series designs, and understand how they can be used to evaluate trends.

- Describe several variations on the basic time series design.

- Describe the strategies for completing a needs analysis in a program evaluation project.

- Understand the purposes and the procedures involved in formative evaluation, summative evaluation, and cost-effectiveness evaluation.

- Identify and describe the ethical problems that often accompany program evaluation research.

As mentioned at the beginning of this text, we would like nothing more than to see you emerge from this methods course with a desire to contribute to our knowledge of behavior by becoming a research psychologist. Our experiences as teachers in this course tell us that some of you indeed will become involved in research, but most of you won't. Many of you will become professional psychologists of some kind, however, working in fields that focus on the development, implementation, and assessment of programs to improve the human condition. For example, as a health psychologist, you might find yourself involved in program to improve the physical and psychological well-being of clients; as a school psychologist, you might be asked to evaluate programs designed to improve student learning; or as an industrial-organizational psychologist, you might help develop programs to improve worker productivity and job satisfaction. As such, you will encounter the worlds of applied research and program evaluation. You may discover you need to do things like:

- Read, comprehend, and critically evaluate research literature on the effectiveness of a program your agency is thinking about implementing.

- Help plan a new program by informing (tactfully) those who are less familiar with research design about the adequacy of the evaluation portion of their proposal.

- Participate in an agency self-study in preparation for an accreditation process.

And if your agency's director finds out you took this course, you might even be asked to design and lead a study to evaluate an agency program.

Beyond the Laboratory

You first learned to distinguish between basic and applied research in the opening pages of Chapter 3. To review, the essential goal of basic research in psychology is to increase our core knowledge about human behavior and mental processes. The knowledge might eventually have a practical application but that outcome is not the prime motivator; knowledge is valued as an end in itself. In contrast, applied research is designed primarily to increase our knowledge about a particular real-world problem, with an eye toward directly solving it. A second distinction between basic and applied research is that while basic research usually takes place in a laboratory, applied research is often conducted in clinics, social service agencies, jails, government agencies, and business settings. There are many exceptions, of course. Some basic research occurs in the field, and some applied research takes place in a lab.

To give you a sense of the variety of applied research, consider these 2015 titles from the prominent *Journal of Experimental Psychology: Applied*:

- Humanizing machines: Anthropomorphization of slot machines increases gambling (Riva, Sacchi, & Brambilla, 2015).

- Goal-oriented training affects decision-making processes in virtual and simulated fire and rescue environments (Cohen-Hatton & Honey, 2015).

- The interactive effects of affect and shopping goal on information search and product evaluations (Fangyuan, Wyer, & Shen, 2015).

These titles illustrate two features of applied research. First, following from our definition, the studies clearly focus on easily recognizable problems (gambling, decision-making in emergency situations, and shopping behavior). Second, the titles demonstrate that, while the prime goal of applied research is problem solving (e.g., how to get firefighters to make good decisions in emergency situations), these studies also further our knowledge of basic psychological processes (e.g., decision making).

Indeed, there is a close connection between basic and applied research, as illustrated by growing field of *translational research*. In Chapter 1, we defined translational research as research that is done for both better understanding of a particular phenomenon as well as for its application to promote physical and psychological well-being. While basic research may serve as the "engine of discovery," driving innovation and deeper understanding of human functioning, it is also important that basic research results apply to situations that enable users of research to inform their practice. Further, to best inform therapeutic interventions, basic research findings need to be *translated* and tested in clinical situations. The National Institutes of Health (NIH) has recognized this need and has made translational research a priority (Woolf, 2008). Broadly speaking, translational research has been called "bench-to-bedside" approaches for translating basic research into interventions and treatments for individuals. In psychology, it has been considered a type of research that can help bridge the science-practice gap (Tashiro & Mortensen, 2006).

Virtually, all applied research has the dual function of addressing applied problems directly and providing evidence of basic psychological phenomena that influence theory development. Furthermore, applied research often is rooted in theories and research findings derived from basic research. One illustration of these points comes from the following example of applied research on the impact of nutritional labeling on perceptions of food health and food choice.

Research Example 33—Applied Research

In Chapter 3, we introduced you to distinction between basic and applied research. On the one hand, basic research can provide us with more knowledge and understanding about various psychological constructs, like attention and memory. On the other hand, applied research can make use of basic research findings and develop empirical studies to both understand and attempt to solve real-world problems, like attention to food labels and making healthy food choices. In a study by Trudel, Murray, Kim, and Chen (2015), basic research is used as a basis for conducting applied research on food preferences and food choices based on consumers' attention to the color-coding of nutrition labels.

In a series of four experiments, Trudel et al. (2015) relied on past basic research demonstrating that traffic light color-coded (TLC) nutrition labels can be useful decision aids for consumers. Green labels should signal "go" for consumers to consume the food, and yellow and red should signal increasing caution in consumption. They wanted to see if such TLC labels are related to how consumers evaluate how healthy a food product is and whether consumers would choose to eat those foods. They also used prior theoretical work on self-regulation of eating behaviors to guide their hypotheses about whether those who were watching their diet versus those that were not would respond differently to TLC labels. Self-regulation is the process by which we try to control our thoughts, emotions, and impulses. With regard to eating behavior, previous research has shown that people rely on external cues to self-regulate their impulses and food intake (Trudel & Murray, 2011). Trudel et al. predicted that dieters would affected by external cues (i.e., TLC food labels) differently than non-dieters, which should result in different processing of nutrition information, different food preferences, and different food choices.[1]

---

[1] Participants answered various questions on a survey, one of which was "Are you currently watching your weight?" (Trudel et al., 2015, p. 258). If participants answered 'yes' to this item, they were classified as dieters, and those who answered 'no' were classified as non-dieters.

Dieters and non-dieters were shown a photo and verbal description of various food products, such as the "Chicken Marbella Sandwich" (Trudel et al., 2015). In the experimental condition, participants saw a nutrition label with various rows color-coded in red, yellow, and green. In the control condition, participants saw a regular black-and-white nutrition label. Then, participants rated how healthy the food items was on a 9-point scale. In Experiment 1, the color coding of the nutrition labels included red (3 rows), yellow (1 row), and green (3 rows). Nondieters rated items as healthy regardless of whether a TLC label was used, whereas dieters rated food items with TLC labels as less healthy than items without TLC labels. Experiment 2 *replicated* the results of Experiment 1 using labels that were color coded either predominantly red or predominantly green. The authors suggested that dieters used the TLC labeling in a way that allowed them to more deeply process nutrition information provided in the labels, leading to more nuanced judgments about the healthiness of the foods. To test this, they conducted a third experiment in which they tested participants' memories for nutrition label information. They found that dieters recalled significantly more information from the food labels when TLC color coding was used than when it was not used. In contrast, non-dieters recalled the same amount of information regardless of whether the labels were TLC color coded. Additionally, dieters accurately recalled more information from the TLC labels than non-dieters.

Trudel et al. (2015) concluded that dieters were more affected by the TLC food labeling. Their first three experiments were laboratory experiments, but they also wanted to see if the effects could be observed outside the laboratory. Experiment 4 was a *field study* where they attempted to replicate their laboratory results with grocery store shoppers. Shoppers at the entrance to a grocery store received a description and either mostly green or mostly red TLC nutrition labels of chocolate candy. They then were offered to sample as many chocolates as they wished from a bowl of 25 chocolates. Next, they rated their perceptions of health of the chocolates on the 9-point scale described above. Trudel et al. found that dieters rated the chocolates as equally healthy, regardless of red or green TLC labels. This effect was slightly different from the results of the laboratory experiments in which dieters showed lower health ratings of food with TLC colored labels than no colored labels. Non-dieters, however, rated the green-labeled chocolates as healthier than the red-labeled chocolates, consistent with the laboratory results. Furthermore, non-dieters took more chocolates to eat than dieters, and especially if the labels were green. Incidentally, the authors also used a moderated *mediation analysis* (see Chapter 9) to demonstrate that shoppers' health evaluations predicted their consumption of chocolate and this depended on whether shoppers were dieters or non-dieters.

In summary, the Trudel et al. (2015) study is an excellent illustration of how applied research can solve real problems while contributing to our knowledge of fundamental psychological phenomena. The authors concluded from their experiments TLC labels influenced food preferences and food consumption and such influences differed between dieters and non-dieters. Non-dieters used the TLC labels as a more explicit guide (stop-go decision making) for evaluating the health quality of foods. Dieters used the TLC labels to more deeply process and remember more nutrition information, which in turn was related to lower health ratings and more self-regulatory control of food consumption.

Applied Psychology in Historical Context

Because psychology in the United States developed in an academic setting, you might think research in psychology traditionally has been biased toward basic research. Not so. From the time psychology emerged as a new discipline in the late 19th century, psychologists in the United States have been interested in applied research and in applying the results of their basic research. For one thing, institutional pressures in the early 20th century forced psychologists to show how their work could improve society. In order to get a sufficient piece of the academic funding pie at a time when psychology laboratories were brand new entities, psychologists had to show the ideas deriving from their research could be put to good use.

Psychologists trained as researchers focused on extending knowledge, but they often found themselves trying to apply basic research methods to solve problems in areas such as education, mental health, child rearing, and, in the case of Walter Miles, sports. Miles was director of the psychology laboratory at Stanford University in the 1920s. Although devoted to basic research throughout most of his career, he nonetheless found himself on the football team's practice field in 1927, as shown in Figure 11.1 (that's Miles in the suit). Stanford's legendary football coach, "Pop" Warner, was known as an innovator, open to anything that might improve his team's performance. Enter Miles, who built what he called a "multiple chronograph" as a way of simultaneously testing the reaction time of seven football players, an offensive line (Miles, 1928). On a signal that dropped seven golf balls onto a cylinder rotating at a constant speed (one ball per player), the players would charge forward, pushing a board that pulled a string that released a second set of golf balls onto the drum. The balls left marks on the cylinder and, knowing the speed of the rotation and the distance between the marks, Miles was able to calculate the players' reaction times. Miles published several studies with his multiple chronograph (e.g., Miles, 1931) and demonstrated its usefulness for identifying the factors that affected a football player's "charging time," but the apparatus never enjoyed widespread use (Baugh & Benjamin, 2006). Nonetheless, it is a good example of an experimental psychologist using a basic laboratory tool— reaction time in this case—to deal with a concrete problem: how to improve the efficiency of Stanford's football team.

Walter Miles made just an occasional foray into applied psychology, devoting most of his life to basic experimental research. Other psychologists, however, while trained as experimental psychologists, turned applied psychology into a career. A prime example is Harry Hollingworth, who entered applied psychology simply to make enough money for his talented wife, Leta, to attend graduate school. The result was a classic study on drug effects, financed by the Coca-Cola Company, whose product had been seized in a raid in Tennessee in 1909 on the grounds that it contained what was considered to be a dangerous drug. Box 11.1 elaborates this fascinating story and describes an early example of a nicely designed double-blind drug effect experiment.

Stanford 1927

The Drs. Nicholas and Dorothy Cummings Center for the History of Psychology, The University of Akron.

FIGURE 11.1
Simultaneously testing the reaction times of Stanford football players, circa 1927 (from Archives of the History of American Psychology, University of Akron, Akron, Ohio).

BOX 11.1 CLASSIC STUDIES—The Hollingworth's, Applied Psychology, and Coca-Cola

In 1911, the Coca-Cola Company was in some danger of having its trademark drink removed from the market or, at the very least, having one of its main ingredients removed from the formula. Under the federal Pure Food and Drug Act, which had been passed 5 years earlier during a time of progressive reform, Coca-Cola stood accused of adding a dangerous chemical to its drink: caffeine. It was said to be addictive (and they sell it to children!), and its stimulant properties were said to mask the need we all have for rest when we become fatigued. In 1909, a shipment of Coke syrup was seized by federal agents in Tennessee. Two years later, Coca-Cola found itself in court, defending its product. Enter Harry and Leta Hollingworth and a research story documented by Benjamin, Rogers, and Rosenbaum (1991).

In 1911, Harry Hollingworth was a young professor of psychology at Barnard College in New York City, anticipating a typical academic career of teaching, doing research, and avoiding committee work. His wife, Leta, also aimed for a professional career as a psychologist. They had married a few years earlier, and the plan was for Leta to teach school in New York while Harry finished graduate studies and began his career. Then Leta would go to graduate school. Unfortunately, Leta soon discovered one of the realities of being a married woman in early 20th century New York: The city's school board did not allow married women to teach (being married was assumed to be a woman's career). Financial difficulties immediately beset the young couple and, when the Coca-Cola Company offered Harry money to examine the cognitive and behavioral effects of caffeine, financial necessity prompted him to agree. To his credit, Hollingworth insisted (and Coca-Cola agreed) on being allowed to publish his results, whether or not they were favorable to the company.

Harry and Leta collaborated on the design for the studies they completed, an elaborate series of experiments that lasted more than a month. With Coca-Cola money, they rented a large apartment in which to conduct the research, with the daily data-collection sessions under Leta's supervision. Five rooms were set up as separate labs, with graduate students serving as experimenters. A variety of mental and physical tests were used, ranging from reaction time to motor coordination. Sixteen subjects were tested. Methodologically, the Hollingworths put into practice several of the concepts you have been studying in your methods course.

- They used *counterbalancing*.

With $N = 16$ and a month's worth of research, you can easily guess that each subject was tested many times. As with any repeated measures design, order effects were controlled through counterbalancing. For example, in one of the studies, participants rotated among five rooms in the apartment, completing a series of tests in each room. The order in which participants were tested in the rooms was randomized, in essence a partial counterbalancing procedure.

- They used a *placebo* control.

Participants were tested after taking pills containing either caffeine or a sugar substance. One set of studies included four groups, a placebo control, and three caffeine groups, each with a different dosage. Hence, the Hollingworths were able to examine not just caffeine effects but also dosage effects.

- They used a *double-blind* procedure.

Subjects did not know if they were receiving caffeine or a placebo, and the experimenters doing the tests in each room did not know if their subjects had taken caffeine or the placebo (Leta, who was in overall command of the testing, knew.)

And the results? Complex, considering the large of number tests used, the dosages employed, a fair amount of individual variation in performance, and the absence of sophisticated inferential statistical techniques (remember from Box 8.3 that nobody was doing ANOVAs before the mid-1930s). In general, no adverse effects of caffeine were found, except that larger doses, if taken near the end of the day, caused some subjects to have difficulty with sleep. Writing several years later in the textbook *Applied Psychology* (Hollingworth & Poffenberger, 1917), Harry wrote that the "widespread consumption of caffeinic beverages . . . seems to be justified by the results of these experiments" (p. 181). As for the trial, Harry testified on behalf of the company, arguing there was no scientific basis for banning caffeine in Coca-Cola. The case against Coke was eventually dismissed (on grounds other than caffeine's effects). One final outcome of the study was that it indeed paid for Leta's graduate studies, with enough money left over for a summer-long European trip. Leta Hollingworth eventually became a pioneer in the study and education of gifted children, probably better known than her husband.

Psychologists at the beginning of the 21st century are as interested in application as were their predecessors at the beginning of the 20th century. That is, they design and carry out studies to help create solutions to real-world problems while at the same time contributing to the basic core knowledge of psychology. However, applied research projects encounter several difficulties not usually found in the laboratory.

Design Problems in Applied Research

From what you have already learned in Chapters 2, 5, and 6, you should be able to anticipate most of the problems encountered in applied research, which include:

- *Ethical dilemmas* (Chapter 2). A study conducted outside of the laboratory may create problems relating to informed consent and privacy. Also, proper debriefing is not always possible. Research done in an industrial or corporate setting may include an element of perceived coercion if employees believe their job status depends on whether they volunteer to participate in a study (see Box 11.3 at the end of this chapter for more on ethics and applied research).

- *A trade-off between internal and external validity* (Chapter 5). Because research in applied psychology often takes place in the field, the researcher can lose methodological control over the variables operating in the study. Hence, the danger of possible confounding can reduce the study's internal validity. On the other hand, external (and specifically, ecological) validity is usually high in applied research because the setting more closely resembles real-life situations, and the problems addressed by applied research are everyday problems.

- *Problems unique to between-subjects designs* (Chapter 6). In applied research, it is often impossible to use random assignment to form equivalent groups. Therefore, the studies often use ex post facto designs and must therefore compare nonequivalent groups. This, of course, introduces the possibility of reducing internal validity by subject selection problems or interactions between selection and other threats such as maturation or history. When matching is used to achieve a degree of equivalence among groups of subjects, regression problems can occur, as will be elaborated in a few pages.

- *Problems unique to within-subjects designs* (Chapter 6). It is not always possible to counterbalance properly in applied studies using within-subjects factors. Hence, the studies may have uncontrolled order effects. Also, attrition can be a problem for studies that extend over a long period of time.

Before going much farther in this chapter, you might wish to look back at the appropriate sections of Chapters 2, 5, and 6 and review the ideas just mentioned. You also might review the section in Chapter 5 about the kinds of conclusions that can be drawn from manipulated variables and subject variables.

SELF TEST

11.1

1. Applied research is said to have a dual function. Explain.
2. Use the example of Miles and the Stanford football team to show how basic research and applied research can intersect.
3. How does applied research fare in terms of internal and external validity?

Quasi-Experimental Designs

Strictly speaking, and with Woodworth's (1938) definitions in mind, so-called true experimental studies include manipulated independent variables and equivalent groups formed by either straight random assignment or matching followed by random assignment. If subjects cannot be assigned randomly, however, the design is called a **quasi-experimental design**. Although it might seem that quasi-experiments are therefore lower in status than "true" experiments, it is important to stress that quasi-experiments have great value in applied research. They do allow for a degree of control, they serve a researcher's goals when ethical or practical problems make random assignment impossible, and they often produce results with clear benefits for people's lives. Thus far, we have seen several examples of designs that could be considered quasi-experimental:

- Single-factor ex post facto designs, with two or more levels

- Ex post facto factorial designs

- P x E factorial designs (the *P* variable, anyway)

- All of the correlational research

In this chapter, we will consider two specific designs typically found in texts on quasi-experimental designs (e.g., Cook & Campbell, 1979): *nonequivalent control group designs* and *interrupted time series designs*. Other quasi-experimental designs exist (e.g., regression discontinuity design), but these two are the most frequently encountered.

Nonequivalent Control Group Designs

In this type of study, the purpose is to evaluate the effectiveness of some treatment program. Those in the program are compared with those in a control group who aren't treated. This design is used when random assignment is not possible, so in addition to the levels of the independent variable, the members of the control group differ in some other way(s) from those in the treatment group—that is, the groups are not equivalent at the outset of the study. You will recognize this as a specific example of ex post facto design in Chapters 7 and 8, a type of design comparing nonequivalent groups, often selected with reference to a subject variable such as age, gender, or some personality characteristic. In the case of the quasi-experimental **nonequivalent control group design**, the groups are not equal at the start of the study; *in addition*, they experience different events in the study itself. Hence, there is a built-in confound that can complicate the interpretation of these studies. Nonetheless, these designs effectively evaluate treatment programs when random assignment is impossible.

Following the scheme first outlined by Campbell and Stanley (1963), the nonequivalent control group design can be symbolized like this:

Experimental group:	O_1	**T**	O_2
Nonequivalent control group:	O_1		O_2

where O_1 and O_2 refer to pretest and posttest observations or measures, respectively, and T refers to the treatment program being evaluated. Because the groups might differ on the pretest, the important comparison between the groups is not simply a test for differences on the posttest, but a comparison of the amounts of change from pre- to posttest in the two groups. Hence, the statistical comparison is typically between the *change scores* (the difference between O_1 and O_2) for each group. Alternatively, techniques are available that adjust posttest scores based on the pretests. Let's make this a bit more concrete.

Suppose the management of an electric fry pan company wants to institute a new flextime work schedule. Workers will continue to work 40 hours per week, but the new schedule allows them to begin and end each day at different times or to put all of their hours into 4 days if they wish to have a 3-day weekend. Management hopes this will increase productivity by improving morale and designs a quasi-experiment to see if it does. The company owns two plants in two very similar U.S. cities, one just outside of Pittsburgh and the other near Cleveland. Through a coin toss, the managers decide to make Pittsburgh's plant the experimental group and Cleveland's plant the nonequivalent control group. Thus, the study is quasi-experimental for the obvious reason that workers cannot be randomly assigned to the two plants (imagine the moving costs, legal fees over union grievances, etc.). The independent variable is whether or not flextime is present, and the dependent variable is some measure of productivity. Let's suppose the final design looks like this:

Pittsburgh plant:	pretest:	average productivity for 1 month prior to instituting flextime
	treatment:	flextime instituted for 6 months
	posttest:	average productivity during the sixth full month of flextime
Cleveland plant:	pretest:	average productivity for 1 month prior to instituting flextime in Pittsburgh
	treatment:	none
	posttest:	average productivity during the sixth full month that flextime is in effect in the Pittsburgh plant

Outcomes

Figure 11.2 shows you four outcomes of this quasi-experiment. All the graphs show the same amount of positive change in productivity for the Pittsburgh plant. The question is whether the change was due to program effectiveness or to some other factor(s). Before reading on, try to determine which of the graphs provides the strongest evidence that introducing flextime increased productivity. Also, refer to the section in Chapter 5 that described threats to internal validity, and try to identify the threats that make it difficult to interpret the other outcomes.

You probably found it fairly easy to conclude that in Figure 11.2a something besides the flextime produced the apparent improvement. This graph makes the importance of control groups obvious, even if it has to be a nonequivalent control group. Yes, Pittsburgh's productivity increased, but the same amount of change happened in Cleveland. Therefore, the Pittsburgh increase cannot be attributed to the program, but it could have been due to several of the threats to internal validity you've studied. *History* and *maturation* are good possibilities. Perhaps a national election intervened between pre- and posttest, and workers everywhere felt more optimistic, leading to increased productivity. Perhaps workers just showed improvement with increased experience on the job.

Figure 11.2b suggests that productivity in Cleveland was high throughout the study but that in Pittsburgh, productivity began at a very low level but improved due to the flextime program. However, there are two dangers here. For one thing, the Cleveland scores might reflect a *ceiling effect* (Chapter 5)—that is, their productivity level was so high to begin with that no further improvement could possibly be shown. If an increase could be seen (i.e., if scores on the Y-axis could go higher), you might see two parallel lines, as in Figure 11.2a. The second problem is that because Pittsburgh started so low, the increase there might be due to *regression to the mean* (Chapter 5) rather than a true effect. In other words, perhaps at the start of the study, productivity was very low for some reason, and it then returned to normal.

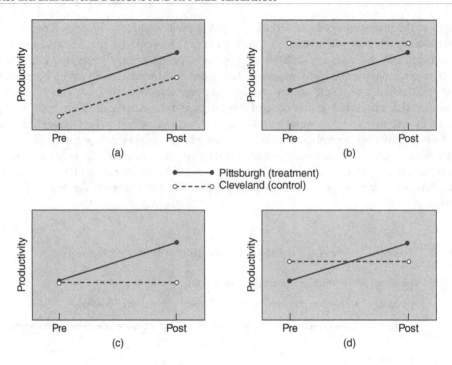

FIGURE 11.2
Hypothetical outcomes of a nonequivalent control group design.

Figure 11.2c seems at first glance to be the ideal outcome. Both groups start at the same level of productivity, but the group with the program (Pittsburgh) is the only one to improve. This may indeed be the case, and such an outcome generally makes applied researchers happy, but a problem can exist nonetheless. Because of the nonequivalent nature of the two groups, it is conceivable that subject selection could *interact* with some other influence—that is, history, maturation, or some other factor could affect the workers in one plant but not those in the other. For example, it's not hard to imagine a Selection x History problem here—some historical event affects the Pittsburgh plant but not the Cleveland plant. Perhaps the knowledge that they are participating in a study motivated the Pittsburgh workers (remember the *Hawthorne effect?*), while Cleveland workers were left in the dark. Perhaps between the pretest and the posttest, the Steelers won yet another Super Bowl, and because workers in Pittsburgh are such avid fans, their general feeling of well-being improved morale and therefore productivity. The Browns, on the other hand, who never win Super Bowls, would be less likely to inspire productivity boosts in the Cleveland plant.

The outcome in Figure 11.2d provides strong support for program effectiveness. Here, the treatment group (Pittsburgh) begins below the control group (Cleveland) yet surpasses the control group by the end of the study. Regression to the mean can be ruled out as causing the improvement for Pittsburgh because one would expect regression to raise the scores only to the level of the control group, not beyond it. Of course, selection problems and interactions between selection and other factors are difficult to exclude completely, but this type of crossover effect is considered good evidence of program effectiveness (Cook & Campbell, 1979).

Regression to the Mean and Matching

A special threat to the internal validity of nonequivalent control group designs occurs when there is an attempt to reduce the nonequivalency of the groups through a form of matching. Matching was first described in Chapter 6 as an alternative to random assignment under certain circumstances, and it works rather well to create equivalent groups if the independent variable is a manipulated variable and participants can be randomly assigned to groups *after* being paired on some matching variable (see Chapter 6 to review the matching procedure). However, it can be a problem in nonequivalent control group designs when the two groups are sampled from populations that differ on the factor being used as the matching variable. If this occurs, then using a matching procedure can enhance the influence of the regression to the mean problem and even make it appear that a successful program has failed. Let's consider a hypothetical example.

Suppose you are developing a program to improve the reading skills of disadvantaged youth in a particular city. You advertise for volunteers to participate in an innovative reading program and select those most in need (i.e., those whose reading scores are, on average, very low). To create a control group that controls for socioeconomic class, you recruit additional volunteers from similar neighborhoods in other cities. Your main concern is equating your experimental and control groups for initial reading skill, so you decide to match the two groups on this variable. You administer a reading skills pretest to the volunteers in your target neighborhood and to the potential control group participants, and use the results to form two groups with the same average score—that is, the matching variable is the reading skills score. Let's say the test has a range from 0 to 100. You decide to select children for the two groups so the average score is 25 for both groups. The treatment group then gets the program and the control group does not; the design is a typical nonequivalent control group design:

Experimental group: pretest reading program posttest
Control group: pretest — posttest

Naturally, you're excited about the prospects of this study because you believe the reading program is unique and will help a lot of children. Hence, you're shocked when these reading scores occur:

Experimental group: pre = 25 reading program post = 25
Control group: pre = 25 — post = 29

Not only did the program not seem to work but also it appears it even hindered the development of reading skills—the control group apparently improved! What happened?

A strong possibility here is that regression to the mean resulting from the matching procedure overwhelmed any possible treatment effect. Remember that the experimental group was formed from those with the greatest need for the program because their skills were so poor. If the reading pretest could have been given to all children who fall into this category (i.e., the population called "very poor readers"), the average score might be quite low—let's say 17. When using the matching procedure, however, you were forced to select children who scored much higher than the mean score from this population of poor readers. Presumably, at least some of the children in this group scored higher than they normally would have on the pretest because no test is perfectly reliable— some degree of measurement error is likely to occur. Therefore, on a posttest, many of these children will score lower (i.e., move back to the mean of 17) simply due to regression to the mean. Let's suppose the program truly was effective and would add an average of 4 points to the reading score. However, if the average regression effect was a loss of 4 points, the effects would cancel each other out, and this would account for the apparent lack of change from pre- to posttest.

For participants in the control group, just the opposite might have occurred. Suppose their population mean score was higher than 25 (35, perhaps). Maybe they were reasonably poor readers to begin with, but not as bad as the experimental group (i.e., they were from a population called "relatively poor readers"). Selecting participants who scored lower than their population mean, in order to produce pretest scores to match those of the experimental group (i.e., 25), could result in a regression effect producing higher posttest scores. For these children, the posttest score would result from the same regression to the mean found in the experimental group, although this time the regression effect would yield an increased score.

Figure 11.3 shows the problem in visual form. Regression and program improvements cancel each other out in the experimental group, while in the control group, regression is the only factor operating, and it pushes the scores toward the higher end. In sum, the reading program might actually have been a good idea, but the matching procedure caused a regression effect that masked its effectiveness.[2]

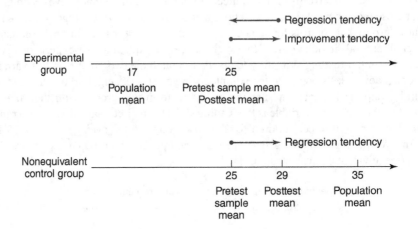

FIGURE 11.3
Hypothetical influences of regression to the mean when matching is used with nonequivalent groups, in an attempt to create equivalent groups.

This type of regression artifact apparently occurred during the first large-scale attempt to evaluate the effectiveness of Head Start, one of the cornerstone programs of President Lyndon Johnson's Great Society initiative in the 1960s (Campbell & Erlebacher, 1970). The program originated in 1965 as an ambitious attempt to give underprivileged preschool children a "head start" on school by teaching them school-related skills and getting their parents involved in the process. By 1990, about 11 million children had participated, and Head Start is now recognized as perhaps the most successful social program ever run by the federal government (Horn, 1990). Yet in the early 1970s, it was under attack for its "failure" to produce lasting effects, largely on the basis of what has come to be known as the Westinghouse study (because the study was funded by a grant to the Westinghouse Learning Corporation and Ohio University), conducted by Victor Cicirelli and his colleagues (1969).

The Westinghouse study documented what it called "fade-out effects"; early gains by children in Head Start programs seemed to fade away by the third grade. The implication, of course, was that perhaps federal dollars were being wasted on ineffective social programs, a point made by President Nixon in an address to Congress in which he explicitly referred to the Westinghouse study. Consequently, funding for Head Start came under attack during the Nixon years. At the same time, the basis for the criticism, the Westinghouse study, was being assaulted by social scientists.

Because Head Start was well under way when the Westinghouse evaluation project began, children couldn't be randomly assigned to treatment and control groups. Instead, the Westinghouse

---

[2] Although the practical and ethical realities of applied research in the field might prevent it, a better procedure would be to give a large group of children the reading readiness test, match them on the test, and randomly assign them to a reading program group and a control group.

group selected a group of Head Start children and matched them for cognitive achievement with children who hadn't been through the program. However, in order to match the groups on cognitive achievement, Head Start children selected for the study were those scoring well above the mean for their overall group, and control children were those scoring well below the mean for their group. This is precisely the situation described in the hypothetical case of a program to improve reading skills. Hence, the Head Start group's apparent failure to show improvement in the third grade was at least partially the result of a regression artifact caused by the matching procedure, according to Campbell and Erlebacher (1970).

In fairness to the Westinghouse group, it should be pointed out they would have disagreed vehemently with politicians who wished to cut the program. Cicirelli (1984) insisted that the study *"did not conclude that Head Start was a failure"* (p. 915; italics in the original), that more research was necessary and that "vigorous and intensive approaches to expanding and enriching the program" (p. 916) should be undertaken. Cicirelli (1993) later pointed out a key recommendation of the Westinghouse study was "not to eliminate Head Start but to try harder to make it work, based on encouraging findings from full-year programs [as opposed to summer-only programs]" (p. 32).

Nonequivalent control group designs do not always produce the type of controversy that engulfed the Westinghouse study. Consider the following two research examples: one is an attempt to increase the physical activity in children during school vacations, and the second is a study of the psychological aftershocks of an earthquake. Although most nonequivalent control group designs use pretest–posttest designs, the second study shows that nonequivalent control group designs do not always use pretests.

Research Example 34—A Nonequivalent Control Group Design

Many health benefits are associated with physical activity, particularly in children. In its FITT plan for physical activity, where FITT stands for frequency, intensity, time, and type, the American Academy of Pediatrics (AAP) recommends daily physical activity that is at least moderately vigorous in intensity (healthychildren.org). However, more access and use of screen-based activities (video games and television) is associated with less physical activity and more sedentary time in children. While there are specific physical activity plans (e.g., FITT) designed to help families increase children's physical activity levels, there are also barriers to access to physical spaces in which children can play. One barrier may be unsafe city streets due to car traffic. In the city of Ghent, Belgium, researchers with the consent of the city council opened up some city streets as car-free spaces where children could play safely.

D'Haese, Van Dyck, Bourdeaudhuij, Deforche, and Cardon (2015) used a nonequivalent control groups design to test whether the opening of "Play Streets" would increase physical activity and decrease sedentary activity during the summer months when children were not in school. Play Streets in Belgium are streets reserved for children's safe play during certain days and times, as determined by city councils. Usually, car traffic is prohibited and the streets are opened during the summer months when children are not in school. D'Haese et al. *operationally defined* their independent variable as neighborhoods where Play Streets had occurred versus not. Thus, the experimental group included children who lived in neighborhoods with Play Streets and the control group included children who lived in comparable neighborhoods but without Play Streets. Importantly, Play Streets occurred on only some summer days in those designated neighborhoods, so the researchers could use a pretest–posttest design to measure physical activity before Play Streets and after Play Streets in the experimental condition. The design looked like this:

Experimental group: pretest   Play Streets   posttest
Nonequivalent control group: pretest   No Play Streets   posttest

Recall that in nonequivalent control group designs, the experimental and control group are not equal at the start, but attempts are made to make the groups as similar as possible. This was the case in the Play Streets study. The two groups were unequal in that they were different city neighborhoods, but D'Haese et al. ensured that the neighborhoods in both groups were similar in terms of walkability of the neighborhoods and the annual household incomes of its residents.

To measure children's physical activity, children wore accelerometers all day including during the 5 hours when Play Streets were open for public use. The accelerometers enabled researchers to record how long children engaged in moderate-to-vigorous physical activity (MVPA). D'Haese et al.'s (2015) results are displayed in Figure 11.4. As you can see, both children in both types of neighborhoods engaged in equivalent levels of MVPA per day before the implementation of Play Streets. After Play Streets, children in the experimental group showed an increase in physical activity, whereas the children in the control group became less physically active.

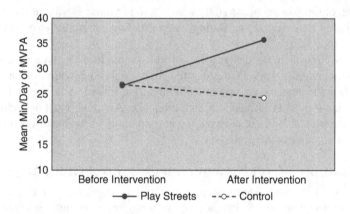

FIGURE 11.4

Changes in (a) physical activity and (b) sedentary activity after implementation of a Play Streets program. Activity recorded during the hours of the Play Streets program. (from D'Haese et al., 2015).

Interestingly, the effects carried over into the entire day. During days when Play Streets were implemented (or not in the case of the control group), children in the Play Streets condition increased their total MVPA from 55 min/day to 67 min/day, whereas children in the control condition decreased their total MVPA from 57 min/day to 53 min/day. Given recommendations that children should engage in physical activity for about 60 min/day, it is evident that use of a program like Play Streets can help provide safe, fun places for children to increase their physical activity to recommended levels.

In addition to using a nonequivalent control group design, D'Haese et al. (2015) also used a *survey method* in which they asked parents' opinions about Play Streets. They asked parents in experimental and control conditions to rate several items on a Likert scale in terms of their level of agreement with various statements. Approximately 60% of parents whose children had access to Play Streets either agreed or strongly agreed that they had the impression that their children played more outside, which was confirmed by children's actual physical activity levels in the experimental group. For parents who were part of the control group (no Play Streets), 76% of parents agreed or strongly agreed that if they had Play Streets that their children would have more social contact with each other. The results of a comparable item for the Play Streets condition showed that 78% of parents reportedly they believed that their children had many friends in the Play Street. The authors concluded that in addition to the health benefits of increased physical activity, social interactions among children can be enhanced with the use of Play Streets. Finally, programs like Play Streets can be very low cost, particularly for low income communities where access to public parks or playgrounds may be limited. In this case, while costs may be low, the benefits to children may be quite high. Later in this chapter, we will explore in more depth *cost-effectiveness analysis* when it comes to a research process called *program evaluation*.

Research Example 35—A Nonequivalent Control Group Design Without Pretests

Nonequivalent control group designs typically include pretests but that is not always the case. Sometimes, these designs occur when an unforeseen opportunity for research makes pretesting impossible. One such event was the 1989 San Francisco earthquake. To James Wood and Richard Bootzin of the University of Arizona, the event suggested an idea for a study about nightmares, a topic already of interest to them (Wood & Bootzin, 1990). Along with colleagues from Stanford University (located near the quake's epicenter), they quickly designed a study to see if the experience of such a traumatic event would affect dream content in general and nightmares in particular (Wood, Bootzin, Rosenhan, Nolen-Hoeksema, & Jourden, 1992). By necessity, they used a nonequivalent control group design. As is generally the case with this design, the groups were nonequivalent to begin with (students from two states); in addition, one group had one type of experience (direct exposure to the earthquake), while the second group had a different experience (no direct exposure).

The experimental group consisted of students from Stanford University and San Jose State University who experienced the earthquake. Nonequivalent controls were college students recruited from the University of Arizona. They did not experience the quake, of course, but they were well aware of it through the extensive media accounts. Shortly after the earthquake event (about a week), all participants began keeping a dream log, which was then analyzed for nightmare content and frequency. Wood et al. (1992) were careful to provide a clear *operational definition* of a nightmare ("frightening dreams with visual content and an elaborated story," p. 220) and to differentiate nightmare from night terrors ("awakening during the night with feelings of intense fear or terror but no memory of a dream," p. 220), instructing subjects to report the former only.

The results were intriguing. Over the 3 weeks of the study, 40% of San Jose students and 37% of the Stanford students reported having at least one earthquake nightmare, while only 5% of the control students at Arizona did (Wood et al., 1992). Of the total number of nightmares experienced by the experimental groups, roughly one-fourth were about earthquakes (27% for San Jose, 28% for Stanford), but virtually, none of the control group's nightmares were about quakes (3% for Arizona). Furthermore, the frequency of nightmares correlated significantly with how anxious participants reported they were during the time of the earthquake.

Well aware of the interpretation problems that accompany quasi-experimental studies, Wood et al. (1992) recognized the dangers inherent in comparing nonequivalent groups. For instance, lacking any pretest (pre-quake) information about nightmare frequency for their participants, they couldn't "rule out the possibility that California residents have more nightmares about earthquakes than do Arizona residents even when no earthquake has recently occurred" (p. 222). If one lives in California, perhaps earthquake nightmares are a normal occurrence. However, relying partly on their general expertise in the area of nightmare research, and partly on other survey data about nightmares (estimates from subjects of pre-earthquake nightmares), the authors argued that the nightmare frequency was exceptionally high in the California group and likely the result of their recent traumatic experience.

Interrupted Time Series Designs

If Wood and his colleagues (1992) could have foreseen San Francisco's earthquake, they might have started collecting nightmare data from their participants for several months leading up to the quake and then for several months after the quake. That would have enabled them to determine (a) if the quake truly increased nightmare experiences for the participants in the quake zone, and (b) if the nightmare frequency peaked shortly after the quake and then returned to baseline. Of course, not even talented seismologists can predict earthquakes, so Wood and his coworkers did the best they could and designed their nonequivalent control group study. If they had been able to take measures for an extended period before and after the event expected to influence behavior, their study would have been called an **interrupted time series design**.

Using the system in Campbell and Stanley (1963) again, the basic time series study can be symbolized like this:

$$O_1 \ O_2 \ O_3 \ O_4 \ O_5 \ \mathbf{T} \ O_6 \ O_7 \ O_8 \ O_9 \ O_{10}$$

where all of the O's represent measured observations of behavior taken before and after T, which is the point at which some treatment program is introduced or some event (e.g., an earthquake) occurs. T is the interruption in the interrupted time series. Of course, the number of measures taken before and after T will vary from study to study and are not limited to five each. It is also not necessary that the number of pre-interruption and post-interruption points be the same. As a general rule, the more data points, the better, and some experts (e.g., Orwin, 1997) recommend at least *50* pre-interruption data points.

Outcomes

The main advantage of a time series design is that it allows the researcher to evaluate **trends**, which are relatively consistent patterns of events that occur with the passing of time. For example, suppose you were interested in seeing the effects of a 2-month antismoking campaign on the number of teenage smokers in a community. The program might include persuasion techniques, peer counseling, showing the teens a smoked-out lung or two, and so on. Assuming you had a good measure of the smoking behavior, you could take the measure a month before and a month after introducing the program and perhaps get the results in Figure 11.5.

Did the program work? There certainly is a reduction in smoking from pre- to posttest, but it's hard to evaluate it in the absence of a control group (i.e., using a nonequivalent control group design). Yet, even without a control group, it might be possible to evaluate the campaign more systematically if not one but several measures were taken both before and after the program was put in place. Consider the possible outcomes in Figure 11.6, which examines the effect of the antismoking campaign by measuring smoking behavior every month for a year before and a year after the program (the solid-line portion of the graphs duplicates Figure 11.5).

Figure 11.7a is a good illustration of how an interrupted time series can identify trends. In this case, the reduction that looked so good in Figure 11.5 is shown to be nothing more than part of a general trend toward reduced smoking among adolescents. This demonstrates an important feature of interrupted time series designs: They can serve to rule out (i.e., falsify) alternative explanations of an apparent change from pre- to posttest.

Two other outcomes that raise questions about the program's effectiveness are seen in Figure 11.6b and 11.6c. In Figure 11.6b, smoking behavior was fairly steady before the campaign

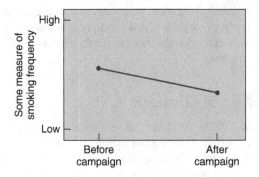

FIGURE 11.5
Incidence of smoking behavior just before and just after a hypothetical antismoking campaign.

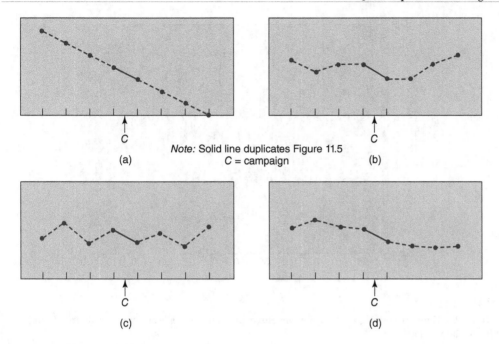

Note: Solid line duplicates Figure 11.5
C = campaign

(a)   (b)

(c)   (d)

FIGURE 11.6
Hypothetical antismoking campaign evaluated with an interrupted time series design—several
possible outcomes.

and then dropped but just briefly. In other words, if the antismoking program had any effect at all,
it was short-lived. In Figure 11.6c, the decrease after the program was part of another general
trend, this time a periodic fluctuation between higher and lower levels of smoking. The ideal
outcome is shown in Figure 11.6d. Here the smoking behavior is at a steady and high rate before
the program begins, drops after the antismoking program is put into effect, and remains low for
some time afterward. Note also in Figure 11.6d that the relatively steady baseline prior to the
campaign enables the researcher to rule out regression effects.

Research Example 36—An Interrupted Time Series Design

An actual example of an outcome like the one in Figure 11.6d can be found in a study of worker
productivity completed at a unionized iron foundry by Wagner, Rubin, and Callahan (1988).
They were interested in the effect of instituting an incentive plan in which workers were treated
not as individuals but as members of small groups, each responsible for a production line.
Productivity data were compiled for 4 years prior to introducing the incentive plan and 6 years
afterward; there were 114 monthly data points. As you can see from their time series graph in
Figure 11.7, productivity was fairly flat and not very impressive prior to the plan but increased
steadily after the plan was implemented and stayed high for some time afterward.

This study also illustrates how those conducting interrupted time series designs try to deal
with potential threats to internal validity. Figure 11.7 certainly appears to show the incentive
plan worked wonders, but there is no control group comparison and the changes could have been
influenced by other factors, including history, instrumentation, and even subject selection.
Wagner et al. (1988) argued that history did not contribute to the change because they carefully
examined as many events as they could in the period before and after the change and could find
no reason to suspect that unusual occurrences led to the jump in productivity. In fact, events that
might be expected to hurt productivity (e.g., a recession in the automobile industry, which
affected sales of iron castings) didn't. The researchers also ruled out instrumentation, which

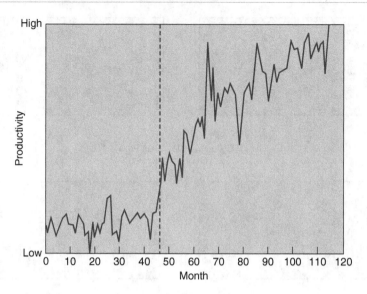

FIGURE 11.7
Interrupted time series design: effect of an incentive plan on worker productivity in an iron foundry (from Wagner et al., 1988).

could be a problem if the techniques for scoring and recording worker productivity changed over the years. It didn't. Third, although we normally think of subject selection as a potential confound only in studies with two or more nonequivalent groups, it can occur in a time series study if significant worker turnover occurred during the time of the new plan; the cohort of workers on site prior to the plan could be different in some important way from the group there after the plan went into effect. This didn't happen in Wagner et al.'s study though. In short, designs like this one, because they lack a control group, are susceptible to several threats to internal validity. These threats often can be ruled out, however, by systematically examining available information, and Wagner and his colleagues did just that.

Variations on the Basic Time Series Design

Sometimes, the conclusions from an interrupted time series design can be strengthened if some type of control comparison is made. One approach amounts to combining the best features of the nonequivalent control group design (a control group) and the interrupted time series design (long-term trend analysis). The design looks like this:

$$O_1\, O_2\, O_3\, O_4\, O_5 \quad \textbf{T} \quad O_6\, O_7\, O_8\, O_9\, O_{10}$$
$$O_1\, O_2\, O_3\, O_4\, O_5 \qquad\quad O_6\, O_7\, O_8\, O_9\, O_{10}$$

If you look ahead to Figure 11.9 in Box 11.2, you will see a classic example of this strategy, a study that evaluated a speeding crackdown in Connecticut by comparing fatal accident data from that state with data from similar states. Another example comes from the aftermath of the Oklahoma City bombing in 1995. This domestic terrorist attack, the bombing of a federal building, killed 168 persons, including 19 children, and injured more than 700. Nakonezny, Reddick, and Rodgers (2004) hypothesized that the resulting feelings of helplessness and insecurity would lead Oklahoma City residents to seek "the comfort and support of familial and marital bonds to restore a sense of structure and security" (p. 91). Focusing on divorce rates in Oklahoma City and in several comparison locations in the state for 10 years before the bombing and 5 years after it, they discovered a significant decline in the Oklahoma City divorce rate for several years following the bombing. Like Figure 11.6b, however, the decline was not lasting; after 5 years, the divorce rate reverted to the normal statewide rate.

A second strategy for strengthening conclusions from a time series study is when a program can be introduced in different locations at different times, a design labeled an **interrupted time series with switching replications** by Cook and Campbell (1979), and operating like this:

$$O_1 \, O_2 \, O_3 \, \textbf{T} \, O_4 \, O_5 \, O_6 \, O_7 \, O_8 \, O_9 \, O_{10}$$
$$O_1 \, O_2 \, O_3 \, O_4 \, O_5 \, O_6 \, O_7 \, \textbf{T} \, O_8 \, O_9 \, O_{10}$$

With this procedure, the same treatment or program is put into place in two locations at two points in time. There is no control group, but the design provides the benefit of a built-in replication. If the outcome pattern in Location 2 matches that of Location 1, the researchers can be more confident about the generality of the phenomenon being studied. This happened in an unpublished study reported in Cook and Campbell (1979). It was completed in the late 1940s and early 1950s, when televisions were just starting to change our lives. A number of Illinois communities were given licenses for new TV stations, but in 1951, there was a freeze on new licenses that wasn't lifted until 1953. That gave researchers an opportunity to study the impact of new televisions on communities at two different times: in the late 1940s, just before the freeze, and right after 1953, with the freeze lifted. Hypothesizing that the new invention would reduce the amount of reading done, researchers studied library circulation data and found support for their concerns about reading. As TVs began infiltrating communities, library circulation dropped, and the pattern was virtually identical during the two times examined.

A third elaboration on an interrupted time series design, again in the absence of a control group, is to measure several *dependent* variables, some expected to be influenced by the interruption, others not expected to change. This was the strategy used in a study by Stolzenberg and D'Alessio (1997). They examined the effect of a California mandatory jail sentencing law, the "three strikes and you're out" policy, on crime rates. The essence of the policy is that jail sentences occur automatically once a person has been convicted of three serious crimes (felonies). Combining data from California's 10 largest cities, Stolzenberg and D'Alessio examined two types of crime rates (i.e., two dependent variables): felonies, supposedly reduced by mandatory sentencing, and misdemeanors (relatively minor crimes). Presumably, misdemeanors would not be affected by the three strikes law. Figure 11.8 shows the results, a good example of the advantages of a time series design. If you look at the curve for serious crimes right after the law was passed, it looks like there is a decline, especially when compared to the flat curve for the misdemeanors. If you look at the felony crime curve as a whole; however, it is clear that any reduction in serious crime is part of a trend occurring since around 1992, well before passage of the three strikes law. Overall, the researchers concluded the three strikes law had no discernible effect on serious crime.

SELF TEST

11.2

1. Why is it said that the nonequivalent control group design has a built-in confound?
2. If nonequivalent groups are used and the groups are matched on a pretest score, the results can be distorted by a _____ effect.
3. Time series designs sometimes include "switching replications." How does this design differ from the basic interrupted time series design?

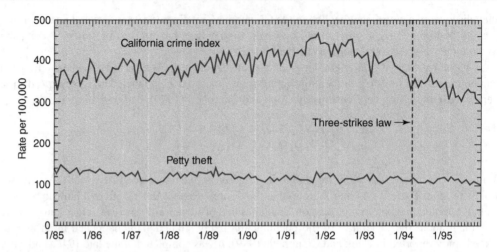

FIGURE 11.8
Interrupted time series using two different dependent measures; the effect of mandatory sentencing on crime rates (from Stolzenberg & D'Alessio, 1997).

Program Evaluation

Applied research that attempts to assess the effectiveness and value of public policy (e.g., California's three strikes law) or specially designed programs (e.g., Meals on Wheels) is sometimes given the name **program evaluation**. This research concept developed in the 1960s in response to the need to evaluate social programs like Head Start, but it is concerned with much more than answering the question "Did program X work?" More generally, program evaluation includes (a) procedures for determining if a need exists for a particular program and who would benefit if the program is implemented; (b) assessments of whether a program is being run according to plan and, if not, what changes can be made to facilitate its operation; (c) methods for evaluating program outcomes; and (d) cost analyses to determine if program benefits justify the funds expended. Let's consider each in turn. First, however, you should read Box 11.2, which highlights a paper by Donald Campbell (1969) that is always included at or near the top of lists of the "most important papers about the origins of program evaluation."

BOX 11.2   ORIGINS—Reforms as Experiments

A 1969 article by Donald Campbell entitled "Reforms as Experiments" is notable for three reasons. First, he argued forcefully that we should have an experimental attitude toward social reform. In the opening sentence, Campbell wrote:

[W]e should be ready for an experimental approach to social reform, an approach in which we try out new programs designed to cure specific social problems, in which we learn whether or not these programs are effective, and in which we retain, imitate, modify, or discard them on the basis of apparent effectiveness. (p. 409)

Second, Campbell's (1969) article helped originate and define the field of program evaluation, and it described several studies that have become classics. Perhaps the best-known example is his description of a study evaluating an effort to reduce speeding in Connecticut (Campbell & Ross, 1968). Following a year (1955) with a record number of traffic fatalities (324), Connecticut governor Abraham Ribicoff instituted a statewide crackdown on speeding, making the reasonable assumption that speeding and traffic fatalities were related. The following year, the number of deaths fell to 284. This statistic was sufficient for Ribicoff to declare that with "the saving of 40 lives in 1956, a reduction of 12.3% from the 1955 . . . death toll, we can say that the program is definitely worthwhile" (quoted in Campbell, 1969, p. 412). Was it?

I hope you're saying to yourself that other interpretations of the drop are possible. For example, history could be involved; perhaps the weather was better in 1956. Even more likely is regression to the mean—324 is the perfect example of an extreme score that would normally be followed by regression to the mean. Indeed, Campbell argued that regression contributed to the Connecticut results, pointing out that "[r]egression artifacts are probably the most recurrent form of self-deception in the experimental social reform literature" (p. 414). Such effects frequently occur in these kinds of studies because interventions like a speeding crackdown often begin right after something especially bad has happened. Purely by chance alone, things are not likely to be quite as bad the following year.

Was regression to the mean all that was involved here? Probably not. By applying an interrupted time series design with a nonequivalent control (comparable states without a crackdown on speeding), Campbell concluded the crackdown probably did have some effect, even if it was not as dramatic as the governor believed. You can see the results for yourself in Figure 11.9.

The third reason the Campbell article is so important is that it gave researchers insight into the political realities of doing research on socially relevant issues. Politicians often propose programs they believe will be effective and, while they might say they're interested in a thorough evaluation, they tend not to be too appreciative of a negative evaluation. After all, by backing the program, they have a stake in its success and its continuance, especially if the program benefits the politician's home state or district. For this reason, politicians and the administrators hired to run programs seldom push for rigorous evaluation and are willing to settle for

favorable research outcomes even if they come from flawed research design. For example, Governor Ribicoff was willing to settle for looking at nothing more than traffic fatalities immediately before and after the crackdown on speeding.

Campbell (1969) recommended an attitude change that would shift emphasis from the importance of a particular program to acknowledging the importance of the problem. This would lead politicians and administrators alike to think of programs as experimental attempts to solve the problem; different programs would be tried until one was found to work. As Campbell put it in the article's conclusion,

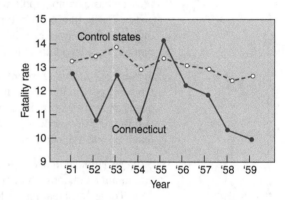

FIGURE 11.9
The Connecticut speeding crackdown, a classic example of an interrupted time series with a nonequivalent control (from Campbell, 1969).

Trapped administrators have so committed themselves in advance to the efficacy of the reform that they cannot afford an honest evaluation. . . . *Experimental administrators* have justified the reform on the basis of the importance of the problem, not the certainty of their answer, and are committed to going on to other potential solutions if the first one tried fails. They are therefore not threatened by a hard-headed analysis of the reform. (p. 428; italics in the original)

Planning for Programs—Needs Analysis

An agency begins a program because administrators believe a need exists that would be met by the program. How is that need determined? Clearly, more is required than just an administrative decision that a program seems to make sense. An exercise program in a retirement community sounds reasonable, but if none of the residents will participate, time and money will be wasted. Before any project is planned in any detail, a needs assessment must be completed.

A **needs analysis** is a set of procedures for predicting whether a population of sufficient size exists that would benefit from the proposed program, whether the program could solve a clearly defined problem, and whether members of the population would actually use the program. Several methods exist for estimating need, and it is important to rely on at least some of these techniques because it is easy to overestimate need. One reason for caution follows from the *availability heuristic*, first introduced in Chapter 1's discussion about ways of knowing. Events that grab headlines catch our attention and become more "available" to our memory. Because they come so readily to mind, we tend to overestimate how often they occur. All it takes is one or two highly publicized cases of children being abandoned by vacationing parents for a call to be made for new programs to fix this seemingly widespread problem. Also, a need for a new program can be overestimated by those in a position to benefit (i.e., keep their jobs) from the program's existence.

As outlined by Posavac and Carey (2010), there are several ways to identify the potential need for a program. These include:

- *Census data.* If your proposed program is aimed at the elderly, it's fairly obvious that its success will be minimal if few seniors live in the community. Census data (www.census.gov) can provide basic demographic information about the number of people fitting into various categories. Furthermore, the information is fine-grained enough for you to determine the number of single mothers under the age of 21, the number of people with various disabilities, the number of older adults below the poverty line, and so on.

- *Surveys of available resources.* There's no reason to begin a Meals on Wheels program if one already exists in the community and is functioning successfully. Thus, one obvious step in a needs analysis is to create an inventory of existing services that includes a description of who is providing the services, exactly which services are being provided, and an estimate of how many people are receiving the services.

- *Surveys of potential users.* A third needs analysis strategy is to administer a survey within the community, either to a broadly representative sample or to a target group identified by census data. Those participating could be asked whether they believe a particular program is needed.

- *Key informants, focus groups, and community forums.* A **key informant** is someone in the community who has a great deal of experience and specialized knowledge about the problem at hand that is otherwise unavailable to the researcher (Gilchrist & Williams, 1999). Such persons include community activists, clergy, people who serve on several social service agency boards, and so on. A **focus group** is a small group (typically 7-9 people) whose members respond to a set of open-ended questions about some topic, such as the need for a particular program (they might also be used to assess a program's progress or its outcome). Focus groups are often used as a follow-up to a community survey, but they also can be used to shape the questions that will appear in a survey. Finally, useful information can sometimes emerge from a **community forum**, an open meeting at which all members of a community affected by a potential program are invited to come and participate. Key informants, focus groups, and forums can all be helpful tools, but the researcher must be careful of weighing too heavily the arguments of an especially articulate (but perhaps nonrepresentative) informant, focus group member, or speaker at a forum.

The past few decades have seen an increased awareness in corporate America that profits are related to worker health. Consequently, companies frequently develop, implement, and evaluate programs for improving the health of their workers. The following study describes a large-scale example that began with a thorough analysis of need.

Research Example 37—Assessing Need in Program Evaluation

A needs analysis project was undertaken by the Du Pont Company prior to starting a program designed to promote healthy behaviors in the workplace (Bertera, 1990). The plan called for a series of changes that would affect over 110,000 employees at 100 worksites. The cost of putting such an ambitious plan into effect made it essential that need be demonstrated clearly.

The Du Pont needs assessment included an analysis of existing data on the frequency of various types of employee illnesses, employee causes of death, and the reasons for employee absence and disability over a 15-year period. One result was that employees making the least amount of money and performing the lowest ranking jobs were the highest on all major categories of illness. That finding told the evaluators that this particular subgroup of workers needed special attention.

Additional indicators that the health promotion program was needed came from a survey of existing company programs for enhancing health. The survey revealed a range of programs run by the medical staffs at the various plants, including programs on weight loss, smoking cessation, stress management, and the like. The programs tended to be one-time lectures or films, however, or counseling during company physical exams; there was minimal follow-up and no systematic evaluation of effectiveness. Employees were also surveyed to determine their knowledge of health-enhancing behaviors, their intention to change things like their eating habits, their self-assessments of whether their own behaviors were health-enhancing or not, and their preferences for a range of health programs.

On the basis of all of this information, Du Pont developed a comprehensive series of programs aimed at improving the health of its workers. These included training programs that went far beyond one-shot lectures, including creation of local employee Health Promotion Activity Committees, recognition and award programs for reaching certain health goals, and workplace climate changes (e.g., removing cigarette vending machines). Also, all workers completed a Health Risk Survey. The results generated a Health Risk Appraisal, which became part of the workers' personnel files and included an individualized plan for promoting healthy behaviors. On the basis of their needs assessment, the Du Pont Company instituted a company-wide program designed to improve workplace health, specifically targeting "smoking cessation, blood pressure control, and lipid control" (Bertera, 1990, p. 316).

Once the needs analysis is complete and the decision is made to proceed, details of the program can be planned and the program begun. Once the program is under way, the second type of evaluation activity begins.

Monitoring Programs—Formative Evaluation

Programs often extend over a considerable period. To wait for a year or so before doing a final evaluation of program effectiveness might be preferable from a methodological point of view, but what if it is clear in the first month that problems exist that could be corrected easily? That is, rather than waiting until the program's completion, why not carefully monitor the progress of the program while it is in progress? This monitoring is called a **formative evaluation**, and according to one analysis (Sechrest & Figueredo, 1993), it is the most common form of evaluation activity.

A formative evaluation can include several components. For one thing, it determines if the program is being implemented as planned. For example, suppose a local crisis hotline decides to develop a program aimed at the needs of young children who are home alone after school while their parents are working. One piece of the implementation plan is to make the hotline's phone number available and well known. A formative evaluation would determine whether the planned advertisements were placed online or in local newspapers at appropriate times and whether mass mailings of stickers with the hotline's number went out as planned. There's no point in trying to evaluate the effectiveness of the program if people don't even know about it.

Another general function of the formative evaluation is to provide data on how the program is being used. Borrowing a term from accounting, evaluators sometimes refer to this procedure as a **program audit**. Just as a corporate auditor might look for inconsistencies between the way inventories are supposed to be managed and the way they actually are managed, the program auditor examines whether the program as described in the agency's literature is the same as the program that is actually being implemented.

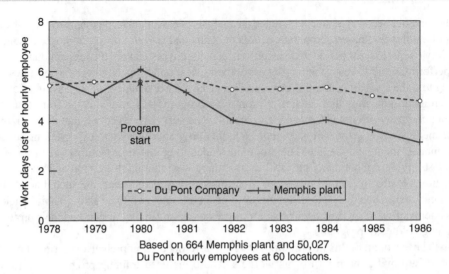

FIGURE 11.10
Effectiveness of a workplace health improvement program, evaluated via time series (from Bertera, 1990).

A final part of a formative evaluation can be a *pilot study* (Chapter 3). Program implementation and some preliminary outcomes can be assessed on a small scale before extending the program. This happened in the Du Pont study. A pilot program at one of the plants, which showed a significant decline in sick days after implementation of the health promotion program, encouraged program planners and led to an elaboration of the program at other sites (Bertera, 1990). As you can see from Figure 11.10, researchers used a time series design, with data collected over 8 years. (*Note*: By 1982, the results were clear enough that executives began expanding the program to other plants.)

Evaluating Outcomes—Summative Evaluation

Politically, formative evaluations are less threatening than **summative evaluations,** which are overall assessments of program effectiveness. Formative evaluation is aimed at program improvement and is less likely to call into question the program's very existence. Summative evaluation, on the other hand, can do just that. If the program isn't effective, why keep it, and, by extension, why continue to pay the program's director and staff? (See what we mean about "threatening?") As Sechrest and Figueredo (1993) stated:

> Summative evaluation and even the rationale for doing it call into question the very reasons for existence of the organizations involved. Formative evaluation, by contrast, simply responds to the question "How can we be better?" without strongly implying the question "How do [we] know [we] are any good at all?" (p. 661)

Despite the political difficulty, summative evaluations are the core of the evaluation process and are an essential feature of any program funded by the federal government. Any agency wishing to spend tax dollars to develop a program is obligated to show those dollars are being used effectively.

The actual process of performing summative evaluations involves applying some of the techniques you already know about, especially quasi-experimental designs. However, more rigorous experiments with random assignment are possible sometimes, especially when evaluating a program that has more people desiring it than space available. In such a case, random assignment in the form of a lottery (random winners get the program; others wind up in a wait list control group) is not only methodologically sound, it is also the only fair procedure to use.

One problem that sometimes confronts the program evaluator is how to interpret a failure to find significant differences between experimental and control groups—that is, the statistical decision is "fail to reject the null hypothesis" Such an outcome is difficult to interpret, as you recall from the discussion in Chapter 4. It could be there just isn't any difference, yet there's always the possibility of a *Type II error* being committed (an effect is real, but your study failed to find it), especially if the measuring tools are not sensitive or reliable. The program might indeed have produced some small but important effect, but the analysis failed to discover it.

Although a finding of no difference can be difficult to interpret, most researchers believe that such a finding (especially if replicated) contributes important information for decision making, especially in applied research. For instance, someone advocating the continuation of a new program is obligated to show how the program is better than something already in existence. Yet, if differences between this new program and one already well established cannot be shown, then it might be wise to discontinue the new program, especially if it is more expensive to implement than the older one. A "fail to reject the null" decision also can help evaluate exaggerated claims made by advocates of a new program. A finding of no difference has important implications for decision making for reasons having to do with cost, and this brings us to the final type of program evaluation activity.

Weighing Costs—Cost-Effectiveness Analysis

Suppose a researcher is interested in the question of worker health and fitness and is comparing two health-enhancement programs. One includes opportunities for exercising on company time, educational seminars on stress management, and a smoking ban. The second plan is a more comprehensive (and more expensive) program of evaluating each worker and developing an individually tailored fitness program, along with financial incentives for achievements like reducing blood pressure and cholesterol levels. Both programs are implemented on a trial basis in two plants; a third plant is used as a control group. Hence, the design is a nonequivalent control group design with two experimental groups instead of just one. A summative evaluation finds no difference between the two experimental groups in terms of improved worker health, but both show improvements compared to the control group. In other words, both health programs work, but the cheap version works just as well as the expensive version. If two programs producing the same outcome differ in cost, why bother with the expensive one?

This corporate fitness example illustrates one type of **cost-effectiveness analysis**: monitoring the actual costs of a program and relating those costs to the effectiveness of the program's outcomes. If two programs with the same goal are equally effective but the first costs half as much as the second, then it is fairly obvious that the first program should be used. A second type of cost analysis takes place during the planning stages for a program. Estimating costs at the outset helps determine whether a program is feasible and provides a basis for the later comparison of projected costs and actual costs.

Estimating costs with reference to outcomes can be a complicated process, often requiring the expertise of a specialist in cost accounting. Thus, a detailed discussion of the procedures for relating costs to outcomes is beyond the scope of this chapter. In addition, it is often difficult if not impossible to put a monetary value on the benefits that might result from the implementation and continuance of a program, especially one involving wellness. Some of the basic concepts of a cost analysis can be discovered by reading Chapter 11 of Posavac and Carey's (2010) fine introduction to program evaluation.

A Note on Qualitative Data Analysis

Chapter 3 introduced the difference between a quantitative analysis (numbers involved) and a qualitative analysis (numbers not so critical), and Chapter 10 elaborated upon qualitative analysis of data from non-experimental designs. Although much of the analysis that occurs in program evaluation is quantitative in nature, there is a great deal of qualitative analysis as well, especially in the first three categories of evaluation just described. Thus, during a needs analysis, quantitative data from a community survey and census data can be combined with in-depth interview information from key informants and focus groups. In formative and summative assessments, quantitative data can be supplemented with a qualitative analysis of interviews with agency workers and clients and with direct observations of the program in action. In short, in program evaluation research, it is seldom a question of whether quantitative or qualitative research is better. Although there has been and continues to be debate about the relative merits of quantitative and qualitative evaluation (e.g., Worthen, 2001), thoughtful program evaluators rely on both.

SELF TEST

11.3

1. When are focus groups and community forums used during a program evaluation?
2. What is a formative evaluation and what is the value of one?
3. What is a summative evaluation, and why does it generate more stress than a formative evaluation?

As first mentioned in Chapter 5's discussion of *external validity*, research in psychology is sometimes criticized for avoiding real-world investigations. This chapter on applied research should make it clear that the criticism is without merit. Indeed, concern over application and generalizability of results is not far from the consciousness of all psychologists, even those committed primarily to basic research. It is evident from psychology's history that application is central to American psychology, if for no other reason than Americans can't help it. Looking for practical applications of research is as American as apple pie.

The next chapter introduces a slightly different tradition in psychological research: an emphasis on the intensive study of individuals. As you will see, just as the roots of applied research can be found among psychology's pioneers, experiments with small N also trace to the beginnings of the discipline. Before moving on to Chapter 12, however, read Box 11.3, which summarizes some ethical problems likely to be encountered when doing program evaluation research.

BOX 11.3   ETHICS—Evaluation Research and Ethics

Whether evaluating programs that provide services to people, conducting studies in a workplace environment, or evaluating a government service, program evaluation researchers often encounter ethical dilemmas not faced by laboratory psychologists. Some special problems include:

- *Informed consent.* People receiving social services are often powerless. When asked to "volunteer" for a study and sign an informed consent form, they may fear that a failure to sign up could mean a loss of services. In situations like this, researchers must take deliberate steps to reassure participants that no coercion will occur.

- *Maintaining confidentiality.* In some research, confidentiality can be maintained by gathering behavioral data from participants but not adding any personal identifiers. In other studies, however, it is necessary for the researcher to know who the participants are. For instance, the researcher might need to repeatedly contact participants, especially if the study is a longitudinal one, or a researcher might want to know who replied to a survey so nonrespondents can be contacted again. In such cases, it is important to develop coding systems to protect the identities of participants. Sometimes, participants in longitudinal studies can use aliases, and survey respondents can send back the anonymous survey and a postcard verifying their participation in separate mailings (Sieber, 1998).

- *Perceived injustice.* Some people might object to being in a control group because they could be missing out on some potentially beneficial treatment. Although most control group members in program evaluation research receive the prevailing treatment rather than none at all, control group problems can still happen. For example, *participant crosstalk* (see Chapter 2 and Box 8.2 in Chapter 8) can occur if control group members discover important information about the program being offered to someone else. Their resentment of "special treatment"

being given to others can seriously affect the outcome. In a study designed to evaluate worksite changes in a coal mine, for instance, control group miners quickly grew to resent those in the treatment group, whom they felt were getting special attention and did not have to work as hard for the same money (Blumberg & Pringle, 1983). The ill will was even directed at the researchers. Control group workers believed them to be in league with the mine owner in an attempt to break the union. The study as originally designed had to be discontinued.

- *Avoiding conflict with stakeholders.* **Stakeholders** are persons connected with a program in which they have a vested interest, including clients, staff, and program directors. Program evaluators must be aware of and take steps to avoid potential conflict. This means being aware of the needs of stakeholders and explicitly addressing them during all stages of the evaluation.

CHAPTER SUMMARY

Beyond the Laboratory

The goal of applied research is to shed light on the causes of and solutions to real-world problems. Like basic research, however, the outcomes of applied research also contribute to general theories about behavior (e.g., the cognitive interview study contributes to our basic knowledge about the influence of context on memory). American psychologists always have been interested in applied research, partly because of institutional pressures to show the "new" psychological science of the late 19th century could be put to good use. Applied research can encounter ethical problems (e.g., with informed consent) and problems with internal validity (e.g., nonequivalent groups), but it is often strong in external validity.

Quasi-Experimental Designs

Research in which participants cannot be randomly assigned to conditions is referred to as quasi-experimental research. Nonequivalent control group designs are one example. They typically compare pretest/posttest changes in a group receiving some treatment with pre/post changes in a control group formed without random assignment. Regression effects can make interpretation

difficult when nonequivalent groups are forced into a degree of equivalency by matching them on pretest scores. In an interrupted time series design, researchers take several measurements both before and after the introduction of the treatment being evaluated. Time series studies enable the researcher to evaluate the effects of trends. Sometimes a nonequivalent control condition, a switching replication, or additional dependent measures can be added to the basic time series design.

Program Evaluation

The field of program evaluation is a branch of applied psychology that provides empirical data about the effectiveness of human service and government programs. Needs analysis studies determine whether a new program should be developed. Census data, surveys, and other community data can help assess need. Formative evaluations determine whether a program is operating according to plan, and summative evaluations assess program outcomes. Cost effectiveness analyses help determine whether a program's benefits are worth the funds invested. Program evaluation research typically combines both quantitative and qualitative methods.

CHAPTER REVIEW QUESTIONS

1. Use the Research Example of traffic signal labeling and food preference and choice as a way of showing how basic research and applied research are related (Trudel et al., 2015).

2. Describe how Hollingworth was able to use fairly sophisticated methodological controls in his applied study of the effects of caffeine.

3. Describe the essential features of a nonequivalent control group design, and explain why Figure 11.2c does not necessarily allow the conclusion that the program was a success.

4. Early program evaluations of Head Start seemed to show that gains made by Head Start children were short-lived; by the third grade, no differences existed between those who had been in the program and those who had not. However, this outcome might have been the result of regression to the mean brought about by the matching procedure used to form the groups. Explain.

5. Describe the Research Example that evaluated whether Play Streets led to increased physical activity in children in terms of why it is a nonexperimental control group, and how researchers tried to equate the groups as much as possible (D'Haese et al., 2015).

6. Describe the essential features of an interrupted time series design and three variations on the basic procedure that can strengthen the conclusions drawn from such a design.

7. Describe two quantitative and two qualitative procedures that can be used when conducting a needs analysis.

8. Distinguish between formative and summative program evaluations. What procedures might be used for each?

9. A finding of "no difference" sometimes occurs in program evaluation research. Explain why this is not necessarily a bad thing.

10. Briefly describe the attributes of the four main types of program evaluation research.

11. Briefly describe the ethical dilemmas that can face people doing program evaluation research.

APPLICATIONS EXERCISES

Exercise 11.1. Identifying Threats to Internal Validity

Threats to internal validity are common in non-experimental studies. What follows is a list of some threats you've encountered in this chapter and in Chapter 5. For each of the hypothetical experiments described, identify which of these threats is most likely to provide a reasonable alternative explanation of the outcome. In some cases, more than one threat could be involved.

Some threats to internal validity:

history	maturation
regression	selection
attrition	selection x history

1. A university dean is upset about the low percentage of freshmen who return to the school as sophomores. Historically, the rate has been around 75%, but in the academic year just begun, only 60% of last year's freshmen return. The dean puts a tutoring program into effect and then claims credit for its effectiveness when the following year's return rate is 65%.

2. Two nearby colleges agree to cooperate in evaluating a new computerized instructional system. College A gets the program and college B doesn't. Midway through the study, college B announces it has filed for bankruptcy (even though it continues to operate). One year later, computer literacy is higher at college A.

3. Twelve women who volunteer for a home birthing program are compared with a random sample of other pregnant women who undergo normal hospital procedures for childbirth. Women in the first group spend an average of 6 hours in labor, while those in the control group spend an average of 9 hours.

4. A 6-week program in managing test anxiety is developed and given to a sample of first-semester college students. Their anxiety levels are significantly lower at the conclusion of the program than they were at the start.

5. A teacher decides to use an innovative teaching technique in which all students will proceed at their own pace throughout the term. The course will have 10 units, and each student goes to unit N after completing unit $N - 1$. Once all 10 units have been completed, the course is over and an A has been earned. Of the initial 30 students enrolled in the class, the final grade distribution looks like this:

16	earned an A
2	failed
12	withdrew from the course during the semester

The instructor considers the new course format an unqualified success.

6. A company decides to introduce a flextime program. It measures productivity for January, runs the program for six months, and then evaluates productivity during the month of June. Productivity increases.

Exercise 11.2. Interpreting Nonequivalent Control Group Studies

A wheel-bearing manufacturer owns two plants, both in Illinois. She wishes to see if money for health costs can be reduced if a wellness program is instituted. One plant (E) is selected for a year-long experimental program that includes health screening and individually tailored fitness activities. The second plant (C) is the nonequivalent control group. Absence-due-to-sickness rates, operationally defined as the number of sick days per year per 100 employees, are measured at the beginning and the end of the experimental year. What follows are four sets of results. Construct a graph for each and decide which (if any) provide evidence of program effectiveness. For those outcomes not supporting the program's effectiveness, provide an alternative explanation for the experimental group's apparent improvement.

Outcome 1	E:	pretest = 125	posttest = 100
	C:	pretest = 125	posttest = 125
Outcome 2	E:	pretest = 125	posttest = 100
	C:	pretest = 100	posttest = 100
Outcome 3	E:	pretest = 125	posttest = 100
	C:	pretest = 130	posttest = 105
Outcome 4	E:	pretest = 125	posttest = 100
	C:	pretest = 110	posttest = 110

Exercise 11.3. Interpreting Time Series Studies

Imagine a time series study evaluating the effects of a helmet law on head injuries among hockey players in amateur city leagues across the nation. Head injuries were significantly lower in the year immediately after the law was passed than in the preceding year. Construct four time series graphs, one for each of the following patterns of results.

1. The helmet law worked.

2. The helmet law seemed to work initially, but its effects were short-lived.

3. The helmet law had no effect; the apparent drop was probably just the result of regression to the mean.

4. The helmet law didn't really work; the apparent drop seemed to reflect a general trend toward reduced violence in the sport.

In the section on interrupted time series designs, we described several variations on the basic design. How might each of those be used to strengthen the hockey study?

Exercise 11.4. Planning a Needs Analysis

You are the head of an advocacy group hired by a school district to develop an anti-bullying program in the public elementary schools in the district. Because you've read this chapter, you respond that a needs analysis should be done. The school superintendent tells you to go ahead and even approves a modest budget for the project. Describe the factors that must be considered before implementing the anti-bullying program in schools and explain the techniques you would use to conduct a needs analysis.

ANSWERS TO SELF TESTS

✓ **11.1**

1. The "dual" functions are solving real-world problems, while contributing to general knowledge about some phenomenon.
2. Miles adapted a basic research methodology, reaction time, to an applied problem, reactions of football linemen.
3. Compared with basic laboratory research, applied research tends to be lower in internal validity and higher in external validity.

✓ **11.2**

1. The groups are nonequivalent; in addition, one group gets one type of treatment, and the other group gets a different treatment (or none at all).
2. Regression.
3. In a switching replication, the treatment program is implemented in two different places and at two different times.

✓ **11.3**

1. During a needs analysis.
2. Formative evaluation assesses a program that is in progress and allows for program improvements to be implemented before the program is completed.
3. Compared to formative evaluations, summative evaluations can eliminate jobs if the result is an ineffective program.

Small *N* Designs

12

PREVIEW & CHAPTER OBJECTIVES

Up to this point in the book, the research strategies you've encountered have tested relatively large groups of participants. We have shown how psychological scientists address methodological problems by creating equivalent groups and avoiding order effects, and how they calculate descriptive statistics, complete inferential analyses, calculate effect sizes and confidence intervals, and draw general conclusions about the effects of independent variables on dependent variables. In this chapter, however, you will encounter a different type of methodology. These studies closely examine either a single individual or a very small group of individuals. Most of the chapter concerns designs that are often called single-subject designs because the behavior of each research subject is considered individually, but they can also be called small *N* designs because they often examine more than just a single individual. The data for these subjects might be combined statistically, but most often the data are described individually, with additional data used for replication purposes. This chapter will also consider research designs called case studies, in-depth analyses of individuals or events. When you finish this chapter, you should be able to:

- Describe examples of classic studies in psychology's history, all using single individuals or a small number of participants, with additional subjects used for replication (e.g., Dresslar, Thorndike).

- Explain how grouping data from large numbers of participants can yield misleading conclusions about behavior.

- Describe practical reasons for doing small *N* research.

- Describe B. F. Skinner's basic philosophy about the proper way to conduct research—the experimental analysis of behavior.

- Describe the essential components of any single-subject design.

- Explain the logic of an A-B-A-B withdrawal design.

- Explain the logic of a multiple baseline design and describe three different multiple baseline procedures.

- Explain the logic of a changing criterion design and relate it to the operant concept of shaping.

- Describe how the alternating treatments design allows comparisons between two levels of an independent variable.

- Describe the criticisms that have been directed at small *N* designs in the operant tradition, and the responses made by defenders of the small *N* tradition.

- Describe the essential features of case study research, and describe how other research methods can be incorporated into a case study.

- Describe the strengths and limitations of case study research.

The small *N* strategy that will occupy the bulk of this chapter is most frequently associated with the philosophy of science developed by B. F. Skinner—you first encountered him in Chapter 1. However, it is important to realize that Skinner was not the first to focus on individual research subjects. Rather, small *N* designs have a long history; in fact, the first experimental psychologists used this approach all the time.

Research in Psychology Began with Small *N*

When psychology emerged as a new science in the second half of the 19th century, statistical analysis was also in its infancy. Galton was just beginning to conceptualize correlations, and inferential techniques like ANOVA did not yet exist. Widespread use of large *N* designs and inferential statistics occurred only after Fisher's work on the analysis of variance appeared in the 1930s (see Box 8.3 in Chapter 8). Before this time, although large *N* studies did occur (some early survey research, for instance), small *N* ruled (Goodwin, 2010).

Some of psychology's pioneers used the smallest *N* possible: They studied their own behavior (e.g., the Ebbinghaus memory studies you encountered in Chapter 7) or the behavior of a single individual (e.g., Watson and Rayner's Little Albert experiment, described in Chapter 2). In Wundt's pioneering laboratory at Leipzig in the late 19th century, small *N* designs were also the dominant strategy. The studies normally involved a very small number of research participants, with the investigator usually serving as one of them. Hence, the separation in role (and status) that exists today between the experimenter giving procedural instructions and a participant following them was not in evidence then. In fact, while in the 1890s, participants were sometimes called *subjects*, they were more likely to be called *observers* because they were typically observing their own behavior and mental processes. Whether to use the term subject or observer was an issue as late as 1930 (Danziger, 1985).

Pioneer experimental psychologists sometimes crudely summarized data (e.g., reported means) from several observers, but more often, they reported the data for each person participating. A nice example of this strategy is a study from the laboratory at Clark University. It was an investigation of "facial vision," the ability to detect the presence of nearby objects even when they cannot be seen. At one time, blind people were believed to have developed this as a special sense to compensate for their loss of vision. Clark University's Fletcher B. Dresslar (1893), however, was able to show the skill had more to do with hearing than with vision.

Figure 12.1 is a picture taken in 1892 of the actual experimental setup. As you can see, a blindfolded person (a graduate student friend of Dresslar's) was seated next to a panel of four 1-foot squares. From left to right, the squares were either open or filled with (a) wood in a latticed design, (b) wood in a solid panel, or (c) wire screening. The panel hung from the ceiling and could be moved by the experimenter (that's Dresslar in the photo) so that each of the squares could be placed next to the blindfolded participant's face. The task was to identify which surface was next to one's face; the participants were Dresslar and two other graduate students.

Courtesy Clark University Archives

FIGURE 12.1
Dresslar's apparatus for studying facial vision, 1892.

Remarkably, all three participants quickly learned to distinguish between pairs of surfaces, as shown in Table 12.1, reproduced from the original article. The data represent the number of right ("R.") or wrong ("W.") responses when making judgments between pairs of surfaces. For example, when comparing the latticed surface with the solid one, F. B. D. (guess who that was) was correct 69 times and wrong just once when the correct answer was "lattice" and was correct 70 out of 74 times when the correct answer was "solid." Similar results occurred for the other two participants.

Notice that while data for all three participants are presented, there are no descriptive statistics combining the three data sets. This is because the strategy was to show the phenomenon occurring reliably for each person, not for the average person—that is, Dresslar tested two additional subjects (O. C. and F. B. D.) in order to *replicate* the initial finding (J. A. B.) twice. This replication strategy is a common feature of today's small *N* designs.

Do the results of Dresslar's study mean facial vision as a separate sense truly exists? No. As a good research psychologist, Dresslar looked for a more parsimonious explanation and for a way to rule out (falsify) the existence of the special facial sense. He found it by making a simple procedural change—he plugged everyone's ears. The result was clear: The "power to distinguish [the panels] was lost entirely" (Dresslar, 1893, p. 349). Facial vision turned out to be the ability to detect slight differences in reflected sound waves.

Studies like the one by Dresslar, featuring data from one or just a few participants, can be found throughout the early years of experimental psychology, but large *N* studies were not completely absent. For example, some could be found in educational psychology and in child study research

Table 12.1 **Data from Dresslar's Study of Facial Vision**

Subject	Open and Lattice				Lattice and Solid				Solid and Wire			
	R.	W.	R.	W.	R.	W.	R.	W.	R.	W.	R.	W.
J. A. B.	65	15	59	25	58	2	56	0	45	0	46	2
O. C.	72	47	74	46	33	13	28	14	21	4	14	9
F. B. D.	53	24	58	17	69	1	70	4	73	0	77	2

Source: Dresslar, 1893, p. 347.

(Danziger, 1985). Such studies featured empirical questions such as "What do elementary school children fear?" and they summarized data from hundreds of children. As you recall from Chapter 9, these so-called "questionary" studies (e.g., Hall, 1883) were among the first to use survey methodology. These large-scale studies with statistical summaries were not without their critics, however. Leta Hollingworth, an early pioneer in the study of gifted children (refer to Box 11.1, which describes the caffeine study she completed with her husband, Harry), wrote that "[i]t has become a fashion in educational research to rush forth hastily with a huge load of paper and pencil tests; to spend an hour or two on a hundred children; to rush hastily home to the adding machine, there to tabulate the performances of the children, not *one* of which has ever been perceived as an individual child" (quoted in Hollingworth, 1943/1990, pp. 114–115, italics in the original).

One famous example of an early small *N* project is worth discussing in detail. Because the research is an important historical predecessor to B. F. Skinner's work on operant conditioning and foreshadowed the coming of behaviorism when it was completed over 100 years ago, it can be considered one of the origins of today's small *N* tradition. Before continuing, please read Box 12.1.

BOX 12.1   ORIGINS—Cats in Puzzle Boxes

Edward L. Thorndike (1874–1959) had a distinguished career as an educational psychologist. However, he is best remembered among research psychologists and historians for his doctoral research, in which he studied how cats escape from puzzle boxes (Thorndike, 1898). The research is important for several reasons. It shows how psychology's pioneers relied on the detailed study of individual research participants, it is a good example of how to use parsimonious explanations for behavior, and it is an early example of the kind of research that paved the way for the development of behaviorism, especially the Skinnerian variety.

Studying Cats One at a Time.

To investigate learning in cats, Thorndike built 15 puzzle boxes, each with a unique escape mechanism. The drawing in Figure 12.2 is Thorndike's sketch of one of these simply constructed boxes ("Box K"). To escape from this box, a cat would have to pull on a string, step on a pedal, and maneuver two side latches (most of Thorndike's boxes were simpler, requiring just one response to escape—his cats had great difficulty with Box K).

Cats were studied individually, and Thorndike described his results cat by cat. The cats learned to escape from the

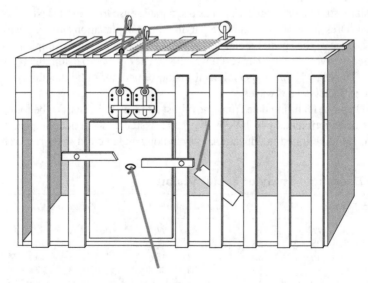

FIGURE 12.2
Thorndike's sketch of "Box K" in his classic studies of cats in puzzle boxes.

boxes through a process Thorndike (1911) called "trial and error, with accidental success" (p. 150) and according to what he named the "Law of Effect" (p. 244). The cats' actions were initially random, and the successful response would eventually occur by accident. Behaviors that worked tended to be repeated ("stamped in" was the phrase Thorndike used), while unsuccessful behaviors were gradually eliminated ("stamped out"). In other words, the effect of a successful behavior was to increase the chances of the behavior occurring on the next trial. The progress of one of Thorndike's cats (no. 10, in Box C, which required a single response) can be seen in Figure 12.3.[1]

Using Parsimonious Explanations.

Thorndike's Law of Effect challenged prevailing ideas about the thinking abilities of animals and provided a more parsimonious explanation of problem-solving abilities. He argued there was no reason to attribute complex thinking processes to animals if their behavior could be explained by a simpler process (i.e., basic trial-and-error learning). Thorndike had little patience with animal researchers who uncritically attributed higher mental processes to animals (e.g., Clever Hans' math skills; see Box 3.2), an attitude shaped by Lloyd Morgan, whose famous statement about

---

[1] On Thorndike's graphs, the *Y*-axis was a measure of time to escape (a vertical millimeter in his original graph meant 10 seconds). As for the *X*-axis, there were no labels, except to note when a significant period passed between his consecutive trials. In Figure 12.3, for example, the small unmarked vertical line (just above the "C") meant a day had elapsed between trials, a "2" was a 2-day gap, "1h" was an hour, and "78" was 78 hours between consecutive trials (Thorndike, 2000, pp. 38–40).

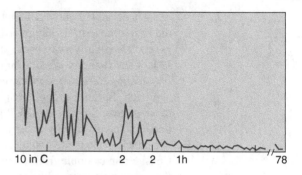

FIGURE 12.3
A record of cat no. 10 learning to escape from Box C (from Thorndike, 1911).

the need for simple yet adequate explanations (Chapter 3) appeared about this time. Thorndike was familiar with Morgan's work and might have heard the Englishman give an invited address on animal learning while visiting Harvard in 1896 (Jonçich, 1968).

Preceding Skinner.

The final point worth noting about Thorndike's puzzle box research is that it represented an experimental approach to the study of learning that paved the way for other behavioral researchers. It also provided a model for learning that eventually took the form of B. F. Skinner's experimental analysis of behavior, which you will encounter later in this chapter. Skinner (1953) acknowledged his debt to Thorndike by referring to the latter's work as being among "the first attempts to study the changes brought about by the consequences of behavior" (p. 59).

Reasons for Small *N* Designs

Despite the popularity of large *N* designs and sophisticated statistical analysis in modern psychology, studies using one or just a few individuals continue to make important contributions to our knowledge of behavior. As you will soon discover, these studies cover the entire range from laboratory to field studies and from basic to applied research. There are several reasons why small *N* designs continue to be used.

Occasional Misleading Results from Statistical Summaries of Grouped Data

The process of summarizing data from large groups of individuals sometimes yields results that fail to characterize the behavior of the individuals who participated in the study. That is, these outcomes can fail to have **individual-subject validity** (Dermer & Hoch, 1999)—the extent to which a general research outcome applies to any one individual subject in the study. Although she didn't use the term, Hollingworth's concern about large-scale educational psychology studies in psychology's early years was, in essence, a concern about individual-subject validity. And the lack of such validity in some large group studies was a central theme in Sidman's (1960) *Tactics of Scientific Research*, considered the classic text on small *N* methodology by advocates of the approach. Because group averages can disguise differences among the individuals composing those groups, Sidman argued, "[g]roup data may often describe a process, or a functional relation, that has no validity for any individual" (p. 274).

A lack of individual-subject validity can produce erroneous conclusions about behavior. Consider an example from a concept-learning experiment with young children as participants. Shown pairs of stimuli like the ones in Figure 12.4, the children pick one of each pair, and they are rewarded (with an M&M perhaps) if they pick the right one. If you look carefully at Figure 12.4, you will see that subjects can pile up the M&Ms if they figure out that "red" is consistently rewarded. Hence, children have to learn to ignore shape (triangle or square or circle) and position (left or right) and focus on color, red in particular. The task is considered learned when the child reaches some criterion score, perhaps 10 consecutive correct choices.

An old controversy in the concept-learning literature concerns the manner in which this type of task is learned (Manis, 1971). According to *continuity* theory, learning is a gradual process of accumulating "habit strength." Each reinforced trial strengthens the tendency to respond to the relevant dimension and weakens responses to the irrelevant dimensions. A graph of this hypothesized incremental learning process should look something like Figure 12.5a. On the other hand, *noncontinuity* theory holds that the children actively try out different hypotheses about the solution during the early trials. While they search for the correct hypothesis, their performance is at chance level (50%), but once they hit on the correct hypothesis, their performance zooms up to 100% accuracy and stays there. Noncontinuity theory predicts that performance should look more like Figure 12.5b.

The history of this issue is long and complicated, with conclusions subject to many qualifications, but part of the resolution hinges on how the data are handled. If data from many participants are grouped together and plotted trial by trial, the result indeed often looks something like

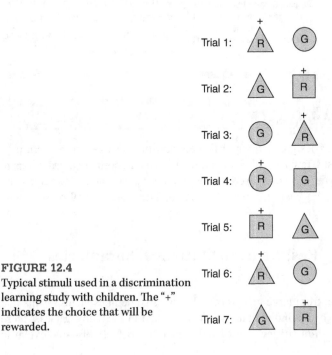

FIGURE 12.4
Typical stimuli used in a discrimination learning study with children. The "+" indicates the choice that will be rewarded.

Trial 1:

Trial 2:

Trial 3:

Trial 4:

Trial 5:

Trial 6:

Trial 7:

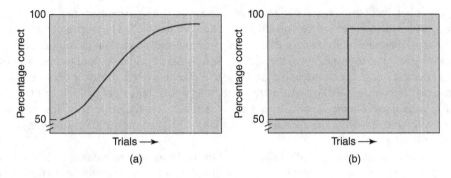

FIGURE 12.5
Concept learning outcomes as predicted by (a) continuity and (b) noncontinuity theory.

Figure 12.5a, and continuity theory is supported. However, a picture more like Figure 12.5b, which supports a noncontinuity theory, emerges when one looks more closely at individual performance, especially on difficult tasks (Osler & Trautman, 1961). Examining performance on trials just before a solution is achieved reveals that accuracy is about 50% (e.g., Trabasso, 1963). After criterion, performance is virtually perfect. That is, individual subjects perform at chance level up to the point when they hit on the correct solution; then their performance improves dramatically. So how does the individual performance illustrated in Figure 12.5b end up as Figure 12.5a when the data are summarized?

The key factor is how long it takes each child to hit on the correct solution; some figure it out quickly, while others take longer. This situation is portrayed in Figure 12.6. As you can see, a series of individual curves, when combined, could easily yield the smooth curve of Figure 12.5a. This is a clear instance of how grouped data can create an impression that is not confirmed by examining the behavior of individual participants. When looking at the group curve, one might reasonably conclude that continuity theory works—a conclusion that, in this case, would be wrong. As a general rule, any researcher using large *N* designs, especially in research in which learning is involved, should at the very least examine the individual data to see if they mirror the grouped data (i.e., to see if individual-subject validity is present).

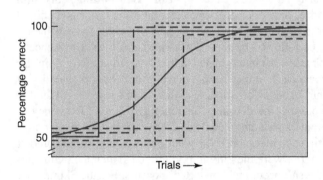

FIGURE 12.6
How grouping data from individual children in a concept-learning experiment can produce a smooth but deceptive learning curve.

Practical and Philosophical Problems with Large *N* Designs

Small *N* designs are sometimes necessary because potential subjects are rare or difficult to find. This can happen in clinical psychology, for example, when a researcher wants to study people with a specific psychological disorder. A related problem can occur in animal research, especially if surgery is involved; the surgical environment is expensive, the procedures are time consuming, and ethical considerations exert downward pressure on the size of *N*. The animal colony itself can be difficult to maintain, with costs in these days of animal rights activism including the expense of a security system. In some cases, the species being studied might be hard to obtain, prohibitively expensive, or require extensive training. For example, the research on teaching sign language to chimpanzees and other apes requires hundreds of hours per animal, and the studies typically extend over many years. In a study teaching sign language to a lowland gorilla (Patterson & Linden, 1981), the ape knew more than 400 signs at age 10; the study began when the ape was just a year old.

Large *N* designs may occasionally fail to reflect the behaviors of individuals, and they may not be feasible even if they are desired, but there are also philosophical reasons for preferring small *N* designs. Those reasons were articulated best by the most famous advocate of this approach, B. F. Skinner (1904–1990). As you might recall from Chapter 4 (in a study used to illustrate ordinal scale data), Skinner was ranked as the most eminent modern-day psychologist in a survey of historians and heads of psychology departments (Korn et al., 1991).

Skinner believed passionately that if psychology were to achieve its goals of predicting and controlling behavior, it must study individuals intensively and derive general principles only after the exhaustive study of separate cases. In other words, psychology should be an *inductive* science, reasoning from specific cases to general laws of behavior. Indeed, Skinner once said it would be better for investigators to "study one rat for a thousand hours" rather than "a thousand rats for an hour each, or a hundred rats for ten hours each" (Skinner, 1966, p. 21). The goal is to reduce random variability by achieving precise control over the experimental situation affecting the single subject. As Skinner (1956) put it, "I had the clue from Pavlov: control your conditions and you will see order" (p. 223). He called this system the "experimental analysis of behavior," and while you should look elsewhere for a thorough discussion of it (e.g., Skinner, 1953), the essentials are worth mentioning here because they provide the philosophical underpinning for the research designs in applied behavior analysis.

The Experimental Analysis of Behavior

For Skinner, the behaviors that most clearly characterize an individual result from that person's learning history, a history based primarily on what he called **operant conditioning**. This form of learning is a "process in which the frequency of occurrence of a bit of behavior is modified by the consequences of the behavior" (Reynolds, 1968, p. 1)—that is, when some behavior occurs in a particular situation, it will be followed by some consequence. If the consequence is positive, the behavior will tend to recur when the individual is in the same situation (or a similar situation) again. Negative consequences, on the other hand, decrease the future probability of the behavior occurring. If a child's tantrum behavior works (e.g., results in a toy), it will tend to be repeated; if it doesn't, it won't. Note that the definition includes the phrase "frequency of occurrence." Skinner believed that in an experimental analysis of behavior, **rate of response** was the most important dependent variable to measure. If the goals of psychology are to predict and control behavior, and for Skinner those were the only important goals, then the main concern is whether a behavior occurs or doesn't occur and how often it occurs. For the Skinnerian, then, the behaviors that characterize our lives are controlled by the environment in which we live. To predict and control behavior, according to Skinner, we must be able to "specify three things: (1) the occasion upon which a response occurs, (2) the response itself, and (3) the reinforcing consequences. The interrelationships among them are the 'contingencies of reinforcement'" (Skinner, 1969, p. 7).

In the laboratory, operant conditioning is most often studied using an apparatus called an *operant chamber*, or *Skinner box*. Figure 12.7 shows a typical one designed for rats (Skinner used rats in his lab, but his favorite subjects were pigeons, who pecked at circular disks in their Skinner boxes). A rat placed in the chamber learns to press down on the lever on the right. When it does so, a food pellet will be released into the food cup (a positive consequence); the rat will become more likely to press the bar again. A negative consequence could be a brief jolt of electricity across the floor grid, which would reduce the chances of future bar pressing behavior.

Once bar pressing behavior is established, it can be brought under the environmental control of stimuli such as the light presented just above and to the left of the bar. If food pellets follow bar presses only when the light is on, the animal quickly learns a simple discrimination: Press when the light is on but don't bother if the light is off. In Skinner's contingencies of reinforcement language, the light being on in the chamber constitutes the "occasion upon which a response occurs," the "response itself" is the bar press, and the food pellet is the "reinforcing consequence."

The rate of bar pressing behavior is recorded and portrayed continuously with an apparatus called a **cumulative recorder**. In a cumulative record, time is presented on the *X*-axis, and bar pressing behavior is recorded at a fixed distance from the *X*-axis every time the animal presses the bar. When and how often a reinforcer follows a response is also recorded, usually as a short, vertical mark. Other events are also recorded, such as when the light goes on and off. Response rate can be assessed simply by looking at the slope of the cumulative record. In the cumulative record in Figure 12.8, for example, the rat is bar pressing rapidly in the first two-thirds of the record (perhaps the cue light in the box is on, and it signals that bar pressing produces food) but is hardly pressing at all in the last third of the record (light off, perhaps).

An extensive portrayal of cumulative records can be found in a book called *Schedules of Reinforcement* (Ferster & Skinner, 1957). As you might recall from your introductory psychology course, a schedule of reinforcement is a rule that determines the relationship between a sequence of behavioral responses and the specific occurrence of a reinforcer. This topic occupied a great deal of

Courtesy of Dr. C. James Goodwin

FIGURE 12.7
An operant chamber for rats.

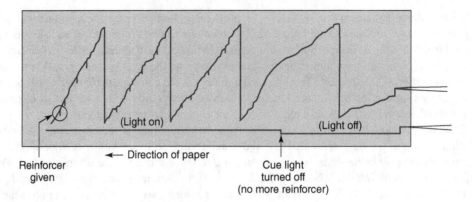

FIGURE 12.8
A hypothetical cumulative record showing both a high (left two-thirds) and a low (right third) rate of responding.

Skinner's time in the 1950s, and the contents of the book provide a perfect illustration of basic research in the experimental analysis of behavior. As Skinner (1984) later described the effort,

> Thousands of hours of data meant thousands of feet of cumulative records. . . . We worked systematically. We would take a protocol and a batch of cumulative records, dictate an account of the experiment, select illustrative records, and cut and nest them in a few figures. In the end, we had more than 1,000 figures, 921 of which went into the book. (p. 109)

In Chapter 1, we used Skinner as an example of how researchers become passionate about their work. The schedules book is a good illustration. The book also exemplifies the small *N* logic: All of the cumulative records in the book show the behavior of individual animals; none show data summary graphs for the "average" rat or pigeon.

The primary publication for basic research in operant conditioning is the *Journal of the Experimental Analysis of Behavior* (*JEAB*), first published in 1958. These titles will give you a sense of what you might encounter there:

> Low-response-rate conditioning history and fixed-interval responding in rats (LeFrancois & Metzger, 1993)

> Pigeons' discrimination of paintings by Monet and Picasso (Watanabe, Sakamoto, & Wakia, 1995)

> Effects of reinforcement history on response rate and response pattern in periodic reinforcement (López & Menez, 2005)

Following Ferster and Skinner's (1957) book, a fair amount of the subsequent basic research in the experimental analysis of behavior concerned the scheduling of reinforcers. For example, the first study just listed, by LeFrancois and Metzger (1993), examined how performance on a "fixed interval" schedule was affected by prior schedules. The details need not concern us, but Figure 12.9, portraying the behavior of two rats in the study, shows that bar pressing on an FI43s (fixed interval schedule of 43 seconds, meaning reinforcement was given for a bar press occurring after 43 seconds) can look very different depending on what preceded it.[2] Skinner often talked about how our current behavior is affected by our "reinforcement history," and this study is a good illustration of the point.

---

[2] The "DRL" in the record stands for **d**ifferential **r**einforcement of **l**ow rates, in this case, a rule that a reinforced bar press would occur only if 20 seconds passed without a bar press occurring.

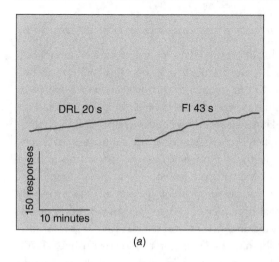

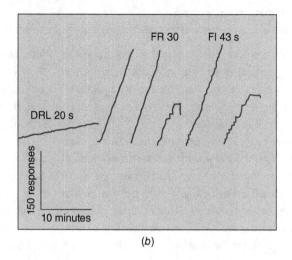

(a)   (b)

FIGURE 12.9
Cumulative records from rats experiencing either (a) DRL→FI or (b) DRL→FR→FI (from LeFrancois & Metzger, 1993).

Applied Behavior Analysis

As Smith (1992) argued, a distinction can be made between two broad categories of scientist. Those representing the "contemplative ideal" focus on trying to understand the basic causes of events in the natural world, while those reflecting the "technological ideal" look for ways to use science to control and change the world. Skinner was firmly in the latter group. Although most of his own research was pure laboratory work, he was always interested in applying the results of an experimental analysis of behavior to real-world problems, and he made important contributions to and recommendations about education, industry, child rearing, and behavior therapy. His ideas even contributed to the NASA space program. On at least two space flights, chimpanzees were given complex operant tasks to learn in space. One psychologist involved in the space project stated that "[e]very technique, schedule, and programming and recording device we used then and subsequently can be traced to [Skinner] or his students" (Rohles, 1992).

Finally, Skinner was not shy about calling for the redesign of society based on operant conditioning principles, a recommendation that made him a controversial figure. To some, his prescriptions for improving the world seemed ominous, and he was accused of trying to turn everyone into rats or pigeons in Skinner boxes. This issue of control is elaborated in Box 12.2, and you should read it carefully and see if you agree with its conclusion before going on to the descriptions of how conditioning principles can be used to solve a variety of applied behavior problems.

BOX 12.2 ETHICS—Controlling Human Behavior

Behaviorists typically describe their goals as the prediction and control of behavior. You might feel a bit uneasy about "control" because it suggests a deliberate attempt to manipulate behavior, perhaps against a person's will. Because of this implication, behaviorists from Watson to Skinner have been accused of seeking dictatorial control via conditioning. For example, when "Cliff's Notes" summarized Skinner's *Walden Two*, a fictional account of a community established on operant principles, it compared the community to George Orwell's nightmare world of *1984* (Todd & Morris, 1992).

(continued)

BOX 12.2   (CONTINUED)

The perception of behaviorist as Big Brother overstates the case but is strengthened when one encounters chapters in Skinner's books with headings like "Designing a Culture" (Skinner, 1953) or superficially reads some of Skinner's statements, usually taken out of context.

The notion that one can and perhaps should act to alter behavior follows from the behaviorist's dictum that much of our behavior is conditioned by our learning history. If our experiences will shape behavior *anyway*, why not ensure that productive behaviors are shaped? This attitude is clearly reflected in two famous quotes. They both imply a more extreme environmentalism than their authors really believed, but each shows an almost mischievous willingness to make controversial statements. The first is a famous claim about child rearing from John Watson, behaviorism's founder:

> Give me a dozen healthy infants, well-formed and my own specified world to bring them up in and I'll guarantee to take any one at random and train him to become any type of specialist I might select—doctor, lawyer, artist, merchant-chief, and yes, even the beggarman and thief. (1924, p. 82)

The second quote is from Skinner's *Walden Two*. Through the voice of the community's founder and perhaps with the wording of Watson's quote in mind, Skinner wrote:

> "What remains to be done?" he said, his eyes flashing. "Well, what do you say to the design of personalities? Would that interest you? The control of temperament? Give me the specifications, and I'll give you the man!" (1948/1976, p. 274)

For Skinner, the controversy over behavior control was a nonissue. It is not a question of deciding whether to control behavior or not, he believed. Behavior *was* controlled by its consequences, period. Given that basic fact, he believed it

followed that effort should be made to create contingencies that would yield productive rather than nonproductive behaviors. Critics remained unconvinced and asked who would be the person deciding which behaviors should be shaped. Skinner believed his critics were missing the point.

One particular manifestation of the controversy over control exists in the clinical environment, where the applied behavior analysis procedures you are about to learn have been quite successful in helping people. One especially controversial procedure has been the use of punishment, including electric shock, to alter the behavior of severely disturbed children. For example, in a study by Kushner (1970), a disabled 7-year-old child (mental age of 2) was treated with electric shock for hand biting. The child frequently bled after biting his hand and had suffered serious infections. Attempts to curb the behavior by having him wear boxing gloves or elbow splints failed. The treatment consisted of placing electrodes on the child's thigh and immediately shocking him every time his hand reached his mouth. The result was an almost immediate decline in the behavior that lasted even when the electrodes were removed.

When procedures like this are used in a study evaluating their effectiveness, has the ethical principle of not harming research participants been violated? Defenders of the use of punishment argue that other procedures often don't work with destructive behaviors like self-biting or head-banging. As long as appropriate safeguards are in place (e.g., other procedures have been tried unsuccessfully, genuine informed consent from parents or guardians has been obtained), the courts have upheld the use of shock "in extraordinary circumstances such as self-destructive behavior that [is] likely to inflict physical damage" (Kazdin, 1978, p. 352).

The applications side of the experimental analysis of behavior is sometimes called **applied behavior analysis**. It includes any procedure that uses behavioral, especially operant, principles to solve real-life behavioral problems. To get a sense of the range of situations in which these principles are used, consider the following recent titles from the *Journal of Applied Behavior Analysis* (*JABA*), a journal founded in 1968, a decade after the creation of *JEAB*:

Teaching empathy skills to children with autism (Schrandt, Townsend, & Poulson, 2009)

Manipulating slot machine preference in problem gamblers through contextual control (Nastally, Dixon, & Jackson, 2010)

Using trained pouched rats to detect land mines: Another victory for operant conditioning (Poling, Weetjens, Cox, Beyene, Bach, & Sully, 2011)

The designs we'll examine in the next section are most frequently applied to clinical settings, but as you can see from this list from *JABA*, the earlier mention of Skinner's applied work, and the designs that follow, operant principles are used in an assortment of circumstances.

> ## SELF TEST
> ### 12.1
>
> 1. Explain why Dresslar's facial vision study is a good example of falsification thinking.
> 2. Explain how Thorndike's puzzle box research illustrates a parsimonious conclusion.
> 3. Those who do research in the experimental analysis of behavior use very small samples and typically do not calculate summary statistics. What strategy do they use instead?

Small *N* Designs in Applied Behavior Analysis

Near the end of their article on fear conditioning in the Little Albert experiment, Watson and Rayner (1920) described several ways in which the fear might be removed. Although they never tried any of these on Little Albert, the attempt to reduce fear using behavioral methods was made a few years later in a pioneering study by Mary Cover Jones (1924), who succeeded in eliminating a fear of rabbits in a 34-month-old boy named Peter. Her strategy was to give Peter his favorite food while placing the rabbit at a distance from him and gradually moving the animal closer, a technique similar to modern-day "systematic desensitization" procedures.

Behavioral approaches to therapy did not immediately flourish following Jones's successful treatment of Peter, but they did become popular beginning in the 1950s and especially in the 1960s and 1970s. The impetus was provided by additional demonstrations of the effectiveness of procedures based on learning principles, along with a developing skepticism of traditional approaches to therapy, especially those relying on Freudian psychoanalytic methods (Eysenck, 1952). In the 1960s, several journals featuring behavioral approaches to therapy appeared, including *Behavior Research and Therapy* (1963) and the *Journal of Applied Behavior Analysis* (1968). With the advent of these journals, research began to appear regularly that included designs showing that a particular method produced a specific behavioral change in a single subject.

Elements of Single-Subject Designs

The essential logic of the single-subject design is simple. Because there are no control groups, the behavior of a single individual must be shown to change as a result of the treatment being applied and not as a result of some other factor. At a minimum, this requires three elements. First, the target behavior(s) must be *operationally defined*. It's not sufficient to say simply that an attempt will be made to reduce a child's disruptive classroom behavior. Rather, the behavior must be precisely defined in terms of easily recorded events, such as speaking out in class while someone else is already speaking, leaving one's chair without permission, and so on.

The second feature of any single-subject design is to establish a **baseline** level of responding. This means the behavior in question must be observed for a period prior to treatment to determine its typical frequency (i.e., normal rate of response, as Skinnerians would say). It is against this baseline level of responding that the effects of a treatment program can be assessed. The third element is to begin the treatment and continue to monitor the behavior. Congratulations if you've noticed this sounds just like the logic of the interrupted time series design described in Chapter 11. In both cases, the goal is to evaluate a treatment against an established baseline.

The simplest single-subject design is sometimes referred to as an **A–B design**, with A standing for baseline and B for treatment. The ideal outcome is for the behavior to change when A changes to B. From your knowledge of threats to internal validity, however, I suspect you may be thinking the A–B design is a weak one. You're right. A change in behavior might be caused by the treatment, but it could also result from a variety of confounding factors, including history, maturation, and even regression to the mean. To reduce the viability of alternative explanations such as these, *withdrawal designs* were developed.

Withdrawal Designs

If a treatment goes into effect and behavior changes, but the change is due perhaps to maturation, history, or regression to the mean, then it is unlikely the behavior will return to its original form if the treatment is subsequently removed or withdrawn. However, if the treatment is withdrawn and the behavior does return to its baseline level, then it is likely the behavior is being affected directly by the treatment and not by some other factor. This is the logic behind the use of a **withdrawal design** (sometimes referred to as a *reversal design*), the simplest of which is an **A–B–A design**. As you might guess, this design begins just like the A–B design, but after the treatment has been in effect for a while, it is withdrawn (the second A).

If behavior changes accompany the introduction and removal of treatment, confidence is increased that the treatment is causing the change. That confidence is further strengthened if reintroducing the treatment brings about another change in behavior. For this reason, researchers prefer an **A–B–A–B design** over the A–B–A design. In effect, the treatment program is evaluated twice (*replication* again). The A-B-A-B design also has the ethical advantage of finishing the study with treatment in place. The ideal outcome, for a behavior that begins with a high rate of occurrence and the goal of treatment is to reduce it (tantrums, for example), is shown in Figure 12.10. Note that for the treatment to be considered successful, the behavior must return to baseline (or close to it) after the withdrawal, and it must change again when treatment is reinstated. When this result occurs, it is difficult to interpret it in any way other than as the successful application of a treatment program. As an example of how this design is actually used, consider the following study of children with ADHD.

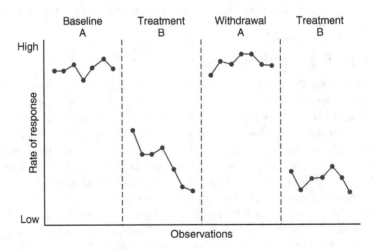

FIGURE 12.10
Ideal outcome of an A–B–A–B withdrawal design.

Research Example 38—An A–B–A–B Design

When you think of attention deficit hyperactivity disorder (ADHD), probably the first treatment that comes to mind is medication, a frequent strategy for dealing with this difficult problem. Those in the applied behavior analysis business, however, first think of nonmedical approaches. A case in point is an ambitious attempt by Flood, Wilder, Flood, and Masuda (2002) to train the schoolmates of children with ADHD to help alter off-task behaviors when doing math problems. In keeping with the general small *N* philosophy, there were only three participants in this study (two boys and a girl), each was studied intensively, and each had significant problems staying on task during school. Each child was 10 years old, diagnosed with ADHD by a primary physician, and not taking medication at the time of the study. "Off-task" behavior was operationally defined in the context of doing math problems as "looking away from the assigned task for 3 s[econds] or more (unless participants were counting on their fingers)" (p. 200). Trained observers hidden on the other side of a two-way mirror recorded these behaviors. To be sure the observers recorded off-task behavior accurately, a second observer was present on 35% of the trials; during these trials, *interobserver reliability* was good—agreement among observers was about 90%.

The treatment in the Flood et al. (2002) study was to pair each ADHD student with a non-ADHD student peer and to have the peer continually reinforce the ADHD student for on-task behavior (e.g., "Wow, we are going fast now," p. 201) and prompt the student when off-task behaviors occurred (e.g., "Let's get moving," p. 201). If the prompting did not get the ADHD subject back on task, the peer confederate "withdrew eye contact and verbal interaction" (p. 201) until the subject returned to the task. As in any A-B-A-B design, baseline was followed by treatment, a withdrawal of the treatment, and then the reintroduction of treatment. As you can see from Figure 12.11, which shows the results for the girl and one of the boys, the off-task behaviors clearly responded to the contingencies; off-task behaviors were quite frequent in the initial baseline, dropped dramatically during treatment, increased again during withdrawal (they labeled it a second "baseline"), and then dropped again during the second treatment period (the outcome for the other boy was essentially the same but included slightly different treatment contingencies). Of importance from an educational standpoint, in addition to showing the change in behavior, the children also solved more math problems during treatment sessions than during baseline sessions. On the other hand, one concern of the researchers was that the study took place in a laboratory environment, rather than a normal school setting, so the extent to which the results might generalize (*external validity*) to the classroom was not clear.

Multiple Baseline Designs

Sometimes, a withdrawal design isn't feasible. For example, if the treatment program involves teaching a particular skill, that skill will remain learned even if the program is terminated. In other words, when the treatment is withdrawn, as in an A-B-A-B procedure, the behavior will not return to baseline but will remain high. A withdrawal design may also present ethical problems and/or practical ones, especially if the behavior being changed is self-destructive (Barlow, Nock, & Hersen, 2009). If the person being treated is a severely disturbed boy who is systematically banging his head against the wall, and an operant procedure manages to stop the behavior, withdrawing the procedure to see if the head banging resumes is difficult to justify. Because this type of research tends to occur in clinical settings, requiring the cooperation of clinical staff, there can be staff resistance to the idea of including the withdrawal of treatment, which might be seen by staff as going backwards ("We just got this behavior stopped and now you want to increase it again?"). Multiple baseline designs help solve these types of practical and ethical difficulties.

In a **multiple baseline design,** several baseline measures are established and then treatment is introduced *at different times*. There is no hard-and-fast rule about the number of baselines

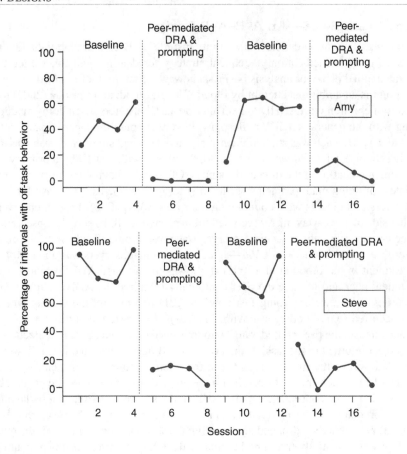

FIGURE 12.11
An A–B–A–B design used by Flood et al., (2002) to increase the on-task behavior of children with ADHD ("Amy" and "Steve").

established per study, but three is typical (Barlow, Nock, & Hersen, 2009). The logic is the same in all cases. If the behavior is responding to the treatment program being examined in the study, then the behavior should change when the program is put into effect, and only then. So, if three different behaviors are being examined and the treatment program is introduced for each behavior at three different times, then the behaviors should change only after the program is introduced for each behavior, and not before. If all three behaviors change when the program is put into effect for the first behavior, then it is difficult to attribute the behavior change to the program; the changes in all three behaviors might be the result of history, maturation, perhaps regression, or some other confound. In general, you can spot a multiple baseline study by looking for several graphs piled on top of each other, with a dotted line moving down from one curve to the next in a stepwise fashion, as in Figure 12.12.

This type of design comes in three varieties. First, multiple baselines can be established for the same type of behavior in several individuals—essentially a replication strategy. This was the approach taken by Wagaman, Miltenberger, and Arndorfer (1993). They developed a training program to help schoolchildren who were experiencing problems with stuttering. Baselines were established for each of eight children, and an effective training began at different times for each. In the second type of multiple baseline design, baselines are established for three different behaviors within a single individual. This strategy was used in an athletic environment by Ward and Carnes (2002), who wished to improve the defensive performance of linebackers. They

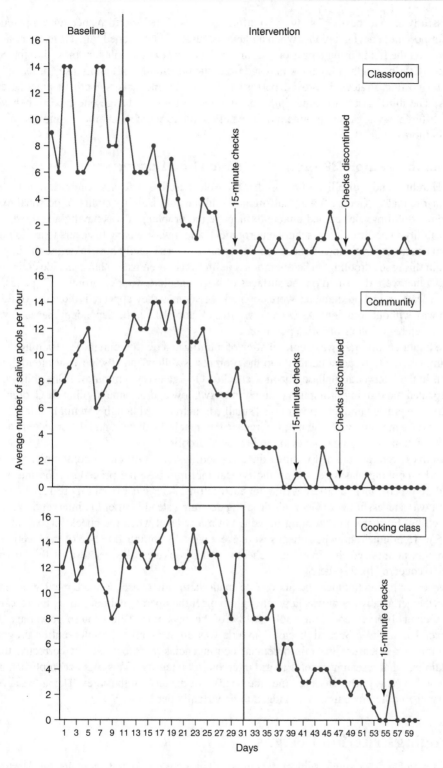

FIGURE 12.12
Data from a multiple baseline across settings study by Kay, Harchik, and Luiselli (2006), designed to eliminate drooling behavior.

successfully used a "posting" strategy to inform players of their performance during practice on three important behaviors: reads (when a player accurately "positioned himself to cover a specified area on the field during a pass or . . . run" p. 2), drops (when a player "moved to the correct position described in the play book in response to the positioning of the offense" p. 2), and tackles. The posting strategy improved performance for the linebackers, both in practice and in games. The third variety of a multiple baseline design tries to change one type of behavior in three different settings (environments). The following Research Example examines this third form in more detail.

Research Example 39—A Multiple Baseline Design

Kay, Harchik, and Luiselli (2006) used a multiple baseline across settings design to help a 17-year-old male ("George") with autism and mild mental disability control a personal hygiene problem—drooling. He seemed unable to manage the problem, it was having an adverse effect on his ability to perform in his school environment, and it was causing his peers to avoid him. As with any such research project, the first issue to resolve was exactly how to define the important terms, in this case "drooling." The operational definition chosen was to have an aide count "pools of saliva that were deposited on the surfaces of his immediate work environment" (p. 25). Only pools at least an inch in diameter were counted. As soon as they appeared, the aide would wipe them away without comment. As you can see from Figure 12.12, the dependent measure was the average number of pools of saliva per hour.

The treatment program was a combination of training and reinforcement. The training involved teaching George to respond correctly to the prompts "swallow" and "wipe your mouth" (with a tissue). In the intervention phase, the aide checked George every 5 minutes. If his chin was wet, she repeated the training prompts, getting him to swallow and/or wipe his chin. If George's chin was dry, she praised him and gave him a "small edible treat." Although you might think the treat would induce more saliva, it did not; George ate the treat immediately, and the procedure actually strengthened his swallowing behavior and reduced drooling.

Baselines were established in three different settings: a classroom, a community vocational site, and a cooking class. Following the typical multiple baseline procedure, the intervention procedure was begun at a different time for each setting. As is clear from Figure 12.12, the intervention was successful, with George's drooling declining steadily after the intervention began in each setting. Furthermore, drooling remained at a low level when the check interval increased from 5 to 15 minutes and when checks were eventually discontinued in two of the locations (the researchers maintained the 15 minute checks in the cooking class because of the "particular hygienic concern" [p. 27] there).

Two other methodological points can be made here. First, because judgment was required about whether a saliva pool was large enough to meet the operational definition, the researchers had a second observer record the pools on 18% of the days of the study. Interobserver agreement was excellent at 96%. Second, because an aide was implementing the intervention program, it was important to ensure the reinforcement contingencies were carried out correctly, thereby maintaining what researchers refer to as "intervention integrity." This was accomplished by the senior author (Kay), who observed the aide on 20% of the days of the study. The aide's accuracy in carrying out the procedures was judged to be virtually perfect at 98%.

Changing Criterion Designs

A third major type of single-subject design is called a **changing criterion design** (Hartman & Hall, 1976), a procedure inspired by the operant procedure of **shaping**, in which a behavior is developed by reinforcing gradual approximations to the final desired behavior. Rats in a Skinner box are "shaped" to bar press, for example, by first reinforcing them for standing next to the bar, then reinforcing them for getting closer, then for standing on their rear feet, and then for touching the bar. Soon after, they are bar pressing for food.

In the changing criterion design, the target behavior is too difficult or complex for the person to reach all at once, so it must be shaped in increments. The procedure begins by establishing the usual baseline. Then a treatment is begun and continued until some initial criterion is reached; then the criterion is made increasingly stringent until the final target behavior is achieved. Health-related behaviors, such as developing exercise or diet programs, are perfect candidates for this type of design. For example, a study by Foxx and Rubinoff (1979) tackled the familiar problem of excessive caffeine consumption by introducing a changing criterion approach. For someone who drinks 15–20 cups of coffee a day, changing immediately to 1–2 cups is probably impossible. Reducing step by step can be effective, however, especially when the person receives specific rewards for reaching a series of gradually more demanding criteria. In Research Example 40, the changing criterion approach was applied to another common problem, that of improving the physical conditioning of out-of-shape children.

Research Example 40—A Changing Criterion Design

It's no secret that "the battle of the bulge" is a major obsession for Americans. What is particularly troubling is the number of children with weight problems: According to the Center for Disease Control (http://www.cdc.gov/), almost 20% of those aged 2 to 19 years old are obese, a percentage that has tripled since 1980. For many children and adolescents, lack of exercise contributes significantly to their weight problems (and the finger exercises of video games don't count as exercise). In a nice example of a changing criterion design that also incorporated elements of the withdrawal design, DeLuca and Holborn (1992) set out to see if the exercise behaviors of three obese and three non-obese 11-year-old boys could be shaped. All of the exercise took place on a stationary bicycle that was programmed to ring bells and flash lights to signal moments when reinforcers had been earned. The study began by establishing the usual baseline. For eight consecutive sessions, each boy was simply told to "exercise as long as you like" (p. 672). After an average baseline level of exercise was established, measured in terms of average cycle revolutions per minute, the first criterion was set at 15% above baseline level. Notice that in line with the small *N* philosophy of focusing on the individual, the first criterion (as well as all subsequent ones) was set not at the same level for all boys, but at a level determined with reference to each boy's starting point.

With the establishment of the first criterion, a variable ratio reinforcement schedule began. The boys were again told to exercise as long as they liked, but the bell would ring and the light would go on when they pedaled at a rate that was, on average, 15% higher than their baseline rate. By getting the bell to ring and light to glow, they accumulated points, allowing them to earn valued prizes (e.g., comic books). After another eight sessions, the criterion increased by another 15% and then increased once more. This was followed by a three-session withdrawal phase, during which the reinforcement contingencies were temporarily suspended. The study then ended with a return to the criterion level in effect just prior to the withdrawal. Figure 12.13 shows the results for four of the boys. Clearly, the level of exercise increased steadily for both the obese and the non-obese boys. Just as clear is that the exercise levels dropped off without the reinforcement contingencies in effect (the withdrawal phase is labeled "BL," for baseline, in the graphs). Note that a possible weakness in the study is the absence of follow-up data. As you might know from your own experiences with exercise programs, it is notoriously difficult to maintain them for any length of time. It would have been nice to find out if the effects of this operant approach were more lasting than is usually the case.

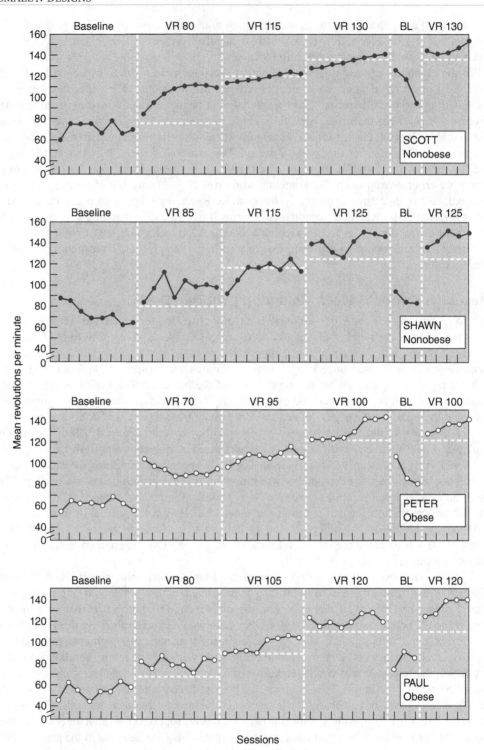

FIGURE 12.13
Data from a changing criterion design to increase the physical conditioning of obese and non-obese 11-year-old boys (from DeLuca & Holborn, 1992).

The DeLuca and Holborn (1992) study illustrates two other points about applied behavior analysis. First, it addresses the question of what constitutes a reinforcer: Some boys might be willing to work for comic books, but others might not. To ensure the boys would be working for outcomes of equal value, DeLuca and Holborn had them complete a "reinforcement survey" at the outset of the study, rating how much they liked certain things on a 10-point scale. Each boy then worked for reinforcers he highly valued. Second, the researchers directly addressed what applied behavior analysts call **social validity** (Wolf, 1978). This type of validity refers to (a) whether a particular applied behavior analysis program has value for improving society, (b) whether its value is perceived as such by the study's participants, and (c) the extent to which the program is actually used by participants (Geller, 1991). DeLuca and Holborn assessed social validity by having each boy, his parents, and his homeroom and physical education teachers complete a "social validation questionnaire" (p. 673), the results of which they described as "uniformly positive." Other indications of program success were anecdotal: All of the boys subsequently participated in track, each of the obese boys convinced his parents to buy him a new bicycle during the program, and all of the boys seemed distressed when the program ended. As previously mentioned, however, the results could have been strengthened with a follow-up 6 months or so later.

Alternating Treatments Designs

The final type of single-subject design we will consider in detail is called the **alternating treatments design**. It has become popular because of its ability to evaluate more than a single treatment approach within the same study. After the usual baseline is established, different treatment strategies (usually two) are then alternated numerous times (a form of *counterbalancing*). The following Research Example shows how this design improved the life of a young girl with autism.

Research Example 41—An Alternating Treatments Design

Lang and his research team (Lang et al., 2009) wished to determine if they could reduce the frequency of a common problem for children with autism: stereotypy. The term refers to the repetitive use of language or, more typically, some dysfunctional motor mannerism (e.g., arm flapping). The child who was the subject of the study was an 8-year-old girl ("Sue") who scored in the "severe autism range" (p. 890) on a standardized rating scale for autism. She seemed unable to play with toys in any normal fashion. When given a toy, all she would do is repetitively spin it on a table; if interrupted, she would scream and fall to the floor.

To change this spin-the-toy stereotypy, Lang et al. (2009) introduced what they called an "abolishing operation component (AOC)" strategy (p. 890) to Sue's therapy. Thinking that attempts to interrupt the stereotypy actually reinforced the behavior, the AOC procedure was to let her spin the toys as much as she wanted, without attention being paid to the spinning. As they described it, "if a child has unrestricted opportunities to engage in stereotyped movement, it is possible that the behavior may eventually lose its reinforcing value, at least for periods of time sufficient to promote the acquisition of new skills" (p. 890). Note that this AOC procedure has a theoretical basis in operant conditioning; it is essentially an operant extinction procedure designed to reduce the probably of response by not reinforcing some behavior.

The two alternating treatments in the therapy program were "play intervention with AOC" and "play intervention without AOC." Half the play intervention sessions were preceded by an AOC period of about 15 minutes (i.e., 15 minutes of Sue doing as much toy spinning as she wanted, without the therapist paying attention to the behavior); the remaining sessions were not preceded by AOC. The play intervention sessions involved exposing the Sue to various conditioning procedures to get her to play normally with a variety of toys—modeling, prompting, and contingent

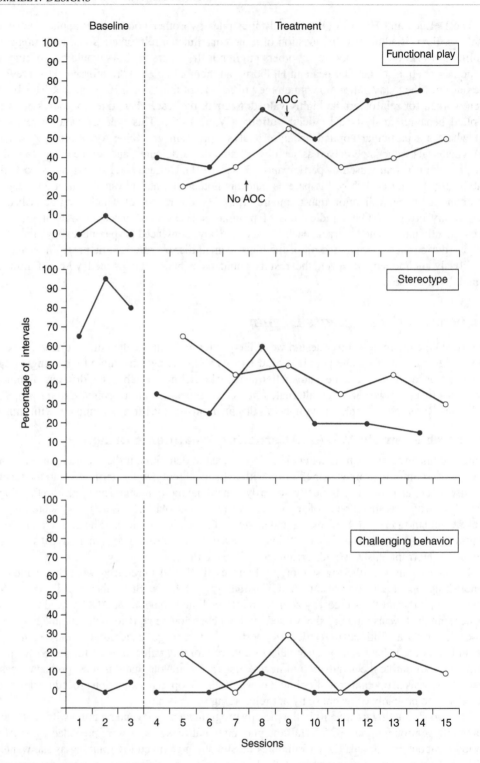

FIGURE 12.14
Data from an alternating treatments design, in a study to reduce stereotypy in an autistic child (from Lang et al., 2009).

reinforcement (e.g., immediate praise for playing properly). Each play intervention session lasted 10 minutes.

During the play intervention sessions, Lang et al. (2009) tracked three behaviors: the stereotypy, what they called "challenging behavior" (screaming and falling on the floor), and functional play. The latter was operationally defined as "independent (i.e., unprompted) use of play materials in a manner consistent with their intended function" (p. 890). Examples were moving a toy train across a table and brushing a doll's hair. As is typical in single-subject studies, several observers recorded these behaviors and interobserver reliability was assessed (and it was high—92% agreement). Changes in these three behaviors can be seen in Figure 12.14.

First, notice the typical strategy of starting by recording baseline behavior: not much functional play, lots of stereotypy, and not a great deal of screaming and falling on the floor. Second, as is typical in an alternating treatments design, you can see by the location of the filled and unfilled squares that the sessions alternated between AOC and non-AOC. Third, it appears the AOC plan worked: Functional play increased, stereotypy decreased, and the only increases in the screaming and falling behaviors occurred during non-AOC.

Although the results of this study supported the AOC concept, Lang et al. (2009) were properly cautious. They recognized, for instance, that the project involved just a single child, so the study needed "replication with other children and in other contexts" (p. 893). They also acknowledged that a withdrawal session or two would have been useful and that there was no follow-up to their study; their project "did not demonstrate sustained improvements in play skills in the absence of the intervention or over time" (p. 893). Nonetheless, they concluded the AOC procedure had some promise for helping children with severe autism.

SELF TEST

12.2

1. What is the methodological advantage of an A-B-A-B design over an A-B-A design?
2. In a multiple baseline design, one variety establishes multiple baselines across several individuals. What are the other two varieties?
3. Which single-subject design best illustrates the operant principle of shaping?

Evaluating Single-Subject Designs

The designs we've been examining have been enormously helpful in assessing the effectiveness of operant and other conditioning approaches to behavior change, and they have improved many lives. They all derive from the behaviorist dictum that if conditions are precisely controlled, then orderly and predictable behavior will follow. They have been found effective in situations ranging from therapeutic behavior change in individuals to community behavior changes in littering. Small *N* designs are not without their critics, however.

The most frequent complaint concerns *external validity*, the extent to which results generalize beyond the specific conditions of the study and replicate consistently. If a particular form of behavior therapy is found effective for a single individual in a specific situation (e.g., George drooling or Sue spinning toys), how do we know the therapy is generally effective for other people with the same or a similar problem? Maybe there was something unusual about the individual who participated in the study. Maybe treatment effects that occur in one setting won't generalize to another (e.g., the ADHD study that may or may not have generalized from the lab to a school environment).

Advocates reply that generalization and replication are indeed evaluated directly in some studies. Wagaman et al.'s (1993) multiple baseline study that helped children overcome stuttering is a good example; the training program took place in the home, but the researchers also assessed the children's performance in school, and were encouraged that the successful outcome at home generalized to the school environment. And the Ward and Carnes (2002) study of linebackers found the improvement in reads, drops, and tackles shown in practice generalized to game performance. Second, although conclusions from single-subject studies are certainly weak if the results aren't replicated, both direct and conceptual replications are common features of this approach. For instance, the use of "differential attention" to shape behavior (i.e., parents attending to their child's desired behaviors and ignoring undesired behaviors) is now a well-established phenomenon, thanks to dozens of small *N* studies demonstrating its effectiveness for a variety of behaviors. Considering just the population of young children, for example, Barlow, Nock, and Hersen (2009) provided a list of 65 studies on the successful use of differential attention published between 1959 and 1978.

Proponents of single-subject designs also point out that external validity is often just as much of a problem for large *N* designs as it is for small *N* designs. For example, a large *N* study on thinking and problem solving using just college students might yield results that would not apply to less verbally fluent groups. And as you might recall from Chapter 5's discussion of external validity, some researchers argue that internal validity is always more important than external validity, and advocates argue that small *N* studies tend to be strong in internal validity in large part to the precision of their *operational definitions*.

Single-subject designs are also criticized for not using statistical analyses but for relying instead on the mere visual inspection of the data. To some extent, this reflects a philosophical difference between those advocating large and small *N* designs. Defenders of small *N* designs argue that conclusions are drawn only when the effects are large enough to be obvious to anyone. In Kay et al.'s (2006) multiple baseline study on drooling, for example, all that was reported was the graph (Figure 12.12) and some simple descriptive statistics (percentage of saliva pools during baseline and treatment). In recent years, however, statistical analyses have begun appearing in research reports of single-subject designs. For example, borrowing from program evaluation research (Chapter 11), some studies have used time series analyses to separate treatment effects from trend effects (Junginger & Head, 1991). Time series analyses also help with the problem of relatively unstable baselines, which can make a visual inspection of a single-subject graph difficult to interpret. Statistical analyses are becoming regular features in the *Journal of the Experimental Analysis of Behavior,* traditionally the purest of the pure Skinnerian journals. One operant researcher lamented that in a survey of articles in the 1989 volume of this journal, he found nearly one-third of the articles used inferential statistics in one form or another and that no more than 10% of the articles included cumulative records (Baron, 1990).

A third criticism of single-subject designs is that they cannot test adequately for interactive effects. As you recall from Chapter 8, one of the attractive features of the factorial design is its ability to identify the interactions between two or more independent variables. Interactive designs for small *N* studies exist, but they are cumbersome. For example, a study by Leitenberg, Agras, Thomson, and Wright (1968) used an A–B–BC–B–A–B–BC–B design to compare two therapy techniques (B and C) and their combination (BC) to help a subject overcome a knife phobia. Notice, however, that technique C never occurred by itself. This required a replication on a second participant, which took the form A–C–BC–C–A–C–BC–C.

One especially important interaction you learned about in Chapter 8 can result from the P x E design, which includes both a subject (P) and a manipulated (E) variable. One type of P x E interaction occurs when the manipulated factor affects one type of person one way but affects others in a different way. The subject variables in P x E designs are, of course, between-subjects variables, but except for multiple baseline across subjects designs, single-subject designs are inherently within-subjects designs. Thus, P x E interactions analogous to the one just described can be found only in single-subject designs through extensive and complicated replications in which it is found that (a) treatment 1 works well with person type 1 but not with person type 2, and (b) treatment 2 works well with person type 2 but not with person type 1.

A final criticism of small *N* designs in the operant tradition concerns their reliance on rate of response as the dependent variable. This approach seldom includes other potentially informative dependent variables, such as reaction times, accuracy, and amount of time spent looking (as in a habituation study). Response rate is certainly a crucial variable, but it is difficult to discount the value of the other measures.

Small *N* research is not confined to the experimental analysis of behavior and applied behavior analysis. Another small *N* research strategy involves studying individuals in great detail by developing case histories or case studies.

Case Study Designs

During the course of their long and happy (and busy) marriage, Charles and Emma Darwin had 10 children. Like many parents, they were especially excited by their firstborn, William, and Dad began keeping highly detailed notes about his son's development. He was motivated in part by his life's consuming passion—evolution, in particular the evolution of emotional expression—but he was also a bit like the modern father who winds up with 400 hours of video for his first child and 4 hours for his second. Detailed diaries weren't kept for the subsequent Darwin children. For William, though, Darwin recorded a wide range of behaviors in great detail and eventually published a report called "A biographical sketch of an infant" (Darwin, 1877). He reported, for instance, that young William was able to visually track a candle at 9 days and reliably produced what we now call the *rooting reflex*: "surface of warm hand placed to face seemed immediately to give wish of sucking" (quoted in Browne, 1995, p. 425). Darwin's account is a pioneering example of a procedure known as the case study method.

A **case study** in psychology normally refers to a detailed description and analysis of a single individual. The method is occasionally referred to as a *case history* because it involves a close analysis of the history of that person's life or a substantial portion of it. Because the description is typically in narrative form, this method is sometimes considered an example of qualitative research, but most case studies also include significant amounts of quantitative data (e.g., results of various personality and aptitude tests). Case studies typically incorporate a variety of methods. For instance, they might involve detailed interviews, both of the person under study and of others who know the person; systematic behavioral observations; psychometric (e.g., IQ test) and physiological (e.g., brain scan) measures; and the incorporation of archival data.

The case study approach is common in clinical work, in which the case of someone with a particular psychological disorder (e.g., depression) is used to illustrate the factors that lead to and influence the disorder and the methods of treatment for it. Case studies are also common in neuropsychology, and our understanding of brain function has been enhanced by studies of those with brain damage resulting from either (a) injury or (b) surgery to help with problem A that produces side effect B. An example of the latter, the case of H.M., is one of psychology's most famous case studies (see Figure 12.15).

H.M. was 27 when he underwent brain surgery in 1953, designed to alleviate the debilitating epileptic seizures he had been experiencing since age 15. After medication had failed to help, H.M. underwent an experimental surgery that destroyed part of his medial temporal lobes,

Jenni Ogden, author of "Trouble in Mind: Stories from a Neuropsychologist's Casebook" OUP, New York, 2012.

FIGURE 12.15
H.M. being tested in the lab in 1986.

including most of his hippocampus. At the time of the surgery, little was known about the hippocampus, except that it seemed to have something to do with the sense of smell. In fact, the hippocampus is an area that contributes to memory storage. The surgery helped reduce H.M.'s seizures dramatically, but it effectively destroyed his ability to form new memories. He was able to retain some memory of his life prior to the surgery, but from 1953 until his death in 2008, he was never able to remember his new experiences. He lived in what the title of an extensive case history of him referred to as the "permanent present tense" (Corkin, 2013) Thus, if you were to meet him, he could carry on a conversation, but if you left the room for a few minutes and then returned, he would have no memory of having met you minutes earlier.

Although you might think that H.M. was just a medical rarity with no significance beyond his individual family tragedy, in fact, the subsequent study of H.M. taught scientists a great deal about the nature of memory. As just one example, consider mirror tracing, a motor learning task in which a subject has to trace the outline of a star, but has to look at the star through a mirror rather than seeing it directly. This is a difficult task, but, working over several days, H.M. was able to show significant improvement (i.e., he learned something new). Yet on each day of the study, H.M. had no memory of having tried the task the day before. This study and others with H.M. enabled researchers to make an important distinction between what is called declarative or explicit memory, and nondeclarative or implicit memory. H.M.'s explicit memory was significantly impaired, but his implicit memory still functioned.

In addition to case studies like those of the famous H.M., resulting from the aftereffects of surgery, other studies occur after brain damage resulting from injury (e.g., as in wartime or in sports) are common. Consider the following Research Example, illustrating the effects of multiple concussions.

Research Example 42—A Case Study

There has been much discussion in recent years of the consequences of repeated head trauma. Most of the examples that make the news occur during football season, when colliding players often suffer concussions, but a sport that produces an even greater frequency of head injury is one in which a primary goal is head injury—boxing. McMicken, Ostergren, and Vento-Wilson (2011) reported a case study of a 36-year-old fighter ("A.B.") who had suffered repeated head trauma during his 15 years of boxing, both as an amateur and as a paid sparring partner. He had been knocked out seven times.

A.B. had been working as a physical education instructor in a substance abuse rehabilitation center. He was referred for assessment to a speech pathologist because his speech was often slurred and inarticulate; by his own admission he sounded drunk, which was affecting his credibility at the rehab center. His supervisor described him as an excellent worker, but his speech was a problem. Because repeated brain trauma is known to produce cognitive impairment, A.B. was first given a battery of cognitive tests that assessed both short-term and long-term memory, judgment, spatial cognition, reasoning, and problem solving. He scored at the 91st percentile or higher on all the tests—so, no cognitive impairment. A.B. was then given several tests for specific language impairment having to do with comprehension; he passed these as well. Physical dexterity was also screened by using a field sobriety test (e.g., touch your finger to your nose). No problem here either. Note the use of *falsification* thinking here—trying to arrive at a diagnosis by ruling out, or disconfirming, alternatives.

The problems for A.B. occurred with tests of articulation. For example, he had trouble producing the normal rhythm in a sentence; he would stress the wrong words or the wrong syllables in a word. He also failed to make clear pauses between words, thereby producing the slurred speech that led others to think he was inebriated. He was diagnosed with *ataxic dysarthria*. Ataxic generally refers to a lack of coordination in muscle movements, while dysarthria is a broad term referring to articulation failure. Ataxic dysarthria, articulation failure due to lack of control over the motor components of articulation, is usually thought to result from damage in the area of the cerebellum, a form of damage that could easily result from the sharp head twisting motions that accompany a sharp blow to the head. And A.B. had lots of experience with sharp blows to the head.

Having identified the most likely diagnosis, speech therapists then developed an articulation training program for A.B. that got him to focus on individual words and to increase the volume of his speech. Another component of the therapy was a form of operant shaping: Training started with individual words, then very brief sentences, and then longer, more typical sentences. At the end of treatment, he had improved significantly on a variety of measures. For instance, one test measured "perceptual intelligibility" (how his speech was understood by others) on a scale from 1 (*unintelligible*) to 7 (*perfectly intelligible*). A.B. scored 3.7 during the assessment period and 5.3 after treatment. The brain damage would probably prevent him from ever scoring a 7, but by becoming more "mindful" of how to articulate words and how to build normal rhythm into sentences, A.B. showed significant improvement and was able to return successfully to work. Nice outcome!

You will notice that the case study of A.B. involved a case history, inclusion of various psychological and neurological tests, the implementation of a treatment (i.e., speech therapy), and an assessment of the effectiveness of the treatment. The comprehensive nature of case studies allows both researchers and practitioners to effectively use data to understand and treat individuals in need of help. This harkens back to our earlier discussion in Chapters 1 and 11 about *translational research*, whose goal is to transform information to improve physical and psychological well-being.

Although case studies in psychology are normally associated with clinical psychology and neuropsychology, experimental psychologists have also completed them, and one of the best-known examples is Alexander Luria's fascinating account of a man who seemed unable to forget anything, seemingly the opposite of H.M. This classic study is detailed in Box 12.3, and if you think that having a nearly perfect memory would solve many of your problems as a student, you'll have second thoughts after reading about "S."

BOX 12.3   CLASSIC STUDIES—The Mind of a Mnemonist

Case histories often document lives that are classic examples of particular psychological types. In abnormal psychology, for example, the case study approach is often used to understand the dynamics of specific disorders by detailing typical examples of them. Case studies also can be useful in experimental psychology, however, shedding light on basic psychological phenomena. A classic example is the one compiled by Alexander Romanovich Luria (1902–1977), a Russian scientist famous for his studies of Russian soldiers who were brain-injured during World War II and for his work on the relationship between language and thought (Brennan, 1991).

The case involved one S. V. Sherashevsky, or "S.," as Luria referred to him, whose remarkable memory abilities gave him a career as a stage mnemonist (yes, people actually paid to watch him memorize things) but also caused him considerable psychological distress. The case is summarized in Luria's *The Mind of a Mnemonist* (1968). Luria studied S. for more than 20 years, documenting both the range of S.'s memory and the accompanying problems of his being virtually unable to forget anything. Luria first discovered there seemed to be no limit on how much information S. could memorize; more astonishing, the information did not seem to decay with the passage of time. He could easily memorize lists of up to 70 numbers and could recall them in either a forward or a reverse order. Also, "he had no difficulty reproducing any lengthy series . . . whatever, even though these had been presented to him a week, a year, or even many years earlier" (Luria, 1968, p. 12).

This is an unbelievable performance, especially considering that most people cannot recall more than seven or eight items on this type of task and that forgetting is the rule rather than the exception. As a student, you might be wondering what the downside to this could possibly be. After all,

it would seem to be a wonderful problem to have, especially during final exam week.

Unfortunately, S.'s extraordinary memory skills were accompanied by severe deficits in other cognitive areas. For example, he found it almost impossible to read for comprehension. This was because every word evoked strong visual images from his memory and interfered with the overall organization of the ideas conveyed by the sentences. Similarly, he was an ineffective problem solver, found it difficult to plan and organize his life, and was unable to think abstractly. The images associated with his remarkable memory interfered with everything else.

Is S. anything more than an idle curiosity, a bizarre once-in-a-lifetime person who doesn't really tell us anything about ourselves? No. He was indeed a very rare person, but the case sheds important light on normal memory functioning. In particular, it provides a glimpse into the functional value forgetting from short-term memory. We sometimes curse our inability to recall something we were thinking about just a few minutes before, but the case of S. shows that forgetting allows us to clear the mind of information that might be useless (e.g., there's no reason to memorize all the items on the menu we just read in a restaurant) and enables us to concentrate our energy on more sophisticated cognitive tasks such as reading for comprehension. Because S. couldn't avoid remembering everything he encountered, he was unable to function at higher cognitive levels.

One final point: It turns out S. was not a once-in-a-lifetime case. Another person ("V.P.") with a similarly remarkable memory was studied by the American psychologists Hunt and Love (1972). Oddly enough, V.P. grew up in a city in present-day Latvia that was just a short distance from the birthplace of Luria's S.

Although case studies usually involve individuals, the term also applies to an analysis of a specific event that is unique in some way. For example, researchers have done case studies of how nearby residents reacted to a nuclear accident at Three Mile Island in Pennsylvania in 1979 (Aronson, 1999) and how people's "flashbulb" memories of the 9/11 attacks change over time (Talarico & Rubin, 2003). In addition, case studies often have a broader meaning in disciplines other than psychology. For example, in sociology, there are case studies of entire communities. A famous example is a 1949 study of adolescents in a small town in Illinois (Hollingshead, 1949). Case studies have also examined social groups (e.g., fraternities), worker groups (e.g., assembly line workers), and religious groups (e.g., Shakers).

Evaluating Case Studies

H.M.'s memory loss, A.B.'s ataxic dysarthria, and S.'s exceptional memory demonstrate the two main strengths of the case study method. First, case studies can provide a level of detailed analysis not found in other research strategies. Second, well-chosen cases can provide prototypical descriptions of certain types of individuals. Having a highly detailed "textbook" description of someone suffering from ataxic dysarthria, for instance, gives clinicians a point of comparison for their own clients. A.B. and S. also illustrate two ends of a continuum, cases that are either common or rare. Head injuries in boxing are common and a detailed case history can shed much light on what can be expected for individuals exposed to repeated head trauma, such as multiple concussions received as a result of other sports injuries or war-related injuries. It is extremely rare for anyone to have memory capacity even approaching that of S., and this case might not seem especially relevant for the rest of us, but the study of S. demonstrated the value of using visual images to improve memory. Further, Luria's description revealed something about the value of normal forgetting from short-term memory.

In relation to theory, case studies can provide inductive support for a theory, they can suggest hypotheses for further testing with other methods, and they can serve the purpose of falsification. Concerning the latter, you already know about one famous example, described in Box 3.2 in Chapter 3. Claims made about the math skills of the horse called Clever Hans were effectively falsified when Pfungst investigated the case.

Case studies also have important limitations, however. First, conclusions drawn on the basis of a single individual may not generalize—that is, there can be problems with *external validity*. The boxer with ataxic dysarthria could turn out to have unique features that would not make him a typical case. Furthermore, it would be inappropriate to conclude that all boxers will develop ataxic dysarthria as A.B. did. Another problem is that ample opportunity exists for the theoretical biases of the researcher to color case study descriptions. Is it so surprising to find unending discussions of unresolved Oedipal complexes and other sexually based problems in case histories written by Freudians?[3] To illustrate, during a session using PsycINFO to find examples for this chapter, we encountered a study called "Ph.D. Envy: A Psychoanalytic Case Study" (Behr, 1992). It described the case of a woman with a "profound and debilitating anxiety around not being able to finish her Ph.D. dissertation. . . . [Her] contempt for those without Ph.D.s and the intense envy of those who possessed them led to the psychical equivalence of Ph.D. envy and penis envy" (p. 99). Would her case be described differently by a non-Freudian? Almost certainly. For instance, a follower of Alfred Adler, who created the concept of an inferiority complex, would probably describe the case in terms of the woman's feelings of inferiority and the frustrated attempts to strive for superiority.

A final limitation of case study methods concerns everyday memory. Participants in case studies of individuals are often required to recall events from the past, and the writers of case histories also have to rely on memories of their encounters with the object of the case. As researchers such as Elizabeth Loftus (1979) have shown repeatedly, memories for the events of our lives are often distorted by circumstances that intervene between the target event and the later recall of it. Take, for example, a New Orleans resident who experienced the devastating Hurricane Katrina in 2005. If asked to describe the experience as part of a case study 10 years later, some of the information would undoubtedly be accurate. After all, people are not likely to forget water filling the entire first floor of their house. However, during the intervening years, the person has (a) experienced the event; (b) seen endless videos, news stories, TV recreations, and photographs of the event;

---

[3] Most historians believe Freud's case histories were written in a way to support his existing beliefs and biases about human nature (Kramer, 2006). In other words, having clear in his mind what he thought should be happening with a patient, he looked for and emphasized any supporting evidence (a form of *confirmation bias*).

(c) listened to countless hurricane stories from friends and relatives; and (d) probably dreamed of the event many times. As Loftus and her research team have demonstrated (e.g., Loftus & Hoffman, 1989), our subsequent memories are often "constructions" of the event itself and of these later occurrences—that is, we now have a memory that incorporates many elements, only one of which is the original event itself. Our memory is by no means a verbatim recording of events.

In sum, case studies are susceptible to bias, they lack control over extraneous variables, and their results may not generalize easily, but they can be useful in generating new research ideas, they can help falsify weak theories, and sometimes they are the only way to document an extraordinary person or event. Case studies that involve multiple methods of inquiry, including interviews, surveys, physical evaluations, and psychological assessments, can be very informative for researchers and practitioners to more fully understand the individual being studied and to propose and implement appropriate treatments to improve one's physical and/or psychological functioning. The case study is an essential and important method for the psychological scientist.

> ## SELF TEST
> ### 12.3
> 1. Single-subject designs have sometimes been criticized on the grounds of external validity. What does this mean, and how do defenders respond?
> 2. What is the essential difference between the case of the boxer with ataxic dysarthria and the case of Luria's mnemonist?
> 3. The case of Clever Hans was described back in Chapter 3 but is used in this chapter to point to a strength of the case study method. Explain.

This chapter has introduced you to a tradition of research in psychology that concentrates on the individual rather than the group. It is an approach ideally suited for some circumstances, such as studying the effects of reinforcement contingencies on behavior and studying individuals in depth. Psychology began with small *N* designs as a method to better understand human behavior. Even though you have now learned about many types of research methods and designs, we end our textbook with small *N* designs to remind you of the importance of the individual in psychological research.

CHAPTER SUMMARY

Research in Psychology Began with Small *N*

Research in psychology's earliest years normally involved a small number of participants, no statistical summaries of data, and, because they had yet to be invented, no inferential statistical analyses. The additional participants served the purpose of replication. Dresslar's facial vision study and Thorndike's research on cats escaping from puzzle boxes are good examples.

Reasons for Small *N* Designs

Individual-subject validity is the extent to which a general conclusion drawn from research with large *N* applies to the individual participants in the study. One reason for favoring small *N* designs is that when summarizing data for a large number of individuals, individual-subject validity can be weak. This occurs in some concept learning research, for instance, in which the summarized data imply gradual learning but an examination of individual behavior implies a more rapid change in performance. Small N designs are also favored when studying participants from rare populations or when practical considerations (e.g., expense) make a large N design impossible.

The Experimental Analysis of Behavior

The philosophical basis for some small N research is the position taken by B. F. Skinner, who argued that if a researcher is able to establish sufficient control over environmental influences, then orderly behavior will occur and can be easily observed (i.e., without statistical analysis). In operant conditioning, behavior is influenced by its consequences and comes under the control of the environment in which it occurs. As a dependent variable, Skinner relied on rate of response. Most of Skinner's work was in basic research (e.g., schedules of reinforcement), but he was a strong advocate for the technological ideal—the practical application of operant principles and techniques to bring about societal change.

Small N Designs in Applied Behavior Analysis

Applied behavior analysis is the application of operant principles to improve behavior. Small N or single-subject designs are used to evaluate the effectiveness of these applied programs. All single-subject designs carefully define terms, establish baselines, and then apply an intervention technique to be evaluated. Withdrawal designs establish a baseline, apply a treatment, and then withdraw the treatment. If the behavior changes along with the changing conditions, it is assumed the treatment was effective in altering the behavior. A-B-A-B designs are preferred over A-B-A designs because the study ends with the treatment in effect and the treatment is tested twice. Multiple baseline designs are often used when withdrawal designs are not feasible or ethical. Multiple baselines can be established for several individuals, several behaviors, or several environmental settings. Changing criterion designs are used when the target behavior must be shaped gradually (e.g., weight loss). Alternating treatment designs allow for the comparison of two or more treatments in a single study. Small N designs have been criticized for being unable to evaluate interactive effects, relying on a single dependent variable, and having limited external validity.

Case Study Designs

Most case studies are detailed analyses of the behavior of single individuals, although some case studies investigate unique events or identifiable groups. They are often used in a clinical setting to study individuals with relatively common disorders (e.g., head injury from boxing) or to analyze of people with rare attributes (e.g., the memory abilities of S.). They can be useful sources of information and can serve to falsify claims and generate hypotheses for further research, but they are subject to the biases of the investigator, memory failures, and lack of generalizability (external validity).

CHAPTER REVIEW QUESTIONS

1. Describe Dresslar's (1893) facial vision study and how the results were presented, and explain why he used three participants instead of just one.

2. Explain why Thorndike's research is a good illustration of the principle of parsimony.

3. Explain what is meant by the concept of individual-subject validity.

4. Use the behavior of a rat bar pressing in a Skinner box to illustrate Skinner's claim that behavior can be predicted and controlled if three main factors are known.

5. Skinner's work is said to reflect the "technological ideal." Explain.

6. Describe the three essential elements of every single-subject design.

7. Describe the essential features of a withdrawal design, and distinguish among these designs: A-B, A-B-A, A-B-A-B.

8. Define a multiple baseline design, explain when it is preferred over a withdrawal design, and describe three varieties.

9. Use the Research Example on exercising for obese and non-obese boys as a way of describing the main features of a changing criterion design. Be sure to work the term "shaping" into your answer.

10. Describe any three ways in which single-subject designs have been criticized. How do advocates for these designs respond?

11. Define the case study method; using the boxer example, describe its strengths and limitations.

12. The case study of a very rare individual can also shed light on normal processes. How do the cases of H.M. and S. illustrate this point?

APPLICATIONS EXERCISES

Exercise 12.1. Designing Self-Improvement Programs

Design a changing criterion program for one of the following self-improvement projects. For each project, be sure to define the target behavior(s) operationally, identify what you would use as reinforcement, and indicate each successive criterion.

1. Increase productive study time.

2. Develop an exercise program.

3. Change to healthier eating behaviors.

4. Improve time management.

Exercise 12.2. Hypothetical Outcomes of Applied Behavior Analyses

For each of the following, sketch hypothetical graphs in the single-subject style that illustrate each of the alternative outcomes.

1. Multiple baseline across three settings:

    a. The treatment program works.

    b. One cannot discount a history or maturation effect.

2. A–B–A–B design

    a. The treatment program works.

    b. It is hard to tell if the program brought about the change or if another factor such as maturation was responsible.

Exercise 12.3. Depicting the Results of Applied Behavior Analyses

For each of the following descriptions and data sets, prepare a graph in the single-subject style that would accurately portray the results. Write a brief conclusion.

1. An A–B–A–B design was used to reduce the number of interruptions made in class by a child whose behavior was disrupting his second-grade class. During treatment, the teacher was instructed to ignore the child's interruptions and to pay special attention to the child when he was behaving productively (e.g., doing class work). The number of interruptions per 1-hour recording session were as follows:

    a. During first A: 12, 12, 7, 6, 6, 9, 8, 10, 9, 11

    b. During first B: 9, 8, 9, 4, 3, 2, 2, 1, 4, 2

    c. During second A: 4, 5, 10, 6, 12, 10, 10, 10, 12, 9

    d. During second B: 9, 9, 2, 1, 1, 1, 0, 3, 4, 1

2. A multiple baseline across persons design was used to improve the foul shooting percentage of three basketball players during practices. A system was used in which successful shots earned points that could later be used to obtain more substantial reinforcers. Each of the following numbers represents the number of foul shots made for each 50 attempted. The underlined numbers are baseline data.

Player 1:	<u>32, 29, 38, 31, 33,</u> 44, 36, 37, 44, 41, 40, 38, 45, 42, 40, 44
Player 2:	<u>30, 32, 28, 30, 30, 40, 35, 32, 33,</u> 38, 40, 45, 44, 44, 42, 44
Player 3:	<u>22, 28, 29, 28, 26, 25, 22, 26, 21, 21, 23, 24,</u> 35, 39, 40, 39

ANSWERS TO SELF TESTS

✓ 12.1

1. By plugging their ears, Dresslar and his colleagues were able to rule out the idea that facial vision involved a special sensory process.
2. Thorndike's trial and error explanation of his cats' behavior was more parsimonious than an explanation attributing rational thought to the cats.
3. They portray the data for each participant, with the additional participants serving the purpose of replication.

✓ 12.2

1. The treatment program (B) is tried not just once but twice (replication occurs)
2. There can also be multiple baselines for different behaviors and for different environments or settings.
3. Changing criterion design

✓ 12.3

1. Some have argued that results from single-subject designs do not generalize beyond the specific situation of the study. Defenders respond that there have been studies that directly test for generalization (e.g., the study on stuttering).
2. The boxer is an example of case involving a common problem, while S. illustrates an extremely rare case (that nonetheless sheds light on normal behavior).
3. A case study can serve the cause of falsification. In the Clever Hans case, the idea that the horse had high-level mathematical skills was falsified.

Epilogue: What I Learned in My Research Methods Course

We sincerely hope that your experience in this research methods course has been a positive and successful one. The course can be difficult, and at times tedious, but we believe strongly that it is the most important one in the psychology curriculum, along with your statistics course (the history of psychology course is right up there too). In the letters of recommendation that we write for our students, both for graduate school *and* for jobs, we always look back to how they did in our research methods courses, and much of the letter will be framed in terms of the kinds of skills developed in that course. We'd like to close the book by (a) listing those skills, some of which we introduced briefly in Chapter 1, and (b) giving you some concrete suggestions about the next steps you can take to become involved in research in psychology.

To become a professional psychologist requires an advanced degree and because graduate study includes a strong dose of research, the undergraduate methods course is an obvious first step toward developing the research skills that will be put to use in graduate school. If you're headed to graduate school, succeeding in this methods course is essential. Yet the majority of undergraduate psychology majors won't go on to earn doctorates in psychology and, as a result, students sometimes question the value of the methods course if their goal is to finish college and get a job. If you're in that category, we'd like to convince you that your chances of getting a decent position and advancing on the job have been improved if you've done well in your methods course. Here's a list of some of the career-enhancing skills you've begun to develop as a result of taking this course. Naturally, if you are heading to graduate school, these skills also apply, and will increase your chances of doing well as you work toward an advanced degree. Here goes:

- Ability to think empirically
  - Frame questions in ways that they can be answered with data.
  - Look for data-based conclusions about the causes of behavior.
  - Recognize that conclusions based on data are "working truths," pending further research and replication; it is important to be willing to change your mind about something, if the data warrant a change.
  - Use logical thinking in the research context, both inductive and deductive varieties.

- Ability to examine claims and information about behavior with a critical eye
  - Be skeptical about unsubstantiated, excessive, and/or simplistic claims.
  - Look out for overly strong (i.e., causal) conclusions based only on correlational data or on insufficient data.
  - Look carefully at graphs to see that they don't mislead, especially by creating deceptive *Y*-axes.
  - Look for alternative and more parsimonious explanations for results being used to support some claim.

- Be skeptical about claims based on questionable evidence (e.g., anecdotal data or glowing testimonials, observations affected by bias, results based on an a very small number of observations).
- Be cautious whenever claims include the word "prove," as in "listening to Mozart has been *proven* to increase your child's IQ".

- Ability to read difficult material for comprehension
  - Be thorough when reading, especially when reading of original research articles.

- Ability to take a vague problem, give it some structure, and work out a systematic plan to solve it
  - Be directly involved in developing, implementing, and completing an empirical research project.
  - Consider "what's next?" thinking when designing the next study, based on the results of one just finished.

- Ability to search efficiently for important information to help solve problems and organize that information coherently
  - Become experienced with PsycINFO and other electronic search tools.

- Ability to organize, summarize, and interpret data
  - Write lab reports and data summaries for data collection exercises.
  - Describe the application of descriptive and inferential statistics to evaluate data collected in labs.
  - Use and correctly interpret SPSS (or other statistical software).

- Improved writing
  - Learning and use the rules for creating the APA-format lab report, which leads writers to be clear, organized, and parsimonious with the language.

- Improved communication skills
  - Create and give oral presentations, posters, lab reports.

- Improved computer skills
  - Use computer statistical packages (e.g., SPSS), graphing software, presentation software (e.g., PowerPoint), and possibly packages or websites that present experiments to be completed by students or help students create surveys.

This is a rather impressive list, and collectively it could be called "research self-efficacy," but note that we prefaced it by writing that you've *just begun to develop these skills*. Skills require practice, so to develop them further, as you continue your career as a psychology major with an interest in research, we would suggest the following:

- Seek out opportunities for independent research with your professors. They will be delighted to have you in their labs, and although you might start by doing routine tasks (e.g., data entry), before long you'll be more deeply involved in projects. By the time you graduate, you will probably be a co-author on a conference poster presentation or two, and you might even have completed one or two studies that reflect your own research ideas and for which you are the lead researcher. If you apply to graduate school in psychology, research experience will be near the top of the list of things that graduate admissions committees expect to see (Landrum & Nelson, 2002).

- Complete an independent research project or a senior thesis, if your school offers them.

- Choose electives likely to have laboratory components. These typically include courses such as Principles of Learning, Cognitive Psychology, Sensation/Perception, and Biopsychology or Neuroscience.

- Go to research conferences and present your research (most likely in poster format). At the very least, you should go to an undergraduate research conference or two. These are small conferences especially designed for undergraduates to present their work. They typically last just a day and feature poster sessions, maybe some oral presentations of research, and an invited address by a prominent researcher. Many schools now have their own "research day," featuring undergraduate research from a variety of departments. Be sure to participate. Even better, submit your work to a regional psychology conference, such as the Southeastern or Midwestern Psychological Association (SEPA, MPA). These are typically 3-day conferences that feature talks by prominent psychologists, lots of poster sessions, and opportunities to meet other student researchers. Third, consider going to one of the national conferences of either the American Psychological Association (August every year) or the Association for Psychological Science (May every year). These are (much) larger versions of the regional conferences. Be careful about timing, however. In order to present your research at these regional or national conferences, you will have to submit your work (typically an abstract) sometime in the fall for presentation the following spring or summer. Hence, it's a good idea to be involved in research no later than your junior year.

- Work hard to meet the requirements for Psi Chi, the national honor society in psychology (www.psichi.org). Besides enhancing your resume, membership gives you special opportunities for research. Psi Chi sponsors several research grants and awards, and at all of the regional and national meetings just mentioned, Psi Chi sponsors poster sessions for research by members and gives out cash awards for high quality posters.

- Submit your work to journals that specialize in undergraduate research. The best known is a journal sponsored by Psi Chi (*Psi Chi Journal of Undergraduate Research*), but others exist. You can find a listing of them, with their website addresses, by looking at Psi Chi's website.

- Find a topic of interest and immerse yourself in it thoroughly. That is, develop a passion for research.

There are enormous gaps in our knowledge of behavior. Hence, there is ample space available for those with the kind of passion and concern displayed by countless researchers of psychological science. What could be better than to have a career that is continually exciting and rewarding and helps us to understand the complexities of behavior and mental processes? The invitation is wide open.

Appendix A
Communicating the Results
of Research in Psychology

In this appendix, you will learn how to:

- Prepare and write an APA-style laboratory report.

- Prepare a professional presentation of your research as either a paper to be read or a poster to be written and organized.

Research Reports and APA-Style

Despite one's specialty within the discipline of psychology, we all share a similar foundation in research methods, statistics, and in the communication of our ideas. Just as statistics is the language researchers use to test hypotheses, the APA writing style allows psychological researchers to communicate with each other using a similar language format. As you begin to learn about APA-style, it will seem to you that the list of seemingly arbitrary rules is endless. Take heart. Practically everything you need to know will be found in this appendix. A Google search (just enter "APA style") will also yield a number of guides, and APA has a brief tutorial. For the primary source, however, the APA's (2010) *Publication Manual* (*PM*) can answer all your format questions. This appendix will teach you the basics and help you learn how to communicate the results of your research, but the *PM* is the ultimate weapon against a botched lab report. Learning and using APA-style is a skill that must be learned and practiced. Like playing piano or driving a car, with enough practice with APA-style, you will become a skilled communicator of psychological research. Before we turn to the details of writing an APA-style research report, let us first explain why we use APA-style when sharing research with the larger psychological community.

There are two reasons for the rules that dictate a consistent format for reporting research in psychology. First, research findings accumulate *external validity* as they are repeated in different labs with different participants and perhaps with slightly varied procedures. In order to replicate a study exactly or make a systematic variation in some procedure, the reader must know precisely what was done in the original study. If the results of a study are written in a known and predictable format, the replication process is made easier. Second, a consistent format makes the review process more efficient and consistent. Thousands of research articles are submitted to dozens of psychological research journals every year. Typically, each article is screened by an editor and then sent to two or three other researchers with expertise in the article's topic. These peer reviewers read the article and send the editor a written critique that includes a recommendation of whether or not the article should be published (most psychology journals reject 70–80% of the articles submitted to them). In the absence of an agreed-on format, the work of the editor and reviewers would be hopelessly complicated. For the purposes of the methods course you are now taking, having a regular format makes it easier for your instructor to grade your lab report fairly.

General Guidelines

One of our beliefs is that the only way to learn how to do research in psychology is to actually do some. The same principle applies to writing. As noted above, writing is a skill like any other, and it improves with practice, assuming one's efforts are followed by useful feedback. Hence, the most basic recommendation we can make is for you to write whenever you can, ask others to read what you've written, and rewrite your work. When writing a lab report, we suggest finding a friend who has already completed the methods course *and* earned a decent grade. As you are writing your report, ask this person to read your work and critique it. Then, use the feedback to improve your writing skill.

Writing Style

The APA-style laboratory report is not the Great American Novel. Therefore, literary devices that might enhance a creative writing exercise, such as deliberately creating an ambiguity to hold the reader's attention or omitting details to arouse curiosity, are out of place in scientific writing. Rather, one should always strive for clarity and simplicity of expression. This is easier said than done, of course, but despite the grain of truth, academic writing is not necessarily stuffy and difficult to follow.

All good writing includes correct grammatical usage. Grammatical errors automatically create ambiguity and awkwardness, so your first step in learning to write a lab report is to be sure you know the basic rules of sentence structure. One problem that seems especially common in scientific writing, perhaps out of a desire to sound objective, is a tendency to overuse the passive voice. Whenever possible, use the active voice, which generally adds clarity and simplifies sentences. To illustrate,

Passive: An investigation of sleep deprivation was done by Smith (1992).

Active: Smith (1992) investigated sleep deprivation.

The *PM* covers this and a number of additional grammatical guidelines on pages 77–86.

In addition to grammatical problems, beginning writers of APA lab reports often use colloquial expressions, or everyday language that may have multiple meanings or diffuse the meaning of a sentence. In this example, "Smith (1992) *looked at* several factors related to sleep deprivation," *looked at* is a colloquial expression that does not accurately describe what Smith did. Instead, "Smith (1992) *examined* several factors related to sleep deprivation" does not include a colloquial expression.

Similarly, beginning writers often use some words inappropriately. For example, although the term *significant* generally means "important" or "meaningful," in a research report, *significant* implies "statistically significant," which has a technical definition relating to the rejection of the null hypothesis (Chapter 4). A reader encountering the word in a research report might assume the technical definition is intended, whether it is or not. To eliminate ambiguity, never use this term in the lab report except when it refers to statistical significance.

Two other common problems with word usage concern the confusion between "affect" and "effect" and the use of plural nouns such as "data." These and related problems are elaborated in Tables A.1 and A.2.

Using Numbers

When reporting numbers, APA prescribes a general rule, which is that the writer should "use numerals to express numbers 10 and above and words to express numbers below 10" (2010, p. 111). Notable exceptions exist, however; here are some of the more common ones.

Table A.1 Effectively Using the Terms "Affect" and "Effect"

One of the most common errors found in student lab reports is the failure to distinguish between the different meanings for the words "affect" and "effect."

affect as a noun means an emotional state; thus
- Because of the pressure of a rapid presentation rate, subjects showed increased <u>affect</u>.

affect as a verb means to influence; thus
- Increasing the presentation rate <u>affected</u> recall.

effect as a noun means the result of some event; thus
- The <u>effect</u> of increasing the presentation rate was a decline in recall.

effect as a verb means to bring about or accomplish some result; thus
- We <u>effected</u> a change by increasing the presentation rate.

A common error is to use "effect" as a verb when "affect" should be used; thus
  Incorrect: Changing to a fixed ratio schedule <u>effected</u> the rat's behavior.
  Correct: Changing to a fixed ratio schedule <u>affected</u> the rat's behavior.
A second common error is to use "affect" as a noun when "effect" should be used; thus
  Incorrect: Changing to a fixed ratio schedule had a major <u>affect</u> on the rat's behavior.
  Correct: Changing to a fixed ratio schedule had a major <u>effect</u> on the rat's behavior.

Table A.2 Plurals of Words with Latin or Greek Origins

The plural forms of many words found in scientific writing derive from their origins in Latin and Greek. A failure to recognize the plural form can lead to a grammatical error of disagreement between noun and verb. The most common example is the word *data*, which refers to more than one piece of information and is the plural of *datum*. Although the term "data" is sometimes found in common usage as a singular noun, the *PM* (p. 96) suggests that it be used only in the plural form.

  Incorrect: The *data was* subjected to a content analysis.
  Correct: The *data were* subjected to a content analysis.

Other examples:

Singular Form	Plural Form
analys**is**	analys**es**
criteri**on**	criteria
hypothes**is**	hypothes**es**
phenomen**on**	phenomena
stimul**us**	stimuli

- In the Abstract, never spell out numbers, even those less than 10, unless the number is the first word in a sentence (and try to avoid making a number the first word in a sentence).

- If a number is part of a measurement unit, use the numeral (e.g., 2-mg dose).

- Use numerals to represent statistical or mathematical information, even if the number is less than 10 (e.g., 6% of the sample. . .).

- Use numerals for times, dates, and ages.

- If a number less than 10 is grouped in a sentence with a number that is 10 or greater, use numerals for both (e.g., "There were 6 stimulus words in the first list and 12 words in the second.").

The complete set of rules about numbers can be found on pages 111–114 of the *PM*.

Reducing Bias in Language

For years, linguists and psychologists interested in language use have investigated the connections between language and thinking. Although the nature of this relationship is a matter of much disagreement, there is a consensus that using language in certain ways can reinforce and perpetuate certain concepts, including stereotypes. The *PM* makes it clear that "[s]cientific writing should be free of implied or irrelevant evaluation of the group or groups being studied" (2010, p. 70).

A common type of bias in language concerns gender. Language that shows gender bias occurs in two varieties. The first is known as a *problem of designation*. This happens when terms include only masculine terminology but are supposed to refer to both males and females. The most common example is the use of *man* when *person* is intended, as in "Man has long been interested in the causes of mental illness." Here are examples of sentences with problems of designation, along with suggested corrections (taken from the 2001 version of APA's *PM*, pp. 70–71). As you can see, the problems can be solved fairly easily by rewording, using plurals, or omitting gender designations altogether.

- The client is usually the best judge of the value of his counseling.
  - *Better:* Clients are usually the best judges of the counseling they receive.

- Man's search for knowledge . . .
  - *Better:* The search for knowledge . . .

- Research scientists often neglect their wives and children.
  - *Better:* Research scientists often neglect their spouses and children.

In addition to problems of designation, some language shows *problems of evaluation*—that is, the terms selected for males and females imply judgments of inequality. For example, a writer describing high school athletes may refer to the *men's basketball team* and the *girls' basketball team* (should be *women's basketball team*). Also, using phrases like *typically male* or *typically female* can promote stereotypical thinking, as can using different descriptors for behaviors that may be identical for males and females (e.g., *ambitious men* but *aggressive women*; *cautious men* but *timid women*).

Gender bias is not the only form of language bias addressed by the *PM*. The manual also urges writers to be cautious about language bias relating to sexual orientation, racial, ethnic, and religious identity, disability, and age. For example (also from the 2001 version of the *PM*, pp. 70–76):

- The sample consisted of 200 adolescent homosexuals.
  - *Better:* The sample consisted of 100 gay males and 100 lesbian adolescents.
  - *Note:* More specific, by identifying the numbers of both male and female participants and avoids the use of the term *homosexual*.

- We studied Eskimos . . .
  - *Better:* We studied Inuit from Canada and Aleuts . . .
  - *Note:* More precise, and shows the variety of native tribes from Canada and Alaska.

- . . . disabled person.
  - *Better:* . . . person with a disability.
  - *Note:* Emphasis is on the person, rather than the disability.

- . . . schizophrenic patients.
  - *Better:* . . . individuals with schizophrenia.
  - *Note:* Emphasis on the person again; the first usage tends to identify the person as the disorder; in addition, the term *patient* should only be used when referring to individuals receiving care in a hospital setting.

Avoiding Plagiarism

In the section in Chapter 2 on scientific fraud, the discussion centered on data falsification, but plagiarism[1] was also mentioned as a serious problem to be avoided. Standard 8.11 of the 2002 ethics code specifically addresses plagiarism, stating simply that "[p]sychologists do not present portions of another's work or data as their own, even if the other work or data source is cited occasionally" (APA, 2002, p. 1070).

The most obvious form of plagiarism is intentionally copying information directly from a source without using quotation marks and then failing to cite the source. The principle is clear: Don't do this under any circumstance, even if the information is from a web page. A second form of plagiarism, sometimes called unintentional plagiarism, is subtler but no less serious. This occurs when writers paraphrase the information, but the sentence structure remains similar to the original source and/or the concepts they describe in the paraphrase clearly belong to the author of that source. Consider the following example. A student is doing a paper on lying and uses a book called *Telling Lies* by Paul Ekman (1985). The student reads the following passage about a situation in which someone is actually telling the truth but is nervous and therefore appears to be lying:

> Another equally important source of trouble, leading to disbelieving-the-truth mistakes, is the Othello error. This error occurs when the lie catcher fails to consider that a truthful person who is under stress may appear to be lying. . . Truthful people may be afraid of being disbelieved, and their fear might be confused with the liar's detection apprehension . . . I have called this error after Othello because the death scene in Shakespeare's play is such an excellent and famous example of it. (Ekman, 1985, pp. 169–170)

The student decides to paraphrase this information and writes the following in a paper:

> Disbelieving-the-truth mistakes are another kind of problem in the accurate detection of lying. The mistake happens when the person trying to catch someone else lying fails to take into account that a truthful person experiencing stress may seem to be lying. This is known as the Othello error, because of the similarity to the death scene in Shakespeare's famous play. Thus, sometimes you could be telling the truth, yet afraid that nobody will believe you. As a result you would appear to be nervous about being detected.

This paraphrasing is an example of plagiarism on two counts. First, the concept, the "Othello error," has clearly been given that name by Ekman. It is his concept, so his book must be cited. Second, the structure and wording of the paraphrasing is too close to the original in several places. Simply taking an author's words and making a few small changes is not original writing: It is plagiarizing. One clear example is when Ekman wrote "This error occurs when the lie catcher fails to consider that a truthful person who is under stress may appear to be lying." The student wrote, "The mistake happens when the person trying to catch someone else lying fails to take into account that a truthful person experiencing stress may seem to be lying."

Thus, any time you use an idea, term, theory, or research finding that belongs to another person, be sure to cite that person's work. To avoid plagiarism, either use direct quotes and clearly attribute the words to the original source, or give credit to the creator of an idea, again by the use of a proper citation. However, note that quoting should be avoided in scientific writing if your intent is to summarize others' work. Instead of quoting, you should paraphrase, and when you paraphrase, do not simply replace some of the original author's words with synonyms you found

---

[1] The term derives from the Latin word *plaga,* meaning a snare or hunting net. The term was eventually applied to the capturing, snaring, or kidnapping of children; thus plagiarism is like "kidnapping" someone's ideas (*Webster's Word Histories,* 1989).

using your computer's thesaurus. Rewrite them in your own words—and still cite the original author, because you will still be using the author's ideas. The writing center at your college or university almost certainly has detailed guidelines for avoiding plagiarism. Go get them. If by some chance the center doesn't have a good set of recommendations, a number of websites provide useful information. One good source is www.plagiarism.org.

Main Sections of the Research Report

The APA-style lab report describing the outcome of an empirical study includes each of the following elements, in this order:

Title page

Abstract

Introduction

Method

Results

Discussion

References

Following the References section, reports may include separate pages for footnotes, tables, and figures (e.g., sketches of apparatus, graphs). In some cases, an appendix (e.g., listing the actual stimulus materials) might be included. Here's how to prepare each main section of the lab report. What follows is what an APA-style research report literally should look like. There are formatting notes in boxes and the content summarizes how to write the APA-style research report.

Running head: SHORT TITLE IS ALL CAPS AND 50 CHARACTERS OR LESS   1

> The **running head** is a heading that will appear 'running' throughout the manuscript in published form. It is created in your word processor's Header option and is a shortened version of the title of your manuscript limited to 50 characters or less (including spaces). The words "Running head" appear only on p. 1 (i.e., the title page of the manuscript, and yes, the 'h' in head is lowercase). The page number should be inserted after the running head on the right-hand side of the page.

Title of Manuscript

Your Name

Your Affiliation

> The title of the article, the name of the person(s) writing the report, and the college, university, or other professional affiliation of the author(s) go about a third of the way down the title page, centered between the margins. The first letters of the primary words in the title are capitalized.
>
> Give some thought to the wording of the article's title, which should range from 10 to 12 words. Take care to avoid beginning your title with phrases like "The Effects of. . ." or "The Relationship between. . ." and instead state what your entire study's overarching results represent. For example, the title "Caffeine Reduces Time-of-Day Effects on Memory Performance in Older Adults" more clearly describes the main message in the study as opposed to "The Effects of Caffeine on Time-of-Day Memory Performance in Older Adults." The title should give the reader a clear idea of the article's content and preview the variables being investigated.

Author Note

> The title page of a manuscript submitted for publication will include an Author Note. This note consists of the complete addresses for the author(s) of the study, acknowledgments (e.g., a grant that supported the research, colleagues who read the manuscript and gave valuable feedback), a description of any special circumstances that might apply (e.g., the study being based on the author's doctoral dissertation), and author contact information (mailing and e-mail addresses). For a lab report you submit in your methods class, your instructor is unlikely to ask you to provide an Author Note. For details on how to format the Author Note, consult the APA *Publication Manual* (2010, p. 24–25).

> You will notice the phrase "Running head" does not appear on this page, nor will it appear anywhere except on p. 1 of your manuscript. Some word processing programs (e.g., Word) have a feature in the Header option to allow this to happen automatically.

> This heading is centered and not boldfaced, unlike other headings later in the manuscript.

Abstract

The **abstract** is the first text material to be read in a research report and normally the last to be written. It is also the *only* part of the article looked at by many readers, who are forced by the sheer mass of information to read the abstract first in order to determine if the entire article is worth examining in detail. Abstracts are reproduced in PsycINFO records. The abstract should be a brief and accurate representation of the entire study. For an empirical study, the abstract contains elements of each of the remaining four major sections (i.e., Introduction, Method, Results, Discussion). Because it must be brief (APA recommends 150–250 words in total; limits vary from one journal to another), it must be carefully prepared—every word counts. To save space, numbers are never spelled out in the abstract unless they begin sentences, and abbreviations are recommended, if appropriate (e.g., "vs." instead of "versus"). The abstract's opening statement is perhaps the most informative. It always includes a statement of the problem, and it usually informs the reader about the individuals tested and/or the variables under investigation. For example, the opening statement from Research Example 12 in Chapter 7 reads, "Human infants learning to stand use visual proprioceptive information about body sway in order to maintain stable posture" (Lee & Aronson, 1974, p. 529). Abstracts are left-justified with no paragraph tab. This abstract includes 237 words.

Keywords: five or six distinct words or phrases that can be used to search for your article in PsycINFO, centered below the text of the abstract

Full Title of Your Report from Your Title Page Centered Here

While page 2 of your APA-style research report is reserved for the Abstract only, page 3 begins the full-blown text of your paper. The Introduction section of the paper comprises the first major section of the APA-style research report and thoroughly describes the problem being studied; by reviewing the pertinent research literature, the Introduction makes clear what is known and not known about the problem. What is unknown or unclear provides the basis for one or more predictions, and these predictions form the hypotheses for the study. Thus, an introduction includes, normally in this order, a statement of the problem, a review of related research literature, and one or more hypotheses to be tested in the study. In a well-written introduction, the author begins by broadly describing the psychological phenomenon of interest. The opening paragraph of a nice introduction should also hook the reader by getting the reader to want to read further. An example of a useful hook is the inclusion of an everyday example of the phenomenon of interest to make it more relatable to the general reader.

After getting the reader's attention, the Introduction includes a review of the existing and relevant research literature and/or theories pertinent to the topic at hand. After reviewing the existing research related to your topic, you should establish a logical rationale for your study. In other words, explain to the reader what gaps exist in the literature and how your research will help fill a gap. The Introduction almost always ends with a clear statement of the specific hypotheses you want to test. Hypotheses should be specific and include the operational definitions of the variables being studied. Below are examples of good and bad hypotheses.

EXAMPLE OF A BAD HYPOTHESIS:

"There is a relationship between self-esteem and depression."

This is more like an empirical question from which theories and hypotheses are later derived.

EXAMPLE OF A GOOD HYPOTHESIS:

"It is hypothesized that there is a negative correlation between self-esteem and depression, such that participants who score low on the Rosenberg Self-Esteem Scale, indicating low self-esteem, will also score low on the Beck Depression Inventory. Furthermore, it is predicted that this correlation will be stronger for women than for men."

An important component of writing APA-style research reports, or any psychology paper for that matter, is proper source citation. When reviewing past research related to the problem at hand, you must furnish reference citations for the studies mentioned; the *PM* provides a specific format for this. Sometimes, the author's name is part of the sentence you are writing. If so, the date of publication follows the name and is placed in parentheses. For example:

Smith (1990) found that helping behavior declined.

If the author's name is not included in the sentence, the name, a comma, and the date are placed in parentheses, usually at the end of the sentence. For example:

In an earlier study, helping behavior declined (Smith, 1990).

If a direct quote is used, the page number is included. However, keep in mind that quotes should be rare when reviewing others' works. For example:

Helping behavior declined when "participants had difficulty determining whether the confederate had fallen onto the live wire" (Smith, 1990, p.23).

OR

Smith (1990) reported that helping behavior declined when "participants had difficulty determining whether the confederate had fallen onto the live wire" (p. 23).

Every work cited in the Introduction (or any other part of the manuscript) must be given a complete reference listing at the end of the paper. You'll learn how that is accomplished shortly in the description of the References section of the report. The *PM* has a thorough guide to citations and can be consulted for virtually any question you may have. Also, APA's format is used in most of your psychology journal articles and textbooks, including this methods text.

Method

This is a first-level heading according to APA and is used to denote the Method, Results, and Discussion sections of an empirical research report.

The Method section includes a detailed account of exactly how you intend to carry out your study. The section begins with the heading "Method" centered and in boldface text, as shown above. Unlike the Introduction, the Method section does not begin on a new page. This section includes descriptions of your participants, what materials you used, and what procedures your participants followed as they participated in your study. The goal is for the Method section to be written in a way that enables other researchers to run the study themselves; thus, it serves as a vehicle for an important part of the replication process described in Chapter 3 and elsewhere. You can think of it as a recipe for your study where you list all of the ingredients and the procedures to cook the perfect experiment.

Participants — This is a second-level heading used in empirical research reports, especially to denote the Participants, Materials, and Procedure subsections in the Method section.

In the Participants (note the boldface again) subsection, you should state how many individuals participated, what kind of individuals they were (e.g., Introductory Psychology students) and how they were selected (e.g., convenience sampling). Present age, gender, and other relevant demographic data here as well. This section is labeled "Participants" or "Subjects" (either is acceptable, but definitely choose "Subjects" if animals are being used in the study).

Materials

Describe in detail all materials used in your study in this subsection. Materials include any tests, equipment, and/or stimuli employed. If you use published materials (questionnaires or surveys) in the study, cite your source; if you created the questionnaire or survey yourself, provide a copy in an appendix. You should describe your testing materials in a way that indicates exactly what you are measuring. The Materials section is much like a listing of the ingredients in a recipe. List all materials with precision and accuracy.

Note any equipment or apparatus here. In the case of standard lab equipment, rather than describing the entire apparatus, the company name and model and/or serial number is sufficient. If this is not possible, describe the equipment in detail. If many pieces of apparatus are used, you may include a separate Apparatus subsection prior to the Materials subsection.

Procedure

Describe in this subsection exactly what you did and how you did it. In other words, provide a detailed description of every event from the beginning until the end of the study. Include experimental and control group assignment to conditions, order or manner of experimental treatment presentation, and a summary of the instructions to the participants. You should include a statement about your research design (e.g., correlational design, 2×2 between-subjects factorial design, etc.).

Results

The Results section is where you show the reader the exact outcome of your study. A well-crafted results section tells a story with the data, and the statistical notation you see in this section is the raw evidence for the claims you make about your data. Provide a concise yet complete verbal description of the results, along with the descriptive and inferential statistics that support the description. Do not attempt to explain why some prediction succeeded or failed; such interpretation belongs in the Discussion section. A good way to organize the Results section is with reference to the sequence of hypotheses in the introduction. For instance, if the Introduction ends with three hypotheses, devote a paragraph of the Results section to each, in the same order as in the intro.

Reporting the Data: Statistics

As you recall from Chapter 4 of the text, descriptive statistics summarize data, and inferential statistics determine whether it is prudent to reject the null hypothesis(es) or not. The most common descriptive statistics reported are means, standard deviations, and correlation coefficients. Typical inferential statistics include t tests, F ratios from ANOVAs, and chi-square (χ^2) tests. The *PM* (2010, p. 34) also encourages the inclusion of effect size calculations, and it is becoming common to see confidence intervals reported as well. Procedures for calculating these analyses (or using SPSS to calculate them) can be found at the Student Companion Site. For now, be aware of two points. First, employ standard abbreviations for statistical terms such as the sample mean (*M*) and standard deviation (*SD*).

Second, the general rule in reporting statistics is to place the descriptive statistics before the inferential statistics in any given paragraph.

In general, the shorthand method for reporting inferential statistics is the same for all types of analysis. It includes the test used (e.g., F), degrees of freedom (e.g., 1 for the numerator of the F ratio and 18 for the denominator), the calculated value of the test (e.g., 12.87), the probability value (e.g., $p = .018$), and the effect size (e.g., Cohen's $d = .22$). Note that the statistical symbols are italicized. You should refer to the specifics of the *PM* to assist you in formatting a Results section, depending on which statistical tests are used. The following paragraphs are examples of how to describe (and format) results from various statistical tests.

An examination of the number of hours of television viewing and the frequency of aggressive acts for each of the 60 children revealed a positive correlation between television viewing and instances of aggressive behavior, $r(58) = .63, p < .05$.

The control group ($M = 14.10$, $SD = 3.14$) appeared to remember more words on the memory test than the drugged group ($M = 12.37$, $SD = 2.14$). However, this difference was tested using an independent groups t test and was shown to be nonsignificant, $t(18) = 1.23, p > .05$. Thus, the data failed to support the notion of a drug effect on memory.

The mean scores for the short, medium, and long retention intervals were 5.92 ($SD = .73$), 10.31 ($SD = 1.03$), and 14.25 ($SD = 1.21$) respectively. A one-way ANOVA revealed a significant effect of retention interval, as hypothesized, $F(2, 34) = 123.07, p < .05$. A post-hoc analysis revealed.

While 60% of the men agreed their map reading skills were strong, only 35% of the women did. A 2×2 chi-square test identified a significant relation between gender and confidence in map-reading skills, $\chi^2 (1, N = 119) = 10.51, p < .05$.

Portraying the Data: Tables and Figures

Descriptive statistics, especially in factorial designs, are often complicated enough that a paragraph-length description of them can be difficult to follow. To avoid the problem, data are often presented in tables and/or figures. **Tables** are row and column arrangements that typically present means and standard deviations or sets of correlations. **Figures** can be graphs, diagrams, flow charts, sketches of apparatus, or photos. Each has specific formatting rules, and you should consult the *PM* for examples of APA-style tables and figures. Although tables and figures appear in published form within the Results section, all tables and figures in the research report you write are placed as separate pages *after* the References section.

It is sometimes difficult to decide whether to use a table or a figure to present the data. In general, a table is preferred if it seems important to report the precise mean scores (on a graph, the exact scores require some guessing) or if any data points are so numerous that a graph would be hopelessly cluttered. On the other hand, graphs can often illustrate a point dramatically; thus, they are especially useful for showing an interaction effect in a factorial study. One certainty is that it is inappropriate to present the same data in two ways—that is, both in a table and as a figure. The most common graph forms are line graphs and bar graphs. As described and illustrated in Chapter 7, line graphs are normally (but not necessarily) used when the variable on the X-axis is continuous; for discrete variables (e.g., gender), bar graphs should always be used.

It is not enough simply to present tables or figures. In the Results section, you must refer the reader to them and point out their important features. Some skill is involved here because you don't want to write a detailed description pointing out every aspect of a table or graph. Thus, in a graph showing a serial position curve in a memory experiment, you might encounter a sentence like this:

> Figure 1 shows that recall was quite high for the first few words of the list, poor for middle words, and almost perfect for the final three words.

Discussion

This is the final section of the text material for your lab report and it serves to tie the entire report together. Begin it with a nontechnical summary of the main results of your study; in other words, tell the reader your main findings without using statistical terminology or jargon. Next, describe the main results with reference to the original hypothesis(es) and then proceed to a broader interpretation of the results of your study. This evaluation includes relating the results to any theoretical points raised in the introduction and trying to explain any failed predictions. The Discussion also addresses the problem of alternative explanations of results. As the author of the article, you will decide on the interpretation that seems most reasonable, but sometimes other alternatives could be conceived. You should mention these alternatives and then explain why you think your explanation is better.

Finally, the Discussion includes an important element of any research program: consideration of the "what's next?" questions you learned about in Chapter 3 of the text. That is, writers usually make suggestions about what the next study should be, given the outcome of the one just completed. This, of course, is a natural consequence of the fact that research always answers some questions but raises others. When you read published journal articles, the Discussion section is a good place to get ideas for your own research.

SHORT TITLE IS ALL CAPS AND 50 CHARACTERS OR LESS 9

References

Unlike the Method, Results, and Discussion sections, the References section starts on a new page with the heading "References" at the top and centered, and no boldface this time. This section consists of an alphabetized (by author) list of all of the sources cited in the lab report. Each item uses a hanging indent, which makes it easier to find specific authors when skimming through a reference page. The *PM* includes a complete set of rules for virtually every type of citation; here are examples of the most common ones:

A journal article with more than one author

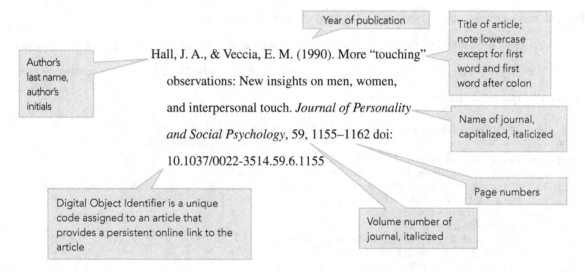

Author's last name, author's initials

Year of publication

Title of article; note lowercase except for first word and first word after colon

Hall, J. A., & Veccia, E. M. (1990). More "touching" observations: New insights on men, women, and interpersonal touch. *Journal of Personality and Social Psychology*, 59, 1155–1162 doi: 10.1037/0022-3514.59.6.1155

Name of journal, capitalized, italicized

Digital Object Identifier is a unique code assigned to an article that provides a persistent online link to the article

Volume number of journal, italicized

Page numbers

A book that is a first edition

Kimmel, A. J. (1996). *Ethical issues in behavioral research: Basic and applied perspectives*. Malden, MA: Blackwell.

A book that is a second edition or later

Kimmel, A. J. (2007). *Ethical issues in behavioral research: Basic and applied perspectives* (2nd ed.). Malden, MA: Blackwell.

A chapter from an edited book

Weiss, J. M. (1977). Psychological and behavioral influences on gastrointestinal lesions in animal models. In J. D. Maser & M. E. P. Seligman (Eds.), *Psychopathology: Experimental models* (pp. 232–269). San Francisco: Freeman.

SHORT TITLE IS ALL CAPS AND 50 CHARACTERS OR LESS   10

Rules for citing references from websites, electronic databases, and so on have been evolving in recent years and are frequently updated. In general, APA recommends that writers "include the same elements, in the same order, as [they] would for a reference to a fixed-media source and add as much electronic retrieval material as needed for others to locate the sources you cited" (2010, p. 187).

One final point is that before turning in an APA-style research report, you should check the citations in the body of your paper against the list in the References section. Make sure (a) every source mentioned in the text of your research report is given a listing in the References section of the paper, and (b) every reference listed in the References section is cited somewhere in the text of your research report.

APA-style is a precise format that allows researchers to easily communicate on common ground with regard to understanding how others do research in a variety of areas in psychology. For a checklist of formatting tips for an APA-style research report, see Table A.3.

Table A.3   APA-Style Checklist for Empirical Research Reports

Have you checked all of the following?

_____ Is your entire paper double-spaced, including References and Tables?

_____ Does the title page follow APA-style, with a title/author/affiliation, running head, and header with page number?

_____ Does the header that will appear on every page of your report include the appropriate page number? [use the "Insert . . . Page Numbers" function]

_____ Does the Abstract appear on page 2?

_____ Does the Abstract follow APA guidelines for length and content?

_____ Does the body of your paper begin on page 3?

_____ Have you cited references in the text according to APA-style?

_____ Does your Introduction begin with your title, centered at the top of page 3?

_____ Do you have the appropriate headings throughout your paper and do they follow APA format for centering and boldfacing?

_____ Are there page breaks between the Introduction, Method, Results, and Discussion sections. If so, THIS IS WRONG!

_____ Are you following APA-style formatting for the Results section?

_____ Do your Tables look exactly like they should, according to the APA _Publication Manual_?

_____ Do you refer to your tables in the text?

_____ Does your References section begin a new page after the body of the text?

_____ Do all your references in the References section match the references cited in the text?

_____ Do your Tables and/or Figures appear as separate pages following your References?

_____ Do you feel relieved that all of these are checked and done?

Presentations and Posters

If you're lucky, you may find yourself in a position to present the results of your research publicly. Opportunities range from a presentation to other psychology students as part of a course requirement to a more formal presentation at a professional conference. For example, as mentioned in the text's Epilogue, sessions for undergraduate research are scheduled at national meetings of the APA and the Association for Psychological Science (APS), and at regional meetings (e.g., that of the Midwestern Psychological Association, or MPA). Also, a number of colleges and universities host conferences specifically for the purpose of presenting undergraduate research.

Tips for Presenting a Paper

Presentations at professional psychology conferences take one of two forms: papers or, more likely, posters. The paper is the more traditional (but rapidly disappearing) format. In a typical 1-hour session (50 minutes, actually), several researchers (usually four) will each read a paper describing their work. If you have this opportunity, here are some recommendations:

1. You will be given a strict time limit—stick to it! A typical limit is 12 minutes, which allows time for 4 papers in the session. If you take 20–25 minutes, the person who is scheduled to go last in the session will hate you forever. Alternatively, you may be cut off by the moderator of the session before you have finished. Either way, going over the time limit is not good.

2. Prepare a one-page handout a friend can distribute to the audience just as you are being introduced. The handout should include the title of the paper, your name, affiliation, and e-mail address, your hypothesis(es), an abbreviated description of the design, the results (usually as a table or graph), and a concise conclusion. Unfortunately, many in the audience will be thinking about what session they are going to attend in the next hour, planning dinner, or rehearsing their own presentation rather than listening carefully to you, so your handout can be an effective way for them to take useful information away with them.

3. If projection equipment is available, and it usually is, take advantage of it. Learn how to use PowerPoint and deliver your presentation that way. If you use PowerPoint, be sure to choose a professional-looking design and avoid cutesy clip-art that detracts from the professionalism and seriousness of your hard work.

4. Prepare a normal lab report and then adapt it to the form of a document to be presented orally, with or without PowerPoint as a visual aid. This means focusing on the essential points and avoiding picky details. For example, although you should include the model name for your apparatus in the lab report, the generic name (e.g., "operant chamber") is fine for an oral presentation. The listener should be clear about the purpose of your study, the essential elements of design and control, the results, and your overall conclusions. Your presentation should be more conversational than in the more formal lab report.

5. Practice your presentation in front of friends. Ideally, have a video made, learn from it (keep it away from your friends so it doesn't wind up on YouTube), and then practice some more. To help with the inevitable anxiety, try to remember that of all the people in the room, you know your project best!

Tips for Presenting a Poster

Poster sessions have the advantage of allowing the presentation of many more research projects per hour than typical paper sessions and, of course, they eliminate the public-speaking anxiety that accompanies a formal paper presentation. They also increase the chances you will meet people with research interests similar to yours. At an effective poster session, you will have a half-dozen good conversations, possibly get ideas for interpreting your results differently, develop ideas for "what's next?" questions, and perhaps exchange e-mail addresses or cell phone numbers.

If you do a poster, you will find yourself in a large room filled with row after row of bulletin boards. On one of these boards, you will arrange a display that enables someone to understand what you have discovered in your research. Some conferences also ask you to prepare copies (usually 50) of a brief version of your poster to be given to those who wish to take one (most of the time, a legal pad for people to write their e-mail addresses on it will do; after you return from the conference, you can send them copies electronically). Here are tips for presenting a good poster:

1. Layout is critically important. Readers of your poster should be able to figure out the essence of what happened in your study in just a minute or two. If their first response is confusion, they will move on to the next poster. Figure A.1 shows you one possible layout, but the particular conference you're attending might have specific rules, so pay attention to them. For instance, some smaller conferences publish all of the abstracts in a booklet given to conference attendees. If so, there's no need for you to include an Abstract on the poster itself. Instead, start with a section called Introduction or Problem Statement.

2. In general, the layout of your poster should be organized and logical. Readers should be able to determine easily the purpose of your study, the method, the results, and your overall conclusions. Notice the order of information on your poster mirrors the order of information in an APA-style research report. Be sure the content of the poster flows easily from left to right.

3. It should be possible to read and understand your poster from a distance of 6 feet. Some universities provide templates for you to use to create your poster. If this service is available, use it! It will likely include an official graphic of the university seal too. Check with your university's library or media center to see if templates are available. Most researchers use PowerPoint to create their posters, using textboxes to contain the main sections of the poster. Your title should be printed in letters about 2 inches high, with your name and

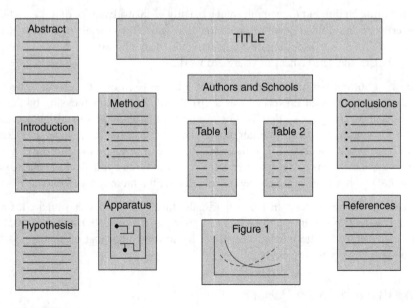

FIGURE A.1
Sample poster layout.

university affiliation a bit smaller. The major headings should be set at about 40 pt., things like figure captions at 28 pt., and text no smaller than 24 pt. Use fonts that are easy to read (e.g., Arial, Geneva, Helvetica). Using color conservatively is OK, but don't overuse it to the point of distraction (e.g., don't create a graph with six colors in it). If you're lucky, your school has a print shop that can place your entire poster onto a single sheet of paper, but you may need to go to a commercial print shop to print your poster. Bring extra pushpins for mounting your poster to the bulletin board; conferences supply pins, but there never seem to be enough.

4. Less is more—edit to the bare bones. Feel free to use bulleted lists instead of long paragraphs, especially for the Method and Results sections. If readers need more precise detail about some aspect of the study, you'll be there to enlighten them.

5. The poster is essentially a visual form of presentation, so use graphics liberally. In addition to tables and graphs, feel free to include drawings of apparatus, photos of the research environment, diagrams of the research design, and so on. Every graphic should tell an important part of the story, and not detract from the content of your research.

6. Finally, your poster should conform to the rules of APA-style, particularly with regard to citing sources, presenting statistical notation, and using headings and subheadings (e.g., Participants, Materials, and Procedure subheadings of the Method).

APPLICATIONS EXERCISES

Exercise A.1   True/False

Six of the following statements about the APA lab report are true. See if you can identify them.

1. After writing the abstract, double space and then immediately begin the Introduction on the same page.

2. On the Title page, the running head functions as an abbreviated title.

3. In the Results section, if you portray your results with a graph, it is also OK to display them in a table because then the reader also gets the exact numbers.

4. The Abstract briefly conveys information from the main sections of the report (Introduction, Method, Results, Discussion).

5. A "what's next" type of paragraph belongs in the Discussion section of the report.

6. Begin each section with a centered label; in the Introduction, for example, the word *Introduction* identifies the section.

7. Each item that appears in the References section should be found somewhere in the lab report itself.

8. The Method section should contain enough information for replication to be possible.

9. In the Results section, to maintain reader interest, it is important to explain and interpret each result right after you report it.

10. The place to operationally define the independent and dependent variables is the Method section.

Exercise A.2   Word Usage

Each of the following lab report sentences contains an error or, at the very least, wording that could be improved. Fix the sentences.

1. 124 male college students were used in the experiment.

2. The data was then subjected to a 2x3 independent groups ANOVA.

3. The instructions had a strong affect on the participants.

4. The criteria for learning was defined as two consecutive errorless runs through the maze.

5. A study of maze learning was conducted by Tolman.

7. The study tried to get at the essence of man's basic need for achievement.

Exercise A.3   Referencing: Sharpening Your APA-Style Skills

Of the following items from a Reference section, one is correct and the remaining seven have exactly one error. Identify the one that is correct and fix the errors in the other seven references.

1. Reynolds, G. S. (1968). *A primer of operant conditioning.* Glenview, IL: Scott, Foresman.

2. Kolata, George B. (1986). What does it mean to be random? *Science, 231,* 1068–1070.

3. Lee, D. N., and Aronson, E. (1974). Visual proprioceptive control of standing in human infants. *Perception and Psychophysics, 15,* 529–532.

4. Miller, A. G. (1972). Role playing: An alternative to deception? *American Psychologist, 27,* 623–636.

5. Geller, D. M. (1982). Alternatives to deception: Why, what, and how? In Sieber, J. E. (Ed.), *The ethics of social research: Surveys and experiments* (pp. 40–55). New York: Springer-Verlag.

6. Bakeman, R., & Brownlee, J. R. (1980). The strategic use of parallel play: A sequential analysis. *Child Development, 51,* 873–878.

7. Brehm, J. (1956). Postdecision changes in the desirability of alternatives. *Journal of Abnormal and Social Psychology, 52(3),* 384–389.

8. Carr, H. A., & Watson, J. B. (1908). Orientation in the white rat. *Journal of Comparative Neurology and Psychology, 18,* pp. 27–44.

Exercise A.4   Main Sections of the Lab Report

In which section of the lab report (Abstract, Introduction, Method, Results, and Discussion) would the following statements most likely be found?

1. We hypothesized that participants given imagery instructions would outperform those given instructions to use rote memorization.

2. There were three different groups in the study.

3. A logical next step would be to add another age group to extend the findings to pre-adolescents.

4. Males recalled 45.6 words ($SD = 2.3$), while females recalled 53.5 words ($SD = 1.9$).

5. The experiment was a 2 (gender) x 3 (instructions) mixed factorial.

6. In an earlier study, Smith (1988) found no such effect.

Appendix B
Answers to Selected End-of-Chapter
Applications Exercises

Chapter 1. Scientific Thinking in Psychology

1.1 Asking Empirical Questions

1. Is God dead?
   Possible empirical questions: To what extent do people of different religious faiths believe in a personal God who is directly involved in their day-to-day lives? For those raised as Christians, did the percentage of them believing in a personal God change over the past 30 years?

3. Are humans naturally good?
   Possible empirical questions: Will people be less likely to donate to charity if they believe their donations will be anonymous? How do believers in different religions react to this question and how do nonbelievers react?

5. What is beauty?
   Possible empirical questions: Do 20-year-old men differ from 40-year-old men in how they define the beauty of a woman? For men of different cultures, which waist-hip ratio in women is considered most beautiful? How do works of art from three artistic traditions vary in ratings of beauty?

1.3 Arriving at a Strong Belief

Authority (parents, priests, ministers, or rabbis; perhaps even Charlton Heston on TV as Moses) is an important factor here. In addition, people might have intense emotional experiences (e.g., while looking upon great natural beauty) they judge to be spiritual in nature. Third, they might use reason to arrive at a belief in God. For instance, they might argue that all events have causes and that ultimately there must be a cause greater than all others (i.e., God).

1.5 Social Cognition and the Psychic Hotline

1. belief perseverance
   After hearing about the "successes" of psychics *repeatedly* on TV infomercials and perhaps from authority figures respected by the individual, a belief might strengthen to the point it is resistant to evidence.

2. confirmation bias
   The individual ignores evidence questioning the validity of psychic predictions and attends only to reports of successful predictions (e.g., those found in supermarket tabloids or reported in great detail by Aunt Edna).

3. the availability heuristic
   A favorable initial belief might be formed if a psychic is consulted in a high-profile police case and appears to make a dramatic break in the case (of course, the hundreds of failed psychic consultations with police don't make the news).

Chapter 2. Ethics in Psychological Research

2.1 Thinking Scientifically About Deception

1. One possible study could examine attitudes toward research and toward psychologists held by students who had been through experiments that either included deception or did not. In addition to the measure of attitudes, students could be asked to rank psychologists, among a number of other professions, on a scale of trustworthiness.

3. One possible study could halt the procedure at different points and ask participants to guess the true purpose of the study.

2.2 Recognizing Ethical Problems

1. This study presents problems relating to consent and privacy violations (unwitting participants could possibly sue for privacy invasions and even bring criminal charges of harassment or criminal trespass); also, without giving consent, one cannot withdraw from the study. To defend the study to an IRB, the researcher would emphasize the importance of understanding how stress affects physiological systems, that the experience was not significantly different from what can happen in any men's room, that proper debriefing would be done, that confidentiality would be maintained (it would not be necessary to know the names of the participants), and that the data would not be used without the person's written permission.

3. This study has serious consent problems and, because participants did not know they were in a research study, they had no knowledge of their right to quit at any time. To defend the study to an IRB, the researcher would stress that the study might provide some understanding of a real historical event and yield insight into people's willingness to engage in unlawful activity; this knowledge could eventually be useful to law enforcement. The researcher would also assure the IRB that a thorough debriefing (perhaps with follow-up) would occur, that strict confidentiality would be maintained, and that data would not be used without the person's written permission.

2.4 Decisions about Animal Research

Galvin and Herzog (1992) found that, in general, men were more likely to approve all of the studies than women were. As for the studies themselves, about 80% (combined male and female data, and estimated from a graph) approved both the "rats" and the "bears" studies, about 55% approved the "dogs" study, about 40% approved the "monkeys" study, and about 20% approved the "mice" study.

Chapter 3. Developing Ideas for Research in Psychology

3.1 What's Next?

1. Possible next studies: Compare male and female drivers; vary the age of the drivers; vary the make (and expense) of the car; replicate the study but add a second group in which the driver is said to be listening to a book on tape instead of talking on a cell phone.

3. Possible next studies: Look at gender differences in this spatial ability; vary experience level by comparing freshmen with seniors; compare distant city locations (learned with reference to maps) with campus locations (learned by walking around campus) that are out of sight from the testing point.

3.2 Replicating and Extending Milgram's Obedience Research

1. The roles of teacher and learner could be varied by gender, yielding four groups: male teacher-male learner; male teacher-female learner; female teacher-female learner; and female teacher-male learner (Milgram did not go to this length, but he did vary the gender of the teacher/subject and found female teachers delivered about the same level of shocks as the male teachers did).

3. One technique used by Milgram (1974) is to give teachers the option of how high to set the shock level; sadists would presumably use high levels. Milgram found teachers continued to deliver shocks (i.e., continued obeying), but they set very low levels, trying to help the learner as much as possible, apparently. They also tried to press the shock lever as quickly as possible, hoping to deliver minimal pain.

3.3 Creating Operational Definitions

1. *Frustration* could be operationally defined as (a) blood pressure elevated 20% over the baseline level for a person or (b) amount of time spent pushing against a blockade to keep a child from a desired toy.

3. *Anxiety* could be operationally defined as (a) level of muscle tension in the shoulders or (b) a person's self-rating of anxiety just before an exam begins, on a scale from 1 to 10.

5. *Memory* could be operationally defined as the number of words recalled after subjects are given an opportunity to memorize a list of words.

Chapter 4. Sampling, Measurement, and Hypothesis Testing

4.1 Scales of Measurement

1. Categories are being used—nominal scale.

3. Rank order is used here—ordinal scale.

5. Nominal scale, assuming the study is set up so it measures whether people help or not (i.e., two categories); could be a ratio scale, though, if the amount of time it takes for someone to help is measured.

7. This is a rank order procedure—ordinal scale.

9. Most psychologists are willing to consider the scales on psychological tests to have equal intervals between choice points—interval scale.

4.2 H_0, H_1, Type I Errors, and Type II Errors

1. H_0: Male and female participants are equally able to detect deception. H_1: Women are better able to detect deception than men, especially when detecting deception in other women (rationale: reading facial expressions of emotion is not a guy thing). Type I error: Females outperform males, when in fact there are no true differences in the ability to judge deception. Type II error: No differences are found in the study, but in fact females are superior to males in judging deception.

3. H_0: depressed = nondepressed in their predictions H_1: predictions of success will be higher for nondepressed than for depressed Type I: nondepressed predictions significantly better

($p<.05$), but no true difference exists Type II: differences in predictions not significant ($p>.05$), but the nondepressed really do have more confidence in their ability to learn a maze.

4.3 Statistical Analysis

For psychology majors: mean = 61.8; median = 61.5; mode = 60; range = 25; standard deviation = 8.07; variance = 65.07; 95% CI: 56.03 to 67.57.

For Philosophy majors: mean = 53.9; median = 53; mode = 51; range = 24; standard deviation = 8.08; variance = 65.21; 95% CI: 48.12 to 59.68.

General conclusion: significantly higher critical thinking scores for psychology majors, probably because of their research methods course → $t(18) = 2.19$, $p = .04$. And the effect size is large ($d = .98$).

Chapter 5. Introduction to Experimental Research

5.1 Identifying Variables

1. There are two independent variables. The first is class; its levels are freshmen and seniors; it is a subject variable. The second is the instruction given to subjects; its levels are "use imagery" and control (no specific instructions); it is a manipulated instructional variable. There are also two dependent variables: confidence ratings (interval scale) and pointing accuracy (ratio scale).

3. There are two independent variables. The first, a manipulated situational variable, is degree of hunger, with two levels operationally defined by the number of hours without food (6 or 12). The second independent variable could be called "tone-food sequencing." Its three levels are (a) tone on and off, then food; (b) tone on, then food; and (c) food, then tone. It is a manipulated situational variable. There are two dependent variables: how long it takes for saliva to begin, and how much saliva accumulates. Both are ratio.

5. There are two independent variables. The first, type of maze, is a manipulated task variable. Its two levels are elevated maze and alley maze. The second variable, type of rat, is a subject variable. Its two levels are wild and lab-bred. There are two dependent variables: number of errors and time to completion. Both are ratio.

7. There are two independent variables. The first is the subject variable of gender (two levels—male, female). The second is the type of stimulus materials used; its two levels are stereotypically male and stereotypically female. It is a manipulated situational variable. The single dependent variable is an accuracy score (total number of correctly identified moved objects), scored on a ratio scale.

5.2 Spot the Confound(s)

1. The independent variable is driver type (four levels, one for each type of driver) and the dependent variable is the distance traveled by a struck golf ball. Confounds are club sequence (the golfers shouldn't all use the clubs in the same order) and golf course hole (some holes might lend themselves to longer distances, if for instance, they are downwind).

Levels of IV	EV1	EV2	DV
Club 1	first to be hit	first hole	distance
Club 2	second to be hit	second hole	distance
Club 3	third to be hit	third hole	distance
Club 4	fourth to be hit	fourth hole	distance

3. The independent variable is memorization strategy (or a similar label), with two levels: imagery and rote repetition. The dependent variable is some measure of recall. Confounds are word type (should all be either concrete or abstract) and presentation mode (should all be either visual or auditory).

Levels of IV	EV1	EV2	DV
imagery	concrete nouns	visual	recall
rote repetition	abstract nouns	auditory	recall

5.3 Operational Definitions (Again)

1. The independent variable is situational ambiguity and, in a helping behavior study, it could be manipulated by staging an emergency (e.g., a person slumped against a wall groaning) and manipulating the level of lighting with perhaps three levels: bright, medium, and dim. These could be operationally defined in terms of some physical measure of brightness. The dependent variable would be helping, which could be operationally defined as occurring whenever a passerby stops and verbally offers aid.

3. One independent variable is level of bowling skill, and it could be operationalized as a bowler's average score. The second independent variable is whether an audience is present or not, and that could be defined easily as a group of people of some fixed number who watch the bowling. The dependent variable is bowling performance, easily defined as one's total score per game.

5. Two independent variables here—whether or not caffeine is ingested and age—and a single dependent variable that could be operationalized as the number of words recalled after studying a list of 30 words for 2 minutes. Caffeine could be operationally defined by having some subjects drink an 8-ounce cup of caffeinated coffee and others drink an 8-ounce cup of decaffeinated coffee. The drinks could be ingested 20 minutes before doing the memory test, to be sure the caffeine has begun to have an effect. Subjects 20–25 years of age could be compared with those 60–65 years old.

Chapter 6. Methodological Control in Experimental Research

6.1 Between-Subject or Within-Subject?

1. The study requires both young and old animals, a between-subjects variable. For each group, some animals would have their visual cortex damaged and others wouldn't, another between-subjects variable.

3. The study involves comparing the exposure therapy procedure with some other procedure or with the absence of a procedure (control group). In either case, this is a between-subjects situation.

5. This study compares problem solving in groups and individually. It could be done as a between-subjects variable, but a within-subjects approach would also be fine and might even be preferable, allowing direct comparison within a specific person of whether problem solving works better in a group or alone.

7. This study compares the degree of suggestibility for two kinds of clinical patients, and because this is a subject variable, it is a between-subjects variable.

6.2 Fixing Confounds

Answers to these items will vary, depending on student creativity. Here are some possible answers.

1. One confound here is club sequence. The first club is always hit first, the second club second, and so on. This is an order effect that must be solved through counterbalancing. Complete counterbalancing would require 24 sequences, which could be easily done by having 24 subjects, each randomly assigned to one of the sequences. The second confound concerns the fact that four holes are used—a different hole for each club. Counterbalancing could be used here as well, if one had no choice but to use four holes. But a better solution would be to have all the balls hit from the same spot, perhaps at a driving range. The study could also include a double blind—neither those running the trials nor the golfers would know which club was hypothesized to be better.

3. The two confounds here, type of word (concrete or abstract) and type of presentation method (seeing the words or hearing them), could easily be controlled by using just one type of word and one type of presentation. Alternatively, both types of words and both types of presentation method could be used, along with the main IV of strategy (imagery versus rote). But it would require having a separate group for each of eight possible combinations of the three variables. As for the main IV of strategy, the instructions to subjects would have to be carefully written to avoid subject bias; if the subjects in the imagery condition are given the impression imagery will be effective, those in the rote repetition condition should also be told their strategy is effective. (In Chapter 8, you will learn that the study would use a 2x2x2 factorial design.)

6.3 Random Assignment and Matching
Matching:

Step 1. Scores on the matching variable—the weights listed in the exercise.

Step 2. Arrange in ascending order:

168, 175, 178, 182, 184, 185, 186, 188, 191, 198, 205, 210, 215, 221, 226, 238

Step 3. Create pairs:

pair 1:	168 and 175
pair 2:	178 and 182
pair 3:	184 and 185
pair 4:	186 and 188
pair 5:	191 and 198
pair 6:	205 and 210
pair 7:	215 and 221
pair 8:	226 and 238

From this point, answers will vary. For each matched pair, flip a coin to see which of the pair is assigned to the weight loss program and which to the control group. Then calculate a mean weight for each. Follow the procedure in the exercise to accomplish random assignment. Then compare the numbers that result from the two procedures. Chances are the two assigned groups will be closer to each other in average weight when the matching procedure is done.

Chapter 7. Experimental Design I: Single-Factor Designs

7.1 Identifying Variables

1. Research Example 11—Independent Groups Design
    Independent variable: note taking strategy (instructional variable)

    > Levels: on a laptop
    > hand-written

    Dependent variable: accuracy (ratio scale of measurement)

3. Research Example 13—Ex Post Facto Design
    Independent variable: traumatic brain injury (subject variable)

    > Levels: injured
    > not injured

    Dependent variable: sarcasm detection score (interval scale of measurement)

5. Research Example 15—Multilevel Independent Groups Design
    Independent variable: amount of bystander intervention (situational variable)

    > Levels: no bystanders present (alone)
    > bystanders present who were able to
    > help
    > bystanders present who were unable
    > to help

    Dependent variable: whether or not child helps (nominal scale of measurement)

7. Research Example 17—Using Both Placebo and Wait List Control Groups
    Independent variable: type of weight loss tape (situational variable)

    > Levels: subliminal tape on weight loss
    > subliminal tape on dental anxiety
    > (placebo control)
    > no tape yet (waiting list control)

    Dependent variable: weight loss after five weeks (ratio scale of measurement)

7.2 Identifying Designs

1. The independent variable is whether or not a person has bulimia; it is a between-subjects variable and a subject variable. The dependent variable is the choice of the body size drawing; assuming equal intervals, it appears to be measured on an interval scale. The design: single-factor, 2-level, ex post facto design. The analysis is an independent samples t test.

3. The independent variable is length of the gratification delay; it is a between-subjects manipulated variable. The dependent variable is how long they continue doing the puzzle; it is a ratio scale of measurement. The design: single-factor, multilevel, independent groups design. The analysis is a one-way ANOVA for independent groups.

5. The independent variable is degree of tattoo coverage; it is a within-subjects manipulated variable. One dependent variable is the judgment about a major; it is measured on a nominal scale (one of five categories). The other dependent variable is the rating scales; depending on the equal interval assumption, this could be either ordinal or interval. The design: single-factor, multilevel, repeated measures design. If an interval scale is assumed, the analysis is a one-way ANOVA for repeated measures.

7. The independent variable is the length of the time limit for each anagram; it is a between-subjects manipulated variable. The dependent variable is the number of anagrams solved, a ratio measure. The design: single-factor, 2-level, matched groups design. The analysis is an dependent samples *t* test.

7.3 Outcomes

1. The independent variable is a discrete variable (type of group in the study), so use a bar graph.

Outcome A. Marijuana impairs recall, whereas subject expectations about marijuana have no effect on recall.

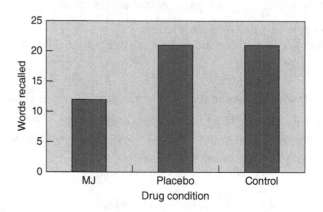

Outcome B. Marijuana impairs recall, but subject expectations about marijuana also reduce recall performance.

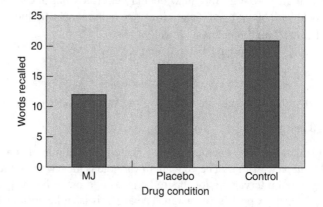

Outcome C. The apparently adverse effect of marijuana on recall can be attributed entirely to placebo effects.

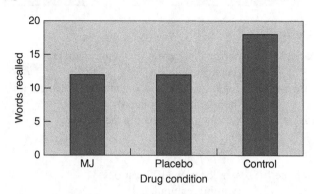

3. The independent variable is a continuous variable (time delay of reinforcement), so a line graph is preferred (a bar graph could be used, however).

Outcome A. Reinforcement delay hinders learning.

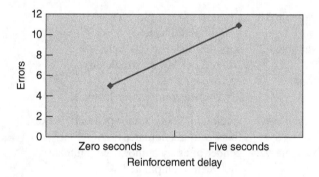

Outcome B. Reinforcement delay has no effect on learning.

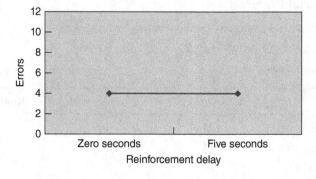

Chapter 8. Experimental Design II: Factorial Designs

8.1 Identifying Designs

1. Independent variable #1:   personality type (A, B, intermediate) (between; subject)

   Independent variable #2:   cognitive task (video game, no video game) (between; manipulated)

   Dependent variable: accuracy in estimating the passage of 2 minutes

   Design: 2 x 3 P x E factorial

3. Independent variable #1:   skin location (10 locations) (within; manipulated)

   Independent variable #2:   visual capacity (blind; sighted) (between; subject)

   Independent variable #3:   time of testing (morning; evening) (between; manipulated)

   Dependent variable: threshold judgments

   Design: 2 x 2 x 10 mixed P x E factorial

5. Independent variable #1:   stimulus color (color; b/w) (within; manipulated)

   Independent variable #2:   stimulus distance (10 feet; 20 feet) (within; manipulated)

   Dependent variable: error score

   Design: 2 x 2 repeated measures factorial

7. Independent variable #1:   labeling of essay author (patient; worker) (between; manipulated)

   Independent variable #2:   gender of essay author (male; female) (between; manipulated)

   Dependent variable: quality ratings

   Design: 2 x 2 independent groups factorial

8.2 Main Effects and Interactions

1. **a.** IV#1:   situational ambiguity (ambiguous, not ambiguous)

   IV#2:   number of bystanders (0, 2)

   DV: time to respond

	0 bystanders	2 bystanders	Row means
Ambiguous	24	38	31
Not ambiguous	14	14	14
Column means	19	26	

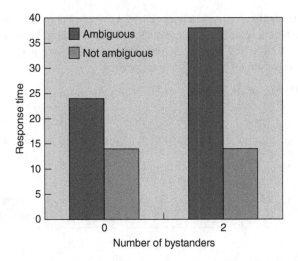

c. There are two main effects and an interaction, but one of the main effects is not relevant. Helping behavior takes longer to occur if the situation is ambiguous, and this is true whether there are 0 (24 > 14) or 2 (38 > 14) bystanders. So the main effect for ambiguity is relevant. There is also a main effect for number of bystanders, but while the number of bystanders affects helping in the ambiguous situation (38 > 24), it is not relevant in the unambiguous situation (14 = 14). So the main effect for number of bystanders is not relevant. The interaction is the key finding and is the reason why the second main effect is not relevant: If the situation is unambiguous, the number of bystanders does not affect helping (14 = 14), but if the situation is ambiguous, helping is slowed by the number of bystanders present (38 > 24).

3. **a.** IV#1:   gender (male, female)

   IV#2:   instructions (male-oriented, female-oriented, neutral)

   DV: problems correct

	Male-oriented	Female-oriented	Neutral	Row means
Males	26	23	26	25
Females	18	24	18	20
Column means	22	23.5	22	

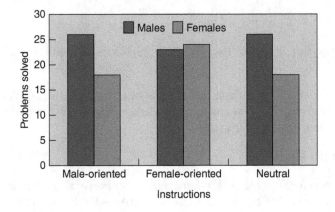

c. There is no main effect for instructions (22 = 23.5 = 22), but there is a main effect for gender (25 > 20) and there is an interaction, which is the key finding. Males outperform females in the neutral condition and when male-oriented instructions are given. With female-oriented instructions, however, no gender difference occurs.

8.3 Estimating Participant Needs

1. 30

3. Cannot be answered without knowing which factor is tested between and which within.

5. 32

Chapter 9. Non-Experimental Design I: Survey Methods

9.1 Deciding on a Survey Method

1. An interview survey would allow respondents to explain their answers.

3. A mail-in survey can be sent to cable TV customers.

5. An online survey (likely posted on Facebook) would best capture participants who are Facebook users.

9.2 Improving Poor Survey Items

1. Have you had an upset stomach lately?

   a. *Upset stomach* could be described more precisely, but the major problem is the lack of precision in the *lately*; does it mean within the past week? month?

   b. After telling the test taker to define *upset stomach* as "nauseated to the point where you think you might vomit but you don't," the item could read:
   Have you had an upset stomach in the last week? If so, how often?

3. In your opinion, how young is the average cigarette smoker?

   a. The *how young* could bias the person toward giving a younger age, and some people might even misinterpret the question as a question about when people first start smoking.

   b. *Better*: In your opinion, what is the average age of a typical cigarette smoker?

5. Most doctors have a superior attitude.

   a. To distinguish physicians from Ph.D.s, it might be better to refer to them as *medical doctors*.

   b. *Superior attitude* is quite vague and ought to be replaced, perhaps with a description of a specific behavior. The item could read: "Medical doctors are often unwilling to explain their recommendations to patients."

9.3 Interpreting Correlations

1. Positive correlation. It could be that dominant mothers never allow their children to develop independence, and they become shy as a result (A → B). However, it could also be that naturally shy children cause their mothers to take more control of the relationship (B → A).

3. Positive correlation. It could be that all of the books in the home were read by the children, making them smarter and therefore better students (A → B). It could be that the third variable of parental attitudes toward learning led to (a) lots of books in the home, and (b) reinforcement for their children being good students (C → A & B).

5. Negative correlation. It could be that getting poor grades increases student anxiety (A → B), but it could also be true that anxious students don't prepare well and don't take tests well (B → A).

7. Positive correlation. This is a third variable problem. The third variable is simply age: The older we get the more milk we are likely to have consumed and, with increased age, the chances of getting some form of cancer increase (C → A & B).

Chapter 10. Non-Experimental Design II: Observational and Archival Methods

10.1 Defining Behaviors for Observational Research

1. Studying in the library: probably need to limit the study to students not using computers and using tables where observation is easy. Studying could be defined as reading any printed material and/or writing notes. In a given 15-minute period, the observers could record total time on task (i.e., studying).

3. Children playing: ages must be defined, as well as cooperative play (children playing next to and interacting with each other) and parallel play (children playing next to each other but not interacting); study could be done in a preschool with observational two-way mirrors, or a video made for later analysis.

5. Couples gazing: There would be some structure to this study, perhaps bringing couples (dating couples and married couples) into the lab and asking them to talk to each other about some defined topic for a fixed period. Their conversations would be taped and later subjected to analysis (i.e., during the interval, the proportion of time spent in mutual gazing).

10.2 Deciding on a Method

1. Naturalistic observation of feeding behavior is warranted.

3. Participant observation can be used in which the female 'participant' in the study would be pretending to use a cell phone or not.

5. Archival research methods would be used to evaluate mental health records.

Chapter 11. Quasi-Experimental Designs and Applied Research

11.1 Identifying Threats to Internal Validity

1. Without a control group, there are several alternative explanations. Because the 60% is way below the normal retention rate of 75% (i.e., an extreme score), regression would be the most

likely threat (65% is heading back in the direction of 75%). History and selection are two other possibilities, but maturation is less likely because two groups of students would be involved in the study.

3. This is most likely a selection problem. The women who volunteer are possibly different in some significant way (e.g., more willing to try new things) from the women selected randomly.

5. Thirty students started the course but only 18 finished it. The problem is attrition, resulting in a group at the end of the course that is systematically different (e.g., more persevering) from those who started the course. This course format might not be effective for the student who needs more direct guidance.

11.2 Interpreting Nonequivalent Control Group Studies

1. It is likely the program worked; absenteeism drops in the experimental plants, but not in the control plant. It is unlikely but possible, however, that a selection x history confound is operating, in which some event affected absenteeism in one plant but not the other.

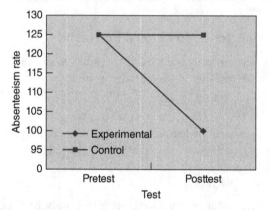

3. There is no evidence the program worked; absenteeism drops in the experimental plants, but it drops by the same amount in the control plant. The decline could be due to any number of confounds but also might be part of a general downward trend that could be revealed in a follow-up study by a time series analysis.

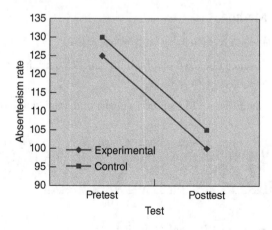

11.3 Interpreting Time Series Studies

1. The law worked.

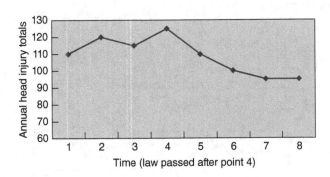

3. Probably a regression to the mean effect.

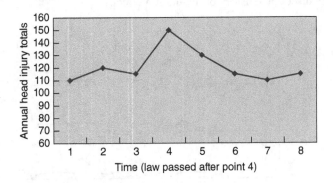

To improve the basic interrupted time series designs, the researchers could (a) use a control group, a league in a city without a helmet law; (b) use a switching replication, comparing with another league that introduced a helmet law at a different time; or (c) add dependent variables not expected to be affected by a helmet law, such as leg injuries.

Chapter 12. Small *N* Designs

12.1 Designing Self-Improvement Programs

1. Increase productive study time: Target behavior could be studying (reading, doing home-work) for 30 consecutive minutes without a break. Reinforcer could be some behavior of value and interest (e.g., time reading a mystery novel). Successive criteria could be in 10-minute intervals, with an interval added each week.

3. Change to healthier eating behaviors: Target behavior could be reducing intake of such junk foods as potato chips and corn chips. Reinforcer could be allowing oneself an extra trip to the golf driving range (assuming golf has reinforcement value!). Successive criteria could be defined in terms of a reduction in the number of ounces of chips consumed per week.

12.2 Hypothetical Outcomes of Applied Behavior Analyses

1. Multiple baseline across three settings:

   a. The treatment program works.

   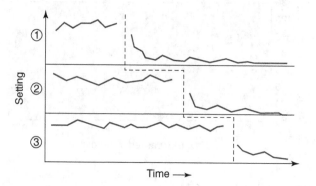

   b. One cannot discount a history or maturation effect.

   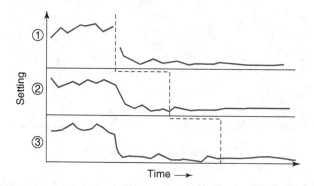

Appendix A. Communicating the Results of Research in Psychology

Exercise A.1   True/False

1. After writing the Abstract, double space and then immediately begin the introduction on the same page.

   • False; the Introduction begins on a new page.

3. In the Results section, if you portray your results with a graph, it is also OK to display them in a table because then the reader gets the exact numbers.

   • False; use a graph or a table, not both.

5. A "what's next" type of paragraph belongs in the Discussion section of the report.

   • True; this is the place for a discussion of potential future research.

7. Each item that appears in the Reference section should be found somewhere in the lab report itself.

   • True; always double-check this.

9. In the Results section, to maintain reader interest, it is important to explain and interpret each result right after you report it.

- False; explanation and interpretation belong in the Discussion section.

Exercise A.2   Word Usage

1. 124 male college students were used in the experiment.

- Numbers beginning sentences must be spelled out fully.

3. The instructions had a strong affect on the participants.

- Should be *effect* not *affect*.

5. A study of maze learning was conducted by Tolman.

- Tolman completed a study on maze learning. (avoid passive voice)

Exercise A.3   Referencing: Sharpening Your APA-Style Skills

1. Reynolds, G. S. (1968). *A Primer of Operant Conditioning.* Glenview, IL: Scott, Foresman.

- Reynolds, G. S. (1968). *A primer of operant conditioning.* Glenview, IL: Scott, Foresman.

3. Lee, D. N., and Aronson, E. (1974). Visual proprioceptive control of standing in human infants. *Perception and Psychophysics,* 15, 529–532.

- Lee, D. N., & Aronson, E. (1974). Visual proprioceptive control of standing in human infants. *Perception and Psychophysics,* 15, 529–532.

5. Geller, D. M. (1982). Alternatives to deception: Why, what, and how? In Sieber, J. E. (Ed.), *The ethics of social research: Surveys and experiments* (pp. 40–55). New York: Springer-Verlag.

- Geller, D. M. (1982). Alternatives to deception: Why, what, and how? In J. E. Sieber (Ed.), *The ethics of social research: Surveys and experiments* (pp. 40–55). New York: Springer-Verlag.

7. Brehm, J. (1956). Postdecision changes in the desirability of alternatives. *Journal of Abnormal and Social Psychology, 52(3),* 384–389.

- Brehm, J. (1956). Postdecision changes in the desirability of alternatives. *Journal of Abnormal and Social Psychology, 52,* 384–389.

Exercise A1.4   Main Sections of the Lab Report

1. We hypothesized that participants given imagery instructions would outperform those given instructions to use rote memorization.

- Introduction

3. A logical next step would be to add another age group to extend the findings to pre-adolescents.

- Discussion

5. The experiment was a 2 (gender) x 3 (instructions) mixed factorial.

- Method

Glossary

A priori **method**   A way of knowing, proposed by Charles Peirce, in which a person develops a belief by reasoning and reaching agreement with others who are convinced of the merits of the reasoned argument.

A–B design   A small N design in which a baseline period (A) is followed by a treatment period (B).

A–B–A design   A small N design in which a baseline period (A) is followed by a treatment period (B) followed by a period in which the treatment is reversed or withdrawn (second A).

A–B–A–B design   Like an A–B–A design except that a second treatment period is established (second B).

Alpha level   The probability of making a Type I error; the significance level.

Alternating treatments design   A small N design that compares, in the same study and for the same participant(s), two or more forms of treatment for changing some behavior.

Alternative hypothesis   The researcher's hypothesis about the outcome of a study (H_1).

Anecdotal evidence   Evidence from a single case that illustrates a phenomenon; when relied on exclusively, as in pseudoscience, faulty conclusions can easily be drawn.

ANOVA   Short for **AN**alysis **O**f **VA**riance, the most common inferential statistical tool for analyzing the results of experiments when dependent variables are measured on interval or ratio scales.

ANOVA source table   A standardized method for displaying the results of an analysis of variance; includes sources of variance, sums of squares, degrees of freedom, mean squares (variance), F ratios, and probability values.

Anthrozoology   A branch of science primarily concerned with examining human–animal interactions.

Application   A goal of science in which basic principles discovered through scientific methods are applied in order to solve problems.

Applied behavior analysis   Research using various methods to evaluate the effectiveness of conditioning procedures in bringing about changes in the rate of response of some behavior.

Applied research   Research with the goal of trying to solve an immediate real-life problem.

Archival data   Data initially collected for a purpose not related to a current research study and then used later for a specific purpose in the current research.

Archival research   A method in which existing records are examined to test a hypothesis.

Assent   To give assent is to say "yes"; in the SRCD code of ethics for research with children, refers to the willingness of the child to participate in the study.

ATI design   Aptitude by treatment interaction design; form of PxE factorial design found in educational research, the goal of which is to examine possible interactions between an aptitude variable (person factor) and a treatment variable (environmental factor).

Attrition   A threat to the internal validity of a study; occurs when participants fail to complete a study, usually but not necessarily a longitudinal study; those finishing the study may not be equivalent to those who started it.

Authority   A way of knowing, proposed by Charles Peirce, in which a person develops a belief by agreeing with someone perceived to be an expert.

Availability heuristic   Social cognition bias in which vivid or memorable events lead people to overestimate the frequency of occurrence of these events.

Baseline   The initial stage of a small N design, in which the behavior to be changed is monitored to determine its normal rate of response.

Basic research   Research with the goal of describing, predicting, and explaining fundamental principles of behavior.

Behavior checklists   Lists of behaviors with predefined operational definitions that researchers are trained to use in an observational study.

Belief perseverance   Unwillingness to consider evidence that contradicts a strongly held view; similar to Peirce's principle of tenacity.

Between-subjects design   An experimental design in which different groups of participants serve in the different conditions of the study.

Biased sample   A sample that is not representative of the population.

Big data   The vast amount of data available in electronic databases that can be extracted and analyzed with the use of advanced data analytic tools.

Bivariate analysis   A statistical analysis investigating the relationship between two variables.

Block randomization   A procedure used in within-subjects design as a counterbalancing procedure to ensure that when participants are tested in each condition more than once, they experience each condition once before experiencing any condition again.

Blocked random assignment   A procedure used in between-subjects designs to accomplish random assignment and ensure an equal number of participants in each condition; ensures that each condition of the study has a subject randomly assigned to it before any condition has a subject assigned to it again.

Carryover effect   Form of sequence effect in which systematic changes in performance occur as a result of completing one sequence of conditions rather than a different sequence.

Case study   A descriptive method in which an in-depth analysis is made of a single individual, a single rare event, or an event that clearly exemplifies some phenomenon.

Ceiling effect   Occurs when scores on two or more conditions are at or near the maximum possible for the scale being used, giving the impression that no differences exist between the conditions.

Changing criterion design   A small N design in which the criterion for receiving reinforcement begins at a modest level and becomes more stringent as the study progresses; used to shape behavior.

Closed question   A type of question found on surveys that can be answered *yes* or a *no* or by marking a point on a scale.

Cluster sample   A probability sample that randomly selects clusters of people having some feature in common (e.g., students taking history courses) and tests all people within the selected cluster (e.g., all students in three of the nine history courses available).

Coefficient of correlation   See *Pearson's* r.

Coefficient of determination   For two correlated factors, the proportion of variance in one factor that can be attributed to the second factor; found by squaring Pearson's *r*.

Cohort effect   A cohort is a group of people born at the same time; cohort effects can reduce the internal validity of cross-sectional studies because differences between groups could result from the effects of growing up in different historical eras.

Cohort sequential design   In developmental psychology research, a design that combines cross-sectional and longitudinal designs; a new cohort is added to a study every few years and then studied periodically throughout the time course of the study.

Community forum   In program evaluation research, a meeting open to community members to discuss the need for, or the operation of, some program.

Complete counterbalancing Occurs when all possible orders of conditions are used in a within-subjects design.

Conceptual replication An attempted reproduction of a study's results in which parts of the procedures of a prior study are purposely changed in order to test predictions similar to those in the original study.

Concurrent validity A form of criterion validity in which a measure is meaningfully related to some other measure of behavior.

Confederate See *Experimental confederate*

Confidence interval An inferential statistic in which a range of scores is calculated; with some degree of confidence (e.g., 95%), it is assumed that population values lie within the interval.

Confidentiality In research ethics, an agreement by the researcher not to divulge the identity of those participating in a research study.

Confirmation bias Social cognition bias in which events that confirm a strongly held belief are more readily perceived and remembered; disconfirming events are ignored or forgotten.

Confound An extraneous variable that covaries with the independent variable and could provide an alternative explanation of the results.

Construct A hypothetical factor (e.g., hunger) that cannot be observed directly but is inferred from certain behaviors (e.g., eating) and assumed to follow from certain circumstances (e.g., 24 hours without food).

Construct validity In measurement, it occurs when the measure being used accurately assesses some hypothetical construct; also refers to whether the construct itself is valid; in research, refers to whether the operational definitions used for independent and dependent variables are valid.

Content analysis A procedure used to systematically categorize the content of the behavior (often verbal behavior) being recorded.

Content validity Occurs when a measure appears to be a reasonable or logical measure of a trait (e.g., as a measure of intelligence, problem solving has more content validity than hat size).

Control group A group not given a treatment being evaluated in a study; provides a means of comparison.

Convenience sample A non-probability sample in which the researcher requests volunteers from a group of people who meet the general requirements of the study (e.g., teenagers); used in most psychological research, except when specific estimates of population values must be made.

Convergent validity Occurs when scores on a test designed to measure some construct (e.g., self-esteem) are correlated with scores on other tests theoretically related to the construct.

Converging operations Occurs when the results of several studies, each employing slightly different operational definitions, nonetheless converge on the same general conclusion.

Correlation See *Positive correlation* and *Negative correlation*.

Correlation matrix A table that summarizes a series of correlations among several variables.

Cost-effectiveness analysis Form of program evaluation that assesses outcomes in terms of the costs involved in developing, running, and completing the program.

Counterbalancing For a within-subjects variable, any procedure designed to control for sequence effects.

Creative thinking A process of making an innovative connection between seemingly unrelated ideas or events.

Criterion validity Form of validity in which a psychological measure is able to predict some future behavior or is meaningfully related to some other measure.

Criterion variable   In a regression analysis, the variable being predicted from the predictor variable (e.g., college grades are predicted from SAT scores).

Critical incidents   Method, used by ethics committees, that surveys psychologists and asks for examples of unethical behavior by psychologists.

Cross-lagged panel correlation   A type of correlational research designed to deal with the directionality problem; if variables X and Y are measured at two different times and if X precedes Y, then X might cause Y but Y cannot cause X.

Cross-sectional study   In developmental psychology, a design in which age is the independent variable and different groups of people are tested; each group is of a different age.

Cumulative recorder   Apparatus for recording the subject's cumulative rate of response in operant conditioning studies.

Data-driven   Describes the belief of research psychologists that conclusions about behavior should be supported by data collected scientifically.

Debriefing   A postexperimental session in which the experimenter explains the study's purpose to participants, reduces any discomfort they felt, and answers any questions they pose.

Deception   A research strategy in which participants are not told all the details of an experiment at its outset; used for the purpose of avoiding demand characteristics.

Deduction   Reasoning from the general to the specific; in science, used when deriving research hypotheses from theories.

Dehoaxing   That portion of debriefing in which the true purpose of the study is explained to participants.

Demand characteristic   A feature of the experimental design or procedure that increases the chances that participants will detect the true purpose of the study.

Demographic information   Data that classifies or identifies individuals (e.g., gender, age, income).

Dependent variable   Behavior measured as the outcome of an experiment.

Description   A goal of psychological science in which behaviors are accurately classified or sequences of environmental stimuli and behavioral events are accurately listed.

Descriptive statistics   Provide a summary of the main features of a set of data collected from a sample of participants.

Desensitizing   That portion of debriefing in which the experimenter tries to reduce any distress felt by participants as a result of their research experience.

Determinism   The assumption made by scientists that all events have causes.

Direct replication   An attempted reproduction of a study's results testing the same type of sample and using the exact procedures and statistical analyses as the original study.

Directionality problem   In correlational research, the fact that for a correlation between variables X and Y, it is possible that X is causing Y but it is also possible that Y is causing X; the correlation alone provides no basis for deciding between the two alternatives.

Discoverability   The assumption made by scientists that the causes of events can be discovered by applying scientific methods.

Discriminant validity   Occurs when scores on a test designed to measure some construct (e.g., self-esteem) are uncorrelated with scores on other tests theoretically unrelated to the construct.

DK alternative   In survey research, when assessing levels of participant knowledge, this is an alternative that means *don't know*.

Double-barreled question   In a survey, a question or statement that asks or states two different things in a single item.

Double blind　A control procedure designed to reduce bias; neither the participant nor the person conducting the experimental session knows which condition of the study is being tested; often used in studies evaluating drug effects.

Ecological validity　Said to exist when research studies psychological phenomena in everyday situations (e.g., memory for where we put our keys).

Effect size　Amount of influence that one variable has on another; the amount of variance in the dependent variable that can be attributed to the independent variable.

Effort justification　After expending a large amount of time or effort to obtain some goal, people giving the effort feel pressured to convince themselves the effort was worthwhile, even if the resulting outcome is less positive than expected.

Empirical question　A question that can be answered by making objective observations.

Empiricism　A way of knowing that relies on direct observation or experience.

Equivalent groups　Groups of participants in a between-subjects design that are essentially equal in all ways except levels of the independent variable.

Error bars　On bar or line graphs, they indicate the amount of variability around a mean; often reflect standard deviations or confidence intervals.

Error variance　Nonsystematic variability in a set of scores due to random factors or individual differences.

Ethics　A set of principles prescribing morally correct behaviors.

Evaluation apprehension　A form of anxiety experienced by participants that leads them to behave so as to be evaluated positively by the experimenter.

Event sampling　A procedure in observational research in which only certain types of behaviors occurring under precisely defined conditions are sampled.

Experiment　A research procedure in which some factor is varied, all else is held constant, and some result is measured.

Experimental confederate　An individual who appears to be a subject in an experiment but is in fact a part of the experiment and in the employ of the experimenter.

Experimental group　In a study with an identified control group, the experimental group is given the treatment being tested.

Experimental realism　The depth to which participants become involved in the experiment; considered more important than mundane realism.

Experimenter bias　Occurs when an experimenter's expectations about a study affect its outcome.

Explanation　A goal of science in which the causes of events are sought.

Ex post facto design　A between-subjects design with at least two groups of participants that uses a subject variable or that creates nonequivalent groups.

External validity　The extent to which the findings of a study generalize to other populations, other settings, and other times.

Extraneous variable　An uncontrolled factor not of interest to the researcher but that could affect the results.

Face validity　Occurs when a measure appears, to those taking a test, a reasonable measure of some trait; not considered by researchers to be an important indicator of validity.

Factor analysis　A multivariate analysis in which a large number of variables are intercorrelated; variables that correlate highly with each other form factors.

Factorial design　Any experimental design with more than one independent variable.

Factorial matrix   A row and column arrangement that characterizes a factorial design and shows the independent variables, the levels of each independent variable, and the total number of conditions (cells) in the study.

Falsification   Research strategy, advocated by Popper, that emphasizes putting theories to the test by trying to disprove or falsify them.

Falsifying data   Manufacturing or altering data to bring about a desired result.

Field experiment   An experiment conducted outside the laboratory; a narrower term than *field research*.

Field research   Research that occurs in any location other than a scientific laboratory.

Figures   In a lab report or description of research, graphs, diagrams, flow charts, sketches of apparatus, or photos.

File drawer effect   A situation in which findings of no difference fail to be published (the studies are placed in one's files); if the number of such findings is large, the few studies that do find a difference and are published produce a distorted impression of actual differences.

Floor effect   Occurs when scores on two or more conditions are at or near the minimum possible for the scale being used, giving the impression that no differences exist between the conditions.

Focus group   A small and relatively homogeneous group brought together for the purpose of participating in a group interview on some topic or, in program evaluation research, to discuss the need for or the operation of a program.

Formative evaluation   Form of program evaluation that monitors the functioning of a program while it is operating to determine if it is functioning as planned.

Frequency distribution   A table that records the number of times each score in a set of scores occurs.

Good subject role   A form of participant bias in which participants try to guess the experimenter's hypothesis and then behave in such a way as to confirm it.

Hawthorne effect   A form of participant bias in which a participant's behavior is influenced by the mere knowledge of being in an experiment and therefore important to the experimenter.

Histogram   Graph of a frequency distribution in bar form.

History   A threat to the internal validity of a study; occurs when a historical event that could affect participants happens between the beginning of a study and its end.

Homogeneity of variance   One of the conditions that should be in effect in order to perform parametric inferential tests such as a *t* test or ANOVA; refers to the fact that variability among all the conditions of a study ought to be similar.

Hypothesis   An educated guess about a relationship between variables that is then tested empirically.

Independent groups design   A between-subjects design that uses a manipulated independent variable and has at least two groups of participants to which subjects are randomly assigned.

Independent variable   The factor of interest to the researcher; it can be directly manipulated by the experimenter (e.g., creating different levels of anxiety in subjects), or participants can be selected by virtue of their possessing certain attributes (e.g., selecting two groups that differ in normal anxiety).

Individual-subject validity   The extent to which the general outcome of a research study characterizes the behavior of the individual participants in the study.

Induction   Reasoning from the specific to the general; in science, when the results of research studies are used to support or refute a theory.

Inferential statistics   Used to draw conclusions about the broader population on the basis of a study using a sample of that population.

Informed consent   The idea that persons should be given sufficient information about a study to make their decision to participate as a research subject informed and voluntary.

Institutional Review Board (IRB)   University committee responsible for evaluating whether research proposals provide adequate protection of the rights of participants; must exist for any college or university receiving federal funds for research.

Instructional variable   Type of independent variable in which participants are given different sets of instructions about how to perform (e.g., given a list of stimuli, groups might be told to process them in different ways).

Instrumentation   A threat to the internal validity of a study; occurs when the measuring instrument changes from pretest to posttest (e.g., because of their experience with the instrument, experimenters might use it differently from pretest to posttest).

Interaction   In a factorial design, occurs when the effect of one independent variable depends on the level of another independent variable.

Internal validity   The extent to which a study is free from methodological flaws, especially confounding factors.

Interquartile range   The range of scores lying between the bottom 25% of a set of scores (25th percentile) and the top 25% of scores (75th percentile); yields a measure a variability unaffected by outliers.

Interrater reliability   The degree of agreement between two or more observers of the same event.

Interrupted time series design   Quasi-experimental design in which a program or treatment is evaluated by measuring performance several times prior to the institution of the program and several times after the program is put into effect.

Interrupted time series with switching replications   A time series design in which the program is replicated at a different location and at a different time.

Interval scale   Measurement scale in which numbers refer to quantities and intervals are assumed to be of equal size; a score of zero is just one of many points on the scale and does not denote the absence of the phenomenon being measured.

Interview survey   A survey method in which the researcher interviews the participant face to face; allows for more in-depth surveying (e.g., follow-up questions and clarifications).

Intraclass correlation   A form of correlation used when pairs of scores do not come from the same individual, as when correlations are calculated for pairs of twins.

Introspection   Method used in the early years of psychological science in which an individual would complete a task and then describe the events occurring in consciousness while performing the task.

IRB   See *Institutional Review Board*.

Key informant   In program evaluation research, a community member with special knowledge about the needs of that community.

Laboratory research   Research that occurs within the controlled confines of the scientific laboratory.

Latin square   Form of partial counterbalancing in which each condition of the study occurs equally often in each sequential position and each condition precedes and follows each other condition exactly once.

Laws   Regular, predictable relationships between events.

Leading question   In a survey, a question asked in such a way that the answer desired by the questioner is clear.

Longitudinal study   In developmental psychology, a design in which age is the independent variable and the same group of people is tested repeatedly at different ages.

Main effect   The presence or otherwise of statistically significant differences between the levels of an independent variable in a factorial design.

Manipulation check   In debriefing, a procedure to determine if subjects were aware of a deception experiment's true purpose; also a procedure that determines if systematic manipulations have the intended effect on participants.

Matched groups design   A between-subjects design that uses a manipulated independent variable and has at least two groups of participants; subjects are matched on some variable assumed to affect the outcome before being randomly assigned to the groups.

Matching   A procedure for creating equivalent groups in which participants are measured on some factor (a "matching variable") expected to correlate with the dependent variable; groups are then formed by randomly assigning to groups participants who score at the same level on the matching variable.

Matching variable   A variable selected for matching participants in a matched groups study.

Maturation   A threat to the internal validity of a study; occurs when participants change from the beginning to the end of the study simply as a result of maturational changes within them and not as a result of an independent variable.

Mean   The arithmetic average of a data set, found by adding the scores and dividing by the total number of scores in the set.

Measurement error   Produced by a factor that introduces inaccuracies into the measurement of some variable.

Measurement scales   Ways of assigning numbers to events; see *Nominal, Ordinal, Interval,* and *Ratio scales.*

Median   The middle score of a data set; an equal number of scores is both above and below the median.

Median location   The place in the sequence of scores where the median lies.

Mediating variable   A controlled (measured) third variable that explains how or why a relationship exists between two correlated variables.

Meta-analysis   A statistical tool for combining the effect size of a number of studies to determine if general patterns occur in the data.

Mixed factorial design   A factorial design with at least one between-subjects factor and one within-subjects factor.

Mixed P x E factorial design   A mixed design with at least one subject factor and one manipulated factor.

Mode   The most frequently appearing score in a data set.

Moderating variable   A controlled (measured) third variable that explains under what conditions does the relationship between two variables exist; also called a moderator.

Multiple baseline design   A small *N* design in which treatment is introduced at staggered intervals when trying to alter (a) the behavior of more than one individual, (b) more than one behavior in the same individual, or (c) the behavior of an individual in more than one setting.

Multiple regression   A multivariate analysis that includes a criterion variable and two or more predictor variables; the predictors have different weights.

Multivariate analysis   A statistical analysis investigating the relationships among more than two variables.

Mundane realism   The degree to which an experiment mirrors real-life experiences; considered less important than experimental realism.

Naturalistic observation   Descriptive research method in which the behavior of people or animals is studied as it occurs in its everyday natural environment.

Needs analysis   Form of program evaluation that occurs before a program begins and determines whether the program is needed.

Negative correlation   A relationship between variables X and Y such that a high score for X is associated with a low score for Y and a low score for X is associated with a high score for Y.

Nominal scale   Measurement scale in which the numbers have no quantitative value, but rather identify categories into which events can be placed.

Nonequivalent control group design   Quasi-experimental design in which participants cannot be randomly assigned to the experimental and control groups.

Nonlinear effect   An outcome that does not form a straight line when graphed; can occur only when the independent variable has more than two levels.

Nonresponse bias   Occurs in survey research when those who return surveys differ systematically (e.g., in political attitudes) from those who don't respond.

Normal curve   A theoretical frequency distribution for a population; a bell-shaped curve.

Null hypothesis   The assumption that no real difference exists between treatment conditions in an experiment or that no significant relationship exists in a correlational study (H_0).

Objectivity   Said to exist when observations can be verified by more than one observer.

Observer bias   Can occur when preconceived ideas held by the researcher affect the nature of the observations made.

Online survey   Survey research conducted over the Internet; can be a survey sent via e-mail or posted on a website or social media site.

Open-ended question   A type of question found on surveys that requires a narrative response rather than a *yes* or *no* answer.

Operant conditioning   Form of learning in which behavior is modified by its consequences; a positive consequence strengthens the behavior immediately preceding it, and a negative consequence weakens the behavior immediately preceding it.

Operational definitions   A definition of a concept or variable in terms of precisely described operations, measures, or procedures.

Operationism   Philosophy of science approach, proposed by Bridgman, holding that all scientific concepts should be defined in terms of a set of operations to be performed.

Order effect   Can occur in a within-subjects design when the experience of participating in one of the conditions of the study influences performance in subsequent conditions; see *Progressive effect* and *Carryover effect*.

Ordinal scale   Measurement scale in which assigned numbers stand for relative standing or ranking.

Outlier   In a data set, a data point so deviant from the remaining points that the researcher believes it cannot reflect reasonable behavior and its inclusion will distort the results; often considered a score more than three standard deviations from the mean.

P × E factorial design   A factorial design with at least one subject factor (P=person variable) and one manipulated factor (E=environmental variable).

Parsimonious   Describing a theory that includes the minimum number of constructs and assumptions in order to explain and predict some phenomenon adequately.

Partial correlation   A multivariate statistical procedure for evaluating the effects of third variables; if the correlation between X and Y remains high, even after some third factor Z has been partialed out, then Z can be eliminated as a third variable.

Partial counterbalancing   Occurs when a subset of all possible orders of conditions is used in a within-subjects design (e.g., a random sample of the population of all possible orders could be selected).

Participant   See *Research participant.*

Participant bias   Can occur when the behavior of subjects is influenced by their beliefs about how they are supposed to behave in a study.

Participant crosstalk   A tendency for people who have participated in a research study to inform future participants about the true purpose of the study.

Participant observation   Descriptive research method in which the behavior of people is studied as it occurs in its everyday natural environment and the researcher becomes a part of the group being observed.

Participant pool   See *Subject pool*

Pearson's *r*   Measure of the size of a correlation between two variables; ranges from a perfect positive correlation of +1.00 to a perfect negative correlation of −1.00; if $r=0$, then no relationship exists between the variables.

Phone survey   A survey method in which the researcher asks questions over the phone.

Pilot study   During the initial stages of research, it is common for some data to be collected; problems spotted in this trial stage enable the researcher to refine the procedures and prevent the full-scale study from being flawed methodologically.

Placebo   In medicine, an inert substance said to have medicinal effect (from Latin meaning "I shall please"); in research, a condition in which subjects believe a treatment is in effect, but it is not.

Placebo control group   Control group in which some participants believe they are receiving the experimental treatment, but they are not.

Plagiarism   Deliberately taking the ideas of someone else and claiming them as one's own.

Population   All of the members of an identifiable group.

Positive correlation   A relationship between variables X and Y such that a high score for X is associated with a high score for Y and a low score for X is associated with a low score for Y.

Posttest   A measurement given to participants at the conclusion of a study after they have experienced a treatment or been in a control group; comparisons are made with pretest scores to determine if change occurred.

Power   The chances of finding a significant difference when the null hypothesis is false; depends on alpha, effects size, and sample size.

Predictions   A goal of psychological science in which statements about the future occurrence of a behavioral event are made, usually with some probability.

Predictive validity   A form of criterion validity in which a measure can accurately forecast some future behavior.

Predictor variable   In a regression analysis, the variable used to predict the criterion variable (e.g., SAT scores are used to predict college grades).

Pretest   A measurement given to participants at the outset of a study, prior to their being treated (or not treated, if in a control group).

Productivity   With reference to theory, the amount of research generated to test a theory; theories that lead to a great deal of research are considered productive.

Program audit   An examination of whether a program is being implemented as planned; a type of formative evaluation.

Program evaluation   A form of applied research that includes a number of research activities designed to evaluate programs from planning to completion.

Programs of research   Series of interrelated studies in which the outcome of one study leads naturally to another.

Progressive effect   In a within-subjects design, an order effect in which the accumulated effects are assumed to be the same from trial to trial (e.g., fatigue).

Protocol   A detailed description of the sequence of events in a research session; used by an experimenter to ensure uniformity of treatment of research participants.

Pseudoscience   A field of inquiry that attempts to associate with true science, relies exclusively on selective anecdotal evidence, and is deliberately too vague to be adequately tested.

Publication bias   The notion that only "statistically significant" results get published and that nonsignificant results do not get published.

Purposive sample   A non-probability sample in which the researcher targets a particular group of individuals (e.g., Milgram using working adults and avoiding college students).

Qualitative research   A category of research activity characterized by a narrative analysis of information collected in the study; can include case studies, observational research, interview research.

Quantitative research   A category of research in which results are presented as numbers, typically in the form of descriptive and inferential statistics.

Quasi-experimental design   Occurs when causal conclusions about the effect of an independent variable cannot be drawn because subjects cannot be randomly assigned to the groups being given different levels of an independent variable.

Questionable Research Practices (QRPs)   Forms of scientific misconduct that may go unnoticed; QRP's range in severity, with falsifying data judged as an extreme form of QRP.

Quota sample   A non-probability sample in which the proportions of some subgroups in the sample are the same as those subgroup proportions in the population.

Random assignment   The most common procedure for creating equivalent groups in a between-subjects design; each individual volunteering for the study has an equal probability of being assigned to any of the groups.

Range   In a set of scores, the difference between the largest value and the smallest value.

Rate of response   The favored dependent variable of researchers working in the Skinnerian tradition; refers to how frequently a behavior occurs per unit of time.

Ratio scale   Measurement scale in which numbers refer to quantities and intervals are assumed to be of equal size; a score of zero denotes the absence of the phenomenon being measured.

Reactivity   Occurs when participants' behavior is influenced by the knowledge that they are being observed and their behavior recorded.

Regression analysis   In correlational research, knowing the size of a correlation and a value for variable X, it is possible to predict a value for variable Y; this process occurs through a regression analysis.

Regression line   Summarizes the points of a scatterplot and provides the means for making predictions.

Regression to the mean   If a score on a test is extremely high or low, a second score taken will be closer to the mean score; can be a threat to the internal validity of a study if a pretest score is extreme and the posttest score changes in the direction of the mean.

Reliability   The extent to which measures of the same phenomenon are consistent and repeatable; measures high in reliability contain a minimum of measurement error.

Repeated-measures design   Another name for a within-subjects design; participants are tested in each of the experiment's conditions.

Replication   The repetition of an experiment; exact replications are rare, occurring primarily when the results of a prior study are suspected to be erroneous.

Representative sample   A sample with characteristics that match those attributes as they exist in the population.

Research participant   A person who takes part in and contributes data to a research study in psychology; see *Subject*.

Research team   A group of researchers (professors and students) working on the same research problem.

Response acquiescence   A response set in which a participant tends to respond positively to survey questions, all else being equal.

Reverse counterbalancing   Occurs in a within-subjects design when participants are tested more than once per condition; subjects experience one sequence and then a second with the order reversed from the first (e.g., A–B–C–C–B–A).

Risk   In the ethical decision making that goes into the planning of a study, the chance that participating in research would have greater costs than benefits to the participant.

Sample   A portion or subset of a population.

Scatterplot   A graph depicting the relationship shown by a correlation.

Science   A way of knowing characterized by the attempt to apply objective, empirical methods when searching for the causes of natural events.

Self-selection problem   In surveys, when the sample is composed of only those who voluntarily choose to respond, the result can be a biased sample.

Serendipity   The process of making an accidental discovery; finding X when searching for Y.

Shaping   Operant procedure for developing a new behavior that underlies the changing criterion design; behaviors are reinforced as they become progressively close to a final desired behavior.

Simple effects analysis   Following an ANOVA, a follow-up test to a significant interaction, comparing individual cells.

Simple random sample   A probability sample in which each member of the population has an equal chance of being selected as a member of the sample.

Single blind   A control procedure designed to reduce subject bias, in which the participant does not know which condition of the study is being tested (the experimenter, however, does know).

Single-factor design   An experimental design with a single independent variable.

Single-factor multilevel designs   An experimental design with a single independent variable and more than two levels of the independent variable.

Situational variable   Type of independent variable in which subjects encounter different environmental circumstances (e.g., large versus small rooms in a crowding study).

Snowball sample   A non-probability sample in which a member of a particular group, already surveyed, helps recruit additional group members through a network of friends; often occurs for surveys of a relatively small group or a group that generally wishes to remain hidden.

Social desirability bias   A type of response bias in survey research; occurs when people respond to a question by trying to put themselves in a favorable light.

Social validity   The extent to which an applied behavior analysis program has the potential to improve society, whether its value is perceived by the study's participants, and whether participants actually use the program.

Stakeholders   In program evaluation research, persons connected with a program that have a vested interest in it; includes clients, staff, and program directors.

Standard deviation   A measure of deviation of a set of scores from the mean score; the square root of the variance.

Statistical conclusion validity   Said to exist when the researcher uses statistical analysis properly and draws the appropriate conclusions from the analysis.

Statistical determinism   An assumption made by research psychologists that behavioral events can be predicted with a probability greater than chance.

Stratified sample   A probability sample that is random, with the restriction that important subgroups are proportionately represented within it.

Subject   A human or animal research participant; humans volunteering for research are now called either *subjects* or *research participants*, while nonhuman animals are typically called *subjects*.

Subject pool   Group of students asked to participate in research, typically as part of an introductory psychology course requirement; sometimes called *participant pool*.

Subject selection effect   A threat to the internal validity of a study; occurs when those participating in a study cannot be assigned randomly to groups; hence the groups are nonequivalent.

Subject variable   A type of independent variable that is selected rather than manipulated by the experimenter; an existing attribute of the individuals chosen for the study (e.g., gender).

Sugging   A marketing strategy in which an attempt to sell a product is made by disguising the sales pitch with what appears to be a legitimate survey; the term is short for **S**elling **U**nder the **G**uise of a survey.

Summative evaluation   Form of program evaluation completed at the close of a program that attempts to determine its effectiveness in solving the problem for which it was planned.

Survey   A descriptive method in which participants are asked a series of questions or respond to a series of statements about a topic.

Systematic variance   Variability that can be attributed to an identifiable source, either the systematic variation of the independent variable or the uncontrolled variation of a confound.

***t* test for independent samples**   An inferential statistical analysis used when comparing two samples of data in either an independent groups design or a nonequivalent groups design.

***t* test for dependent samples**   An inferential statistical analysis used when comparing two samples of data in either a matched groups design or a repeated-measures design.

Tables   In a research report, summaries of data or descriptions of research design laid out in a row and column arrangement.

Task variable   Type of independent variable in which participants are given different types of tasks to perform (e.g., mazes that differ in level of difficulty).

Testing   A threat to the internal validity of a study; occurs when the fact of taking a pretest influences posttest scores, perhaps by sensitizing participants to the purpose of a study.

Thematic analysis   A method of identifying and analyzing patterns of responses (or themes) within qualitative data.

Theory   A set of statements that summarizes and organizes existing information about a phenomenon, provides an explanation for it, and serves as a basis for making predictions to be tested empirically.

Third variable problem   The problem of drawing causal conclusions in correlational research; third variables are uncontrolled factors that could underline a correlation between variables X and Y.

Time sampling   A procedure in observational research in which behavior is sampled only during predefined times only (e.g., every 10 minutes).

Time series design   See *Interrupted time series design*.

Translational research   A form of research that is done for both better understanding of a particular phenomenon as well as for its application to promote physical and psychological well-being.

Trends   Predictable patterns of events that occur over time; evaluated in time series studies.

Type I error   Rejecting the null hypothesis when it is true; finding a statistically significant effect when no true effect exists.

Type II error   Failing to reject the null hypothesis when it is false; failing to find a statistically significant effect when the effect truly exists.

Unobtrusive measures   A measure of behavior that can be recorded without participants knowing that their behavior has been observed.

Validity   In general, the extent to which a measure of X truly measures X and not Y (e.g., a valid measure of intelligence measures intelligence and not something else).

Variance   A measure of the average squared deviation of a set of scores from the mean score; the standard deviation squared.

Wait list control group   Control group in which participants aren't yet receiving treatment but will eventually; used to ensure that those in the experimental and control groups are similar (e.g., all seeking treatment for the same problem).

Withdrawal design   A small N design in which a treatment is in place for a time and then removed to determine if the rate of behavior returns to baseline.

Within-subjects design   An experimental design in which the same participants serve in each of the conditions of the study; also called a *repeated-measures design*.

Written survey   A survey method in which the researcher creates a written questionnaire that is filled out by participants.

Yoked control group   Control group in which the treatment given a member of the control group is matched exactly with the treatment given a member of the experimental group.

References

Abramovitz, C. V., Abramovitz, S. I., Roback, H. B., & Jackson, M. C. (1974). Differential effectiveness of directive and nondirective group therapies as a function of client internal-external control. *Journal of Consulting and Clinical Psychology, 14*, 849–853.

Adair, J. G. (1973). *The human subject: The social psychology of the psychological experiment*. Boston: Little, Brown.

Adams, J. S. (1965). Inequity in social exchange. In L. Berkowitz (Ed.), *Advances in experimental social psychology* (pp. 267–299). New York: Academic Press.

Adler, T. (1992, September). Debate: Control groups—bad for cancer patients? *APA Monitor, 23*(8), 34.

Adler, T. (1992, November). Trashing a laboratory is now a federal offense. *APA Monitor, 23*(10), 14.

Ainsworth, M., Blehar, M., Waters, E., & Wall, S. (1978). *Patterns of attachment*. Hillsdale, NJ: Erlbaum.

Allen, M. W., & Wilson, M. (2005). Materialism and food security. *Appetite, 45*, 314–323.

Alogna, V. K., Attaya, M. K., Aucoin, P., Bahnik, S., Birch, S., Birt, A.R., . . . Zwaan, R. A. (2014). Registered replication report: Schooler & Engstler-Schooler (1990). *Perspectives on Psychological Science, 9*, 556–578.

American Heritage dictionary of the English language (3rd ed.) (1992). Boston: Houghton-Mifflin.

American Psychological Association (1953). *Ethical standards of psychologists*. Washington, DC: Author.

American Psychological Association (1973). *Ethical principles in the conduct of research with human participants*. Washington, DC: Author.

American Psychological Association (1982). *Ethical principles in the conduct of research with human participants*. Washington, DC: Author.

American Psychological Association (1985). *Guidelines for ethical conduct in the care and use of animals*. Washington, DC: Author.

American Psychological Association (2001). *Publication manual of the American Psychological Association* (5th ed.). Washington, DC: Author.

American Psychological Association (2010). *Publication manual of the American Psychological Association* (6th ed.). Washington, DC: Author.

American Psychological Association (2002). Ethical principles of psychologists and code of conduct. *American Psychologist, 57*, 1060–1073.

Anastasi, A., & Urbina, S. (1997) *Psychological testing* (7th ed.). Englewood Cliffs, NJ: Prentice Hall.

Anderson, B., Silver, B., & Abramson, P. (1988). The effects of race of the interviewer on measures of electoral participation by blacks. *Public Opinion Quarterly, 52*, 53–83.

Anderson, C. A., & Bushman, B. J. (2001). Effects of violent video games on aggressive behavior, aggressive cognition, aggressive affect, physiological arousal, and prosocial behavior: A meta-analytic review of the scientific literature. *Psychological Science, 12*, 353–359.

Anderson, C. A., Lindsay, J. J., & Bushman, B. J. (1999). Research in the psychological laboratory: Truth or triviality? *Current Directions in Psychological Science, 8*, 3–9.

Anderson, J. E. (1926). Proceedings of the thirty-fourth annual meeting of the American Psychological Association. *Psychological Bulletin, 23*, 113–174.

Anderson, T., & Kanuka, H. (2003). *E-research: Methods, strategies, and issues*. Boston: Houghton Mifflin.

Animal Welfare Act of 1966, 7 U.S.C. §§ 2131-2156 (2013). Retrieved from http://www.aphis.usda.gov/animal_welfare/downloads/Animal%20Care%20Blue%20Book%20-%202013%20-%20FINAL.pdf

Anonymous advertisement (1881, October). *Phrenological Journal, 73*, old series, 3–4.

Arnett, J. J. (2008). The neglected 95%: Why American psychology needs to become less American. *American Psychologist, 63*, 602–614.

Aronson, E. (2007). *The social animal* (10th ed.). New York: Worth.

Aronson, E., & Mills, J. (1959). The effects of severity of initiation on liking for a group. *Journal of Abnormal and Social Psychology, 59*, 177–181.

Aronson, E., & Mettee, D. (1968). Dishonest behavior as a function of different levels of self-esteem. *Journal of Personality and Social Psychology, 9*, 121–127.

Asch, S. (1956). Studies of independence and conformity: A minority of one against a unanimous majority. *Psychological Monographs, 70* (Whole No. 416).

Atkinson, J. W., & Feather, N. T. (1966). *A theory of achievement motivation*. New York: Wiley.

Azar, B. (2002, February). Ethics at the cost of research? *APA Monitor, 33*(2), 38–40.

Babkin, B. P. (1949). *Pavlov: A biography*. Chicago: University of Chicago Press.

Bahrick, H. P. (1984). Semantic memory content in permastore: Fifty years of memory for Spanish learned in school. *Journal of Experimental Psychology: General, 113*, 1–29.

Bakan, D. (1966). The influence of phrenology on American psychology. *Journal of the History of the Behavioral Sciences, 2*, 200–220.

Bandura, A. (1986). *Social foundations of thought and action: A social cognitive theory*. Englewood Cliffs, NJ: Prentice Hall.

Bandura, A., Ross, D., & Ross, S. A. (1963). Imitation of film-mediated aggressive models. *Journal of Abnormal and Social Psychology, 66*, 3–11.

Barber, T. X. (1976). *Pitfalls in human research*. New York: Pergamon Press.

Barlow, D. H., Nock, M. K., & Hersen, M. (2009). *Single case experimental designs: Strategies for studying behavior change*. Boston: Allyn & Bacon.

Baron, A. (1990). Experimental designs. *The Behavior Analyst, 13*, 167–171.

Baron, R. M., & Kenny, D. A. (1986). The moderator-mediator variable distinction in social psychological research: Conceptual, strategic, and statistical considerations. *Journal of Personality and Social Psychology, 51*, 1173–1182.

Baugh, F. G., & Benjamin, L. T., Jr. (2006). Walter Miles, Pop Warner, B. C. Graves, and the psychology of football. *Journal of the History of the Behavioral Sciences, 42*, 3–18.

Baumeister, R. F. (2008). Free will in scientific psychology. *Perspectives on Psychological Science, 3*, 14–19.

Baumeister, R. F., Vohs, K. D., & Funder, D. C. (2007). Psychology as the science of self-reports and finger movements: Whatever happened to actual behavior? *Perspectives on Psychological Science, 2*, 396–403.

Baumrind, D. (1964). Some thoughts on ethics of research: After reading Milgram's "Behavioral study of obedience." *American Psychologist, 19*, 421–423.

Baumrind, D. (1985). Research using intentional deception: Ethical issues revisited. *American Psychologist, 40*, 165–174.

Beauchamp, T. L., & Childress, J. F. (1979). *Principles of biomedical ethics*. New York: Oxford University Press.

Beck, A. T., Steer, R. A., & Brown, G. K. (1996). *Manual for the Beck Depression Inventory-II*.

Behr, W. A. (1992). Ph.D. envy: A psychoanalytic case study. *Clinical Social Work Journal, 20*, 99–113.

Beisecker, T. (1988). Misusing survey research data: How not to justify demoting Christine Craft. *Forensic Reports, 1*, 15–33.

Belmont Report (1979). The Belmont Report: Ethical principles and guidelines for the protection of human subjects of research. Retrieved from http://www.hhs.gov/ohrp/policy/belmont.html

Benedict, J., & Stoloff, M. (1991). Animal laboratory facilities at "America's Best" undergraduate colleges. *American Psychologist, 46*, 535–536.

Benjamin, L. T. Jr., Cavell, T. A., & Shallenberger, W. R. (1984). Staying with initial answers on objective tests: Is it a myth? *Teaching of Psychology, 11*, 133–141.

Benjamin, L. T., Jr., Rogers, A. M., & Rosenbaum, A. (1991). Coco-Cola, caffeine, and mental deficiency: Harry Hollingworth and the Chattanooga trial of 1911. *Journal of the History of the Behavioral Sciences, 27*, 42–55.

Bensley, D. A. (2008, February). Can you learn to think more like a psychologist? *The Psychologist, 21(2)*, 128–129.

Bertera, R. L. (1990). Planning and implementing health promotion in the workplace: A case study of the Du Pont Company experience. *Health Education Quarterly, 17*, 307–327.

Bhattacharjee, Y. (2013, April 26). The mind of a con man. *New York Times Magazine*. Retrieved from http://www.nytimes.com/2013/04/28/magazine/diederik-stapels-audacious-academic-fraud

Blumberg, M., & Pringle, C. D. (1983). How control groups can cause loss of control in action research: The case of Rushton coal mine. *Journal of Applied Behavioral Science, 19*, 409–425.

Boesch-Achermann, H., & Boesch, C. (1993). Tool use in wild chimpanzees: New light from dark forests. *Current Directions in Psychological Science, 2*, 18–21.

Boorstin, D. J. (1985). *The discoverers*. New York: Vintage Books.

Boothby, E. J., Clark, M. S., & Bargh, J. A. (2014). Shared experiences are amplified. *Psychological Science, 25*, 2209–2216.

Boring, E. G. (1950). *A history of experimental psychology* (2nd ed.). Englewood Cliffs, NJ: Prentice Hall.

Brady, J. V. (1958, April). Ulcers in "executive" monkeys. *Scientific American, 199*, 95–100.

Brady, J. V., Porter, R. W., Conrad, D. G., & Mason, J. W. (1958). Avoidance behavior and the development of gastroduodenal ulcers. *Journal of the Experimental Analysis of Behavior, 1*, 69–72.

Bramel, D., & Friend, R. (1981). Hawthorne, the myth of the docile worker, and class bias in psychology. *American Psychologist, 36*, 867–878.

Bransford, J. D., & Johnson, M. K. (1972). Contextual prerequisites for understanding: Some investigations of comprehension and recall. *Journal of Verbal Learning and Verbal Behavior, 11*, 717–726.

Brantjes, M., & Bouma, A. (1991). Qualitative analysis of the drawings of Alzheimer's patients. *The Clinical Neuropsychologist, 5*, 41–52.

Braun, V., & Clarke, V. (2006). Using thematic analysis in psychology. *Qualitative Research in Psychology, 3*, 77–101.

Brehm, J. W. (1956). Postdecision changes in the desirability of alternatives. *Journal of Abnormal and Social Psychology, 52*, 384–389.

Brennan, J. F. (1991). *History and systems of psychology*. Englewood Cliffs, NJ: Prentice Hall.

Bridgman, P. W. (1927). *The logic of modern physics*. New York: Macmillan.

Broadbent, D. E. (1958). *Perception and communication*. New York: Pergamon Press.

Brotsky, S. R., & Giles, D. (2007). Inside the "Pro-ana" community: A covert online participant observation. *Eating Disorders, 15*, 93–109.

Browne, J. (1995). *Charles Darwin: Voyaging*. Princeton, NJ: Princeton University Press.

Bryan, J. H., & Test, M. A. (1967). Models and helping: Naturalistic studies in aiding behavior. *Journal of Personality and Social Psychology, 6*, 400–407.

Burger, J. (2009). Replicating Milgram: Would people still obey today? *American Psychologist, 64*, 1–11.

Burks, B. S., Jensen, D. W., & Terman, L. (1930). *Genetic studies of genius, Vol. 3. The promise of youth: Follow-up studies of a thousand gifted children*. Stanford, CA: Stanford University Press.

Bushman, B. J., & Anderson, C. A. (2009). Comfortably numb: Desensitizing effects of violent media on helping others. *Psychological Science, 20*, 273–277.

Byrne, G. (1988, October 7). Breuning pleads guilty. *Science, 242*, 27–28.

Campbell, D. T. (1969). Reforms as experiments. *American Psychologist, 24*, 409–429.

Campbell, D. T., & Erlebacher, A. (1970). How regression artifacts in quasi-experimental evaluations can mistakenly make compensatory education look harmful. In J. Hellmuth (Ed.), *Compensatory education: A national debate* (pp. 185–210). New York: Brunner-Mazel.

Campbell, D. T., & Ross, H. L. (1968). The Connecticut crackdown on speeding: Time series data in quasi-experimental analysis. *Law and Society Review, 3*, 33–53.

Campbell, D. T., & Stanley, J. C. (1963). *Experimental and quasi-experimental designs for research.* Chicago: Rand-McNally.

Carpenter, S. (2012, March 30). Psychology's bold initiative. *Science.* Retrieved from http://www.sciencemag.org/content/335/6076/1558

Carr, H. A., & Watson, J. B. (1908). Orientation in the white rat. *Journal of Comparative Neurology and Psychology, 18*, 27–44.

Casler, K., Bickel, L., & Hackett, E. (2013). Separate but equal? A comparison of participants and data gathered via Amazon's MTurk, social media, and face-to-face behavioral testing. *Computers in Human Behavior, 29*, 2156–2160.

Cattell, J. M. (1895). Proceedings of the third annual meeting of the American Psychological Association. *Psychological Review, 2*, 149–172.

Ceci, S. J., & Bruck, M. (2009). Do IRBs pass the minimal harm test? *Perspectives on Psychological Science, 4*, 28–29.

Chen, F., Wyer, R. J., & Shen, H. (2015). The interactive effects of affect and shopping goal on information search and product evaluations. *Journal of Experimental Psychology: Applied, 21*, 429–442.

Cherry, E. C. (1953). Some experiments on the recognition of speech, with one and with two ears. *Journal of the Acoustic Society of America, 25*, 975–979.

Christensen, L. (1988). Deception in psychological research: When is its use justified? *Personality and Social Psychology Bulletin, 14*, 664–675.

Christenson, C. V. (1971). *Kinsey: A biography.* Bloomington: Indiana University Press.

Cialdini, R. B. (2009). We have to break up. *Perspectives on Psychological Science, 4*, 5–6.

Cicirelli, V. G. (1984). The misinterpretation of the Westinghouse study: A reply to Zigler and Berman. *American Psychologist, 39*, 915–916.

Cicirelli, V. G. (1993). Head Start evaluation. *APS Observer, 6*(1), 32.

Cicirelli, V. G., Cooper, W. H., & Granger, R. L. (1969). The impact of Head Start: An evaluation of the effects of Head Start on children's cognitive and affective development. *Westinghouse Learning Corporation, OEO Contract B89–4536.*

Cohen, J. (1988), *Statistical power analysis for the behavioral sciences* (2nd ed.). Hillsdale, N.J.: Lawrence Erlbaum.

Cohen, J. (1994). The earth is round (p < .05). *American Psychologist, 49*, 997–1003.

Cohen, F., Solomon, S., Maxfield, M., Pyszczynski, T., & Greenberg, J. (2004). Fatal attraction: The effects of mortality salience on evaluations of charismatic, task-oriented, and relationship-oriented leaders. *Psychological Science, 15*, 846–851.

Cohen, S., Tyrell, D. A., & Smith, A. P. (1993). Negative life events, perceived stress, negative affect, and susceptibility to the common cold. *Journal of Personality and Social Psychology, 64*, 131–140.

Chen, F., Wyer, R. J., & Shen, H. (2015). The interactive effects of affect and shopping goal on information search and product evaluations. *Journal of Experimental Psychology: Applied, 21*, 429–442.

Coile, D. C., & Miller, N. E. (1984). How radical animal activists try to mislead humane people. *American Psychologist, 39*, 700–701.

Collins, G. (2011, April 7). Medicine on the move. *New York Times*, A23.

Converse, J. M., & Presser, S. (1986). *Survey questions: Hand crafting the standardized questionnaire.* Newbury Park, CA: Sage.

Cook, T. D., & Campbell, D. T. (1979). *Quasi-experimental design and analysis issues for field settings.* Chicago: Rand-McNally.

Cook, A. F., & Hoas, H. (2011). Protecting research subjects: IRBs in a changing research landscape. *IRB: Ethics & Human Research, 33*, 14–19.

Cooper, H., Hedges, L.V., & Valentine, J. C. (Eds.). (2009). *The handbook of research synthesis and meta-analysis* (2nd ed.). New York, NY: Russell Sage Foundation.

Cooper, M. L. (2006). Does drinking promote risky sexual behavior? *Current Directions in Psychological Science, 15*, 19–23.

Corkin, S. (2013). *Permanent present tense: The unforgettable life of the amnesiac patient, H. M.* New York, NY: Basic Books.

Cornell, E. H., Heth, C. D., Kneubuhler, Y., & Sehgal, S. (1996). Serial position effects in children's route reversal errors: Implications for police search operations. *Applied Cognitive Psychology, 10,* 301–326.

Coulter, X. (1986). Academic value of research participation by undergraduates. *American Psychologist, 41,* 317.

Crocker, J. (2011). The road to fraud starts with a single step. *Nature, 479,* 151.

Cronbach, L. J. (1957). The two disciplines of scientific psychology. *American Psychologist, 12,* 671–684.

Cronbach, L. J., Hastorf, A. H., Hilgard, E. R., & Maccoby, E. E. (1990). Robert R. Sears (1908–1989). *American Psychologist, 45,* 663–664.

Crowley, K., Callahan, M. A., Tenenbaum, H. R., & Allen, E. (2001). Parents explain more often to boys than to girls during shared scientific thinking. *Psychological Science, 12,* 258–261.

Crum, A. J., & Langer, E. J. (2007). Mind-set matters: Exercise and the placebo effect. *Psychological Science, 18,* 165–171.

D'Haese, S., Van Dyck, D., De Bourdeaudhuij, I., Deforche, B., & Cardon, G. (2015). Organizing "Play Streets" during school vacations can increase physical activity and decrease sedentary time in children. *International Journal of Behavioral Nutrition and Physical Activity.* Published online 2015 Feb 13. doi: 10.1186/s12966-015-0171-y

Dallenbach, K. M. (1913). The measurement of attention. *American Journal of Psychology, 24,* 465–507.

Damasio, A. R. (1994). *Descartes' error: Emotion, reason, and the human brain.* New York: Avon Books.

Damisch, L., Stoberock, B., & Mussweiler, T. (2010). Keep your fingers crossed! How superstition improves performance. *Psychological Science, 21,* 1014–1020.

Danziger, K. (1985). The origins of the psychological experiment as a social institution. *American Psychologist, 40,* 133–140.

Darley, J. M., & Latané, B. (1968). Bystander intervention in emergencies: Diffusion of responsibility. *Journal of Personality and Social Psychology, 8,* 377–383.

Darwin, C. (1872). *The expression of the emotions in man and animals.* London: Murray.

Darwin, C. (1877). A biographical sketch of an infant. *Mind, 2,* 285–294.

de Bruin, A., Treccani, B., & Della Sala, S. (2015). Cognitive advantage in bilingualism: An example of publication bias. *Psychological Science, 26,* 99–107.

DeAngelis, T. (2008, September). Information gold mines. *GradPSYCH, 6*(3), 20–23.

Delaney, P. F., Verkoeijen, P. L., & Spirgel, A. (2010). Spacing and testing effects: A deeply critical, lengthy, and at times discursive review of the literature. In B. H. Ross (Ed.) *The psychology of learning and motivation: Advances in research and theory (Vol. 53)* (pp. 63–147). San Diego, CA: Elsevier Academic Press.

DeLuca, R. V., & Holborn, S. W. (1992). Effects of a variable-ratio schedule with changing criteria on exercise in obese and nonobese boys. *Journal of Applied Behavior Analysis, 25,* 671–679.

DeLucia, P. R., & Griswold, J. A. (2011). Effects of camera arrangement on perceptual-motor performance in minimally invasive surgery. *Journal of Experimental Psychology: Applied, 17,* 210–232.

Dennis, W. (1941). Infant development under conditions of restricted practice and of minimum social stimulation. *Genetic Psychology Monographs, 23,* 143–189.

Department of Health and Human Services (1983). Federal regulations for the protection of human research subjects. In L. A. Peplau, D. O. Sears, S. E. Taylor, & J. L. Freedman (Eds.), *Readings in social psychology* (2nd ed.). Englewood Cliffs, NJ: Prentice Hall.

Dermer, M. L., & Hoch, T. A. (1999). Improving descriptions of single-subject experiments in research texts written for undergraduates. *Psychological Record, 49,* 49–66.

Dewsbury, D. A. (1990). Early interactions between animal psychologists and animal activists and the founding of the APA committee on precautions in animal experimentation. *American Psychologist, 45,* 315–327.

Diener, E., & Crandall, R. (1978). *Ethics in social and behavioral research.* Chicago: The University of Chicago Press.

Diener, E., Fraser, S. C., Beaman, A. L., & Kelem, R. T. (1976). Effects of deindividuation variables on stealing among Halloween trick-or-treaters. *Journal of Personality and Social Psychology, 33,* 178–183.

Diener, E., Matthews, R., & Smith, R. (1972). Leakage of experimental information to potential future subjects by debriefing subjects. *Journal of Experimental Research in Personality, 6,* 264–267.

Dillman, D. A., Smyth, J. D., & Christian, L. M. (2009). *Internet, mail and mixed-mode surveys: The tailored design method* (3rd ed.). New York: Wiley.

Domjan, M., & Purdy, J. E. (1995). Animal research in psychology: More than meets the eye of the general psychology student. *American Psychologist, 50,* 496–503.

Donnerstein, E. (1980). Aggressive erotica and violence against women. *Journal of Personality and Social Psychology, 39,* 269–277.

Drews, F. A., Yazdani, H., Godfrey, C. N., Cooper, J. M., & Strayer, D. L. (2009). Text messaging during simulated driving. *Human Factors: The Journal of the Human Factors and Ergonomics Society, 51,* 762–770.

Dresslar, F. B. (1893). On the pressure sense of the drum of the ear and "facial-vision." *American Journal of Psychology, 5,* 344–350.

Dunlap, R. E., Van Liere, K. D., Mertig, A. G., & Jones, R. E. (2000). Measuring endorsement of the New Ecological Paradigm: A revised NEP scale. *Journal of Social Issues, 56,* 425–442.

Dunn, T. M., Schwartz, M., Hatfield, R. W., & Wiegele, M. (1996). Measuring effectiveness of Eye Movement Desensitization and Reprocessing (EMDR) in non-clinical anxiety: A multi-subject, yoked control design. *Journal of Behavior Therapy and Experimental Psychiatry, 27,* 231–239.

Ebbinghaus, H. (1964). *Memory: A contribution to experimental psychology* (H. A. Ruger & C. A. Bussenius, Trans.). New York: Dover. (Original work published 1885)

Edlund, J. E., Sagarin, B. J., Skowronski, J. J., Johnson, S. J., & Kutter, J. (2009). Whatever happens in the laboratory stays in the laboratory: The prevalence of participant crosstalk. *Personality and Social Psychology Bulletin, 35,* 635–642.

Eichstaedt, J. C., Schwartz, H. A., Kern, M. L., Park, G., Labarthe, D. R., Merchant, R. M., . . . Seligman, M. E. P. (2015). Psychological language on Twitter predicts county-level heart disease mortality. *Psychological Science, 26,* 159–169.

Ekman, P. (1985). *Telling lies: Clues to deceit in the marketplace, politics, and marriage.* New York: W. W. Norton.

Elkins, I. J., Cromwell, R. L., & Asarnow, R. F. (1992). Span of apprehension in schizophrenic patients as a function of distractor masking and laterality. *Journal of Abnormal Psychology, 101,* 53–60.

Elmes, D. G., Kantowitz, B. H., & Roediger, H. L., III. (2006). *Research methods in psychology* (8th ed.). Belmont, CA: Wadsworth.

Epley, N., Akalis, S., Waytz, A., & Cacioppo, J. T. (2008). Creating social connection through inferential reproduction: Loneliness and perceived agency in gadgets, gods, and greyhounds. *Psychological Science, 19,* 114–120.

Eron, L. D., Huesman, L. R., Lefkowitz, M. M., & Walder, L. O. (1972). Does television violence cause aggression? *American Psychologist, 27,* 253–263.

Eysenck, H. J. (1952). The effects of psychotherapy: An evaluation. *Journal of Consulting Psychology, 16,* 319–324.

Faden, R. R., & Beauchamp, T. L. (1986). *A history and theory of informed consent.* New York: Oxford University Press.

Fancher, R. E. (1990). *Pioneers of psychology* (2nd ed.). New York: W. W. Norton.

Farrington, A., & Robinson, W. P. (1999). Homelessness and strategies to identify maintenance: A participant observation study. *Journal of Community and Applied Social Psychology, 9,* 175–194.

Faurie, C., & Raymond, M. (2004). Handedness, homicide and negative frequency-dependent selection. *Proceedings of the Royal Society.* Retrieved from www.isem.univ-montp2.fr/GE/Adaptation/bibliographie/fauriePRSLB2004.pdf

Feinberg, J. (1974). The rights of animals and unborn generations. In W. T. Blackstone (Ed.), *Philosophy and environmental crisis* (pp. 43–68). Athens: University of Georgia Press.

Feingold, A. (1992). Good-looking people are not what we think. *Psychological Bulletin, 111,* 304–341.

Fernald, D. (1984). *The Hans legacy.* Hillsdale, NJ: Erlbaum.

Ferster, C., B., & Skinner, B. F. (1957). *Schedules of reinforcement.* New York: Appleton-Century-Crofts.

Festinger, L. (1957). *The theory of cognitive dissonance.* Stanford, CA: Stanford University Press.

Festinger, L. (1999). Reflections on cognitive dissonance: Thirty years later. In E. Harmon-Jones & J. Mills (Eds.), *Cognitive dissonance: Progress on a pivotal theory in social psychology* (pp. 381–385). Washington, DC: American Psychological Association.

Festinger, L., Riecken, H. W., & Schachter, S. (1956). *When prophecy fails*. Minneapolis: University of Minnesota Press.

Fink, A. (1995). *How to ask survey questions*. Thousand Oaks, CA: Sage.

Finkel, E. J., & Eastwick, P. W. (2008). Speed-dating. *Current Directions in Psychological Science, 17*, 193–197.

Fischman, M. W. (2000). Informed consent. In B. D. Sales & S. Folkman (Eds.), *Ethics in research with human participants* (pp. 35–48). Washington, DC: American Psychological Association.

Fisher, C. B., & Fyrberg, D. (1994). Participant partners: College students weigh the costs and benefits of deceptive research. *American Psychologist, 49*, 417–427.

Fisher, R. A. (1925). *Statistical methods for research workers*. London: Oliver & Boyd.

Fisher, R. A. (1951). *The design of experiments* (6th ed.). New York: Hafner. (Original work published 1935)

Fiske, S. T. (2009). Institutional Review Boards: From bane to benefit. *Perspectives on Psychological Science, 4*, 30–31.

Flood, W. A., Wilder, D. A., Flood, A. L., & Masuda, A. (2002). Peer-mediated reinforcement plus prompting as treatment for off-task behavior in children with attention-deficit hyperactivity disorder. *Journal of Applied Behavior Analysis, 35*, 199–204.

Flourens, P. (1978). Phrenology examined (C. D. Meigs, Trans.). In D. N. Robinson (Ed.), *Significant contributions to the history of psychology. Series E. Volume II*. Washington, DC: University Publications of America. (Original work published 1846)

Folkman, S. (2000). Privacy and confidentiality. In B. D. Sales & S. Folkman (Eds.), *Ethics in research with human participants* (pp. 49–57). Washington, DC: American Psychological Association.

Forrest, D. W. (1974). *Francis Galton: The life and work of a Victorian genius*. New York: Taplinger.

For scientists, a beer test shows results as a litmus test (2008). Retrieved from www.nytimes.com/2008/03/18/science

Forsyth, A. J. M., & Lennox, J. C. (2010). Gender differences in the choreography of alcohol-related violence: An observational study of aggression within licensed premises. *Journal of Substance Abuse, 15*, 75–88.

Fowler, F. J., Jr. (1993). *Survey research methods* (2nd ed.). Newbury Park, CA: Sage.

Fowler, F. J., Jr. (1998). Design and evaluation of survey questions. In L. Bickman & D. J. Rog (Eds.), *Handbook of applied social research methods* (pp. 343–374). Thousand Oaks, CA: Sage.

Foxx, R. M., & Rubinoff, A. (1979). Behavioral treatment of caffeinism: Reducing excessive coffee drinking. *Journal of Applied Behavior Analysis, 12*, 335–344.

Fraysse, J. C., & Desprels-Fraysee, A. (1990). The influence of experimenter attitude on the performance of children of different cognitive ability levels. *Journal of Genetic Psychology, 151*, 169–179.

Freng, S., Webber, D., Blatter, J., Wing, A., & Scott, W. D. (2011). The role of statistics and research methods in the academic success of psychology majors: Do performance and enrollment timing matter? *Teaching of Psychology, 38*, 83–88.

Friedman, H, S., Tucker, J. S., Schwartz, J. E., Tomlinson-Keasey, C., Martin, L. R., Wingard, D. L., & Criqui, M. H. (1995). Psychological and behavioral predictors of longevity: The aging and death of the "Termites." *American Psychologist, 50*, 69–78.

Frith, H., & Gleeson, K. (2004). Clothing and embodiment: Men managing body image and appearance. *Psychology of Men & Masculinity, 5*, 40–48.

Fulero, S. M., & Kirkland, J. (1992, August). *A survey of student opinions on animal research*. Poster presented at the annual meeting of the American Psychological Association, Washington, DC.

Fung, S., & Leung, A. S. (2014). Pilot study investigating the role of therapy dogs in facilitating social interaction among children with autism. *Journal of Contemporary Psychotherapy, 44*, 253–262.

Gallup, G. G., & Beckstead, J. W. (1988). Attitudes toward animal research. *American Psychologist, 43*, 74–76.

Gallup, G. G., & Eddy, T. J. (1990). Animal facilities survey. *American Psychologist, 45*, 400–401.

Gallup, G. G., & Suarez, S. D. (1985a). Alternatives to the use of animals in psychological research. *American Psychologist*, *40*, 1104–1111.

Gallup, G. G., & Suarez, S. D. (1985b). Animal research versus the care and maintenance of pets: The names have been changed but the results remain the same. *American Psychologist*, *40*, 968.

Galton, F. (1869). *Hereditary genius*. London: Macmillan.

Galton, F. (1872). Statistical inquiries into the efficacy of prayer. *Fortnightly Review*, *12*, 125–135.

Galton, F. (1874). *English men of science: Their nature and nurture*. London: Macmillan.

Galton, F. (1948). An inquiry into human faculty and its development. In W. Dennis (Ed.), *Readings in the history of psychology* (pp. 277–289). New York: Appleton-Century-Crofts. (Original work published 1883)

Galvin, S. L., & Herzog, H. A. (1992). The ethical judgment of animal research. *Ethics & Behavior*, *2*, 263–286.

Geller, D. M. (1982). Alternatives to deception: Why, what, and how? In J. E. Sieber (Ed.), *The ethics of social research: Surveys and experiments* (pp. 40–55). New York: Springer-Verlag.

Geller, E. S. (1991). Editor's introduction: Where's the validity in social validity? *Journal of Applied Behavior Analysis*, Monograph #5, 1–6.

Gibson, E. J. (1980). Eleanor J. Gibson. In G. Lindsey (Ed.), *A history of psychology in autobiography. Volume 7* (pp. 239–271). San Francisco: W. H. Freeman.

Gibson, E. J., & Walk, R. D. (1960). The "visual cliff." *Scientific American*, *202*, 64–71.

Gilchrist, V. J., & Williams, R. L. (1999). Key informant interviews. In B. F. Crabtree & W. L. Miller (Eds.), *Doing qualitative research* (2nd ed.) (pp. 71–88). Thousand Oaks, CA: Sage Publications.

Gillham, N. W. (2001). *A life of Sir Francis Galton: From African exploration to the birth of eugenics*. New York: Oxford University Press.

Gillespie, R. (1988). The Hawthorne experiments and the politics of experimentation. In J. G. Morawski (Ed.), *The rise of experimentation in American psychology* (pp. 114–137). New Haven, CT: Yale University Press.

Gilligan, C. (1982). *In a different voice: Psychological theory and women's development*. Cambridge, MA: Harvard University Press.

Gladue, B. A., & Delaney, H. J. (1990). Gender differences in perception of attractiveness of men and women in bars. *Personality and Social Psychology Bulletin*, *16*, 378–391.

Godden, D. R., & Baddeley, A. D. (1975). Context-dependent memory in two natural environments: On land and under water. *British Journal of Psychology*, *66*, 325–331.

Goodall, J. (1978). Chimp killings: Is it the man in them? *Science News*, *113*, 276.

Goodall, J. (1990). *Through a window: My thirty years with the chimpanzees of Gombe*. Boston: Houghton Mifflin.

Goodman, J. K., Cryder, C. E., & Cheema, A. (2013). Data collection in a flat world: The strengths and weaknesses of Mechanical Turk samples. *Journal of Behavioral Decision Making*, *26*, 213–224.

Goodwin, C. J. (2010). Using history to strengthen a research methods course. *History of Psychology*, *13*, 196–200.

Goodwin, C. J. (2012). *A history of modern psychology* (4th ed.). New York: Wiley.

Goosens, N. A. M. C., Camp, G., Verkoeijen, P. P. J. L., Tabber, H. K., & Zwaan, R. A. (2014). The benefit of retrieval practice over elaborative study in primary school vocabulary learning. *Journal of Applied Research in Memory and Cognition*, *3*, 177–182.

Grant, H. M., Bredahl, L. C., Clay, J., Ferrie, J., Groves, J. E., McDorman, T. A., & Dark, V. J. (1998). Context-dependent memory for meaningful material: Information for students. *Applied Cognitive Psychology*, *12*, 617–623.

Greenberg, J., Pyszczynski, T., & Solomon, S. (1986). The causes and consequences of a need for self-esteem: A terror management theory. In R. F. Baumeister (Ed.), *Public and private self* (pp. 189–212). New York, NY: Springer-Verlag.

Grose, P. (1994). *Gentleman spy: The life of Allen Dulles*. Boston: Houghton-Mifflin.

Guéguen, N., & Ciccotti, S. (2008). Domestic dogs as facilitators in social interaction: An evaluation of helping and courtship behaviors. *Anthrozoös*, *21*, 339–349.

Hagemann, N., Strauss, B., & Leißing, J. (2008). When the referee sees red. *Psychological Science*, *19*, 769–771.

Haggbloom, S. J., Warnick, R., Warnick, J. E., Jones, V. K., Yarbrough, G. L., Russell, T. M., . . . Monte, E. (2002). The 100 most eminent psychologists of the 20th century. *Review of General Psychology, 6,* 139–152.

Hall, G. S. (1883). *The contents of children's minds on entering school.* New York: Kellogg.

Harris, B. (1979). Whatever happened to Little Albert? *American Psychologist, 34,* 151–160.

Hartman, D. P., & Hall, R. V. (1976). The changing criterion design. *Journal of Applied Behavior Analysis, 9,* 527–532.

Hartwig, M. K., & Dunlosky, J. (2012). Study strategies of college students: Are self-testing and scheduling related to achievement? *Psychonomic Bulletin & Review, 19,* 126–134.

Henle, M., & Hubbell, M. B. (1938). "Egocentricity" in adult conversation. *Journal of Social Psychology, 9,* 227–234.

Henrich, J., Heine, S. J., & Norenzayan, A. (2010). The weirdest people in the world? *Behavioral and Brain Sciences, 33*(2–3), 61–83.

Herringshaw, A. J., Ammons, C. J., DeRamus, T. P., & Kana, R. K. (2016). Hemispheric differences in language processing in autism spectrum disorders: A meta-analysis of neuroimaging studies. *Autism Research.*

Herzog, H. (1993). Human morality and animal research. *The American Scholar, 62,* 337–349.

Herzog, H. (2010). *Some we love, some we hate, some we eat: Why it's so hard to think straight about animals.* New York: Harper-Collins.

Herzog, H. (2011). The impact of pets on human health and psychological well-being. *Current Directions in Psychological Science, 20,* 236–239.

Hilgard, E. R. (Ed.). (1978). *American psychology in historical perspective.* Washington, DC: American Psychological Association.

Hilgard, E. R. (1987). *Psychology in America: A historical survey.* San Diego, CA: Harcourt Brace Jovanovich.

Hilgartner, S. (1990). Research fraud, misconduct, and the IRB. *IRB: A Review of Human Subjects Research, 12,* 1–4.

Hite, S. (1987). *Women and love.* New York: Knopf.

Hobbs, N. (1948). The development of a code of ethics for psychology. *American Psychologist, 3,* 80–84.

Hogan, T. P., & Evalenko, K. (2006). The elusive definition of outliers in introductory statistics textbooks for behavioral sciences. *Teaching of Psychology, 33,* 252–256.

Holahan, C. K., Sears, R. R., & Cronbach, L. J. (1995). *The gifted group in later maturity.* Palo Alto, CA: Stanford University Press.

Holden, C. (1987, March 27). NIMH finds a case of "serious misconduct." *Science, 235,* 1566–1577.

Hollingshead, A. B. (1949). *Elmstown's youth.* New York: Wiley.

Hollingworth, H. L. (1990). *Leta Stetter Hollingworth: A biography.* Bolton: Anker Publishing Co. (Original work published 1943)

Hollingworth, H. L., & Poffenberger, A. T. (1917). *Applied psychology.* New York: D. Appleton.

Holmes, D. S. (1976a). Debriefing after psychological experiments. I. Effectiveness of postdeception dehoaxing. *American Psychologist, 31,* 858–867.

Holmes, D. S. (1976b). Debriefing after psychological experiments. II. Effectiveness of postexperimental desensitizing. *American Psychologist, 31,* 868–875.

Holmes, D. S., McGilley, B. M., & Houston, B. K. (1984). Task-related arousal of Type A and Type B persons: Level of challenge and response specificity. *Journal of Personality and Social Psychology, 46,* 1322–1327.

Horn, J. L. (1990, October). Psychology can help kids get a Head Start. *APA Monitor, 21*(9), 3.

Hothersall, D. (1990). *History of psychology* (2nd ed.). New York: McGraw-Hill.

Hubel, D. H. (1988). *Eye, brain, and vision.* New York: Scientific American Library.

Hubel, D. H., & Wiesel, T. N. (1959). Receptive fields of single neurons in the cat's striate cortex. *Journal of Physiology, 148,* 574–591.

Huesmann, R., & Dubow, E. (2008). Leonard D. Eron (1920–2007). *American Psychologist, 63,* 131–132.

Huff, D. (1954). *How to lie with statistics.* New York: W. W. Norton.

Hull, D. B. (1996). Animal use in undergraduate psychology programs. *Teaching of Psychology, 23*, 171–174.

Hunt, E., & Love, T. (1972). How good can memory be? In A. W. Melton & E. Martin (Eds.), *Coding processes in human memory* (pp. 237–260). Washington, DC: V. H. Winston.

Hunt, R. R., & Ellis, H. C. (2004). *Fundamentals of cognitive psychology* (4th ed.). New York: McGraw-Hill.

Infurna, M. R., Reichl, C., Parzer, P., Schimmenti, A., Bifulco, A., & Kaess, M. (2016). Associations between depression and specific childhood experiences of abuse and neglect: A meta-analysis. *Journal of Affective Disorders, 190*, 47–55.

Inzlicht, M., & Ben-Zeev, T. (2000). A threatening intellectual environment: Why females are susceptible to experiencing problem-solving deficits in the presence of males. *Psychological Science, 11*, 365–371.

James, W. (1950). *Principles of psychology.* Vol. *1.* New York: Dover. (Original work published 1890)

Jenkins, J. G., & Dallenbach, K. M. (1924). Minor studies from the psychological laboratory of Cornell University: Oblivescence during sleep and waking. *American Journal of Psychology, 35*, 605–612.

Ji, L., Peng, K., & Nisbett, R. E. (2000). Culture, control, and perception of relationships in the environment. *Journal of Personality and Social Psychology, 78*, 943–955.

John, L. K., Loewenstein, G., & Prelec, D. Measuring the prevalence of questionable research practices with incentives for truth telling. *Psychological Science, 23*, 524–532.

Johns, M., Schmader, T., & Martens, A. (2005). Knowing is half the battle: Teaching stereotype threat as a means of improving women's math performance. *Psychological Science, 16*, 175–178.

Jonçich, G. (1968). *The sane positivist: A biography of Edward L. Thorndike.* Middletown, CT: Wesleyan University Press.

Jones, J. H. (1981). *Bad blood: The Tuskegee syphilis experiment.* New York: Free Press.

Jones, M. C. (1924). A laboratory study of fear: The case of Peter. *Pedagogical Seminary, 31*, 308–315.

Jump, P. (2011, November 28). Scholars analyze a case of massive research fraud. *Inside Higher Ed.* Retrieved from https://www.insidehighered.com/news/2011/11/28/scholars-analyze-case-massive-research-fraud

Junginger, J., & Head, S. (1991). Time series analyses of obsessional behavior and mood during self-imposed delay and responsive prevention. *Behavior Research and Therapy, 29*, 521–530.

Karnes, E. W., & Leonard, S. D. (1992). Graphoanalytic and psychometric personality profiles: Validity and Barnum effects. In B. L. Beyerstein & D. F. Beyerstein (Eds.), *The write stuff: Evaluations of graphology—the study of handwriting analysis* (pp. 436–461). Buffalo, NY: Prometheus Books.

Karpicke, J. D. (2012). Retrieval-based learning: Active retrieval promotes meaningful learning. *Current Directions in Psychological Science, 21*, 157–163.

Karpicke, J. D., & Grimaldi, P. J. (2012). Retrieval-based learning: A perspective for enhancing meaningful learning. *Educational Psychology Review, 24*, 401–418.

Kaufman, A. S., & Kaufman, N. L. (1983). *KABC: Kaufman Assessment Battery for Children. Interpretive manual.* Circle Pines, MN: American Guidance Service.

Kay, S., Harchik, A. E., & Luiselli, J. K. (2006). Elimination of drooling by an adolescent student with autism attending public high school. *Journal of Positive Behavior Interventions, 8*, 24–28.

Kazdin, A. E. (1978). *History of behavior modification: Experimental foundations of contemporary research.* Baltimore: University Park Press.

Keltner, D., Ellsworth, P. C., & Edwards, K. (1993). Beyond simple pessimism: Effects of sadness and anger on social perception. *Journal of Personality and Social Psychology, 64*, 740–752.

Kendall, M. G. (1970). Ronald Aylmer Fisher, 1890–1962. In E. S. Pearson & M. G. Kendall (Eds.), *Studies in the history of statistics and probability* (pp. 439–447). London: Charles Griffin.

Kent, D. (1994). Interview with APS president-elect Richard F. Thompson. *APS Observer, 7*, 4, 10.

Kim, K., & Spelke, E. S. (1992). Infants' sensitivity to effects of gravity on visible object motion. *Journal of Experimental Psychology: Human Perception and Performance, 18*, 385–393.

Kimmel, A. J. (2007). *Ethical issues in behavioral research: A survey.* Malden, MA: Blackwell.

Kinsey, A. C., Pomeroy, W. B., & Martin, C. E. (1948). *Sexual behavior in the human male.* Philadelphia: W. B. Saunders.

Kinsey, A. C., Pomeroy, W. B., Martin, C. E., & Gebhard, P. H. (1953). *Sexual behavior in the human female*. Philadelphia: W. B. Saunders.

Kirk, R. E. (1968). *Experimental design: Procedures for the behavioral sciences*. Belmont, CA: Brooks/Cole.

Kitayama, S., Markus, H. R., Matsumoto, H., & Norasakkunkit, V. (1997). Individual and collective processes in the construction of the self: Self-enhancement in the United States and self-criticism in Japan. *Journal of Personality and Social Psychology, 72*, 1245–1267.

Kline, R. B. (2004). *Beyond significance testing: Reforming data analysis methods in behavioral research*. Washington, DC: American Psychological Association.

Kohlberg, L. (1964). Development of moral character and moral behavior. In L. W. Hoffman & M. L. Hoffman (Eds.), *Review of child development research* (Vol. *1*). New York: Sage.

Kolata, G. B. (1986). What does it mean to be random? *Science, 231*, 1068–1070.

Koocher, G. P., & Keith-Spiegel, P. (1998). *Ethics in psychology: Professional standards and cases* (2nd ed.). New York: Oxford University Press.

Korn, J. H. (1988). Students' roles, rights, and responsibilities as research participants. *Teaching of Psychology, 15*, 74–78.

Korn, J. H. (1997). *Illusions of reality: A history of deception in social psychology*. Albany: SUNY Press.

Korn, J. H., Davis, R., & Davis, S. F. (1991). Historians' and chairpersons' judgments of eminence among psychologists. *American Psychologist, 46*, 789–792.

Kornell, N., & Bjork, R. A. (2007). The promise and perils of self-regulated study. *Psychonomic Bulletin & Review, 14*, 219–224.

Kramer, P. D. (2006). *Freud: Inventor of the modern mind*. New York: Harper Collins.

Kraut, R., Olson, J., Banaji, M., Bruckman, A., Cohen, J., & Couper, M. (2004). Psychological research online. *American Psychologist, 59*, 105–117.

Kroeger, K. A., Schultz, J. R., & Newsom, C. (2007). A comparison of two group-delivered social skills programs for young children with autism. *Journal of Autism and Developmental Disorders, 37*, 808–817.

Kruger, J., Wirtz, D., & Miller, D. T. (2005). Counterfactual thinking and the first instinct fallacy. *Journal of Personality and Social Psychology, 88*, 725–735.

Krupat, E. (1975). Conversation with John Darley. In E. Krupat (Ed.), *Psychology is social: Readings and conversations in social psychology*. Glenview, IL: Scott, Foresman.

Kruta, V. (1972). Marie-Jean-Pierre Flourens. In C. C. Gillespie (Ed.), *Dictionary of scientific biography* (*Vol. V*). New York: Scribner's.

Kuhn, T. S. (1970). The function of dogma in scientific research. In B. A. Brody (Ed.), *Readings in the philosophy of science* (pp. 356–373). Englewood Cliffs, NJ: Prentice Hall.

Kushner, M. (1970). Faradic aversive controls in clinical practice. In C. Neuringer & J. L. Michael (Eds.), *Behavior modification in clinical practice*. New York: Appleton-Century-Crofts.

Kuther, T. L. (2006). *The psychology major's handbook* (2nd ed.). Belmont, CA: Wadsworth.

Landrum, R. E., & Chastain, G. (1999). Subject pool policies in undergraduate-only departments: Results from a nation-wide survey. In G. Chastain & E. R. Landrum (Eds.), *Protecting human subjects: Department subject pools and Institutional Review Boards* (pp. 25–42). Washington, DC: American Psychological Association.

Landrum, R. E., & Nelson, L. R. (2002). The undergraduate research assistantship: An analysis of the benefits. *Teaching of Psychology, 29*, 15–19.

Lang, R., O'Reilly, M., Sigafoos, J, Lancioni, G. E., Machalicek, W., Rispoli, M., & White, P. (2009). Enhancing the effectiveness of a play intervention by abolishing the reinforcing value of stereotypy: A pilot study. *Journal of Applied Behavior Analysis, 42*, 889–894.

Langer, E. J., & Rodin, J. (1976). The effects of choice and enhanced personal responsibility for the aged: A field experiment in an institutional setting. *Journal of Personality and Social Psychology, 34*, 191–198.

Lawton, C. A. (1994). Gender differences in wayfinding strategies: Relationship to spatial ability and spatial anxiety. *Sex Roles, 30*, 765–779.

Leak, G. K. (1981). Student perception of coercion and value from participation in psychological research. *Teaching of Psychology, 8*, 147–149.

Lee, D. N., & Aronson, E. (1974). Visual proprioceptive control of standing in human infants. *Perception and Psychophysics, 15*, 529–532.

LeFrancois, J. R., & Metzger, B. (1993). Low-response-rate conditioning history and fixed-interval responding in rats. *Journal of the Experimental Analysis of Behavior, 59*, 543–549.

Leitenberg, H., Agras, W. S., Thomson, L. E., & Wright, D. E. (1968). Feedback in behavior modification: An experimental analysis. *Journal of Applied Behavior Analysis, 1*, 131–137.

Lepper, M. R., Ross, L., & Lau, R. R. (1986). Persistence of inaccurate beliefs about the self: Perseverance effects in the classroom. *Journal of Personality and Social Psychology, 50*, 482–491.

Licht, M. M. (1995). Multiple regression and correlation. In L. G. Grimm & P. R. Yarnold (Eds.), *Reading and understanding multivariate statistics* (pp. 19–64). Washington, DC: American Psychological Association.

Loft, S., Smith, R. E., & Bhaskara, A. (2011). Prospective memory in an air traffic control simulation: External aids that signal when to act. *Journal of Experimental Psychology: Applied, 17*, 60–70.

Loftus, E. F. (1979). *Eyewitness testimony.* Cambridge, MA: Harvard University Press.

Loftus, E. F., & Hoffman, H. G. (1989). Misinformation and memory: The creation of new memories. *Journal of Experimental Psychology: General, 118*, 100–104.

Loftus, E. F., & Ketcham, K. (1991). *Witness for the defense: The accused, the eyewitness, and the expert who puts memory on trial.* New York: St. Martin's Press.

López, F., & Menez, M. (2005). Effects of reinforcement history on response rate and response pattern in periodic reinforcement. *Journal of the Experimental Analysis of Behavior, 83*, 221–241.

Lorenz, K. (1966). *On aggression.* New York: Harcourt Brace Jovanovich.

Lotufo, P. A., Chae, C. U., Ajani, U. A., Hennekens, C. H., & Manson, J. E. (1999). Male pattern baldness and coronary heart disease: The physician's health study. *Archives of Internal Medicine, 160*, 165–171.

Ludwig, T. D., & Geller, E. S. (1997). Assigned versus participative goal setting and response generalization: Managing injury control among professional pizza deliverers. *Journal of Applied Psychology, 82*, 253–261.

Luria, A. R. (1968). *The mind of a mnemonist.* New York: Basic Books.

MacLeod, C. M. (1991). John Ridley Stroop: Creator of a landmark cognitive task. *Canadian Psychology, 32*, 521–524.

MacLeod, C. M. (1992). The Stroop task: The "gold standard" of attentional measures. *Journal of Experimental Psychology: General, 121*, 12–14.

Mangione, T. W. (1998). Mail surveys. In L. Bickman & D. J. Rog (Eds.), *Handbook of applied social research methods* (pp. 399–427). Thousand Oaks, CA: Sage.

Makel, M. C., Plucker, J. A., & Hegarty, B. (2012). Replications in psychology research: How often do they really occur? *Perspectives on Psychological Science, 7*, 537–542.

Manis, M. (1971). *An introduction to cognitive psychology.* Belmont, CA: Brooks/Cole.

Marean, G. C., Werner, L. A., & Kuhl, P. K. (1992). Vowel categorization by very young infants. *Developmental Psychology, 28*, 396–405.

Mayer, F. S., & Frantz, C. M. (2004). The connectedness to nature scale: A measure of individuals' feeling in community with nature. *Journal of Environmental Psychology, 24*, 503–515.

McClelland, D. C. (1961). *The achieving society.* Princeton, NJ: Van Nostrand.

McClelland, D. C., Atkinson, J. W., Clarke, R. A., & Lowell, E. L. (1953). *The achievement motive.* New York: Appleton-Century-Crofts.

McCord, D. M. (1991). Ethics-sensitive management of the university human subject pool. *American Psychologist, 46*, 151.

McDonald, S., & Flanagan, S. (2004). Social perception deficits after traumatic brain injury: Interaction between emotion recognition, mentalizing ability, and social communication. *Neuropsychology, 18*, 572–579.

McGraw, K. O., Tew, M. D., & Williams, J. E. (2000). The integrity of Web-based experiments: Can you trust the data? *Psychological Science, 11*, 502–506.

McGraw, M. (1941). Neural maturation as exemplified in the changing reactions of the infant to pin prick. *Child Development, 12*, 31–42.

McMicken, B. L., Ostergren, J. A., & Vento-Wilson, M. (2011). Therapeutic intervention in a case of ataxic dysarthria associated with a history of amateur boxing. *Communication Disorders Quarterly, 33*, 55–64.

Meissner, C. A., & Brigham, J. C. (2001). A meta-analysis of the verbal overshadowing effect in face identification. *Applied Cognitive Psychology, 15*, 603–616.

Merikle, P. M., & Skanes, H. E. (1992). Subliminal self-help audiotapes: A search for placebo effects. *Journal of Applied Psychology, 77*, 772–776.

Middlemist, R. D., Knowles, E. W., & Matter, C. F. (1976). Personal space invasions in the lavatory: Suggestive evidence for arousal. *Journal of Personality and Social Psychology, 33*, 541–546.

Milgram, S. (1964). Issues in the study of obedience: A reply to Baumrind. *American Psychologist, 19*, 448–452.

Miles, W. R. (1928). Studies on physical exertion I: A multiple chronograph for measuring groups of men. *American Physical Education Review, 33*, 379–387.

Miles, W. R. (1930). On the history of research with rats and mazes: A collection of notes. *Journal of General Psychology, 3*, 324–337.

Miles, W. R. (1931). Studies in physical exertion II: Individual and group reaction time in football charging. *Research Quarterly, 2*(3), 5–13.

Miles, W. R. (1933). Age and human ability. *Psychological Review, 40*, 99–123.

Milgram, S. (1963). Behavioral study of obedience. *Journal of Abnormal and Social Psychology, 67*, 371–378.

Milgram, S. (1974). *Obedience to authority: An experimental view*. New York: Harper & Row.

Mill, J. S. (1843). *A system of logic, ratiocinative and inductive, being a connected view of the principles of evidence, and the methods of scientific investigation*. London: Longmans, Green.

Mill, J. S. (1869). *The subjection of women*. London: Longmans, Green, Reader, Dyer.

Miller, G. A. (1969). Psychology as a means of promoting human welfare. *American Psychologist, 24*, 1063–1075.

Miller, N. (1985). The value of behavioral research on animals. *American Psychologist, 40*, 423–440.

Miller, W. R., & DiPilato, M. (1983). Treatment of nightmares via relaxation and desensitization: A controlled evaluation. *Journal of Consulting and Clinical Psychology, 51*, 870–877.

Mills, W. (1899). The nature of animal intelligence and the methods of investigating it. *Psychological Review, 6*, 262–274.

Minton, H. L. (1987). Lewis M. Terman and mental testing: In search of the democratic ideal. In M. M. Sokal (Ed.), *Psychological testing and American society, 1890–1930* (pp. 95–112). New Brunswick, NJ: Rutgers University Press.

Minton, H. L. (1988). Charting life history: Lewis M. Terman's study of the gifted. In J. G. Morawski (Ed.), *The rise of experimentation in American psychology* (pp. 138–162). New Haven, CT: Yale University Press.

Mitchell, G. (2012). Revisiting truth or triviality: The external validity of research in the psychological laboratory. *Perspectives on Psychological Science, 7*, 109–117.

Mook, D. G. (1983). In defense of external invalidity. *American Psychologist, 38*, 379–387.

Morell, V. (1995). *Ancestral passions: The Leakey family and the quest for humankind's beginnings*. New York: Simon & Schuster.

Morgan, C. L. (1903). *Introduction to comparative psychology*. London: Walter Scott.

Morgan, F. W. (1990). Judicial standards for survey research: An update and guidelines. *Journal of Marketing, 54*, 59–70.

Moses, S. (1991, July/August). Animal research issues affect students. *APA Monitor, 22*(7), 47–48.

Mowrer, O. H., & Mowrer, W. M. (1938). Enuresis—a method for its study and treatment. *American Journal of Orthopsychiatry, 8*, 436–459.

Mueller, P. A., & Oppenheimer, D. M. (2014). The pen is mightier than the keyboard: Advantages of longhand over laptop note taking. *Psychological Science, 25*, 1159–1168.

Murphy, G. L. (1999). A case study of a departmental subject pool and review board. In G. Chastain & R. E. Landrum (Eds.), *Protecting human subjects: Departmental subject pools and institutional review boards* (pp. 131–156). Washington, DC: American Psychological Association.

Murray, H. A. (1943). *Thematic apperception test*. Cambridge, MA: Harvard University Press.

Myers, D. G. (1990). *Social psychology* (3rd ed). New York: McGraw-Hill.

Myers, D. G. (1992). *Psychology* (3rd ed.). New York: Worth.

Nakonezny, P. A., Reddic, R., & Rodgers, J. L. (2004). Did divorces decline after the Oklahoma City bombing? *Journal of Marriage and Family*, *66*, 90–100.

Nastally, B. L., Dixon, M. R., & Jackson, J. W. (2010). Manipulating slot machine preference in problem gamblers through contextual control. *Journal of Applied Behavior Analysis*, *43*, 125–129.

National Research Council (2011). *Guide for the care and use of laboratory animals* (8th ed.). Washington, DC: The National Academies Press. Retrieved from http://www.nap.edu/openbook.php?record_id=12910&page=R1

Neale, J. M., & Liebert, R. M. (1973). *Science and behavior: An introduction to methods of research*. Englewood Cliffs, NJ: Prentice Hall.

Neisser, U. (1976). *Cognition and reality*. San Francisco: W. H. Freeman.

Nickell, J. (1992a). A brief history of graphology. In B. L. Beyerstein & D. F. Beyerstein (Eds.), *The write stuff: Evaluations of graphology—the study of handwriting analysis* (pp. 23–29). Buffalo, NY: Prometheus Books.

Nickell, J. (1992b). Handwriting: Identification science and graphological analysis contrasted. In B. L. Beyerstein & D. F. Beyerstein (Eds.), *The write stuff: Evaluations of graphology—the study of handwriting analysis* (pp. 42–52). Buffalo, NY: Prometheus Books.

Nolan, S. A., & Heinzen, T. E. (2012). *Statistics for the behavioral sciences* (2nd ed.). New York: Worth.

Norcross, J. C., Hanych, J. M., & Terranova, R. D. (1996). Graduate study in psychology: 1992–1993. *American Psychologist*, *51*, 631–643.

Nuremberg Code. (1949). *Trials of war criminals before the Nuremberg Military Tribunals under Control Council Law No. 10*, Vol. 2, pp. Washington, D.C.: U.S. Government Printing Office.

O'Brien, T. P., Walley, P. B., Anderson-Smith, S., & Drabman, R. S. (1982). Naturalistic observation of the snack-eating behavior of obese and nonobese children. *Addictive Behaviors*, *7*, 75–77.

Orne, M. T. (1962). On the social psychology of the psychology experiment: With particular reference to demand characteristics and their implications. *American Psychologist*, *17*, 776–783.

Orwin, R. G. (1997). Twenty-one years old and counting: The interrupted time series comes of age. In E. Chelimsky & W. R. Shadish (Eds.), *Evaluation for the 21st century* (pp. 443–465). Thousand Oaks, CA: Sage Publications.

Osler, S. F., & Trautman, G. E. (1961). Concept attainment II: Effect of stimulus complexity upon concept attainment at two levels of intelligence. *Journal of Experimental Psychology*, *62*, 9–13.

Parsons, H. M. (1974). What happened at Hawthorne? *Science*, *183*, 922–932.

Patten, M. L. (1998). *Questionnaire research: A practical guide*. Los Angeles: Pryczak.

Patterson, F. G., & Linden, E. (1981). *The education of Koko*. New York: Holt, Rinehart, & Winston.

Peck, F. S. (1978). *The road less traveled*. New York: Simon & Schuster.

Peterson, L., Ridley-Johnson, R., & Carter, C. (1984). The supersuit: An example of structured naturalistic observation of children's altruism. *Journal of General Psychology*, *110*, 235–241.

Plötner, M., Over, H., Carpenter, M., & Tomasello, M. (2015). Young children show the bystander effect in helping situations. *Psychological Science*, *26*, 499–506.

Plotz, D. (2000, June 4). Greens peace. *New York Times Magazine*, *32*, 37.

Plous, S. (1996a). Attitudes toward the use of animals in psychological research and education: Results from a national survey of psychologists. *American Psychologist*, *51*, 1167–1180.

Plous, S. (1996b). Attitudes toward the use of animals in psychological research and education: Results from a national survey of psychology majors. *Psychological Science*, *7*, 352–358.

Plous, S., & Herzog, H. (2001). Reliability of protocol reviews for animal research. *Science*, *293*, 608–609.

Poling, A., Weetjens, B., Cox, C., Beyene, N. W. Bach, H. & Sully, A. (2011). Using trained pouched rats to detect land mines: Another victory for operant conditioning. *Journal of Applied Behavior Analysis*, *44*, 351–355.

Pollick, A. (2007). IRBs: Navigating the maze. *APS Observer*, *20*(10), 16–21.

Popper, K. R. (1959). *The logic of scientific discovery*. New York: Basic Books.

Posavac, E. J., & Carey, R. G. (2010). *Program evaluation: Methods and case studies* (8th ed.). Englewood Cliffs, NJ: Prentice Hall.

Rauscher, F. W., Shaw, G. L., & Key, K. N. (1993). Music and spatial task performance. *Nature, 365*, 611.

Redelmeier, D. A., & Tibshirani, R. J. (1997). Association between cellular-phone calls and motor vehicle collisions. *The New England Journal of Medicine, 336*, 453–458.

Resnick, J. H., & Schwartz, T. (1973). Ethical standards as an independent variable in psychological research. *American Psychologist, 28*, 134–139.

Reynolds, G. S. (1968). *A primer of operant conditioning*. Glenview, IL: Scott, Foresman.

Reynolds, R. I. (1992). Recognition of expertise in chess players. *American Journal of Psychology, 105*, 409–415.

Riva, P., Sacchi, S., & Brambilla, M. (2015). Humanizing machines: Anthropomorphization of slot machines increases gambling. *Journal of Experimental Psychology: Applied, 21*, 313–325.

Roberts, N. P., Roberts, P. A., Jones, N., & Bisson, J. I. (2015). Psychological interventions for post-traumatic stress disorder and comorbid substance use disorder: A systematic review and meta-analysis. *Clinical Psychology Review, 38*, 25–38.

Robinson, E., Kersbergen, I., Brunstrom, J. M., & Field, M. (2014). I'm watching you. Awareness that food consumption is being monitored is a demand characteristic in eating-behavior experiments. *Appetite, 83*, 19–25.

Rockefeller, J. D. IV. (1994). Is military research hazardous to veterans' health? Lessons spanning half a century: A report examining biological experimentation on U.S. military. Retrieved from *www.trufax.org/trans/roc00.html*

Rodin, J., & Langer, E. J. (1977). Long-term effects of a control-relevant intervention with the institutionalized aged. *Journal of Personality and Social Psychology, 35*, 897–902.

Roediger, R. (2004). What should they be called? *APS Observer, 17*(4), 5, 46–48.

Roediger, H. L., III, & Karpicke, J. D. (2006). Test-enhanced learning: Taking memory tests improves long-term retention. *Psychological Science, 17*, 249–255.

Roediger, H. L., & McDermott, K. B. (1995). Creating false memories: Remembering words not presented in lists. *Journal of Experimental Psychology: Learning, Memory, and Cognition, 21*, 803–814.

Rogelberg, S. G., & Luong, A. (1998). Nonresponse to mailed surveys: A review and guide. *Current Directions in Psychological Science, 7*, 60–65.

Rogosa, D. (1980). A critique of cross-lagged correlation. *Psychological Bulletin, 88*, 245–258.

Rohles, F. H., Jr. (1992). Orbital bar pressing: A historical note on Skinner and the chimpanzees in space. *American Psychologist, 47*, 1531–1533.

Romanes, G. J. (1886). *Animal intelligence*. New York: D. Appleton.

Rosenberg, M. J. (1969). The conditions and consequences of evaluation apprehension. In R. Rosenthal & R. L. Rosnow (Eds.), *Artifact in behavioral research* (pp. 280–349). New York: Academic Press.

Rosenthal, R. (1966). *Experimenter effects in behavioral research*. New York: Appleton-Century-Crofts.

Rosenthal, R. (1979). The file drawer problem and tolerance for null results. *Psychological Bulletin, 86*, 638–641.

Rosenthal, R. (1991). *Meta-analytic procedures for social research*. New York: Sage Publishers.

Rosenthal, R. (1995). Writing meta-analytic reviews. *Psychological Bulletin, 118*, 183–192.

Rosenthal, R., & Fode, K. L. (1963a). Three experiments in experimenter bias. *Psychological Reports, 12*, 491–511.

Rosenthal, R., & Fode, K. L. (1963b). The effect of experimenter bias on the performance of the albino rat. *Behavioral Science, 8*, 183–189.

Rosnow, R. L., Goodstadt, B. E., Suls, J. M., & Gitter, A. G. (1973). More on the social psychology of the experiment: When compliance turns to self-defense. *Journal of Personality and Social Psychology, 27*, 337–343.

Rozin, P., Kabnick, K., Pete, E., Fischler, C., & Shields, C. (2003). The ecology of eating: Smaller portion sizes in France than in the United States help explain the French paradox. *Psychological Science, 14*, 450–454.

Rucci, A. J., & Tweney, R. D. (1980). Analysis of variance and the "second discipline" of scientific psychology: A historical account. *Psychological Bulletin, 87*, 166–184.

Ryan, L., Hatfield, C., & Hofstetter, M. (2002). Caffeine reduces time-of-day effects on memory performance in older adults. *Psychological Science, 13*, 68–71.

Sanford, E. C. (1914). Psychic research in the animal field: Der Kluge Hans and the Elberfeld horses. *American Journal of Psychology, 25*, 3–31.

Schaie, K. W. (2005). *Developmental influences on adult intelligence: The Seattle Longitudinal Study*. New York: Oxford University Press.

Schaie, K. W. (1988). Ageism in psychological research. *American Psychologist, 43*, 179–183.

Schlagman, S., Schulz, J., & Kvavilashvili, L. (2006). A content analysis of involuntary autobiographical memories: Examining the positivity effect of old age. *Memory, 14*, 161–175.

Schneirla, T. C. (1929). Learning and orientation in ants. *Comparative Psychology Monographs, 6 (No. 4)*.

Schoeneman, T. J., & Rubanowitz, D. E. (1985). Attributions in the advice columns: Actors and observers, causes and reasons. *Personality and Social Psychology Bulletin, 11*, 315–325.

Schooler, J. W., & Engstler-Schooler, T. Y. (1990). Verbal overshadowing of visual memories: Some things are better left unsaid. *Cognitive Psychology, 22*, 36–71.

Schrader, W. B. (1971). The predictive validity of the College Board Admissions tests. In W. H. Angoff (Ed.), *The College Board Admission Testing Program*. New York: College Entrance Examination Board.

Schrandt, J. A., Townsend, D. B., & Poulson, C. L. (2009). Teaching empathy skills to children with autism. *Journal of Applied Behavior Analysis, 42*, 17–32.

Schuman, H., & Presser, S. (1996). *Questions and answers in attitude surveys: Experiments on question form, wording, and content*. Thousand Oaks, CA: Sage.

Scott-Jones, D. (2000). Recruitment of research participants. In B. D. Sales & S. Folkman (Eds.), *Ethics in research with human participants* (pp. 27–34). Washington, DC: American Psychological Association.

Sears, D. O. (1986). College sophomores in the laboratory: Influences of a narrow data base on psychology's view of human nature. *Journal of Personality and Social Psychology, 51*, 515–530.

Sechrest, L., & Figueredo, A. J. (1993). Program evaluation. In L. W. Porter & M. R. Rosenzweig (Eds.), *Annual Review of Psychology. Volume 44* (pp. 645–674). Palo Alto, CA: Annual Reviews.

Shea, C. (2011, November 13). Fraud scandal fuels debate over practices of social psychology. *The Chronicle of Higher Education. Retrieved from http://chronicle.com/article/As-Dutch-Research-Scandal/129746/*

Sheldon, W. H. (1940). *The varieties of human physique: An introduction to constitutional psychology*. New York: Harper & Row.

Sheldon, W. H. (1942). *The varieties of temperament: A psychology of constitutional differences*. New York: Harper & Row.

Shepard, R. N., & Metzler, J. (1971). Mental rotation of three-dimensional objects. *Science, 171*, 701–703.

Shook, N. J., & Fazio, R. H. (2008). Interracial roommate relationships: An experimental test of the contact hypothesis. *Psychological Science, 19*, 717–723.

Shute, V. J. (1994). Learners and instruction: What's good for the goose may not be good for the gander. *Psychological Science Agenda, 7*(3), 8–9, 16.

Sidman, M. (1960). *Tactics of scientific research*. New York: Basic Books.

Sieber, J. E. (1998). Planning ethically responsible research. In L. Bickman & D. J. Rog (Eds.), *Handbook of applied social research methods* (pp. 127–156). Thousand Oaks, CA: Sage.

Sieber, J. E., & Saks, M. J. (1989). A census of subject pool characteristics. *American Psychologist, 44*, 1053–1061.

Sigall, H., & Ostrove, N. (1975). Beautiful but dangerous: Effects of offender attractiveness and nature of the crime on juridic judgment. *Journal of Personality and Social Psychology, 31*, 410–414.

Silverman, I. (1975). Nonreactive methods and the law. *American Psychologist, 30*, 764–769.

Simola, J., Kuisma, J., Öörni, A., Uusitabo, L. & Hyönä, J. (2011). The impact of salient advertisements on reading and attention on web pages. *Journal of Experimental Psychology: Applied, 17*, 174–190.

Simmons, J. P., Nelson, L. D., & Simonsohn, U. (2011). False-positive psychology: Undisclosed flexibility in data collection and analysis allows presenting anything as significant. *Psychological Science, 22*, 1359–1366.

Simons, D. J., & Holcolme, A. O. (2014). *Registered replication reports: A new article type at Perspectives on Psychological Science 27*(3). Retrieved from: http://www.psychologicalscience.org/index.php/publications/observer/2014/march-14/registered-replication-reports.html

Simons, D. J., Holcombe, A. O., & Spellman, B. A. (2014). An introduction to the registered replication reports at Perspectives on Psychological Science. *Perspectives on Psychological Science, 9*, 552–555.

Singer, P. (1975). *Animal liberation*. New York: Avon.

Skinner, B. F. (1953). *Science and human behavior*. New York: Free Press.

Skinner, B. F. (1966). Operant behavior. In W. K. Honig (Ed.), *Operant behavior: Areas of research and application* (pp. 12–32). New York: Appleton-Century-Crofts.

Skinner, B. F. (1969). *Contingencies of reinforcement*. Englewood Cliffs, NJ: Prentice Hall.

Skinner, B. F. (1976). *Walden Two*. New York: Macmillan. (Original work published 1948)

Skinner, B. F. (1979). *The shaping of a behaviorist*. New York: New York University Press.

Skinner, B. F. (1984). *A matter of consequences*. New York: New York University Press.

Small, W. S. (1901). Experimental study of the mental processes of the rat. *II. American Journal of Psychology, 11*, 133–165.

Smith, D. (2003, January). What you need to know about the new code. *APA Monitor, 34*(1), 62–65.

Smith, L. D. (1992). On prediction and control: B. F. Skinner and the technological ideal of science. *American Psychologist, 47*, 216–223.

Smith, S., & Sechrest, L. (1991). Treatment of aptitude x treatment interactions. *Journal of Consulting and Clinical Psychology, 59*, 233–244.

Smith, S. S., & Richardson, D. (1983). Amelioration of deception and harm in psychological research: The important role of debriefing. *Journal of Personality and Social Psychology, 44*, 1075–1082.

Smoll, F. L., Smith, R. E., Barnett, N. P., & Everett, J. J. (1993). Enhancement of children's self-esteem through social support training for youth sport coaches. *Journal of Applied Psychology, 78*, 602–610.

Society for Research in Child Development. (1996). Ethical standards for research with children. *SRCD directory of members*, 337–339.

Sokal, M. M. (1992). Origins and early years of the American Psychological Association, 1890–1906. *American Psychologist, 47*, 111–122.

Spelke, E. S. (1985). Preferential looking methods as tools for the study of cognition in infancy. In G. Gottlieb & N. Krasnegor (Eds.), *Measurement of audition and vision in the first year of postnatal life* (pp. 323–363). Norwood, NJ: Ablex.

Sprinthall, R. C. (2000). *Basic statistical analysis* (6th edition). Boston: Allyn and Bacon.

Spurzheim, J. G. (1978). Outlines of phrenology. In D. N. Robinson (Ed.), *Significant contributions to the history of psychology. Series E. Volume II*. Washington, DC: University Publications of America. (Original work published 1832)

Steele, K. M., Ball, T. N., & Runk, R. (1997). Listening to Mozart does not enhance backwards digit span performance. *Perceptual and Motor Skills, 84*, 1179–1184.

Steele, K. M., Bass, K. E., & Crook, M. D. (1999). The mystery of the Mozart effect: Failure to replicate. *Psychological Science, 10*, 366–369.

Sternberg, R. J., & Grigorenko, E. L. (1999). A smelly 113° in the shade (Or, why we do field research). *APS Observer, 12*(8), 10–11, 20–21.

Stoeber, J., Childs, J. H., Hayward, J. A., & Feast, A. R. (2011). Passion and motivation for studying: Predicting academic engagement and burnout in university students. *Educational Psychology, 31*, 513–528.

Stolzenberg, L., & D'Alessio, S. J. (1997). "Three strikes and you're out": The impact of California's new mandatory sentencing law on serious crime rates. *Crime and Delinquency, 43*, 457–470.

Strayer, D. L., Cooper, J. M., Turrill, J., Coleman, J., Medeiros-Ward, N. & Biondi, F. (2013). *Measuring cognitive distraction in the automobile*. Washington DC: AAA Foundation for Traffic Safety

Strayer, D. L., & Drews, F. A. (2004). Profiles in driver distraction: Effects of cell phone conversations on younger and older drivers. *Human Factors*, *46*, 640–649.

Strayer, D. L., & Johnston, W. A. (2001). Driven to distraction: Dual-task studies of simulated driving and conversing on a cellular telephone. *Psychological Science*, *12*, 462–466.

Strayer, D. L., Turrill, J. Coleman, J., Ortiz, E. V., & Cooper, J. M. (2014). *Measuring cognitive distraction in the automobile II: Assessing in-vehicle voice-based interactive technologies.* Washington DC: AAA Foundation for Traffic Safety.

Stroop, J. R. (1992). Studies of interference in serial verbal reactions. *Journal of Experimental Psychology: General*, *121*, 15–23. (Original work published 1935)

Sullivan, D. S., & Deiker, T. E. (1973). Subject-experimenter perceptions of ethical issues in human research. *American Psychologist*, *28*, 587–591.

Talarico, J. M., & Rubin, D. C. (2004). Confidence, not consistency, characterizes flashbulb memories. *Psychological Science*, *14*, 455–461.

Tashiro, T., & Mortensen, L. (2006). Translational research: How social psychology can improve psychotherapy. *American Psychologist*, *61*, 959–966.

Tavris, C. & Bluming, A. (2008). Taking the scary out of breast cancer stats. *APS Observer*, *21*(9), 16–17.

Taylor, D. W., Garner, W. R., & Hunt, H. F. (1959). Education for research in psychology. *American Psychologist*, *14*, 167–179.

Taylor, S. J., & Bogdan, R. (1998). *Introduction to qualitative research methods: A guidebook and resource* (3rd ed.). New York: Wiley.

Teigen, K. H. (1994). Yerkes-Dodson: A law for all seasons. *Theory and Psychology*, *4*, 525–547.

Terman, L. M. (1925). *Genetic studies of genius, Vol. 1. Mental and physical traits of a thousand gifted children.* Stanford, CA: Stanford University Press.

Terman, L. M., & Oden, M. H. (1947). *Genetic studies of genius, Vol. 4. The gifted child grows up: Twenty-five years' follow-up of a superior group.* Stanford, CA: Stanford University Press.

Terman, L. M., & Oden, M. H. (1959). *Genetic studies of genius, Vol. 5. The gifted group at mid-life: Thirty-five years' follow-up of the superior child.* Stanford, CA: Stanford University Press.

Thomas, E. (1995). *The very best men.* New York: Simon & Schuster.

Thorndike, E. L. (1898). Animal intelligence: An experimental study of the associative processes in animals. *Psychological Review Monographs*, *2* (*No. 8*).

Thorndike, E. L. (1899). A reply to "The nature of animal intelligence and the methods of investigating it." *Psychological Review*, *6*, 412–420.

Thorndike, E. L. (1911). *Animal intelligence: Experimental studies.* New York: Macmillan.

Titchener, E. B. (1906, June 6). *Letter to L. N. Wilson.* Wilson Papers, Clark University, Worcester, MA.

Todd, J. T., & Morris, E. K. (1992). Case histories in the great power of steady misrepresentation. *American Psychologist*, *47*, 1441–1453.

Tolman, E. C. (1959). Principles of purposive behavior. In S. Koch (Ed.), *Psychology: A study of a science. Volume 2: General systematic formulations, learning, and special processes* (pp. 92–157). New York: McGraw-Hill.

Tomas, V. (Ed.). (1957). *Charles S. Peirce: Essays in the philosophy of science.* New York: Liberal Arts Press.

Tomlinson-Keasey, C. (1990). The working lives of Terman's gifted women. In H. Y. Grossman & N. L. Chester, (Eds.), *The experience and meaning of work in women's lives* (pp. 213–239). Hillsdale, NJ: Lawrence Erlbaum.

Trabasso, T. (1963). Stimulus emphasis and all-or-none learning in concept identification. *Journal of Experimental Psychology*, *65*, 398–406.

Trafimow, D., Madson, L., & Gwizdowski, I. (2006). Introductory psychology students' perceptions of alternatives to research participation. *Teaching of Psychology*, *33*, 247–249.

Trafimow, D., & Marks, M. (2015). Editorial. *Basic and Applied Social Psychology*, *37*, 1–2.

Triandis, H. C. (1995). *Individualism and collectivism.* Boulder, CO: Westview Press.

Trudel, R., & Murray, K. B. (2013). Self-regulatory strength amplification through selective information processing. *Journal of Consumer Psychology, 23*, 61–73.

Trudel, R., Murray, K. B., Kim, S., & Chen, S. (2015). The impact of traffic light color-coding on food health perceptions and choice. *Journal of Experimental Psychology: Applied, 21*, 255–275.

Tryon, R. C. (1929). The genetics of learning ability in rats: Preliminary report. *University of California Publications in Psychology, 4*, 71–89.

Tversky, A., & Kahneman, D. (1973). Availability: A heuristic for judging frequency and probability. *Cognitive Psychology, 5*, 207–232.

Tweney, R. D. (1987). Programmatic research in experimental psychology: E. B. Titchener's laboratory investigations, 1891–1927. In M. G. Asch & W. R. Woodward (Eds.), *Psychology in twentieth-century thought and society* (pp. 34–57). New York: Cambridge University Press.

Ulrich, R. E. (1991). Animal rights, animal wrongs and the question of balance. *Psychological Science, 2*, 197–201.

Ulrich, R. S. (1984). View through a window may influence recovery from surgery. *Science, 224*, 420–421.

van Kammen, W. B., & Stouthamer-Loeber, M. (1998). Practice aspects of interview data collection and data management. In L. Bickman & D. J. Rog (Eds.), *Handbook of applied social research methods* (pp. 375–397). Thousand Oaks: CA: Sage.

Vandehey, M. A., Marsh, C. M., & Diekhoff, G. M. (2005). Providing students with instructors' notes: Problems with reading, studying, and attendance. *Teaching of Psychology, 32*, 49–52.

Vohs, K. D., & Schooler, J. W. (2008). The value of believing in free will: Encouraging a belief in determinism increases cheating. *Psychological Science, 19*, 49–54.

Wagaman, J. R., Miltenberger, R. G., & Arndorfer, R. E. (1993). Analysis of a simplified treatment for stuttering in children. *Journal of Applied Behavior Analysis, 26*, 53–61.

Wagner, J. A., III, Rubin, P. A., & Callahan, T. J. (1988). Incentive payment and nonmanagerial productivity: An interrupted time series analysis of magnitude and trend. *Organizational Behavior and Human Decision Processes, 42*, 47–74.

Walker, A. J. (1996). Couples watching television: Gender, power, and the remote control. *Journal of Marriage and the Family, 58*, 813–823.

Ward, P., & Carnes, M. (2002). Effects of posting self-set goals on collegiate football players' skill execution during practice and games. *Journal of Applied Behavior Analysis, 35*, 1–12.

Wason, P. C., & Johnson-Laird, P. N. (1972). *Psychology of reasoning: Structure and content.* Cambridge, MA: Harvard University Press.

Watanabe, S., Sakamoto, J., & Wakia, M. (1995). Pigeons' discrimination of paintings by Monet and Picasso. *Journal of the Experimental Analysis of Behavior, 63*, 165–174.

Watson, J. B. (1907). Kinesthetic and organic sensations: Their role in the reactions of the white rat to the maze. *Psychological Review Monograph Supplements, 8 (No. 33).*

Watson, J. B. (1913). Psychology as the behaviorist views it. *Psychological Review, 20*, 158–177.

Watson, J. B. (1924). *Behaviorism.* New York: W. W. Norton.

Watson, J. B., & Rayner, R. (1920). Conditioned emotional reactions. *Journal of Experimental Psychology, 3*, 1–14.

Webb, E. J., Campbell, D. T., Schwartz, R. D., Sechrest, L., & Grove, J. B. (1981). *Nonreactive measures in the social sciences* (2nd ed.). Boston: Houghton Mifflin.

Webster's word histories. (1989). *Springfield*, MA: Merriam-Webster.

Weindling, P. J. (2004). *Nazi medicine and the Nuremberg Trials: From medical war crimes to informed consent.* New York: Palgrave Macmillan.

Weiss, J. M. (1968). Effects of coping response on stress. *Journal of Comparative and Physiological Psychology, 65*, 251–260.

West, S. G., Gunn, S. P., & Chernicky, P. (1975). Ubiquitous Watergate: An attributional analysis. *Journal of Personality and Social Psychology, 32*, 55–65.

Westman, M., & Eden, D. (1997). Effects of respite from work on burnout: Vacation relief and fade-out. *Journal of Applied Psychology, 82,* 516–527.

Wilhite, H., & Ling, R. (1995). Measured energy savings from a more informative energy bill. *Energy and Buildings, 22,* 145–155.

Wilkinson, L., & APA Task Force on Statistical Inference. (1999). Statistical methods in psychology journals: Guidelines and explanations. *American Psychologist, 54,* 594–604.

Williams, L. E., & Bargh, J. A. (2008). Experiencing physical warmth promotes interpersonal warmth. *Science, 322,* 606–607.

Winston, A. S. (1990). Robert Sessions Woodworth and the "Columbia Bible": How the psychological experiment was redefined. *American Journal of Psychology, 103,* 391–401.

Wirth, J. H., & Bodenhauser, G. V. (2009). The role of gender in mental-illness stigma: A national experiment. *Psychological Science, 20,* 169–173.

Witkin, H. A., & Goodenough, D. R. (1977). Field dependence and interpersonal behavior. *Psychological Bulletin, 84,* 661–689.

Witt, L. A., & Nye, L. G. (1992). Gender and the relationship between perceived fairness of pay or promotion and job satisfaction. *Journal of Applied Psychology, 77,* 910–917.

Witte, R. S., & Witte, J. S. (2014). *Statistics* (10th ed.). Hoboken, NJ: Wiley.

Wolf, M. M. (1978). Social validity: The case for subjective measurement, or how behavior analysis is finding its heart. *Journal of Applied Behavior Analysis, 11,* 203–214.

Wood, J. M., & Bootzin, R. R. (1990). The prevalence of nightmares and their independence from anxiety. *Journal of Abnormal Psychology, 99,* 64–68.

Wood, J. M., Bootzin, R. R., Rosenhan, D., Nolen-Hoeksema, S., & Jourden, F. (1992). Effects of the 1989 San Francisco earthquake and content of nightmares. *Journal of Abnormal Psychology, 101,* 219–224.

Woodworth, R. S. (1938). *Experimental psychology.* New York: Henry Holt.

Woolf, S. H. (2008). The meaning of translational research and why it matters. *JAMA, 299*(2), 211–213.

Word, C. O., Zanna, M. P., & Cooper, J. (1974). The nonverbal mediation of self-fulfilling prophecies in interracial interaction. *Journal of Experimental Social Psychology, 10,* 109–120.

Worthen, B. R. (2001). Whither evaluation? That all depends. *American Journal of Evaluation, 22,* 409–418.

Wundt, W. (1904). *Principles of physiological psychology* (5th ed.) (E. B. Titchener, Trans.). New York: MacMillan. (Original work published 1874)

Yerkes, R. M., & Dodson, J. D. (1908). The relation of the strength of stimulus to rapidity of habit formation. *Journal of Comparative Neurology and Psychology, 18,* 459–482.

Zajonc, R. B. (1990). Leon Festinger (1919–1989). *American Psychologist, 45,* 661–662.

Zezima, K. (2010, September 13). *For many, "washroom" seems to be just a name.* Retrieved from www.nytimes.com/2010/09/14/us

Index